INTRODUCTION TO PSYCHOLOGY

DOING PSYCHOLOGY ON YOUR OWN

Larry Vandervert

Excerpts from:
Psychology: Lectures and Study Guide
Third Edition
by Lois McDermott
University of Washington

Pearson
Custom
Publishing

Cover art: "Mann auf einer Leiter," by Quint Buchholz.

Printed in the United States of America

10 9 8 7 6 5 4 3 2 1

Please visit our website at www.pearsoncustom.com

ISBN 0–536–02756–0

BA 990414

PEARSON CUSTOM PUBLISHING
160 Gould Street/Needham Heights, MA 02494
A Pearson Education Company

Copyright Acknowledgments

Grateful acknowledgment is made to the following sources for permission to reprint material copyrighted or controlled by them:

Photo 1.1 "B.F. Skinner," courtesy of Liaison Agency, Inc.

Photo 1.2 "Sigmund Freud," courtesy of Associated Press/ World Wide Photos.

Photo 1.3 "Carl Rogers," courtesy of Corbis-Bettmann.

Photo 1.4 "Researcher," courtesy of World Bank Photo Library.

Photo 1.5 "Elephant," courtesy of PhotoDisc, Inc.

Photo 2.1 "Autonomous Mobile Robot," courtesy of American Honda Motor Co., Inc.

Figure 2.6 "All Thinks, Great and Small," by permission of Hans Moravec, reprinted from ROBOT, 1998, Oxford University Press.

Photo 2.35 "Brain," courtesy of Visuals Unlimited.

Figure 3.1 "Man Sitting on a Stool," courtesy Carol Donner, reprinted from Scientific American, April 1992.

Photo 3.9 "Boy Doing Arithmetic on Blackboard," courtesy of Silver Burdett Ginn.

Photo 4.1 "Cliff House on Seal Rock," courtesy of Corbis-Bettmann.

Photo 4.3 "Emotional Reaction of Cat to a Threat," courtesy of Photo Researchers.

Photo 4.4a "Man yelling in anger," courtesy of Tony Stone Images.

Photo 4.4b "Angry Mandrill," courtesy of Tony Stone Images.

Photo 4.17 "Rat with Damaged Hypothalamus," by permission of Dr. Neal E. Miller, photo by J. A. F. Stevenson.

Photo 4.20 "Facial Expressions," courtesy of Dr. Paul Ekman.

Photo 4.21 “Man Jumping,” courtesy of FPG International LLC.

Photo 5.6 “Operant Conditioning” courtesy of Life Magazine, Time Warner, Inc.

Photo 5.11 “Variable Ratio Schedule of Reinforcement,” courtesy of PhotoEdit.

Photo 5.14 “Learning Through Observation,” by permission of Will Hart.

Photo 5.15 “Three Children Studying,” courtesy of Merrill Education.

Photo 6.27 “Young Girl Painting,” by permission of Omni-Photo Communications, Inc.

Photo 7.8 “Social Loafing,” courtesy of PhotoEdit.

Photo 7.9 “Milgram Obedience,” courtesy of Alexandra Milgram.

Photo 7.13 “Compliance,” courtesy of PhotoEdit.

Photo 7.14 “Man with Boy in Park,” courtesy of PhotoDisc, Inc.

Photo 8.1 “Mohandas Gandhi,” courtesy of the Associated Press.

Photo 8.4a “Albert Einstein,” courtesy of Corbis-Bettmann.

Photo 8.4b “Eleanor Roosevelt,” courtesy of Corbis-Bettmann.

Photo 8.4c “Martin Luther King, Jr.,” courtesy of Associated Press/ World Wide Photos.

Photo 8.14 “Girl Smiling,” courtesy of Pearson Education/ Prentice Hall College Division.

Photo 9.4 “Agoraphobia - Crowd,” courtesy of Photo Researchers, Inc.

Photo 9.5 “English Soccer Riot,” courtesy of Associated Press/ World Wide Photos.

Photo 10.1 “Agoraphobia – Girl Looking out Window,” courtesy of PhotoEdit.

Photo 10.6 “Group discussion,” courtesy of Pearson Education/ Prentice Hall College Division.

CONTENTS

PREFACE

Preparing to Understand and Use Your Psychology Textbook

What Is the Best Way to Learn About Psychology?

A New Emphasis in Introductory Psychology

Textbooks are starting points for much learning and thinking. Today psychologists know a great deal about how learning and thinking can be improved. What can psychology tell us about how to organize a textbook that would produce the greatest advancements in your knowledge?

We are beginning to understand that the human brain attempts to organize everything that comes its way into cognitive map-like representations of objects, relationships, and ideas.[1] The modeling process begins in a prehistoric part of the brain that helped creatures find their ways around in the world. This old part of the brain is called the *hippocampus,* and its mapping and modeling functions reach into the most advanced learning and thinking portions of the brain called the *cerebral cortex.* Figure 1 shows how the hippocampus reaches into the cerebral cortex of the brain.

In human beings, even the printed words you are now reading become organized in a model or map-like manner. Your brain does this because it is the most powerful way for it to learn and to think. A cognitive model or map integrates knowledge into a single, coherent, and complete picture. "Unconscious" cognitive processes also operate in this fashion. You will study evidence of both conscious and unconscious integrative processes in the chapters of this book.

[1]In all animals, including humans, the brain creates cognitive models of its surroundings in its complex neural networks. In the human cultural activity of science, as well as everyday activity, a variety of models with differing levels of complexity are involved in learning, thinking, and creativity. Children learn by playing with toys which are simple models of the things they represent. As we grow older we learn to think about complex relationships like the change of seasons through models of the earth's relationship to the sun. Brilliant scientists like Albert Einstein create symbolic mathematical models of the universe. It is our view that the quality of your learning, thinking, and creative work is dependent on the completeness and accuracy of the cognitive models you have acquired.

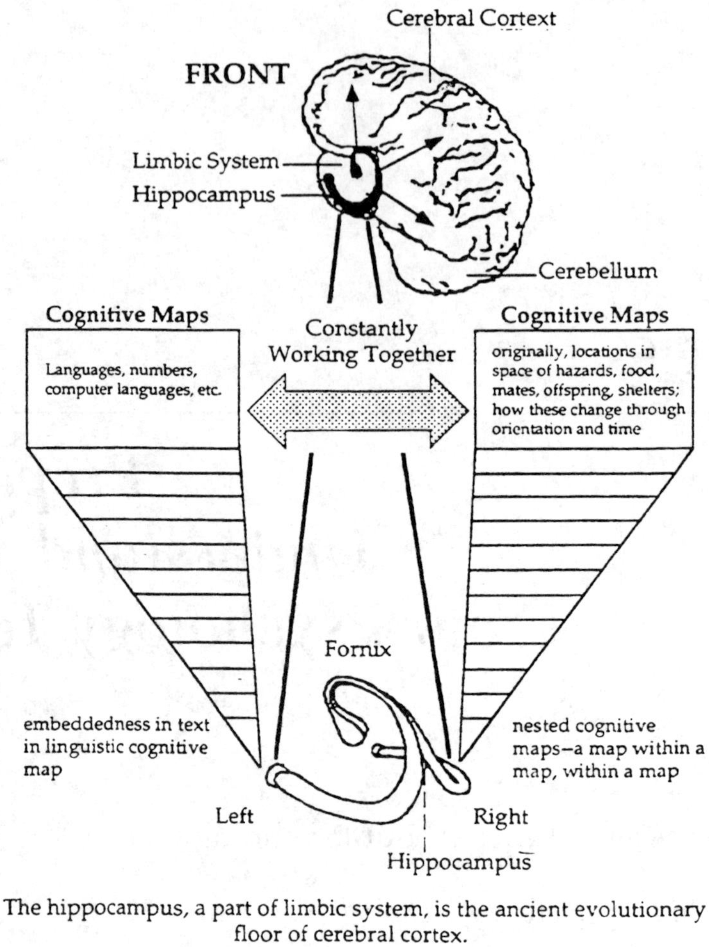

Figure 1 Your brain makes maps of everything you learn.

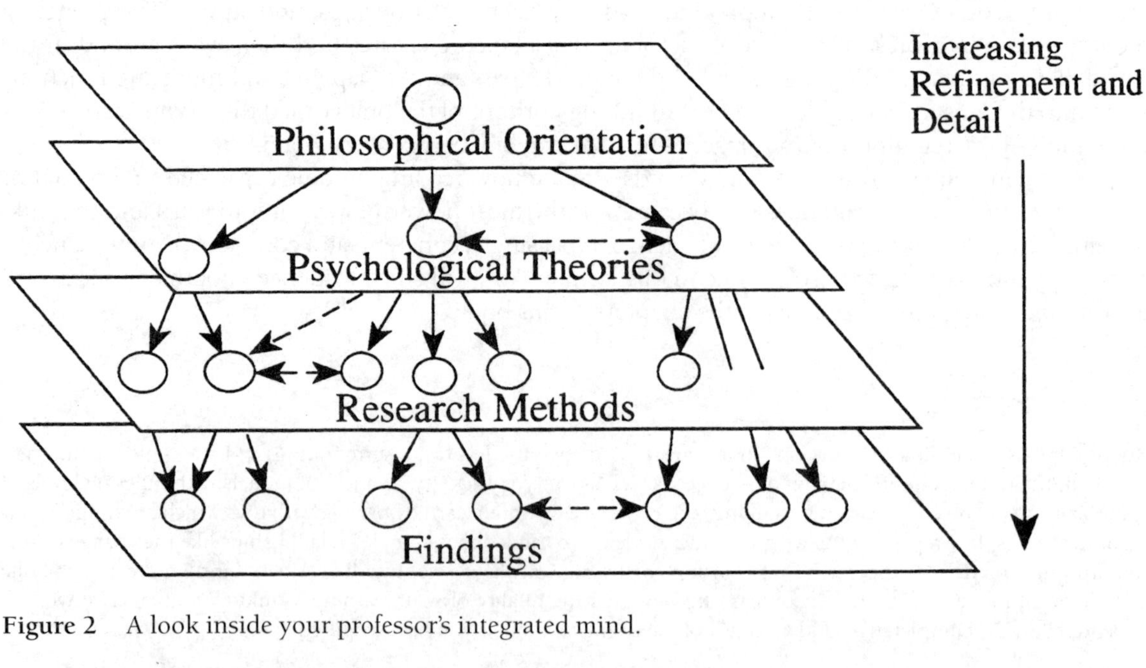

Figure 2 A look inside your professor's integrated mind.

Why Is Science So Powerful? The Maps of Psychology: Theories, Research Methods, and Data

It has often been pointed out that theories are like maps. Theories are explanatory frameworks very much like maps that provide powerful guidance to help us find our way while learning new ideas, and guiding our thinking about complex topics. For example, Sigmund Freud's theory about dreams and the unconscious mind provides an integrative picture that helps us make sense of the fascinating "territory" of our dreams.

Psychological researchers who study how knowledge becomes organized by the brain have discovered that "experts" like your psychology professor have acquired a framework of knowledge that is different from that of students. Figure 2 illustrates in a simple way how the theories of psychology are part of a large, interrelated system of knowledge that consists of clear relationships among four levels of ideas, procedures, and findings.

The four levels of knowledge are like four maps stacked on top of one another with each lower one having increased detail. Your professor is an expert who has clear, well-organized models and map-like understandings of the many theories in psychology and their related methods and data.

On the other hand, because of traditional testing procedures, beginning students of psychology tend to acquire only *unrelated* collections of what are called "routes." A **route** is a fixed, inflexible way of getting from one place to another. In the case of learning and thinking, a route is a fixed, inflexible way of solving problems—*especially in solving new problems never before encountered.* (Psychologists and teachers often call the ability to solve new kinds of problems "critical thinking.") While the brain organizes even routes into mini-map structures, they are fragmented and usually unrelated to one another. They therefore are of limited use and can lead to a great deal of confusion. For example, let's say you're in the city of New York for the first time, and you ask a passerby how to get to the Empire State building. You are given the following route:

Go down this street until you get to the fourth traffic light. Then take a left and go until you come to the cathedral; take a right and go about a mile.

What happens if you forget *any* portion of the route? What happens if you encounter road construction halfway along the way that detours you off in the opposite direction? You'll probably become lost all over again! Have you ever felt that way during an exam? While routes like the one described above are useful in special, limited situations that occur on the spur-of-the-moment, they are very inefficient for learning and thinking **critically** about any **new** situation or any **overall** situation.[2] How many routes could be described for the entire city of New York? Zillions! However, if you had a single, one-page map (or, perhaps, an architectural model) of the city, it would show you all of the possible routes at a glance—you need never get lost no matter what might happen. Are you beginning to get the picture?

How Can You Learn to Think Like a Scientist? Psychology: An Integrative Introduction

Taking all of the foregoing ideas into consideration, I have organized the chapters of this textbook in a new way. Each of the chapters is organized in an integrative fashion—much like you saw illustrated in Figure 2. As you learn and think about psychology, you will learn to organize its ideas and applications in a similar integrative fashion. You will be learning to **think** like a scientist while you are learning science. You will **not** be asked simply to memorize a bunch of easily forgotten, nearly meaningless, and unrelated facts (routes) about psychology.

[2]In many college exams students are tested in terms of routes they have learned. Nearly all multiple-choice, true/false, and essay exams require students to learn and memorize mostly unrelated routes of knowledge. This situation is unfortunate because it actually tends to move the students away from the professor's map-like organization of knowledge that has been formed on the basis of many years of education and experience.

At the same time each of the chapters is organized so that it is very compatible with the time-honored SQ3R study method. You may be familiar with this powerful approach to study. The SQ3R study method is quite similar to the organization of scientific knowledge that you see depicted in Figure 2. It encourages you to develop map-like cognitive models in whatever you study. In fact, this is why the SQ3R method works so well. In many ways it is nearly as powerful a method as scientific method itself.

How Does SQ3R Help You Develop Cognitive Models of Psychology?

Briefly, SQ3R means that study should **always** start with a **S**urvey of the material at hand. This is the way a scientist begins study. Then **Q**uestions about the material are posed. An easy way to generate questions is to simply turn the chapter headings into questions. Headings can be turned into questions either by you or by the textbook. Sometimes it is helpful to have textbook authors pose the questions, because they know exactly what they want you to learn and can choose the appropriate questions carefully. Scientists, too, ask questions to be answered, and they are guided in their choice of questions mostly by their theories. ***R***eading, then becomes an ***active search*** for answers. In science, too, reading and researching is a constant search for answers and connections. ***R***eciting is a time for self-assessment on the section of the chapter you have just completed. It is ***not*** a time for regurgitating the text as it is written. Reciting is an opportunity for you to formulate and mull over in your own terms what you have learned. Put ideas into your own words, think of everyday examples that are familiar to you, and draw diagrams or pictures to show how subpoints are related. Recitation, although scientists don't call it by that name, is critical in science.[3] It is the time when the scientist reflects on what has been learned, and implications and connections are sought. **R**eview is the time to bring it all together in a bird's-eye view. In addition to reviewing everything from the steps above, this is the time to seek a sense of the overall organization of the chapter.

Larry Vandervert
September, 1999

[3]After extensive reading scientists mull over and reflect on what they have been studying and learning. This helps organize new material with what they already know. It is a critical period for the scientist, because it often leads to discovery and invention.

1

The Ideas and Methods of Psychology

In Greek mythology there is the wonderful story of Eros and Psyche (Cupid and Psyche in Roman myth). Psyche, the daughter of a king, was the most beautiful mortal the world had ever seen. She was so beautiful that even Aphrodite, the Greek goddess of love, became jealous of her and in anger sent her son Eros, god of love, to punish the mortal. But Eros secretly had her whisked off to a magnificent palace and, not wanting Psyche to know of his admiration (and his identity), visited her only at night. After a time, Psyche became curious as to the identity of her delightful but unseen husband. Psyche awoke in the middle of the night, lit a lamp, and held it above her husband's face. She was delighted at what she saw—the charming face of Eros himself! But as she gazed, a drop of hot oil fell upon the god's bared shoulder. Eros quickly awakened. He was angry that Psyche had not shown faith in him.

The palace vanished and Psyche was alone. Psyche again had the anger of Aphrodite upon her. In an attempt to satisfy Aphrodite, she agreed to complete various ordeals. Psyche succeeded in overcoming them, some unseen force seemed to help her.

Finally, feeling that Psyche had atoned for her loss of faith in him, Eros, who had secretly continued to love and watch out for her, went to Zeus (god of heavens) and asked that he and Psyche be reunited. Zeus not only consented to this but made Psyche immortal. Aphrodite soon forgot her anger and jealousy. Eros and Psyche married and joyously celebrated on Mt. Olympus.

What Is the Subject Matter of Psychology?

The classic story of Eros and Psyche is very enlightening about the early Greek idea of *psyche*—the emblem of the soul and of immortality. The idea of Psyche is the beginning of our quest to understand the subject matter of psychology. The beautiful Greek maiden Psyche represented in myth the breath and drive of desire and love. The word psyche originated in the interplay of the Greek language, and Greek myths.

The word psyche in ancient Greek looked like this: The first letter (psi—pronounced si) is often used as a symbol to represent psychology. The *Oxford English Dictionary* defines the earliest meaning of the word psyche:

> . . . the animating principle in man and other living beings, the source of all vital

> activities, rational and irrational, the soul or spirit in distinction from its material vehicle . . . p. 1549

The equating of the animating principle in all living things and the soul is quite different from the Western idea of the Christian soul. The powerful Greek mind of Aristotle (McKeon, 1947) provided the best analysis of the Greek idea of soul or psyche. Aristotle described different levels of the animating force. The lowest level of the force of psyche was self-nutrition. Self-nutrition was the only level of psyche of which plants were capable. The highest level of psyche was mind or thinking, and only human beings were capable of this level of animation.

You can see that the idea of psyche originated in attempts to explain the then mysterious, unseen force(s) which underlie virtually everything in human experience, perception, motivation, emotions, thoughts, and yes, even love. These forces are depicted in the ordeals of the maiden Psyche. In more modern times, psychology's subject matter has moved away from the idea of the soul, and to the idea of the *mind* as the animating principle behind experience and behavior.

Can Science Study the Mind?

Ultimately, the human *psyche* or mind constitutes the subject matter of psychology. The *ology* portion of the word psychology suggests, however, that psychology should conduct its business in a scientific fashion. And, science requires *objectivity* rather than simply *subjectivity.* The problem is that the mind does not seem to be a public event, but rather a private and subjective one. In other words, while each of us has a mind, it is pretty much a private affair. People around us really have little idea about what we are feeling or thinking about, although they can and usually do speculate about what is going on in our heads. But, certainly, no one has ever objectively observed the minds of other people or animals.

The fact that the mind is the ultimate subject matter for psychology, and, at the same time, is not directly and objectively observable presents psychology with an interesting problem:

> How can psychology scientifically study the mind when the stuff of the mind (its contents and processes) are not directly available to scientific study?

While this is a very critical problem for psychology, it does have many solutions. As you will see, it is the great abundance of these solutions which makes psychology interesting, exciting, controversial, and at times, it must be admitted, a bit confusing.

How Can Such a Diverse Field as Psychology Be Described?

One way to describe what the scientific study of the mind includes would be to simply make a list of all of the chapters and topics in this textbook. For example, the mind is what the nervous system does (Chapter 2); the mind perceives a world (Chapter 3), the mind is conscious and dreams (Chapter 4), and so forth. At the same time what is common to all of these topics is that they involve the objective study of behavior and *cognition.* This leads directly to a definition of psychology. *Psychology is the scientific study of human and animal behavior and cognition.* (Why animals are included in the definition of psychology will be explained in a moment.)

What Are the Four *Integrated* Ways in Which Psychology Studies Human and Animal Behavior and Cognition?

Each of the sciences, whether it be, for example, physics, chemistry, biology, or psychology consists of four different, yet thoroughly integrated levels of research activity. It is pointed out in your student preface that these levels of research activity are like four similar maps stacked on top of one another. These four maps include the following:

1. Philosophical Orientation
2. Theories
3. Research Methods
4. Research Findings

As we go from one "map" to another, the only thing that changes is the degree of refinement that is possible. In scientific research this is like "zooming-in" on geographical maps of finer and finer scales. If you understand clearly what these four maps are all about and how they are related to one another, you should have little trouble understanding how everything in this textbook is interrelated.

To make these four ways of thinking about and exploring science clear to you, let us apply them to a real situation. Since you probably have some knowledge about biology, and since biology and psychology are closely related disciplines, we will use an example from that science. As you probably know, the essential subject matter of biology is life. This is how the four integrated research activities would apply to "life:"

A Persisting PHILOSOPHICAL Question About Life: "How did life begin?"

One might take the view that life began as a purely natural event. For example, perhaps life came into being long ago as the result of a complex chemical situation or *"primordial soup,"* as it is often called. This special situation, the theory might continue, was unique in that it resulted in a "first cell-like form" that had within it a capability to reproduce itself. This would be a small start toward a *theory of evolution.* This view offers the beginning of an explanation of how life got started and then over the ages developed into a variety of forms.

Methodological Zoom-In (Procedures and instruments are developed to make certain observations.) Single cells are usually small. And, we might expect the earliest ones to be very small. Also, their fossils might be broken into even smaller fragments. Finally, it would seem logical to guess that the earliest cells would be found in the earliest (oldest) rock formations—the Precambrian. Therefore, we might develop a procedure of microscopic analysis of Precambrian rock fossils.

Empirical Zoom-In (The methods provide findings that support the theory.) Many fossil traces of plant and animal life dating back to previous geological times seem to support a natural evolutionary explanation of life.

Persisting Philosophical Questions in Psychology

Now we can apply the four integrated research activities to psychology. You have seen earlier that the ultimate subject matter of psychology is the "animating principle in man . . . ," as distinguished from the body. It might be apparent to you now that what this really means is that this principle or mind is the subject matter of psychology at the philosophical level. You recall we asked the question, "What is the mysterious principle in us that thinks, asks questions, and, like Psyche herself, loves?" There are many other interesting questions for psychology at the philosophical level:

1. Are humans the only creatures which truly have a mind?
2. Will computers someday "think" the way the mind thinks?
3. How does your mind control your body—or *not* control it?
4. How does your brain give rise to your every day experience?
5. Do human beings have free will?

As you might guess, a great deal has been written in the exciting area of *philosophical psychology.*

Psychology at the Theoretical Level

How Are the Principles of Evolution Related to Psychology?

Our earlier biological example of the four integrated ways of thinking about psychology was no mere accident. Modern psychology is thoroughly biologically based, and most psychologists would agree it is likewise thoroughly *evolutionary.* There are many ways to think about the role of evolutionary theory in psychology. First, human behavior and cognition are thought to be developmentally continuous with subhuman forms of life. For example, the neural networks in your brain that give rise to all behavior and cognition work in the same ways in all animals—from fish, to birds, to humans. Second there is not a chapter or topic in this book that does not presuppose the influence of evolutionary processes. This means that whether we are talking about human learning, development, or personality, for example, change arises continuously from pre-existing levels or forms in objectively understandable ways. In fact, the principles of evolution provide an underlying framework for the definition of psychology provided earlier, and they connect psychology with other sciences.

How Do the Principles of Evolution Provide an Integrating Framework for Psychology?

The *general principles of evolution,* then, are an overall set of integrating of principles that underlies most of the other more specialized theories in psychology. The general principles of evolution are so pervasive in modern psychology and are taken for granted by so many psychologists, they more or less reside in the background of the more traditional theories in psychology.

For now, we can list several important principles of evolution that provide an underlying framework for psychology. Important principles of evolution:

1. Describe the normal distribution of behavioral and cognitive characteristics across people.
2. Describe basic and objective mechanisms of change in behavior and cognition.
3. Describe how a person's behavior and cognition develop over a life time.
4. Describe connectednesses and commonalties in behavior and cognition across species.
5. Provide scientifically based connections with other sciences, for example, biology, chemistry, anthropology, linguistics, ethology, and sociology that help in understanding the nature of human and animal behavior and cognition.

We will return to the principles of evolution many times in this book, and will point out their connections with the traditional topics and theories in psychology.

When and How Did the Traditional Theories in Psychology Develop?

The mind is so incredibly complex (it somehow provides us with the entirety of our reality), and because it seems so elusive to direct observation, many views of mind have seemed plausible during the history of psychology. While the basis for modern psychology may have started with Aristotle over 2,400 years ago, it has been only in the last hundred years or so that new views of mind have begun to offer solutions to the problem of its objective study.

By late in the nineteenth century many psychologists of mind had begun studies in a *"new" psychology*—in laboratories. More and more, mind was being studied scientifically. But this required that mind not be studied directly, but *indirectly.* The trend was toward laboratory study of external indicators of mind's activities. These included such observations as the relationship between conditions in the environment and the reactions or responses of both animals and human beings. The development of the new psychology was greatly influenced by the then equally new theory of evolution.

Since scientists could not study the privacy of mind directly, they began to devise views of mind that permitted them to study *outward* expressions of mind. In a sense, these theoretical solutions to attaining objectivity in psychology tended to put mind itself only where science could—out of direct view, and in a "black box." Since we cannot observe mind directly, the scientists were saying, let us take the view that we can learn nearly as much about psyche—the animating principle, by studying only its physiology and the behavior it produces (or which produces it).

What Are the Traditional Psychological Theories?

Today, the thinking of most psychologists is influenced by some combination of five fairly distinct views about how to go about the work of psychology (see Figure 1.1). These theoretical approaches to psychology each offer important insights and understandings concerning your world of experience.

The Behavioral View

Behaviorism, as this view came to be called, represents an extreme response to attaining objectivity in psychology. Since mind is not directly observable in public fashion, this approach suggests that we place all aspects of mind into a box and study only behavior that is undeniably observable. For behaviorism this includes only the behavior of the environment and the behavior of organisms. Since the environment consists of *stimuli* (S), and behavior consists of *responses* (R), this approach has been called S-R psychology.

B.F. Skinner

B.F. Skinner became the most notable proponent of behaviorism. He ingeniously reduced the fundamentals of the environment down to carefully controlled pleasant and unpleasant stimulus variables within his *operant conditioning apparatus.* In a similar fashion, behavior has been reduced to very fundamental responses such as the concisely defined *bar-pressing behavior* of, for example, white rats. Since these stimulus and response variables, and various relationships between them, are the only interests of behaviorism, and since any activities which might be going on inside the organism are thought to be irrelevant, behaviorism can be called a black-box approach to the study of mind.

Behaviorists do not have an interest in explaining, diagramming, or building brain-like machines which might help show or tell us what is going on inside the black box. We usually refer to these internal activities as consciousness, or free-will or experience. Behaviorists deny the importance of these mind-like activities, and in the extreme, even deny them a casual role in human activity or even their existence. While few psychologists today would consider themselves extreme behaviorists, the view has provided psychology with many valuable insights into human and animal behavior. For example, much can be learned by carefully analyzing the effects of the passing environment on your own behavior. Starting right now, begin to notice the degree to which your behavior seems to be the result of passing stimuli, or previous experiences with specific environmental situations. You will probably find that the ongoing "flow" of your behavior is greatly influenced by the "unplanned" coincidences of stimuli and responses you happen to encounter (for example, if someone interrupts you in the middle of a thought, you may not be able to recall what you were thinking about). Behaviorists like B.F. Skinner suggest there are only three things that are controlling your behavior at any given moment: (1) the *genetic endowment* you received from your two parents, (2) your *past responses to stimuli,* and (3) your *present situation.* Perhaps there is more to you, but no matter how we might feel about the behavioral view, it has shown the reasonableness of an objective and totally measurable approach to the study of "mind."

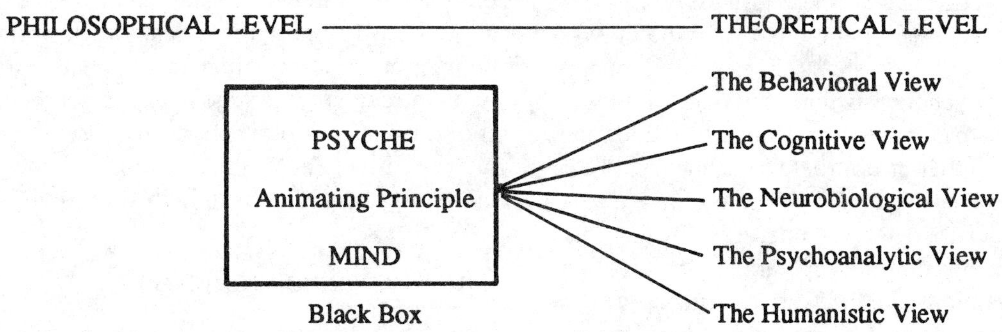

Figure 1.1 Five Approaches to Psychology

The Cognitive View

Cognition has come to refer to the mental processing of perceptions, memories, and information—in a word, thinking. The cognitive view differs from the behavioral view in its desire to understand the mental processing which its proponents feel must certainly go on inside the black box of the behaviorist. The cognitive psychologist says there can be more to the objective study of the mind than simply S's (stimuli) and R's (responses). Therefore, they believe it is just the explaining, diagramming, and building of machine models, for example, that might show or tell us what is going on inside the box. **The Student Preface of this textbook is an example of the application of the cognitive view to learning and thinking.**

So, what does go on inside the black box? As you might guess there have been many suggestions. As an *analogy,* if you were asked to explain what goes on inside a video game or a computer (without taking it apart), what would you say? Think about this question for a few minutes. You would probably produce diagrams, internal structures, mechanisms, and stages of game activity. What you were asked to do is essentially the same as what the cognitive psychologist might attempt to do with the behaviorist's black box.

A particularly promising form of cognitive psychology involves the most complex machine diagrams of all. Within the inter workings of digital computers there exists a rich source of ideas for cognitive psychology—structures, stages, diagrams, mechanisms, operations, schemes, and maps. Computing *systems* seem to be able to accomplish many of the things nervous systems are able to do. For example, computers read-in, remember, calculate, solve problems, and report back. It is important, however, to keep in mind that most cognitive psychologists draw distinctions between the operations of computer systems and nervous systems. For example, many cognitive psychologists point out that computers don't have passions and do not make commitments. Whether or not these capacities will be a matter of extensiveness of programming remains to be understood. At any rate, it is obvious that the study of computer-operations analogies to mind operations will be a very exciting approach to the study of mind during future decades. We believe that the development of computing systems is a boundless source of cognitive *modeling* that will provide more and more answers to questions about a variety of topics in psychology.

The Neurobiological View

The more we learn about the human nervous system, the more we understand the close relationship between its activities and behavior and cognitive processes. For example, the *bioelectrical* activity of the brain as measured by the *electroencephalograph* (EEG) is directly related to whether you are asleep, awake, or problem solving. We know also that certain parts of the brain control specific types of behavior in specific parts of the body. In addition, one side of the cerebral cortex seems to be largely responsible for one type of information processing related to speech, and the other side of the cortex to other features of cognition and behavior.

What types of neurological activity underlie the various behavioral and mental events of your daily life? What is happening in your brain when you learn, remember, or are in love? These are questions psychologists within the neurobiological approach are beginning to answer. In certain ways the nervous system itself presents us with a black box. That is, when brain tissue and chemistry are examined directly we find no worries, no pains, no loving, no light of day, no sounds, no mind. In this special sense, cognitive psychology's study of diagrams of systems is not essentially different from the neurobiologist's study of the nervous systems. A person's private world of experience is not directly observed in either case. But information processes are observed or inferred in both. An interesting area of investigation that studies how artificial systems can learn, remember, solve problems, and maintain themselves is called *cybernetics.* This *comparative study* of biological and machine systems gives us clues about how the brain might do its work, and is, of course, at the same time much related to the work of cognitive psychologists. Cybernetics is the study of control mechanisms of systems that are much like the original idea of psyche—the animating principles in all living things.

The Psychoanalytic View

The *psychoanalytic view* of psyche begins to move us away from the very highly scientific ori-

Sigmund Freud

entation of the approaches we have thus far examined. Sigmund Freud, who gave us the psychoanalytic view, was arguably the greatest single overall contributor to our understanding of the animating principles which underlie human behavior and cognition. Freud's methods were both subjective and objective. He was subjective in that much of his theorizing was strongly flavored by the analysis of his own personal mental life (self-analysis), and objective in that he developed a scientific approach to the study of unconscious behavior.

Freud's explanation of human behavior is one of complex psychodynamics or psychological forces controlled by *unconscious* forces. The rules of behavior adopted by civilization force human beings to *repress* many of their biological drives that had served the human species well before it became highly civilized.

As Freud developed his psychoanalytic *clinical* methods two of his most important themes were constantly revised: his work on dreams (*The Interpretation of Dreams,* 1900) and the drives of sexuality and aggression, key drives of human behavior. Freud felt the dream to be "the royal road to the unconscious." During sleep, he thought repressed material reached a harmless perceptual level of expression and relief—the dream.

In his essays on sexuality Freud introduced the concept of sexual drive *sublimation.* Rather than expressing our sexual drives directly, society may require us to repress them so that they express themselves in dreams, in *neurotic behavior,* or culturally acceptable behavior, such as the arts, science, or philosophy. Freud felt that civilized people are discontented, unhappy, and stressed beneath their appearances because so many natural urges (mostly sexual) cannot be directly expressed. He postulated that the more a particular society thwarts direct expressions of these instinctual drives the more the members of that society are discontented.

While few psychologists today would embrace all of what Freud had to say about human psychodynamics, his work had widely influenced thought in nearly every discipline which studies the nature of humanity. Freud's feelings about man's instinctual urges of aggression led him to be fearful for the future of humankind. For example, he felt the brutality of wars to be an expression of man's natural instincts. However, Freud wanted us to openly attempt to understand how the dynamics of the repressed material of the unconscious is affected by civilization so that we might free our intellects to become what we can become—to mature beyond the present "childhood" of humankind.

The Humanistic View

Thus far, the approaches to understanding psyche that have been described have not stressed the role of the individual person's phenomenal world as the significant animating principle in their life. How much of your behavior is the result of you being you—a unique being in the world? How free is the unique animating principle of you to become what you can become? This is an important question for humanistic psychology. This emphasis on the special meaning of the individual makes the animal and machine studies of other approaches seem somewhat irrelevant.

Much of humanistic psychology is concerned with how people perceive and feel life as they come to understand themselves and others and to

Carl Rogers

become the person they can. For example, the educational system in which people find themselves has a profound effect on what they ultimately become. And, naturally, humanistic psychology has much to say about education. Humanistic psychology touches us all in this area, and what it has to say about education reveals much about this approach. Humanistic psychologist Leo Buscaglia has written a good deal in critical areas of education. In his important little book entitled simply *Love* (1972) he has this to say:

> Education should be the process of helping everyone to discover his uniqueness, to teach him how to develop that uniqueness, and then to show him how to share it because that's the only reason for having anything. Imagine what this world would be like if all along the way you had people say to you, "It's good that you're unique; it's good that you're different. Show me your differences so that maybe I can learn from them." But we still see the process again and again of trying to make everyone like everybody else.

Carl Rogers, widely known for a special approach to *psychotherapy* which he called *patient-* or *client-centered therapy,* has developed a student-centered approach to teaching. By centering the direction, content, and structure of teaching on students, Carl Rogers (1961) has been able to bring out and develop the uniqueness of each of his students. Because, as Leo Buscaglia has pointed out, much of our experience with being a high school student has traditionally not been aimed at bringing out the uniqueness of each person, most college students encounter a difficulty with *student-centered teaching.* Students who expect to be told what to study are usually at a loss at first when this job is put into their hands. But humanistic psychologists have found that once the students come to truly feel accepted in this situation, they are on the road to develop themselves as persons and self-directed learners. One of Carl Rogers' 1961 students, Samuel Tenenbaum, who was a professor himself at the time, put the experience of finally adjusting to student-centered teaching in these words: "In the process, we all felt elevated, freer, more accepting of ourselves and others, more open to new ideas, trying hard to understand and accept." There are few who would disagree that these are important goals of any type of education.

How Should You Think About the Various Views or Approaches to Psychology?

We have briefly described five of the traditional major views or theories of modern psychology. Each of these views holds a part of the truth in explaining the animating principles of mind and each helps in understanding human behavior and cognition. It would be a mistake to rigidly categorize the men and women who represent the various approaches. Each of these scientists, practicing psychologists, and students of human behavior has broad understandings of psychology. The behaviorist probably understands what the humanist is trying to say, and the humanist probably understands what the behaviorist is saying. It is just that, for the time being, psychologists who strongly represent a particular point of view feel that it is best to focus their attention on what concerns them most in order to contribute the most to our understanding.

However, you (or any animal) always act as a whole. As you interact with the environment (behaviorism), you think (cognitive approach), your behavior is the function of biochemical activities (neurobiological approach), you are influenced by forces of which you are not immediately aware (psychoanalytic approach), and you are a unique, striving human being (humanistic approach). This means that while there have traditionally been many more or less separate views of the principles which animate behavior, we can't really take the psyche of human beings apart as it seems the various views would have us do. Each of the views represents a necessary part of the intricate puzzle which underlies human behavior and cognition. So, it will be a great advantage if we conceive psychology's views of the person from an *integrated perspective*—to view them as forming an integrated whole, to view them as they really are.

What Special Outlooks and Hopes Does the Author Bring to Psychology?

An integrative perspective approach will certainly help us bring together the traditional views of psychology, but it will do much more. It is my desire to help you understand how everything in psychology fits together. My approach is an integrative and unifying one that focuses attention on the basic concepts and underlying principles that apply throughout the entire body of knowledge of psychology.

The Common Organization of Knowledge in Psychology

Each of the chapters in this book has been organized in a common way—according to the four integrative levels of scientific activity presented near the beginning of this chapter. These four levels stretch across the various chapters of this book so that all of the *persisting philosophical questions, theories, methods and findings* appear and reappear in a variety of interrelated contexts—*as they really do in psychology.* This commonalty across chapters will integrate basic concepts and underlying principles among what otherwise would series of more or less seemingly unrelated chapters.

Will this sort of integrative organization really work in helping you understand psychology? Yes, it will. College teachers and psychologists have found that integrative organization helps students more clearly think about and remember psychology, because it is the way your professor does it! I am simply letting you in on your professor's "secret"—the great secret of scientific understanding and thinking. Your Student Preface describes how your professors organize their knowledge in terms of cognitive modeling and mapping.

How Is Research in Psychology Conducted?

At the research methods level in psychology the theory that is adopted also suggests the conditions under which the observations will be made.

Researcher

Studying the Individual: The Case Study Research Method

You may recall that the psychoanalytic view and the humanistic view stressed the importance of studying the individual rather than people in general. The study of a single subject (person) can be carried out in a very scientific manner, with the theory giving directions as to just what will be studied and under what conditions or circumstances. This may or may not include an intensive study of a person's personal story of history.

Interesting examples of *case studies,* or case reports, as they are often called, come from studies of *"retarded savants"* and *"autistic savants."* Two of the reasons these particular studies can be so interesting are: (1) the behavior reveals a phenomenally unique world of experience, and (2) since psychology has not yet developed satisfactory explanations for the savant behavior, it offers a good testing ground for the theories or views that attempt to make such explanations.

The retarded savant has always been regarded as something of a psychological curiosity. The literature mentions only a handful of such people, often children who, although they possess extraordinary abilities in some narrowly limited area, are generally felt to be "demented." These special skills do not usually depend upon abstract reasoning and include caloric calculation, such as the ability to tell the day of the week of a particular date in any year; mathematical manipulation, usually done without resorting to paper and pencil and with amazing rapidity; demonstration of amazing powers of recall or musical *precocity* where memory function is the general basis for the precocity; and occasionally exceptional ability in art. This paper will list both the extraordinary abilities and the results of the psychological tests given to a very unusual idiot savant, but that is not its sole intent. What appears to be lacking in the literature is a developmental *anamnesis* of a case, a report of one of these unusual cases as a person, to give a framework through which the talents and personality of the patient can be made understandable in the light of psychoanalytic theory. Finally, because this particular patient has raised some special questions regarding the role of abstract thinking and creativity, some ideas about the creative process are discussed.

Harriet G., the person this case study was about, had more than one savant ability. Her most profound performances were in musical skills:

> She does not practice, and even though she had not been near the instrument for seven months when I first heard her play, she performed adequately. This ungainly, awkward, inelegant lady, this overgrown five-year-old, became absolutely transformed when I asked her to perform for a seminar at Boston State Hospital. She sat down demurely, stared quietly at the keyboard until we all grew silent, then brought her hands slowly to the keyboard and let them rest a moment. Then she nodded her head and began to play with all the feeling and movement of a concert performer. For that moment in time she was another person.

Detailed study of the individual savant may provide very interesting information:

> One Christmas day when she (Harriet G.) was 35 she announced to the family that she had a dream in which she had seen her father die. This was the first dream that she had ever reported and that day her father died just before the family was to sit down to Christmas dinner.

We will return to retarded savants, and autistic savants and the case method in Chapter 12.

Correlational Research Methods

Sometimes it is interesting and valuable to study the relationship between things which seem to happen together more often than one would expect by chance alone. For example, it may seem to you that the brightest students in each of your classes always is the egg-head type, wears glasses and doesn't exactly look like a movie star. Or it may seem to you that people are friendlier on sunny days than they are on rainy ones. But, is either of these relationships true? There are methods that will help you answer these questions.

Let us take a specific example of a *correlational study.* Have you ever wondered whether or not the moon has an effect on the behavior of human beings? Many people have. After all, who hasn't heard the story of the werewolf and the full moon? Perhaps you have heard people say, "Boy, with the crazy things people are doing tonight, there must be a full moon!" Is there a relationship between the phases of the moon and human behavior? Although this is a very controversial area of study in psychology, a few researchers are convinced there is!

Working within what they call biological tides theory, Arnold Lieber and Carolyn Sherin (1972; Lieber, 1978) have carefully studied the relationship between the phases of the moon and extreme aggressive behavior—homicide. These researchers studied the moon phases which were present when nearly 2,000 homicides were committed. Figure 1.2 illustrates the findings of their study, and many similar to it. While these are not as yet conclusive, there does seem to be a complex and meaningful relationship between the phases of the moon and human behavior. During the new-moon and full-moon phases, when the gravitational pull of the moon and sun combine, there seems to be a significant increase in the number of homicides. The biological tides theory directs our attention to the possible effects of the new and full moons because this is when the strong spring tides occur in the oceans. Perhaps something like the spring tides also occurs in the biology of the human body. Because causal effects are not shown in correlational studies, these methods are often surrounded with controversy of one sort or another. Sometimes we do not have the knowledge to perform causal type studies, as the case of the phases of the moon. The correctional study is extremely valuable in psychology and can give us predictive information concerning human behavior. It also provides a rich source of ideas which may eventually become studies where causal effects can be shown between variables.

Studying Behavior in the Natural Setting: Naturalistic Observation Research

When behavior is studied in its natural setting many things are happening at once. It is almost impossible to determine what is related to what unless one has some idea what to look for. While it may provide more description than explanation, even in the naturalistic observation method a theory or point of view is critically helpful. For example, if someone sets about to observe the behavior of baboons in their natural setting, that person must have some idea about

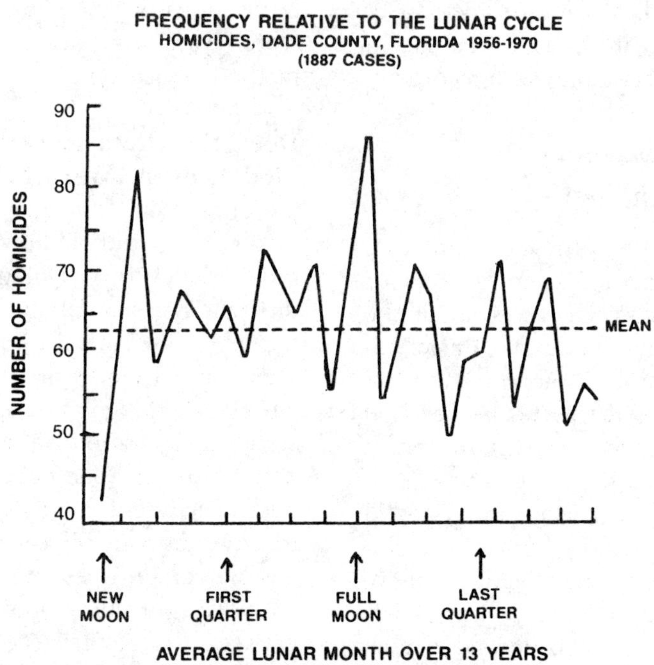

Figure 1.2 Frequency of Lunar Homicides, Dade County, Florida, 1956–1970

why studying baboons might be important. Why would a psychologist be interested in baboons? The theory involved helps to answer this question. For example, Jane Goodall is working within a general theory framework of the theory of evolution when she:

1. records certain field observations under certain conditions—and does not record certain other observations.
2. draws certain parallels to humans, for example in the tool-using analogy.

Proto-tool-using behavior among chimpanzees would only be an observation worth recording if some sort of theory were tying complex tool-using behavior among humans to simple forms of tool-using behavior among chimps. Evolutionary theory is just such a theory. Likewise the "social behavior" of baboon troops would not necessarily be recorded, or even noticed, if the field observer were not assuming some sort of evolution of social behavior. Being in the field is an excellent way to observe and collect unified systems of information. The wholeness of events is fractured as little as possible.

Human children are also studied in the natural setting of various environments. In studying how relationships form between children and how play behavior is developed, they might be studied on the playground as a natural setting. Again, these studies require some sort of theory to guide the researcher as to what is and is not a significant observation worth recording.

Research in the Laboratory: Experimental Psychology

Up to this point examples of research methods discussed have not permitted researchers or clinicians to make *causal inferences* about the variables being studied. For example, David Viscount could not show that Harriet G.'s savant behavior was caused by her particular personal history, especially with her mother (although there are single subject case reports where cause can be inferred). Arnold Lieber and Carolyn Sherin also could not show that the moon causes homicides, and Jane Goodall cannot show a causal link between chimps using tools and human beings using tools. However, much research in psychology does permit causal inferences to be made between variables.

In studies done in the laboratory a great deal of *control* over variables is possible. Variables of the environment and of the person or organism can be controlled to the point where only one type of variable is left free to vary. In laboratory situations the basic job of the researcher's methodology is to establish conditions so that the variation in only one type of variable precedes the behavior to be observed.

For this methodological framework we can define "cause" in the laboratory situation as follows:

> "If variation in variable-one and *only* variable-one can be observed to precede variation in variable-two, then variation in variable-one may be said to *cause* the variation in variable-two."

Another way to put this is to say variable-two *depends* on a variation of variable-one. For this reason variable-two, the behavioral variable, is usually referred to as the *dependent variable*. Variable-one, because it is varied by the researcher or clinician, has been called the *research variable*, the *experimental variable*, and often, the *independent variable*. Since in the laboratory methodology the behavior truly depends on the variation of the research variable, it seems best to refer to environmental and organismic variables as dependent variables. Outside of the methodological arrangements of some type of control these terms don't really apply. In other words, research variables and dependent variables are methodological terms.

Does the Brain Actually Make Cognitive Models of the World? An interesting example of studying behavior in the laboratory has involved the study of how the brain makes cognitive models of the things in the world. Many different types of laboratory studies have supported the idea that the brain is a natural pattern seeker and a model maker. For example, Kosslyn (1985) designed experiments that required student subjects to scan distances in their imaginations on an island they had studied previously. The findings of these experiments showed that the amount of scanning time required to answer certain questions about objects on the island was directly proportional to the distances between the objects (see Figure 1.3). Kosslyn concluded that when we think our imaginations use little models of the real world.

VARIATION IN EITHER ONE ENVIRONMENTAL VARIABLE OR ONE ORGANISMIC VARIABLE (VARIABLE — 1) → Precedes and leads to → VARIATION IN A BEHAVIORAL VARIABLE (VARIABLE — 2)

Figure 1.3 Controlling Variables in Psychological Research

More recently Bower (1994) has used computers that simulate brain activities to perform experiments that combine the cognitive and neurobiological approaches we discussed earlier. Bower has attempted to find out how the brain actually thinks and solves problems. He concluded that, "We're basically model-driven systems. We have this model running inside (our heads) of what the world's like, and we (our brains) collect data accordingly" (p. 29). The implication of these experiments is that without models our brains could not think and solve problems at all! This same idea is discussed in the Student Preface of this book.

If we insert the particulars of Kosslyn's laboratory study of imagination into the methodological definition of "cause" offered earlier, it would look like this:

> "If variation is distance between objects, and only variation in distance between objects can be observed to precede variation in scanning time, then distance between objects may be said to cause the variation in scanning time."

You can see how important it is for the researcher to be sure that all other variables that might somehow affect scanning time are controlled by the laboratory methodology. The problem of truly naming and controlling all possible variables that might lead to changes in the dependent variable is the fundamental problem for laboratory studies.

What Are Intervening Variables? There is one general class of variables which must be mentioned. You will recall that in the cognitive, psychoanalytic, and humanistic views there has been a very strong emphasis upon what might be going on inside the black box to account for the observed relationship between the environment and behavior, or the person and his/her behavior. These "goings-on" inside the black box also can be thought of as variables. For example, when you say, "John has a good memory" or "John has a high intelligence," you are talking about things which go on inside of him (his nervous systems). You cannot see his memory or his intelligence, but you know he has them. And you know memory and intelligence vary, both within John and between John and other people you know. Variables of this type, which seem to account for the relationship you see between John and his behavior, or the environment and his behavior, are called *intervening variables.* As you might guess, intervening variables have a lot to do with the particular view or theory which proposes their nature. For example, the cognitive view might suggest processes, levels, and diagrams to show how memory intervenes to explain behavior; on the other hand, the neurobiological view might suggest the intervening properties of ribonucleic acid (RNA) as an intervening variable. Figure 1.4 illustrates the relationship between research, intervening, and dependent variables.

Clinical and Experimental Research: How Are They Different?

There are two fundamental methodological approaches in psychology. The one you have probably heard the most about is usually called *clinical psychology* or *differential psychology.* This approach is essentially interested in human differences and human problems. Most psychologists work as professionals or do research in clinically related areas. The second approach, which you probably have heard little about, is usually called experimental psychology. *Experimental psychology* has the aim of establishing law-like knowledge of human and animal behavior which would apply to everyone, rather than a particular individual. An experimental psychologist might be just as interested in the behavior of rats as in yours. With the clinical psychologist, your personal behavior would always be the ultimate concern.

So, we actually have two types of psychology—one interested in human differences, and

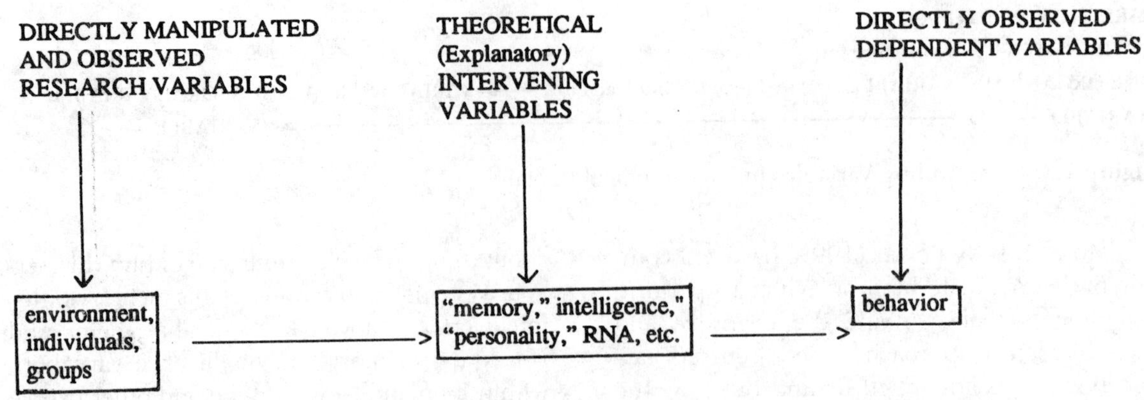

Figure 1.4 Relationship Between Research, Independent and Dependent Variables

one in law-like knowledge—which would apply similarly to everyone and in most cases to animals. The differences between these two types of psychology can also be shown in the illustration of theory fundamental methodological approaches to the study of behavior. In the differential or clinical model (Figure 1.5) attention is focused upon the person or organismic variable as the independent variable. The methodology sets up the situation so that environmental variables are held constant. On the other hand, in the experimental model (Figure 1.6) attention is focused upon the environmental variable as the independent variable. Of course, in both of these models the dependent variable is the behavioral variable. An example of each of these models will help remove their abstractness. The first example will illustrate how clinical psychologists might study or determine differences in intelligence. In Figure 1.7, you can see that IQ is a function of the person or organism taking the intelligence evaluation. You can see also that the environmental sources of variation have been held constant by administering to each person exactly the same IQ test, under the same circumstances (the test *is* the environment). IQ is a function of the person (IQ score = f(person)). The second example (Figure 1.8) will illustrate how an experimental psychologist might determine a law-like relationship between the color of an emergency light and reaction time. A

The Differential or Clinical Model

$S^1 \longrightarrow O^1 \longrightarrow R^1$

$S^1 \longrightarrow O^2 \longrightarrow R^2$

$S^1 \longrightarrow O^3 \longrightarrow R^3$

$R = f(0)$

Figure 1.5 Behavior Is a Function of Person or Organismic Variation; Environment Is Held Constant

The Experimental Model

$S^1 \longrightarrow O^1 \longrightarrow R^1$

$S^2 \longrightarrow O^1 \longrightarrow R^2$

$S^3 \longrightarrow O^1 \longrightarrow R^3$

$R = f(S)$

Figure 1.6 Behavior Is a Function of Environment Variation; Person or Organismic Behavior Is Held Constant

S^1(IQ test) ——>O^1(John) ——>R^1(IQ = 115)

S^1(IQ test) ——>O^2(Mary) ——>R^2(IQ = 118)

S^1(IQ test) ——>O^3(Paul) ——>R^3(IQ = 140)

Figure 1.7 I.Q. as a Function of Intelligence Evaluation

research psychologist working in laboratories for the National Aeronautics and Space Administration (NASA) might want to know if an astronaut's reaction time could be improved by using appropriately colored warning lights on the instrument panel. It does not matter who the astronaut is.

If this were an actual experiment, you could see that reaction time (RT) is a function of the environmental variable (hue of emergency light). The organismic or person variable was, in effect, held constant by using *randomized groups* (r-groups). Also, if this had been an actual experiment, we perhaps would have discovered a law of behavior (at least for humans). This law might be something like this: The shorter the electromagnetic wavelength of a visual signal of color, the shorter the reaction time in emergency situations. Might this hypothetical experiment be in any way related to the color/muscle strength experiment? What types of environmental and person or organismic variables should be controlled in laboratory study of the effects of hue on muscle strength? We will return to various research methods many times in later chapters. It is very important for you to realize that, using a little ingenuity, any of the topics which were discussed in this research methodology section,—the "retarded savant," the effects of the moon phases on behavior, chimpanzee behavior in the natural setting, or the effect of color on muscle strength,—could be studied using nearly any of the methodologies. For example, how might you study the effect of the phases of the moon on behavior using the case study method? Why might you wish to undertake such a study?

How Are the Research Findings in Psychology Expressed?

At the *empirical* level, each of the five major views of psychology directs us to pay attention to certain observable events and not so much to others. For example, recall that the behavioral view focuses nearly exclusively on observable stimulus and bioelectric events such as those measured by the EEG. It is important to realize that all of the five major views must come face-to-face with the problem of attaining objectivity at the empirical level. That is, each view, whether it be the behavioral or the humanistic, must suggest what we are to observe as acceptable evidence for its explanations of human behavior. Also, each view usually tells us what is or is not to be accepted as support.

Since we have pictured the mind contained within a black box, we may note that psychologists who hold various views have to find empirical support for themselves from three general sources. The following terms and examples will be very important to you throughout this book—as they are throughout psychology.

Objectively Observable Psychology

Variables of the Environment: How Does the Environment Vary?

Stimuli: Stimulus variables include variations in lighting, sounds, temperature, odors, tastes, etc. Essentially, any part of the environment, or its complex arrays that you might become aware of, could be called a stimulus variable.

S^1(red light) ——>O^1(r-group) ——>R^{RT} = .6 sec.

S^2(green lt.) ——>O^1(r-group) ——>R^{RT} = .4 sec.

S^3(blue lt.) ——>O^1(r-group) ——>R^{RT} = .2 sec.

Figure 1.8 Reaction Time as a Function of Environmental Variable

Variables of Persons: How Do People Vary?

Person or Organic Variables: Organismic variables include variations in organism characteristics like height, weight, sex, hair color, eye color (obviously, genetic endowment), educational background (or experimental conditioning background in the case of animals), personal experiences and personal perceptions, attitudes, vales, etc. Essentially, any characteristic of the person or organism.

Variables of Behavior and Cognition: How Does What We Do Vary?

Response Variables: Response variables include variations in speaking, writing, walking, standing still, blinking, etc. Essentially, any observable movement or activity of a person or organism. As you will discover later, it is very important to include neurobiological events, such as those which are measured by the EEG, as response variables.

Each of the five major views of psychology puts a different emphasis upon the importance of these sources of variation. Each forms empirically grounded *operational descriptions* of the various aspects of behavior and cognition. Since in real-life situations involving the whole person, stimuli, the person and his responses are in constant interaction, all these are integrated in the operational descriptions. These aspects of behavior and cognition which are thus operationally described include the many you would expect psychology to include, for example, personality, memory, learning, thinking, and intelligence. As an example of how these operational descriptions actually look, let us see how "love" (since we started this chapter with the love of Eros and Psyche) has been operationally described. At the one extreme the humanistic psychologist may offer a very *open* empirical operational description of love. He or she may even wish to refer to the description as nonscientific. Leo Buscaglia (1972), a humanistic psychologist, has offered this description:

> Love is a learned, emotional reaction. It is a response to a learned group of stimuli and behaviors. Like all learned behavior, it is affected by the interaction of the learner with his environment, the person's learning ability, and the type and strength of the reinforces present; that is, which people respond, how they respond and to what degree they respond to his expressed love. Love is a dynamic interaction, lived every second of our lives. Therefore, it is everywhere at every time. For this reason, I am put off by the phrase, "to fall in love." I do not believe that one falls *in* or *out* of love. One learns to react in a particular way to a certain degree to a specific stimulus . . . It seems more accurate to say one *grows* in love . . . Man is either constantly *growing* in love, or dying. Therefore, his actions as well as his interactions will change throughout his life. (pp. 90–91)

This humanistic approach to love can be described in terms of stimuli, responses, and person variables.

Let us compare the humanistic operational description to a cognitive one. Social psychologist Zick Rubin (1970) has operationally described love as ". . . an attitude held by a person toward a particular other person, involving predispositions to think, feel, and behave in certain ways toward that other person." Romantic love, within this theory, is thought to consist of three measurable components:

1. *Affiliative and dependent need*—for example, "If I could never be with ____, I would feel miserable."
2. *Predisposition to help*—for example, "If ____ were feeling badly, my first duty would be to cheer him/her up."
3. *Exclusiveness and absorption*—for example, "I feel I can confide in ____ about virtually anything."

To help determine whether or not the above three components could really gauge romantic love, Rubin measured the degree to which couples with high scores on the love scale gazed into one another's eyes versus the gazing done by low scoring couples. The study of eye gazing both supported the idea that the romantic love was actually being measured and that people in love do tend to gaze into one another's eyes more than those not in love.

It should be clear from the comparison of the humanistic view and the cognitive view on the aspects of the empirical variables of psychol-

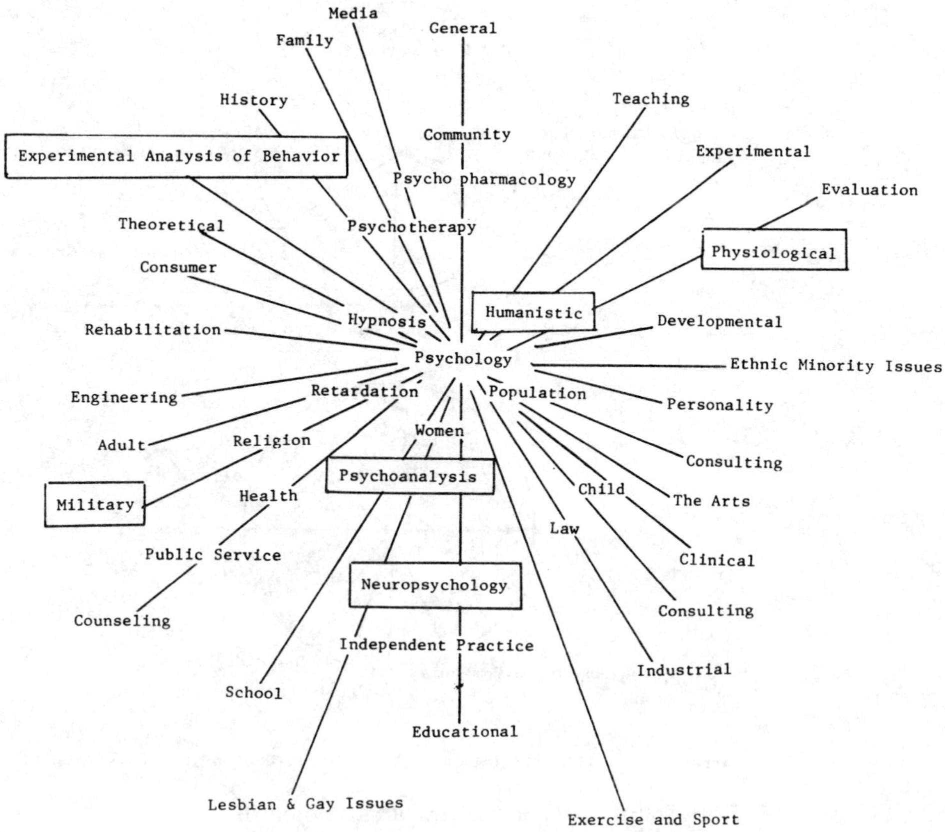

Figure 1.9 Divisions of the American Psychological Association

ogy, that they both attempt to operationally describe the topic of love. Since both have these organizational similarities, we can see that while the approaches to love are slightly different, they have many things in common.

The love example illustrates what a unified systems view can offer. At the empirical level, note how the variables of the environment, the person, and the behavior, are used (methodology) in operational descriptions. This will permit you to see many parallels throughout the differ-

The Place	The Work
Air Force Human Resources Laboratory	Aircrew Training Effectiveness Personnel Qualifications Tests Visual Displays and Image Generators Artificial Intelligence
Army Institute for Behavioral and Social Sciences	Manpower and Personnel Human Factors Education and Training Simulation and Training Devices
Central Intelligence Agency (CIA)	Psychological Research Psychological Assessment Industrial/Organizational Psychology Human Factors Psychophysiology

Figure 1.10 Aspects of Military Psychology

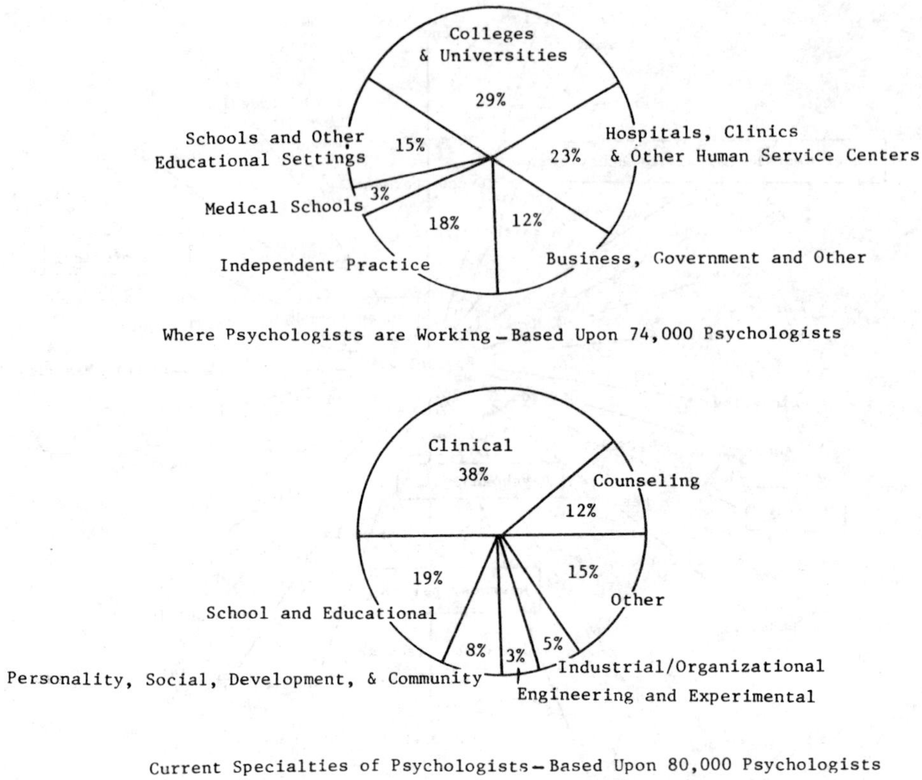

Figure 1.11 Current Work Settings and Specialties of Psychologists

ent units of this book. These parallels are so important to your understanding of psychology that a simplified and more complete explanation of how topics can be operationally described is presented in Appendix A of this book.

Part Two: Applications of Psychology

In the first part of this chapter you have learned that there are many views within psychology, and you learned that the methods of study psychologists use a great variety of human and animal activities. These discussions provided you with some indirect examples of the kinds of things psychologists do in their work. This part of the chapter will give more direct examples of psychologists' work. First, we will examine the actual specialties of psychologists in the United States and their work settings. Second, we will briefly examine the literature of psychology. Together, these two descriptions will provide a global indication of the kinds of things psychologists do.

Specialties in the Application of Psychology

When many people think about what psychologists do, they likely think of the classic example of a person lying on a couch being "analyzed" by a psychologist or a *psychiatrist.* To some degree this picture of a psychologist at work is true. However, the great majority of psychologists do other sorts of things in their work.

What Are Some of the Professional Careers in Psychology?

The largest organization of professional psychologists is the American Psychological Association (APA), some 72,000 members strong. These psychologists belong to a variety of subgroups or divisions of the APA. Figure 1.9 illustrates the 47 current divisions of the APA. You can begin to appreciate the very broad variety of work specialties of psychologists. Note that divisions of the experimental analysis of behavior, physiological and comparative, clinical neuropsychology, psychoanalysis, and humanistic psychology are included. These divisions are closely related to the five traditional views within psychology. The Division for the Experimental Analysis of behavior would include psychologists who hold the more behavioristic and cognitive views. The Division of Military Psychology may be especially puzzling to you. Figure 1.10 presents examples of what military psychologists do. It is worth noting the Army Research Institute employs the greatest number of research psychologists in the United States. The great number of research psychologists employed by the military attests to the critical importance of both *pure research psychology* and *applied psychology*. Figure 1.11 provides an overall picture of what psychologists do and where they work.

An Integrated Approach to Psychology in the Real World

The true test of any way of thinking about psychology (or anything else) is to ask, how does it work in the real world? In this regard, how has the adoption of an integrated applied approach fared in the real world? Does a unified approach really help? The answer is clear. Integrated approaches have become the major trend where psychology meets the real world—*because they work best even in the most complex situations.*

Diagnosis and Treatment in Psychology and Psychiatry

In *psychiatry* the unified systems approach has become a major trend (Kaplan & Saddock, 1985) because it offers a real way of taking into account "the complexities of a very difficult field." In addition, the American Psychiatric Association has adopted a standard way of diagnosing mental disorders in terms of five interrelated axes (elements) of systems. This standard diagnostic approach represents a unified systems approach. The details of the diagnostic system are presented in Chapter 9.

Fitting Human Beings to Complex Machine Systems in Engineering Psychology

In engineering psychology a unified systems approach has been the usual approach for many years. But as *man-machine relationships* (including you sitting in front of a word processor) have become more and more complex, a unified systems approach is the only approach that works.

Bringing It All Together

Psychology has the incredible task of understanding the human mind through the scientific study of human and animal behavior and cognition. Many views and methods on how to accomplish this task have contributed to our present understanding. We hope our integrated approach to psychology helps clarify and integrate this overall picture of modern psychology.

The work of psychology touches every area of human activity in a great diversity of work settings. As psychology is applied to more and more complex human problems, it becomes more and more necessary to take into account the whole human being in his or her whole situation. An integrated approach will offer the best framework through which psychology can achieve this goal.

Each of the chapters of this book have been organized much like the first one. After a brief overview story is presented which captures a major idea for the chapter, the persisting philosophical questions at hand will be posed, then the traditional views will be presented, finally followed by the standard methods and findings that naturally flow from them.

Glossary

analogy: A similar or parallel situation or relationship.

anamnesis: Information about patients and their background that might be helpful in understanding the onset of their disorder.

applied psychology: Research and work in psychology may be undertaken for pure reasons, that is, for the advancement of knowledge, or for applied reasons, that is, to help solve some particular human problem.

autistic savants: Persons who, even though they have some mental disability or disorder, have an extremely high degree of some specific ability. These special abilities may involve spectacular memory, mathematical calculation, art, or musical performances.

behaviorism: A theoretical explanation of mind based on objectively observable behavior.

bioelectrical activity: All biological activity contains a measurable electrical component.

black box: The mind may be thought of as a black box. Nothing is really known about what is going on inside the black box in an objective sense, therefore we are left only to speculate about how "mind" operates.

case studies: A study method which helps to explain a single individual or group (such as a family). All available pertinent information, for example, medical tests and psychological test results, are brought to bear in understanding the case.

causal inferences: The idea that one thing or event makes another thing or event occur.

cerebral cortex: The more recently developed or evolved outer "bark" of the brain where great detail in thought and action occur.

client-centered therapy: Therapy that emphasizes the potential of self-direction in patients to solve their own problems. Clients are helped to mobilize their own psychic resources.

clinical: Concerning the diagnosis and treatment of individual patients.

clinical psychology: A general research method and orientation which attempts to show the relationship between the person or group and behavior.

cognition: A general term for the processes by which an organism gains awareness and knowledge.

consciousness: In humans, awareness of the environment and of the self, and the distinction between them.

control: In research, the manipulation of either the environment or people to insure that a given behavior is the result of only its selected aspects.

correlational study: A study of the relationship between two things or variables.

cybernetics: The comparative study of control mechanisms in machines and in organisms.

dependent variable: The behavior or response under study in psychological research that depends upon some aspect of either the environment or the person(s).

differential psychology: See clinical psychology.

electroencephalograph: A technique used to measure the electrical activity emanating from various parts of the brain. The technique can detect the degree to which the brain is aroused, and brain disturbances.

electromagnetic spectrum: The entire spectrum of wavelengths of electromagnetic radiation. Visible light, with all of its possible colors, is the result of the impingement of this spectrum upon the visual system.

experimental psychology: A general research method and orientation which attempts to show the relationship between the environment and behavior.

experimental variable: The aspect of the environment or person(s) that is manipulated by the researcher so that the observed behavior is the result of only selected aspects of the environment or person(s).

general systems theory: A holistic or unifying view of all the sciences. Unification comes about through organizational principles common to all sciences or theoretical views in general.

genetic endowment: The genetic makeup an organism receives from its parent(s).

humanistic psychology: An approach in psychology which emphasizes the wholeness and uniqueness of each individual. Each person is thought to be capable of self-direction.

idiot savants: See autistic savants.

independent variable: See experimental variable.

information processing: Processes that reduce uncertainty in a course of action for either a machine or an organism.

instinctual drives: Strong inherited motivational and emotional tendencies which are unconscious in origin.

intervening variables: Aspects of psyche which are postulated to account for the relationships between the environment or the person and behavior. Like psyche, these variables are not directly observable, although their neurobiological bases may be.

man-machine relationships: Any system in which human beings and machines interact to perform a function.

mind-body problem: The problem of determining how the mind is interrelated to the body.

mind-science problem: Mind is not open to observation. Science requires that its subject matter be open to observation. Therefore, science cannot directly study mind.

natural phenomenon: Any thing or event which occurs in nature.

neurobiological activity: Biological activities of nerve cells in the brain that carry out its perceptual and behavioral processes.

neurotic behavior: The behavior of a person (or animal) who has unwarranted fears or anxieties of certain situations.

new psychology: Psychology that in the late nineteenth century began to move away from a general "armchair" approach to a more scientific laboratory-based approach.

objectivity: Open to observation by anyone, therefore free from bias.

operational descriptions: A statement of the operations necessary to objectively observe what is meant by a term. This procedure permits the scientific study of the term.

Oxford English Dictionary: A many-volumed dictionary that contains the history of the usage of English words since they first appeared in written form.

past responses to stimuli: The complete history of interactions between an organism and its environment(s).

person or organismic variables: Ways in which people or organisms differ from one another.

phenomenal world: The world as the individual subjectively experiences it.

precocity: Very rapid or early development.

present situation: The present environment as it is perceived moment by moment by an organism.

pressing of a bar: In laboratory animal studies, the animal would press a small bar to obtain a reward. Bar pressing is objectively observable behavior.

proto-tool using: Earliest or primitive tool using.

psyche: The illusive animating principle in all living things—the mind.

psychiatrist: A licensed physician who practices the prevention, diagnosis, and treatment of mental disorders.

psychiatry: A specialty within the medical sciences which deals with the prevention, diagnosis, and treatment of mental disorders. Both biological and psychotherapeutic techniques are used.

psychoanalysis: Sigmund Freud's analysis of the psyche that includes the development of the relationships of psychological forces from earliest childhood.

psychotherapy: The treatment of mental disorders through any psychological technique. These techniques can include everything from simply talking with the patient to psychoanalysis and "faith cures."

pure psychology: See applied psychology.

randomized groups: A sample of people or animals that has been selected from their representative groups at random. This helps to insure that samples are equivalent.

repress: To stop from entering consciousness.

research variable: See experimental variable.

stimuli: Any physical events which lead to or cause activity in a sense organ.

student-centered teaching: Teaching techniques which emphasize the potential of self-direction in students to learn on their own. Students are helped to mobilize their own learning resources.

subjectivity: Open to observation only by an individual, therefore bias is possible.

sublimation: The redirection of primitive energies into socially acceptable channels.

system: The set of persisting (and usually orderly) interrelationships between parts or elements of a whole.

theory of evolution: The theory that all presently living things developed through a process of selection from other preexisting species.

unconscious: A region or portion of the psyche of which the person is unaware. It is thought to strongly influence behavior.

unified perspective: To view all possible influences and their interrelationships which might affect a person's behavior.

Ideas and Methods: Doing Psychology on Your Own

Lois McDermott

Basic Concept #1—Two Big Ideas

The logo for this course is the elephant. Throughout the lectures you will hear reference to our "encounter with the elephant." The icon of the elephant comes from the Hindu proverb about the search for truth. One day three blind pilgrims were on the path searching for enlightenment when they encountered an obstacle in their path. Upon examination of the obstacle, the first blind seeker exclaimed that they had stumbled upon a dangerous serpent that must be avoided. The second insisted that an enormous wall that must be scaled blocked their way. The third lamented that they had lost their way in a jungle of vines and palms that must be slashed through. Soon, an enormous argument ensued among the pilgrims about the true nature of their encounter. Eventually, a sighted pilgrim passing by paused to listen to the arguments of the blinded (narrow-minded) pilgrims. At last, impatient with the brawl, the sighted one exclaimed, "Behold, the elephant." At that moment the scales fell from the blinded eyes of the pilgrims. The first realized that his "dangerous serpent" was the tail, the second knew that his "brick wall" was the flank and the third grasped that his "palm jungle" was the trunk and ears of the elephant. The moral of the story is that without vision and tolerance for many diverse perspectives, we are unlikely to find the truth about our experience—"We will fail to behold (comprehend) the elephant" (i.e., the true nature of things).

Theory in Psychology. Since the birth of psychology, many learned scholars have struggled with the enormous task of describing, predicting and explaining the human psyche (for our purposes, the "elephant"). In the ensuing hundred years, six major theoretical perspectives have emerged—biological, psychodynamic, behavioral, cognitive, humanistic, and sociocultural. Theory is the **first big idea** in Chapter 1. The purpose of theory is to provide an encompassing explanation of empirical data. In the proverb, the claim of the second blind pilgrim that his experience of firmness, breadth, and height of the obstacle was a "wall to be scaled" was his **theory** about the nature of the obstacle. From theory comes hypothesis testing and then, hopefully, some truth.

In this course we will be looking at eight major aspects of human experience—*consciousness, motivation, learning, cognition, social behavior, personality, psychological disorders,* and *treatment of disorders.* We can think of each of these aspects as a part of our "elephant." Furthermore, there have been different schools of thought (theories) driving the investigation of each of these subjects. In each case we will look at the major theories that have been used to organize the empirical data. In this way you will have the opportunity to "listen" to the arguments of modern day truth-seekers (e.g., psychologists) about the nature of personality, or motivation, or consciousness. Of course as the proverb would teach us—we need to think of the theories as complementary truths, not mutually exclusive truths; as emerging truths, not absolute truths. We need to keep in mind that the best explanation of any aspect of human experience will be able to encompass the valuable contributions of all of these theories.

Some are impatient to know "which theory is true?" Theories are neither true nor false. Theories are judged by: (a) how well they explain the bulk of current data, (b) how well they can encompass future data, and, (c) how well they provide a useful guide for further inquiry. As we progress in the course we will discuss the ascendance and decline of certain theoretical explanations of the human psyche and experience. We will examine how some theories seem useful for explaining some phenomena but are poorly developed with regard to others. This first lesson in psychological theory, is just that—a first introduction. My goal, however, is that by the end of the course these theories will feel like useful rules of thumb that you can use when you ask questions about the "nature of the elephant."

As students of psychology progress in their education they typically find that they are drawn to one or two theoretical approaches, strongly object to others and are indifferent to the remaining. Most people who become professional psychologists eventually become "schooled" in a certain theoretical approach and gradually lose understanding or appreciation of others. From time to time professional psychologists from different theoretical perspectives get into a row about some feature of human nature or behavior. This often results in further empirical research—collecting data to test or refute some hypothesis generated from a certain theoretical approach. This brings us to the **second big idea**—namely the use of the scientific method to extend our understanding of human nature and behavior.

Method in Psychology. Psychology is defined as the scientific study of the behavior, emotions and mental processes of sentient organisms. Many disciplines such as philosophy, literature, art, and religion delve into the nature and behavior of humans, as well. However, psychology is a field of study that uses the scientific method to do so. Sometimes the research findings of psychologists seem like little more than common sense; sometimes they seem counter to common sense. The **scientific method** is designed to provide us with a certain kind of truth—empirical truth. Philosophy, art, literature and religion also provide "truth" but of an entirely different sort. Because psychology is based on empirical research that requires us to quantify and measure the things we study, psychology cannot undertake the study of some very interesting questions. The other disciplines are designed to address those. However, as you work your way through this course, I hope that you will discover this "empirical approach" to be a powerful, useful way to understanding many important aspects of human nature and behavior (see Appendix A). Some of you may come to prefer the scientific method more than the approaches offered by other disciplines and decide to make a career in psychology.

Psychology Today. As we look to the 21st century it is likely that some of the current perspectives will endure, some decline and all together new ones will emerge.

Psychology, as it is based in empiricism, is destined to grow and change. As we near the end of this century we see the decline of the *humanist* perspective except in the clinical domain. We see the hegemony of *behaviorism* being nudged, nay, thrust aside by the new age of the *cognitive* perspective. The *psychodynamic* perspective, with its origins in Freud's psychoanalytic theory, is leaving psychology and university academia and taking up residence in psychiatry and/or free standing psychoanalytic institutes. The new thinkers in psychology have rejected it as "unscientific" and thus not worthy of a place in the discipline of psychology. The *biological* perspective (biopsychology), the very foundation of modern psychology, is abandoning psychology and headed for newly forming departments of behavioral neuroscience, genetics, physiology and/or endocrinology.

The science of psychology continues to be "mathematized." Ever increasing sophistication in mathematics and statistics are required to keep pace. Computer modeling of social, developmental and physiological phenomena are becoming ever more common. Many new psychology majors are dismayed by the amount of mathematics and natural science required for a BS in psychology and entry into graduate school, to say nothing of the statistics requirements for a Ph.D.

Unit Focus. This unit will introduce you to the five theoretical perspectives on the study of behavior and mental processes and to the research methods that have been prominent in the 20th century. The goal will be to convince you that scientific truth does lie in rigorous method and that psychology does direct inquiry. There is no value free research in psychology—all is done to support or refute a particular hypothesis and in doing so to enhance or degrade a particular view of the human psyche (i.e., theoretical perspective). If all goes well some observant "sighted" seeker of truth will be there when needed to resolve the squabbles of those without the capacity for vision (integration).

Study Objectives

1. Learn the five dominant theoretical perspectives in psychology—biological, psychodynamic, cognitive, behavioral, humanistic.
2. Use these perspectives to explain some social problem such as the high violent crime rate among teenage males.
3. Distinguish between scientific research and armchair psychology (e.g., the common sense, hindsight bias of the lay person).
4. Compare and contrast the three different purposes and goals of psychological research (i.e., description, prediction, and explanation of causation).
5. Learn the different methods used to collect data for each type of research (e.g., descriptive, predictive, explanative) and give examples.

Key Terms

analogy
anamnesis
applied psychology
case studies
causal inferences
cerebral cortex
consciousness
control
correlational study

autistic savants
behaviorism
bioelectrical activity
black box
electromagnetic spectrum
experimental psychology
experimental variable
general systems theory
genetic endowment
humanistic psychology
idiot savants
independent variable
information processing
instinctual drives
intervening variables
man-machine relationships
mind-body problem
mind-science problem
natural phenomenon
client-centered therapy
clinical
clinical psychology
cognition
neurobiological activity
neurotic behavior
new psychology
objectivity
operational descriptions
Oxford English dictionary
past responses to stimuli
personal or organismic variables
phenomenal world
precocity
present situation
pressing of a bar
proto-tool using
psyche
psychiatrist
cybernetics
dependent variable
differential psychology
electroencephalograph
psychiatry
psychoanalysis
psychotherapy
pure psychology
randomized groups
repress
research variable
stimuli
student-centered teaching
subjectivity
sublimation
system
theory of evolution
unconscious
unified perspective

Problem Set 1

1. Gail is interested in how many students in her psych class are Asian or African American, Judeo-Christian or other, male or female, ESL or native English speakers. She asks each student to fill out a questionnaire about these issues.

   1a. What type of research approach is Gail using?

2. Bob wonders if UW students drink more lattés when it's rainy. He obtains the daily January sales records of several latté carts and coffee houses in the U District, as well as the daily weather records for January and compares the sales records with the weather records each day.

   2a. What type of research method is Bob using?

3. What kind of correlation (positive, negative, or zero) would you expect to find between:

   3a. Family income and number of bathrooms in the home?

   3b. Time spent watching TV and time spent reading books?

   3c. Number of umbrellas open and inches of rainfall?

   3d. Level of anxiety and desire to give a speech?

   3e. Age (infancy to age 40) and hours of sleep per 24 hours?

   3f. Favorite color and number of years of education completed?

4. Dr. B asserted that individuals who have depressed relatives (for example, parents or grandparents) are at an increased risk for becoming depressed themselves. Dr. B argued that this is probably due to a "depression gene" which is inherited. Dr. B based her findings on a careful study of three generations of the descendants of depressed people. This study revealed that close relatives of depressed people were more likely to become severely depressed themselves, while distant relatives were more likely to become only mildly depressed themselves.

   4a. What type of research method is Dr. B using?

   4b. Does Dr. B's research involve IV and DV?

   IF YES, what is the IV? What is the DV?

   4c. What is Dr. B's theoretical perspective?

5. Dr. C asserted that people become depressed because they have learned to behave in certain depressed ways. As an example, she cited a case study in which the depressed husband was pampered by his wife and children every time he felt down or "blue." At these times, his wife would prepare his favorite meals and serve them to him in bed, while the children would take care of all of the yard work for him. Dr. C concluded that the husband was being rewarded for being depressed, so naturally he continued to be depressed.

   5a. Which type of research method is Dr. C using?

   5b. Does Dr. C's research involve IV and DV?

   IF YES, what is the IV? What is the DV?

   5c. What is Dr. C's hypothesis?

   5d. What is Dr. C's theoretical perspective?

6. Dr. D asserted that individuals who have experienced early neglect and trauma when they were infants are likely to develop unconscious conflicts which can cause depression. Dr. D asserted that her conclusions were based on her impressions of depressed clients whom she has seen in therapy.

   6a. What type of research method is Dr. D using?

   6b. Does Dr. D's research involve IV and DV?

   IF YES, what is the IV? What is the DV?

   6c. What is Dr. D's hypothesis?

   6d. What is Dr. D's theoretical perspective?

7. Dr. E asserted that certain thinking habits cause depression. He described a study involving 30 college students. At the beginning of the study, the students' level of depression was measured on a scale of 1 to 10, with 1—"not depressed" and 10—"severely depressed." The students were randomly assigned to one of three groups. Group 1 received several lectures telling them that they were ultimately the ones who were responsible for themselves, and that they should blame themselves for every failure, no matter how small. (For example, if they were caught in a traffic jam, this would be their own fault.) Group 2 received several lectures on the types of trees and shrubs found on campus. Group 3 received no lectures. After 1 week, Dr. E measured all of the students' level of depression a second time, using the same scale as before.

   RESULTS: Students in Group 1 were much more depressed at the end of the study, compared to the beginning. No change occurred for the students in Groups 2 and 3. Dr. E concluded that habitually blaming oneself for failure leads to depression.

   7a. What type of research method is Dr. E using?

   7b. Does Dr. E's research involve IV and DV?

   IF YES, what is the IV? What is the DV?

   7c. What is Dr. E's hypothesis?

   7d. What is Dr. E's theoretical perspective?

   7e. Why did Dr. E include Group 2?

   7f. In other words, Dr. E included Group 2 in order to control for a possible ______ variable.

   7g. Groups 2 and 3 are both examples of ______.

8. Dr. Nguyen was also at the conference on depression. He had noticed that more UW students are depressed in the winter than in the summer, and wondered if this was related to the fact that Seattle's winters are characterized by days of very little sunlight. If so, perhaps depressed students who are exposed to "extra" sunlight would become less depressed. At first, he planned to simply expose depressed students to light and see what happens to their mood. However, he thought that depressed students who were told to do something which would help them might become less depressed just because of the "extra attention" they received, rather than because of the actual effects

of whatever they did. This made Dr. Nguyen realize that he had to design a more complicated experiment.

During November, Dr. Nguyen gave all of his students the Beck Depression Inventory (a standard questionnaire which measures level of depression) in order to measure their level of depression. 40 students scored as depressed. Dr. Nguyen divided these 40 students on a "first come, first serve" basis into 4 groups. The students in Group 1 were each given a special bank of high-intensity, full-spectrum lights (similar to natural sunlight) and instructed to sit in front of the lights for 30 minutes each evening. Group 2 was given the same light apparatus but normal-strength household bulbs were used. The students in Group 3 were told to sit in the same location in their home for 30 minutes each evening. The students in Group 4 were not contacted until after the study was over and therefore didn't receive any instructions. Each week, Dr. Nguyen contacted the students in Groups 1, 2, and 3 to make sure that they were all carrying out their instructions. After one month, all 40 students took the Beck Depression Inventory again, and Dr. Nguyen compared their scores before and after the experiment.

RESULTS: The students in Group 1 were significantly less depressed at the end of the experiment. The students in Groups 2 and 3 showed no change, while the students in Group 4 became slightly more depressed.

8a. What is Dr. Nguyen's theoretical perspective?

8b. What is his research hypothesis?

8c. What type of research is this?

8d. What kind of statistics can he use?

8e. What is the IV?

8f. What is the DV?

8g. Groups 2, 3, and 4 are each examples of ______.

8h. Why did Dr. Nguyen include Group 2?

8i. Why did Dr. Nguyen include Group 3?

8j. Why did Dr. Nguyen include Group 4?

8k. In other words, Dr. Nguyen included Groups 3 and 4 to control for the effects of two possible ______ variables.

8l. What serious flaw do you see in Dr. Nguyen's design?

9. The last person to present her findings at the depression conference was a student named Donna Donnabother. She had noticed that some of her friends felt less depressed when they exercised regularly, and decided to conduct an experiment to see if this was true of other people as well.

   She placed an announcement in the waiting room of several health clinics and health stores, soliciting volunteers to participate in a study of exercise and depression. When subjects called, she had them come to a room at the University and take the Beck Depression Inventory. Subjects who scored as "moderately depressed" were put into the study. She let these subjects choose which group they would like to participate in: Group 1, which involved aerobic classes three times a week at a posh health club, and Group 2, which involved weight lifting at the University once a week with a 1-on-1 training coach.

   To provide a control group for her study, Ms. Donnabother asked students in her Psych 101 class "who have been feeling depressed lately" to take the Beck Depression Inventory. Students who scored "moderately depressed" were selected for the control group.

   At the end of three months, every subject in both exercise groups and in the control group were interviewed by clinical psychology graduate students who were enrolled in a course that was training them to assess depressive symptoms in adults.

RESULTS: Subjects in Group 1 were much less depressed at the end of the study. Subjects in Group 2 were also much less depressed at the end of the study. Subjects in Group 3 were somewhat more depressed at the end of the study than they were at the beginning. Ms. Donnabother presented her findings at the conference, and concluded that exercise reduces depression.

The psychologists at the conference raised numerous criticisms about Ms. Donnabother's research design. Some of the psychologists raised questions about the reliability, validity, and generalizability of her study. Others asserted that there were several possible confounding variables in her study. Still others questioned the quality of her control group. Finally, some psychologists criticized the ways in which Ms. Donnabother operationalized her IV and DV. List the flaws in Ms. Donnabother's study.

See Appendix C for answers to problem set.

2

The Nervous System and Behavior

The Robot: Human Equivalence by 2010?

In Woburn, Massachusetts (and elsewhere), quiet developments are taking place which will doubtlessly change our concepts of everything we know. In the words of a preeminent researcher in the science of robotics, Dr. Hans Moravec (1998), Carnegie-Mellon University, who is behind many of these developments: "It is clear to me that we are on the threshold of a change in the universe comparable to the transition from non-life to life." Think about that for a moment. Please do not read on! Read that quote again.

What could Hans Moravec possibly be talking about? What could be a change as fundamental as the change from non-life to life? A Honda research team has developed, and continues to develop, autonomous mobile robot systems that can already do many of the things you can do. Figure 2.1 is an illustration of one of the advanced Honda robot systems that helps, and in some cases replaces, humans.

The number of autonomous functions the free-roaming robots can perform is incredible. In a typical day on the job the robot can move about prison corridors mapping its "beat" just as any new human guard on the job must be shown his beat. Once mapping is completed, the robot "knows" its way around. The robot's sensory systems can detect the presence of human beings by vision and by odor. This information can be processed by the robot's limited computer brain even in unstructured and unmapped circumstances, and the information can be sent on to other robots and to humans in a central control room. The robot guard can ask a series of questions to provide information about an intruder and can then decide what limited action might be taken under the circumstances. Since the robot is almost indestructible (a distinct advantage over its human counterpart), it can take quite a beating and still receive, process, and transmit information. This, of course could be very valuable during a prison riot or if the robot were in the process of neutralizing explosives. The robot will attempt to retreat if it senses it is being battered or "hurt." Finally, the robot is able to sense and track its own internal states of well-being. For example, if it needs to replenish its autonomous energy source it again "knows" it should go to one of the recharge outlets it has mapped in its brain. This is much the same way you replenish your autonomous energy source when you know you are hungry.

How does the Honda-P3 accomplish all of these amazing human-equivalent feats? You may know more about what is involved than you might have thought. How many of the terms in Table 2.1 are familiar to you?

Table 2.1 Equivalent Robot Functions

1. sonar range finder	used to navigate submarines and ships, and to detect objects
2. infrared (heat) and ultrasonic sensors	used to detect objects and human presence
3. ammonia sniffer	used to detect humans
4. voice synthesizer	allows robot to issue questions and commands
5. waterproofed and bulletproofed	to withstand a fierce beating
6. internal electrical sensors	enables robot to know when it's batteries are low it is hungry or is being abused
7. computer	allows for sophisticated processing programs

Obviously, it takes a great deal of effort and knowledge to make all of these systems work together as a robot. P3 autonomous robot systems require that engineering experts from many areas work together as much as possible. A P3

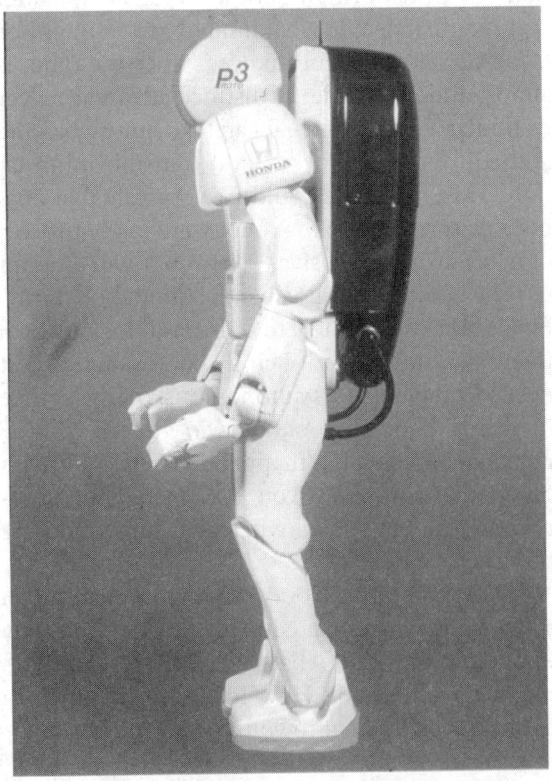

Figure 2.1 Autonomous Mobile Robot

Table 2.2 Engineering Robot Designers

1. hardware and software designers (brain and brain processes)
2. mechanical design engineers (body characteristics)
3. power and control systems specialists (brain decision paths)
4. computer scientists (machine cognition *algorithms*)
5. artificial intelligence scientists (cybernetic analyses)
6. electronic security measures experts (human engineers)

robot requires the cooperation of at least the experts listed in Table 2.2. This cooperative effort represents a general systems team approach the one described in Chapter 1. Autonomous robot systems could not be developed without taking a systems approach.

Certainly all of these experts and all of this sophisticated technology costs a great deal of money. Would you like to have a P3 robot, designed to be a personal guard and friend, who would help you with your studies?

What Does the Robot Have to Do with the Nervous System?

You might have guessed that the point of all this is that the development of autonomous mobile robot systems is leading quickly toward that "... change comparable to the transition from nonlife to life." This change involves the creation of robot systems with human nervous system *equivalence!* Hans Moravec very convincingly argues that this is bound to occur within the next 20 years. His arguments are based essentially upon two themes. First, the historical development of *machine intelligence* system's memory and speed predicts human equivalence within that time. Second, the evolution of human intelligence capabilities has occurred in the particular way that it has because of pre-man's and man's mobility.

This second theme is very important for psychology and is amazingly simple. Any organism that survives by moving about must evolve a *general intelligence* which win allow it to function (and survive) in an environment which is greatly varied and ever full of surprises. The development of vision, for example, in higher *invertebrates* and *vertebrates* has been the common evolutionary response to this situation. Recently, Moravec and over 200 of his colleagues at Carnegie-Mellon University were asked by the Defense Department to develop a sophisticated "seeing" robot system by the year 1992 (Lerner, 1985). This "autonomous robot system is supposed to be able to guide itself at full speed both down a highway and cross-country, doing reconnaissance for a battlefield commander when he needs it." On the other hand, organisms that are *sessile,* like shellfish, encounter much less variety and more repetitive conditions. This environment with repetitive survival requirements is better met with more specialized forms of behavior rather than generalized intelligence.

In the same way that roving animals tend to evolve higher general intelligence capabilities, Moravec feels that the best way to develop higher general intelligence in machine system processing (computers) is to do it within the survival needs of a roving machine like an autonomous mobile robot. Existing computers are like clams in that their essential linearity is a response to repetitive tasks. Computers (and their programs) which must solve problems relative to moving about in an unpredictable environment will have to evolve (through their engineers) higher generalized intelligence. This is exactly what the "on the job" P3 mobile robot would be up against! Through efforts of engineers it seems very probable that we will have human equivalence within the next 20 years.

The great step analogous to the change from nonlife to life Moravec suggests will result from the attainment of human equivalent machine intelligence. This step will see the replacement of the most complex behaving systems with information processing systems—what we generally call intellect or mind. Once human equivalence is reached, machine intelligence will evolve itself (under our guidance at first) at an accelerated rate. It, and not us, will be responsible for the dissemination of intelligence (including our own) throughout the universe.

Implicit in this possibility of human equivalence would be a slight modification of the operational description of psychology itself. Psychology might then be redefined as the "scientific study of human, animal, and machine behavior." (All might be considered behaving systems that perform according to common laws which, in turn, govern the behavior of complex information processing systems.)

Toward a Philosophy of the Brain

In Chapter 1, I stated that my bias was that of a systems approach to mind and behavior. In this chapter on the nervous system and behavior you will be introduced to the primary *functional* system of psychology. The characteristics of this system mediate both mind and behavior. The ultimate question for psychology concerns just how this system's activities give rise to all consciousness and all of our actions. And can other information processing mediums, like machines, give rise to consciousness?

In terms of this question of consciousness the nervous system is still pretty much of a black box. That is, the ideas of input—processing—output is really all we have as a definition for consciousness before we study the details of the biochemistry of the nervous system. For example, we do not understand how the brain gives light and color to the visual world. All of the things you see have a counterpart and place in your brain. As the great Nobel laureate in physiology, Sir John Eccles, stated it so much better:

> There is general agreement among neuroscientists that every conscious experience—every perception, thought, and memory—has as its material counterpart some specific *spatio-temporal* activity in the vast *neuronal* network of the cerebral cortex and *subcortical nuclei,* that is woven of neuronal activities in space and time in the 'enchanted loom' so poetically described by Sherrington. (1970, pp. 4–5)

Yet, in that very place in time where you are doing the seeing another observer can see only relatively uninteresting brain tissue. The intact brain is dark and essentially colorless. How is it possible to have both the vibrant color and light, and the darkness in the same place at the same time? So, at this philosophical level, mind or consciousness remains a puzzle. We will get partial answers to this mystery in our discussion of theoretical approaches to the nervous system and behavior.

Theoretical Approaches to the Brain and Nervous System

At the theoretical level we must examine some views that help explain how the brain and the rest of the nervous system give rise to the *experiential world* and behavior coordinated with it. You have been introduced to Hans Moravec's view (the evolution of intelligence in organisms that move about versus those that don't) that is very helpful in understanding how the perplexing relationship might have come about in the first place.

There are other views which help us understand conceptually how the nervous system might be producing experience and the related purposive behavior. Recall from Chapter 1 that the major views within psychology differ somewhat in the degree to which they feel we should consider conscious experience or the related behavior. Remember, for example, the behaviorist is not so interested in how the brain produces conscious experiences as he might be in how it produces behavior. However, in keeping with the real philosophical question for psychology, we will consider the whole continuum from perceiving, through thinking, and externally observable behavior.

Three Ways to View How the Nervous System Does Its Unique Work

There are numerous views of how the brain and the rest of the nervous system perform. I have chosen views with three considerations in mind. First, they are illustrative of the nervous system as a system—a system of interrelated activities. Second, these views will actually help explain how the system does its work. And, finally, you will find these views very interesting.

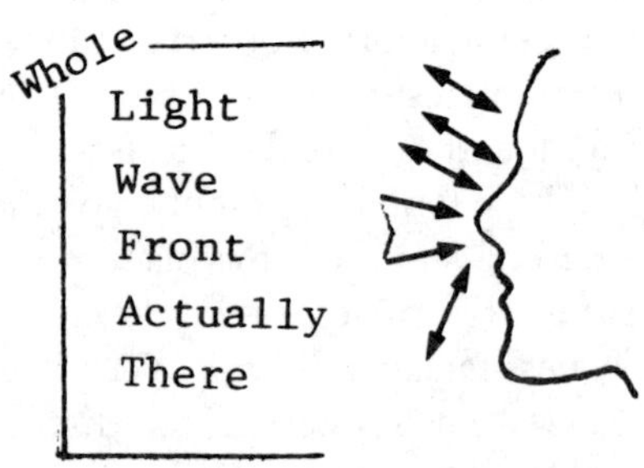

Figure 2.2 Photographic Light Wave

View One: Does the System Make Holograms *of the Outside World?*

The most intriguing view of how the tissue of the nervous system does its job comes by way of a systems analogy to the science of *holographic imagery* production (Karl Pribram, M. Nuwer & R.J. Baton 1974; Karl Pribram 1982). You might be aware that a hologram is a specially prepared film that can be used to produce a very real, very detailed three-dimensional image. The preparation of a hologram and the holographic image is conceptually quite simple.

A comparison with regular photographic ideas would be one way to begin understanding holograms. In a standard photograph, light information is recorded on the film on a two-dimensional *point-by-point* basis only, thus recording only one view of the image. This can be accomplished by simply focusing the light information from the outside world on the film (or just on the back of a darkened chamber). So, in the photograph a person's nose, for example, is recorded only on one area of the film (or one area of the back of a dark chamber). When you look at the person on the developed negative you can see his nose from only one angle—dead-on usually. However, you know that in the real world a person's nose can be seen from countless angles. How nice it would be to expose a photographic film so that the entire unfocused real world of light wave fronts could be recorded and then developed so that you could see *into* the photo just as you see into the real world. In holograms the entire unfocused real world of light is recorded so that you can later see a replica of the originally photographed scene. With the proper equipment, film, and procedures a hologram image is difficult to distinguish from a real scene. But how are holograms made? And how might the brain do the same sort of thing?

Any image consists of the *amplitude* of the light waves (this makes areas appear darker or lighter), the *frequencies* of the light waves (this gives the image its colors), and the *phase* of the light waves (gives the impression that the image has depth). These characteristics of light waves are illustrated in Figure 2.3. Anytime we can record all three of these aspects of waves, we will see a color 3D image.

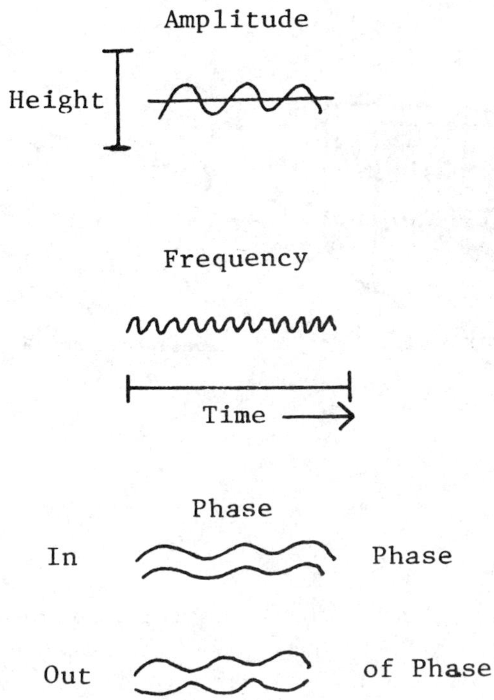

Figure 2.3 Characteristics of Light Waves

Figure 2.4 Film Interference Patterns

The holographic view of how the brain produces visual experience, and all other experience as well, proposes that the brain too is capable of making holograms. In the brain, however, there is no film, and there is no laser. How might the brain produce holograms? In the brain there are billions of communicating nerve cells (neurons) and trillions of interconnections that form complex networks or patterns of bioelectrical charge. It is thought that these complex patterns represent, for example, visual experiences that are very similar to the frequency, amplitude, and phase aspects of a visual scene. These networks of neurons would contain constructive and destructive patterns of *excitatory* (+) and *inhibitory* (–) electrical potentials (see Figure 2.4).

Figure 2.5 is a simplified illustration of the reconstruction (or "illumination") of a wave front for the apple *in the brain*. It should be mentioned that while the holographic view may not depict exactly how the brain produces experience, it does, in fact, produce, for example, 3D images in some way. An important fact that supports the holographic theory is that if you cut a regular photograph in half, you lose half of the photograph. If you cut a regular hologram in half, you still have interference information from every part of the original object. This fact is valuable in understanding how the brain functions because it has similar organizational and functional characteristics. For example, certain mappings in the brain, are reproduced *redundantly* and large areas of the brain can be removed without removing a section of conscious awareness. Obviously, the information you do have in your brain is spread redundantly throughout it in some fashion.

This analysis tells us a little bit about how the images of consciousness might be constructed. Perhaps we have partially answered the enigma of light (or sound, etc.) in the brain. Holograms can be made of any wave forms: light, sound, or wave phenomena.

The holographic model also helps us describe the tremendous and versatile memory capacities of the brain. Not only does this include memories of dates, names, and the like, but the staggering memory processes required for the brain's regulation of "automatic" activities including maintenance of homeostasis, reflexes, walking, etc. It has been estimated that holographic capacity for storage of information could reduce the space required for the Library of Congress (holdings in the tens of millions, including graphics and manuscripts of all sorts) to the size of a sugar cube! If x-ray wave lasers were used, the dimensions would be significantly further

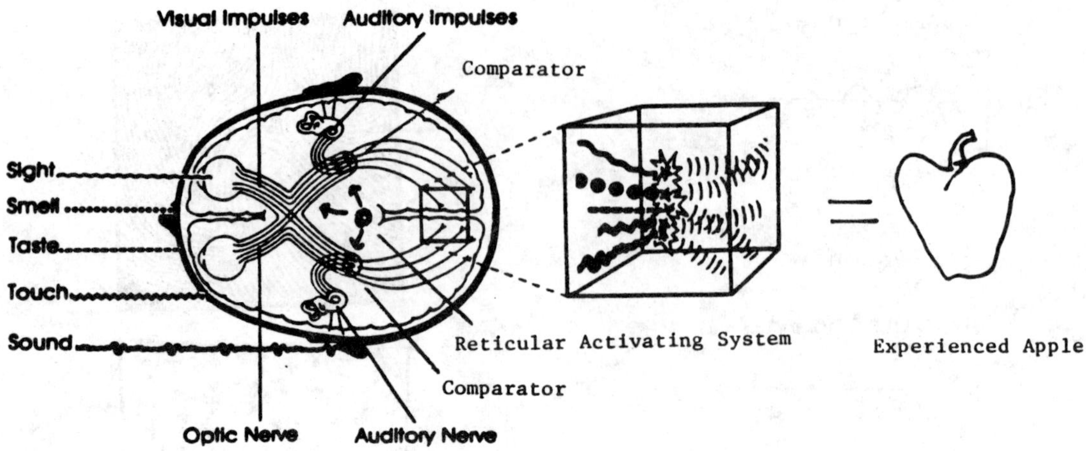

Figure 2.5 Reconstruction of a Wave Front

reduced. X-ray waves are perhaps 1,000 times smaller (shorter) than light waves. The hologram may help explain how imagination is constructed in our thinking.

The hologram is a helpful way to view how the brain and the rest of the nervous system does its work. If we could combine the visual capacity of hologram input with holographic memory storage into a robot's vision system, it might "see" the world as well as you do, perhaps better. Next, we might tie these together with holographic storage of millions or billions of computer programs and—C3PO! While you may not actually see C3PO in your lifetime, there is little doubt that you will see robot systems of that complexity and ability.

View Two: Is the System Complex Enough to Make Holograms?

It is appealing to suppose that the brain and the rest of the nervous system gives rise to human consciousness simply out of its tremendous complexity. Brain scientists (David Hubel, 1979; Edelmant, Mountcastle, 1978; Nauta & Fiertag, 1986) tell us that the brain is estimated to consist of between 10 billion and 1 trillion communicating cells (neurons). Each of the billions of cells in the brain is interconnected with many others. Each cell receives information from perhaps 1000 connections or so and passes on about 1000 connections. In addition to the structural complexity, there is great functional or operating complexity. For example, each brain cell can discharge information anywhere from 1 to 1000 times a second! This discharge rate depends on what other connections are doing. Next, there are as many as 50 chemical transmission messengers which might be involved in the communication of information between cells. These can function in a variety of ways to control information states between cells within 1/10,000th of a second.

Here is a simple way of thinking about this complexity. The number of storage and processing states the human brain is capable of would be $2^{50,000,000,000}$. This represents fifty billion brain cells each capable of being "on" or "off" at any given moment. It has been calculated that this number would take 450 years to write out at one digit per second! So, the actual number of possible states in the brain would be a number nearly 15 billion digits long! If this number were typed out it would fill 6,667 books the size of this book!

Hans Moravec has compared speed and memory capacities in a number of systems (see Figure 2.6). In this sort of analysis, too, the brain's complexity is staggering. Your brain whizzes through information 10,000 times faster than a Cray-2 computer—the world's fastest. A Cray-2 chugs along at up to a billion instructions per second.

We have been discussing "thought processes(ing)" and complexity. Recent research is showing that memory and learning are largely due to cell information patterning, which takes place where the messengers do their work at interconnection sites. It has been estimated that

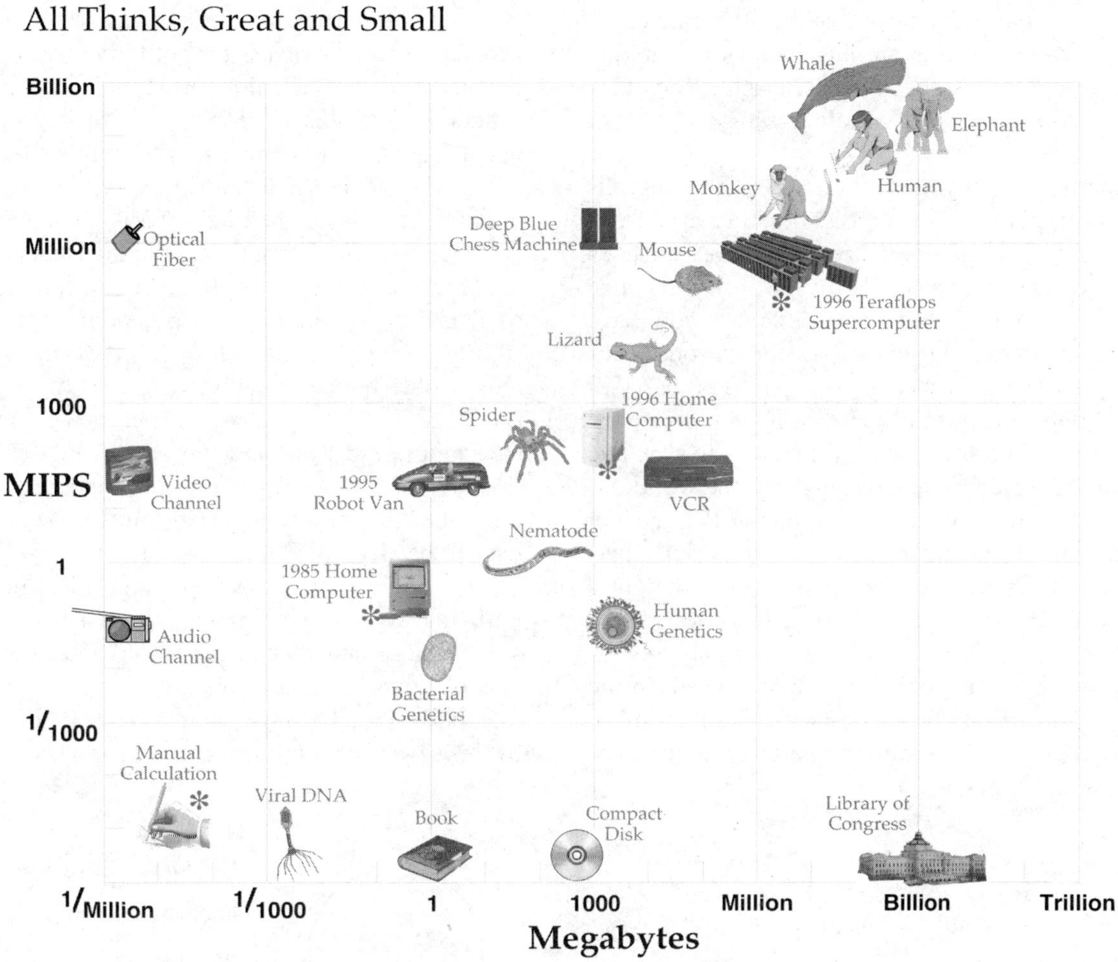

Figure 2.6 Think Power: Computing Speed and Memory of Some Animals and Machines

there are about 1 quadrillion of these in the brain.

But, again, even if we accept the idea that the digits for the number of information states possible in the brain would fill 6,667 textbooks with numbers, we have to ask how these trillions upon trillions of patterns give rise to consciousness. This level of complexity would certainly complement the holographic view.

View Three: Two Interacting Subsystems

Recently, Elkhonon Goldberg and Louis Costa (1981) have carefully studied the way the two halves of the brain differ in the manner in which they acquire and use various descriptions of the world. They refer to these as differing "descriptive systems." These include the following:

1. *Natural languages* (English in the case of your present reading).
2. *Specialized languages* which exist explicitly in culture such as formal mathematical languages, musical notation, and the rules and processes of games (chess, for example) communicated via special notation. Next time you play a card game, you will be using this sort of descriptive system when you say, "My queen beats your jack."
3. *Idiosyncratic* descriptive systems which, according to Goldberg and Costa ". . . develop in an individual during the acquisition of new tasks (or in the processing of previously

> unknown classes of stimuli) . . ." In the case of your present processing, these idiosyncratic strategies are likely providing unique impressions, speculations, insights, and questions about what you are reading.

The left half of your brain tends to have its cells organized in a way to process best the natural languages and the specialized languages such as words and numbers that do not usually change their meanings. For example, once you have learned to read music well, it is pretty routine for you to read most sheet music. On the other hand, the right side of your brain has its cells organized in a way to process better your own idiosyncratic way of organizing and dealing with the world.

The left half of the brain, the left *cerebral hemisphere,* shows mostly an *intraregional* pattern of brain cell connectivity, while the right a mostly *interregional* pattern of connection. These patterns are shown in Figure 2.7. Hypothetically, the intramodal structure of the cells in the left half of the brain provides the anatomical basis for input—output patterns that have become routine. Conversely, the intermodal structure of cell relationships in the right half provides a superior basis for both orientation to novelty in incoming information, and the idiosyncratic assemblage of new descriptive systems. Figure 2.7 illustrates on the simplest level that highly routinized descriptive system work could efficiently be handled by cells in a single purpose area of the brain. When you ask a person his name (under normal circumstances), there is little reason to draw upon other specialized groupings of cells. However, if you asked what would happen if a gun were discharged in the space shuttle as part of an experiment, a new (not routine) analysis and synthesis would have to take place. Not only would information from a number of areas be required, but they would have to be assembled in a new way.

Of course, in actual situations like these both halves of the brain would participate in some way. When your name is asked, the right half of your brain is probably always piecing together a parallel impression. And, obviously, the space shuttle question requires sophisticated

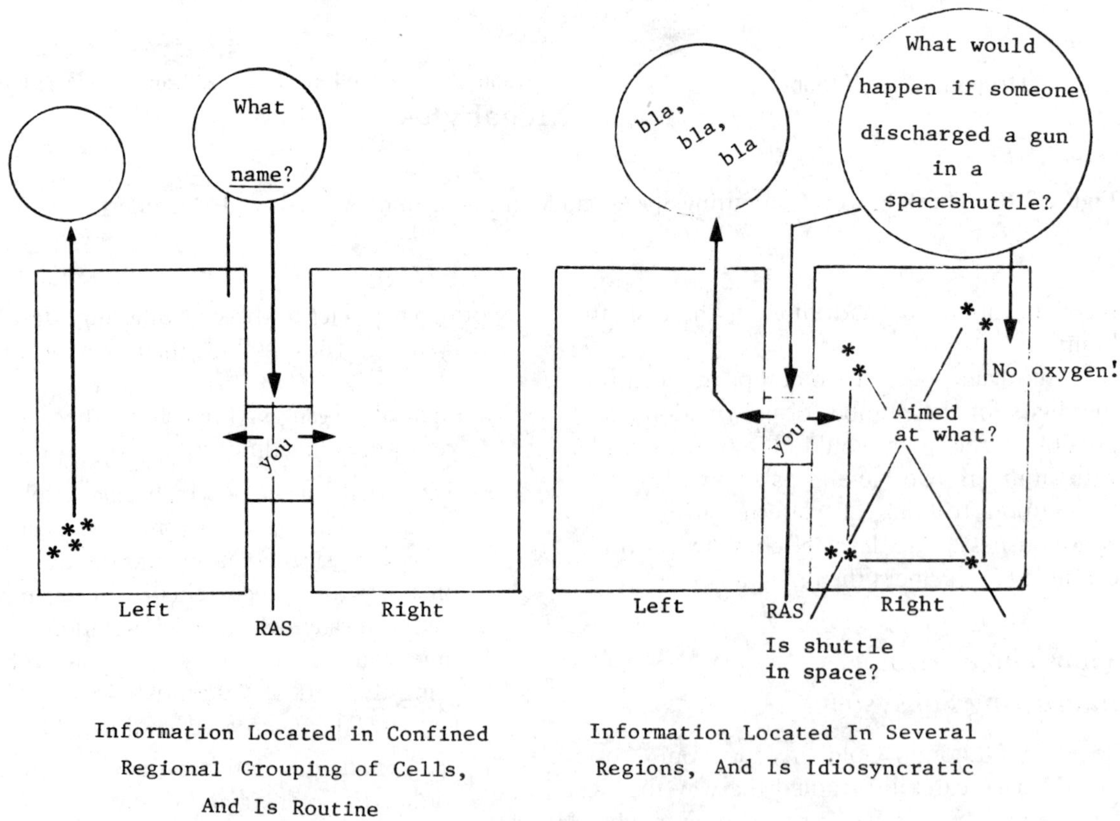

Figure 2.7 Diagram of Types of Work in the Brain

use of both natural and specialized languages. However, in these situations one half or the other would tend to actually lead in meeting the demands at hand.

Can this view help us understand how the brain produces conscious experience? One way to interpret these different "wiring" plans of the two halves of the brain would be to conclude that the whole brain really consists of two types of computers. One half generally runs on programs already written, and the other usually writes new programs and program segments as needed as we go through life. Later in this chapter you will learn about people who have had the two hemispheres of their brains surgically cut-off from one another. The study of these people has led researchers to conclude that these people have a sort of "double consciousness." Perhaps each side of the brain has its own consciousness. Or, perhaps one half is conscious and the other more unconscious. For an excellent discussion of the idea of relating the two hemispheres of the brain to the question of consciousness, I recommend Sally Springer and Georg Deurtsch's (1985) book, *Left-brain, Right-brain*.

So far you have, seen three views of how the brain might be related to the production of experience and behavior. How close to the truth these views are remains a delightful mystery. Now that you have some ideas about how to view the brain, you are in a position to appreciate the significance and relevance of what we know about the brain. So, we can now turn to the empirical brain and some of the methods of its study.

The Empirical Brain

There are at least three good reasons to study the brain. First, without some understanding of the structure and functions of the brain and the rest of the nervous system we would not be able to evaluate the many views of the brain. Second, a modern, detailed understanding of the brain will help as understand both normal and abnormal everyday behavior. And, third, while we do not know exactly how the brain and the rest of the nervous system gives rise to consciousness, a great deal is known. Let us find out what we know about the nervous system that will help us clarify the theoretical and practical mysteries.

The Neuron

Neurons are the communication cells of the nervous system. Many people have made the point that organisms like the ant or the shark must be very well adapted to their place in the environment because they have remained relatively unchanged for millions of years. The neuron is even better at what it does. The neuron is essentially the same in organisms from the simplest to the most complex producing the units of information in an information system.

What is information? Think about information you have. What time is your psychology class? It's at 9:30 A.M.? Information is knowledge. Information makes you more sure about things. If you need information about where your psychology instructor is, and you are told he is either in his office or in his classroom, you are *uncertain* about where he is. I can reduce this uncertainty for you with one piece of information—he is not in his office. What is essential for information to be information is that it must reduce uncertainty.

The Neuron and Information

Information can take on countless (probably infinite) appearances. Figure 2.8 illustrates a few common appearances of information systems. These use differing patterns of things or events to reduce uncertainty by the use of the command to "ADD." Some scientists believe that collections of neurons reduce uncertainty through patterns similar to those seen in computer machine language. This is so because individual neurons are either in a resting state or "0," or in a state of firing an impulse or "1." An important idea in General Systems Theory is that all of these information systems are homologous, that is, one may be transformed into another and accomplish the same function. The point here is that systems that reduce uncertainty can take any form—as long as the rules of the system are systematic and consistent. The information in people's faces is sometimes misleading. One of the reasons for this is that some of the rules governing facial information are inconsistent with what the person is actually thinking. You will recall that the left and right sides of the cerebral

Morse Code	. — — — . . — — . .
Computer's Machine Language	000110000000
English	ADD

Figure 2.8 Three Different Information Systems

cortex seem to use different types of languages or notational systems. What we were really seeing there is the use of two different types of information systems that have some degree of systematic relationship to one another. Each has the job of reducing uncertainty.

Now let's look at some of the rules neurons follow as they pass information throughout the nervous system (communicate). There are about 50 billion cells in the human brain. There are many different types of neurons, perhaps 1,000, each serving slightly different roles in their jobs of interconnecting information. However, regardless of the connectivity role a particular neuron might have, the basic technique of communicating among them is amazingly consistent. In fact, we can illustrate the transfer of information among all neurons with one basic model. Figure 2.9 depicts two impulses traveling along a neuron's *axon*. These pulses of information are about one hundredth of a second apart. Most neuron axons are not actually "naked" like the one depicted. An *insulating sheath* (see Figure 2.10) allows the impulse to "jump" from one *node of Ranvier* to the next. This latter means of conduction speeds the impulse along its way. (It should be noted that both the sodium and potassium ions are positive in charge. Therefore, the interior of the axon is only relatively negative with respect to the exterior. There are several ways to understand this situation. For example, different metals carry different degrees of charge and since sodium ions are about 30 percent smaller than potassium ions, there can be more of these positive charges to a given space.)

Some have likened this process of the electrochemical impulse to a fuse rapidly burning along the neuron's axon. However, this analogy gives you the impression that something has burned away. This is not the case at all! While this may describe the impulse "front," it does

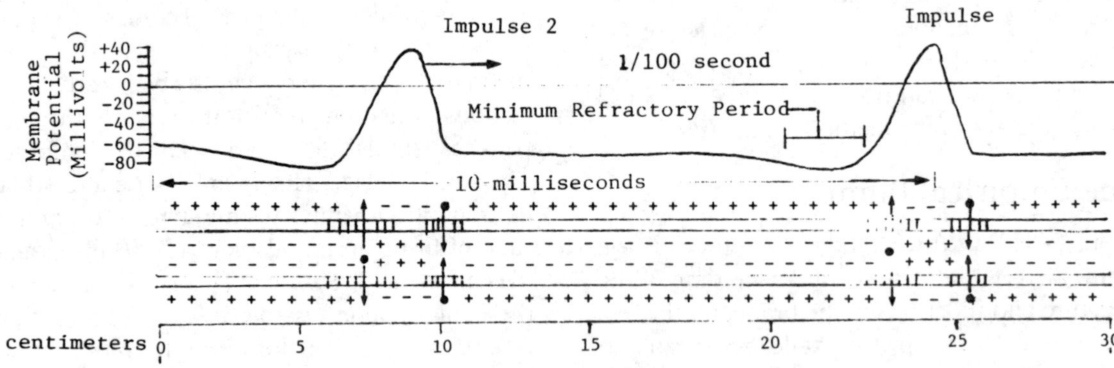

Propagation of Nerve Impulse along the axon coincides with a localized inflow of sodium ions (NA +) followed by an outflow of potassium ions (K +) through channels that are "gated," or controlled, by voltage changes across the axon membrane. The electrical event that sends a nerve impulse traveling down the axon normally originates in the cell body. The impulse begins with a slight depolarization, or reduction in the negative potential, across the membrane of the axon where it leaves the cell body. The slight voltage shift opens some of the sodium channels, shifting the voltage still further. The flow of sodium ions accelerates until the inner surface of the membrane is locally positive. The voltage reversal closes the sodium channel and opens the potassium channel. The outflow of potassium ions quickly restores the negative potential. The voltage reversal, known as the action potential, propagates itself down the axon. After a brief refractory period a second impulse can follow. The impulse propagation speed is that measured in the giant axon of the membrane.

Figure 2.9 Propagation of a Nerve Impulse

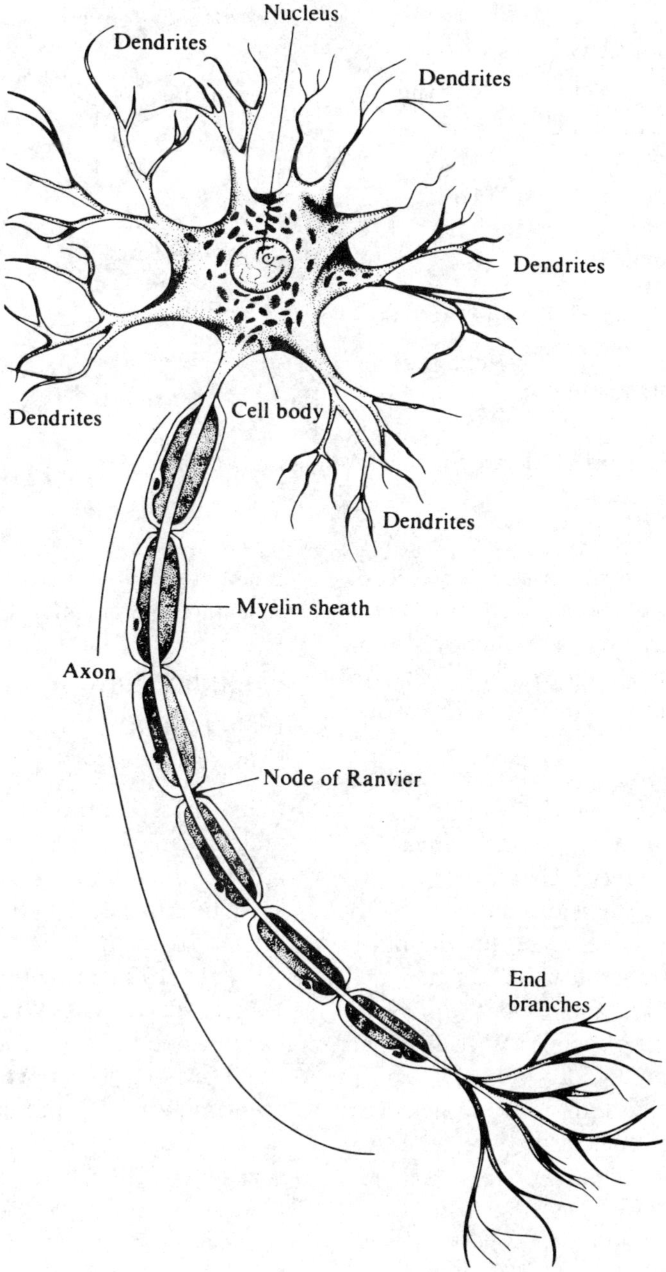

Figure 2.10 The Neuron

not describe the process. If we do use the fuse idea, then it must be a fuse that immediately renews itself as it burns along its way—a living, self-healing fuse.

Actually, the process of electrochemical activity of the nerve impulse is much more like a "wet" battery (like the one in your car). Figure 2.11 illustrates the constant discharging when the car's system requires it, and then recharging by reversing the flows of ions (as in the neuron) in its *electrolyte* (as in the axon). In the diagram, the three stages of rest, discharge, and recharge are compared to the "wet" battery like the one in your car and to the "wet" neurons like the ones in your head. The axon is turned to a vertical position.

Notice that in both cases the electric charge is carried by *ions.* You have probably learned that electricity consists of the flow of *electrons.*

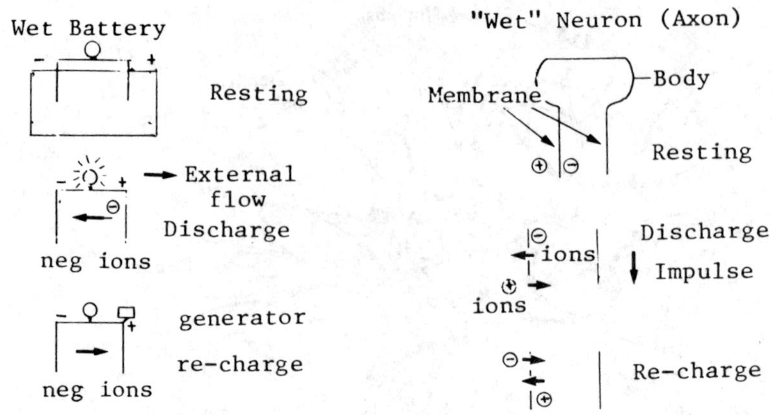

Figure 2.11 Comparisons of Electrochemical Activity

This is not the case in batteries. It is true of course that external wires attached to either a battery (like the one going to the light bulb) or to an axon (like ones going to a volt meter to measure axon activity) involve current carried by electron flow.

So, in a sense, you have about 50 billion tiny wet batteries in your head all communicating through these little impulses. Remember though, the neuron battery recharges so fast that it can pulse (turn the light on and off) up to 1000 times a second. And, each time the pulse turns the light on, it does it with the same consistent brilliance. This fact about impulses, called the all-or-none principle, since it either fires or it doesn't, is a key idea in how the neuron uses information. As long as you understand that we are using an analogy between the wet battery and the transmission of neuronal impulses, I should point out that these neuron batteries are extremely small—neuron sized. The entire energy output of the brain's billions of neurons has been estimated to be about that of a 20 watt light bulb! The world's most advanced computer running on 20 watts!

The nerve impulse with its variety of rates is essentially the way neurons communicate with one another. The impulse is the information system which underlies all communication in the nervous system and all consciousness in the brain. The nerve impulse underlies the natural languages of the left cerebral hemisphere and the idiosyncratic languages of right hemispheres. The impulse itself is of the same nature whether it is involved in the production of seeing, smelling, or thinking.

Complex Patterns of Impulse Generation: Synapses

While it is true that the nerve impulse is essentially the same throughout the nervous system and amazingly carries all information, the generation of these impulses is even more intriguing.

The synaptic conduction of impulse information between neurons offers a good basis for the chemical explanation of many behaviors. When we try to explain learning or memory, for example, on the basis of the impulse alone (with its all-or-none action) we make little progress. In the same way the impulse alone does not help much in understanding abnormal behavior associated with such diseases as *epilepsy, schizophrenia,* or the effects of drugs such as *cocaine.* The study of synaptic activity is critical to understanding all of these. Additionally, understanding synapses might shed some important light on the three theoretical views (holography, complexity, and differences in the cerebral hemispheres) discussed earlier.

Surprisingly, neurons in communication don't actually touch one another. There is always a space or gap between communicating neurons. You will recall that the information signal transported along the axon was electrical. At the synapse, however, the nature of information transmission is mostly chemical. Chemicals released into the synaptic space between the neuron supplying the information and the neuron receiving the information may either tend to cause the recipient neuron to pulse (excite it) or not to pulse (inhibit it). There are perhaps 50 or 60 of these chemical transmitters. There may be as many as 1000 to 10,000 dendrites, cell body "antennas" receiving these excitatory or inhibitory messages. And these messages may be coming from 100 to 1000 other neurons.

The cell body of the neuron more or less "averages" all of these incoming synaptic messages. If there are a greater number of excitatory messages, and the excitation is great enough, the neuron will discharge down the axon. If the number of inhibiting messages are greater, the neuron will not discharge even though there are excitatory influences present. Obviously the timing of these exciting and inhibiting chemical influences is important to impulse rate—the essential carrier of information. Recall that there are probably about one quadrillion synapses in your brain.

The way in which transmitter chemicals excite or inhibit neurons is conceptually quite simple. The transmitter substance can cross the synaptic gap (Figure 2.12) in as little as 1/10,000 of a second. Once the chemical is in the gap area and has either contributed to inhibition or to excitation, the gap must be chemically cleaned or cleared to its original state. If this were not the case, normal information state (impulse rates) changes would be altered.

The chemical cleaning or clearing of the synaptic gap is accomplished in two fundamental ways: (1) *enzyme destruction* of the released transmitter substance, or (2) the *reuptake* of the released transmitter substance. The quick enzyme destruction of certain transmitter chemicals occurs by changing the substance to chemicals

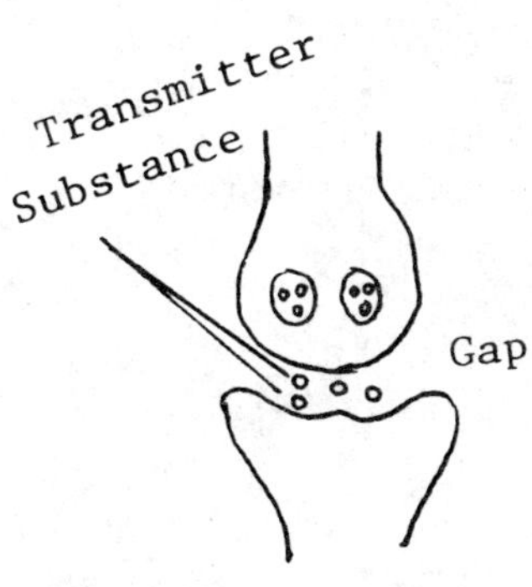

Figure 2.12 Synaptic Gap

inert to synaptic transmission. The reuptake process involves *presynaptic vesicles* that vacuum up or recapture transmitter substance molecules that were released milliseconds earlier.

As we suggested earlier, the synaptic areas are now thought to be the place most likely responsible for the production and changes in learning and memory. Whenever a person learns something new, certain synaptic connections are being re-ordered in terms of strengths and weaknesses. This occurs through a complex modification of the dynamics of transmitter substance release. So, as you read this text, chemical relationships between neurons in your brain are changing. And, in turn, these changes underlie new aspects of consciousness and of your thinking.

In a similar way the modulation of synaptic chemistry can help explain much about abnormal behavior. What causes diseases such as schizophrenia, why does *curare* immobilize the skeletal muscles, and why does cocaine have the effect on people it has?

Schizophrenia: A Case of Too Much Receptance of a Transmitter Chemical. Schizophrenia, as you might know, is a disease of the mind marked by withdrawal from reality as the rest of us seem to know it. Thinking tends to follow confused patterns unpredictably. It now appears that schizophrenia is the result of too much brain activity involving the transmitter *dopamine*. It appears that people with schizophrenia have a neural defect or too many postsynaptic receptors for dopamine. Antipsychotic drugs (schizophrenia is a *psychotic* disorder) somehow make the postsynaptic membrane less sensitive to dopamine-mediated transmission. The phenothiazine antipsychotic drugs greatly reduce the symptoms of schizophrenia. Schizophrenia is a major world health problem and has many clinical appearances. We will return to more about schizophrenic disorders in Chapter 9.

Curare: A Case of Blocking the Effects of a Transmitter Chemical. Curare has long been used by primitives of South America in the hunting of wild game. Curare brings down the game by acting as a powerful poison which stops muscle action. In a lethal dosage muscles involved in respiration stop and death results.

Curare molecules just happen to be very similar to molecules of *acetylcholine,* a muscle stimulator. Curare, therefore, mimics acetylcholine in postsynaptic receptors. Unfortunately, while the curare can take the place of acetylcholine, it does not stimulate muscle activity. The curarized animal (or person) may want to move, but when it tries, nothing happens.

Cocaine: A Case of Blocking Reuptake. Cocaine comes from the leaves of the coca plant of South America. Today, millions of mountain natives chew coca leaves for their comforting (nonhallucinogenic) effects. This practice is a more or less normal cultural practice and is centuries old. Leaf chewing is probably not harmful. A daily consumption of a few leaves contains little actual cocaine, and additionally contains other buffering ingredients. Of course, cocaine sniffed or injected is destructive in many ways, and is addictive.

Cocaine greatly stimulates the central nervous system. The effective and cognitive effects of this stimulation include elation, feeling of enhanced physical and mental abilities, and tireless energy. Cocaine's stimulating effects come about because its molecules interfere with the normal reuptake of neurotransmitter chemicals. Synaptic gap areas remain filled with stimulating transmitter molecules. Postsynaptic excitatory firing rates become greater than normal.

The Brain and Other Organizational Aspects of the Nervous System That Control Behavior

Up to this point we have discussed some of the theories which might produce behavior and consciousness, and we have examined the fundamental processes related to the neuron and its communicative activities. Now we will discuss the larger organizational aspects of the nervous system.

In discussing the neuron, we stated the on/off/integration functions which we might find in computer counterparts in the P3 Robot; the larger organization of the nervous system can nicely be compared to its control system. Figure 2.13 outlines the macroscopic architecture of the nervous system. The nervous system (control system) is constantly involved in an input—processing—output—*feedback loop.* At the microscopic level, too, there are millions of feedback loops in the brain (Edelman, 1978). Input is the only channel through which we can generally know about the outside world (outside the nervous system). Output is the only

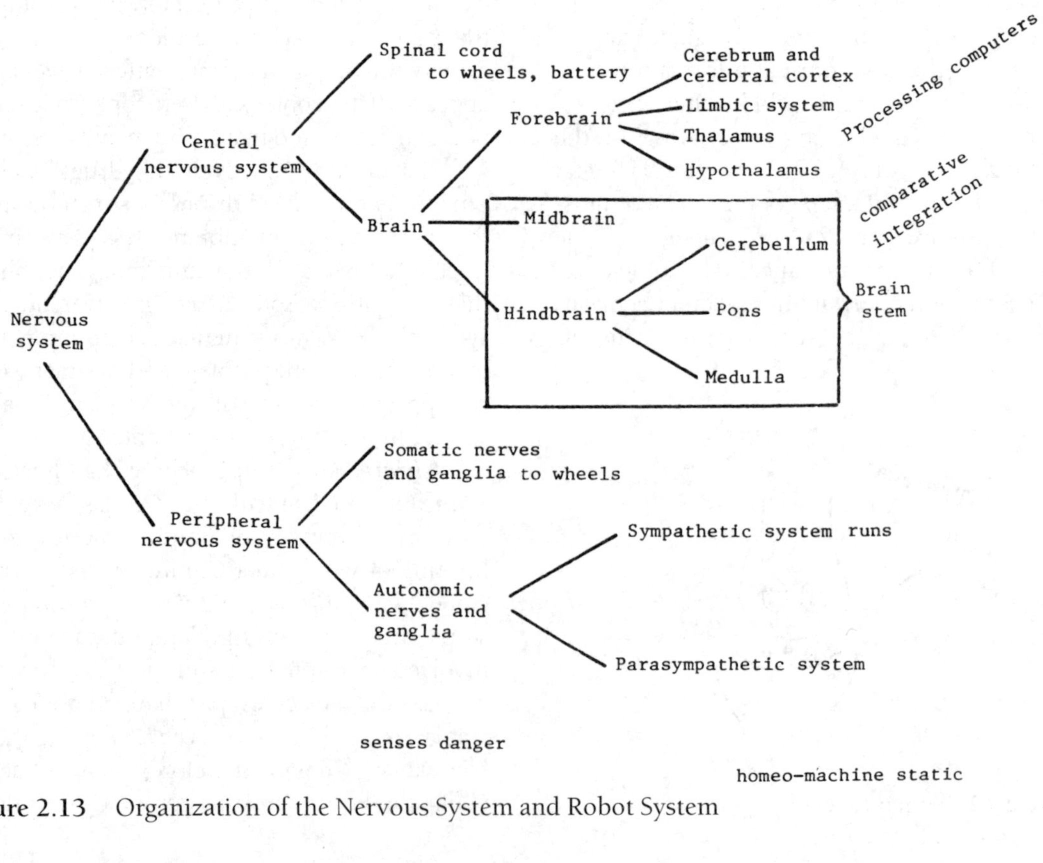

Figure 2.13 Organization of the Nervous System and Robot System

way we can respond to and influence the outside world. In between, there is processing of everything necessary to keep the loop consistently intact—all thought, perception, emotions, states of equilibration, etc.—so that the system can survive.

Without the feedback idea included in the organizational model the robot would not be able to adjust its relationship to its environment of inputs. The robot would run into walls, fall down stairs and so on, just like you would without feedback. So as we examine the organization of the nervous system keep in mind that the purpose of any nervous system (human or animal) is to maintain some consistent relationships within itself and between its own behavior and the environment. It does this through a never-ending stream of trial and error feedback.

The Central Nervous System

The central nervous system (CNS) includes the *brain* and the *spinal cord* and nothing more. Essentially, you can think about these as central processing functions of the organizational feedback loop. You might think about the central nervous system as being roughly equivalent to the computer(s) that process information for the robot. The spinal cord could represent an extension of processing activities down into the robot body with small local feedback loops. For example, if the robot batteries are low, the decision to recharge might be made by one of these loops even if some of the central processing had to be involved in getting the robot to the recharge station.

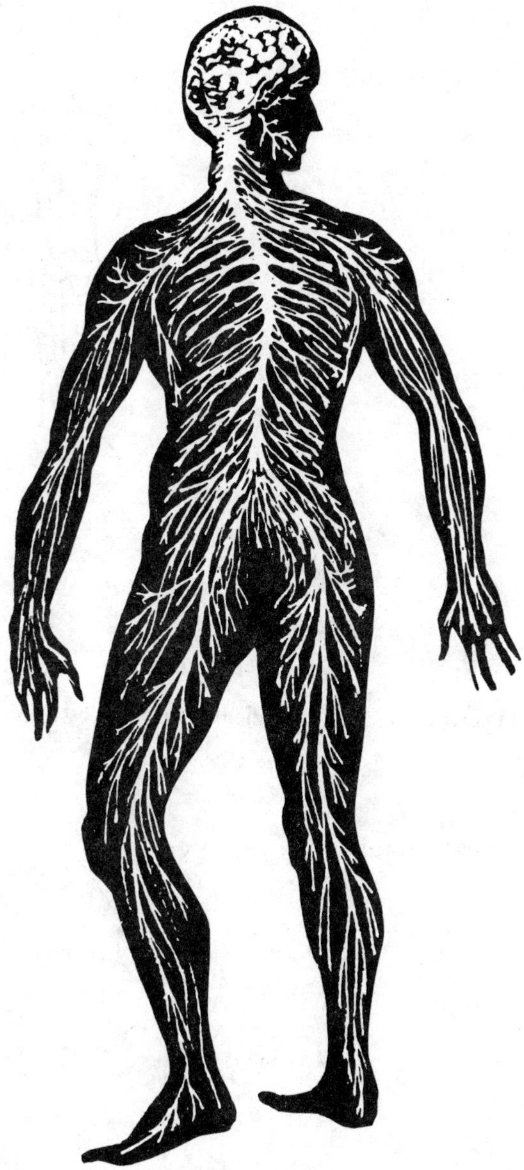

Figure 2.14 Central Nervous System

The Peripheral Nervous System

The *peripheral nervous system* provides the input and output innervation to (a) the external world (the *somatic division*), and to (b) the internal world of the body (the *autonomic division*). Normally, we find it quite easy to think about examples of feedback organization involving the CNS for the somatic division of peripheral innervation (like driving a car), but not for the autonomic division. In fact, the term autonomic originally came from the idea of self-governance—not under the control of the central nervous system. However, we know now the autonomic division also represents an organizational feedback loop involving the CNS as does the somatic division. In the brain the cerebral cortex, for example, constantly exercises modulations over the activities of the "autonomic" functions through a feedback system.

Somatic Division. A good example of the somatic division's feedback organization is either a knee-jerk reflex response loop or a CNS controlled voluntary activity such as kicking a ball. In Figures 2.15 and 2.16 a message from some small portion(s) of the cortex is transmitted along down the spinal cord to a particular loop of nerve cells in the spinal cord. The loop

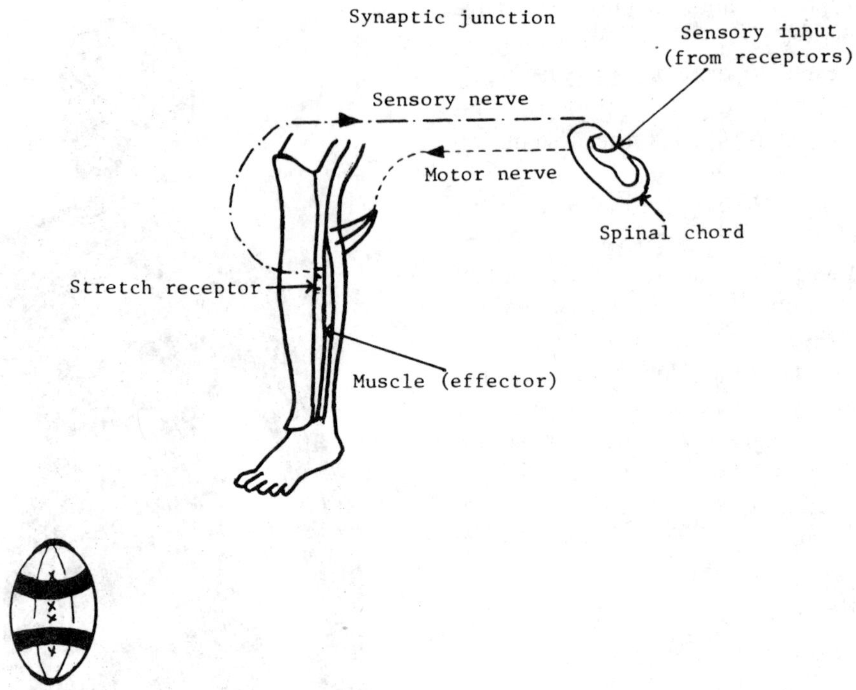

Figure 2.15 Physiological Feedback System

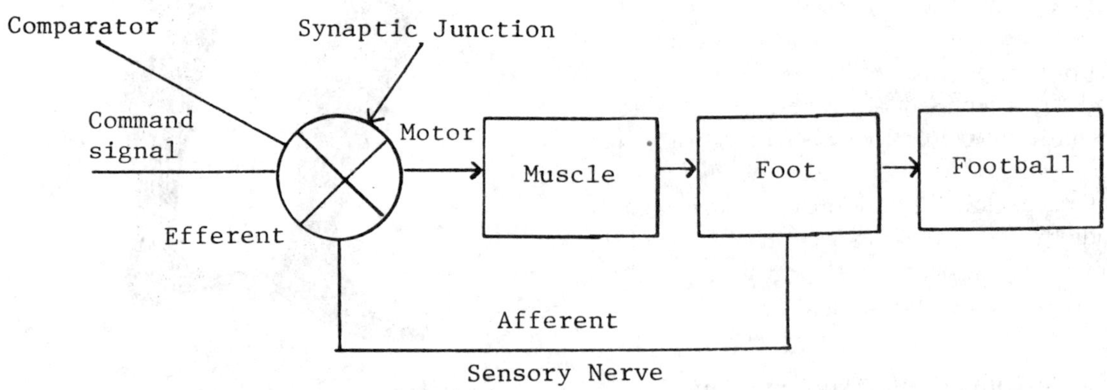

Figure 2.16 Block Diagram of Physiological Feedback System

contains a motor output *efferent nerve,* a sensory *afferent nerve,* and a processing synaptic junction (local comparator). If there were only an output message, neither the spinal cord at the reflex level nor the cortex would "know" how, when and where the action had taken place. We could suppose that a person whose comparator had been damaged because the toes had been anesthetized, might complete the loop with visual information. This is a regular part of the total feedback organization, as are numerous other loops.

Autonomic Division. In the autonomic division of the nervous system (ANS), the feedback organizational loop is of course present, but is a little harder to keep track of. There are four essential ideas which will help us in this regard. First, the autonomic system in itself is an efferent system. In other words, the system itself is completely motor. Remember, that the somatic system, on the other hand, is clearly both sensory and motor. Second, the autonomic system in the majority of the cases dually innervates its motor-effected organs. This means that a part of the ANS excites the particular organ and another part of the ANS inhibits that same organ. Third, the feedback sensory or afferent nerves involved in ANS feedback loops are not a part of the ANS itself. These feedback afferent nerves find their way back to the CNS, the cortex, and other parts of the brain by other routes. Fourth, largely because of the automatic homeostatic equilibrating nature of the autonomic system and the circuitous routing back to mainly *subcortical* centers, voluntary control of the ANS is weak—but its potential is certainly there.

The ANS serves the internal organs of the body. Figure 2.17 shows these organs and where the appropriate efferent nerves leave the spinal cord. The *sympathetic* fibers which prepare and sustain you for "fighting or fleeing" in emergency situations all leave the central portion of the spinal cord. The *parasympathetic* fibers that maintain efficient use of available body energy (homeostatic) leave either the head or the tail of the spinal cord.

To get an idea of the specific function of the two organizational subsystems of the ANS, examine Table 2-4. The sympathetic "fight or flight" system should not be thought of strictly as an excitation system, nor the parasympathetic "maintaining" as an inhibition system. It can be seen that in some cases the sympathetic system excites an organ (sweat glands), and inhibits other glands (salivary glands). And the parasympathetic effectors excite the salivary glands but inhibit heart action.

Most of the organs are dually innervated. This provides very positive homeostasis. However, a few organs, like the sweat glands, are excited to secrete and therefore cool you in an emergency, but when the emergency has passed, the sympathetic stimulation simply stops. The parasympathetic system is not needed to "shut off" this glandular activity.

While it may appear that the efferent control of the inner environment is hopelessly on automatic pilot maintaining the efficient use of body energy as you go about your daily affairs, this is not the case at all. The cortex gains some degree of control of many of the organs of the ANS through experience. Some of this

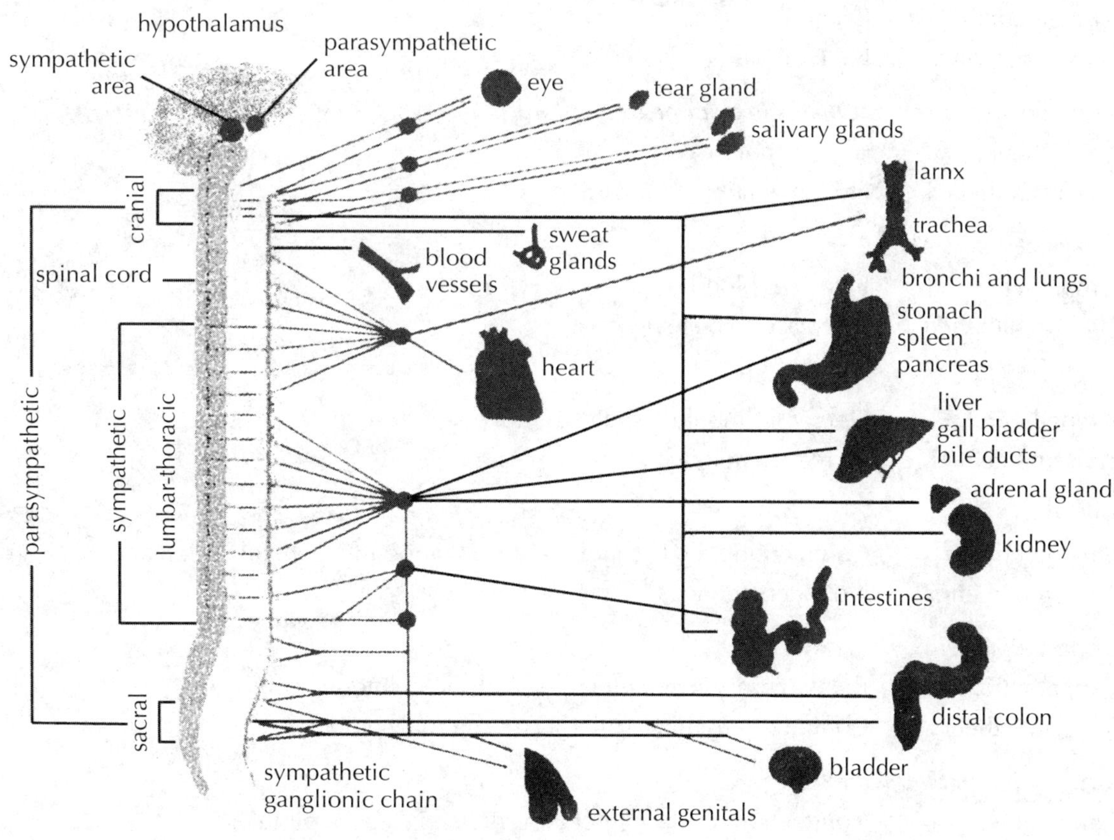

Figure 2.17 The Autonomic Nervous System

Table 2.4 Functions of the Autonomic Nervous System

Sweat Gland	
Sympathetic:	Stimulates secretion
Parasympathetic:	No innervation
Salivary Gland	
Sympathetic:	*Vasoconstriction,* which decreases salivary secretion
Parasympathetic:	Stimulation of salivary secretion and *vasodilation*
Lungs (bronchial tubes)	
Sympathetic:	Dilation
Parasympathetic:	Constriction
Heart	
Sympathetic:	Increases rate and strength of contraction; dilates coronary vessels that supply blood to heart muscle cells
Parasympathetic:	Decreases rate and strength of contraction, constricts coronary vessels
Blood Vessels, Skin	
Sympathetic:	Constriction
Parasympathetic:	No innervation for most (vasodilation occurs if sympathetic innervation ceases or decreases)
Blood Vessels, Skeletal Muscle	
Sympathetic:	Dilation
Parasympathetic:	No innervation
Blood Vessels, Visceral Organs (except heart and lungs)	
Sympathetic:	Constriction
Parasympathetic:	No innervation for most
Liver	
Sympathetic:	Increases blood sugar
Parasympathetic:	Decreases blood sugar
Stomach	
Sympathetic:	Decreases motility (speed of movement)
Parasympathetic:	Increases motility
Spleen	
Sympathetic:	Contraction and discharge of stored blood into general circulation
Parasympathetic:	No innervation
Urinary Bladder	
Sympathetic:	Relaxes muscular wall; increases tone in internal sphincter
Parasympathetic:	Contracts muscular wall; relaxes internal sphincter
Arrector Pili of Hair Follicles	
Sympathetic:	Contraction results in erections of hairs ("goose pimples")
Parasympathetic:	No innervation

cortical modulation is helpful to you, some is not. For example, at exam time you may worry too much, which often causes sympathetic arousal and only hinders you—you feel nervous. And certainly you know that you have learned a good deal of control over bladder and bowel releases, which should ordinarily occur with natural bladder and bowel pressures. If these pressures become great at inappropriate times you can cortically control them for a time.

In additional ways, you have learned to adapt to threatening situations which might evoke the "fight or flight" responses. For example, as a child you may have been frightened by the sight of a dog, but as you grew up and had more and more experiences with dogs you learned that you did not have to be prepared to fight them, or flee from them. This shows that processes of the higher centers in the cortex have modified the original reaction. Thus, spies and poker players have learned to suppress any fight or flight related responses. They must attempt to keep the sympathetic nervous system from making them tremble, or perspire; they have learned to remain cool under "fire."

So, there are a great number of examples of cortical control or modulation of the ANS. But, we can take this further. In fact, it is likely that given the right circumstances, the thinking cortex could probably learn modulation of any portion of the ANS. This would require the systematic introduction of our essential organizational nervous system control—feedback.

Biofeedback and the Cortical Modulation of the ANS

Psychologists have developed methods of systematically studying how the cortex can learn to modify ANS activity. We will discuss just how this learning takes place later in Chapter 5. Voluntary control over activities of the ANS is difficult to learn because the system is normally and mostly under the control of parts of the brain (*thalamus* and *hypothalamus*) that operate on an unconscious homeostatic level. However, while the ANS is totally efferent there are afferent nerve fibers that feed back to the cortex and other parts of the brain. In other words, the feedback loop organization is present, but in terms of voluntary processes it is normally weak.

What is needed to improve cortical modification of the ANS is a strengthening of the sensory or afferent element of the organizational feedback loop. One way to do this is to simply provide additional sensory feedback from another correlated source. For example, it would be pretty difficult for you to use the weak conscious feedback of vasodilation and correlated skin temperature increase to learn to modify those activities. If, however, we simply amplify either one of these, we would be strengthening the afferent and sensory part of the organizational loop. Figure 2.18 shows how additional, stronger afferent information gets back to the CNS. It is quite easy to use skin temperature as a correlated measure of local vasodilation (the more warm blood present, the warmer the skin). The amplifier might contain a very sensitive meter which visually deflects with each

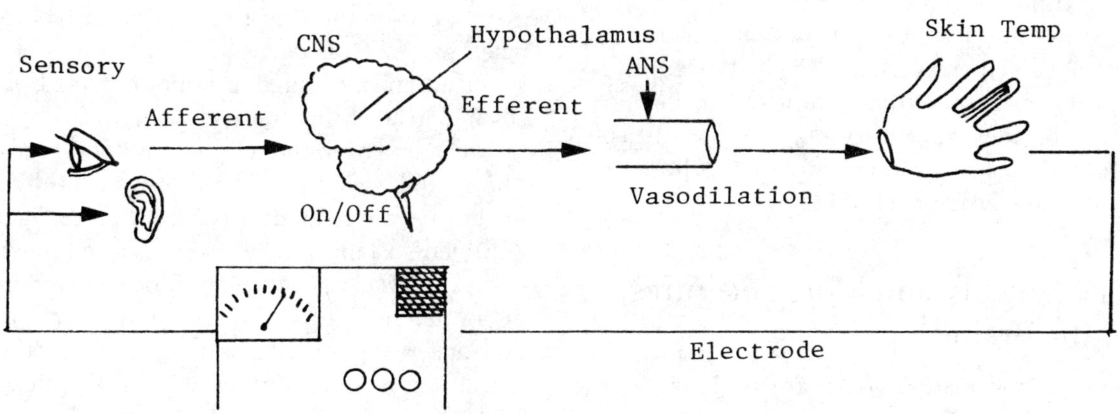

Figure 2.18 Organization of a Feedback Loop

change of, say, ½₀th of a degree. Also, the amplifier might emit a sound each time the ½₀ of a degree deflection occurred. This is now a much stronger feedback loop with the eyes and ears a part of the afferent portion of the organizational loop. This strengthening of the loop with amplified biological information has been called *biofeedback.* Using biofeedback, most people can learn to control their skin temperature at will.

This system and biofeedback clearly demonstrates the constant organizational loop of information in the nervous system. Theoretically, biofeedback should permit the cortical modification of any portion of the ANS.

The Organization of the Brain and the Spinal Cord: More Details

You already know a lot about general aspects of the CNS. Now, you can put what you know to work as we place the brain and spinal cord into organizational loops with their environments.

The Spinal Cord. The spinal cord, running up and down the interior of the spinal vertebrae, can be thought of as a communications trunk line which provides a communications loop between the brain and periphery of the body lying below the head. We have discussed the somatic and autonomic nervous systems in this regard. And earlier, you saw how spinal loops mediate both voluntary and reflexive behavior. In the head itself motor and sensory activity are functions of the *cranial nerves.*

The Brain. The empirical brain, too, is best understood in terms of systems of organizational loops. This approach will consist of sensory input features, processing features, and motor output features in the way in which they are tied together. Because of the particular physical organization of the brain it will be best for us to consider the sensory and motor features of the brain together and then move to how the processing areas are related to them.

The Sensory and Motor Features of the Brain

Sensory information comes to the brain from the outside world through the five senses. These include vision, hearing (audition), smell (olfaction), taste (gustation), and touch (the somatic senses including temperature and pain). There are other sensory information channels or modalities that provide mostly unconscious sensory information.

All of the sensory information (except smell) is relayed to appropriate areas of the brain through a subcortical area called the thalamus. Sensory information travels to three important sensory areas in the brain. These include the *visual cortex, auditory cortex,* and the *somatosensory* (body) area.

Nearly all motor commands originate in the brain. Sensory information is on the incoming side of processing; motor information is on the outgoing side. Motor output is controlled by the *primary motor cortex.* The somatosensory areas and the primary motor cortex are adjacent to one another and more or less parallel one another in terms of representational mapping of body areas (see Figure 2.19). Messages from the motor cortex move through areas below the cortex (including the thalamus) and the spinal cord to produce behavior.

The *cerebellum* is often described in terms of automatic control of learned muscle movements—such as walking. However, the cerebellum contains a representation of sensory and motor areas where it acts, not so much as a command center (as in the case of the primary motor area), but as a monitoring and coordinating center. When you dance, play the piano, etc., all pretty much without thinking about what you are doing, the cerebellum is coordinating visual, auditory, muscular, and vestibular activities (to mention a few). In fact, even reading this page is a delicate symphony of coordinated sensory and motor activity. You move your head and your eyes in unison for sensory input closely coordinated with processing.

The sensory-related and motor-related processing areas of the brain are somewhat conveniently adjacent to the sensory and motor areas. The central fissure provides a convenient dividing line for understanding processing (see Figure 2.20). For example, there are two concentrations of speech-related areas. One, Broca's area (after discoverer Paul Broca) is involved in the production of speech—speech output, and the other, Wernicke's area (after discoverer Carl Wernicke), is involved in receiving speech—speech input. Knowing the general sensory related/motor re-

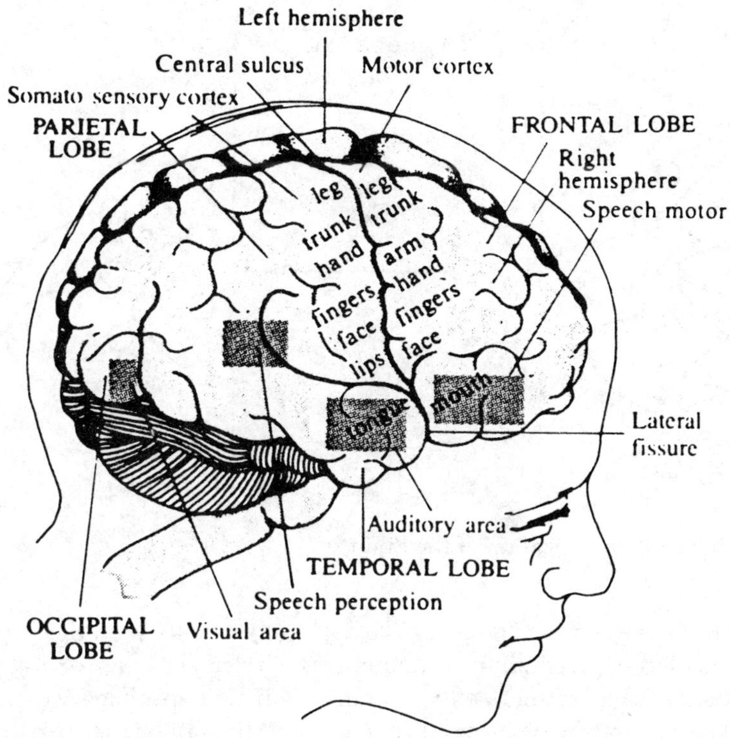

Figure 2.19 Lobes of the Cerebral Cortex

lated areas of processing in the brain, you might have already guessed that Broca's area is located forward of the central fissure and Wernicke's areas behind the fissure. Incapacity of either of these speech areas does not necessarily involve the other.

The Organization of Processing

What is processing? This is the area in our study of the nervous system where we have the least detailed understanding. A good deal is known about the input and output sides of processing, much less is known about what goes on between.

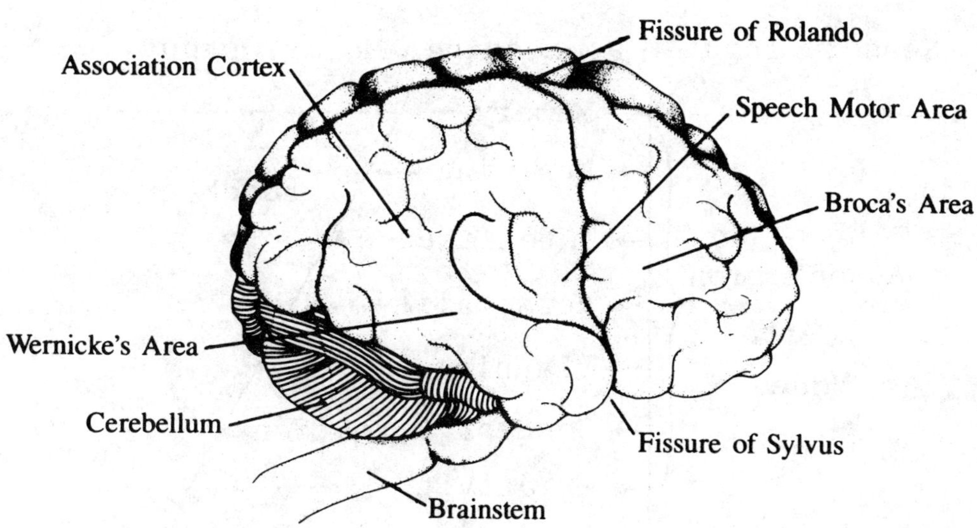

Figure 2.20 Location of Broca's and Wernicke's Areas

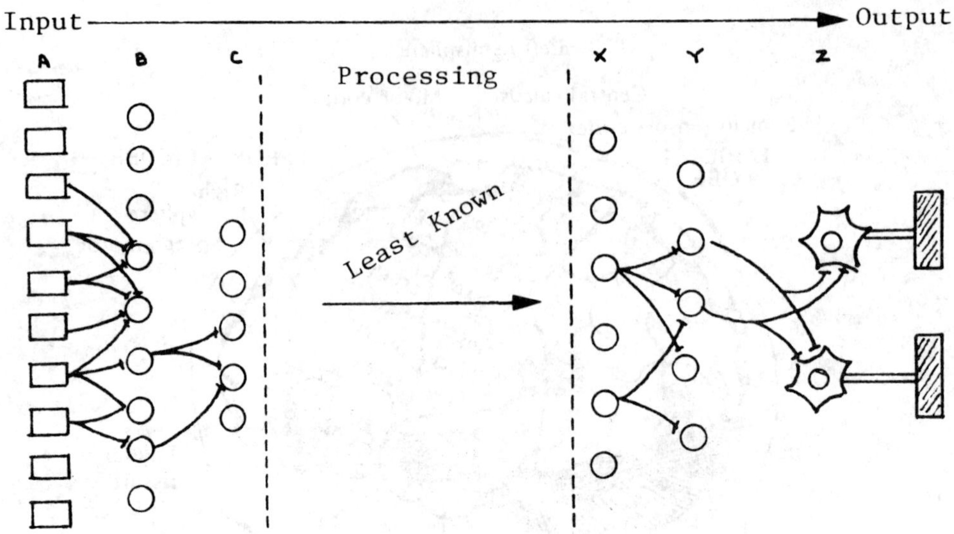

Figure 2.21 Overall Organization of the Brain

Figure 2.21 illustrates this idea. The way I like to think about what lies between input and output is that it is whatever organizes input and output into a survival relationship involving both growth and equilibration (Edelman, 1978, 1985). These are the jobs of the processing computers of the robot (the robot learns more about its environment constantly). The study of how these processing jobs are done in humans and animals comprises most of the subject matter of psychology. Figure 2.22 illustrates how topics in psychology are related to processing.

Processing takes place in what are called the *association areas* of the brain. It would be helpful for you to recall the "association connectedness" differences in processing between the two cerebral hemispheres we discussed earlier. That particular difference in organization of processing is probably the most general difference in cerebral association areas. However, there are more specific sensory/motor association area related to both hemispheres.

Each cerebral hemisphere contains processing areas that are adjacent to the related primary sensory area. It can be seen in Figure 2.23 that the visual cortex sends information into an adjacent perceptual processing area. Complex processing involving combinations of sensory information,

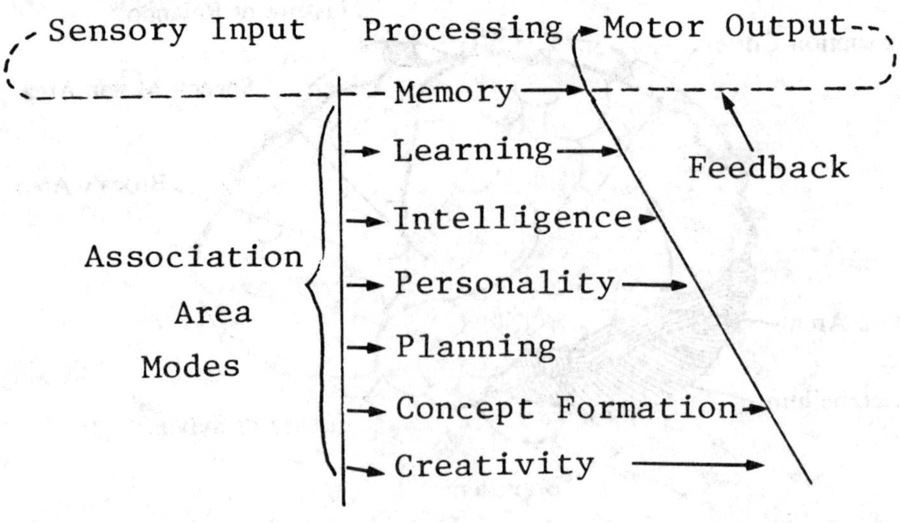

Figure 2.22 Processing Functions of the Brain

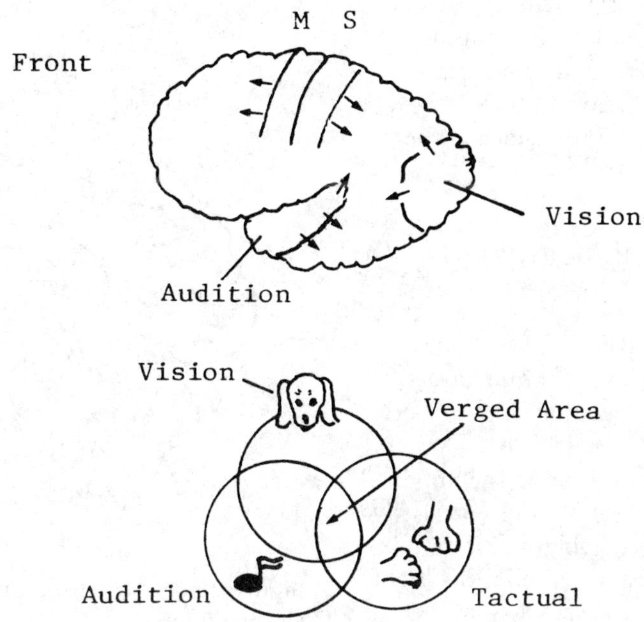

Figure 2.23 Specific Sensory/Motor Areas of Brain Hemispheres

say, audition, vision, and tactile (as when you are dancing) tend to occur where the sensory lobe areas junction or merge.

Just as the areas behind the central fissure are the sensory cortexes and the sensory association or processing areas, in each cerebral cortex motor association areas are found the frontal portions adjacent to the primary motor cortex (see Figure 2.24).

Obviously, the sensory association areas must be richly interconnected with the motor association areas and the cerebellum. If you will think about dancing again for a moment, you not only experience complex sensory input, but complex motor performance. While much of this motor output is automatic with balance coordinated by the cerebellum, you must also usually maneuver between and around other

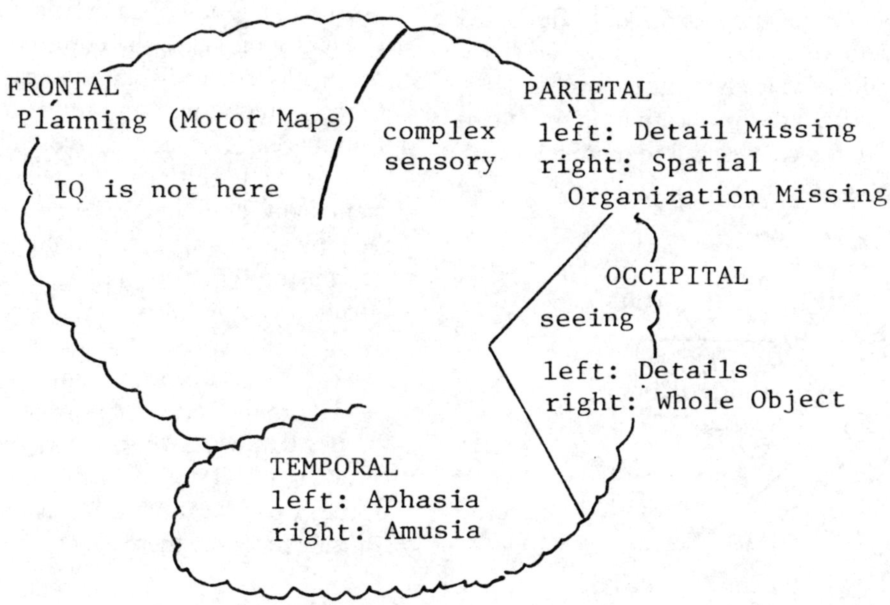

2.24 Cerebral Cortex Motor Association Areas

dancers, as seen in Figure 2.25. The motor association areas in the frontal lobe in conjunction with sensory information guide you through. There might be an occasional planned (not automatic) dip at the end of the dance—frontal motor association area.

The Older Subcortical Areas and Temperature Regulation

Much of the control of your behavior goes on not at a conscious level, but at an unconscious level. Think about the regulation of your body temperature. An organizational feedback loop in your brain maintains your core body temperature at about 98.6°F. Various parts of your body depart from 98.6° considerably. For example, your finger tips are probably at about 85° right now (unless you are cramming for an exam, then they might be at 75°; sympathetic arousal). The subcortical areas of your brain carry out a variety of bodily and behavioral activities. Figure 2.26 and Table 2.5 show the location of some of these areas and describes them.

With two of these subcortical bodies, the brain stem and the hypothalamus, we can easily illustrate the organizational feedback loop involved. These feedback loops are *negative feedback loops* because the activity of the loop is decreased as the activity is increased. The loop negates any variation from a setpoint in the comparator of the loop. A household thermostatic system operates this way as do loops discussed previously in this chapter. Negative feedback overall produces a steady state. In positive feedback loops, which don't concern us in this chapter, production increases lead to more increases, and any decreases lead to more decreases. The

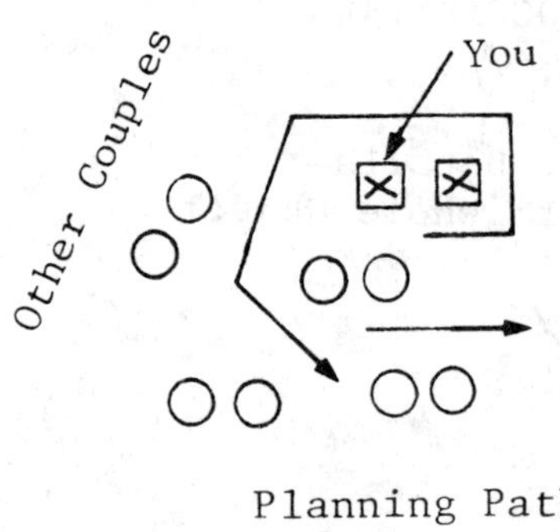

Figure 2.25 Paths of Dancing Couples

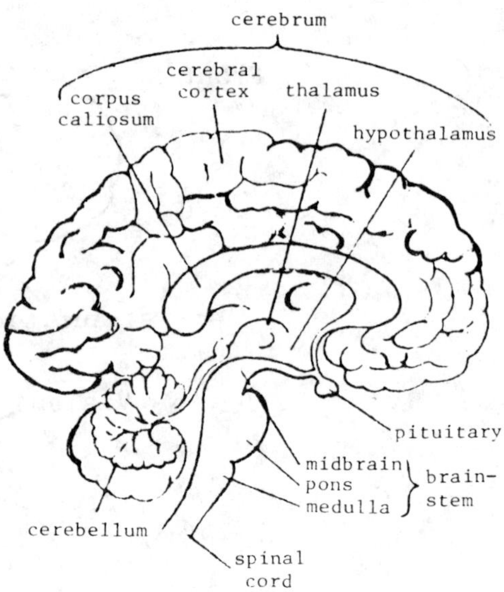

Figure 2.26 Structural Functions of the Human Brain

following examples of temperature regulation are of the negative type (Figures 2.27 and 2.28).

The Reticular Activating System (RAS) Within the brain stem is the reticular activating system (RAS). As in Table 2.5 you can see the RAS is a brain arousal coordinator. If the RAS only aroused the brain in a positive loop fashion, you would either "explode" with information or shut down into sleep for a lack of it. However, the RAS operates as a negative feedback alert loop. This organization is described in Figure 2.27.

This loop keeps the cortex in control of an informational steady state. Normally, a ringing phone would arouse you to get up and answer it. In this case the message would be going right through the larger loop. If however, you had an exam in one hour you might decide (cortex) that the phone call was not important. Somehow the straight-through pattern has to be altered on direction of the cortex. The smaller loop between sensory, RAS, and cortex can keep the normal arousal pattern from occurring and it can ignore the sensory information. Earlier, we discussed how the cortex can learn to ignore certain stressful incoming messages and arousal of the ANS. The RAS is intimately involved in learning to ignore these events or situations.

The Hypothalamus The hypothalamus is a very small aggregate of brain tissue, but it

Table 2.5 Structural Divisions of the Human Brain

Brain stem:	Stalk of brain; enlarged, knobby extension of spinal cord; consists of medulla, pons (bridge), and midbrain. Contains all nerve fibers that pass between spinal cord and higher brain centers and nuclei involved with many autonomic reflexes and RAS.
Function:	Transmission of signals between spinal cord and higher brain centers; control of heartbeat, respiration, some other autonomic functions. Different levels of arousal, sleep and wakefulness, depending on circumstances both learned and unlearned; switch for cerebral hemisphere arousal level role.
Corpus callosum:	Nerve fibers between hemispheres.
Function:	Exchange of information between hemispheres.
Thalamus:	Two egg-shaped masses of gray matter below cerebral hemispheres.
Function:	Main relay center between brain stem and cerebrum; nuclei sort and process sensory information before transmission to cortex.
Hypothalamus:	Small mass (about 4 grams) below thalamus, above pituitary.
Function:	Controls pituitary; integration center for sex drive, anger, hunger, thirst, pleasure, temperature regulation; source of ADH and oxytocin.

plays very critical roles in the overall homeostatic operations of the body. The hypothalamus controls and acts as a switchboard for the internal environment much as the thalamus above it acts as a switchboard for the incoming information headed for the cortex. The hypothalamus controls the *pituitary gland* (see Figure 2.28) not through axonal synaptic transmission as we have discussed up to this point, but through the release of hypothalamic "brain hormones."

Table 2.6 is a list of principal endocrine glands, what *hormones* are secreted, and their effects. Earlier, in the discussion of the autonomic portion of the peripheral nervous system, you learned how the brain influenced the internal environment in terms of "fight or flight" responses and their reductions. Now, with the addition of the hypothalamus and its regulation of the endocrine system, our picture of the nervous control of the internal environment is more complete.

Organizational Aspects of the Entire Nervous System There are two reasons I have chosen the regulation of body temperature as our final example of nervous system organization. First, all aspects of the nervous system's

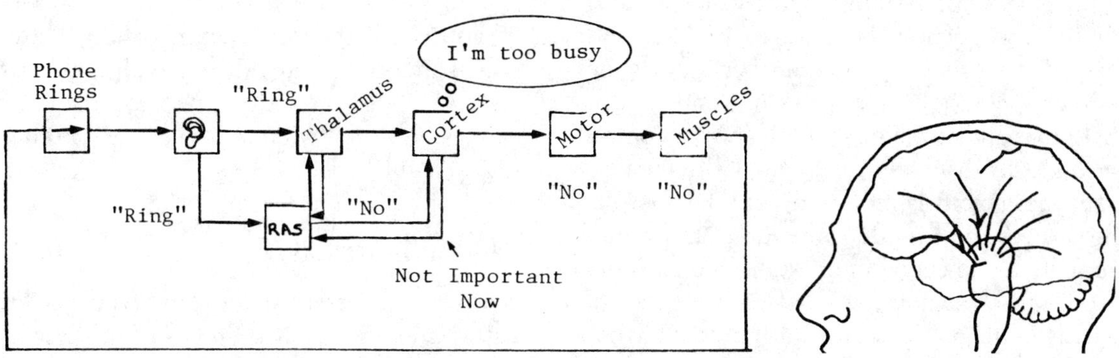

Figure 2.27 The Reticular Activating System

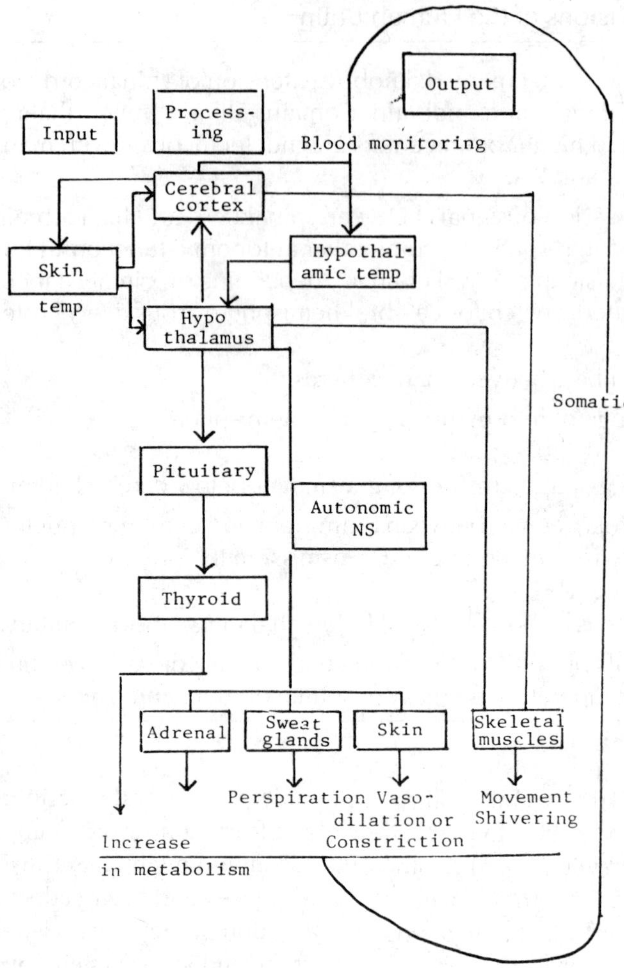

Figure 2.28 The Hypothalamus Regulation of Body Temperature

control can be illustrated in a simplified manner. Second, it puts all of this organized activity into some simple feedback loops.

The regulation of human body temperature so that it hovers right around 98.6°F or 37°C requires that the system be able to respond to both excesses of heat (hot days, rooms, etc.) and of cold. In either case we can begin with the temperature receptors in the skin. It can be seen that the hypothalamus used every control means at its disposal to rectify any discrepancy from the hypothalamic setting of 98.6°F. (During a fever the hypothalamus does its job not through malfunction but through a higher negative feedback setting.) Note the convergence of activity at the bottom of the diagram. The hypothalamus attempts equilibrium through voluntary, involuntary, and hormonal means.

The Methodological Study of the Nervous System's Relationship to Behavior

By now you know a great deal about the nervous system and behavior. You are now in a position to appreciate the significance of the methods which are used to provide you with that knowledge. This treatment of methods cannot be exhaustive, but it will introduce you to both historical and recent attempts.

The Cellular Level

Neurons are essentially microscopic, so filled with variety, and with many supporting and connective glial cells. There are nine times more *glial cells* than nerve cells in the CNS. It is hard

Table 2.6 Some of the Principal Endocrine Glands

Gland	*Hormone*	*Principal Action*
Pituitary, anterior lobe	Growth hormone (somatotropin)	Stimulates bone and muscle growth, inhibits oxidation of glucose, promotes breakdown of fatty acids
	Prolactin	Stimulates milk production and secretion in "prepared" gland
	Thyroid-stimulating hormone (TSH)	Stimulates thyroid
	Adrenocorticotropic hormone (ACTH)	Stimulates adrenal cortex
	Follicle-stimulating hormone (FSH)	Stimulates ovarian follicle, spermatogenesis
	Luteinizing hormone (LH)	Stimulates corpus luteum and ovulation in female, interstitial cells in male
Hypothalamus (via posterior pituitary)	Oxytocin	Stimulates uterine contractions, milk ejection
	Antidiuretic hormone (ADH, vasopressin)	Controls water excretion
Thyroid	Thyroxine, other thyroxinelike hormones	Stimulate and maintain metabolic activities
	Calcitonin	Inhibits release of calcium from bone
Parathyroid	Parathyroid hormone (parathormone)	Stimulates release of calcium from bone, promotes calcium uptake from gastrointestinal tract, inhibits calcium excretion
Adrenal cortex	Cortisol, other cortisol-like hormones	Affect carbohydrate, protein, and lipid metabolism
	Aldostrerone	Affects salt and water balance
Adrenal medulla	Epinephrine and norepinephrine	Increase blood sugar, dilate some blood vessels, increase rate of heartbeat
Pancreas	Insulin	Lowers blood sugar, increases storage of glycogen
	Glucagon	Stimulates breakdown of glycogen to glucose in the liver
Ovary, follicle	Estrogens	Develop and maintain sex characteristics in females, initiate buildup of endometrium
Ovary, corpus luteum	Progesterone and estrogens	Promote continued growth of endometrium
Testis	Testosterone	Supports spermatogenesis, develops and maintains sex characteristics of males

to say what you are looking at even with a microscope. *Staining techniques* have provided good methods by which to study individual neuronal structures by microscope.

By using the *Golgi staining technique* (after discoverer Camillo Golgi—1875), about 1 out of 100 neurons is completely stained (set off) from the others. No one knows why the Golgi method works or why it stains only a particular few neurons. It seems unlikely that the staining occurs on a chance or random basis. The Golgi procedure tells us not only how various neurons are structured, but by inference the number of neurons per standard cubic amount of brain tissue. This has led to our estimates for the entire brain.

The Functional Brain Level

Historically, much has been learned about the functions of areas of the brain by observing the behavioral changes that occur in people who have lost known brain areas due to accidents or illness. This is a little like waiting until your car won't start, and then searching around under the hood to find out what the problem is. Using this method, a novice could eventually learn the functions of all sorts of things under the hood. However, this method could take forever, and it could lead to some very wrong conclusions. It would be more accurate and speedy to simply systematically remove parts one at a time and observe the results in car performance.

When it comes to the brain and the rest of the nervous system, this simple plan can be carried out in many ways. Brain "parts" can be removed, destroyed, *electrically monitored* (remember the neuron is like a tiny battery), and *electrically stimulated* to fire. You have already seen how transmitter chemicals and hormones in the brain inhibit or stimulate neurons to fire.

All of these methods and more are used to study the nervous system functions and their interactions. Since the nerve impulse is essentially the same throughout the animal kingdom, and brains of different species have similar organizational patterns, most of these methods can be applied to animals. These studies can directly help us understand human brain function.

The Interaction Level

Recent studies and recently developed methodologies have helped researchers close in on the details of the relationship between brain processing activity and the input and output involved. Three very important developments include the *tachistoscopic* presentation of stimuli to *"split-brain"* patients; the electroencephalographic study of brain *lateralization* in normal subjects and the use of *positron emission tomography* (PET) in the study of brain lateralization. All of these methods are extensively used in the study of other aspects of brain function. The study of brain lateralization and *hemisphericity* has been used in each example because it so clearly illustrates the methods and the brain functions.

The Tachistoscopic Presentation of Visual Information: Lateralization of Function. Epilepsy involves various forms of involuntary seizures. In some epileptics motor area seizures are so pronounced and so regular they become a threat to life itself. For many of these individuals the seizures do not respond to medication. By the 1960s animal studies had led to the hypothesis that these seizures might be restricted to motor areas in one cerebral hemisphere by surgically cutting the *commissures* that connect the two hemispheres (Bogen & Vogel, 1962). Since the seizure must start somewhere, if the commissures were cut it would not reach the other side of the brain. Several severe epileptic patients had their commissures surgically cut, and thus became what have been termed "split-brain" patients. While the outcomes of these operations varied from patient to patient in terms of arresting the seizures, the cutting of the commissures seemed to have little effect on their everyday behavior.

The evaluation of the patients in terms of functional outcomes, i.e., behavioral, psychological, and neurological, was first carried out by Michael Gazzaniga (1967) and Roger Sperry (1968) and their coworkers. Using tachistoscopic presentation of stimuli these researchers discovered many interesting things about the functions of each side of the cerebral cortex. Using knowledge of how the visual system puts information into each side of the brain, a methodological setup was invented that allowed researchers to selectively put information into either side of the patient's brain.

When the patient's eyes are focused in as shown in Figure 2.29 and information is presented for only ⅒ of a second, information from the left visual field goes only to the right visual

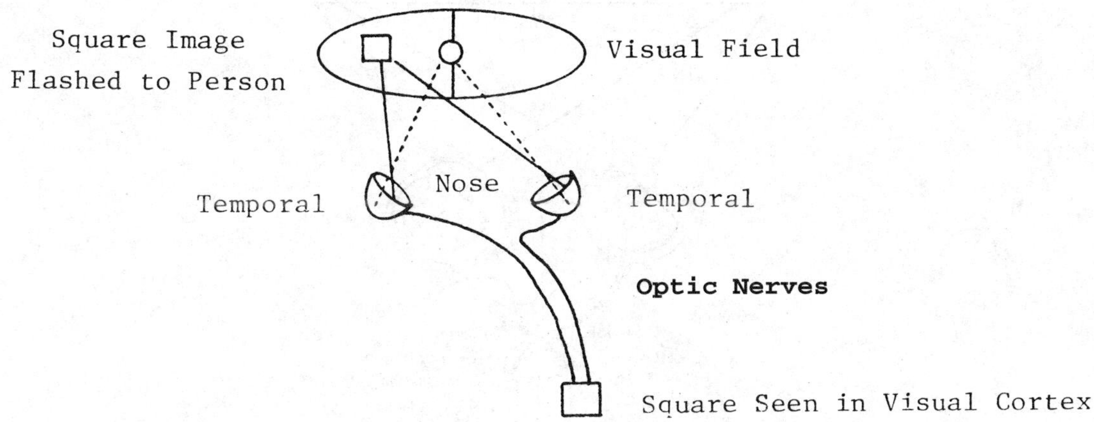

Figure 2.29 Diagram of Cambered Eyes, Visual Field, and Right Side of Optic Nerve

cortex. Note that with the eyes cambered and fixed on the center of the screen, the image of the square falls only on the temporal (temples) side of the retina of the right eye, and on the nasal (nose) side of the left eye. Now notice that the nasal image of the square crosses over to the right side, and the temporal square stays on the right side. This puts the square only into the right visual cortex. Note, too, that the corpus callosum commissure has been surgically cut. This keeps the square restricted to the right side of the brain. In a normal person the square would immediately be transferred to the other side so that both halves of the cortex would have the information. What if the person moves his eyes? He doesn't. Since information is presented for only 1⁄10th second, there is too little time for the person to shift his gaze. By the time he does, the information is gone.

This was a rather creative invention of methodology to study functional effects of hemisphere deconnection. Roger Sperry shared the Nobel Prize in physiology in 1981 for this and much subsequent work in this area. The essential findings (there were many more) presented in 1968 are listed in Figure 2.30. Patients, for example, seemed to be blind to words presented in the left visual field and therefore to the right hemisphere. On the other hand, words presented to the right visual field and therefore to the left visual cortex were readily described by the patients.

It is very reasonable now to assume that speech or writing might simply be an appearance of highly routinized groups of neurons and spacial (spatial) constructions with simply an appearance of intermodal connectivity in the right hemisphere. When looking at Figure 2.30, realize that the left side of the brain controls the right side of the body and vice-versa.

Electroencephalographic Measurement: Lateralization of Function. The brains of all animals produce a continuous measurable output of tiny electrical signals. Your brain is doing it right now. The electroencephalograph (EEG) and the record it produces, the electroencephalogram, provide measures of this activity. Since electrical sensors can be placed virtually anywhere on the scalp, and since the extracellular electrical activity levels immediately beneath them is what is measured, the electroencephalographic method can be used to determine the general level of activity in any part of the brain.

As with any electrical signal, EEG signals from the brain vary in terms of both frequency and amplitude. Each of these measures indicates what the brain in a particular area is doing. The frequency of the EEG is related to the predominant number of times, in a given period of time (usually a second), neurons are firing. This firing or impulse rate is related to the general arousal level in the area being monitored. Figure 2.31 shows some sample frequencies along with the correlated arousal level in the area. The higher the frequency, the higher the arousal level. Actually, this is not an unexpected correlation. The more excited a neuron becomes with information, the higher the frequency of its impulse activity.

The EEG's wave forms are very complex (as is the issue involved). They do not occur as

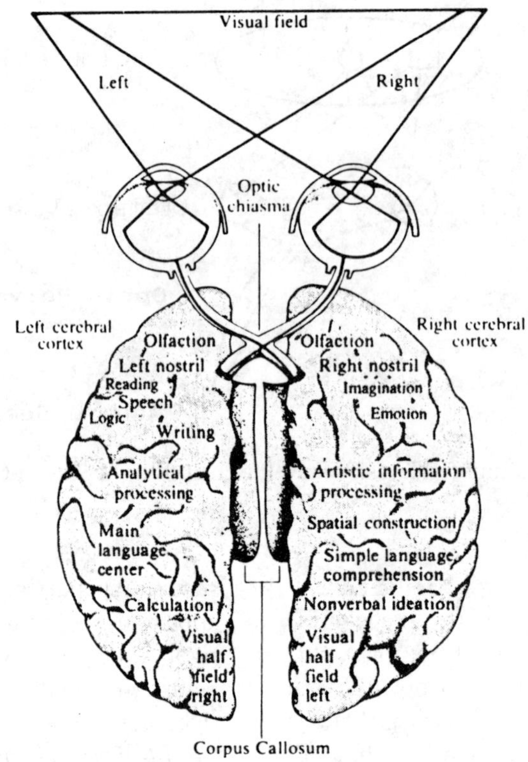

Figure 2.30 Essential Lateralization Findings of M. Gazzaniga and R. Sperry

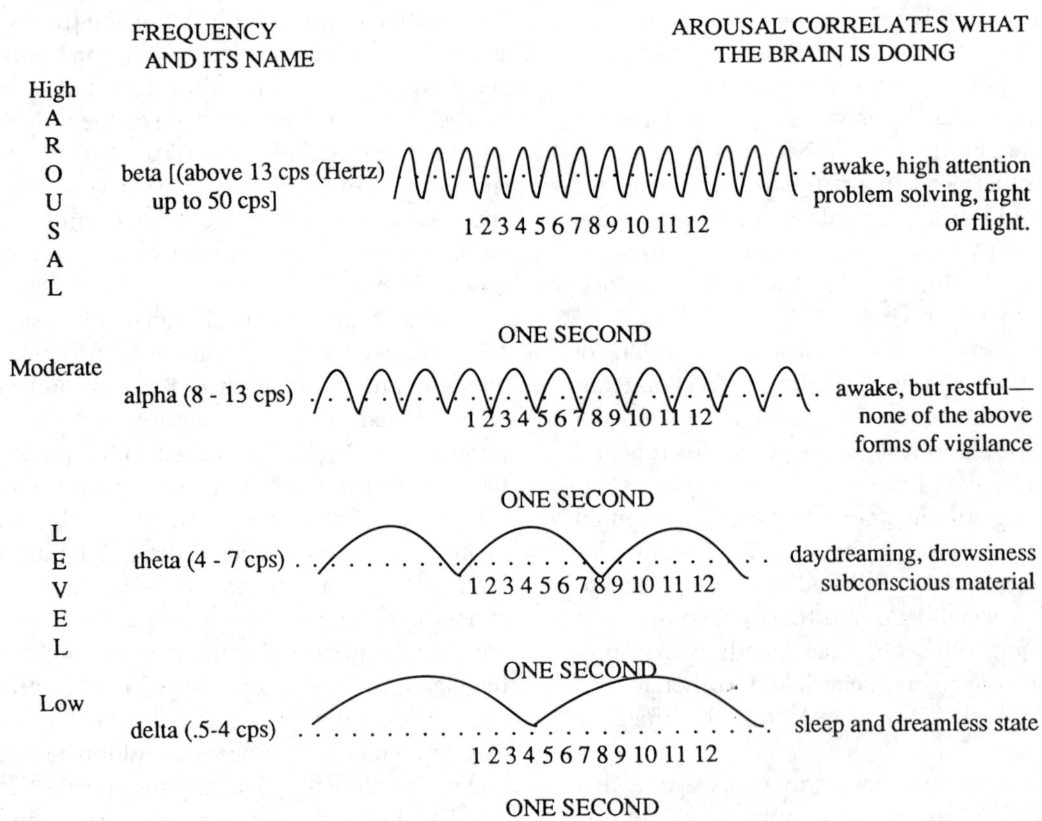

Figure 2.31 Types of Frequencies

distinctly as my frequency diagrams would lead you to believe. The diagram shows the only predominant frequency at any given moment; the one with the greatest electrical power or amplitude. The amplitude refers to the height of the waves and is measured in voltage strength (Figure 2.32). Typically the amplitude varies between 20 and 100 microvolts (millionths of a volt). While the frequency of EEG waves is associated with arousal level, amplitude is related to the number of local neurons firing in *synchrony*, or in unison. Figure 2.33 shows a highly simplified idea of how neurons might fire in synchrony (A) or in *asynchrony* (B) (out of unison). There are thousands or millions of neurons involved in most EEG measurements, but situation (A) would produce a higher amplitude. It should be noted that in general the EEG does not measure the action potential pulsing down axons but measures correlated extracellular activity. However, the case of high synchrony probably represents an exception to this and does measure the action potentials (pulses). The idea of voltage synchrony and asynchrony is analogous (perhaps homologous) to the constructive and destructive wave interference patterns involved in the exposure of a hologram.

If the brain had little or no EEG activity, it would be one indication of brain death in a body that is still functioning. In this measurement of brain death, the entire brain is not dead. Subcortical centers, like the brain stem, would still be functioning. However, brain death determination is very complex, requiring much more than just low or no amplitude activity. The EEG is only a part of brain death determination.

The EEG can be used to study the lateralized functions of the cerebral hemispheres. David Galin and Robert Ornstein (1972) studied the EEG records of the left and right cerebral cortexes while normal college students carried out various tasks. They reasoned that if the left hemisphere was responsible for speech and writing, and the right for spatial construction as Roger Sperry had found with split-brain patients, it should show up in the EEG records of normal people. It was found that this was true.

When a student subject was asked to write a letter, his left hemisphere (electrodes on left scalp) produced more beta waves and the right hemisphere (electrodes on the right scalp) produced more alpha waves during the writing task. Then, when a subject was asked to put together a design of blocks (a spatial task), the EEG record reversed. Now, the right hemisphere produced more beta and the left more alpha.

These studies using EEG methodologies have helped corroborate the notion that the

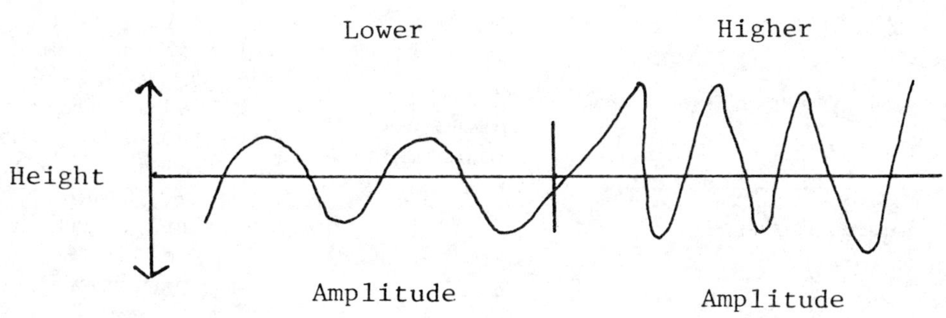

Figure 2.32 Amplitude

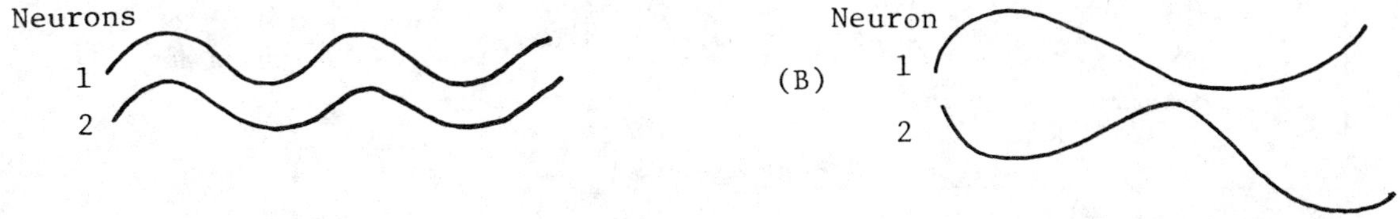

Figure 2.33 Simplified Version of Neurons Firing

brains of normal people, as well as those of split-brain patients, are lateralized and specialized for particular functions during daily activities. Now we will move on to a very recent methodology which corroborates even further the idea of laterality of functions and supports aspects of all of our discussions of hemisphericity.

Positron Emission Tomography (PET): Lateralization of Function. The number one source of food for brain activity is *glucose.* As neurons do their work, they burn up glucose. Positron emission tomography allows us to at least see where and to what degree groupings of neurons are working—while they work. This measure is possible because along with the glucose a radioactive substance has been included. As the working neurons consume the glucose, positrons are set free (decay). When these freed positrons (antimatter) meet freely occurring electrons (matter), they annihilate one another. The result of this mutual annihilation is the release of two energy rays that can be systematically detected and related to their sources of might. Sophisticated computer programs reconstruct the location and degrees of glucose consumption throughout the slice (tomo) of brain being monitored by energy ray detectors.

In the drawings of computer-constructed images in Figure 2.34, you can see both where activity is occurring and to what degree with different types of sensory input. This method gives us more details about how the hemispheres are lateralized and specialized for functions and how they work together Notice that non-musicians tend to process new (to them) music on the right side of the brain. Musicians, for whom much music has become routinized, tend to process the information on the left side. This corroborates what we learned earlier concerning the interconnectedness of neurons in the left versus the right cerebral hemispheres. Also, note that language and music seem to be lateralized.

Due to its great cost and great complexity, positron emission tomography is still pretty much of a research tool available to only a very fortunate few researchers. However, I think you can see that PET will become a very important tool with which to study the nervous system and behavior.

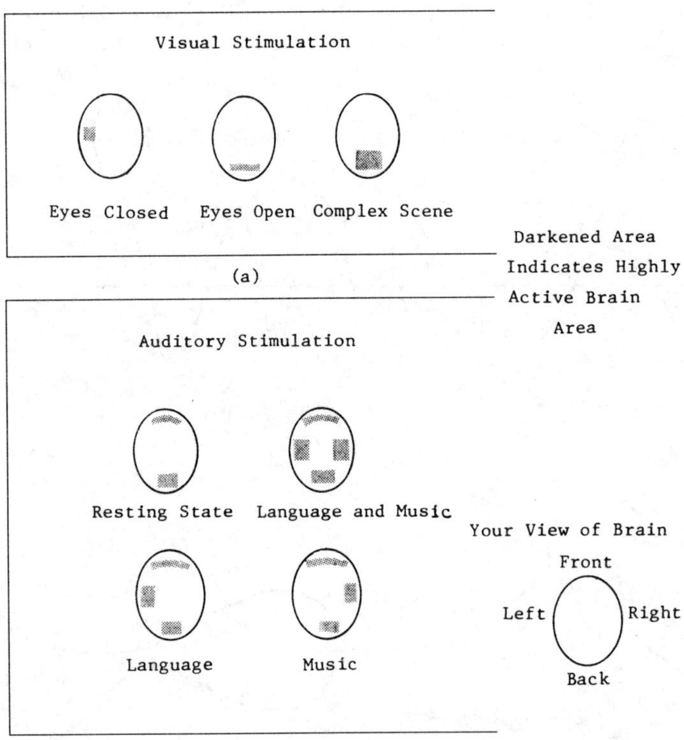

When a subject is visually stimulated (a) glucose metabolism is greatest when viewing a complex scene. Recall that the visual projection areas are located in the back of the brain. When subjects are presented with various auditory stimuli (b) various parts of the brain begin high glucose metabolism. The high levels of activity seen in the frontal areas of the brain probably resulted from the fact that these subjects were told that the more they could remember about the experiment, the more they would get paid for their participation. Perhaps the frontal areas of the brain are planning strategies for recall and rehearsing information.

Figure 2.34 Diagram of Brain Function Using Positron Emission Tomography

Bringing It All Together

The philosophical, theoretical, empirical, and methodological treatments presented in this chapter for thinking about the brain and behavior all fit together. The interrelatedness of these four levels of analysis is a crucial element for a general systems view and the understanding it can provide. And, it will be the important overriding concern in all chapters which follow.

The interplay of the four levels of analysis produce a constantly emerging understanding of how behavior can come about, and how the brain can give rise to consciousness. It seems likely to me that within the lifetimes of most readers of this text that mind and brain will somehow come together. It seems certain that with advances in biochemistry, in computer systems, holography, and methods like PET, we are poised on the threshold of great advances in this area. We can go back to Hans Moravec's statement in the beginning of the chapter. Perhaps Dr. Moravec is right—human equivalence by 2010. When the control systems in autonomous robots merge in ability with the control systems in humans, then what will you and I do? We will return to this question in Chapter 6.

Glossary

acetylcholine: A neurotransmitter that is responsible for muscle activity.

afferent: Nerve fibers that carry information toward the CNS.

algorithm: Any set of rules for performing translational or transformational operations (including mathematical, mechanical, linguistic, neurobiological, metaphorical, etc., ones) which link problems, input data, and solutions. The long division algorithm is a set of rules which provides one way of solving long division problems.

amplitude: The power of any wave of energy. This power is indicated by the height of the wave(s).

association areas (of the brain): Areas of the cortex that receive information from the primary sensory and motor cortexes of the brain. These areas are involved in learning and perceiving.

asynchrony: The rising and falling of energy waves at differing times.

auditory cortex: The portion of the cortex where "hearing" is located.

autonomic division (of the peripheral nervous system): The self-regulating portion of the peripheral nervous system that innervates smooth muscles and glands.

autonomous mobile robot: A self-directed, free-moving, self-contained robot system.

axon: The major conduction tube which takes information (an impulse) away from the cell body of a neuron.

biofeedback: A method of feeding back the amplified output of a person's (or animal's) autonomic nervous system so that the person becomes aware of it, and can learn to control its behavior.

brain: The portion of the nervous system that is enclosed in the skull.

cerebellum: A part of the brain that is involved in balance and coordination. It integrates many motor and sensory systems in body movement.

cerebral hemispheres: The major two rounded parts of the brain that are located above the brain stem.

cocaine: A stimulating drug that is made from the leaves of the coca plant.

commissures: Communicative nerve networks between the two hemispheres of the brain.

comparator: A device or process which permits a system to determine its precoded information state, and whether or not deviations from that precoded state occur. In holography the standard reference permits the recording and recreation of the entire visual information state of a film negative.

cranial nerves: Nerves which control sensory and motor activities in the head. These nerves do not rise from the spinal cord, but are present directly in the brain.

curare: A poison that has a paralytic action on the body.

dopamine: A neurotransmitter found in many parts of the brain. An overabundance of this chemical seems related to the mental disorder schizophrenia.

efferent: Nerve fibers that carry information away from the CNS.

electrically monitored: The measurement of the electrical activity of neurons or larger portions of the brain.

electrically stimulated: Neurons, groups of neurons, or larger portions of the brain stimulated into activity by the application of electric current.

electrolyte: A chemical substance that carries electrical current by the movement of ions.

electron: A fundamental subatomic particle that carries a negative electric charge. Electricity is often described as a flow of electrons in a conductive medium.

enzyme destruction: The altering of transmitter chemicals by enzymes so that they will no longer function as transmitters.

epilepsy: A nervous system disorder that involves involuntary muscle seizures.

equivalence: Like, but not the same. Many machines perform tasks much in the ways humans do. These machines include everything from pliers to computers.

excitatory: Causing a process to begin or to continue. With inhibition, one of the two fundamental nervous system processes.

experiential world: The perceived world of conscious experiences, thoughts, images, and awareness of experience.

feedback loop: The loop or path of processes or elements that inputs the loop's activities. This "looping back" of a system's output permits it to maintain a steady state.

frequency: The number of waves which occur within a given amount of time to produce energy. The more waves that occur, for example within a second, the higher the frequency of that wave.

general intelligence: Problem-solving capacities in animals or machines that may be applied to a broad variety of problems.

glial cells: Neuronal supportive cells in the central nervous system.

glucose: A simple sugar important in releasing energy.

Golgi staining technique: A chemical process which brings about 1 out of 100 neurons into clear view.

hemisphericity: Refers to the idea that individual people tend to be either mostly "right-brained" or mostly "left-brained."

hologram: The whole (holo) record (gram) of a visual scene recorded on a film negative that, when illuminated properly, will produce a three-dimensional image of the original visual scene.

holographic imagery production: The photographic production of three-dimensional images.

hormones: Chemicals secreted by endocrine glands that give rise to various activities in cells throughout the body.

hypothalamus: Regulates a broad variety of bodily adjustments, including the activities of the autonomic nervous system, emotional behavior, motivated behavior, thirst, hunger, sexual behavior, body temperature, and endocrine activities (through the pituitary gland).

idiosyncratic languages: Languages which are personal to each individual. These are personal sets of rules of thinking which occur when the individual confronts a novel situation.

inhibitory: Stops a process from continuing. With excitation, one of the two fundamental nervous system processes.

innervation: To supply with nerves. The excitation of muscles and glands by nerves.

insulating sheath: Most axons are insulated from the surrounding chemical environment. This sheath also sets the conditions for the transmission of an impulse in "jumps" along the axon.

interregional: Taking place between regions of the brain.

intraregional: Taking place within a region of the brain.

invertebrates: Animals which have no skeletal backbone, such as worms or octopi.

ions: An atom or group of atoms that may carry either a positive or negative electrical charge. In substances, electrical current may be carried by ion movement.

lateralization: The study of which side of the brain performs which function.

machine intelligence: The capacities of machine systems, like computers, to solve problems and to "learn."

mapping: The process of learning (acquiring) perceptual and memory information about the territory in which a machine or animal must perform tasks.

natural languages: Languages which have developed for general use by the members of a culture. Examples would include English, German, Chinese, etc.

negative feedback loop: A feedback loop in which any variations from a setpoint are negated. This permits the body or system to maintain a state of balance.

neuronal: Of neurons—neurons are the communication(ing) cells of the brain and the rest of the nervous system.

neurons: The communication(ing) cells of the nervous system.

nodes of Ranvier: Points along the insulating sheaths of axons that maintain the conduction of "jumping" impulses.

parasympathetic (division of the autonomic nervous system): Activates normal, non-stressed states of homeostasis in the glands and smooth muscles of the major body cavity. Often works in opposition to activations of the sympathetic division of the autonomic nervous system.

peripheral nervous system: All parts of the nervous system except for the brain and spinal cord.

phase: The degree to which different energy waves are in step with one another. If they rise and fall together, they are in phase. If one wave rises while another falls, they are out of phase.

pituitary gland: The master endocrine gland. It controls hormone secretions that influence other endocrine glands throughout the body.

point-by-point: In regular photography, parts or points of light information selected through the camera's aperture or opening that fall on parallel points of the film negative. Only a small portion of the light from the original scene is recorded on the film.

positron emission tomography: A method of studying the activities of the living brain as it does its work.

presynaptic vesicles: Within the terminal buttons of the axon are small vesicles that store transmitter chemicals for future use.

primary motor cortex: The major area of the cortex that is involved in the control of bodily movement.

psychotic disorder: A broad class of severe mental disorders that includes severe mood disorders, several forms of schizophrenia, and paranoia.

redundantly: In excess of what is needed—an overabundance.

reuptake: A process of clearing the synaptic gap of transmitter chemicals after the transmission of a signal across the gap. The presynaptic vesicles draw the previously released transmitter chemicals back into them.

schizophrenia: A mental disorder that influences nearly all aspects of a person's functioning. There is a general loss of contact with the reality the normal person perceives, and behavior is accordingly disturbed.

sessile: An organism which is permanently attached (for example, to a rock), and is not free to move about.

somatic division (of the autonomic nervous system): Includes the nerve supply to the skeletal muscles (voluntary) and the sensory nerves that lead into the CNS.

somatosensory: The major area of the cortex that receives sensory information from the body.

spatio-temporal: In space and time.

specialized languages: Languages which have developed for the use of specialized groups of people in a culture. Examples would include mathematics, musical notes, and rules of games.

spinal cord: The portion of the central nervous system encased in the backbone. It is the major communication link between the brain and the rest of the body.

split-brain patients: Severe epileptic patients who have had the communicative nerve networks between the two cerebral cortexes surgically cut.

staining techniques: Chemicals applied to brain or nervous system tissue to permit clear viewing of individual neurons and their various structures.

standard reference: See comparator.

subcortical: Below the cortex of the brain. Usually refers to the older centers of the brain, including the thalamus, hypothalamus, pituitary gland, and the brain stem.

subcortical nuclei: Older (in an evolutionary sense) centers of the brain that are deep inside the brain and control its basic functions.

sympathetic (division of the autonomic nervous system): Activates the fight or flight patterns of responses when the person or organism is stressed. This system mobilizes the energies of the body in the face of either real or perceived threats.

synchrony: The rising and falling of energy waves in unison.

tachistoscopic: The rapid presentation of stimuli.

thalamus: A processing center for all sensory information (except for smell) on its way to the cerebral cortex.

vasoconstriction: The contraction of blood vessels.

vasodilation: The expansion of blood vessels.

vertebrates: Animals which have skeletal backbones, such as mice or human beings.

visual cortex: The portion of the cortex where "seeing" is done.

Biopsychology: Doing Psychology on Your Own

LOIS MCDERMOTT

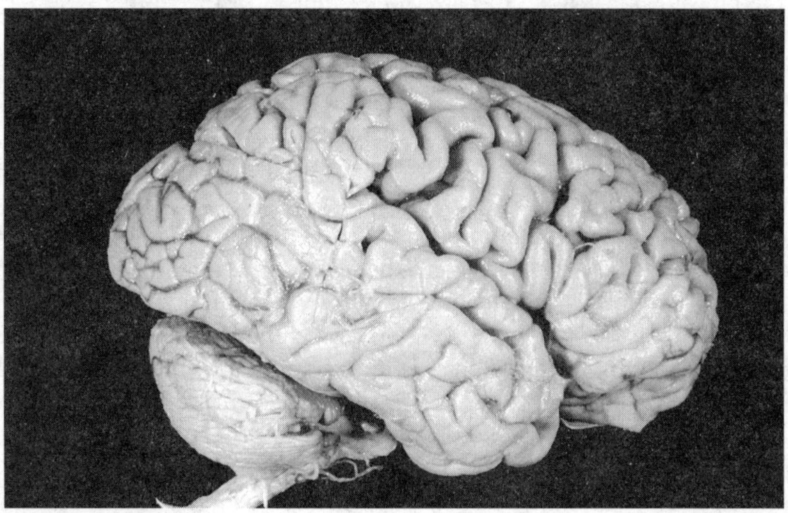

Basic Concept #2—Two Big Questions

Beginning students of psychology are often quite surprised, even dismayed, by the widespread infiltration of biology into the study of psychology. Psychology, i.e., the study of behavior and mental processes of sentient organisms, has always been a natural science. To ignore this fact is to grossly misunderstand the nature of the study of psychology. Ancient Greek philosophers of science, Plato and Aristotle (to later be joined by European philosophers, Descartes and Locke) began to think about and debate the **mind-body** question and the **nature-nurture** question centuries ago. The two big questions in biopsychology are: (1) how is the psyche determined by the interaction of nature (biological functions) and nurture (environmental experience)? And, (2) to what extent is the mind (psyche) the same as the body (brain) or separate from the body? These same questions continue to intrigue psychologists and the lay public alike. Often these questions enter political and religious debates. Is homosexuality a choice or is it innate? Are the cognitive capabilities of females different from males and if so, is the difference due to hormones and genetics or rearing and social structure? These questions have been with us for hundreds of years and the search for answers to these and many more like them continues today in the subfields of biopsychology called neuroscience, physiological psychology, behavioral genetics, sociobiology, and behavioral evolution, to name the most prominent.

Neuroscience. The function of the brain has intrigued humans for millennia. It was suggested initially that it was nothing more than a radiator to allow the cooling of the body. In fact, the brain does control temperature regulation, but not as a radiator. It was also suggested that the body contained four distinct vapors (humors) which gave rise to four personality styles, i.e., sanguine (blood), melancholic (black bile), choleric (yellow bile) and phlegmatic (phlegm). In fact, there are neurochemicals (i.e., hormones and neurotransmitters) in our brain and body that do play an important role in mood and personality—e.g., endorphins, estrogen, testosterone, and a host of neurotransmitters (most of which are yet to be discovered and described). As awareness of specific brain areas emerged the search for the soul was on. The first stop was the pineal gland, which turned out to be involved in the control of our biorhythms while areas of the frontal cortex appeared involved in control of intention and thus perhaps "free will."

Evolution and Genetics. With the advent of Darwin's Theory of Evolution and the discovery of genes, chromosomes and the double helix, focus shifted to the role of evolution and genetics in the nature of Man. It was some time before the female of the species was included in the study of humans. Today the Human Genome Project is underway to identify and describe the millions of genes that comprise the 46 strands of human DNA.

The study of the minds and brains of the wounded on European battlefields during the 19th century fueled knowledge of the mysteries of the mind-brain connection. In the 20th century researchers increasingly turned to the vivisection of animals for knowledge to be extrapolated to the human mind and brain. As we move into the 21st century, the development of sophisticated imaging techniques (e.g., MRI, PET, CAT scans) allow us to "see" the brain in action as the mind is involved in a host of activities. Originally the claim was made for biological **determinism**—i.e., "**biology as destiny**." At the close of this century a new view holds sway, namely, **biological interactionism.** One of the most important discoveries of the modern age of biopsychology is the fact that experience plays an enormous role in the development of brain structure. Ninety percent of the synaptic connections in the adult brain are not present at birth—but arise from experience with the environment. In addition, we now know that all genetic predispositions come to fruition, if—and only if, the environment is optimal for their development. Findings such as these have replaced the view of biological determinism of the human psyche with the concept of biopsychosocial interactionism. The question is no longer nature *or* nurture but nature *and* nurture.

Unit Focus. In this unit on biopsychology the focus will be on the neuroscience of the human psyche. You will be introduced to the structure and function of the nervous system at the level of the neuron, and the structures of the brain. We will focus on the higher order processes that are unique to human and non-human primates. These processes are highly evolved in the two hemispheres of the cerebral cortex of primate brains. To explore these processes you will be introduced to patients who have either suffered traumatic brain damage or undergone therapeutic surgeries that have changed the function of their brains in interesting ways that provide insight into the working of the most amazing organ of the human body.

Study Objectives

1. Learn the parts of the neuron and how they are involved in neurochemical transmission across the synapse. Understand the role of neurotransmitters (NT) in brain function.
2. Learn the structure and function of the various divisions of the nervous system.
3. Learn about the evolution of the triune brain, and which functional areas are found in each layer. Learn how we judge the intelligence of the brains of animals on the phylogenetic scale.
4. Learn the structures and their functions found in the two cerebral cortical hemispheres.
5. Learn the research (e.g., patients with brain damage) that establishes the occurrence of hemispheric laterality in the human brain.
6. Be familiar with the research on "split brain patients" and the implication for our sense of a unitary self.
7. Understand how to interpret findings of brain differences that are correlated with behavioral differences.

Key Terms

acetylcholine
afferent
algorithm
amplitude
association areas (of the brain)
asynchrony
auditory cortex
autonomic division
autonomous mobile robot
axon
biofeedback
brain
cerebellum
cerebral hemispheres
cocaine
commissures
comparator
cranial nerves
curare
dopamine
efferent
electrically monitored
electrically stimulated
electrolyte
electron
enzyme destruction
epilepsy
equivalence
excitatory
experiential world
feedback loop
frequency
general intelligence
glial cells
glucose
Golgi staining technique
hemisphericity
hologram
holographic imagery production
hormones
hypothalamus
idiosyncratic languages
inhibitory
innervation
insulating sheath
interregional
intraregional
invertebrates
ions
lateralization
machine intelligence
mapping
natural languages
negative feedback loop
neuronal
neurons
nodes of Ranvier
parasympathetic (division of the autonomic nervous system)
peripheral nervous system
phase
pituitary gland
point-by-point
positron emission tomography
presynaptic vesicles
primary motor cortex
psychotic disorder
redundantly
reuptake
schizophrenia
somatic division (of the autonomic nervous system)
somatosensory
spatial-temporal
specialized languages
spinal cord
split-brain patients
staining techniques
sandard reference
subcortical
subcortical nuclei
sympathetic (division of the autonomic nervous system)
synchrony
tachistoscopic
thalamus
vasoconstriction
vasodilation
vertebrates
visual cortex

Problem Set #2: Biopsychology

1. Match parts of the neuron (cell body, vesicles, axon, terminal, synapses, dendrite, receptors) with the following:
   a. NT released into space called ______
   b. NT synthesized in ______
   c. NT released from ______ which are located in the ______
   d. postsynaptic activity caused by binding of NT on post-synaptic ______
   e. action potential travels down ______
   f. portion of neuron which may be wrapped in myelin is ______
2. If you were being attacked by a pack of wild dogs, what role would each of the following play in your defense and survival?
   a. occipital cortex
   b. hypothalamus
   c. precentral cortex
   d. frontal cortex

e. parietal cortex
f. amygdala
g. limbic system
h. Broca's area
i. ANS
j. somatic NS
k. temporal lobes
l. adrenal glands
m. reticular activating system
n. endorphins

3. Name the part of the nervous system (CNS, somatic NS, ANS, SNS, PSNS) involved with the following:
   a. directs voluntary movements of skeletal muscles
   b. spinal column
   c. transmit sensory information from body surface and muscles to brain
   d. increases heart rate, slows digestion, dilates pupils
   e. calms the body after danger has passed
   f. prepares the body to respond to danger or threat
   g. controls the secretions of glands and the muscles of internal organs
4. While you are writing answers to these questions which brain areas perform the following functions?
   a. sensing how tightly you are holding the pen
   b. causing you to tighten or loosen your grip on the pen
   c. noticing the shape of the marks you are making
   d. keeping good postural control as you write
   e. keeping you alert and involved as you work
   f. noticing whether the marks are actually "words"
5. Damage to which area of the brain would most likely give rise to the following symptoms?
   a. hearing loss
   b. neglect syndrome
   c. disruption of normal breathing
   d. inability to voluntarily move the L arm
   e. movements such as walking are jerky and uncoordinated
   f. inability to recognize these marks as words
   g. cannot form spoken words, although can understand speech
   h. inability to feel the weight of shoe on your R foot
   i. disturbed hormone balance in your body
   j. loss of appetite for food or sex
   k. loss of problem solving abilities, e.g., "judging" and "planning"
6. Jerry has had a commissurotomy to give him relief from epilepsy. In an experiment using a tachistoscope various pictures or words were flashed in portions of the visual field. When asked to say what he had seen, Jerry said "Bench." When asked to select an object from behind a screen he selected a toy car. What two images must have been projected respectively to the LVF vs. RVF? Why? Which hand did he use? Why?

7. In a second experiment the picture of a NAIL was projected to both visual fields. When asked to "match" the image by selecting from a collection of alternatives, Jerry used his ______ hand to point to a snake and his _______ hand to point to a hammer. Why did his two hands make different matches?
8. In a final experiment, the picture of a snowman and house covered with snow was flashed to one visual field and a picture of a chicken foot was flashed to the other. Jerry picked different responses with his left and right hand. When Jerry was asked to explain why he made his two responses he said "I saw a snow scene and picked the snow shovel, and I guess you have to keep the chickens inside during a snow storm."
   a. What was flashed in the right visual field?
   b. Which hand chose the shovel?
   c. What does the comment "and I guess you have to keep the chickens inside during a snow storm" illustrate about hemispheric function?

See Appendix C for answers to problem set.

3

Consciousness

What Is Consciousness?

Consciousness (everyday awareness) is fundamental to psychology, because it constitutes the evolutionary flooring from which human behavior and cognition arose. Human beings share consciousness with lower animals, and its presence in them is hundreds of millions of years old. Dinosaurs, for example, were doubtlessly quite aware of their surroundings. But, what ***is*** consciousness, and how is it related to the distinctly "human mind," and human thought? While these questions are still very much open, we believe that the best approach to answering them lies in the study of the evolution of consciousness and cognition in both animal and human nervous systems. Therefore, in the beginning of this chapter we will present our view of how the nervous system generates consciousness, and, then, provide examples of how behavior and simple cognition in lower animals seem to show many signs of the emergence of the human mind and thought.

How Can the Experience of Phantom Limbs Help Us Understand the Nature of Consciousness?

People who have lost limbs or have been born without them very often continue to experience the presence of the nonexistent limb. A person missing an arm or a leg may cause pain to be felt just where the limb would normally be. Or, the person may actually experience a "normal" presence of the missing limb as you feel the presence of, say, your hands or feet (Figure 3.1).

Ron Melzack (1992), who has studied the neurological bases of phantom limbs perhaps more than anyone, has proposed that the reason people experience phantom limbs (and phantom seeing and hearing) is because the brain comes into being with a complete pattern of the body in it. Then, throughout life the brain continuously generates this whole body pattern in a *feedforward* fashion to indicate "that the body is intact and unequivocally one's own." After a person suffers the loss of a limb, the brain continues to generate a complete body pattern, and thus the experience of limbs that actually no longer exist.

Melzack has proposed that the body pattern is continuously generated in three major brain circuits. These circuits produce: (a) the sensation of the body and its movements (the *somatosensory system*), (b) emotion and motivation (the *limbic system*), and (c) cognition that includes one's recognition of the self in relation to sensory input (regions of the cortex, especially of the *parietal cortex*). We interpret the

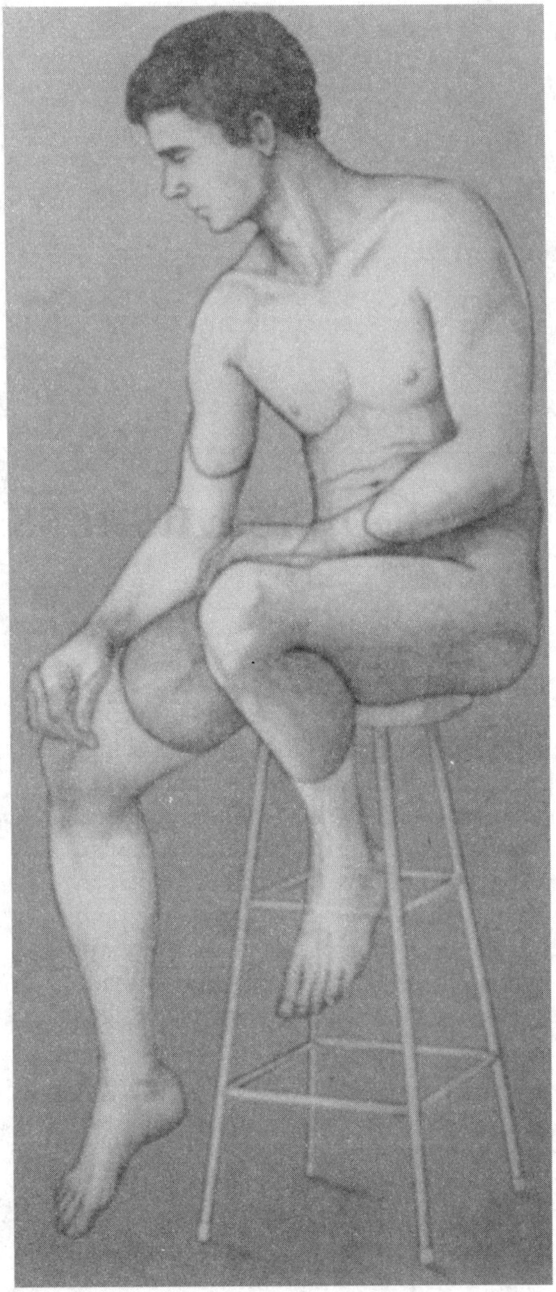

Figure 3.1 Typical examples of phantom limbs reported by patients are combined in this human figure. Some parts of the phantom are felt especially vividly (*highlighted areas in transparent limbs*). The phantom limb is perceived as perfectly real to the patient, who describes it as being in various positions and often reports feeling pain in it.

combined feedforward activity of these brain circuits to ***be*** the fundamental experience of conscious awareness (Vandervert, 1995, 1999). According to this view, consciousness would be the totality of the experience of your body as it is continuously fed forward in anticipation of change in the environment. It should be understood that much, perhaps most, of this activity takes place without complete awareness in normal, everyday experience (Figure 3.2).

To What Degree Are Animals Conscious?

Do Animals Think?

To understand the idea of consciousness as it exists in psychology today, we must consider systems of consciousness as they might occur in both humans and animals. Much of what is accepted in psychology rests upon the fact that animals, like humans, have nervous systems with their respective neurons, synapses, and some well-developed cortexes. Animals perceive, learn, have memories, communicate, have emotions, are motivated, and exhibit a good deal of social behavior. In other words, we have come to accept a certain limited parallel between these systems as they operate in humans and in animals. But what are the limits of this comparative approach? We know humans are conscious only because we ourselves are humans. We think, use and create languages, have dreams, and so forth, but are these parts of animal consciousness? Can we learn anything about consciousness from studying the behavior of animals—the same way we have learned so much about the nervous system?

The broadest and most thorough approach to the question of consciousness has become what has been termed by Donald R. Griffin (1978, 1985) as *cognitive ethology*. Cognitive ethology is the comparative study of consciousness and awareness of all animal species. Recent scientific books on consciousness in animals and its possible relationships to human consciousness include Griffin's *Animal Thinking* (1984), and Stephen Walker's *Animal Thought* (1983). Comparative studies along these lines may ultimately help lead us to the heart of psychology and point to ways in which we may deal directly with the idea of mind on a scientific basis.

As you read the following circumstantial evidence on the nature of animal consciousness and thought, proceed open-mindedly, as would an ethologist, making careful observations followed by analysis.

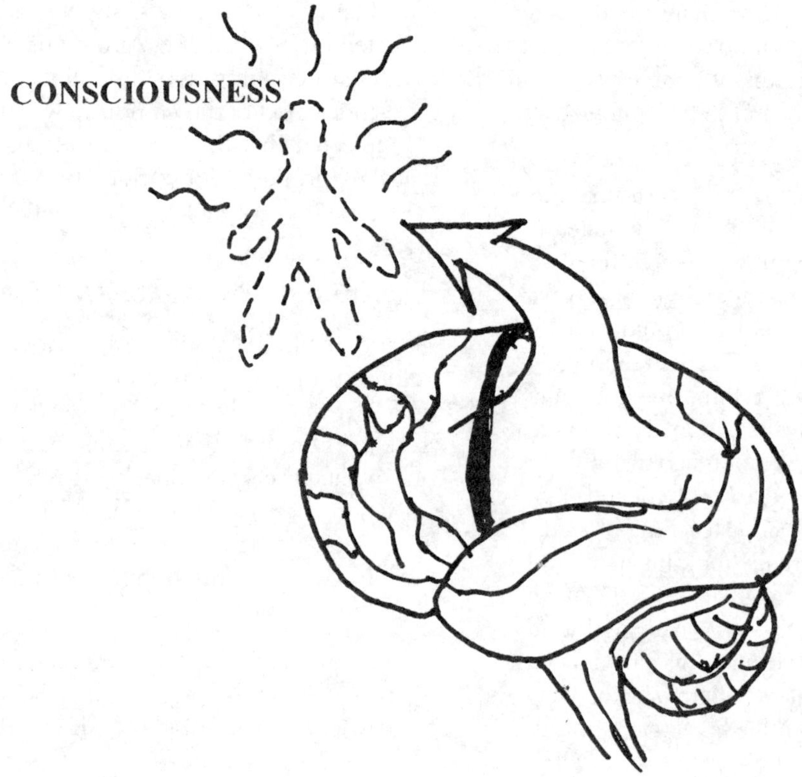

Figure 3.2

Do Animals Dream?

Nearly everyone has observed a sleeping cat or dog that suddenly begins to twitch its paws, its whiskers, and, if observed carefully, move its eyes under its eyelids as if following the action of a dream. Perhaps you have wondered, is it really having a dream?

When animals twitch, and move their eyes while they are asleep, it usually appears that they are doing animal sorts of things—eating, biting, or running. Since the motor-sensory maps in cat and dog brains are laid out adjacently, as they are in humans, it seems that some sort of sensory images likely accompany the observed twitching of the sleeping animals. It has been found by T. Allison and H. Van Twyver (1970) that the EEG record of sleep (slow waves) and dreaming (faster waves) in birds and mammals are in general the same as for humans.

Further, Michael Jouvet (1979) found that when a portion of the cat's brain stem is destroyed, the automatic behavior restrictions that prevent an animal from acting out its dreams are removed. In this case the cat's dream behavior takes on all of the appearances of a cat fully awake. The cat's behavior follows its dreaming of a complex interaction with its environment. It seems that cats and other animals do, in fact, dream.

Do Animals Use Languages?

Human consciousness involves the creation and use of languages primarily for two-way communication between people. There are many examples of one-way animal communication: barking, pawing at a door, and so forth. But, can animals learn to communicate needs, desires, and possibly thoughts to other animals using two-way symbolic systems? Can they learn simple languages as we understand languages to be?

In the 1960s Allen and Beatrix Gardner began teaching and studying the use of American Sign Language (ASL) in an infant chimpanzee they named Washoe (Gardner & Gardner, 1971). Washoe acquired a very large number of signs, and when later joined by other, younger chimps she began to teach them signs she had learned (Fouts, Fouts & Van Cantfort, 1989).

When Washoe's own infant died, a ten-month-old chimp was found to replace it to help ease her grieving. The infant's name was Loulis and Washoe adopted him. What followed may surprise you:

> After the first eight days that Washoe and Loulis were together he began to imitate his first sign. . . . From our video recordings we found that Washoe was doing some very subtle teaching, in that she would initially orient, then sign COME, then approach him, and then retrieve him. She gradually faded this so that she stopped retrieving him then she stopped approaching him and finally all she had to do was orient and sign. She also did some active teaching of signs. In one case she actually took his hand and molded it into the sign for FOOD in an appropriate context. . . . What we found was that Loulis acquired his signs from Washoe and some of them she actively taught him. He used his signs to communicate with his fellow chimpanzees as well as with humans. (Fouts & Fouts, 1994, p. 32)

This amounts to a cultural transmission of the signing language. But what do chimps sign or "talk" about? Do they sign about some of the same things humans talk about?

> In one study we recorded over 5,200 instances of chimpanzee signing. This signing was analyzed into different categories. The majority of signing by the chimpanzees occurred in the three categories of 'play,' 'social interaction,' and 'reassurance'; these accounted for over 88 percent of the chimpanzee to chimpanzee conversations. The remaining 12 percent was spread across the categories of 'feeding,' 'grooming,' 'signing to self,' 'cleaning' and 'discipline.' An interesting aspect of these findings was that they indicated that the chimpanzees used their signs primarily for various types of social interaction. (Fouts & Fouts, 1994, p. 33)

Do Animals Pretend or Deceive?

Pretending for us humans takes a lot of work and a lot of thinking. We have to guide our behavior in a way that we know will mislead another person. This requires that we must be able to imagine what others are imagining about a certain situation and then make the pretense look good. Good pretending is what human actors are noted for; it takes concentration, empathy, and understanding in addition to imagination.

> A provocative report of animal deception comes from ethologist Jane Goodall-van Lawick's observation of chimpanzees in the wild: Figan, an adolescent male in Tanzania's Gombe Stream National Park, learned that he could lead adult males away from the banana pile by striding purposely into the woods. The others followed him off; he then returned by another route to gobble unmolested. Even Figan occasionally got his comeuppance. Once when he had led a group of chimps from the camp, he returned to find yet another high-ranking male installed at the banana pile. "Figan stared at him for a few moments," Goodall later recounted, "then flew into a tantrum, screaming and hitting the ground." (Goodall-van Lawick, 1971, p. 97)

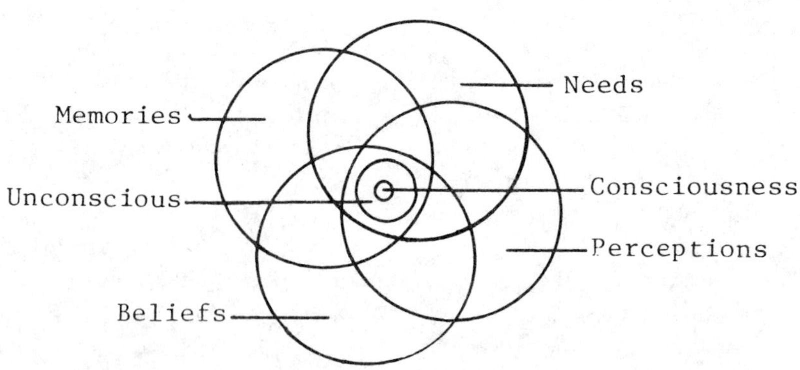

Figure 3.3 Consciousness Maintains Boundaries by Integrating the Systems of Information

This is not an isolated report of deception occurring among apes.

Two young male chimpanzees, Loulis and Dar, that are housed with Washoe regularly, use the tactic of deception in play:

> What Loulis signed about with Dar was mainly play. They would request tickle and chase games from each other. However, when the game became too rough and one of them was hurt they would then sign to Washoe for comfort with HUG/LOVE signs and other solicitations of reassurance. When they fought we even observed Loulis apparently blaming Dar for the commotion. The two boys were screaming and fighting when Washoe rushed in, as she usually did to stop the fights, Loulis signed to her 'GOOD GOOD ME' and then screaming pointed at Dar. Washoe would then discipline Dar. After several months of this Dar apparently caught on to the tactic and would throw himself on the floor when he saw Washoe enter the room and begin to cry and sign a frantic 'COME HUG' to her, whereupon she would comfort Dar. Then she would scold Loulis with a bipedal swagger toward him signing 'GO THERE' to him, pointing to the over-head exit tunnel for the room. (Fouts & Fouts, 1994, p.33)

There are many other provocative examples of animal behavior that lead psychologists to wonder about the conscious mental life of animals. Many animals use tools, solve problems, go through their own peculiar stages of cognitive development (see stages of cognitive development, Chapter 6).

Persisting Philosophical Questions About Consciousness

Our descriptions of animals dreaming, deceiving, and using language have opened the subject of consciousness and thought to more critical examination. Examples of animal consciousness that parallel human examples can help us begin to understand and define just what consciousness involves. The ancient Greeks grappled with this same question, and, as you learned in Chapter 1, developed a theory about the nature of consciousness. Do only humans have minds? Since we can accept the idea that animals have nervous systems, perceptions, and so forth, does consciousness also fit in? How does it fit in? We do not yet have complete answers for these questions. However, Donald R. Griffin has offered us a way to think about consciousness and thinking in a broad philosophical perspective:

> Within a range of circumstances for which they have been adapted in the course of evolution, insects in general, and honeybees in particular, display abundant evidence of versatile behavior that would be interpreted as resulting in conscious thinking if it occurred in our own species. If learning and adjustment of behavior to changing circumstances are criteria for conscious thinking, honeybees, weaver ants, and other insects satisfy these criteria reasonably well—within the range of circumstances for which they have been adapted in the course of evolution. Of course the scope of insect versatility seems very limited from our human perspective, but this difference may be a quantitative rather than a qualitative difference in kind. Honeybees may think consciously about what is important to them and about those challenges and solutions that lie within their competence. Can we be certain that human thinking is capable of dealing with all contingencies? When viewed from a cosmic perspective, are our most highly trained and well informed leaders behaving in a wholly rational fashion in response to the threat of nuclear warfare? Or are we following time-worn behavior patterns that have been adaptive in the past under radically altered circumstances? In some future century might *paleoethnologists* from another galaxy compare our behavior to that of wasps that continue to lay eggs in a nest where they fall through holes the animal could easily repair? (1985, p. 476)

Consciousness and thinking in honeybees may sound far-fetched; however recent experiments have provided evidence that honeybees form and use **cognitive maps** of their territories (Gould, 1986). The use of cognitive maps in organisms is usually considered a form of thinking.

Theories of Consciousness

At the level of theory, consciousness presents psychology with a unique problem. It is not sufficiently understood to suppose that proponents of the traditional views would all be addressing the same topic. For example, we cannot be sure that when the behaviorists express their views of consciousness they are addressing the same phenomena as would be, for example, the neurophysiologist. The meaning of consciousness *itself* is still somewhat in a state of philosophical controversy. The traditional views in psychology might include differing philosophical orientations toward the topic of consciousness and therefore be talking about different things.

Residing in the area between the simple conscious awareness and the complexities of the human mind and human thought are many special features of consciousness and cognition that all theorists regardless of their particular view tend to take into consideration. The following areas offer especially important continuing insights toward our scientific understanding of consciousness and thinking: the study of language systems and the duality of consciousness in the two hemispheres of the brain; the study of dreams, biofeedback, hypnosis, mind (or consciousness) altering drugs, and running all through these topics, the findings of cognitive ethology.

The balance of this chapter is about these areas of study that make special contributions to our overall understanding of consciousness. Each of the following study areas of psychology can offer us understandings about consciousness. Where relevant evidence is available we will discuss how these studies might possibly also apply to animal consciousness.

How Are the Special Varieties of Consciousness Studied, and What Has Been Found?

What Is Meant by the Duality *of Consciousness?*

In Chapter 2 we discussed the use of the tachistoscopic method in the study of the lateralized function of the two hemispheres of the brain. These same studies and many others provided new insights into the nature of consciousness. One of the earliest conclusions from this body of research was that each of the two disconnected hemispheres of the brain seemed to contain its own consciousness—a duality of consciousness (Sperry, 1968).

In the split-brain laboratory study if, for example, two different stimuli are presented at the same time to the right and left visual fields, say the letter A on the right, and the letter B on the left, each hemisphere sees a different stimulus. Then, if the person is asked to draw with his *left* hand (controlled by right hemisphere) what has been seen, the letter A is immediately drawn. However if the person is asked what he or she has drawn, they will reply "a B" (see Figure 3.4). The left hemisphere does not know what the right hemisphere has been doing!

This "double consciousness" extends beyond the person simply being aware of different stimuli in each hemisphere; each hemisphere also seems to have its own wishes and intentions. During the testing of these subjects there would often be spontaneous ". . . frowning, wincing, and negative head shaking" (Sperry, 1968, p. 732) as the right hemisphere, knowing a correct answer, but unable to talk, would hear the left hemisphere making obviously mistaken verbal replies. Sperry (1968) summarized the apparent duality of consciousness in the split-brain subjects as follows:

> [There is] . . . an apparent doubling in most of the realms of conscious awareness. Instead of the normally unified single stream of consciousness, these patients behave in may ways as if they have two independent streams of conscious awareness, one in each hemisphere, each of which is cut off from and out of contact with the mental experiences of the other. In other words, each hemisphere seems to have its own separate and private sensation; its own perceptions; its own concepts; and its own impulses to act, with related volitional, cognitive, and learning experiences. (p. 724)

Later study (LeDoux, Wilson, & Gazzaniga, 1977) of a split-brain subject who was able to communicate his right hemisphere choices, feelings, and intentions by arranging Scrabble letters provided additional evidence for double consciousness in split-brain subjects. Their subject, P.S., would be asked the stem of a question

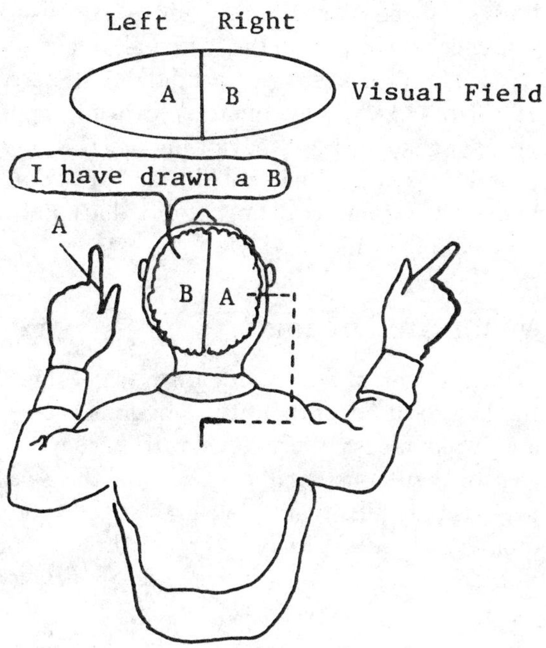

Figure 3.4 Split-brain Laboratory Study

verbally with the key word left out. Then the key word would be flashed to either the right or left hemisphere. When asked about the choice of a job, for example, the left hand spelled out "automobile race" for the right hemisphere (Figure 3.5a). However, P.S.'s left hemisphere indicated that he would like to be a draftsman (Figure 3.5b)!

It appears that in split-brain subjects at least there exists dual consciousness(es). But does a normal person have, as it were, two minds? David Galin and Robert Ornstein (1972, and Ornstein, 1978) have analyzed the activities of the two hemispheres in normal people using the *electroencephalograph.* They have concluded that normal people continually alternate between the cognitive modes of the two hemispheres, depending on the task at hand, as they go about their daily activities. While we cannot conclude from these studies that normal people have the sort of dual consciousness apparent in split-brain people, it does appear that the location of our attention shifts from one hemisphere to another. And there are researchers who have argued that dual consciousness is normal in all of us. For example, Roland Puccetti (1981) has proposed that since each hemisphere must separately register whatever is being seen, therefore two images, a single observing stream of consciousness would see everything in duplicate. But, we don't see things in duplicate. Therefore the argument goes, we must have two consciousnesses each seeing a single representation

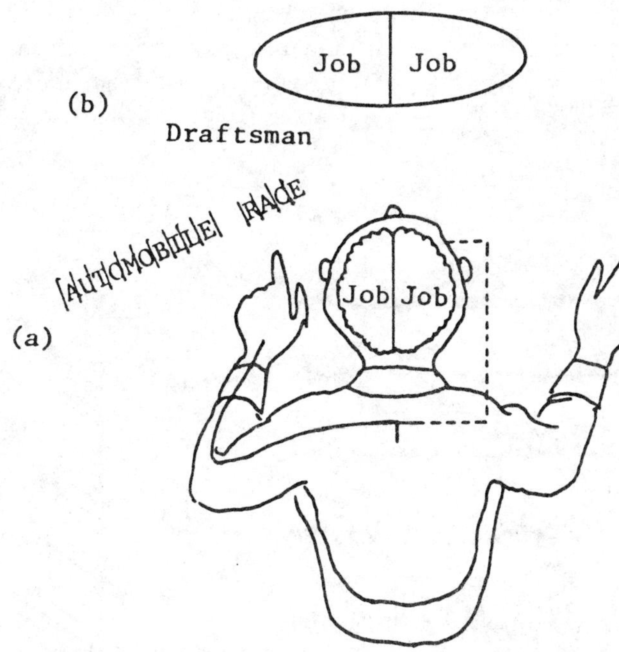

Figure 3.5 Evidence of Dual Consciousness in Split-brain Subjects

of the visual world. Pucceti's view is only a speculation, but an interesting one.

There is evidence that seems to be leaning in the direction of dual consciousness in normal human beings—there are really two of you in your skull. But, if our consciousness is dual, why does it seem to have a single unity? Concluding 20 years of research and reflection on split-brain subjects, Michael Gazzaniga (1983) has suggested that the left hemisphere speaks for the whole brain even though it does not itself constitute the whole brain:

> The emerging picture is that our cognitive system is not a unified network with a single purpose and train of thought. A more accurate metaphor is that our sense of subjective awareness [the seeming that we are a single unity] arises out of our dominant left hemisphere's unrelenting need to explain actions taken from any one of a multitude of mental systems that dwell within us. . . . These systems, which coexist with the language system, are not necessarily in touch with the language processes prior to a behavior. Once actions are taken, the left, observing these behaviors, constructs a story as to the meaning, and this in turn becomes a part of the language system's understanding of the person. (pp. 535–536)

Examples of what Gazzaniga said in his final sentence can be seen often in the split-brain subject's behavior. The verbal, left side of split-brain subjects, upon observing a surprising response on the part of the left hand, might say, "Now, I know it wasn't me that did that" (Sperry, 1968, p. 733). How often do we all, upon observing surprising behavior in ourselves, find ourselves saying, "That's not like me," or " I don't know what came over me," or "I don't know why I did that, I just did"?

What Are Dreams?

William Dement and N. Kleitman (1957) were the first to discover that just as periods of sleep and wakefulness present us with regular cycles of conscious awareness, within the sleep period are regular nightly cycles of *higher cortical arousal.* These cycles of cortical arousal are directly associated with cycles of dream activity.

The Stages and Cycles of Dream Consciousness

The electroencephalograph (EEG) was described in some detail in Chapter 2. The EEG record varies with the level of conscious arousal in the subjects—human and animal alike. In Figure 3.6 it can be seen that the falling of arousal is in a sense similar in idea to the falling arousal levels as presented in Chapter 2. However, in the case of falling asleep it is more a matter of the slow delta waves becoming steadily more predominant in the EEG record. For example, when 20 to 50 percent of the waves are the slow delta waves, you are in stage-3; when over 50 percent are

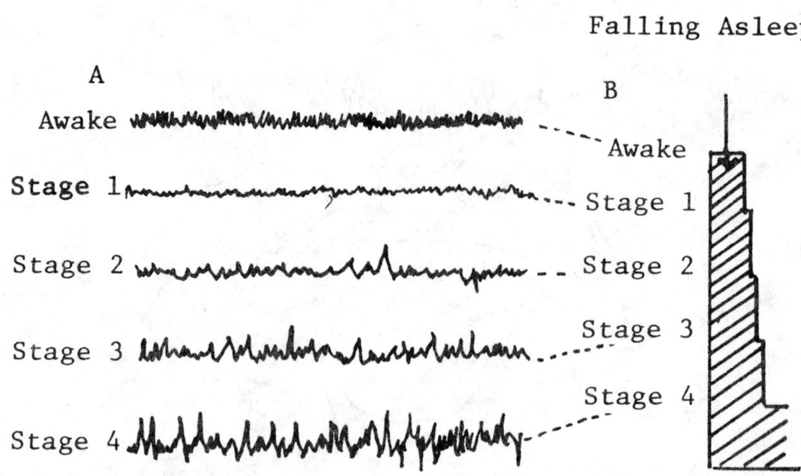

Figure 3.6 EEG Record of Delta Waves in Falling Asleep

delta, you are at stage-4 sleep. Typically, it takes about 30 to 40 minutes for you to reach the low level of arousal of stage-4. Then the nightly cycles begin.

The cycles of arousal for an entire night of dreaming are shown in Figure 3.7. You dream about every 90 minutes every night. We have included the cycles of arousal that occur even during the day to give you an overall perspective of this *ultradian rhythm* (Kripke & Sonnenschein, 1978; Chase 1979; Broughton, 1986; Rossi, 1986). Notice the daytime cycles also run on 90 minute cycles. Not long after you have descended to stage-4 sleep (typically about 15 minutes) you begin to move toward wakefulness in a kind of reverse falling asleep.

Rapid Eye Movements

Upon the first cyclic return to stage-1 sleep, *rapid eye movements (REMs)*. If you simply ask a friend to close his eyelids and then move his eyes around as though he were watching a tennis match, you'll see REMs. Along with this paradox of sleep behavior there are others during REM episodes: the heart speeds up, respiration becomes irregular, and blood pressure increases. If you refer to the table of the autonomic sympathetic activities (Chapter 2) you will see that arousal in the nervous system during REM extends beyond the eye movements and the brain wave activity. For all practical purposes the sleeper at this point seems to be following a fast action movie—of which they are a part! William Dement and Nathaniel Kleitman (1957) would suggest, in fact, they probably are having such a dream. If the person is awakened during the REM period he will usually be able to report some sort of dream. The work of Michael Jouvet (1979) on *oneiric behavior* in cats cited earlier where the cat acts out a dream pattern would tend to support the idea that REMs are to some degree following a dream. Note, however, that W.D. Foulkes (1962) has found that people who are in *non-rapid eye movement (NREM)* stages also often report dreams if awakened. Consciousness is probably always to some degree present at some level in the brain whether you are awake or asleep! It seems quite possible that just as alertness waxes and wanes slightly during daytime wakefulness (see Figure 3.7 with a full 24 hours of arousal cycles), it waxes and wanes but does not go "off" at any time during sleep.

The fact that due to the presence of REMs the sleeping person seems to be dreaming, and *also* displays dramatic changes in sympathetic nervous system activity is indeed *paradoxical*. Thus the REM periods are often interchangeably called *paradoxical sleep*. REM periods typically occur five to seven times each night, and with each cycle they get longer and more involved. You might expect the later and longer REM period dreams to concern older, more significant, and more emotional content.

Why Do We Dream?

Animals without significant cortex development such as fishes and reptiles do not exhibit REMs or paradoxical sleep. On the other hand, the

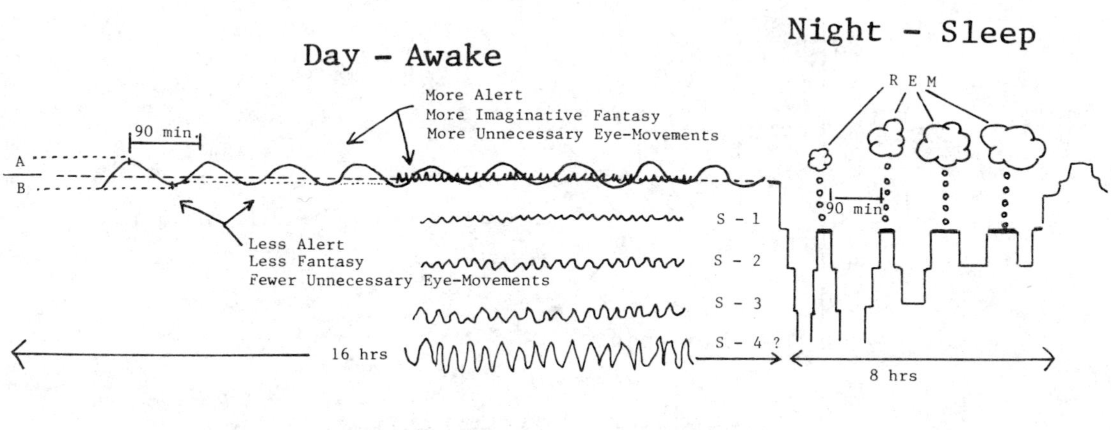

Figure: 90 minute cycles of arousal level over 24 hr. periods (M. Chase, 1979)

Figure 3.7 Cycles of Arousal

warm-blooded birds and mammals do. Among animals that do exhibit REMs, those that have the longest normal sleep periods also spend the most time in REM. What animal spends the most time in REM? According to Michael Jouvet "the world champion in dreaming" is the domestic cat with about 180 to 200 minutes each day! Humans are in REM about half that time (about 100 minutes a night). The amount of REM that any species exhibits depends upon the maturity of the subject's brain. Jouvet says, "The brain is almost constantly dreaming when the most complex nervous structures are under development *in utero* or *ex utero*" (1975, p. 517). So as the animal or person gets older and older they very significantly spend less and less time in REM. In Figure 3.8 are the percentages of time the cat, rat, and guinea pig spend in REM as they mature. The newborn cat or rat spends about 90 percent of the time in REM during sleep. The cat and rat brains are very immature at birth. The guinea pig, on the other hand, which has a brain that is almost fully mature at birth, has only an amount of REM near the adult level. The amount of REM in the guinea pig 20 days before birth is about the same as the newborn rat. In humans brain development also closely parallels the amount of time spent in REM. Table 3.1 illustrates this relationship.

It appears that dreaming prior to birth probably takes up a considerable portion of the time. If there is indeed dream content with these REMs of the pre-full term infant, either in utero or ex utero, one wonders what the dream content might be! After you have read the account of Carl G. Jung and the *collective unconscious* in Chapter 10, ask yourself if Jung could possibly have been right!

Table 3.1 Age (level of brain development) in humans and amount of time spent in REM

Age	*Percent of Sleep Time in REM*
10 week premature infant	80%
2–4 week premature infant	60%
full-term newborn	50%
2 years	30–35%
10 years and on	about 25%

Note: From "Physiology of Sleep and Dreaming" by D. D. Kelly, 1981, in *Principles of Neural Science* by E. R. Kandel & T. H. Schwartz (Eds.), New York: Elsevier/North-Holland.

On the basis of these relationships between brain maturity and the amount of time spent in REM, and the fact that more complex brains learn more complex things (have more cortex) and exhibit REM, Jouvet has proposed that *innate* patterns of motor behavior are being laid down and integrated in the brain during REM. This process allows the cortex of the human infant, for example, to engage in the motor/sensory sucking reflex upon birth. Later it prepares brain circuitry for sitting, walking, speech, abstract reasoning, etc. This *genetic programming*

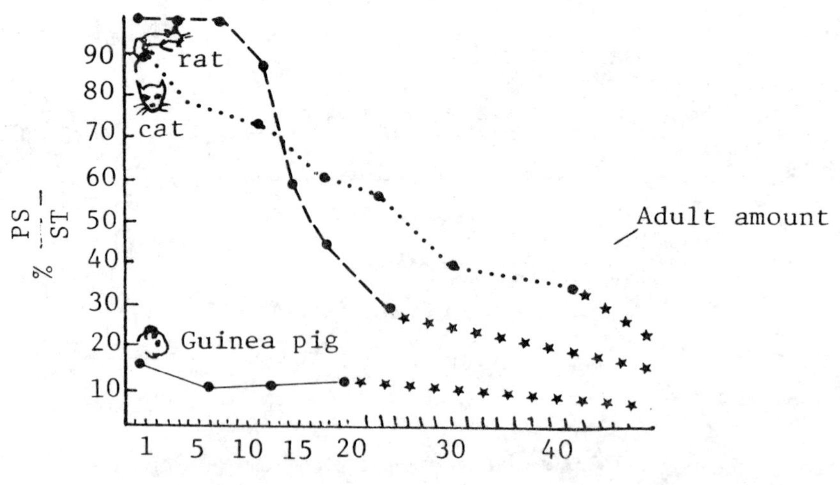

Figure 3.8 Percentages of Time Spent in REM

of the brain provides two flexibilities. First, the REM programming prepares the motor cortex with sensory schemes before the time when they are actually required (the instinctual pattern develops at a particular time). Second, demands of several actual potential environments can be organized into complex motor patterns. This genetic programming process leads one to the conclusion that the integration of motor behavior during REM is primary—and the experience of the dream is secondary. According to this theory you dream because you twitch, you do not twitch because you dream. In support of this notion, K. Sakai and R. Cespuglio (1976) have found that REMs precede any brain activity that might be related to "seeing the dream" by about 20 milliseconds. Jouvet is not alone in his explanation of why we dream.

J. Alan Hobson and Robert McCarley (1977; Hobson, 1988) have proposed a similar explanation which they call the activation-synthesis model of dreams. In order to make sense of spontaneous activations of lower-level brain processes, the content of a dream is "made-up" by higher cortical cognitive processes. This does not mean that dreams are not meaningful. On the contrary, as genetic programming takes into account the organism's experiences with the environment at the neurological level, dream activity should be very meaningful.

How Meaningful Are Dreams?

We perhaps will never know what sorts of experiences accompany REMs in animals and human fetuses. However, much is known about the content of human dreams. Table 3.2 lists the features present in reported dreams of college students. Recall that dream mentation reports come from subjects who are in both REM and NREM. REMs and autonomic sympathetic behavior of paradoxical sleep are associated with emotional and visual content, and physical movement. On the other hand, NREM is more associated with "thinking content." Nightmares occur not during REM sleep as one might expect, but during the NREM stages 3 and 4. In addition, sleep walking does not occur during REM periods. This makes sense because during REM, motor systems are suppressed so that the dreamer does not act out dreams. It seems possible that some sort of mentation is occurring all through sleep at some level.

In classic work Calvin Hall (1966) analyzed thousands of dream reports and has concluded that most of our dreams fall within one of the following categories:

> THE HUMAN TRIANGLE: The average number of dream characters, including the dreamer, is three. If the dreamer is a male, it includes two men and a woman, and vice versa. One may dream of being left out of the triangle.
>
> FREEDOM VERSUS SECURITY: This is the dream representation of growing up and becoming independent versus a regression to the comforts of staying or going home. One may dream of tearful departures from loved ones by strange means.
>
> THE MORAL CONFLICT: Hall said, "We are all sinners in our dreams" (p. 152). Many of our dreams involve us doing things we would not think of doing in real life.
>
> THE CONFLICT OF THE SEX ROLES: Regardless of whether we are males or females, we all have characteristics of both. This is true in both the biological and cultural senses. In dreams we sometimes experience confusion about our sexuality—we may find ourselves dressed in peculiar ways in dreams.
>
> LIFE VERSUS DEATH: The balance between life and death is a deep concern to all people. As we get older, dream content begins to reflect this concern. This often includes dreams of the younger years.

Obviously these five categories of dreams are closely related to things we think about daily. But, why are dreams often so bizarre? Hall offers this explanation:

> The function of dreaming, as we have said many times, is to reveal what is in the person's mind, not to conceal it. Dreams may appear enigmatic because they contain symbols, but these symbols are nothing more than pictorial metaphors, and like the verbal metaphors of waking life their intention is to clarify rather than to obscure thought. What is the difference between a person awake exclaiming, "He's a majestic individual," and a person asleep conjuring up the image of a

Table 3.2 Common Dreams of College Students

Dream	Percentage of Students Total	Male	Female
Falling	83	80	85
Being attacked or pursued	77	77	78
Trying repeatedly to do something	71	68	75
School, teachers, studying	71	60	84
Falling, with fear	68	62	73
Sexual experiences	66	93	36
Arriving too late	64	60	67
Eating delicious food	62	57	67
Being frozen with fright	58	53	64
A loved person is dead	57	49	67
Being locked up	56	55	58
Finding money	56	61	50
Swimming	52	47	58
Snakes	49	43	55
Being on verge of falling	47	52	41
Being inappropriately dressed	46	39	54
Dead people as though alive	46	40	53
Being smothered	44	42	47
Being nude	43	48	37
Fire	41	33	50
Failing an examination	39	34	44
Flying through air	34	32	35
Seeing self as dead	33	33	34
Being tied up	30	28	34
Killing someone	26	38	11

king? There is no difference except in the medium of expression. The verbal metaphor expressed by the adjective "majestic" and the dream image of a king represent the same conception. (1966, p. 215)

How Are Biofeedback and Meditation Related to Consciousness?

Meditation as a variation of consciousness probably involves a focused or "expanded" awareness. A question might be, expanded to where? While meditators make all sorts of claims for meditation, the major claim is that it provides a road to "inner peace"—which should free the consciousness for "higher" consciousness. Religious and philosophical issues put aside, the suggested expansion to higher states of consciousness through meditation will have to await further refinements in the scientific assessment of consciousness for verification. On the other hand, in terms of the brain, meditation does offer a means of expanding consciousness toward the control of autonomic nervous system functions (see Chapter 2). This sort of control of consciousness is not at all mysterious. Just sit back comfortably, gently close your eyes, breathe deeply, and concentrate on a suitable thought or sound for 15 minutes or so. (Transcendental meditation is described here. Some forms of meditation do not involve the relaxation of the somatic muscles. Maulavi is a form of meditation which is accompanied by the vigorous dancing of the "whirling dervishes.") With consciousness turned inward, all sorts of changes occur in autonomically innervated body activities. Arousal levels as indicated by heart rate, *electrodermal activity,* skin temperature, respiration, blood pressure, *electromyographic activity,* oxygen consumption, blood flow, and biochemical changes occur. In answer to our earlier question, "expansion to where?" one might refer to this type of meditation as an expansion of conscious control to the autonomic nervous system which, of course, is usually mostly under involuntary control.

How does meditation produce this unique expansion of consciousness into the autonomic realm? David Holmes (1984) has found that all of these profound effects on the arousal levels of the ANS can be produced simply by relaxing! If one takes 15 minutes to just relax, all of the same changes in heart rate, etc. will occur. Meditation simply sets the stage and occasion for some good periods of relaxation. In other words, whether one wishes to achieve this "expansion of consciousness" by becoming a meditator or by simply learning to really relax (and making provisions for it in one's daily schedule) is a toss-up in terms of benefits! This is true, Holmes found, in terms of either general lowering of arousal or lowering it in the face of threatening situations (see phobias, Chapter 13). What about the higher levels of consciousness claimed by the meditator? This could be a true claim in a sense. After all, if people draw their attention away from the heated anxiety of job, school, etc., and focus it inward, they may see things more clearly. This could simply help give needed perspective on life, and might even allow the *creative incubation* process to occur. But all of this will occur whether you meditate or simply take time off to relax (like going fishing) in an equal proportion.

The above sort of expansion of awareness or consciousness "inward" is no more clearly seen than in *biofeedback* learning (see Chapters 2, 5). Biofeedback not only permits a systematic approach to the relaxation of arousal functions, but permits it in a very selective way. And, recall from Chapter 2 that since the entire internal environment (body) is innervated, theoretically much of the entire "inner world" could potentially come under conscious, cortical control.

At the level of consciousness (rather than physiology as in Chapter 2, or learning as in Chapter 5), biofeedback can be explained in terms of the learning of the conscious control of minute *coverants* (more on these in Chapter 13). Taking the idea of these coverants as "operants of the mind" from Lloyd Homme (1965) we might assume, at least in the case of biofeedback, that conscious thoughts are emitted responses. They too should therefore be *operantly conditionable.* Since coverants can be observed only in private consciousness, the person having them must see to it that certain desired coverant thoughts are rewarded, so that they become more likely. Or, if the desired thoughts are so minute that the person is not totally aware of them, their effects can be immediately *amplified* so that their relationship to relaxing or other behaviors can be learned. In biofeedback, specific coverants cannot be directly amplified and rewarded, but classes of coverants (thoughts) can be. For example, thoughts related to relaxation (imagining yourself on a warm, sandy beach soaking up the sun, etc., "warm coverants") can be feedback rewarded via *EEG, EMG,* or skin temperature feedback. The reward for the coverants or thoughts of relaxation can be simply knowing that you are in fact connecting your thoughts with relaxation.

Animal Biofeedback?

"Do animals purposefully relax using a variety of mental states in the process?" While animal meditation will have to remain a puzzle, animal biofeedback does not.

Barry Gruber, Paul J. School, and Edward Taub (1981) have taught monkeys to self-regulate a variety of autonomic nervous system functions. Once the animals learn how an automated display of lights will reward them for temperature and EMG regulation, they can regulate them at will. Humans must also be taught how to use the light displays and sound displays of biofeedback amplifiers. Animals, then, seem to emit some sort of coverant consciousness which can be conditioned through biofeedback training. It is important to realize that coverants in humans are likely quite different from those in animals.

What Can Hypnosis Tell Us About Consciousness?

At times particular events in which you are participating may seem to take on a life of their own. Think about being at a dance, a sporting event, a movie, a play, or in a very heated argument. The situation, the crowd, almost seem to "hypnotize" you (and everyone else) so that you may find yourself saying things, doing things, or believing things that later may puzzle you. In a way you have been hypnotized. You have willingly, while fully awake, *dissociated* yourself from your everyday global and ongoing pattern of consciousness. Some of these dissociations can have horrible results (like the soccer game out of hand), others perhaps only a little embarrassing.

Edwin G. Boring (1950), Martin Orne and Gordon Hammer (1975) have said the effects of hypnosis have been evident since ancient times. The healing and trance-like "spirit possessions" seen in both primitive and some modern religions are examples of hypnotic dissociations. The non-religious use of hypnosis was "discovered" by Franz Anton Mesmer. Mesmer, and followers that surrounded him, led people in the late 1700s to believe, much like people at a sporting event, that magnetism, and later his own personal "animal magnetism," could help cure all sorts of ailments. While Mesmer's techniques did not have much to do with modern hypnosis, the fundamental effects of *suggestion* on his patients did. Mesmer, interestingly, did not have any idea why his magnetism approach worked on people. But his work did help popularize a study of the effects of suggestion.

British physician James Braid in 1843 came to apply the term *hypnosis* to this ancient phenomenon. Braid, as a scientist, did not believe in what he saw the Mesmerists doing in public demonstrations. But at one demonstration the evidence that hypnosis was "real" was so convincing that he completely changed his mind on the matter. Because of the relaxed state of mesmerized subjects Braid referred to the state as a type of sleep. Braid "described the mesmeric trance as a 'nervous sleep' and invented for the underlying doctrine the term neurohypnology. In general, the prefix of the term came to be dropped, a change which led to the words hypnotic, hypnotize and hypnotism" (Boring, 1950, p. 124). Braid spent the rest of his life attempting to understand the physiological basis of hypnosis. Only recently some progress has been made in this direction. For example, David Spiegel, Steven Cutcomb, Ren Chuan, and Karl Pribram. (1985) have found that the EEGs of hypnotized subjects show a different information processing pattern in the occipital region of the brain when they are blocking out visual stimuli that are actually present.

While each of the varieties of conscious discussed in this chapter has its unique aspects, some thoughts on their similarities will help us get a better perspective. Hypnosis is an altered state of consciousness that has relaxing and dissociation in some form in common with dreaming, meditation, and biofeedback. Dissociation is seen in dreams in the fact that they represent a part of consciousness that is separate from everyday awareness. The meditator attempts to separate his conscious experience of the outer world from his inner consciousness—although the dissociation boundary between these states of consciousness may be thinner than in the case of dreams. In biofeedback, the dissociation component is absent and the process is guided by consciousness. At the other extreme, dissociation underlies a class of mental disorders (see Chapter 12). The idea of dissociation is the same in these disorders, but because the dissociation is out of control of the person's everyday consciousness it causes disabling mental problems.

It is helpful to arrange dissociative states of consciousness in terms of a hierarchy of this element that is so critical in understanding these altered states of consciousness. This arrangement of altered states of consciousness by degree and control of dissociative is based upon *neodissociative* analysis of consciousness control like that proposed by Ernest Hilgard:

> While hypnosis dramatizes the existence of dissociative phenomena, neodissociation theory serves to call attention to many empirical problems and nonhypnotic top-

> ics in which dissociative aspects are also prominent. The ultimate aim of neodissociation theory is to achieve a coherent understanding of these diverse phenomena. (1976, pp. 168–169)

Hilgard's multiple cognitive control systems approach to dissociation(s) is really a systems perspective on consciousness. Table 3.3 provides a hierarchy of dissociation beginning with the guided dissociations of biofeedback, meditation, and hypnosis, to the out-of-control dissociation of the mental disorders. We could add to this hierarchy the type of dissociation that occurs at various events like those listed at the beginning of this section on hypnosis.

How Is Hypnosis Described?

Hypnosis is not sleep even though one might get that impression from popular descriptions. Hypnotized persons do not exhibit the EEG behavior of sleep, rather they are consciously aware of their surroundings. In addition to the critical idea of dissociation, hypnotized persons are affected in many other ways. The left column of Table 3.4 lists some of these effects. In the col-

Table 3.3 Degrees of Dissociation in Various Altered States of Consciousness

Altered State	*Degree of Relaxation*	*Degree of Dissociation*
BIOFEEDBACK	From light to profound	Can be great. Totally guided by the subject. Can return to everyday consciousness at will.
MEDITATION	Light to profound	Can be profound. Totally guided by the subject. Can return to everyday consciousness at will.
HYPNOSIS	Light to profound, a usual part of induction	Can be profound. Usually guided by a hypnotist. Subject can return to everyday consciousness at will.*
SUGGESTION	Variable, depending upon context	Can be profound. Usually guided by complex external contexts, e.g., sporting event, movie, doctor's office or prescription, etc. Subject may have difficulty returning to everyday consciousness at will.
DREAMING	Stages of sleep including both REM and NREM	A normal state of extreme dissociation.**
DRUGS	Variable depending upon specific drug	Can be profound. Minimal guidance by the subject.
DISSOCIATIVE AND RELATED DISORDERS***	Not relevant	Complete, out-of-control episodes of dissociation during everyday wakeful consciousness, or see fugue.

*Once hypnotized the subject may have real difficulty with challenges such as "try to open your eyes," or "you cannot remember your own name (even if you try to)," or ignoring post-hypnotic suggestions. However, these examples do not necessarily indicate any unmanageable dissociation for the subject. See Orne and Hammer (1975) for a discussion of these phenomena. Some theorists do not make a distinction between suggestion and hypnosis, others do.

**A dreamer does not usually decide what to dream about, or to quit a dream, or to change its ongoing scenario. Rather he, or she, spontaneously becomes aware of them due to other dream related events (paradoxical activity or a dream researcher). One can, however, learn to manipulate dreams quite well (see Stephen Laberge, 1985).

***See dissociative disorders such as fugue, and, although not classified as dissociative disorders by the DSM-III, phobias. Obsessive compulsive disorders contain elements of consciousness separation.

Table 3.4 Hypnotic Phenomena and Effects

Hypnotic Phenomena	*Hypnotic Effects*	*Possible Reasons for Effect*
1. Automatic Writing*	Dissociation**	When conscious attention is distracted, ingrained habits may continue to function without subject's awareness.
2. Girl thinks she is at home alone (see Gibson below)	Dissociation	(same as reason above)
3. Age-Regression**	Memory enhancement	Anxiety that may interfere with memory retrieval is reduced.
4. Dentist completes dental work without anesthesia	Relief from pain or change in emotional state	Subject expects change; subject reacts only to actual pain or emotional state rather than to expected pain or emotions. Another possibility is that pain is actually blunted by stimulated neurological mechanism.
5. Subject is deluded into thinking he is a great singer—and acts accordingly	"Unusual" behavior	Subject feels such behavior is expected or wishes to please hypnotist by being a "good subject" (social pressure).
6. A lemon tastes sweet	Sensory or perceptual changes	Perceptual mechanisms may actually change, or subject may lie, either consciously or unconsciously, in order to be a "good subject."
7. Girl disrobes (see Gibson below)	Disinhibition	Subject can now place responsibility for acts elsewhere (on hypnotist).
8. After coming out of hypnotic suggestion hypnotist taps a pencil—subject, seemingly for no reason, takes off shoe.	Posthypnotic suggestion	Subject unconsciously learns association between two events so that later, when one event occurs, the second event is acted upon or is brought to mind.

*If subjects are asked to write meaningful sentences while discussing another topic, they will do this and later be surprised to see what they have written. Automatic drawing also can be elicited.

**Although portions of earlier experiences may be recalled, age-regression reports may not be accurate. Subjects under hypnosis have highly imaginative memories and can be quite convincing in their age-regression performances. Subjects can also be induced to give very convincing age-progression performances.

***While dissociation is traditionally associated with unconscious vis-à-vis conscious motives and activities, biofeedback and meditation provide examples of dissociation with more manipulable boundaries. This is illustrated in the learned control of dreams in the lucid state.

umn at the right of the table are some interpretations of these effects that are drawn from everyday processes of suggestion. These explanations have been provided by Theodore X. Barber (1969) who is skeptical that hypnosis represents a special state of consciousness. Barber's explanations are based upon behavioral and cognitive aspects of everyday consciousness—good imagination, positive attitude, motivation, expectations, and willingness. Essentially Barber has attempted to demystify hypnosis as a scientifically unmanageable state of mind.

In biofeedback and meditation the person guides their own relaxation and degree of dissociation. In hypnosis these processes are usually under the guidance of another person—the hypnotist. In a limited sense, then, it is the will of the hypnotist that returns you to everyday consciousness. However, this external will is really under the guidance of the person's own will. Hypnotized people will not do things that go against their basic beliefs. This is not as simple as it might sound. British psychologist and hypnotist H.B. Gibson explains:

> There is a well-known story which is quoted by various writers, concerning a young woman who was being demonstrated in a somnambulistic state by Charcot when he was called out of the lecture theatre. He asked his assistant to carry on. This young man, taking advantage of the absence of his professor, thereupon suggested to the young woman that she should strip off all her clothes. As the story goes, this young woman, being of a modest type who would not normally appear nude before a gallery of strangers, came out of her trance, slapped the face of the impertinent young doctor, and flounced from the room. This anecdote is often cited to make the point that the hypnotized person is not a robot, but an individual with personal standards which are not to be flouted. If this is the case, then is the possibility of hypnosis being used for criminal purposes, as suggested by Bjornstrom and others, groundless?
>
> Well, if the young doctor who wanted the girl to strip herself in public had possessed an adequate knowledge of hypnosis he would have proceeded otherwise, and perhaps attained his object. . . . He could have suggested, for instance, that she was quite alone. . . . Having blotted out consciousness of other people being present, the hypnotist might then have induced hallucinations of time and place and suggested to the girl that she was at home and about to take a bath. The girl might then have proceeded to remove all her clothes, for there is nothing immodest about stripping to take one's bath. Thus, while it is not reasonable to expect hypnotized persons to transgress against their own normal standards of conduct, hypnosis can be used to get people to perform an overt act which is contrary to their own general inclinations by temporarily distorting their perception of reality. (1977, pp. 133–134)

As in biofeedback and meditation, hypnotic induction narrows the focus of attention of the subject. In the case of hypnosis it is under the guidance of the hypnotist. This narrowing of attention can be helped along in several ways. The hypnotist may ask the subject to gaze at a particular point, or simply to concentrate upon what the hypnotist is saying. How well the person responds to the suggestions of the hypnotist depends upon the person. Some people are very suggestible, others are not at all. About 5 to 10 percent of people cannot be hypnotized, about 15 percent are easily hypnotized, and everybody else is somewhere in between. To help the hypnotist determine how suggestible a particular subject is, he can test for susceptibility. Table 3.5 lists items that are used to determine how suggestible a person might be. The mosquito hallucination (item #3) involves the hypnotist suggesting to the subject that a mosquito is buzzing around and lands on the subject's forehead. If the subject is susceptible at this level, he might grimace and brush or swat at an imaginary mosquito.

How Widely Is Hypnosis Used Today?

Although hypnosis has experienced periods of acceptance and non-acceptance, it has in recent times grown in both respect and use. In 1970 a division of the American Psychological Association, Psychological Hypnosis, was created. A study by this division has found that between 1974 and 1978 the number of graduate programs in clinical psychology, dentistry, and medical schools offering courses in hypnosis had doubled! Medical hypnosis continues to be more and more widely used (Patricia Long, 1986, Wilkes, 1986). Today the major uses of hypnosis include psychotherapy and the control of pain (Spiegel, 1987).

Can Animals Be Hypnotized?

In hypnosis a certain set of circumstances and events leads a person into an altered state of suggestion. Likewise, certain circumstances and events will lead animals into trance-like altered states of behavior (here we must infer any altered states of consciousness, although you will see shortly that there is some evidence for the altered state of consciousness in animals).

Everyone has heard that certain animals, for example, rabbits, "freeze" when danger is near.

Table 3.5 Stanford Hypnotic Susceptibility Scale, Form C

Item	*Criterion of Passing*
0. Eye closure during induction	(Noted, but not scored)
1. Hand lowering (right hand)	Lowers at least 6 inches in 10 seconds
2. Moving hands apart	Hands 6 inches or more apart after 10 seconds
3. Mosquito hallucination	Any acknowledgment of effect
4. Taste hallucination (sweet, sour)	Both tastes experienced and one strong or with overt movements
5. Arm rigidity (right arm)	Less than 2 inches of arm bending in 10 seconds
6. Dream	Dreams well, experience comparable to a dream
7. Age regression (school fifth and second grades)	Clear change in handwriting between present and one regressed age
8. Anosmia to ammonia	Odor of ammonia denied and overt signs absent
9. Arm immobilization (left arm)	Arm rises less than 1 inch in 10 seconds
10. Hallucinated voice	Subject answers voice realistically at least once
11. Negative visual hallucination	Reports seeing only two boxes of three boxes
12. Posthypnotic amnesia	Subject recalls three or fewer items before "Now you can remember everything"

Source: Weitzenhoffer and Hilgard (1962).
Note: This scale is used in conjunction with a brief attempted induction of hypnosis, during which the subject is observed and rated on performance on the above 12 items. The hypnotist suggests each item and notes if the subject responds to the suggestion. The possible score is 12.

But there are also reliable examples of stroking, eye-gazing, and suddenly putting animals on their backs that make them lapse into an immobilized state. F.A. Volgyesi (1966), a world expert on these sort of "hypnotic" events in animals, puts animals into trances. Amazingly, poking such animals with pins, for example, does not provoke a response!

While proponents of the idea of real animal hypnosis like Volgyesi and J. Hoskovec (1969) do not claim to be able to get a rabbit running around acting like a chicken, they do believe that somewhere down in the older brain structures the brain mechanism that causes animals to become immobile, etc., is also a component mechanism in some human hypnosis. For example, the hypnotist's challenge of "Try to open your eyes," or "You cannot move your arm," or "You will not feel the pain," etc., may be related to the same mechanism which underlies the animal trances. Human versions of trances are simply made more complex due to the great amount of uncommitted cortex. And, of course, most human varieties of hypnosis, including self-hypnosis, do not involve trance-like immobilization.

On the other hand, researchers such as S.C. Ratner (1967), and G.G. Gallup (1974) believe that the manipulable trance behavior in animals is a simple evolutionary survival tactic. If the animal either plays dead or doesn't move, a predator either may not see him or lose interest.

Gallup does at least see the possibility that animal and human hypnosis might somehow be related:

> It could be argued that the presumed similarity between human and animal hypnosis has done more to retard research than to provide a useful explanatory framework. But perhaps when the status of hypnotic events in humans has been clarified, the analogy will become more useful. (1974, p. 839)

One phenomenon which might demonstrate that animals are more open to suggestion than simple instinctual traces is *learned helplessness.* In this situation an animal might learn that it cannot escape a punishing shock, for example. If then the animal is permitted an escape route, it will not even try to escape. It seems that the animal has accepted a condition of helplessness. One might regard this as a sort of suggestion that has been transmitted to the animal not by words, but deeds. Further, it has been found that some animals (within the same species) take the suggestion of helplessness quite easily, while others escape as soon as an escape route is permitted. This might be a matter of differences in susceptibility to altering the cognitive state of the animal—an altered state of consciousness. H.B. Gibson's (1977) book includes a full chapter on hypnosis in animals, along with critical discussion.

Theories of Incorrect Perception—Illusions in Consciousness

We have been discussing theories of sensation. Now, we will examine theory mechanisms that are fundamental to perceptual consciousness. This will involve a discussion of perceptual *constancies.* Nearly all of the time the constancies permit us to perceive the world in meaningful and *veridical* ways. However, under certain circumstances the influences of the constancies actually mislead us. We then perceive *illusions.*

Perception Constancies

Things and events around you seem to stay themselves even though the *proximal* images or impressions of them on your receptors are the farthest things from themselves from moment to moment. For example, next time you are walking about the campus hold your thumb and forefinger close to your eye and measure the height of a person, say, 20 feet away. You'll notice that the image between your thumb and finger is only perhaps an inch tall. However, your perception of that person is as full-sized. Most of the time you can't even imagine that the image is so small.

So, while the image of particular objects on your retina varies tremendously depending on your distance from them, the objects seem to stay the same size. This control of expectancy is called size constancy. Figure 3.9 shows that even though the image pattern varies in size, the percept size stays constant. Another way to put this is that as a person approaches you on the street, he doesn't seem to increase in size. He stays constant no matter what the distance.

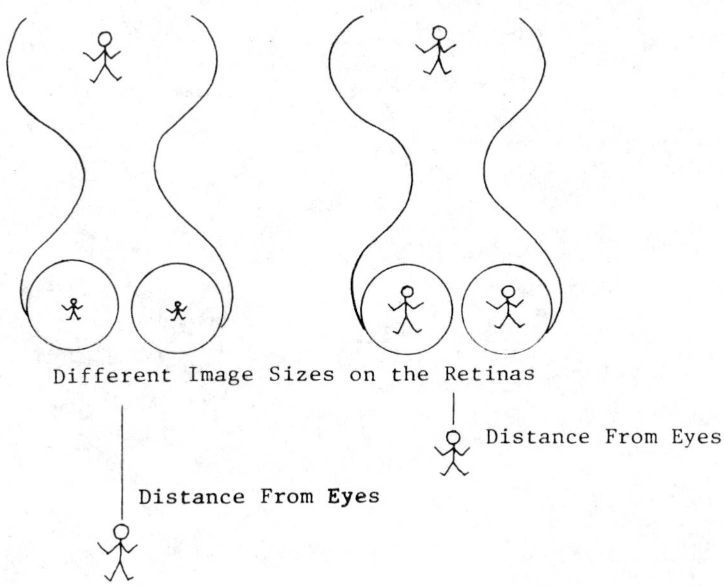

Figure 3.9 Size Constancy

In addition to size constancy there are many other functional constancies which allow you to move through your environment (and have it move about you) so that there are not too many surprises. It would be a surprise if occasionally the person 20 feet away actually turned out to be an inch tall!

Shape constancy refers to the fact that objects no matter how viewed seem to remain the same shape. Look at this book you are reading from several different angles. No matter how you view it, it still looks like your psychology book. You are experiencing shape constancy. Try to make your psychology book not look like your psychology book! It is nearly impossible to break this constancy.

Color constancy refers to the fact that objects appear to be the same color even though viewed under different lighting conditions. Your friend Ralph does not seem to suddenly have a tan when you see him in night light or a semidarkened room. Color constancies can break down much easier than either size or shape constancies.

Other constancies include other aspects of the changes that occur in your sense→perceptual relation to your environment. These include brightness, motion, and position. The purpose and principles underlying all of the constancies are the same. This is another way the modalities work in harmony.

Illusions

It should come as no surprise that illusions or incorrect perceptions occur in some relation to the necessary distorting mechanisms that underlie the constancies. Barbara Gillam (1980) has evaluated several approaches to explaining illusions and has concluded that illusions are most likely related to the functional constancies.

Illusions are not veridical perceptions based upon differing proximal information (images) as are the constancies—but are pretty much the reverse. Illusions involve incorrect perceptions based upon veridical information. Figure 3.10 shows this "reverse" nature of an illusion. Compare this with the illustrations of the constancies. Note that the two horizontal lines are actually equal in length in the eyes, but the perception is incorrect—it's an illusion.

Now look at the illusions that appear in Figure 3.11. Notice how they are all relatable to the constancies. This does not rule out the possibility that physiological aspects of the visual system, or the effects of eye motor activity might contribute to the percept error.

Constancies, themselves, are in a sense illusions (recall the power of the shape illusion on your textbook) and can themselves cause percept errors if conditions are right. Because your brain has to distort things in order to provide everyday useful veridical perceptions from a variety of

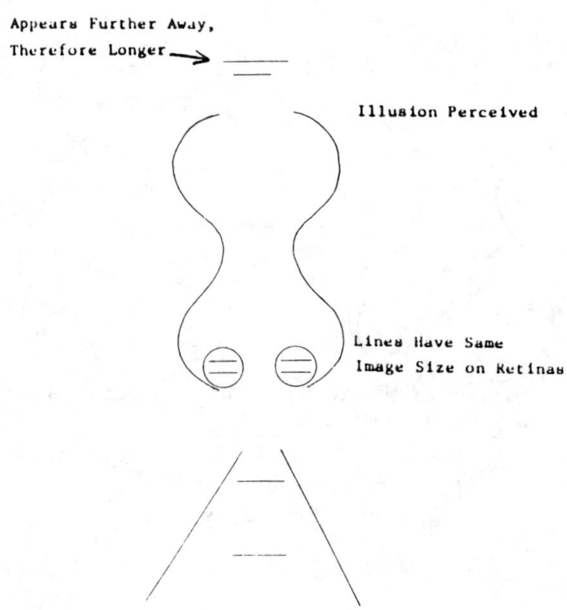

Figure 3.10 Reverse Nature of Illusions

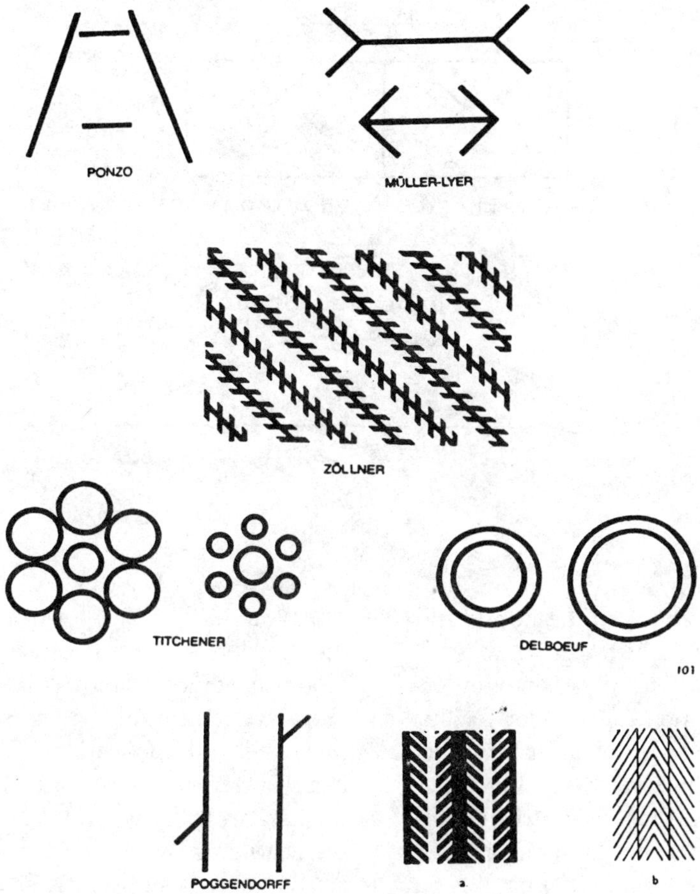

Figure 3.11 Types of Illusions

images, it risks that distortion will at times mislead it. This is the very thing that is at work in the Ponzo illusion. The railroad tie #2 looks further down the track (an everyday constancy cue), but since the ties in the Ponzo drawing are really the same size, your constancy processing system loses the risk, and tie #2 seems longer.

An example of a Ponzo-type illusion that you have seen often is the *moon illusion.* Even though the moon on the horizon appears much larger than when overhead, their images are actually the same size (see Figure 3.12a). Measure them next time you have a chance. However, Lloyd Kaufman and Irvin Rock (1962) have theorized the moon on the horizon appears further away (like railroad tie #2 did) than does the moon overhead. Therefore size constancy processing loses the bet again and powerfully creates the illusion that the moon on the horizon is much larger. This particular moon illusion theory is partly based upon the fact that people tend to perceive the overall spatial environment in a rather distorted way. Figure 3.12b shows what Kaufman and Rock found. People tend to report that the horizon judgment involves greater distances than overhead ones.

Time Illusions

There are other illusions related to the constancies that we listed earlier. One type of illusion that occurs daily in our life might slip our notice because there is no single particular constancy related to it. These are the time illusions. As you have probably experienced, time does not always seem to pass at the same rate. There's an old saying "How time flies when one is having fun." We can add to this another common experience. "How time drags when one is bored." There is no doubt that subjective time experience varies a great deal depending on what we are doing.

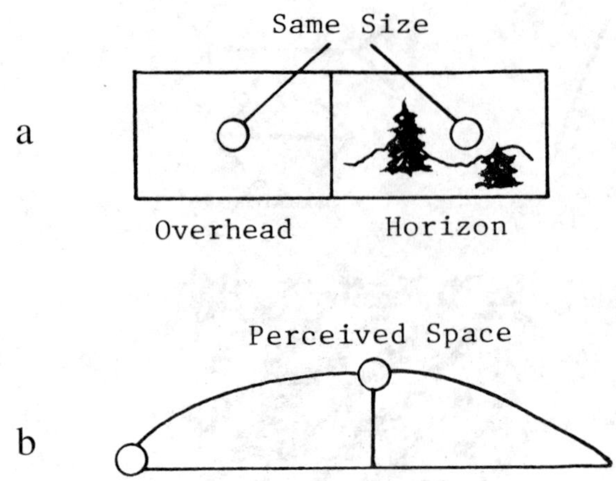

Figure 3.12 Moon Illusion

Psychologists who have studied time illusions have their counterparts to the Ponzo and the other visual illusions. Although they are a little more involved, they are very easy to understand. The Tau and Kappa effects refer to illusions based upon time-space relationships. *Tau Effect* is an illusion concerning spacing judgments based upon time intervals between stimuli, and *Kappa Effect* is a time judgment based upon the spacing of stimuli. The Kappa illusion is of primary interest to us as a time illusion.

Figure 3.13 shows that subjective time undergoes an expansion simply by separating the lights which both go on one second apart by a greater distance. The more the stimuli are spaced, the longer the time interval seems—even though it is the same.

So, what explanation do we have for this illusion? Is there a constancy behind this one? Bill Jones and Yih Lehr Huang (1982) (amplifying the work of D.R. Price Williams) have theorized that people impute some degree of constant motion between the stimuli. This brain constancy says, "It takes longer to go a greater distance if one is going at a constant speed." This makes sense. The subjects in these experiments don't actually "see" a motion between the stimuli in the Kappa effect illusion. The imputing is done in an automatic and formal sense. The constant motion between the lights is perceived in the same way the other constancies are—immediate, automatic, and formal. Think again about the shape constancy of your psychology textbook. It, too, is automatic.

There are also Tau and Kappa effect illusions for audition and for touch. Since it seems the illusion occurs because of the imputed motion-distance relationship, time illusions are likely generalizations of size and shape illusion processes (misapplications) we discussed earlier. The Kappa illusion illustrates the idea that time seems to fly when we are active, and time seems to drag when we are bored. When we are active external stimuli are spaced more closely together per objective unit of time, and when we are bored external stimuli tend to be spaced further apart.

Consciousness Beyond Consciousness?

One of the "theoretical level proofs" of the existence of *Extrasensory Perception (ESP)* involves predictions made using various powers of the binomial. It is important to realize that this approach to testing for the existence of ESP does not offer proof at the empirical level of analysis. That is, the approach does not establish the existence of an *empirical referent* for ESP. In order to establish such a basis for ESP, we would have to discover the four criteria required for any type of perception. These four criteria include (1), a measurable energy continuum, (2), a receptor cell, (3), a separate pathway to the CNS, and (4), a unique experience. In Table 3.8 these criteria are shown as they relate to 10 sensory-perceptual channels. With this very important warning in mind, let us see how the theoretical support for ESP is established.

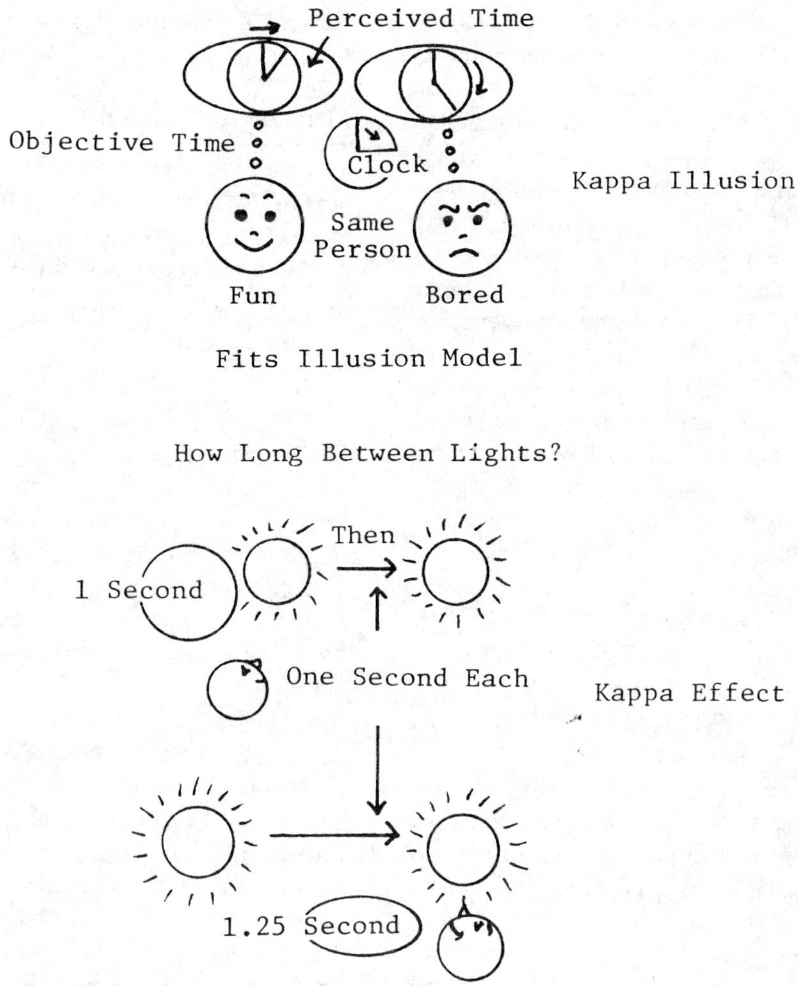

Figure 3.13 Kappa Illusion

Before we begin, you might be interested to know whether psychologists teaching in colleges and universities believe in the possibility of ESP. A recent survey (Wagner & Monnet, 1979) found that 34 percent of teaching psychologists felt that it was a very likely possibility, and 34 percent felt that it is an impossibility, with the rest somewhere in between. Table 3.6 shows how college professors in the natural sciences and the arts compare with psychology professors.

One obvious difference between psychology professors and professors from all other fields is in the percentage that feel ESP is impossible. Do the psychology professors know something about ESP the others don't? No, they don't. Psychology teachers are probably more cautious in their attitudes toward ESP simply because it is a puzzling subject within their own field.

As you are probably aware, ESP involves the idea that some people (perhaps all people) are able to respond directly to something in the external world that seems not due to sensory information or inference. We might conduct an experiment which would test whether or not subjects can determine, "read" or guess what is being chosen randomly by a machine or experimenter. So that a binomial probability analysis could be performed on the subject's performance, we would want to control the number and types of "stimuli" the machine might randomly select. Many early experimental studies of telepathy (a direct response to someone else's mental activity) and of clairvoyance (a direct response to an object or event not explainable by perception, memory, or inference) used what are often called ESP-cards (Zener cards, after Karl Zener) to control the stimuli the machine or experimenter might select (Bowles & Hynds, 1978). There are five different symbols on the cards: a star, three wavey lines, a plus sign, a square, and a circle. You may have seen these.

What would you think if someone were able to guess which of the ESP cards the machine had selected six times in a row? How likely would this high level of accuracy be by chance alone? The expanded binomial can tell very easily the exact chance of guessing correctly (or incorrectly) six times or any number of times. It can just as easily tell you the exact chance of guessing correctly or incorrectly in any combination. Table 3.7 shows how it can be done.

So, if the five different ESP cards are used, and say, six guesses are made, the binomial would be rewritten like this: $(\frac{1}{5} + \frac{4}{5})^6$. Again, this simply says that because there are five different cards, the chances of guessing correctly each time you guess is *a* or $\frac{1}{5}$, and the chance of guessing wrong each time you guess is *b* or $\frac{4}{5}$. Four of the possible responses you could make out of the five will turn out to be wrong ones each time you guess.

Now, simply expand $(\frac{1}{5} + \frac{4}{5})^6$. You will find that this binomial when expanded looks like this:

$$\left(\frac{1}{5}\right)^6 + 6\left(\frac{1}{5}\right)^5\left(\frac{4}{5}\right) + 15\left(\frac{1}{5}\right)^4\left(\frac{4}{5}\right)^2 + 20\left(\frac{1}{5}\right)^3\left(\frac{4}{5}\right)^3 + 15\left(\frac{1}{5}\right)^2\left(\frac{4}{5}\right)^4 + 6\left(\frac{1}{5}\right)\left(\frac{4}{5}\right) + \left(\frac{4}{5}\right)^6$$

P all 6 correct (first term); P 4 correct and 2 incorrect (third term); P all 6 incorrect (last term)

$$= .000064 + .000536 + .01536 + .08192 + .24576 + .393216 + .262144$$

$$= 1.00 \text{ (of course)}$$

P means "probability" or chance

Table 3.7 Method for Determining Correct Guesses

In the binomial $(a + b)^N$:

1. *a* can represent the probability (chance of a *correct* guess by chance alone).
2. and *b* can represent the probability of an *incorrect* guess by chance alone.
3. and, finally, *N* is simply the *number* of times you make a guess.

Each term represents a possible combination of correct and incorrect guesses out of the six guesses you made. You can see that the chance of guessing correctly six times in a row with five cards would be $(\frac{1}{5})^6$ or exactly .000064 as a decimal, or about one time out of 15,625—not too likely by chance alone. Also, you can see that getting them all wrong by guessing is much more likely (.262144)—about 1 time out of 4. All of the other possible combinations can be determined by simply looking at the appropriate exponents. For example, the chance of getting four correct (as) and 2 wrong (bs) out of six guesses is determined by noting the term where *a* has the exponent 4 and *b* has the exponent 2. This term is 15 $(\frac{1}{5})^4$ $(\frac{4}{5})^2$ and is equal to .01536, or about one chance out of 65. There are more direct ways in the algebra of combinations to make these same calculations. If you were guessing a large number of times—like 25 or 30 times—you would find expanding the binomial a hopelessly large task. However, the point here is to see the graphic relationship of the expanded binomial and Pascal's Triangle to the symmetry of a normal bell-shaped curve, and how probability can be determined.

Table 3.6 Academic Field and Attitude Toward ESP

ESP is:	*Natural Sciences*	*Arts*	*Psychology*	*All Professors*
a fact	10%	31	5	16
likely	46	48	29	49
an unknown	15	8	10	11
remotely possible	28	11	22	19
impossible	3	2	34	4

Adapted from Wagner & Monnet (1979)

Why ESP Seems to Exist

You may now be wondering how the use of the binomial could help "prove" the existence of ESP. Once the binomial has established exactly what the chance outcomes should be for experiments with ESP cards, we are in a position to evaluate the meaning of a very interesting phenomenon. Some subjects' scores deviate greatly from pure chance as determined by the

Table 3.8 Summary Chart of Empirical Bases of Sense→Perception

Measurable Energy Continuum	*Receptor Cell*	*Pathway to CNS*	*Unique Experience*
1. Modality: Vision Electromagnetic Spectrum (400–700nm)	rods, cones	optic nerve	seeing
2. Modality: Audition Vibrational Energy (20–20,000 cps)	hair cells	auditory nerve	hearing
3. Modality: Gustation Molecules in Solution (saliva)	microvilli (taste buds)	cranial nerves	smell
4. Modality: Olfaction Molecules in Solution (mucus) (from volatile substances molecular weight 30–300)	cilia (Olf. epithelium)	cranial nerve	smell
5. Modality: Touch Mechanical Distortions (min. .00004´)	free nerve ends Pacinian corpusule	slow & fast fibers	touch
6. Modality: Pain Intense Mechanical/Thermal (relation between fast and slow fiber information and descending CNS modulation)	free nerve ends	slow & fast fibers	hurting
7. Modality: Temperature Thermal Stimuli above and below "physiological zero"	free nerve ends	slow & fast fibers	warm, hot cool, cold
8. Modality: Organic Mechanical and Chemical in Viscera	free nerve ends	slow & fast fibers (some direct to thalamus)	feelings in viscera (some emotional)
9. Modality: Kinesthetic Body Motions (mechanical)	free nerve ends (muscles, tendons, joints)	slow & fast fibers	body movements
10. Modality: Vestibular Body Axis Motions (mechanical)	hair cells in the cranial nerve semicircular canals		linear/ angular accelerations

binomial! (Rao, 1984). It has been found that certain people are able to score (guess) far above that the binomial would predict. Furthermore, they are able to do this consistently. For example, one experiment used five cards and gave subjects 25 chances to guess. Out of the 25 guesses we would expect subjects to average about five correct guesses. However, many subjects were able to average as high as seven correct guesses. One subject was even able to average 18 correct guesses. The chances against such a performance by chance alone are incredible! They are so incredible it would not be reasonable at all to chalk it up to chance. It is further interesting that certain people consistently score far below what the binomial would predict (Schmeidler and McConnell, 1958). What can these strange experimental outcomes possibly mean? Some interesting theoretical conclusions are possible. There is little doubt that something is behind these consistent deviations from chance (Rhine, Pratt, Smith, Stuart, and Greenwood 1966, p. 191). What is this something? It is ESP. But what is ESP? As of yet we do not know.

How Do Drugs Affect Consciousness?

The brain is a biological system. Anything that goes into the brain system altering its biochemistry will in some way alter consciousness. In Chapter 2 you learned how drugs can affect the nervous system at the synapses. In Chapter 13 you will explore how psychotropic drugs can alter the brain chemistry of people with mental disorders to help them function normally.

Since the effects of drugs on consciousness will be taken up in other chapters, and since here we are aiming at understanding aspects of normal consciousness in normal situations the discussion will be brief. Table 3.9 describes briefly how the major classes of drugs affect consciousness.

Table 3.9 Psychoactive Drugs Commonly Involved in Drug Abuse

Drugs	*Usage*	*Conscious Effects*
Sedatives		
Alcohol (ethanol)	Reduce tension Facilitate social interaction "Blot out"	feelings of warmth, expansiveness, toward alterations in mood extremes, "blackouts" or lapses of memory
Barbiturates Nembutal (pentobarbital) Seconal (secobarbital) Veronal (barbital) Tuinal (secobarbital and amobarbital)	Reduce tension Induce relaxation and sleep	feelings of relaxation, physical and intellectual weariness
Stimulants		
Amphetamines Benzedrine (amphetamine) Dexedrine (dextroamphetamine) Methedrine (methamphetamine)	Increase feelings of alertness and confidence Decrease feelings of fatigue Stay awake for long periods	increased alertness, wards off feelings of fatigue reduces appetite
Cocaine (cocoa)	Decrease feelings of fatigue Increase endurance Stimulate sex drive	can accentuate sexual processes, feeling of peace and contentment

Table 3.9 *(continued)*

Drugs	*Usage*	*Conscious Effects*
Narcotics		
Opium and its derivatives Opium Morphine Codeine Heroin	Alleviate physical pain Induce relaxation and pleasant reverie Alleviate anxiety and tension	euphoric "rush" often compared to sexual orgasm (about 60 seconds), feelings of relaxation and euphoria, followed by craving for more
Methadone (synthetic narcotic)	Treatment of heroin dependence	satisfies craving of narcotics
Psychedelics & Hallucinogens		
Cannabis Marijuana Hashish Mescaline (peyote) Psilocybin (psychotogenic mushrooms) LSD (lysergic acid diethylamide-25)	Induce changes in mood, thought, and behavior "Mind expansion"	changes in reality, alterations in subjective time, sensory enhancements, feelings of well-being, enhanced enjoyment of sexual intercourse, things intellectually clearer, laughter and giggling inappropriately intense or prolonged. distorts and enhances imagery, mind is expanded, alterations of consciosness may either be positive or negative for the subject
PCP (phencyclidine)	Induce stupor	
Antianxiety drugs		
minor tranquilizers Librium (chlordiazepoxide) Miltown (meprobamate) Valium (diazepam) Others, e.g., Compoz (scopolamine)	Alleviate tension and anxiety Induce relaxation and sleep	

Bringing It All Together

While each of the topics discussed in this chapter represents an area of study within psychology in its own right, these topics have in common psychology's continuing interest in understanding the conscious underpinnings of behavior and cognition. In Ernest Hilgard's (1980) review of *Consciousness in Contemporary Psychology*, the underlying theme was this return by psychologists to considerations of mind and consciousness. At the same time psychologists and researchers from other disciplines are attempting to understand consciousness in terms of the evolution of the nervous system (Edelman, 1992; Vandervert, 1995, 1999). The studies of animal consciousness are part of this broad trend in psychology.

The work of the cognitive ethologists cannot help but improve our understanding of just what it is we mean by consciousness. The theory section emphasizes that it would be difficult to have a chapter on "consciousness" without forming some basic idea of what consciousness is. As we improve our idea of consciousness we will be getting directly at the heart of psychology.

Glossary

abstraction: A concept or idea that is produced by distilling countless observations down to a few or a single common element(s).

anecdotal reports: Reports that are based upon casual rather than preplanned systematic observation.

cognitive ethology: The comparative study of human and animal cognition and consciousness that may include findings derived from observations in either the laboratory or in natural settings.

cognitive maps: A mental picture or representation of an area or a process that allows an organism to accomplish certain tasks. The organism need not have been previously trained and may find new ways of doing things based upon the mental picture or map.

collective unconscious: Images and concepts that are inherited in all members of a species. Even though these are unconscious, it is thought they do influence behavior in many ways.

coverants: Elements of thoughts or mental images which, if rewarded, will become more likely in the future; if not rewarded, they will become less likely.

creative incubation: A process that is thought to occur when a person takes his or her mind off of a problem with which they have been working. Solutions to the problem may then seem to "pop" up unexpectedly.

dissociation: A process by which an organism becomes separated from a certain portion of its environment, or where certain elements of consciousness or personality become separated from one another.

electrodermal activity: Electrical activity of the autonomic nervous system that can be measured at the skin.

electromyographic activity: The electrical activity of the muscles. It can be a reflection of either autonomic or somatic activity.

ethology: The comparative study of animals in their natural settings.

ex utero: Out of the uterus—after birth.

genetic programming (of the brain): The gene-directed structuring of the brain so that it controls bodily functions, including its own, both before and after birth.

feedforward: Response in anticipation of discrepancy between a future actual state of affairs and a present state.

higher cortical arousal: The cortex being active or awake.

hypnosis: A technique employed in suggestion, or a state of suggestibility that may be self-induced.

innate: Inherited or inborn.

in utero: In the uterus—before birth.

isomorphy: Similar or identical in structure or function.

learned helplessness: Because of repeated lack of success, an organism learns that attempts at some particular task are hopeless, and are, therefore, not even tried.

meditation: Steady reflection, or behavior that focuses the mind.

metaphor: The comparison of one category of things or events with another that seems similar in nature.

neodissociative: A newer and broader idea that views various types of dissociation as having common bases.

nonrapid eye movement (NREM): Periods of sleep that do not contain rapid eye movements.

NREM: See nonrapid eye movement.

oneiric behavior: A technical term for behavior related to dreaming.

operantly conditionable: Voluntary behavior that can be learned though a series of rewards and punishments.

paradoxical sleep: During REM many bodily activities, including the electrical activity of the brain, seem to "wake up." Yet the person is sound asleep.

phenomenal: The causative effects of sense experience upon behavior.

rapid eye movements (REM): The movements of the eyes beneath the eyelids during sleep. They indicate that a dream is in progress.

REM: See rapid eye movements.

suggestion: The transmission of a belief or expectancy without the use of argument, command, or coercion.

ultradian rhythm: Any biological rhythm that occurs on less than a daily cycle.

zeitgeist: The flavor, spirit, or trends of the times.

Consciousness: Doing Psychology on Your Own

Lois McDermott

Basic Concept #3— The Puzzle of Consciousness

Psychology is the study of sentient organisms. Conscious awareness of the world within and/or the world without is central to our concept of a sentient being. What then could be more central to the study of psychology than the study of consciousness?

However, the study of **normal consciousness** (everyday awareness of reality) has proved to be very difficult. Consciousness has been a tricky concept to define and reduce to numbers via operational definitions. The study of normal consciousness has tended to occur through the study of sensation and perception and thinking and memory processes. From this line of research it becomes exceedingly clear that our sense of conscious awareness is constructed both by extracting information from the outside world (through our senses) and by extracting information from the world inside our minds (through memory and thinking). However, even with regard to the world of the senses, our mind imposes its own order on our awareness of reality. While it is likely that all of us are processing the external world in largely similar ways, it must be recognized that our individual conscious awareness of reality is a product of our own mind.

Some of what psychologists have discovered about normal consciousness has been extrapolated from the study of **dissociative states**—states of consciousness that deviate from the norm by altering and/or splitting off (dissociating) some aspects of awareness from other aspects. There has been great interest in the altered states of awareness found in **sleeping, dreaming, hypnosis, psychoactive drugs states** (which will be dealt with in this unit) and **meditation, dissociative disorders** and certain **disease states** (which will be dealt with at a later point). The research has been motivated by an interest in these altered states, not only for their own sake but also, for what they reveal, by comparison, about normal consciousness. There has also been an examination of the purported altered state of consciousness associated with **paranormal perceptions** (ESP).

Unit Focus. For as long as we have had access to the writings of ancient peoples, we have known that humans have an eternal fascination with the experience of dreaming. Humans throughout recorded history have been mystified, intrigued and terrified by their dreams and have relied upon dreams as a basis for making decisions and taking action. It should not be surprising then, that some psychologists, beginning with Freud's *Interpretation of Dreams,* have had a long-standing interest in unraveling the mysteries of dreaming and of sleep itself. After all, the sleep state of consciousness comprises fully one-third of our lives.

The invention of the electroencephalograph (EEG) and other recording devices (EKG, EMG) made it possible to establish operational definitions for some aspects of normal consciousness, the sleeping states of consciousness, and many of the other dissociative states. Hans Berger, the inventor of the EEG, was the first to establish that different states of consciousness (cognitive states) are associated with identifiable brain wave patterns. From that point forward, the psychology of consciousness (especially sleep and dreaming) has been dominated by the study of the brain's neurophysiology and neurochemistry—correlates of conscious awareness.

This unit is designed to introduce you to the study of consciousness—all sorts of consciousness (e.g., waking, dreaming, hypnosis, and drug states). First we examine how our waking state of consciousness is created by the workings of the mind (i.e., the internal perceptual process)—our reality is a function of the mental processes we inherited from our ancestors and developed through experience. We do not extract information from the environment; we create information out of the raw materials of the senses. After examining the best-understood state of consciousness—the sleep state—we will have a glimpse at some very intriguing states of altered consciousness.

Study Objectives

1. Learn the different definitions of consciousness.
2. Compare the "conscious" of the left and right hemispheres.
3. Learn the physiology of sleep and dreaming.
4. Compare and Contrast the two basic types of sleep—(e.g., HVS vs. LVF, NREM vs. REM, PSNS vs. SNS, quiet vs. active sleep states).
5. Learn the three main models of dreaming and create a synthesis model.
6. Distinguish between myth and fact with regard to hypnosis, psychoactive drug states, near-death experience and paranormal perceptions.

Key Terms

abstraction
anecdotal reports
cognitive ethology
cognitive maps
collective unconsciousness
coverants
creative incubation
dissociation
electrodermal activity
electromyographic activity
ethology
ex utero
genetic programming (of the brain)
feedforward
higher cortical arousal
hypnosis
innate
in utero
isomorphy
learned helplessness
meditation
metaphor
neodissociative
nonrapid eye movement (REM)
NREM
oneiric behavior
operantly conditionable
paradoxical sleep
phenomenal
rapid eye movements (REM)
REM
suggestion
ultradian rhythm
zeitgeist

Problem Set #3: Consciousness

1. It is the night before a big psych test. You are studying hard, planning to pull an all-nighter. Suddenly you find yourself rowing across Red Square on a huge pencil. You can no longer fight the current and you get swept down the drain. You hear an air raid siren (actually your alarm clock just went off). You land in the gunner's position in a WWII spit fire airplane. Giant mark-sense forms shaped like airplanes are attacking you from all directions. When you awaken you are in despair, realizing you have been sleeping and not studying.
   a. This dream is characteristic of which sleep stage?
   b. What characteristics of the dream support your answer?
   c. Draw an illustration of what your EEG activity might look like during this dream, defining amplitude and frequency.
   d. What other physiological signs would be consistent with this stage of sleep?
   e. What is the minimum amount of time you were asleep?
2. Indicate which of the following features are characteristic of (unique to) stage 5 sleep as opposed to stages 1–4.
   a. penile erection and vaginal lubrication
   b. synchronized brain waves
   c. irregular heart rate, rapid shallow respiration
   d. sleep walking
   e. lengthening duration as night progresses
   f. PGO spikes
   g. increased duration during periods of physical activity
   h. decreased duration as aging occurs
   i. complete loss of muscle tone
   j. awakenings
   k. realistic, emotionally neutral cognitions
3. Of the various beliefs that are commonly held about hypnosis list two that are supported by research data and four that are most likely false.
   a. two true ideas?
   b. four false ideas?
4. Paranormal perceptions are defined as ______.

5. List and define three types of ESP.
6. Despite numerous anecdotes, TV shows, newspaper stories about cases of ESP, there is still scientific skepticism about ESP. Why?
7. List the drugs which fit into each of the following categories and describe the general changes in conscious function of each of the categories.
   a. stimulants
   b. depressants
   c. hallucinogens
8. What are some of the misconceptions about drug addiction? What are some of the effects of the most common drugs in society (i.e., alcohol, nicotine)?

See Appendix C for answers to problem set.

4

Motivation

Can You Achieve Anything You Desire?

We begin this chapter with the picture seen below. Take a few minutes to write a story about this picture. Using your creative imagination, make up a story that is as vivid and dramatic as you can manage. So that you can compare your story with the stories written by some of my own students and those in your psychology class, David Atkinson (1958) has provided some rather loose guidelines.

Figure 4.1

Write for just about one minute on each of the four story guidelines listed in Table 4.1.

Table 4.1 Guidelines for Story

1. What is happening? Who is the person? (one minute)
2. What has led up to this situation? That is, what has happened in the past? (one minute)
3. What is being thought? What is wanted? By whom? (one minute)
4. What will happen? What will be done? (one minute)

You have just expressed a great deal about what motivates you and how much emotion is involved. You will learn later, in Chapter 8, *Personality,* that many needs can be measured by asking people to make up stories like yours. Let us evaluate some stories looking for the expression of a particularly interesting need or motive for college students—the *need to achieve.*

Do you want to achieve great success in life? Do you want to be at the top of whatever it is that you do? You probably do, although not everyone is so motivated, and this desire has little to do with ability. But the big question is, will you succeed? Is there some way psychology can help tell you in advance whether or not your motivation will get you there? The answer is an emphatic yes! The secret to predicting the likelihood that you will be a success is in your little story. It is a simple matter of knowing what to look for.

What to Look for When Thinking About the Need to Achieve

Whenever you read stories about someone who has been very successful, her story usually goes something like the following: she worked very hard at being successful for many years, (2) she had very high standards set for her own behavior, (3) she overcame many obstacles, and (4) she accomplished something unique. Think about Abraham Lincoln, Eleanor Roosevelt, or Mohandas Gandhi for example. While we don't have to be world famous to be "at the top of the heap," the story behind success is usually very much the same. Think of anybody you know who is at least a mild success and I'll bet their story has at least these four parts to it.

These are also some of the things we would look for in evaluating the amount of achievement motivation expressed in your story. Let's take a look at a story written by one of my own students. She wrote for one minute on each of the story guidelines I gave you earlier.

The Achievement Imagination of Dianne Schmitt. What is happening? Who is the person?

"The man in the picture is awaiting a boat from the sea. He is a member of the underground resistance—castle is vacant in background except for resistance (group)."

What has led up to this situation? What has happened in the past?

"The castle is an old fortress and serves as meeting place for underground to send messages/supplies/people out by sea."

What is being thought? What is wanted? By whom?

"The man is anxious for the boat to appear. Perhaps they have been detected. All lights are out in the castle except for a signal light awaiting the boat."

What will happen? What will be done?

"Signal will at last be received from the boat and broadcast answer back from the castle. The man, much relieved, will begin escorting the people to escape down the steps to the boat."

What does this story tell us about Dianne's desire to achieve? If we go back to the common grounds all stories of achievement are likely to have, we can score the amount of achievement-related need that Dianne's story expresses. McClelland, Atkinson, Clark and Lowell (1953) provided us with just such a way to determine expressions of long term involvement, high standards, overcoming obstacles, and doing something unique.

According to McClelland's system, we should give the story one point for each of the achievement related ideas listed in Table 4.2.

Does Dianne express a need to achieve? Yes, she does. Quite a lot. Her little story got one of the three highest scores in an introductory psychology class of 60 students! From this we might predict that Dianne will be an achiever. She wasn't really telling us about the man in the picture; she was unconsciously telling us about herself! Will she actually succeed? Time will tell, but it is likely.

Table 4.2 Achievement Motivation

McClelland's Achievement Ideas	*Dianne's Score*
1. Is story about achievement?	YES = +1 (the resistance has a job to do)
2. Stated need or desire to achieve?	NO = 0
3. Identified person (hero) leading the action?	NO = 0
4. Anticipation of a good ending if hard work is done?	YES = +1 (man much relieved, escorts people)
5. Anticipation of a poor outcome even if hard work is done?	YES = +1 (perhaps detected)
6. Expression of a personal obstacle which the hero of the story must overcome?	NO = 0
7. Expression of an environmental obstacle with which the hero must contend?	NO = 0
8. Something that nurtures or helps the hero?	NO = 0
9. Positive feeling about the achievement?	YES = +1 (man much relieved, happy ending)
10. Negative feeling about not having achieved?	NO = 0
11. Main overall theme about achievement?	YES = +1 (the work of the resistance group dominates the story)
TOTAL = 5 points	

How did your story score? Many of the student stories I score show little or no *achievement motivation*. What does this mean? It depends on what you have in mind for yourself. While achievement motivation measured in this way is related to achievement in life in general, it is not much related to college grades (an aspect of college success), because in this exercise you were asked to be highly imaginative; positive and negative feelings were important in the scoring.

If you really want to be a high achiever in life, you can learn to use your achievement-related imagination to get you there. A great deal of what a person does in life is the direct result of how he imagines himself in the world—and what you imagine is mostly learned! This is precisely the point of the exercise of having you tell an imaginative story about the picture.

You can think of the following exercise as a brief achievement motivation training program. Look at the picture in Figure 4.2. Now go back to the items we used to evaluate our stories. Write an imaginative story that would get a score of 11 points—if scored by one of your fellow classmates. Although you can take more than four minutes to write your story, work as quickly as you can. Try to find a picture or two with ambiguous situations in them—more or less like the ones you have seen in this section. See if you can write imaginative 11-point stories for all these new pictures.

Figure 4.2

You will find that you will begin to think about situations more in terms of long-term involvement, high standards, obstacles you might encounter, and unique accomplishments. Since we tend to act as we imagine things to be, you may find yourself understanding what it takes to achieve whatever you really want.

Toward a Philosophy of Emotion and Motivation

Emotion and motivation are highly related concepts. Here we will try to understand their relationship. The term *motivation* refers to the initiation, direction, strength, and persistence of behavior as an organism moves from its needs to its satisfactions (goals). *Motives* refer to all of the external and internal conditions that determine motivation. *Emotion* refers to all of the various feelings that accompany motivation. These feelings include fear, anger, disgust, surprise, joy, sadness, and many more.

The Relationship Between Emotion and Motivation

Let's go back for a moment to Dianne Schmitt's little story about the activities of the underground resistance. Her story not only contained tips about motivations, but also about emotions. We almost intuitively assume that motivation has to do with whatever energizes or drives, and directs our behavior toward certain goals. Dianne writes, for example, of a man who is a member of the resistance and ends up rescuing people. This is motivated behavior. But also notice that Dianne has given the man feelings that are an integral and necessary part of the desire to rescue, *The man is anxious for the boat to appear.... The man, much relieved, will begin escorting* . . . These are emotions.

If you go back to the scoring plans for the level of achievement motivation in the stories, you can see that points are given for feelings as well as for strivings and goals. For example, points are given for either anticipations of good (happy) or poor (sad) outcomes, and points are given for either positive or negative feelings about the achievement. If the man in Dianne's imagination (really Dianne) was striving for something, any anticipation of not achieving the goal would necessarily involve negative feelings that he would be energized to avoid; any anticipation of achieving the goal would necessarily involve positive feelings that he would be energized toward. This relationship between emotion and motivation makes sense to Dianne's imagination—and it makes sense to us.

So, here we have in a very highly cognitively originated story of motivation, with no emotion in the four story guidelines or the pictures themselves. This tells us something about how closely the two must parallel in daily life. Most psychologists who study emotion, or motivation, or both, agree that our feelings and what we seek are closely bound together. For example, here is how some leading motivation psychologists have expressed this relationship. Robert Beck in the second edition of his book *Motivation: Theories and Principles* (1983) writes in the preface, "The emotion chapter is explicit recognition of the greater need to integrate 'emotional' and 'motivational' concepts and phenomena." Another motivation psychologist, Eva Dreikurs-Ferguson (1976), tells us why Beck is right:

> Since they are not operationally defined in a unique way, emotion and motivation . . . are not behaviorally distinguishable, . . . the position adopted in this book is that emotion and motivation at this point in the history of psychology are interchangeable constructs, because no adequately validated distinction yet exists between them. Until such a distinction is possible, there is no value in calling the same phenomena by two separate names. (p. 92)

The point of Dreikurs-Ferguson's description of the relationship between emotion and motivation can be seen in Dianne's story. For example, would the man who was a member of the resistance bother rescuing people if he had no feelings? On the other hand, would the man worry about being detected if he was not a member of the resistance with plans to rescue people?

How We Should Think About the Relationship Between Emotion and Motivation

Silvan Tomkins (1980) has suggested that affects or feelings act as *analogic amplifiers* of motives.

And he feels that affects are the primary innate motivating mechanisms. Think, for example, of the effect of terror or fear. This general affective analogue can amplify motives related to all sorts of situations. You can fear flunking out of college, losing your job, or being turned down for a date. Without this parallel amplification by affect (fear in this case), nothing gets done—like getting homework done! Tomkins says, "The affect system is therefore the primary motivational system because, without its amplification, nothing else matters and, with its amplification, anything else can matter!" (p. 147). At any rate, we should think of emotion and motivation as *mutually causal*. That is, their relationships are governed by countless positive and negative feedback loops involving many parts of the nervous system. *Positive feedback loops* are related to the mounting and sometimes seemingly out of control nature of emotions and motivation, for example, in romance and war. *Negative feedback loops* are related to the fact that in our daily lives, emotions and motivations do not push our bodies beyond their limits.

In regard to our example of achievement motivation, what could be the key primary affect which results in high (amplified) scores in our student stories? Is it fear, loving, sadness? David C. McClelland (1985) suggests that the emotional incentive (amplifier) of interest and surprise at novelty are the emotional amplifiers of achievement motivation. In other words, if you feel very curious about what is going on in the picture, your imaginative story will be about achievement.

We should think of emotions and motives as interacting systems of conditions that get as to do things. Emotions as indications of naturally evolved incentives to behave are intricate amplifiers of drives that propel us toward goals.

In our discussions of possible explanations of emotion and motivation, we will systematically examine the physiological, learning, and cognitive theories. We will see the similarity between emotion and motivation from each of these points of view. So, for example, when we discuss the physiological theories of motivation, we can reflect back on what we learned about the physiology of emotions.

Theories of Emotion

Physiological Bases for Emotion. Where do emotions come from in the first place? You are familiar with Charles Darwin's theory of evolution. When most people think about the theory of evolution they think in terms of the anatomy of the bodies of various animals, including man. According to Darwin, just as bodies evolve, so do brain structures, behavior patterns, and even minds. They are all interrelated as evolutionary processes unfold.

Emotions and their expressions then have come about because they have had survival value. Darwin's book *The Expression of the Emotions in Man and Animals* (first published in 1872) directly addressed the evolution of the emotions. If you think about the way animals express emotions of fear and anger, for example, you can appreciate how these emotional expressions would enhance their chances of survival. Figure 4.3 shows a cat reacting to a threatening dog. The facial expression, the posture, and the erect hair should all convince the dog of the cat's intentions.

Several modern theorists have continued with the evolutionary approach. Especially interesting has been the work of theorists who have studied emotional expression in the face.

Figure 4.3 Emotional Reaction of Cat to a Threat

In Figure 4.4 for example, Irenaus Eibl-Eibesfeldt (1971) illustrates facial expressions of anger similarity across species, cultures, and age groups. Note that people who are under stressful conditions commonly unconsciously tense the frontalis muscles of the face (forehead) and the trapezius muscles of the upper back. Now, look back at Darwin's cat!

If these expressions of emotions have evolved and are innate, then there must be representations of these in the nervous system. In Chapter 2 we were introduced to the autonomic nervous system (ANS) and its involvement in the fight and flight reactions. This is a part of the neurology of emotion, and we will return to it in the empirical section. Our knowledge of the involvement of the ANS in emotional behavior gives us an opportunity to examine two traditional ways of thinking about just how we experience emotions and where in the nervous system they originate.

The Emotional Sequence of Events

Think about the last time you felt intense emotions. Perhaps you were watching a very sad movie, you were in an argument, or you were about to get some important exam results. What is the sequence of events in your nervous system that results in your feelings?

Common Sense Sequence. In the example of the sad movie, a *common sense sequence of emotion* would indicate you first felt sadness at the death of your hero and therefore cried as shown in Figure 4.5.

James-Lange Sequence. However, there are other ways to look at this situation. The early American psychologist William James would have us change the order of events a little. James felt that the feeling of sadness occurred only because changes in the body had occurred first. And you feel these changes. So, the *James-Lange sequence* of events would indicate the tears occurring first, followed by feelings of sadness as shown in Figure 4.6. As James put it in 1890: "Common sense says we lose our fortune, are sorry and weep; . . . (my) hypothesis . . . is that we feel sorry because we cry, angry because we strike, afraid because we tremble. . . ." Carl Lange (1885, 1967), a Danish physiologist, independently suggested this same sequence of events some time later. Now this idea is referred to as the James-Lange theory.

The James-Lange theory is a descriptive theory with not a lot of neurological facts to back it up—except maybe the sheer existence of the

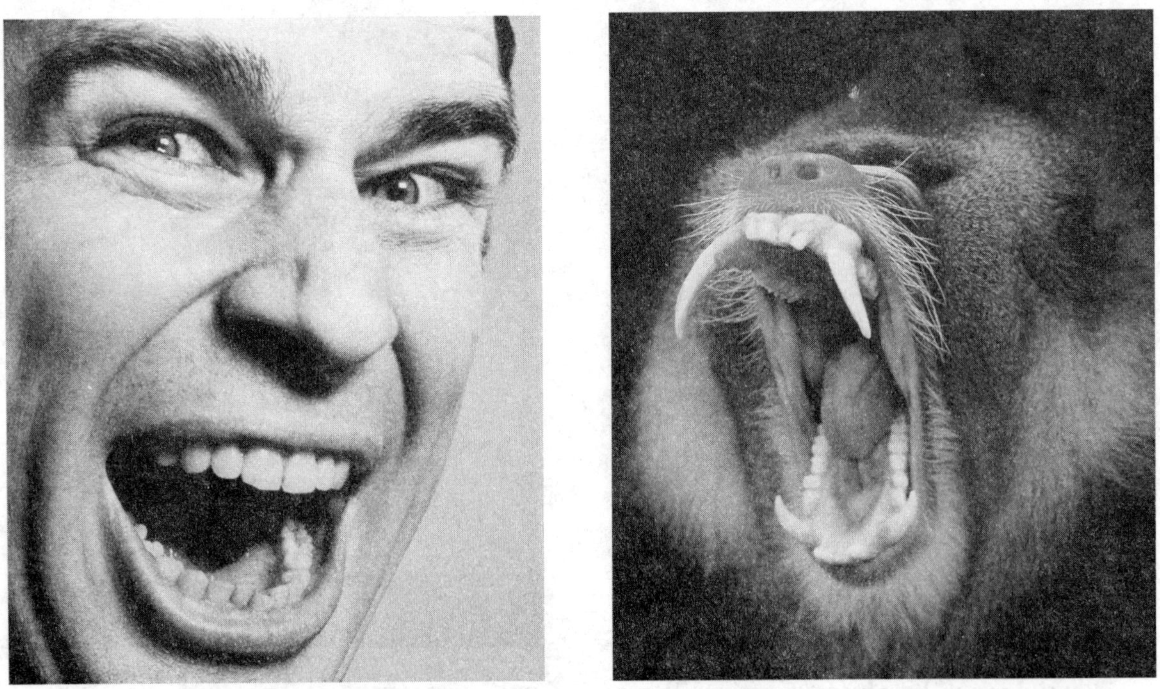

Figure 4.4 Eibl-Eibesfeldt's Facial Expressions

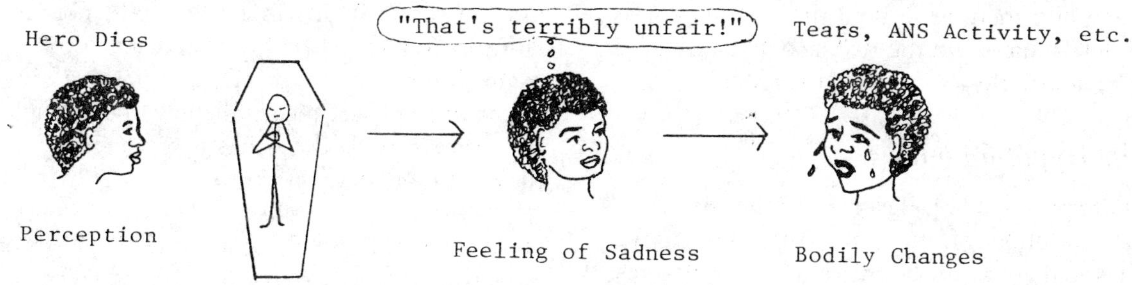

Figure 4.5 Common Sense Sequence

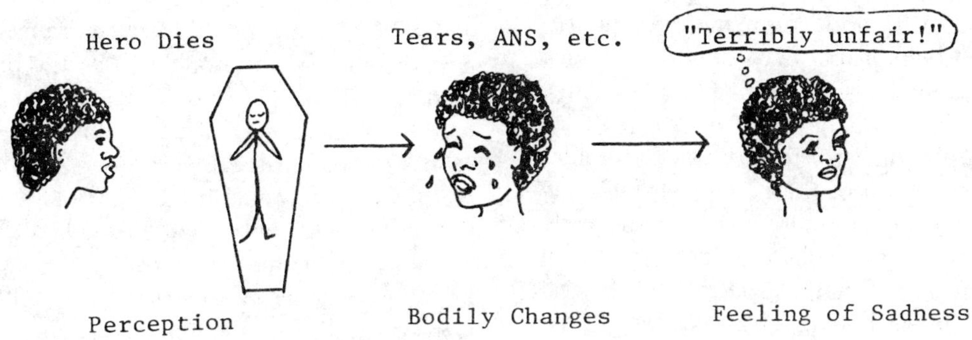

Figure 4.6 James-Lange Sequence

ANS and its activities. For example, a broad variety of felt emotions, fear, rage, joy, etc., all have very similar ANS activities. The basic problem with James' approach is that the ANS, as a system, apparently does not have the capacity to give rise to the great variety of emotions as we experience them.

Cannon-Bard Theory of Emotion. Walter Cannon (1927), drawing on research by Philip Bard, was responsible for showing in many ways that the ANS and *viscera* were not capable of giving rise to the variety of emotions we actually feel. He proposed a sequence of events (Figure 4.7) that switched the origin of the emotions from the ANS and its activity to the hypothalamus in the brain (see Chapter 2).

Here, we see incoming information routed through the limbic system structures in the

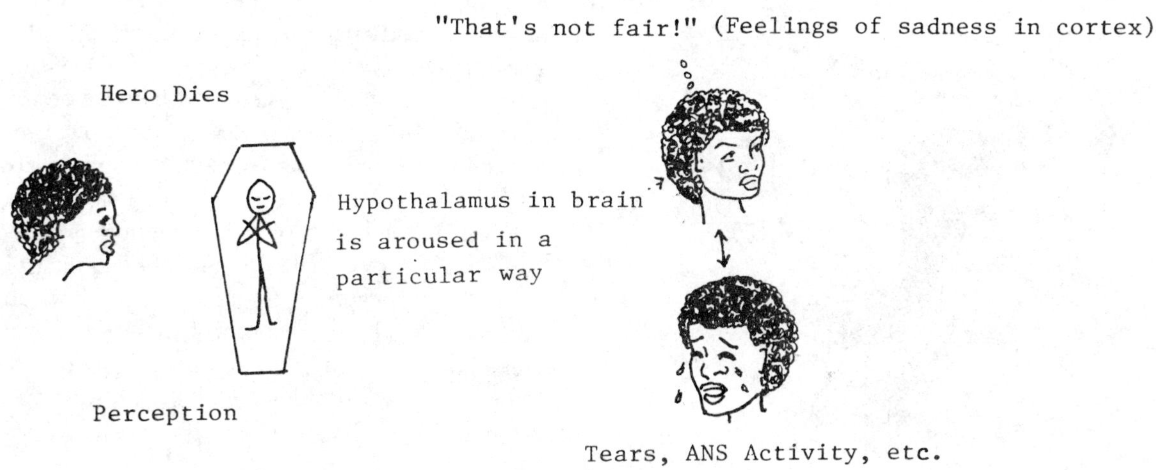

Figure 4.7 Cannon-Bard Sequence

brain, and then on to both the cerebral cortex for felt sadness and the ANS activity and motor behavior (in this case related to crying).

The Hypothalamus

Neurologist Paul MacLean (1975) has described the evolution of the brain through survival phases that produced three brain structures. These include (1) the oldest, the *reptilian brain phase* (before mammals), (2) the older mammals phase, the *paleomammalian brain phase* (before higher mammals), and (3) the more recent *neo-mammalian brain phase*. According to this idea our brain really consists of three brain systems. Figure 4.8 illustrates these.

Notice that most of the cortex of the older mammalian brain is associated with what we now call *limbic system* structures. During the early mammalian survival phase, crude emotional expressions and feelings played key survival roles. The limbic system, which is a part of the inheritance of the brain, is still the site of the origins of emotional experiences (feelings). Lower animals, of course, do not have the amount of cortex of humans, so their feeling portion of the emotions are not so varied or distinct as ours.

Learned Bases of Emotion

In Chapter 5, we saw how learning involves the influences of environmental reinforcers—both pleasurable and aversive. The influence of the positive reinforcers, negative reinforcers, and punishments is not limited to effects on behavior, but also extends to feelings or emotions. How do you feel when you receive an "A" on an exam (a positive reinforcer)? If a positive reinforcer did not feel nice somehow, there would be no increase in the behavior required to get them, or more of them.

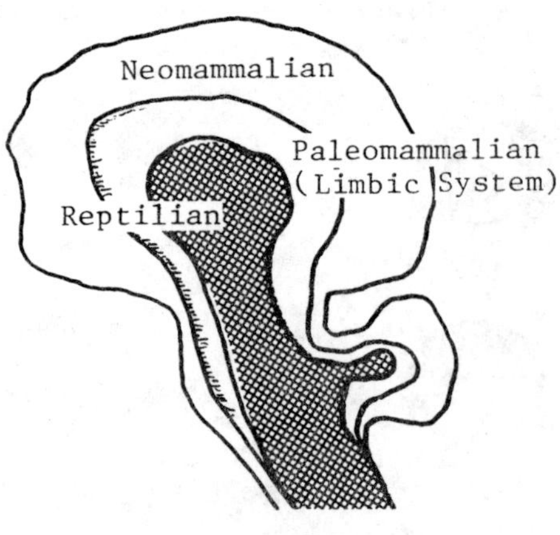

Figure 4.8 MacLean's Evolutionary Brain System

Behaviorist J.R. Millenson (1967) has suggested that the presentation or termination of powerful primary or secondary reinforcers has predictable emotional as well as behavioral effects. Table 4.3 shows the possible emotions and the Pavlovian (CS–UCS) relationships suggested by Millenson. In this scheme, anger, anxiety, and elation are thought to be the primary emotions. The others would be experienced by mixing positive and negative reinforcers into more complex occurrences. For example, a child sneaks a cookie from the cookie jar, eats the cookie, and subsequently is scolded. Which emotion might this both positive and negative learning sequence give rise to? Right, apprehension—next time, in the same situation.

This analysis of how the environment triggers various emotions is quite speculative. However, it does set the stage for a learning explanation of emotion which is much more solidly based. This new theory, called the *opponent-process theory,* asks that we reformulate the very idea of what a reinforcer (positive or negative) really is. The opponent-process theory originated in the opposing-process theory of color vision.

The Opponent-Processes Theory of the Course of Feeling States

Richard L. Solomon and John D. Corbit (1974) have proposed that this opponent-process idea also applies to many of your emotions. The visual system and the limbic system both operate on the basis of opposing processes. Have you ever noticed that when you are elated, you eventually "come down"? And when you do come down you may feel a little bored, or as if something is missing. Or, on the other hand, after the anguish or mild terror of preparing for an exam, you have an extremely good feeling. Both of these emotional events are very similar to a course of seeing red, stopping the red stimulus (looking away) and seeing green. Solomon and Corbit give this example:

> A woman at work discovers a lump in her breast and is immediately terrified. She sits

Table 4.3 Primary Emotional Operations

Common names of emotion	*Effects on ongoing operant activity*	*Pavlovian pairing operation*
Terror Anxiety Apprehension	Suppression of positively reinforced operants. Facilitation of negatively reinforced operants.	Stimulus followed by negative reinforcer.
Rage Anger Annoyance	Increases in magnitude of certain operants. Reinforcing value of attack and destruction raised.	Stimulus followed by termination of a positive reinforcer.
Ecstasy Elation Pleasure	Enhancement of certain operants. Little information available.	Stimulus followed by a positive reinforcer, or by the termination of a negative reinforcer.

*Adapted from Millenson (1967)

> still, intermittently weeping, or she paces the floor. After a few hours, she slowly regains her composure, stops crying, and begins to work. . . . She manifests the symptoms usually associated with intense anxiety. While in this state she calls her doctor for an appointment. . . . The doctor makes his examination. He then informs her that there is no possibility of cancer, that there is nothing to worry about, and that her problem is just a clogged sebaceous gland requiring no medical attention.
>
> A few minutes later, the woman leaves the doctor's office, smiling, greeting strangers, and walking with an unusually buoyant stride. Her euphoric mood permeates all her activities as she resumes her normal duties. . . . A few hours later, however, she is working in her normal, perfunctory way. Her emotional expression is back to normal. She once more has the personality immediately recognizable by all of her friends. Gone is the euphoria, and there is no hint of the earlier terrifying experience of that day. (p. 119)

The emotional experience sequence is directly analogous to the color situation. The opposing processes are at work whether the environmental stimulus is a positive reinforcer or a negative reinforcer. In the story above, we started with a negative situation, that is, with the opposing-process elation. We could just as well have illustrated the course of emotional experience by starting with a positive stimulus situation, that is, with an opposing-process of distress, craving, or loneliness.

Reinforcers in this theory can take on broader dimensions. A reinforcer is not simply something pleasant or unpleasant and thereby controlling behavior. The effects of reinforcers, both positive and negative, often have this complex triphasic effect on behavior and on feelings.

Cognitive Influences on Emotion

A whole audience can watch a person being beaten over the head with a mallet, and be rolling in the aisles with laughter. We can do this sort of thing because our cognitions can interpret situations in a variety of ways. The reason the people in the theater are laughing, instead of being mortified or outraged, is simply because they're watching the Three Stooges, and they "know" the man isn't really getting hurt.

Is it possible that the high (fun) level of arousal that occurs while watching the Three Stooges is the same high level of arousal you'd have if you thought the man was really being beaten over the head with a mallet? The only difference between the two situations would be the interpretation you put on the situation and the label you gave it. If you were to interpret the situation to be a comedy, you would laugh even if the man's head and arms were coming off. If on the other hand you had interpreted the same situation as a tragedy, you would have cried, or gotten angry. Sometimes comedy and tragedy are so thoroughly mixed in a movie, for example, we are not sure what or how we should feel. If you happen to come in in the middle of such a film, you may have a hard time figuring out how you should interpret what you are seeing. The whole point of these examples is that cognition certainly plays a role in felt emotions.

Just how much does cognitive interpretation influence what we feel? Some cognitive theorists have attempted to show that a single type of arousal associated with ANS arousal can give rise to different felt emotions depending on what the person interprets the situation to be. This view of emotion is generally referred to as *attribution theory* (Schachter & Singer 1962). The emotions you feel in a given situation depend on what you perceive is happening.

D.G. Dutton and A.P. Aron (1974) conducted an interesting little experiment that measured the degree of sexual interpretation of a high anxiety-arousing situation. They stationed an attractive female investigator near the exits of two public park bridges. One bridge was sturdy and low to the ground, the other one was very shaky and over 200 feet above a canyon! As men exited the bridges, the female investigator would ask them if they would participate in a psychology experiment. They were asked to write a short story about a picture much like the one at the beginning of this chapter. The attractive experimenter also told the men that if they wanted to know the results of the experiment, they could telephone her, and provided them with a number to call.

Dutton and Aron found that the men who had just crossed the high, precarious bridge, and were therefore high in anxiety, wrote of more sexual imagery in their stories than the other men who had just exited the low, safe bridge. They were also much more likely to telephone the woman later to get the results of the experiment. Apparently, according to these researchers, the presence of the attractive investigator led the high-anxiety men to interpret their arousal as sexual interest. On the other hand, what would the opponent-process theory suggest might be the explanation for the outcome of this experiment? Recall the woman's social gregariousness after the doctor told her she had nothing to worry about. Could these men have been similarly relieved to be off the bridge?

Stanley S. Schachter and Jerome E. Singer (1962) have taken the question of the role of cognitive interpretations into the laboratory for study. Rather than measuring the effects of an arousal state in subjects who had just crossed high, frightening bridges, they simply injected certain subjects with epinephrine. This adrenal gland drug produces ANS arousal (either naturally or by injection) which is similar to that produced by frightening experiences.

In one of Schachter and Singer's experiments, some subjects were told that the injection (supposedly a new vitamin compound) would cause certain physiological reactions; other subjects were not told what to expect. Then, all of the subjects were put in a situation where a research confederate would either act happily or angrily. The only interpretation reasonable for these subjects was either the happy-arousing situation or the anger-arousing situation they had been exposed to. The results indicated that those subjects not told what to expect experienced either the happy or the angry emotions depending upon the confederate to which they were exposed. On the other hand, the subjects who were told what to expect for the drug injection did not interpret their reactions in accordance with the behavior of the confederate researchers.

Figure 4.9 shows the outcome of this interesting experiment. These results support the idea that a single epinephrine state (ANS state) can be interpreted as two rather different emotions on cognitive interpretive processes. While Schachter might be over-emphasizing the role of cognition in emotion a bit, it does appear that cognitive processes can and do play a regular and important role in what emotions are experienced.

Going back to the example of the Three Stooges, I think you can now appreciate that the emotions we experience are greatly influenced by what we think is happening. At the same time, recent evidence does indicate that the different emotions have subtly differing physiological processes related to them. Paul Ekman, R.W. Levenson, and W.V. Friesen (1983) have found, for example, that heart rate change and right finger temperature change differ slightly for each of six emotions. Figure 4.10 summarizes their findings. Although the differences are very small, they are significant enough to say that dif-

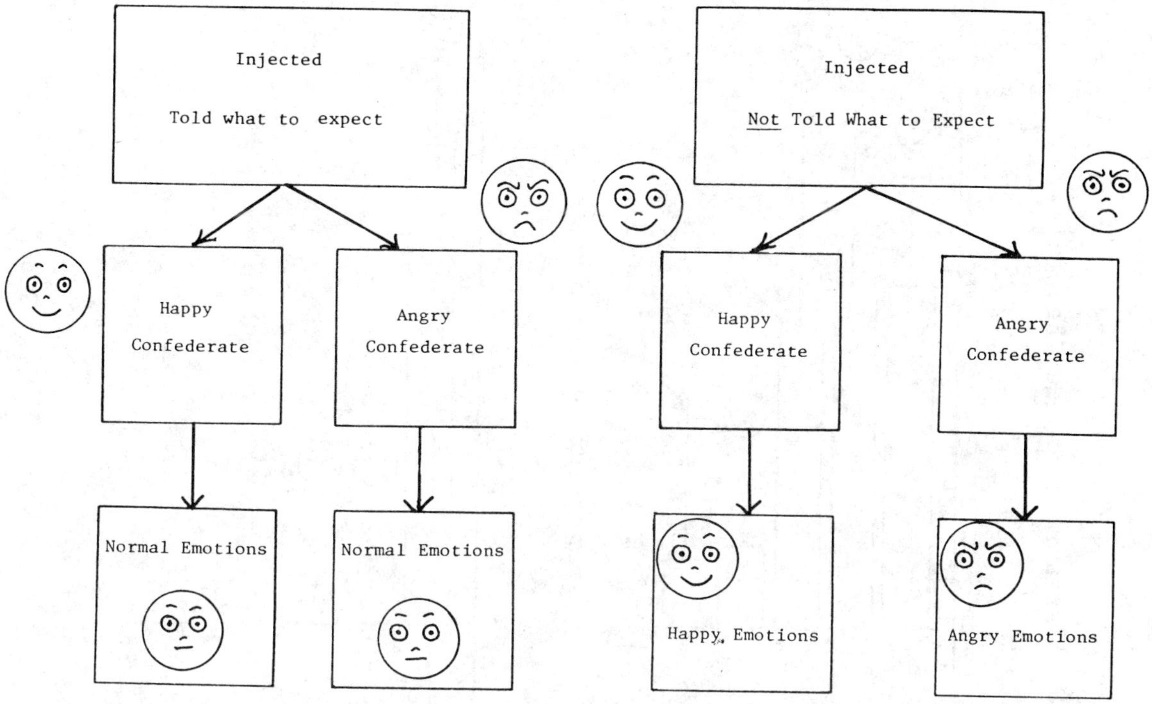

Figure 4.9 Diagram of Schachter-Singer Experiment

ferent emotions may have slightly different physiological bases.

Theories of Motivation

When we read of a man who has just gone over Niagara Falls in a barrel we can't help but ask ourselves, "Why on earth would anybody want to go over Niagara Falls in a barrel?" Earlier, we were concerned with the feelings of the man in Dianne's story. Now we are interested in why Dianne imagined about the "resistance forces and of rescuing people."

Physiological Explanations of Emotions

Human motivation has been explained in terms of *instincts.* William McDougall (1908) carefully defined instincts in terms of (1) incentives, (2) emotions, and (3) drives. *Incentives* are certain stimuli that an animal tends to notice. If the mother bear tends to notice anything which might threaten her cubs, emotional arousal will occur. This was thought by McDougall to be at the core of the instinct. Finally, there is a *drive* to seek a goal. The mother bear's behavior is energized. She may attack the threatening situation.

McDougall was careful to state instincts in general terms, that is, to reduce the number of proposed innate propensities of animals and humans down to reasonable common denominators. You will see shortly that the instinct idea has continued to influence modern thinking about the biological basis of motivation.

Homeostasis and the Reduction of Imbalances in the System

Homeostasis is a constant process that attempts to maintain the internal environments of all living things (Fletcher, 1942). The goal of homeostatic processes is very similar to the thermostatic processes which maintain a room temperature close to, say, 68°F. In the same way that the negative feedback system of the thermostat keeps the room temperature at about 68° or that of a freezer at 20°, recall from Chapter 2 that the hypothalamus is largely responsible for maintaining a human body temperature of about 98.6°F. The entire body chemistry is similarly maintained by homeostatic processes.

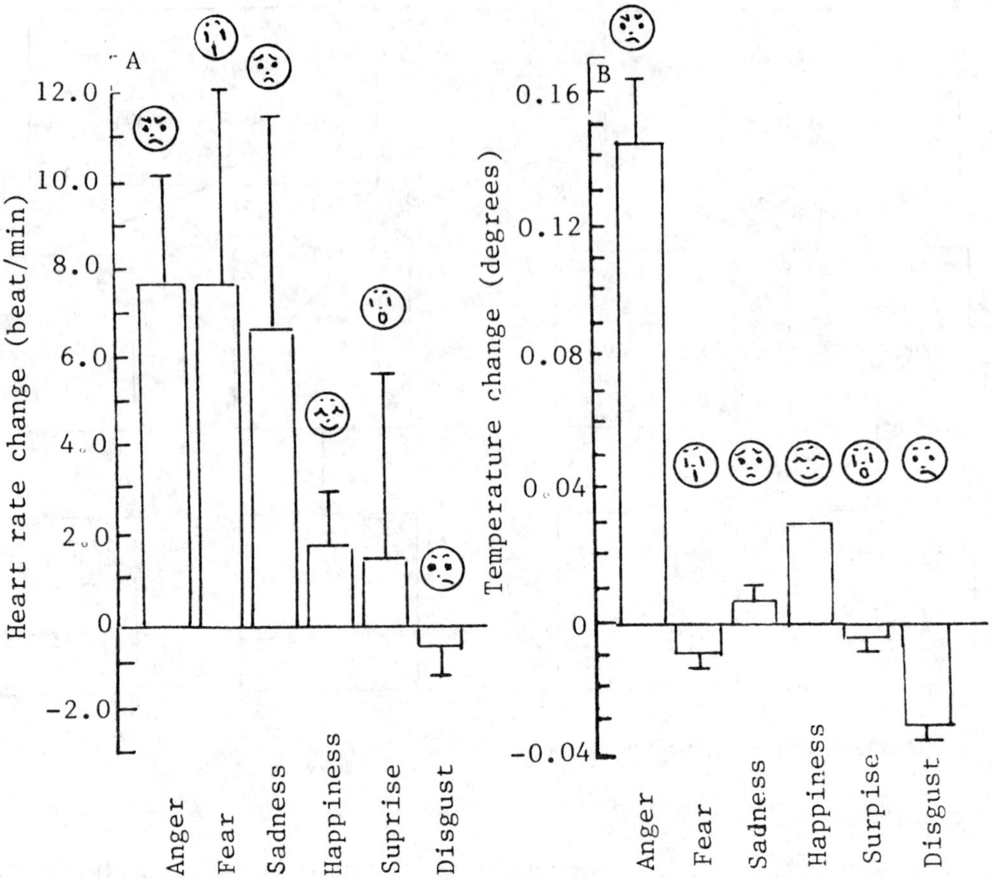

Changes in (A) heart rate and (B) right finger temperature during the directed facial action task. For heart rate, the changes associated with anger, fear, and sadness were all significantly greater (P 0.05) than those for happiness, surprise, and disgust. In finger temperature, the change associated with anger was significantly different (P 0.05) than that of all other emotions.

Figure 4.10 Physiological Reactions to Emotion

What is important to us here is that the maintenance of these homeostatic "steady states" requires a great deal of body behavior, that is, internal and external activity. While much of the temperature regulatory behavior is automatic, some is not. The cerebral cortex may "feel cold," and motor activity like jumping around may occur voluntarily. Also, of course, through learning, appropriate clothing may be donned. This is motivated behavior in relation to homeostasis.

Why do people have, as McDougall put it, a food-seeking propensity? Eating and drinking behaviors are a part of the *equilibration* of energy, minerals, vitamins, fluids, and so forth needed to maintain the internal environment. While the idea of homeostasis suggests the idea of *equilibrium,* from our motivational perspective we are more interested in equilibration. Think again about maintaining a room temperature of 68°F. On a very cold day, the actual temperature in your home may vary between 67° and 69° all day long with the furnace going on and off dozens of times. That's a lot of behavior, that's equilibration. If we thought the heating system with its controls, energy source, thermostat and wiring were alive, we would attribute motivated behavior to its activities. In the same way we can think of homeostasis as being an optimum state of equilibration with a *set-point* for body conditions. However, the motivational concern is in seeing how this is related to the great amounts of food eating, food procuring, food selecting, food growing, food thoughts, and food fantasies behavior.

Much motivated behavior can be understood in terms of tension reduction in relation to homeostasis. However, the appropriateness of the application of this explanation to all forms of behavior, while inviting, is unclear or perhaps unfounded. Sexual behavior, for example, does not seem to be regulated by homeostasis. There seems to be no actual necessity to engage in sexual activity in order to survive (except at the species level), as there is a necessity to engage in eating. The complete motivation of behavior beyond the physiological needs related to hunger, thirst, rest, core body temperature, etc., probably lies beyond homeostasis.

Beyond Instincts and Homeostasis: Natural Incentives

Animals and humans have evolved within the context of a natural environment. Both emotion and motivation have developed within this context. *Ethologists* carefully study the natural behaviors of animals and principles derived from these studies clearly have implications for human behavior.

Instincts and Releasing Stimuli. In a now classic example, Nikolass Tinbergen (1952) has provided the following description of the interplay between instinctive patterns of behavior and their natural environmental context.

Tinbergen studied the three-spined stickleback (a small fish) in its natural courting and mating-related behavior. As this sequence of events is described, notice how the stickleback behavior and the environmental context (including other sticklebacks) are interrelated. First, in the spring the male sticklebacks set up a mating territory by chasing away all possible threatening intruders, whether male or female. Second, the territory established, nest building occurs. The male binds together weeds on the water bottom. Third, after completion of the nest building, the underside of the male stickleback slowly changes color from a dull grey to a bright red. Fourth, the territory is now open to others. Whenever an egg-swollen female enters the territory, the male courts her with a zigzag motion, and she follows him to his nest. Fifth, he places his head in the nest so that she sees the opening. Sixth, she enters the nest. Seventh, the male prods at the base of the female tail. This behavior induces the female to lay her eggs. This courting sequence is repeated from three to five times with different females. Eighth, the male's urges to mate wane, and the bright red color begins to fade. Ninth, the male keeps fresh oxygen-rich water flowing through the eggs by fanning the nest. He does this until the eggs hatch. Tenth, the male stays with the young until they are large enough to join with schools of other fish.

I have purposely taken you through this sequence step-by-step. Each step involves a change in stimulus/organism relations that releases the next step in the instinctive pattern of behavior. The change in stimulus acts as signs along the way to release certain innate behavior. This sequence of signs approach helps answer such questions as why is the male clearing the territory, why is he building a nest, etc.

Ethological studies of human behavior strongly suggest that much human behavior is also released by certain sign stimuli. Irenaus Eibl-Eibesfeldt (1971), whose work we discussed earlier in relation to similar emotional facial expressions across species, has suggested the idea of human cuteness as a releaser for picking up and cuddling of infants by adults. This cuteness sign we probably share with other animals. Figure 4.11 shows how the young and the adult compare across species. The head, the eyes, and the forehead of the young are proportionately larger, the nose (or beak) is more upturned. These same cuteness signs may also carry over toward adult attractiveness.

The territoriality exhibited by the stickleback has many counterparts in human behavior. We tend to mark off space that is "ours" especially when a particularly important task or situation is at hand. We mark off a territory for eating, shelter, work, sexual behavior, needed relaxation, etc. Paul MacLean (1975) attributes these behaviors to the older reptilian parts of our brains. On the other hand, when simply riding a bus or attending a movie we rather willingly allow territorial boundaries to be disrupted. But even then there are sign stimuli limits which, if crossed, will lead to discomfort and territorial behavior

Physiological Processes and Higher Motives. Both homeostasis and the idea of instinct releasers fall somewhat short of helping us understand the complexities of many higher

Figure 4.11 Young and Adult Facial Features

forms of human behavior. For example, what is behind Dianne Schmitt's story of high achievement motivation? Is there any way we can relate achievement motivation and other higher motives to physiological processes?

Motivation psychologist David McClelland (1985) has suggested an explanation that brings together emotions, *sign stimuli* (releasers), and learning. McClelland refers to the "turn on" effects of sign stimuli (like the egg-swollen female stickleback) as *natural incentives.* Although more subtly affected than animals by sign stimuli, he argues that human emotions can be used as indications of natural incentives in humans.

For example, McClelland theorizes that basic sign stimuli, like small variations in stimuli from what is expected, later develop into the complex and cognitive motives—like achievement motives.

A Learning Explanation of Motivation: Opponent-Process Theory

In Chapter 5 on *Learning,* we will discuss Edward Thorndike's description of how discomfort or satisfaction following an animal's response gives direction to the development of behavior. This will be a description of how reinforcement drives the direction of behavior. Thorndike also described the energizing force.

> A kitten, three to six months old, if put in [a] box when hungry, a bit of fish being left outside, reacts as follows: it tries to squeeze through between the bars, claws at the bars, and at loose things in and out of the box, reaches its paw out between the bars, and bites at its confining walls. Some one of these promiscuous clawing, squeezing, and bitings turns around the wooden button and the kitten gains freedom and food. By repeating this experience, the kitten gradually comes to omit all the useless clawing, etc., and to manifest only the particular *impulse* [italics added] (e.g., to claw hard at the top of the button with the paw, or to push against one side of it with the nose) which has resulted successfully. It turns the button around without delay whenever put in the box.

The word *impulse* in Thorndike's description is important in the description of learning. Without the drive energizing behavior, no learning would occur, and no new behavior would be acquired.

One thing traditional learning explanations of motivation have had difficulty with has been why drive increases with learning, and why both animals and humans engage in behavior which is at first aversive or punishing. Earlier, we discussed the opponent-process theory of motivation with its implications for emotions. There we saw how the opponent-process idea could be used to explain emotions. In this section we will see that the opponent-process theory of motivation offers a new source of motivation that builds on its idea and also requires experience with positive and negative reinforcers.

An Example of Acquired Motivation Involving Aversive Stimuli. There are many examples of things we do that at first are very aversive. But we freely do these things, and we keep on doing them, often at an accelerated rate. Thorndike's statement (Chapter 5) about the effects of satisfaction and discomfort leaves us a little puzzled about what drives behavior toward aversive activity. For example, why do people willingly take up parachuting? Why do they willingly put their bodies into excruciatingly hot sauna baths? Why do they willingly climb aboard terrifying rides at amusement parks? All of these activities are initially aversive, and yet we not only do them, our interest in them accelerates over time.

The opponent-process theory of acquired motivation closely parallels the example of opposing emotions we saw earlier. Richard Solomon (1980), drawing on S.M. Epstein's example of the course of emotions among military parachutists, describes the events:

> During the first free-fall (before the parachute opens), even the bravest men show a fearful reaction. Their eyes may bulge, their lips retract, they may yell, their bodies curl forward, and their autonomic nervous systems are in a high state of excitation. There may even be involuntary urination. After they have landed safely, they go through a short period during which they look stunned and stony-faced and do not talk much. Then, after a few minutes, they begin to chatter and enter into lively social interaction with peers. The after-reaction appears to last about 10 minutes.

This example illustrates an opponent-process in Figure 4.12. The opponent-process B (elation) continues on after the novice parachutist lands. The emotional course of events is shown in Figure 4.13.

Finally the parachutist gains acquired motivation.

> After many parachute jumps, the signs of affective habituation are clear, and the fearful reaction is usually undetectable. Instead, the parachutists look tense, eager, or excited, and during free-fall they report a thrill. After a safe landing, there is evidence of a withdrawal syndrome. The activity level is very high, with leaping, shouting, rapidly shifting social interactions, voluble talk, and general euphoria. This period, often described as exhilaration, decreases slowly in time, but often lasts for 2–3 hours. Indeed, I was once told by a sport parachutist that his "high" lasted eight hours. A new, positive source of reinforcement is now available, one that could never have eventuated without repeated self-exposures to an initially frightening situation to which the subject then becomes accustomed. (pp. 697–698)

So, the initial jump ends in a mild state of elation. After many jumps the parachutists get used to the jumping part of the emotion, and the opposing process, elation, has increased dramatically (Figure 4.14). People who jog, take sauna baths, etc., experience the same increase of postexperience euphoria over time. Figure 4.15 shows how the opponent process (in this case related to euphoria) increases with experiences. This elation and its increase becomes, in and of itself, a powerful source of motivation to move toward an initially aversive situation—hence, acquired motivation.

An Example of Acquired Motivation Involving a Pleasant Stimulus. It is quite easy to explain why people do pleasant things—it

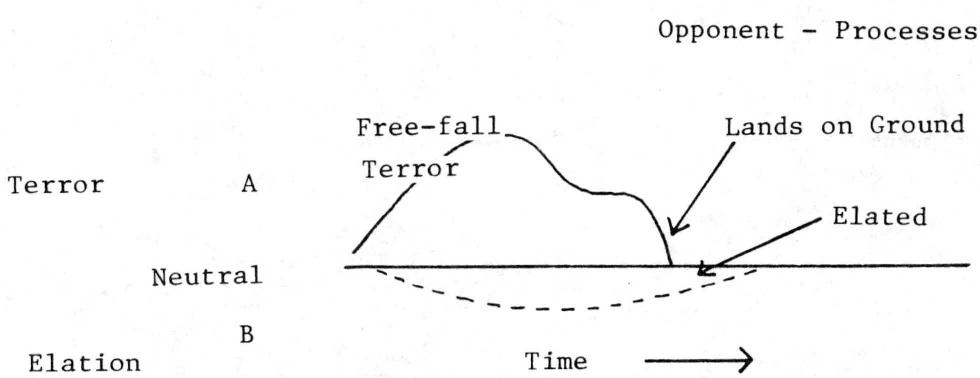

Figure 4.12 Example of Opponent-Process

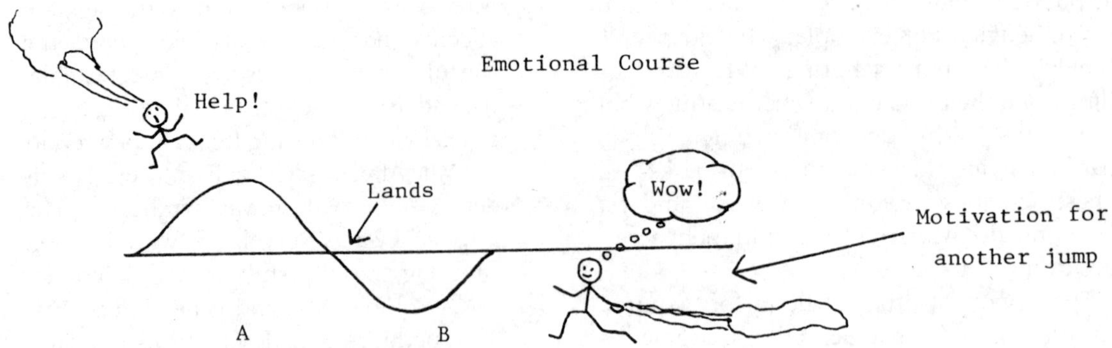

Figure 4.13 Process of Acquiring Motivation

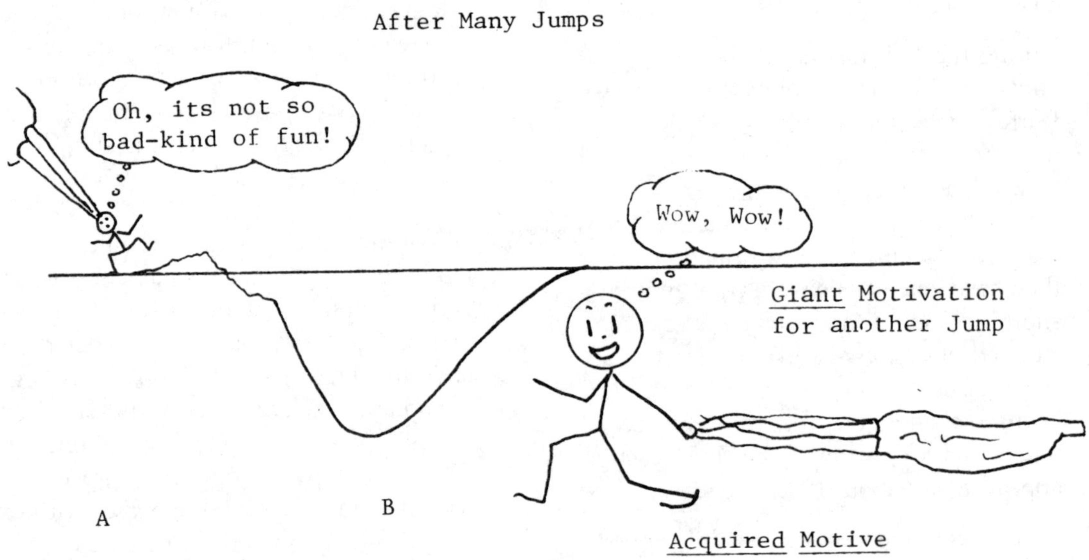

Figure 4.14 Acquired Motivation

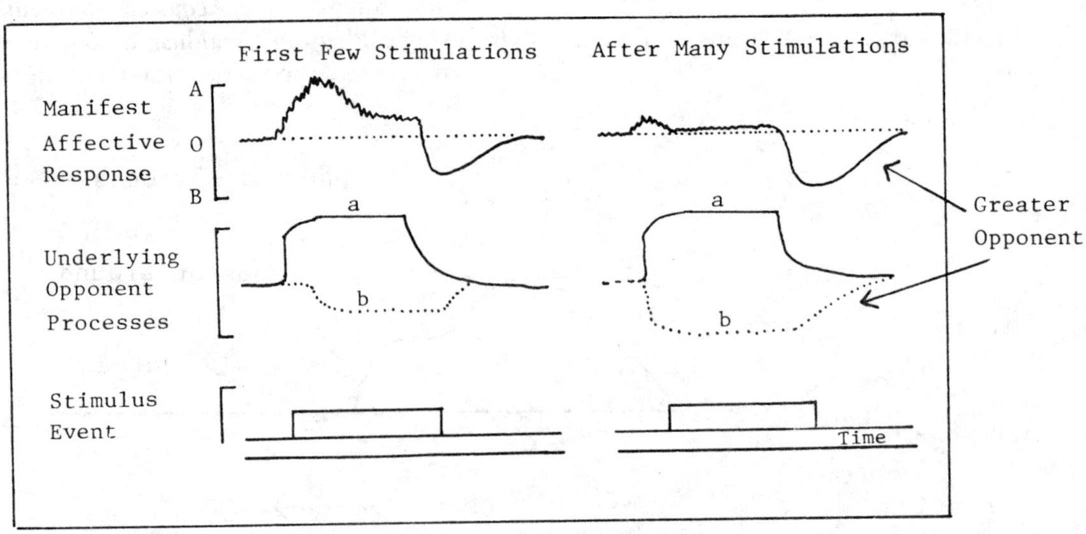

Figure 4.15 Comparison of Novel Unconditioned Stimuli

feels good! And so it is easy to explain why people, for example, eat potato chips. But, why is there so much truth in the advertising that says, "I'll bet you can't eat just one"? An acquired motive can be either positive or negative. Solomon (1980) describes the course of events when people come to use opiates:

> The first doses of an opiate (if the dosage is in the right size) produce a potent pleasure called the rush, followed by a less intense state of euphoria. . . . The rush has been characterized by people as an intense sexual pleasure felt all over the body, all at once. When the drug loses its effect because of metabolic destruction, the user goes into a state of mild discomfort with both physiological and psychological aspects. The physiological aspect includes runny eyes and nose, abdominal pains, clammy skin, and muscular malaise. The psychological aspect is called craving and refers to an aversive state. Most organisms will perform an operant if it will get rid of an aversive state. Thus, drug users tend to redose because this is the surest and quickest way to get rid of the physiological and psychological aspects of withdrawal aversiveness. A slower way is merely to let time go by because the withdrawal aversiveness will slowly die away; but this method is less preferred. (p. 696)

Solomon continues with a description that parallels the increased euphoria of the parachutist—but here it is an increased craving and hurting!

> If self-doses are frequently repeated, however, two correlated changes in effect then occur. (a) The rush is no longer experienced and euphoria is often absent (loss of euphoria); and (b) the withdrawal syndrome becomes much more intense, both physiologically and psychologically, and its duration lengthens dramatically. Thus the positive reinforcer loses some of its power, but the negative reinforcer gains power and lasts longer. . . . Thus the motivation in drug use changes gradually, with successive doses, from positive to aversive control. The user not only becomes more drug tolerant but also becomes more intolerant of drug termination or absence. (p. 696)

Now just as the parachutist habituated to jumping, the opiate user habituates to the drug. The high decreases, but the opponent-process of aversive craving and hurting gets out of hand. Note that with the parachutists the negative reinforcers lost some of their power as more jumps were taken, but the positive reinforcer (elation) gained power and lasted longer. We now better understand an acquired motivation that takes many lives each year. The opponent-process theory helps answer the question of why do people willingly jump out of airplanes, take drugs, etc. Can you think of other acquired motives that fit the opponent-process idea? There are a great many.

A Cognitive Theory of Motivation

As you know by now, cognitive explanations of behavior emphasize thought processes in determining the way you behave. Consider how we go about explaining the occurrence of everyday personal events. For example, if you saw someone get up during the middle of the class, collect his things, and walk out, to what would you attribute this behavior? Does the student have an important appointment for a job interview, does he have to leave because he is ill, or is he just bored with the class? Without anyone knowing the reason, if as soon as the person left, you asked others to what they attributed the student's behavior, you'd probably get several different explanations. The point is, people do attribute the behavior of others (and of objects) to something and, they do this whether they know the real reasons or not. Understanding this can lead to important cognitive explanations of why people behave the way they do.

Attribution Theory. Attribution theory is an explanation of how cognitive factors influence your behavior (Heider, 1958; Kelly and Michela 1980). If you attributed the student's leaving the class to boredom, a *situational attribution,* you might be tempted to go to the instructor after class and compliment him on his lecture to make him feel better. On the other hand, if you attributed his departure to illness, a *dispositional attribution,* you might raise your hand and say to the instructor, "Do you think someone should see if (the student) is okay?" In other words, the things you attribute the causes of behavior to, whether you are right or wrong, have a lot to do with the reasons of your behavior. Attribution theory is an important cognitive theory in psychology, and we will return to this approach in more detail in Chapter 7, *Social Behavior,* and in Chapter 8, *Personality,* where George Kelly's theory of personal constructs is an alternative way of expressing the ideas of attribution theory.

Attribution Theory and Achievement Motivation. Attribution theory and achievement motivation are closely related (Zajonc, 1980). If we now go back to the picture at the beginning of this chapter, we have a situation that is actually quite similar to the student leaving in the middle of class. Anyone would naturally attribute some explanation as to what might be going on in this picture. What sorts of attributions did Dianne make about what was happening, who the person was, etc.? Did she make attributions of a mostly situational or a mostly dispositional nature?

If you examine the kinds of things we gave Dianne points for, you can see that the achievement-motivated person attributes challenges, persistence, an optimistic view of outcomes, dispositional causes to the scene, etc. This is an example of how Dianne's cognitions (attributions in this case) influences her behavior—her story writing, and probably her future! It helps us understand why she does, what she does.

An Overall Structural Model of Motivation

As with the overall emotion model, the motivation model, as well as offering some explanation, allows us to get a perspective on the topic.

Abraham Maslow's Structural Motivational Hierarchy. We have discussed physiological, learning, and cognitive aspects of motivation. Abraham Maslow has structured a hierarchy of motivation so that we might consider how these various aspects of motivation might be related to

Table 4.4 Maslow's Need Hierarchy

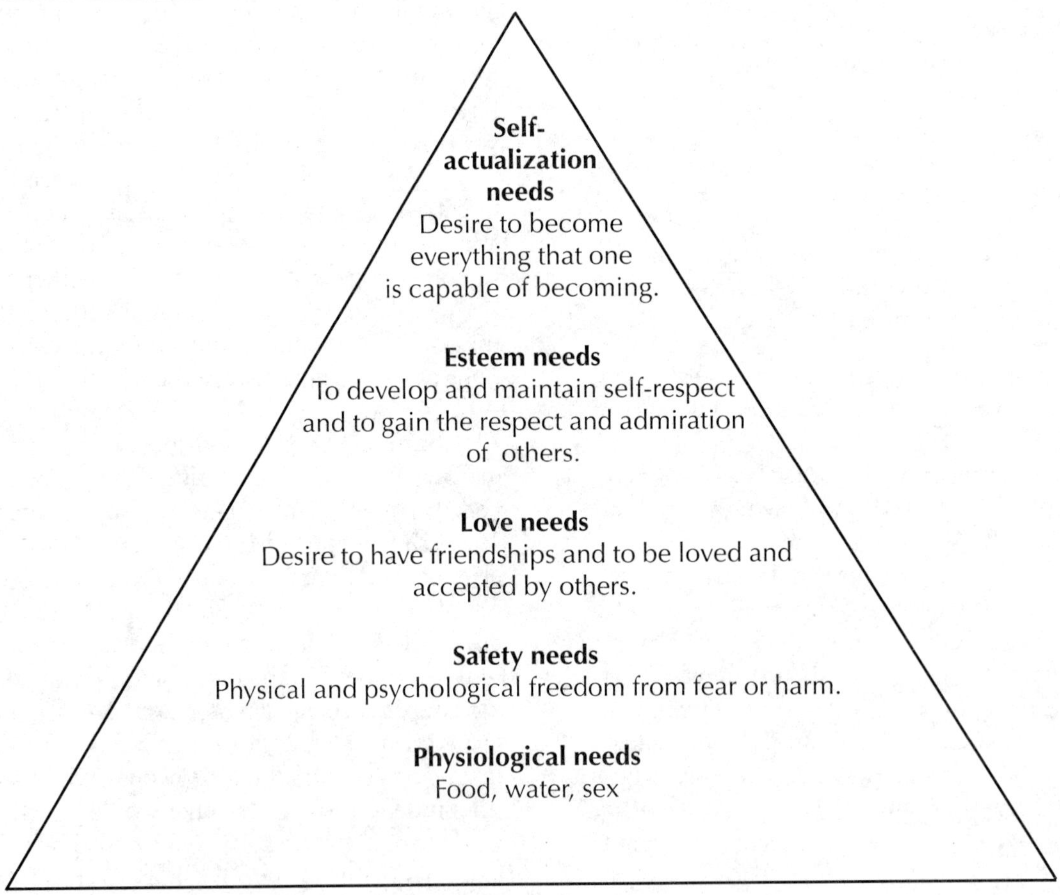

one another. In Table 4.4 is an organization of human needs proposed by Abraham Maslow (1943). These needs are thought to energize and organize the direction and persistence of behavior.

The hierarchical order of the needs is meant to convey the idea that the lower needs organize behavior until the need is met. When a level of need is met, a higher level automatically begins to organize behavior around those needs.

Many college students are highly motivated by the love-related needs. The resulting organization of behavior involves a lot of group activity, friendships, parties, dates, etc. This behavior often gets in the way of grade-earning behavior. But the married students (not necessarily older), for whom the love-related needs are more likely met, are more organized by the esteem and *self-actualization* needs.

While Maslow's need hierarchy is intuitively inviting, it does not have much empirical support (Wahba & Bridwell). While it is easy to understand that a person badly in need of water, for example, will have his behavior organized to get some above all else, it is just as easy to cite examples of people who have starved themselves to death for a cause. The self-actualization need, here, dominates the physiological needs.

Clayton Alderfer (1972) has proposed revisions of Maslow's structural model in what he calls *ERG theory*. The ERG approach consists of only three fundamental needs: Existence, Relatedness, and Growth (ERG). Table 4.5 shows the relationship of this ERG model to Maslow's hierarchy. Notice that the ERG model is not a hierarchy. This model allows several needs to organize behavior simultaneously, and there is no restriction on the order of need activation. This model is empirical in origin, and so is quite well-founded. It does fit the idea that people will starve themselves, give up their lives, etc., for a cause, or undergo great physiological deprivation while mountaineering or exploring.

Table 4.5 Alderfer's ERG Theory

Alderfer	*Maslow*
Growth	Self-actualization needs
Relatedness-Growth	Esteem needs
Relatedness	Love needs
Existence	Safety Needs
	Physiological needs

But, Maslow's model remains popular. Perhaps the empirically truer model of motivation (ERG) does not fit our everyday attributional explanation of motives themselves. Maslow's model may come close to how the average person in his daily routines attributes causes in the world, and is therefore hard to dismiss.

Final Notes to the Theory Section

The opponent-process theory of motivation, which includes a description of the course of emotion, illustrates how emotion and motivation are constant partners in explaining behavior. The opponent-process theory can be related to both learning (for a broader understanding of what is involved in reinforcers), and to physiology (the possible link with endorphins in the opponent process, related to stimuli that are initially aversive).

Empirical and Methodological Aspects of Emotion and Motivation

The empirical and methodological aspects of emotion and motivation are treated together. There are two reasons for this approach. First, the amount of empirical information (at least for the first course) is rather meager. Second, prominent methods are so closely related to the structuring of the meaning of the empirical counterparts of emotion and motivation one cannot always be reasonably viewed without the other. This echoes the sentiment of Eva Dreikurs-Ferguson. In other words, there are few general methods that apply to many aspects of either emotion or motivation.

Hunger and Obesity

Think about being hungry. And next time you're just dying for a pizza, ask yourself this question, what part of me is hungry? If we can answer this question, we can establish the empirical basis for one of the most fundamental emotions/motivations.

Are you hungry in the mouth? Actually, you probably are a little. H.D. Janowitz and M.I. Grossman (1949) implanted dog's throats with tubes so that when they ate, the food did not go to the stomach but simply fell out. The dogs did quit eating after a time. However, as you might guess, they resumed eating sooner than non-implanted control group dogs for whom the food went directly to the stomach.

Are you hungry in the stomach? Again, yes, you are hungry in your stomach. Walter Cannon (1934) measured the relation between hunger pangs and the contraction of the stomach. To do this, he had subjects swallow a tube with a balloon on the end. The balloon was then comfortably inflated. Whenever the stomach contracted, then, air was gently forced out through the tube. At the same time, the subjects reported their hunger pangs by pressing a key. The methodological setup is shown in Figure 4.16. What was discovered was that the contractions and the pangs were correlated. However, people who have had their stomachs removed still report normal desire for food. Obviously, the correlation, which Cannon found, was just that—correlation and not causal relationship.

Do you feel hungry in your brain? Studies so far have led us in that direction. Actually, this should not seem too surprising. After all, perception of the external environment occurs in the brain, why not the perception of the internal environment? Recent studies have focused on the hypothalamus as the control center for feeding. Just as the limbic system and hypothalamus control emotions and body temperature regulation, it is actually the cortex that is largely responsible for the feeling of emotion and the feeling of warmth, this is true also for hunger. At any rate it would seem impossible to study any behavior in animals that retained only a hypothalamus—they would no longer be alive.

A Hypothalamic Set-Point. Since the hypothalamus seems to control eating behavior—both turning it on and turning it off—the idea of a set-point for each person has been hypothesized by Richard E. Kessey and Terry Powley (1975). The set-point might be considered to be a part of the idea of homeostasis that we discussed earlier. As Geen, Beatty, and Arken (1984) describe it:

> The basic idea of set-point theory is quite simple. Feeding is viewed as one of the

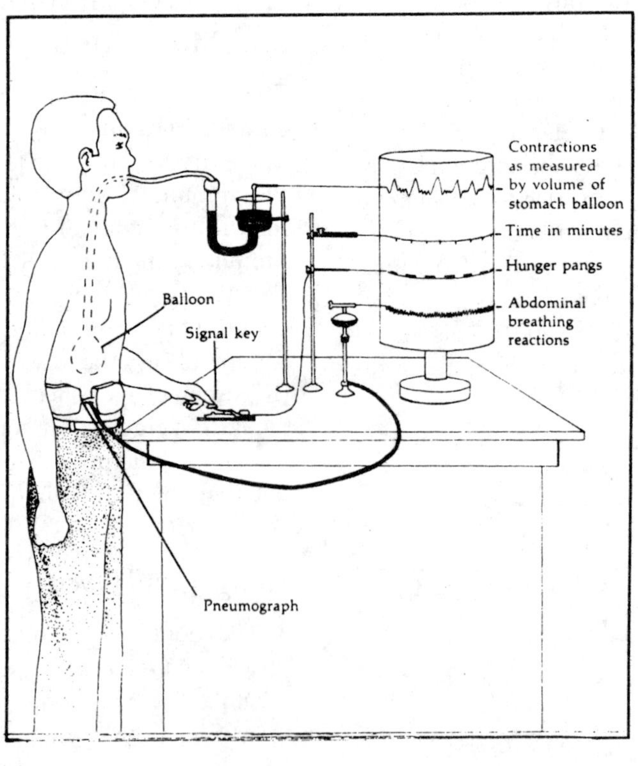

Figure 4.16 Apparatus Used in Cannon's Research

many responses, both behavioral and physiological, that the organism makes to defend a certain level of body weight (or fat, because this is the most easily varied body store). The body weight level that is defended is presumed to be determined by a host of factors, including the individual's genetic background, sex, and possibly his or her early feeding experience. From the perspective of set-point theory, ventromedial hypothalamic (VMH) and lateral hypothalamic (LH) lesions raise and lower the setpoint for body weight. (pp. 69–70)

So, if a person's set-point is high, a higher body weight is defended (tolerated) by the hypothalamic controls—at a lower set-point, a lower body weight is defended. Table 4.6 illustrates this idea.

While the evidence is solid, the set-point idea is a hypothesis—it has not actually been found in the hypothalamus. Set-point theory may explain a part of what is behind obesity, as illustrated in the rat in Figure 4.17 with VMH lesions (high set-point). There are other metabolic processes related to obesity as well.

Figure 4.17 Rat with Damaged Hypothalamus

Higher Level Needs: Affiliation and Power

You will recall that in Maslow's need hierarchy, hunger was one of the basic physiological needs and placed at the bottom of the hierarchy. With the warnings of the ERG model in mind, we will now move up the hierarchy to *affiliation needs* and *power needs*. The need for affiliation leads us to want to be with someone, to join groups, go to parties, etc. The need for power leads us to want to control others.

As was the case with the achievement need, affiliation and power need levels can be measured by analyzing the stones people write or tell about pictures depicting ambiguous situations. In fact, the same stories which were earlier evaluated could now be evaluated for aspects of needs for affiliation and power.

The General Adaptation Syndrome (GAS) and Emotion/Motivation

In the opponent-process theory of motivation and the accompanying emotions, we talked about their parallel course of events and how new motives can be acquired. This course of events can either go from positive to negative or

Table 4.6 Set-Point Hypothesis

B	Heavy	Damage to VM part of hypothalamus (high set-point)	overeating
O			
D			
Y			
W	Normal	Normal Hypothalamic set-point	normal eating
E			
I			
G			
H	Thin	Damage to lateral part of hypothalamus (low set-point)	less eating
T			

vice versa. Either of these situations place great biochemical demands on the body in regard to homeostatic equilibration. Both the opiate rush/euphoria of the drug user, and the frightening free-fall of the novice parachutist are stressful to the body and cause a great deal of autonomic nervous system and endocrine system activity.

The General Adaptation Syndrome (GAS)
In either case, these activities follow a general adaptive pattern of equilibration which involves both motivation and emotion. Following is the description of the course of this adaptive pattern as it was described by Hans Selye.

Selye's *general adaptation syndrome (GAS)* can be illustrated by an example of swimming in 65°F water on an 85° day in a 98° body. This should keep the hypothalamus busy. There are three physiological (and psychological) phases of this syndrome (see Figure 4.18):

1. Alarm Reaction: There are two phases to this reaction. First, physiological shock, then physiological countermeasures.
   a. Shock Phase: You are lying on a beach. It is pleasantly warm (85°). Your body is equilibrating to maintain about 98°. This is not great stress. Then you decide to go for a swim. The water is 20° degrees cooler than the air temperature (and 33° cooler than your body temperature). You have done this before, and you can't decide whether to just jump in and get the shock phase over with, or to wade in slowly (little shocks).
   b. Countermeasures: Once that shock is over, you slowly feel you are adjusting to the water. This is the result of the physiological counter to the shock. Your body's chemistry and activity is rapidly changing.
2. Stage of Resistance: Soon you adapt to the cool water. Your body is operating at higher than normal resistance to cold levels. The water now curiously feels good, and, depending on the water temperature, may feel good to you for some time. But all the while, the higher resistance level comes at a

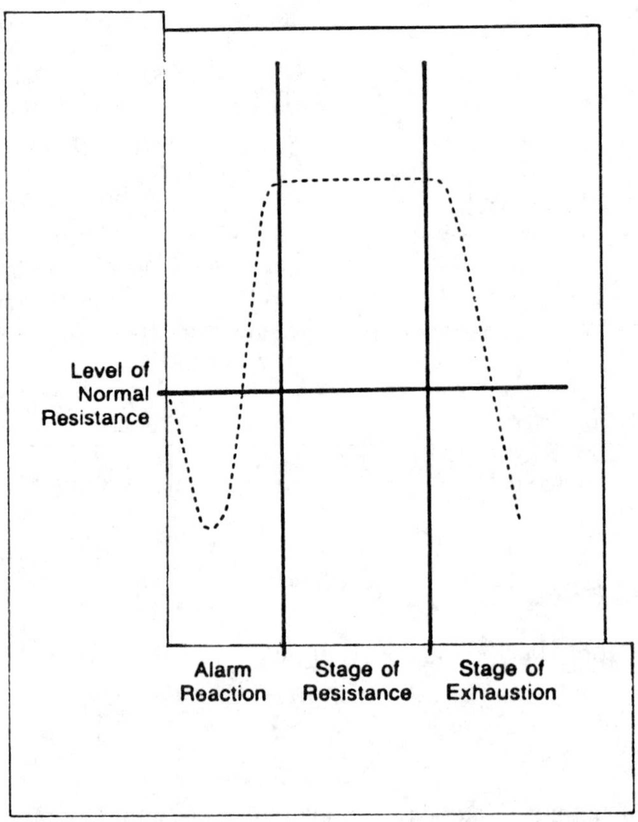

Figure 4.18 General Adaptation Syndrome

price—the higher arousal is slowly taking a toll on your body reserves.

3. Stage of Exhaustion: After some time in the water your body has had enough. If the water is very cold, the state of resistance will be very short, and the stage of exhaustion will come on quite quickly. You may again feel chilled. The body temperature is dropping and can no longer be easily maintained. You leave the water, wrap the warm beach towel around you and shiver. If this stage of exhaustion had continued on too long, you might have died from hypothermia.

Let's assume that you didn't perish! Instead, you swam around for twenty minutes, got out of the water and dried off. Now, according to the opponent-process theory, you would have felt refreshed after this aversive dip in the cold water because your body would be on a natural high. Richard Solomon (1980) has suggested that during the habituation period (physiological countershock and stage of resistance) the brain produces endorphin substances that make you feel good in the cold water. The brain concentration of these substances lingers after you get out of the cold water (stressor).

During the course of the GAS there is a parallel course of motives and feelings. The course of events described in the opponent-process theory goes beyond, but includes, Selye's general adaptation pattern of events. Selye's adaptable pattern would occur in much the same manner if, instead of cold water, you got into a hot tub at, say 110°F. It's hot at first, then feels very pleasant. In the first case (cold water) the autonomic nervous system and the endocrine system help to keep the body warm; in the hot tub, they must help to keep the body cool. How do you feel after a session in a hot tub? Great!

Obviously, as R.S. Lazarus (1980) has pointed out, the body's response to cold water and to hot water would not be autonomically or hormonally the same—quantitatively or qualitatively. One does not perspire in cold water. But, overall, GAS would be clearly recognizable as would the effects of the opponent-process.

Everyday Stresses. Our first examples of the GAS involved physical attacks on the body's equilibration. However, the same model can be applied to the cognitive stresses as well. That is, things you believe to be stresses are stresses. This is an attributional process. The person who goes from one stress to another may "burn out" with classes, job, study, classes, job, study—taking no time off and becoming perhaps exhausted. They can only maintain the stage of resistance for so long, especially if stresses are piled upon one another so that stages of resistance become shorter. New stresses push the body to exhaustion quite quickly.

Earlier, in the swimming example, we mentioned that during the stage of resistance a toll was being taken of the body's reserves (to keep the body warm). Everyday cognitive stresses cause the same sort of depletion. As the body's reserves are diminished, the body becomes progressively more vulnerable to certain diseases. Selye (1956) called these "diseases of adaptation." These diseases do not involve any particular germ, but rather the body's own reaction to stress. The body's reaction during resistance seems to encourage certain maladies. These include headaches, high blood pressure, sinus attacks, allergic reactions, and emotional disturbances.

It is difficult for the average person to know just how much stress he, or she, is actually responding to. The mobilization of energy during the stage of resistance (as when in cold water) can make everything seem to be just fine. However, both pleasant and aversive stimuli require special equilibration responses from the body.

To help determine how much stress one was being exposed to, and the likelihood of when one might become ill, Thomas Holmes and Richard Rahe (1967) developed the stress rating scale shown in Table 4.7.

Notice that the *Social Readjustment Rating Scale* contains both positive and negative life events. Any change makes adjustment necessary. This fits in well with both our earlier discussion of the opponent-process examples and our discussion of Selye's GAS. Both positive and negative events require adaptive measures be taken by the body, and if continued for long periods of time can result in illness.

The Lie Detector and the Autonomic Nervous System

One of the most complex categories of emotions and motivations is that related to lying. And, to make things worse, we often behave, both inter-

Table 4.7 Life Events and Weighted Values

HOW TO USE: Add up value of Life Crisis Units for Life Events experienced in two-year period.
0 to 150—No significant problems
150 to 199—Mild life crisis (33 percent chance of illness)
200 to 299—Moderate life crisis (50 percent chance of illness)
300 or over—Major life crisis (80 percent chance of illness)

Life Event	*Value*	*Life Event*	*Value*
Death of spouse	100	Change of responsibility at work	29
Divorce	73	Son or daughter leaving home	29
Marital separation	65	Trouble with in-laws	29
Jail term	63	Outstanding personal achievement	28
Death of close family member	63	Wife beginning or stopping work	26
Personal injury or illness	53	Beginning or ending school	26
Marriage	50	Revision of habits	24
Fired from work	47	Trouble with boss	23
Marital reconciliation	45	Change in work hours	20
Retirement	45	Change in residence	20
Change in health of family	44	Change in schools	20
Pregnancy	40	Change in recreation	19
Sex difficulties	39	Change in social activity	18
Gain of new family member	39	Change in sleeping habits	16
Change in financial state	38	Change in number of family get-togethers	15
Death of close friend	37		
Change of work	36	Change in eating habits	15
Change in number of arguments with spouse	35	Vacation	13
		Minor violations of law	11
Foreclosure of mortgage	30		

SOURCE: Adapted from T.H. Holmes and R.H. Rahe, The Social Readjustment Rating Scale. *Journal of Psychosomatic Research. 11* (August 1967) 213. Reprinted with permission from the authors and Pergamon Press Ltd.

nally and externally, as if we are hiding something when we are falsely accused. In this situation we may experience all sorts of ANS-related activity—blushing, frustration, perspiration, rapid heart beat, etc.

The idea of associating lying with the ANS is an old one. In their recent evaluation of lie-detecting methodology, Benjamin Kleinmuntz and Julian J. Szucko (1984) offer this example:

> Consider the Bedouins of Arabia, who until quite recently required conflicting witnesses to lick a hot iron; the one whose tongue was burned was thought to be lying. The Chinese, it is said, have a similar method for detecting lying: Suspects were forced to chew rice powder and spit it out; if the powder was dry, the suspect was guilty. A variation of this test was used during the inquisition. The suspect had to swallow a "trial slice" of bread and cheese; it stuck in the suspect's palate or throat, he or she was not telling the truth. These more recent methods reflect the belief that

emotionality is associated with lying. The hot iron, sticky rice, and dry bread and cheese tests all probably reflect changes in the suspect's flow of saliva, which tends to be diminished in situations of high stress. If the volume of the suspect's flow is decreased, then he or she is frightened and therefore must be telling a lie. Thus the fear that is aroused in the suspect, who, it is assumed, is aware of lying, activates the sympathetic branch of the autonomic nervous system, which in turn diminishes the salivation, thereby drying the tongue and palate. . . . Contemporary polygraphic practice, too, relies on similar reasoning and physiological notions. (pp. 766–767)

The *polygraph* measures blood pressure, pulse, respiration, and perspiration (GSR). Perspiration is measured by change in electrical resistance (or alternatively, conductance) at the surface of the skin. Figure 4.19 shows the effects of sympathetic stimulation in the ANS. These fight or flight related responses are measured directly or indirectly by the polygraph.

The Case of Fay. Kleinmuntz and Szucko report on the criminal case of Floyd Fay:

> . . . (T)his case was recently reported in *Criminal Defense* (Cimmerman, 1981). It deals with Floyd Fay, also known as Buzz, who was charged with aggravated murder in a shooting case and was convicted on the basis of the lie detector. A summary of the details follows. . . .
>
> According to Cimmerman's account of the case, Floyd Fay was named as the hold-up man who mortally wounded Fred Ery in an Ohio carry-out robbery attempt. Several hours before dying of his wounds, Ery had said, "It looked like Buzz, but it couldn't have been." Fred died about 5 hours later after losing much blood and receiving large doses of Demerol. During that 5 hour period, he became more certain of his assailant, stating numerous times "Buzz did it."

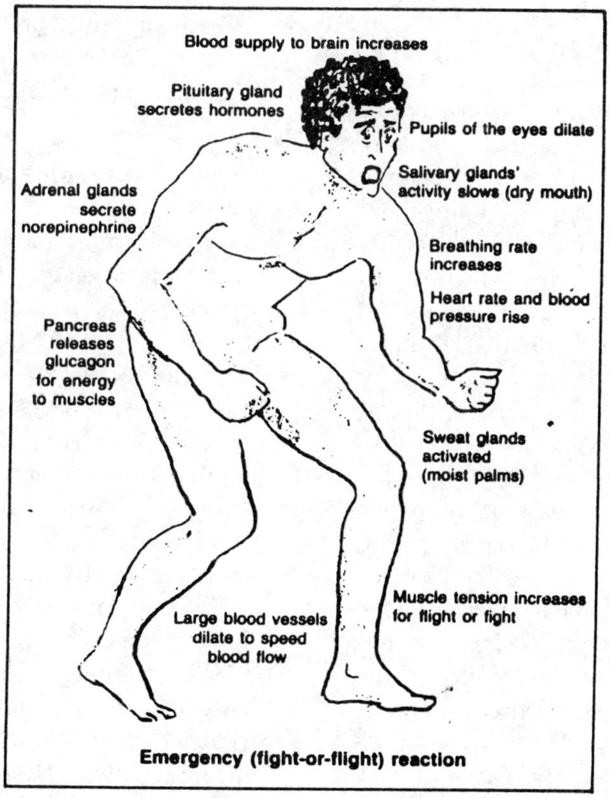

Figure 4.19 Physiological Arousal in Emotion

> . . . On his polygraph he [Fay] was judged to be deceptive in regard to his knowledge of and involvement in the Ery killings. A similar judgment was rendered on the second polygraph. . . . Fay was quickly convicted of murder and sentenced to life in prison.
>
> Somewhat less convinced now than at the outset of his trial that "they'll let me go tomorrow," Fay began what turned out to be a two-and-a-half-year prison term. With the aid of diligent county public defender, Adrian Cimmerman, Fay appealed his conviction. After extensive investigative work and a chance tip by an informant, Fred Ery's real assailant was tracked down, apprehended, and convicted.
>
> An addendum to the Fay case is germane to the main topic of this article. During his stay in prison and perhaps due to the false conviction based on the strength of the polygraph test. Fay became something of an expert on the polygraph test. Particularly, he learned enough about the implausible theory that underlies modern polygraphy so that he became an expert at beating it, a feat that the principal textbook on polygraphy (Reid & Inbau, 1977) claims to be improbable. In fact, most spokespersons of the polygraph industry in the United States deny that anyone can beat a lie detector test administered by a qualified examiner. One psychologist-polygrapher, Raskin, has even been quoted (Lykken, 1981a, p. 20) as stating that 95.5 percent of hardened criminals behind bars can be detected as deceptive by the lie detector. Given these statistics, one would not expect Fay to learn how to beat the control question polygraph test, a lesson that can save a prisoner from being transferred to a maximum security prison for violations of prison rules. But Fay coached 27 inmates scheduled to take polygraph examinations; all freely admitted to him that they were guilty of the offenses charged (usually drug offenses). After about 20 minutes of instruction, 23 of the 27 managed to pass, that is, to beat the lie test (Lykken, 1991a). Quite embarrassing, we believe. It turns out, then, that the technique is not only highly fallible, it is also fakeable.

As D.T. Lykken (1981), a leading polygraph method researcher, has recently concluded, ". . . the polygraph pens do no special dance when we are lying."

Does the polygraph really detect lying? At the present time this is a controversial issue in psychology. Beside the fact that theory bases for polygraph lie-detection are lacking, one practical problem with lie detection methods based on the polygraph is that they very often conclude that people who are telling the truth are lying and vice versa (Saxe, Dougherty & Cross, 1985). For the people involved and for psychology this is a totally unsatisfactory state of affairs. The American Psychological Association (APA) has recommended that polygraphs not be used in the workplace (Polygraphs, 1987):

> It is inevitable that innocent people are going to be hurt by the continued use of polygraphs. In fact, over 50 percent of those selected by polygraphs in the workplace will be falsely accused of dishonesty in situations that will affect their jobs, their chances for promotion, and their future employment. (p. 1)

Facial Expressions and Emotions. Recent research on the relationship between facial expressions and emotions might provide some clues on how we might improve the lie detector method. At the beginning of the theoretical section on emotions we examined the survival value of certain facial expressions. The idea was that facial expressions have evolved, in part, to mirror the emotional state of the animal—and thus indicate to other animals whether advance or withdrawal is expected. In this respect, we could think of the face as an extension of the limbic system and cerebral cortex activity. Recall how the face fits into the motor and sensory areas of the cerebral cortex, Chapter 2. The motor and sensory mapping of the face in the cerebral cortex is related to the limbic system and the ANS in feedback loops. Much of this organization is apparently innate (Konner, 1987).

Paul Ekman, Robert W. Levenson, and Wallace V. Friesen (1983) have shown that simply

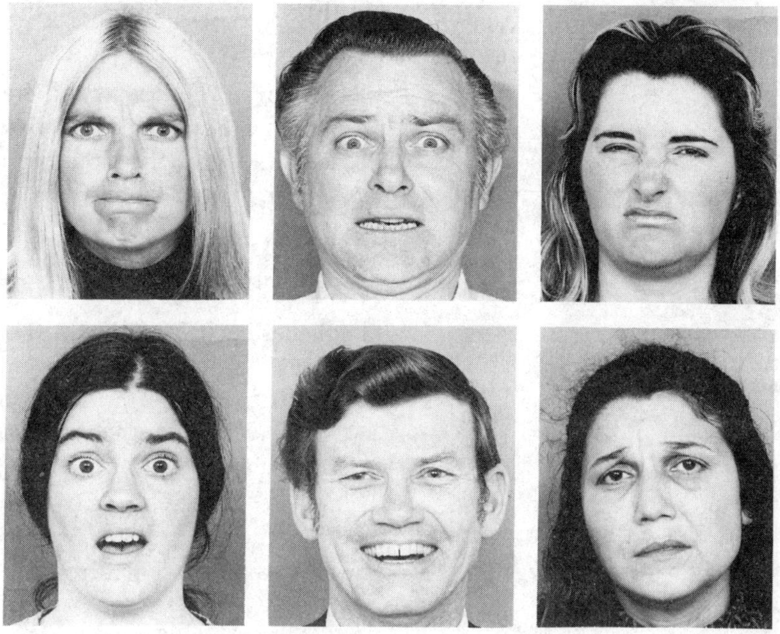

Figure 4.20 Facial Expressions Faked by Actors

donning a particular faked facial expression causes ANS activity that is different for each expressed emotion. Figure 4.20 shows an actor faking facial expressions. These expressions, themselves, cause different ANS responses. So, when you feel low, smile; even if it's faked it could have good effects on your body. You might want to refer back to Ekman's detailed findings which were presented earlier (Figure 4.10). The point for you here is that these findings indicate that the feedback loops involving expression of the face and the brain are fairly basic. The faked motor-sensory information apparently "fools" the limbic structures into activating the appropriate ANS arousals.

Silvan Tomkins has suggested that basic emotional facial expressions are universal in our species, and that facial expressions give rise to our emotional feelings. This *facial feedback hypothesis* is somewhat controversial, but is partially supported by Ekman's findings. I guess the thing to do during the lie detector test is to smile continuously! It is probable that the sequence involves fairly strong innate feedback loops including the muscles and the skin of the face, the cerebral cortex, the limbic system, and the ANS.

Silvan S. Tomkins (1980) does seem to be right about the universality of facial expressions themselves. Carroll E. Izard (1979) and Paul Ekman have both shown that facial expressions are interpreted similarly by both literate and nonliterate people from a variety of cultures. Paul Ekman and Harriet Oster (1979) have concluded that the following emotions have universal facial expression: "In sum, there is unambiguous evidence of universality only for the expressions of happiness, anger disgust, sadness, and combined fear/surprise." Further study might reveal universal facial expressions for other emotions.

Bringing It All Together

At the beginning of this chapter you were introduced to the idea of achievement motivation and how you might develop your own desire to achieve through imagination. This chapter idea has a good deal in common with the chapters on *learning* and on *memory.* In the chapter on learning you saw how powerful learning by mutation can be. The principles of social learning helped explain how very great talent comes about.

Almost any great skill can, to a great extent, be learned. The more you know about your own cognitive nature (meta cognition) the more likely you will become what Maslow has referred to as the self-actualizing person. When asked what is one of the lessons of psychology, this one ranks very high.

Glossary

achievement motivation: The tendency for a person's behavior to be directed toward succeeding. See need to achieve.

affiliation need: One of several human needs that were proposed by Henry Murray and his colleagues. This need guides behavior toward relating to and cooperating with others and toward remaining loyal to friends.

analogic amplifier: Processes running parallel to motives that increase motivation.

attribution theory: The view that people try to explain the behavior of others (or their own) in relation to personal qualities or situational factors.

Cannon-Bard Theory of Emotion: The sequence of events in emotions is that first we perceive the positive or negative elements in a situation, then this information is channeled to the hypothalamus, and finally simultaneously is sent to the cerebral cortex (feelings) and the ANS (physiological and behavioral aspects of emotions).

common sense sequence of emotion: The sequence of events in emotions is that first we perceive the positive or negative elements in a situation, then have feelings about the situation, and finally these lead to physiological and behavioral aspects of the emotion.

dispositional attribution: Explaining the behavior of others on the basis of personal qualities.

drive: A psychological or physiological arousal that moves an organism toward or away from a goal.

emotion: The feelings that accompany behavior which moves an organism from need states (such as hunger) to goals (such as eating).

equilibration: The process and activities required to maintain stable states in cells, organs or in the entire body.

equilibrium: A stable or steady state in cells, organs, or in the entire body.

ERG theory: The view that there are three fundamental human needs: existence, relatedness, and growth. None of these needs is thought to be a "higher" need than the others.

ethologists: Scientists who study animals in their natural environments.

facial feedback hypothesis: The idea that the muscles of the face directly influence activities of the ANS. This suggests, for example, that if you smile, the smile alone will make you feel better.

GAS: See general adaptation syndrome.

general adaptation syndrome: A standard pattern of bodily reactions to stress. This pattern of bodily reactions adapts the body to the stressful events by maintaining a stable state in the face of the stress. These reactions take a toll on bodily resources.

homeostasis: The maintenance of an equilibrium or stable state in cells, organs, or the entire body.

incentive: An external stimulus or goal which can move behavior either toward or away from it. See also motives.

instinct: Motivation that is based upon an inborn pattern of behavior.

James-Lange Sequence of Emotion: The sequence of events in emotions is that first we perceive the positive or negative elements in a situation, then this leads to physiological and behavioral aspects of the emotion which finally give rise to feelings.

limbic system: A grouping of brain regions, including parts of the hypothalamus, and the thalamus, that are involved in emotional expression and other behavior required for the preservation of the species. (See paleomammalian brain).

motivation: A general term used to explain the initiation, direction, strength, and persistence of behavior. Motivation is inferred from these characteristics of behavior.

motives: Ideas assigned as the basis for motivation. These would include, for example, needs, incentives, goals, and expectations.

mutually causal: Related things or events that causally influence one another. Mutual causality is found among the subsystems of all systems.

natural incentives: See incentives.

need to achieve: One of several human motives or needs that were proposed by Henry Murray and his colleagues. This need guides behavior to succeed and to excel, and to accomplish something difficult.

negative feedback loop: Feedback loops that contain a predetermined steady or stable state which the loop maintains. Any departures in the output of the loop from the steady state are "negated" or removed as output is checked by the preset, predetermined comparator in the loop.

neomammalian brain: The brain structure that evolved only in humans. This "new" mammal brain is involved with abstract reasoning, invention, and religion.

opponent-process theory (of emotion and motivation): The view that during the course of emotional and motivational events, two opposing physiological processes are simultaneously occurring. If a person is elated, then the chemical processes, which will lead to more depressed feelings, are simultaneously occurring. This view was directly derived from the opponent-process view of color vision.

paleomammalian brain: The brain structure that evolved in early mammals, for example, horse and cat families. The "old" mammal portions of the brain that are involved in nurturing of the young, dreaming, and playing games.

polygraph: A device that measures pulse rate, blood pressure, respiration, and perspiration in lie-detection.

positive feedback loops: Feedback loops wherein the output of the loop either increases or decreases further output in an uncontrolled fashion. In the former, the unchecked increases in output may cause the system to "fly apart." In the latter, the unchecked decreases, making output smaller and smaller, may shut the system down.

power need: One of several human needs that were proposed by Henry Murray and his colleagues. This need guides behavior toward controlling others or one's environment. This behavior may include the use of suggestion, seduction, persuasion, or restraint.

reptilian brain: The brain structures that evolved during the era of the reptiles. The "older" portions of the brain that are involved in territorial behavior, sleep-waking behavior, ANS functions.

self-actualization: The view of humanistic psychologists, such as Abraham Maslow, that the highest human need is to become all that one is capable of becoming.

set-point: A predetermined stable or steady state that is maintained by negative feedback loops. See negative feedback loop, homeostasis.

sign stimuli: Specific stimuli that give rise to particular emotion or motivational states.

situational attribution: Explaining the behavior of others on the basis of situational circumstances.

social readjustment rating scale: A scale of life events that have either positive or negative effects on people. All of these events represent life changes and are therefore stressful. Each life event is quantitatively scaled in terms of its degree of stress.

viscera: The organs enclosed in the major body cavities.

Motivation: Doing Psychology on Your Own

Lois McDermott

Basic Concept #4—Two Big Ideas

Not many people are aware of the things that "push" and "pull" them to do what they do. Why are *you* going to college? You could probably write a long list of reasons. But would your list include any of the *psychological processes* that you learned about in this chapter? How many students would ascribe their behavior and thinking about college to the two big concepts in this chapter—*achievement motivation* and *Maslow's hierarchy of needs?*

Now, with your new concepts of motivation, when you look around the classroom you can sort of see with x-ray vision into the kinds of motives that propel people to attend class, get good grades, hold part-time jobs, *and* throw a party now and then. People do all of these things because they are identifiable psychological processes of motivation at work. And the good news is that people can *learn* to strongly influence these processes, not only in themselves, but in others.

Motivation is a need or desire that energizes and directs our behavior toward or away from some goal object. When we awaken each day we are pushed and pulled in many different directions—toward the bathroom, kitchen and health club; toward school, work and play. We now understand that human motives fall into 2 very different categories—the "pushes" called **drives,** and the "pulls" which are called **incentives.** The study of drives originates in the biological perspective on motivation—it is a look at innate, cyclical, homeostatic needs (e.g., hunger, thirst, novel experience, reproduction, and warmth). The result of motivation in these cases is satiation (satisfaction). This perspective looks at the role of genetics, hormones, fixed action patterns, and neurochemistry in the many drive states known to date.

The study of incentives is rooted in the cognitive, behavioral, and sociocultural perspectives on motivation—it is a look at learned, chaotic, environmentally induced desires (e.g., fame, wealth, beauty, admiration, achievement, and sexual desirability). The result of motivation in these cases is a never-ending quest for more and more. This perspective looks at the role of punishments and rewards, expectations and beliefs, and social norms, in the many incentive states known to date.

Unit Focus. In this unit there will be a heavy focus on the motives that energize and direct your behavior and thinking toward achievement. It is obvious that achievement is basic to human life. That is, beyond air, water, food and so on, how we achieve in school, work, personal relationships, and recreations is what life is all about. Both the achievement motive and Maslow's need hierarchy address the most important "high-end" aspects of our lives.

Study Objectives

1. Learn how to write a high achievement motivation story about yourself.
2. Learn how emotion and motivation are interrelated.
3. Understand how Maslow's need levels direct behavior and thinking in a stepwise fashion.

Key Terms

achievement motivation
affiliation need
analogic amplifier
attribution theory
Cannon-Bard Theory of Emotion
common sense sequence of emotion
dispositional attribution
drive
emotion
equilibration
equilibrium
ERG theory
ethologists
facial feedback hypothesis
GAS
general adaptation syndrome
homeostasis
incentive
instinct
James-Lange Sequence of Emotion
limbic system
motivation
motives
mutually causal
natural incentives
need to achieve
negative feedback loop
neomammalian brain
opponent-process theory
paleomammalian brain
polygraph
positive feedback loops
power need
reptilian brain
self-actualization
set-point

sign stimuli
situational attribution
social readjustment rating scale
viscera

Problem Set #4: Motivation

1. Using Maslow's hierarchy of needs, identify each of the following as being examples of Basic Needs (B), Psychological Needs (P), or Actualizing (A).
   a. quenching thirst, satisfying hunger
   b. striving to gain respect from peers
   c. writing poetry for spiritual fulfillment
   d. finding a nice apartment in a safe neighborhood
   e. striving to feel part of a community
   f. raising bonsai as a quest toward inner peace
   g. seeking sexual intimacy
   h. realizing your full potential as a human being
   i. going to church to please one's parents
   j. joining a sorority/fraternity to be with friends
2. Using the eleven scoring guidelines for achievement motivation, write an 11-point story for the picture that appears at the beginning of this chapter (Figure 4.1). Then, score your story according to the scoring guidelines.
3. Identify the motives which are considered drives, as opposed to incentives.
   - money, sex, thirst, sleep, pain avoidance, fame, thinness, achievement, praise
4. The following terms refer to Hunger Motivation. Which of these are characteristic of incentives? of drives?
   - internal, chaotic, set point, overweight, free-feeding, anorexia, glycogen, cyclical, acquired, ideal weight, normal weight, homeostasis, dieting, satiation, LH, VmH
5. George lost his way while backpacking and has been forced to survive on fewer than 50 percent of the calories he normally eats. If he remains in this predicament for four weeks we would expect:
   a. his body weight to ______
   b. his activity level to ______
   c. his metabolism to ______
   d. his interest in food to ______
   e. his feelings of hunger to ______
   f. his mental processes to ______
6. Match the following characteristics with the eating styles. Anorexia (A), Bulimia (B), Chronic Dieting (CD), Normal Eating (N)—more than one may apply
   a. always on current fad "weight loss program"
   b. eating in a free-feeding situation
   c. denial of eating problem, which is obvious to others
   d. maintain body weight 15 percent below normal through self-imposed starvation
   e. chronic fear of fat
   f. permanently lowered metabolism
   g. frequent, secret binges and purging
   h. eating in response to biological cues of hunger and satiety

i. most typical eating pattern in college women
j. more common in males than females
k. feeling cyclic loss of control
l. distorted body image
m. insignificant weight loss
n. dental, GI problems
o. hyperactivity
p. experienced calorie restriction as children

7. Which eating disorder does Anika most likely have? Label the specific symptoms which indicate she has this disorder.

   Anika's family noticed that Anika never seemed to actually eat anything, even though she often prepared the family elaborate meals. At dinner time she always reported lack of hunger, claiming she had been "tasting" during the preparation. If cajoled to join the family she carefully counts out 15 grains of rice, four or five mushrooms and one bite of fish which she would push around in her bowl as if she were eating. When not studying to keep her straight-A average as a high school sophomore, Anika would be exercising—race walking, cycling, swimming, even jumping up and down in the shower if she felt desperate for some activity. She dropped from 110 pounds to 75 pounds, but she still felt fat. One day she fainted at school and was rushed to the emergency room, a heart arrhythmia was discovered and she was hospitalized in the cardiac care unit. She feels her family is making a big deal out of nothing and is resisting the attempts from the staff psychologist to get her into therapy.

See Appendix C for answers to problem set.

5

Learning and Conditioning

The Opportunity to Learn How to Learn

This chapter on *learning* and *conditioning* presents a wonderful opportunity! At the end of this chapter you may look upon your experience as a student in ways you never have before. Here you will be given the opportunity to learn how to learn! Figure 5.1 depicts how through the long years of your schooling you have learned about history, chemistry, biology, etc. You have not yet been taught how to learn. You, as a learner, have not been the center of attention. Rather, the contents of these subject-matter areas of knowledge have traditionally been the focus of your school activities and experiences.

But this situation has been largely due to the fact that little had been known about how learners learn. Psychology now understands much about how people learn. We can begin to reformulate knowledge and the ways we think about it, in terms of learning principles rather than mysterious "lumps" of knowledge the learner can only hope to understand. When Isaac Newton was making his contribution to the invention of calculus, he did not do it with the learner in mind. Newton didn't say to himself, "Gee, I wonder if students will be able to learn calculus?" His only real concern was whether or not his calculus could be used to accurately describe certain events. This situation is true of most of what you are asked to learn in school—especially in college. It is difficult, if not impossible, to think of any bit of knowledge that was originally invented or discovered with the learner in mind except perhaps the psychology of learning. The primary goals have always been ones of integrity and descriptive powers of the subject—not the learner.

How This Can Be Changed

Psychology has provided great insights about how people learn. Therefore, many subjects have been reformulated with the learner in mind (see Figure 5-2). Some of these reformulations may be familiar to you. Table 5.1 contains a brief list of some of the more effective reformulations (Gnitecki, 1982; Kearsley, Hunter & Seidel, 1983).

Eight Principles of Learning

Principles of learning have been used to systematically modify the traditional subject-centered approaches on the left, so that they become the

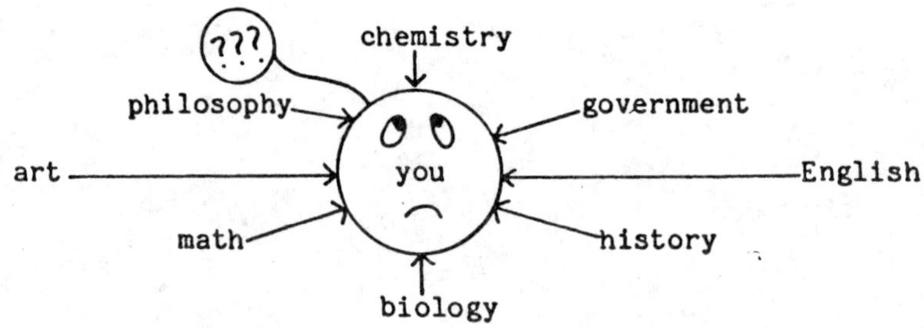

Subjects Demanding That You Somehow Learn About Them

Figure 5.1 Traditional Learning Principles

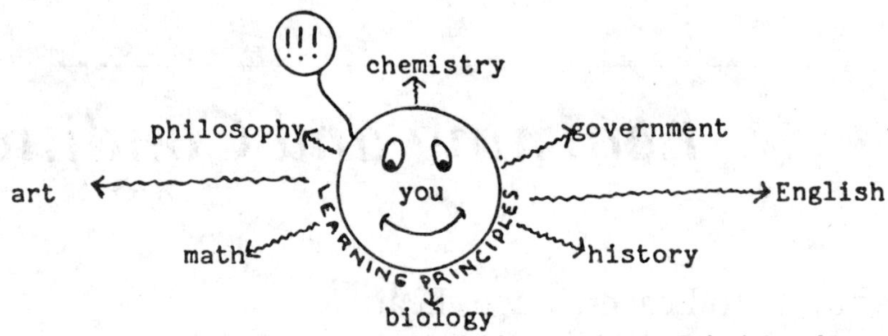

Subjects Reformulated into Learning Activities Based upon Principles of Learning

Figure 5.2 Reformulated Learning Principles

Table 5.1 Traditional Subject-Centered Approaches versus Reformulated Learner-Centered Approaches

Traditional Approaches	*Reformulated Approaches*
1. Traditional textbooks	1. *Programmed textbooks*
2. Typical learning approaches used by most students	2. Learning approaches used by top students
3. Typical classroom activities	3. *Computer-assisted instruction* and special learning labs
4. Traditional popular literature	4. The new literature approach (very difficult topics made understandable for the layperson)

reformulated learner-centered approaches on the right. Thousands of studies of animals and humans within the methods of the behavioral views of psychology have resulted in part in the following principles:

1. Learning is facilitated if the learner knows the consequences of his or her behavior.
2. The more often a certain behavior is rewarded, the more likely it is to reoccur in that situation.
3. If reward does not follow the learner's behavior, the likelihood of that behavior occurring in that situation decreases.
4. Reward should rapidly follow the behavior you would like to learn. Delay of reward will slow your rate of learning.
5. Complex material (like calculus) can always be broken down into smaller and smaller steps (approximations).
6. Complex behavior (to match complex material like doing calculus problems) can be shaped through a process of successive approximations.
7. Reward has the tendency to motivate the learner. If the learner's behavior is rewarded, he becomes more active in that situation,

and this increases the likelihood of even more reward.

8. Learning is facilitated when the learner makes overt responses.

Now, let us apply these principles of learning to you. You're going to begin to transform yourself from being a typical student to being a top student. If you already are a top student maybe you will find out why you are. You can apply the lessons of these principles to any subject, be it algebra or history. Using these programming principles, B.F. Skinner (1984) has recently convincingly argued that schools could teach traditional subjects in half the time they presently do.

PRINCIPLE 1: The Importance of Knowing the Consequences of Your Behavior

As you study your textbooks for exams how often do you know the consequences of your reading behavior? Do you remember what your English teacher has been telling you for years about paragraphs? Each paragraph covers a topic. This means that if you are reading a chapter with 30 paragraphs in it, you have 30 topics to deal with, and 30 convenient opportunities to provide yourself with consequences! If you will simply ask yourself what the point of each text paragraph is, you will be providing yourself with the critical feedback you need to learn.

PRINCIPLES 2 & 3: Reward Increases Reading Behavior and No Reward Decreases It

How often do you receive a reward as you read? Probably not very often when reading a textbook. Many textbooks, like Newton's calculus, were not written to pique your interest. On the other hand, a good novel is. The rewards you receive as the novel unfolds are its passions, compassions, tragedies, and comedy that spark your reading behavior—you simply can't put the book down!

The rewards in reading a textbook are the organized knowledge it provides. A powerful advantage of providing feedback for each paragraph is that most of the time the average student is able to recall and understand information on a paragraph-by-paragraph basis. This in itself supplies a constant source of reward. And this reward, in turn, increases the chances of further reading.

PRINCIPLE 4: The Importance of Immediate Reward

It is an extremely important principle of learning that there be a close connection between doing something correctly, and immediately knowing that it is correct. You may be familiar with housebreaking a dog. Not only must your poor pet learn to control normally involuntary systems, but he must learn when and where.

The dog should be rewarded as a "good dog" or scolded as a "bad dog" immediately upon the occurrence of the behavior. Catching the animal in the act helps him more quickly make the connection between his attempts at control and location. In the same way if your reading behavior is not rewarded soon after it occurs you may have trouble making the appropriate connections. Again, the simple act of asking yourself what each paragraph is saying right after you read it provides the immediate reward necessary for accurate learning.

PRINCIPLES 5 & 6: Successive Ideas of the Textbook and the Successive Steps of Learning

There is no theoretical reason to think that complex textbook material and the complex behavioral demands that go with it cannot be broken down into smaller and smaller learning steps. Actually, when you read paragraph by paragraph, you am taking the advantage of breaking complex material down into manageable topics. But what happens when you come to a paragraph that you do not understand? You must always remember that that particular paragraph can be broken down into smaller topic steps. As you can guess, there is no limit to how far this process can go. If you stay with it, you can learn almost anything!

PRINCIPLE 7: Reward Increases Your Interest

You might ask yourself why you like the particular subjects you do like. One explanation based upon the principles of learning is simply that you learn to like what you are rewarded for. If you do well in math you probably like math. If you carefully apply the principles of learning we have been discussing, two things should happen. First, you will mysteriously start liking more of the courses you are taking. But, secondly, and maybe even more importantly, you will start enjoying learning itself. You will be learning to learn!

PRINCIPLE 8: Overt Responses Tend to Facilitate Learning

Finally, it is important to know that the more active you become as you learn and read the more you will likely learn. As you read, it is very helpful to discuss the material with others, draw diagrams to illustrate concepts, perform little experiments concerning what you are reading, etc. To the extent you can create your own lab experiences for each of your courses, you will facilitate all of your learning.

Putting the Principles All Together

We have applied a few simple behaviorial principles of learning to you. Think about a few implications of what you have learned. How might you write a better textbook? Is that top student really a genius or is he simply letting the principles of learning work for him? How might we design a computer-assisted program to take into account our principles of learning? In the "new literature" very complex topics are made understandable by the average person. What principles of learning can you see at work in the new literature approach? One very common study method is called the SQ3R method (see Francis Robinson (1970) in the suggested reading at the end of this chapter). SQ3R stands for Survey, Question, Read, Recite, and Review. What is involved in this method of textbook study should be obvious. Which behavioral principles of learning are included in this very popular method of study? What additional cognitive principles are included in it?

There is probably no such thing as a difficult subject. Perhaps only the amount of time you have been given and the ways it has been presented to you have made subjects seem difficult. Have you ever noticed that once you do learn something, it suddenly seems simple? That's because it really is simple. It is the process of learning that can at times be difficult—and it really never has to be. Again, you will see some very convincing evidence for this at the end of this chapter and in Chapters 6 and 8.

Toward a Philosophy of Learning

At the philosophical level, learning presents us with the question: How is it that we and other animals change in relation to our environment? How is it, as William Verplanck (1957) puts it, that we came to exhibit a change in behavior (or neurobiological functions, or cognitive structure) between two successive exposures to the same environment? This is the essential problem of learning. How should we view this process? In the theory section to follow, the phenomena of learning could be approached in terms of any of the traditional views. Table 5.2 provides some indications of how we might proceed.

Although a discussion of all of these views of learning would provide us with a complete story of learning, it would also take us beyond the scope of the introductory course. Since a major goal of this chapter is learning how to learn, we will focus our attention upon the behavioral and

Table 5.2 Approaches to Learning

1. *The Neurobiological View:* we would describe changes in the brain that occur as a result of successive exposures to various environmental conditions.
2. *The Psychoanalytic View:* we would describe changes in the hypothesized id, ego, and superego, relationships that occur as the result of longer developmental exposures to various environmental conditions. Here, the family, school, and therapy environments could all be described in terms of learning.
3. *The Humanistic View:* we would describe the development of the person as an autonomous learner in student-centered learning.
4. *The Behavioral and Cognitive Views:* we would describe the evolution of behavior as the result of successive exposures to various environmental conditions.

cognitive views. These views are readily applied by students to their own learning and are easily related to a systems perspective.

A Theoretical Model: Learning as the Evolution of Behavior: A Systems Perspective

Most views or theories within psychology are actually analogies to those that have been helpful in arriving at explanations in other disciplines. In the case of learning, a very helpful theory model has been that of the *Theory of Evolution.* At the philosophical level the Theory of Evolution presents us with a similar question: How is that plants and animals over generations change in relation to their environments? The Darwinian evolution of biological systems, and the evolution of psychological systems of individuals through learning share many principles. Therefore, some of the key ideas of evolutionary theory can be applied to learning principles and processes to help us think about them in a more holistic perspective. These key ideas are listed in Table 5.3.

Table 5.3 Key Ideas of Evolutionary Theory and of Learning Principles

1. Both have a wide and normal distribution.
2. Both share the process of natural selection.
3. Both have factors that lead to the extinction of their characteristics.

The General Model: Evolution

Let us briefly examine the above principles. Harvard University professor emeritus Ernst Mayr tells us that the modern theory of evolution ". . . stands today as the organizing principle of biology." (1978) And since psychology is most often considered to be a subfield of biology, we should study these principles. Recall that this is an advantage of a systems approach.

Wide Distribution of Characteristics of Systems. When we talk about the evolution of the species in relation to the evolution of behavior that occurs through learning, we can refer to species evolution as evolution-1, and to learning as evolution-2. In evolution-1, it is essential first that there be variation in the members of the species. For example, people, animals, and plants show great variation across members. How do people vary? In every way you can think about them. This is true for all living things. In general, these variations take on a standard sort of arrangement or *normal distribution* (see Figure 5.3). When the great mathematician Karl Pearson (1893) was developing early notions on the mathematics of evolution, which laid much of the groundwork for behavioral statistics, he noted that even the breadths of foreheads of Naples crabs varied in a normal distribution. We will return to the concept of a standard of variation in some detail in the statistical appendix.

Natural Selection. A second essential idea in evolution-1 involves the process of *natural*

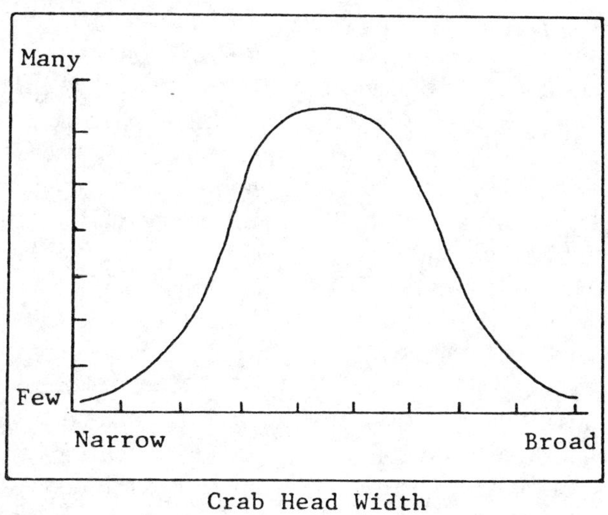

Figure 5.3 Normal Curve Distribution

selection. You have probably heard the expression "survival of the fittest." This is an outcome of the process of natural selection. Out of all of the variations a species exhibits, some members, because they are quicker, smarter, more resistant to disease or predators, or their foreheads are broader, will have a better chance of reproducing their kind. Natural selection and the survival (reproducibility) of the fittest are really two sides of the same coin. The concept of natural selection will be extremely helpful in understanding learning processes.

Extinction. Finally, for our purpose, the process of evolution-1 includes the idea of *extinction.* Extinction means that those members of a species which do not survive to reproduce tend to come to an end.

A Dynamic Bridging of the Gap Between Evolution and Learning

Just as the theory of evolution describes changes in *species* in relation to the environment, the model can be used conceptually to describe some of the details involved in the principles and processes of behavior evolution in the individual—learning. On forming this analogy, let us begin with a *theory* level definition of learning. We have already noted that learning involves *changes in behavior upon two successive exposures to the same environment.*

Defining Learning. It is certainly no accident that we can compare learning processes to evolutionary ones. In 1859 Charles Darwin had insisted upon a continuity across species. For example, he had suggested that humans may not be alone in their ability to reason. Darwin felt that the human mind itself had evolved, and that mental processes had come about in a similar manner in both humans and animals. An investigator who helped formulate much of the early basis for modern behavioral learning theory was Edward L. Thorndike. Thorndike was well aware of Darwin's views, and in 1898 published his doctoral thesis, entitled *Animal Intelligence: An Experimental Study of the Associative Processes in Animals.* This was clearly a Darwin-inspired thesis. So impressed with Darwin's insights about how behavior comes about in species, Thorndike later wrote at length on *Darwin's Contributions to Psychology* (1909) in glowing terms.

What Thorndike discovered through careful observation much as Darwin had proceeded was something in the learning process that was similar to Darwin's selection process. Upon carefully observing many animals, Thorndike came to the conclusion that behavior change was the result of changing the environment in desired ways. Thorndike stated this idea in the *Law of Effect.*

> The Law of Effect is that: Of several responses made to the same situation, those which are accompanied or closely followed by satisfaction to the animal will, other things being equal, be more firmly connected with the situation, so that, when it recurs, they will be more likely to recur; those which are accompanied or closely followed by discomfort to the animal will, other things being equal, have their connections with that situation weakened, so that, when it recurs, they will be less likely to occur. The greater the satisfaction or discomfort, the greater the strengthening or weakening of the bond. (1911, p. 244)

If you look closely at the statement of this law you will see analogies to each of the essential ideas of evolution.

In Thorndike's classic methodology, a cat is placed in a puzzle-box where at first it exhibits a great variety of behaviors. As the many variations occur, some, like lifting a paw near the door latch, allows the cat to escape. After repeated imprisonment inside the puzzle-box, the amount of time the cat needs to escape gradually shortens. The behavior of lifting the paw has been progressively selected to solve the problem at hand. This (natural) selection has proceeded in accordance with the law of effect, the effect being the door opening upon the appropriate behavior. So, it was not necessary, Thorndike felt, to suppose that animals think or reason. Animal learning was felt to be simply the result of connections or associations between an animal's behavior in a situation and changes (consequences) in the environment. While Thorndike was able to demonstrate the law of effect, the question of whether or not animals think or reason was really not conclusively answered by this demonstration. As you will see later in this chapter, cognitive psychologists have contributed additional views to this situation.

With the effect dynamic or the selection of behavior in mind, we will discuss a theoretical definition of learning. Imagine how the neurobiologists might want to replace the law of effect with the progressive and orderly development of neuronal connections. For example, W.M. Cowan (1985) and Gerald Edelman (1985) would suggest a natural selection process occurring among neurons. The details of how evolution would apply in these other views of learning would require as to include additional and more sophisticated dynamic principles of evolution. These would not be a reasonable expectation for the first course in psychology.

Empirical Definition of Learning. A definition that I find very helpful in describing learning is that provided by Gregory Kimble (1961):

> Learning is a relatively permanent change in behavior potentiality, that occurs as a result of reinforced practice or experience with the environment.

As this definition stands, it is an empirical one.

Theoretical Definition of Learning When the idea of reinforced practice is meant to be the law of effect and causes behavior change, we have a theoretical definition of learning.

The following definition of learning, while not universally accepted, tells us what learning is and gives us guidance as to what it is not. In this regard, there are four very critical aspects to this very succinct definition.

1. The learned change is relatively permanent. This allows us to exclude all of the momentary physiological changes that occur in you daily, such as being hungry, thirsty, or tired; being startled, or becoming fearful of noises in the night; bodily changes as the result of circadian rhythms, e.g., blood sugar level, hormone levels.
2. A change in behavior potentiality is involved in learning. It may be years before much of what you have learned actually appears in your behavior. Up to that time, it will only have been a potential to behave. Also, this term recognizes, in a way, the fact that you can learn a great deal simply by observing others. You don't actually have to act while watching someone else execute many procedures. For this reason many psychologists prefer to expand the definition to include reinforced experience or observations. You will see the importance of adding these additional independent variables to the definition later in the chapter when we discuss social or observational learning.
3. *Reinforcement* of some sort is necessary for learning to occur. In this particular definition the role of reward is emphasized as the mechanism that results in learning. We should expand the idea of reinforcement to include *negative reinforcement.* As Thorndike (1911) points out, an animal will work hard to avoid an unpleasant situation or stimulus. *Punishment* (the delivery of an unpleasant stimulus) is also a mechanism of behavior change.
4. Practice is the occasion for some degree of learning to occur. Practice can include the actual occasion of behavior, imagination, or observation (see 2).

Putting the Theoretical Notion of Learning to Work

The theoretical definition is not all there is to learning. In the balance of this chapter we will describe basic methodologies through which the idea of learning has been studied and what has been found. These methods are usually referred to as conditioning procedures.

Methods Used in Studying Learning

Classical Conditioning

Evolution-1 has provided animals and human beings with a great number of reflexes. Reflexes provide more or less unconscious or involuntary adaptive measures that help ensure survival. A simple operational description of the idea of a *reflex* would be as follows:

> A reflex involves an inborn, stereotypical response to a particular type of stimulus. It is therefore based upon an inborn wiring pattern in the nervous systems of all members of a species. Reflexive wiring patterns involve both the somatic (for example, knee jerk and eye blinking) and autonomic (for example, salivation and pupillary

dilation and contraction) divisions of the peripheral nervous system.

While reflexes represent inborn wiring patterns in the nervous system, and inborn stimulus response correlations, they are modifiable through learning. Examples of the modification of reflexes through learning include biofeedback techniques (Chapter 2), the learned aspects of the experience of pain and meditation (Chapter 3), and classical conditioning.

The modifiability of reflexes greatly broadens their survival value. That is, a modifiable reflex is of much greater survival value to a given creature than a simple one-purpose unmodifiable one.

In the laboratory methodology, the reflex modification form of learning has been referred to as respondent *classical conditioning*. Most of the earliest laboratory studies of classical conditioning were conducted by the Russian physiologist, Ivan P. Pavlov (1927). Pavlov's place in psychology is very important; he discovered a great deal about how learning occurs. The implications of his work for psychology are treated in some detail within the discussion of Soviet psychology in Chapter 15.

Pavlov's (1927) basic method was very simple. He used the unlearned salivary response to the stimulus of food in dogs as the reflex for study. The fact that this reflex was open to learning modification was discovered quite *serendipitously*. Pavlov began to notice that events taking place prior to giving dogs food, a part of another research problem, would cause them to begin salivating. Subsequently, all sorts of stimulus events were presented to the dogs prior to giving them food. In each case the dogs would begin to salivate with the appearance of the stimulus prior to the food. This situation was organized into a standard laboratory methodology for the study of this phenomenon. The classical arrangement of this standard laboratory method (Anrep, 1920) was as follows (see Figure 5.4):

> A dog was loosely harnessed in a restraint apparatus. The dog's parotid gland (large salivary gland in cheek) was cut so that saliva could be collected externally and accurately measured. Next, a tuning fork was sounded, and 7 or 8 seconds later a small measure of dry, powdered food was placed before the dog. At the beginning of the lab procedure the dog would only salivate during eating. But gradually, after many repetitions of the procedure, the dog would begin to salivate at the sound of the tone.

The dog had been conditioned (and had learned) so that it now behaved differently. It can be seen that this new behavior prepares the dog to more effectively deal with conditions in its environment.

Classical learning is very important to you every day of your life. Any time events are paired over and over again (as with the dog) you are potentially being classically conditioned. Think about some events that always seem to precede good feelings in yourself. Think about how you feel when you see someone coming toward you with a smile on her face—and what happens next. On the other hand, negative feelings can be

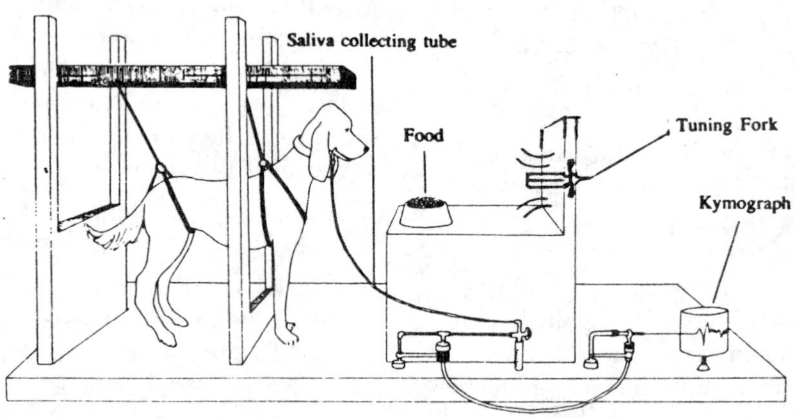

Figure 5.4 Classical Conditioning

classically learned. How do you feel when you see someone coming toward you with a frown? How do you feel when you hear sad music? If, as you were growing up, sad music was always paired with the coming of Christmas, that music would make you feel warm inside. This should help us appreciate why widely different cultures can enjoy such a variety of music and activities during the same holidays.

You will see later, classical learning and conditioning can produce abnormal behavior, superstitious behavior, change buying attitudes through advertising, be used in the treatment of mental disorders, and strongly influence your everyday behavior.

Classical Conditioning Procedures and Examples

Before going on, you should have some familiarity with the empirical aspects of the classical conditioning methods. These empirical level considerations will allow you to more clearly identify elements in everyday events which are involved in this type of learning. There are four critical empirical elements involved in classical conditioning and learning.

1. The *Unconditioned Stimulus* (UCS) A stimulus that at the beginning of a procedure results in a regular, correlated, and measurable response. In the classical Pavlovian procedure, it was the food.
2. The *Unconditioned Response* (UCR) This is the response to the Unconditioned Stimulus. In Pavlov's classical procedure, this response was the dog's salivating. The UCS→UCR constitutes a reflex.
3. The *Conditioned Stimulus* (CS) The conditioned stimulus is referred to as a *neutral stimulus* in relation to the Unconditioned Response at the beginning of the procedure. This is the tone stimulus in Pavlov's classical procedure. Remember, the UCR here is the salivary response of the dog. (The CS is not totally neutral—just in relation to the UCR. The CS, being a stimulus, usually elicits some sort of response—like orienting to it.) To be considered a CS the stimulus cannot elicit the UCR at the start of procedures. The tone did not elicit the salivary response at the start of the procedure.
4. The *Conditioned Response* (CR) When the dog has learned to salivate *to the* CS, the response is technically a Conditioned Response. The UCR is the response to the UCS, the CR is the response to the CS. The UCR and the CR, both salivary responses in Pavlov's classical procedure, differ in subtle ways.

Classical Conditioning: A Christmas Example If we put all four of these empirical elements into the procedural stages diagrammatically it would appear as in Table 5-4.

You might question whether or not this Christmas example constitutes the stable UCS→UCR correlation required for classical conditioning to take place. It is of course true that the songs don't always precede the highly rewarding activities associated with Christmas by Pavlov's (1972) 7 or 8 seconds. Actually, it has been found that classical learning will occur as the result of a number of timing arrangements in the pairing of the CS and UCS. Figure 5.5 shows some of the possibilities that have been investigated.

Some classical learning probably occurs as the result of any of these temporal pairing arrangements. And, certainly, in the case of Christmas music and Christmas get-togethers all of them occur. However, one of the pairing arrangements seems to work best in forming the learning, and one of them seems to be least effective. If you thought the *delayed conditioning* arrangement was best, you were correct. This arrangement was the one used in the classical procedure of Pavlov where a tone was employed as the CS. *Backward conditioning* results in little if any classical learning.

Classical learning has a great deal to do with the acquisition and maintenance of involuntary, habitual behavior. As further examples of how habits might be formed in relation to regular pairings of stimuli we should briefly discuss the ideas of *higher-order classical conditioning* and of *stimulus generalization*.

Higher-Order Conditioning Pavlov discovered that once a CR had been established, to elicit a neutral CS an additional CS could be conditioned to elicit the CR. This higher-order procedure is illustrated in Table 5.5.

I think you could easily construct a diagram for the procedures of third- and fourth-order

Table 5.4 The UCS → UCR Correlation

BEFORE ANY REGULAR PAIRING	UCS ——————————	>UCR
	people getting together with smiles and laughter to exchange gifts, (especially significant to children), and have a good time	good feelings of acceptance, love, warmth, belonging, etc.
BEFORE ANY REGULAR PAIRING	CS ——————————	>
	the songs "White Christmas," "Jingle Bells," etc.	no response particularly related to the UCR (above). It is difficult to tell at what age the CS is still neutral.
DURING REGULAR PAIRING OF CS & UCS	CS ————>UCS ————	>UCR
	the songs people getting together, etc.	good UCS feelings of warmth, etc.
	These two stimuli come together in a variety of temporal arrangements.	
FOLLOWING THE YEARS OF REGULAR PAIRING	CS ——————————	>CR
	the songs	generalized feelings of warmth, optimism, etc.

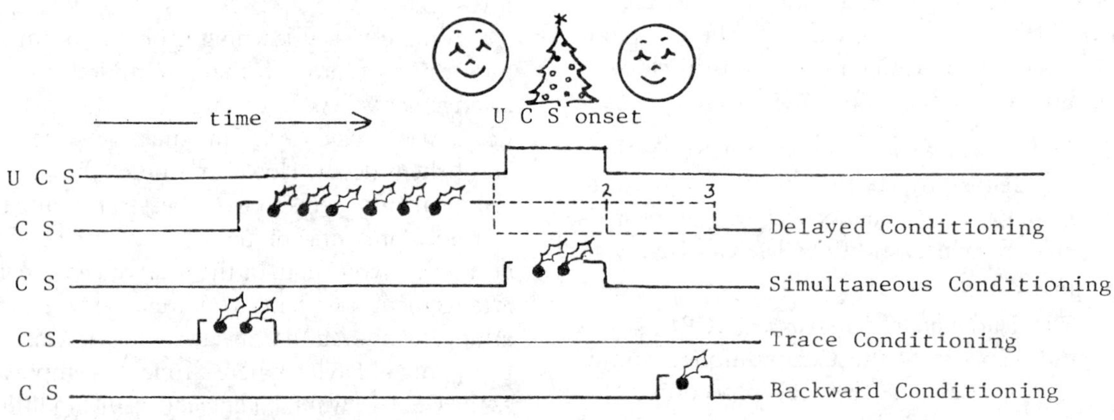

Figure 5.5 Arrangement for Pairing CS and UCS
The upward movement of a line represents the point in time when the stimulus is presented. The downward movement of a line represents the point in time when the same stimulus is terminated. In delayed conditioning the CS may be terminated at any one of three general points in time (see 1, 2, 3 on the delayed conditioning line). Delayed conditioning is so named because this procedure results in a delay in the appearance of the CR over the more simultaneous conditioning methods.

conditioning. Remember to leave the UCS out once CS^1 has been firmly established. While Pavlov did not have much luck in establishing higher orders of classical learning in the laboratory procedure, that was largely because the reward (UCS) was omitted after the first order of conditioning was established. When the reward is omitted, extinction, as Pavlov called it, of the learned response occurs. This extinguished behavior disappears from the overt behavior distribution. It may undergo *spontaneous recovery* to the overt level after some time has passed and eliciting conditions occur. Can you think of analogies to extinction and this "spontaneous recovery" in evolution of the species? Pavlov may have had trouble with higher-order condi-

Table 5.5 Higher Order Conditioning

first-order conditioning	
STABLE UCS UCR	Food (UCS) → Salivation (UCR)
PAIR CS UCS	Tone (CS) → Food (UCS) → Salivation (CR^1)
CS ELICITS CR	Tone (CS) → Salivation (CR)
second-order conditioning	
CS^2 IS PAIRED WITH CS^1	
Black Square (CS^2)	→ Tone (CS^1) → Salivation (CR^1)
Note that the original UCS (reinforcer) is not used in higher-order conditioning.	
AFTER SEVERAL PAIRINGS	
Black Square (CS^2)	→ Salivation (CR^2)

tioning, but in everyday life higher-order conditioning is very important in the acquisition and maintenance of many habitual behaviors and their potentialities. In everyday life second- and third-order CS's regularly occur with the UCS also occurring. Again, as in the case with the Christmas example, we need only look for regular pairings of stimuli in the environment for potential higher orders of conditioning.

Advertising. You may have noticed how television advertisements for automobiles, while they might change slightly, always pair the same sort of stimulus events. For example, depending on the type of car being advertised, there is a regular pairing of car and $/success, or the car and romance/success, or the car and dependability/success. This is just a little more complicated than the Christmas example. In advertising, the UCS of the generalized and stable rewards of money, romance, and security are used to condition you in a classic manner to make connections (unconscious and involuntary habits) between these UCS's and a product—a car in this case (Staats & Staats, 1958). The entire higher-order procedure might look as it appears in Table 5.6.

The point in pairing these stimuli over and over (often for many years) is to get you to habitually and unconsciously connect brand-name X with a CR^2 that has some of the important elements of the above UCR. Have you ever wondered why a new brand-X car just somehow "turns you on"? Is it a coincidence that young people often say things like, "Wow, what a sexy car!" Or, they might be heard saying, "Boy, what a tough machine!" They often apply elements of these exclamations to members of the opposite sex. Perhaps, the unconscious is revealing its years of experience with this sort of constant pairings that occur in advertisements.

While we have used the example of the higher-order conditioning of sexual attractiveness to automobile brand names, we could just as easily illustrate how some cars are advertised with the financial-success-oriented individual in mind. Have you ever noticed how some makes of cars are always parked in front of mansions in their ads? This sort of advertising is not necessarily dishonest; it simply is taking advantage of one of the fundamental ways we learn.

Table 5.6 Paired Repeatedly Since Your Childhood

CS^2 →	CS^1 →	UCS →	UCR
(car brand X)	(new car)	(romance symbol)	(subtle sexual and/or affiliative responses)

Stimulus Generalization

When a dog is conditioned to salivate to the sound of a tone (CS), he is also learning to respond to stimuli that are similar to the tone. For example, Pavlov found that any tone-like sound would also elicit the conditioned response of salivating. This fact is called stimulus generalization. It is very likely that much of the popular music we like is partly a matter of stimulus generalization. The music of Christmas, patriotic music, church music, and, for our Western culture, classical music themes are probably anchor CS's which, when generalized, make certain new pieces of music sound attractive. If you listen carefully to some of the popular music you like, you may hear some of this stimulus similarity. The process of stimulus generalization is constantly going on and it too leads to habitual and unconscious patterns of behavior.

The Learning of Phobias. A widely known example of stimulus generalization involves the experimental induction of *phobia* in an infant. The story is that of 11 months old Albert B., commonly known as "little Albert." John B. Watson (1920), the founder of American behaviorism, wanted to know if a human infant could be conditioned to fear something that was neutral in regard to fear (UCR) at the beginning of conditioning. Watson used a sudden loud sound which can cause you to be startled and to panic for a moment as a fear-eliciting UCS. Such a sudden loud sound would result in a sympathetic (involuntary) response. As the neutral stimulus, Watson used a white rat. Diagrammed, the procedure appears in Table 5.7. After seven pairings of these stimuli, Little Albert learned the sympathetic fear response to the white rat. Eventually, not only would Little Albert produce the fear response to the white rat, but to stimuli that were similar in appearance to it. Five days after conditioning Little Albert to fear the white rat, Watson presented other similar stimuli, for example a rabbit, Santa's mask, Watson's own gray hair, etc., to the infant. Albert showed the fear response to all of these stimuli (see Table 5.8). A stimulus generalization had occurred.

If you did not know that Little Albert had been conditioned to fear a white rat and about the phenomenon of stimulus generalization, you would probably be very puzzled when Little Albert would cry and pull away from the rabbit's foot on your key chain. And, assuming little Albert were capable of self-reflection, he, too, would be puzzled by his fear of the rabbit's foot. Remember, the original condition and the generalization take place at an unconscious level. It is an unreasonable reaction. But, then, people exhibit all sorts of unreasonable fears. You may know someone who is afraid to ride in elevators or afraid to fly in commercial airplanes. These unreasonable fears (phobias) are habitual and unconscious reactions to riding in elevators and airplanes (or simple reaction to real or imagined

Table 5.7 Induction of a Phobic Response

CS →	UCS →	UCR
white rat →	sudden loud sound →	fear response

Table 5.8 Stimulus Generalization

gray hair
rabbit
white rat (CS) ⟶ fear (UCR)
cotton wool
dog

(The curve around the CS's is used to illustrate the idea that as stimuli become less similar to the original CS, they elicit less of a fear response.)

elevator or airplane disasters). Stimulus generalization and classical conditioning of fear response offer one explanation for the origin of phobias. And it is likely that a great many occur in this way. People with phobias are usually puzzled by their own behavior.

In this regard, a reversal of the conditioning process which produces phobias can be used to relieve them. This process called systematic desensitization will be discussed in Chapter 10.

Instrumental Conditioning

Certainly, concepts of the processes of evolution are helpful in appreciating and understanding the survival of modified reflexes—for example, in unconsciously salivating preparatory to receiving food, or in unconsciously avoiding an electric shock. However, the fundamental evolutionary dynamic of natural selection can be demonstrated even more clearly in operant or *instrumental conditioning*. As B.F. Skinner (1981) pointed out, operant conditioning represents variation and selection in progress.

At the beginning of this chapter you were introduced to a plan that would help you to learn how to learn—to get voluntary control over your learning processes. Several principles of how you could become the instrument of your own learning were illustrated. Instrumental conditioning differs methodologically from classical conditioning, in that the animal's or person's behavior is instrumental in producing a reward or in avoiding punishment. Another way to look at this distinction is that instrumental conditioning involves voluntary learning. Think about the difference in Little Albert becoming fearful of a white rat and in your learning to apply the principles of learning at the beginning of this chapter. If we diagram the empirical variables related to the idea of behavior of the animal or person producing a reward, it would appear as in Table 5.9.

Much of the laboratory methodology for instrumental conditioning has been carried out by B.F. Skinner (1953). Skinner prefers to refer to instrumental conditioning as operant conditioning because the organism operates upon the environment or influences the environment rather than the other way around.

In the typical laboratory setup, an animal is placed in an operant conditioning apparatus or Skinner box (see Figure 5.6) where it emits a wide range of behavior. In evolutionary parallel, this coincides with the distribution of organism characteristics. Just as there are positive and negative consequences for certain organism

Table 5.9 Instrumental Conditioning

freely emitted behavior (potential CR's)	→	positive or negative consequences (UCS's)	→	situational cues (CS's)

Figure 5.6 Operant Conditioning

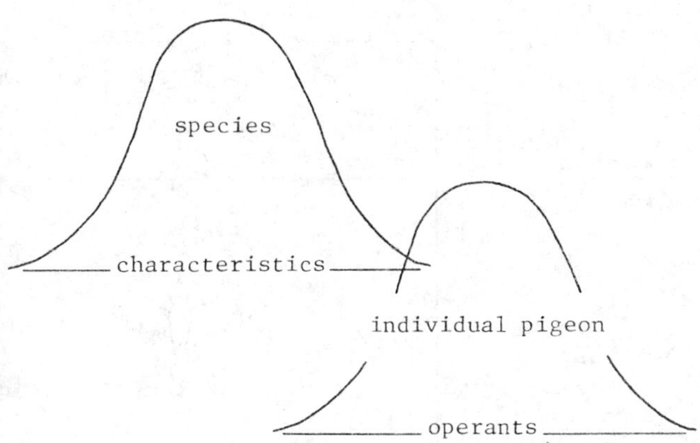

characteristics in the Darwinian model, for example, quickness, weight, etc., there are positive and negative consequences for behaviors in the distribution of freely emitted operants. If an operant is followed by a positive environmental effect UCS (reward just as in classical method), then the likelihood of that behavior being reproduced in that situation increases (see Thorndike's law of effect). The behavior has been selected in accordance with its effect. In the same way, organismic characteristics are naturally selected because they help lead to reproducibility of another sort. In operant methods the above procedure is called reward training. Recall that one of the principles of learning was that "the more often a certain behavior is rewarded, the more likely it is to recur in that situation." We have already encountered the role of "consequences," the first learning principle in the definition of instrumental learning. Complex instrumental behavior does not occur by a simple one-step process of response selection as described above. Just as in species evolution, most instrumental learning involves a long series of *successive approximations* toward some final behavior pattern or behavioral capability. Using the principles of learning you will probably not become a top student overnight. Descriptively, the process of successive approximations toward some final behavior pattern is called shaping.

Instrumental Conditioning Procedures and Examples. Let us say you would like to instrumentally condition a pigeon to turn a full circle to receive a food reward. You might wait some time before the pigeon would perform a smooth full circle as it walked around the food source so that you could reward his behavior. However, because of a simplified rule version of the law of effect, you can reward a series of small approximations to turning a circle and get the same result. This version of the law of effect can be stated as follows: "The behavior that immediately precedes a reward (no matter what the behavior is) will become more likely in that situation." An illustration of this process will be helpful. Figure 5.7 represents a schematic diagram of an instrumental conditioning apparatus with a pigeon that has been taught to eat from a food cup. This training is very easy due to the simplicity of the response required and the hunger of the pigeon. At the beginning of reward training the pigeon will likely spend a good deal of time orienting toward the food cup. This is represented by the peak of the normal curve. His behavior excursions around the food cup will be somewhat haphazard (response generalization), but will *distribute normally.* When the pigeon steps in the desired direction (say clockwise) you can reward the pigeon with a food pellet by pressing a button on your remote control switch (see Figure 5.8).

Now, a new distribution of behavior excursions will occur. This is the direct result of the law of effect as stated in our simplified rule. This new distribution is depicted in Figure 5.9.

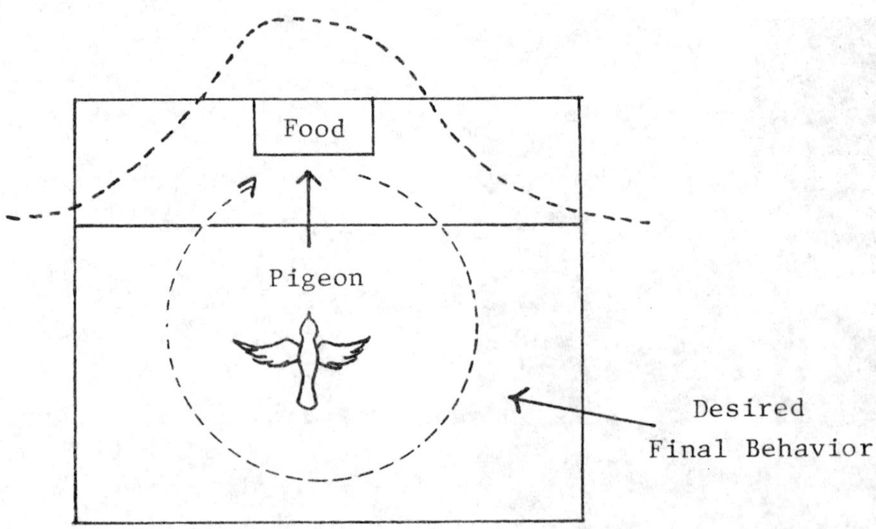

Figure 5.7 Goal of Instrumental Conditioning

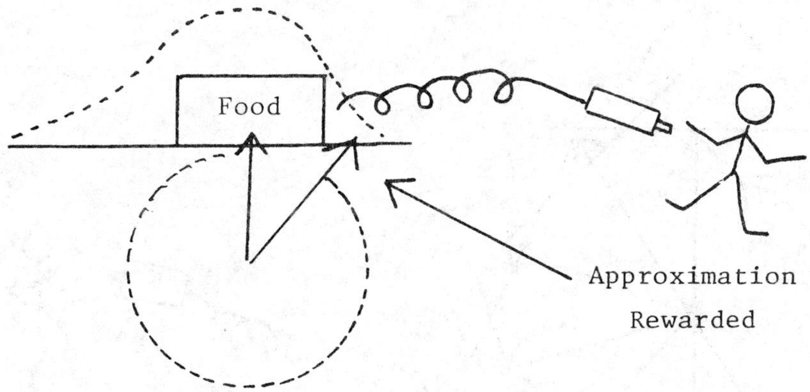

Figure 5.8 Beginning Reward Training

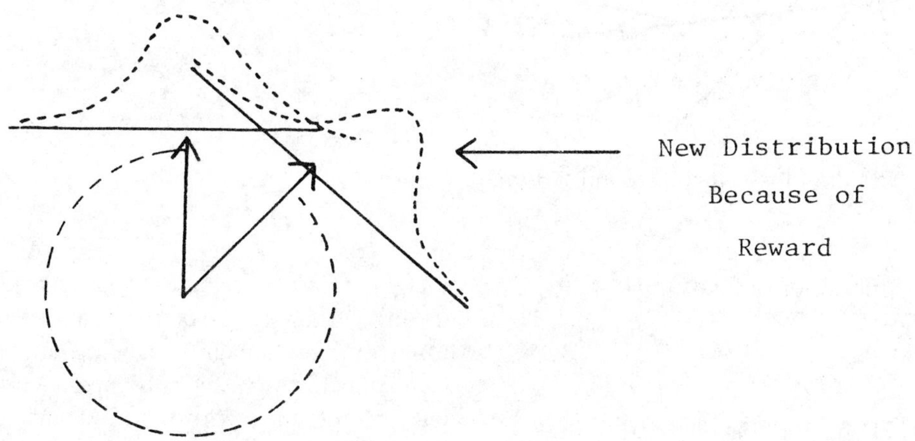

Figure 5.9 Behavior as a Result of Law of Effect

A selection process of turning a circle has started. Now that the approximations distribution has moved a little in the clockwise direction, the pigeon is more likely than before to go even further in that direction. Next, when an approximation of, say, a quarter turn clockwise occurs, which it now likely will, another food reward is given. Figure 5.10 shows simplified approximations, continuing clockwise until the pigeon is over halfway around the circle. Then it is likely she will continue turning all the way since it is shorter than going back.

So, here we have seen the "evolution" of a behavior pattern—a natural selection by successive approximations to turn a circle. Much of your behavior occurs in just this fashion. We can summarize the process of conditioning a pigeon to turn a circle by reiterating the principles of learning. You should be able to identify each of the eight principles appearing in Table 5.10 that occurred during the conditioning of the pigeon.

Other Effects of Instrumental Learning and Conditioning

The principles of behavioral conditioning and learning go on producing their effects whether we purposely control procedures or not. Sometimes these principles result in the development of behavior that was not intended or even imaginable. Three classic examples of this include the learning of *superstitious behavior,* the learning of *learned helplessness,* and the effects of *scheduled reward.*

Superstitious Behavior. Recall that we found that a simple implication of the law of effect was that whatever behavior immediately precedes reward will become more likely in that situation in the future. What would happen if a

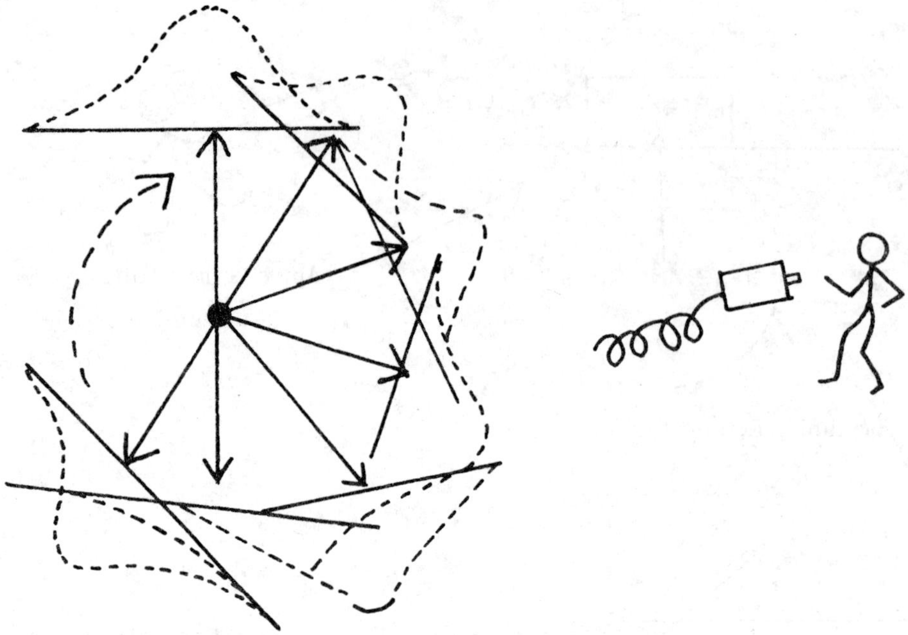

Figure 5.10 Result of Instrumental Conditioning

Table 5.10 Principles of Learning

1. consequences
2. reward
3. decrease in behavior (this might be a little difficult)
4. reward rapidly follows
5. complex material
6. complex behavior
7. motivated
8. more overt behavior enhances learning

reward suddenly began to appear on a regular basis no matter what you (or the pigeon) happened to be doing at the moment? During the time this regular reward occurred, you might accidentally be doing anything. So, according to our law of behavior, whatever it was you were doing just prior to the delivery of the reward would become more likely in that situation. However, this behavior would have nothing to do with the appearance of the reward. This is a conditioned behavioral superstition.

This simple law of behavior might well help explain why rituals like dancing and chanting have become superstitious behaviors. One can imagine rain occurring on a fairly regular basis during certain times of the year. At the same time, one can imagine dancing and chanting types of behavior also occurring on a heightened level during times of drought (behavior tends to become more variable when a particular reward is withheld). It becomes fairly likely that the dancing and chanting overlay on routine patterns of behavior will accidentally just precede a badly needed downpour. A spurious correlation of events undoubtedly plays some role in reinforcing superstitious behavior.

Learned Helplessness. Laboratory studies on the phenomenon of learned helplessness have great implications for our understanding of human behavior. People who have encountered unpleasant (aversive) stimuli over and over with no chance of escape often come to the conclusion that they cannot change the situation (Seligman, 1957). They learn to suffer and bear it. This situation is like the learning of superstitions, in that spurious correlations maintain control over behavior. Perhaps the better we understand these subtle principles, the more likely we will be able to control them.

In the laboratory demonstration of learned helplessness, a dog might be placed in an apparatus where electric shock can be administered through grids on the floor. The dog is restrained in a harness from any chance of escape. If the dog is shocked repeatedly, it will eventually cease its attempts to escape. Now, even if the dog had been trained to avoid shocks before, he will not attempt any move to avoid the shocks (Overneier & Seligman, 1967). It is as if the no-escape training has removed his hope—the dog has learned helplessness.

At the cognitive level in humans, learned helplessness is a case of what has been referred to as a *self-fulfilling prophecy* (Merton, 1948) or expectancy (Rosenthal & Jacobson, 1968). The prophecy or expectancy that escape is impossible for the dog is fulfilled. The notion of learned helplessness helps to explain where some of the negative prophecies come from in the first place.

Students often feel that they cannot earn an "A" in a particular college course. They feel that they have always been "C" students and cannot earn "As." This may be a version of learned helplessness. Years and years of mild punishment, with no chance of escape from school experiences, can take a great toll. Traditional school practices almost make it mandatory that a large portion of each class receives "Cs" and that some even fail! Asking you to learn how to learn is asking you to see through any small degree of teamed helplessness that may be hindering your progress. If you say, "Oh, these principles can't help me learn," you may be admitting to a little learned helplessness. Later in this chapter we will discuss the development of great talent, which involves, in part, a positive prophecy that is stage-by-stage fulfilled—learned success!

Scheduled Reward. As is evident from your everyday activities, reward does not have to occur for you to learn each thing you do. How many times will you comb your hair "just right" to receive an occasional approving glance, a compliment, or to avoid a negative comment? Once learned, your behavior is maintained with very little actual reinforcement.

Psychologists have put a great deal of effort into studying just these situations involving partial *schedules of reinforcement.* Actually, partial reward may be more effective than 100 percent continuous reward. See Figure 5.11. As you learn about the effects of partial schedules of reinforcement, see if you can discover why superstitious behavior is so persistent.

These interesting patterns of partial reinforcement could take many different forms, but four common schedules have been widely studied. Two of them are schedules based upon the passage of time before a reinforcer is made available, and two of them are based upon the number of responses the animal (or person) makes before a reinforcer is received.

Figure 5.11 Variable Ratio Schedule of Reinforcement

Schedules Based Upon the Passage of Time

Regular Intervals of Time Before a Reinforcer Is Available. Some reinforcers become available according to a regular time schedule. For example, seasons of the year, meals, college exams, the mailcarrier's rounds make available regularly timed rewards. Because of the regularity of reward timing, your behavior need only become active to receive a reward just before the regular available time. If you have a college exam every three weeks, you know you need only study just before the exam to receive the reward of a passing grade. Your behavior in this case is responding to what is usually called a *fixed-interval schedule* of reinforcement. If we graph the amount of study time you put in daily when exams are occurring on a fixed-interval schedule of three weeks, it might appear as shown in Figure 5.12. Descriptively, the effect of little output following reinforcement and a great deal just before reinforcement is available is called *scalloping*. If we place an animal on a fixed-interval schedule of reinforcement, his behavior pattern will show the same sort of scalloping.

Irregular Intervals of Time Before a Reinforcer Is Available. Some reinforcers become available according to an irregular time schedule. Examples include those associated with pop quizzes, a hunter waiting for a deer to come down to a stream for water, and air traffic controllers awaiting an out-of-place "blip" to appear on their radar screens. Let's examine the example of the deer hunter. A deer may appear 10 minutes after the hunter takes her position overlooking the stream or three hours later. The hunter doesn't know when a reward will become available. The only way she can be sure to be able to take advantage of it is to closely observe behaviors. If the hunter takes a nap, even for a few minutes, she may miss her chance. In this situation the hunter's behavior is responding to what is called a *variable-interval schedule* of reinforcement. Here, there are few if any scallops in the behavior pattern. The rate of emitted behavior is very constant as is the rate of response.

Schedules Based Upon the Number of Responses Emitted

Regular Number of Responses Before a Reinforcer Is Delivered. There are many situations in life where a regular and known number of responses will produce a reward. Every child who has shoveled snow from the walkways of neighbors or has mowed lawns during the summer to make extra money has been influenced by how a regular number of responses results in a reward. Each time a walk is shoveled or a lawn mowed the child receives his pay. Piece workers in factories must complete a regular number of items requiring a regular

SCHEDULES OF REINFORCEMENT

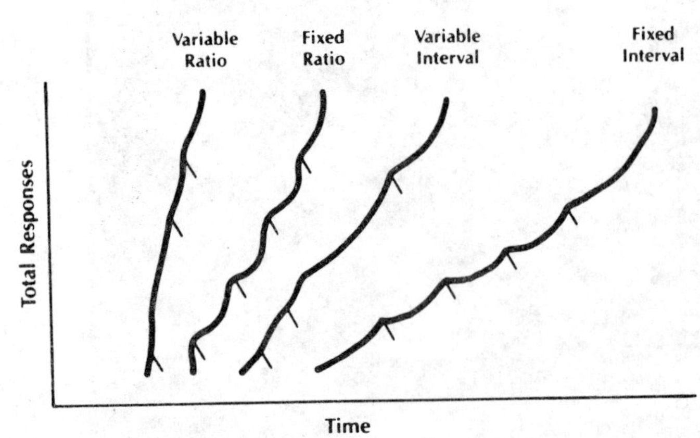

Variable Ratio
Ratio of responses to reinforcements is varied. (Example: Pigeon is reinforced after four responses, eight responses, two responses, 10 responses, etc.) Note the high response rates and lack of pauses produced by this schedule.
Fixed Ratio
Ratio of responses to reinforcements is fixed and regular. (Example: Pigeon is reinforced after every fourth response.) Note the pause after each reinforcement, which is characteristic of fixed-ratio schedules.
Variable Interval
The delivery of reinforcement is contingent upon both passage of time and occurrence of a response, but the length of time is varied rather than fixed. (Example: Pigeon is reinforced after the first response following the passage of one minute, then after the first response following the passage of three minutes, then after the first response following the passage of two minutes, etc.) Leads to very stable and uniform response rates.
Fixed Interval
The delivery of reinforcement is contingent upon both the passage of time and the occurrence of a response. (Example: Pigeon is reinforced after the first response following the passage of one minute, after the first response following the passage of another minute, etc.) The scalloped shape is typical of fixed-interval schedules.

Figure 5.12 Schedules of Reinforcement

number or responses to receive pay. In these instances behavior is influenced by what is called a *fixed-ratio schedule* of reinforcement. A certain number of responses must be made before reinforcement is delivered. Fixed-ratio schedules of reinforcement result in a high rate of response and in very small scallops (you lose money if you rest).

Irregular Number of Responses Before a Reinforcer Is Delivered. There are a very many situations in life where reinforcement depends upon an irregular number of responses. The person or animal is never quite sure how many responses he must make before he will receive a reward. Have you ever played a game of chance? Such games include lotteries, bingo, and slot machines in Las Vegas. These situations present you with what is called a *variable-ratio schedule* of reinforcement. Because you are never quite sure if and when the next response will be rewarded, you produce a very high rate of behavior. This helps explain why people will stand in front of slot machines for hours hoping the next dollar will bring riches. But is this "strictly chance" gambling the only behavior that is influenced by variable-ratio schedules of reward? Actually, the variable-ratio schedule probably influences the most sublime of human behavior. Every inventor, every writer who must make an indeterminant number of responses before receiving a reward is influenced by this schedule of reinforcement. Thomas A. Edison worked long hours, reached many dead ends, but the rewards came—he just never knew when to expect them. From his experience came his famous quote "Genius is 1 percent inspiration and 99 percent perspiration."

Classical and Instrumental Conditioning: A Theoretical Meeting

When we described classical and instrumental (operant) conditioning, we examined different methods of studying the empirical variables of learning. An important question to consider is whether or not these two methodologies constitute two types of learning or is learning simply learning no matter how many methodologies are invented to study it?

There are very helpful ways to think about this problem. An examination of two of them will give us greater insights into learning. In this regard we will examine the learned cortical control of the autonomic nervous system—biofeedback, and the phenomenon of *secondary reinforcement.*

Biofeedback. As you learned in Chapter 2, biofeedback learning can involve the cortical control of the autonomic nervous system. This learned voluntary control of involuntary nervous activity seems to involve classical and instrumental methods in some sort of homogenization of conditioning procedures. Certainly, classical UCS–UCR relations are involved in the control of the ANS. And just as certainly instrumental freely emitted behavior—UCS–CS relations are involved by using cortically emitted approximations (recall the ideas of "coverants," Chapter 4) to acquire some desired final behavior.

In a simplified diagram of a biofeedback learning loop (Figure 5.13), voluntary control has been reduced to the idea of the law of effect. If the result of emitted intention or image is positive (+), it is likely repeated. It is "ON." If the result of an emitted intention or image is negative (feedback goes wrong direction) (–) or zero, it is likely not repeated. It is "OFF." The resultant. efferent innervation of the ANS learning, for example, sympathetic reduction and vasodilatation in the skin, constitutes a reflex or involuntary relationship. Here the two methodological approaches come together on a component basis. If there are actually two types of learning, they can learn to work together very nicely and very quickly. This situation appears to support the findings of Neal E. Miller (1978) that the conditioning methodologies cannot be shown to reveal two underlying types of learning. It is critical to the theoretical aspects of learning separate from the methodological definitions.

Secondary Reinforcement. Most complex human behavior, like earning grades in college or earning money so you can live the life you want, seem to be a matter of instrumental learning. In fact, at the beginning of this chapter you were introduced to some tips on learning how to learn, and these tips involve instrumental learning. It seems fairly obvious that earning grades or earning money is accomplished through trial and error learning. However, there is a small problem with all of this: the grades, the money,

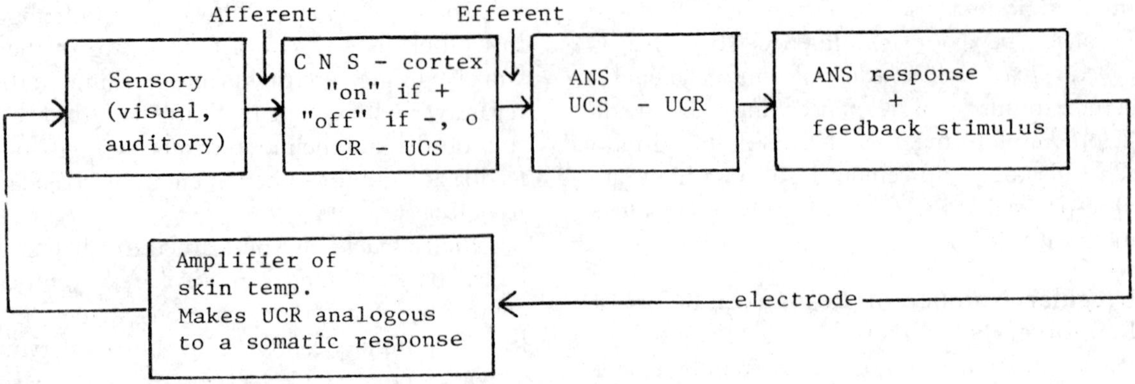

Figure 5.13 Feedback Learning Loop

etc., are not *primary reinforcers* (like food, water, comfort, avoiding pain), they are secondary reinforcers.

Why is it that you will work so hard for a little piece of paper (grades or money)? They have no value of and in themselves. How is it that little pieces of paper gain such powerful control over your behavior and thoughts in the first place? Did you emit certain behavior and as a result receive them?

The most obvious solution to our problem is that these little pieces of paper have become classically conditioned to the primary reinforcers. Just as Pavlov's dogs learned to salivate to a tone (which they could not eat), you have been classically conditioned to work and study for little pieces of paper. Why? Because the little pieces of paper became unconsciously connected with food, comfort, and the avoidance of pain.

Table 5.11 Example of Classical Conditioning

CS ⟶	UCS ⟶	UCR
money	food	hunger relieved

Every time you buy something needed or even think about how your grades are preparing you for a chance at a good job (or are avoiding the pain of a flunking grade), the neutral stimulus (piece of paper) is being paired with a UCS of some kind (primary reinforcer).

So, again we see the two methodologies merging almost inextricably. As you go about your daily learning experiences, CS's, UCS's, UCR's, and CR's are combined in all sorts of marvelous ways and that is learning. The classical and operant methodologies are very convenient ways to help us make sense of this very complex phenomenon.

Toward a Behavioral-Cognitive View of Learning

The classical and operant approaches to the psychology of learning are behavioristic ones. Behaviorism has a long history in the study of learning and has helped us to clearly identify it. However, we must strive to put as much theoretical pressure to bear as possible if we are to achieve a really comprehensive picture of learning—to approach a general systems theory level of understanding. To help us to do this we examine one more level of theoretical complexity in our study of learning. We will now use what you know about learning to help understand a cognitive view of learning—learning through the observation of models—*social learning*.

There are at least two significant ideas which emerge concerning the importance of the phenomena associated with social learning. First, with the heavy attention to movies, television, and highly arousing models, social learning effects take on a critical role in our learning. How do models we observe on television since early childhood affect our adult behavior? We will discuss this issue in some detail in the chapter on social psychology. Second, social learning theory seems to fit well into our general systems view through a continuation of the parallels with evolutionary theory. Philippe Rushton (1982) has proposed that the analogy continues through the concepts of sociobiology. Sociobiology is essentially the idea that much social behavior is innate and has evolved through the survival of useful social patterns of behavior. These would include the general fact and phenomena of social learning. That is, just as evolution (a biological theory) is clearly related to classical and operant learning, so is sociobiology related to social learning. In Chapter 7 on social psychology we will return to sociobiology in some detail.

Social Learning Theory and the Development of Talent

You have learned that the behavioristic methodologies are essentially tied in with the law of effect. These methods focus upon learning that occurs as the result of direct environmental consequences. However, much of what we learn is not learned by "doing" and then receiving immediate consequences. Rather, it is accomplished simply by observing others. If, as a child, you see someone fall out of a tree and get hurt, you learn something. You don't have to climb a tree and then fall from it to see if it also hurts you. You can imagine or anticipate that it hurts. In reinforcement terms the reward is anticipatory. Obviously, models can greatly facilitate our learning. Every day, you may spend a great deal of time at the Student Union (SU) just watching people. You are silently learning a great deal you may later put to use in very subtle ways. A lot of what you learn are subtleties of body language. I can remember when I was a young boy attending my favorite cowboy movies. I would watch every detailed move of the hero. Then at the end of the movie, I would strut out of the theater as if I were the hero. I could almost feel his presence controlling my movements.

Five Phenomena of Social Learning

Observational learning is not just a general cognitive concept. All of the concepts within the behavioristic approach are systematically taken into account in social learning theory, but this does not mean there is point-by-point agreement. Albert Bandura (1977) has described five critical modeling phenomena:

1. Learning Through Observation

   We spend a great deal of time watching other people do things. For example, you might watch someone, either in real life or on television executing a dive. Then at some later time, you execute the same dive. You have learned through observation. Unfortunately, some negative behaviors like cigarette smoking have strong components of observational learning.

2. Learning Creative Patterns of Behavior Through Observation

   You not only observe single individuals executing a certain act, you observe many people doing the same sort of thing and the way they do it may differ greatly from model to model. For example, if you are learning to dance, you probably watch all sorts of interesting styles. Your style may be a completely new style, not just an imitation of one of the several styles you have seen. This process of observing many *heterogeneous models* certainly facilitates the development of innovation in many areas of life.

3. Learning to Inhibit Behavior Through Observation

   If you have learned a certain type of behavior and then see someone else punished for it, that behavior may become inhibited through observation. This often happens when you join a new group, or enlist in the military. Behavior you used to get away with in one group may be punished in others. If you have joined a new team, and the coach screams at one of the players for not executing a move properly, you will not make the same mistake. You will inhibit the errant behavior.

4. Learning to Disinhibit Behavior Through Observation

   This type of observational learning has the opposite effect of learning inhibition through observation. If you ever watched someone get away with something you normally would not do because you're inhibited, and then because they got away with it, you try it, an inhibition has been disinhibited through observation. This type of observational learning can have profound good and bad effects. Very often good creative models (like your speech teacher) can free you from inhibitions to realize your potential for public speaking. On the other hand, during the anarchy of riots, disinhibited looting behavior (watching others get away with it) can become rampant!

5. The Social Diffusion of Innovation Through the Observation of Members of Society at Large

   If all social learning occurred only on an individual basis, important social innovations would spread very, very slowly. Moreover, *homogeneous trends* would be much less likely. Think about our society's great interest in nationwide trends and fashions like jogging and the importance of sound nutrition. These trends spread very quickly through observational learning, and television has accelerated the spread of social innovation. In 1983, people observing the sales of Cabbage Patch Dolls on TV reports pitched this social innovation into an overnight frenzy.

Of course, there are moderating influences on these social learning phenomena. Some of these are the same ones that modify the other learning models we have discussed earlier. Some are unique to social learning theory. These modifying limitations (with biological overtones) include four cognitive processes that are the result of influences on the person in his or her social learning. Obviously, this is quite a different focus from the strictly behavioristic view of learning. The four cognitive processes include *attention, retention, motor reproduction,* and *motivation.*

Four Cognitive Processes of Social Learning

Attention means you must observe a model. If you don't observe you will not learn. There are two important ideas here. First, if a model just happens to be present, there is some likelihood you will observe and learn. Second, different people, because of their unique past learning history, may attend to different aspects of the same model. The retention process refers to the fact that if a model is attended to, there must be a representation of the model's performance in some sort of memory—a picture image, a verbal description, a motor representation, etc. If you observe someone showing you how to use a complicated piece of machinery, but are so fearful that you won't be able to perform when asked, none of the retention processes may have had a chance to form an adequate memory. So, when the person asks you to execute what has been shown to you, you somehow can't seem to pull it off. Motor reproduction means your nervous system must have the component skills to

Figure 5.14 Learning Through Observation

produce the observed behavior. A three-year-old child does not have the component skills in his neurology or his cognitive capacities to imitate someone adequately driving a car. Motivation refers to the fact that even if all of the above processes are adequate for observational learning to occur, reinforcement of some sort is still required. If the person cannot anticipate that imitating the observed behavior will result in either external reward or self-satisfaction he will not learn the observed behavior. Think of all the behavior you observe going on around you each day. For example, you may observe an argument between a male and a female student. You may attend carefully (the guy's a jerk!), you may retain a clear picture of the observed behavior (he said cruel things to his girlfriend in front of others), and you have the component skills to produce or replicate the behavior (you could say the same thing to your girlfriend), BUT, the motivation is missing.

The Learning and Conditioning of Famous People

Recent research at the University of Chicago by Benjamin Bloom (1985) and his colleagues on world-famous concert pianists, Olympic swimmers, tennis players, and research mathematicians is showing that careful attention to learning principles and observational learning are usually the keys to developing talent (often to the level of genius)—not necessarily genetics! Professor Bloom's life of study has led him to conclude that most human beings (98 percent) are born with fantastic potential—a potential of being world famous!

What are the circumstances that tend to produce great talent? Here described by Maya Pines (1982) are the factors Bloom and his colleagues have discovered in studying the development since early childhood of 120 world-famous people.

1. Parents who greatly value and enjoy either music, sports, art or intellectual activity and view it as a natural part of life, so that the child learns its language as easily as he learns to speak.
2. Parents who believe in the work ethic.
3. A first teacher who is warm and loving, who makes the lessons seem like games and lavishes rewards. This teacher need not be highly skilled. For the pianists, it was a neighborhood teacher; for the mathematicians, it was usually their own father. But the instruction must be given on a one-to-one basis, and the parents must take great interest in it.
4. A second teacher who emphasizes skills and self-discipline. Again, the instruction must be individualized. For the mathematicians, the best teacher is one who answers their questions, gives them books to read and lets them work independently.
5. A gradual change in the child and his family as both realize the progress the child has been making. They now begin to focus their resources on the developing talent.
6. Access to what Professor Bloom calls a "master teacher"—one of the rare experts who knows how to train top professionals and open the right doors for them. Some families traveled 2,000 or 3,000 miles to find such a teacher or coach. No sacrifice in time, money or effort seemed too great.

Each of these factors can be seen in the principles of learning, especially that of observational learning. Table 5.12 lists a few, keyed with the number of the conditions above.

It can be seen that Bloom's description of how the individual, his behavior, and the environmental conditions interact to produce the development of human potential. The "evolution" (through successive stages or approximations) of great talent in the individual represents a blend of all we have said about the formation

Table 5.12 An Evolution Through Successive Stages of Final Talent

1. The importance of available models
2. The importance of learning cognitive level motivation
3. The importance of a model and reinforcement
4. The importance of motor reproduction
5. The importance of sustained cognitive motivation
6. The importance of modeling and learning to disinhibit behavior through observation.

of habitual patterns of behavior, instrumental learning, and the undeniable influence of social or observational learnings. Perhaps now you are a little more convinced that you really can learn how to learn, and that most people have the potential to do great things. In Chapter 6 you will study new trends in measurement of ability that are directed toward determining particular areas of highest potential a person has.

Bringing It All Together

In addition to understanding the study of learning psychology, this chapter contains important personal messages for all students. First, your learning performances can, over time, be greatly improved by understanding the principles of learning. The skills (both mental and physical) we achieve are best looked upon as the result of slow evolutionary development through learning processes. Second, much of everyday behavior that we don't think of as "learned," such as liking certain Christmas music, is in fact to a great extent learned. An understanding of learning development will help you help your own children optimize what they can become. We will return to this idea in the chapters on memory, human development, personality, and creativity and intelligence.

Glossary

backward conditioning: In classical conditioning, a procedure where the conditioned stimulus follows the unconditioned stimulus.

classical conditioning: A laboratory procedure for the study of learning that is based upon reflexes or reflex-like behavior. Equivalent terms include Pavlovian conditioning and respondent conditioning.

computer-assisted instruction: The use of computers (usually desktop) to assist the student in having a variety of interactive experiences and feedback in learning tasks.

conditioned response: The response to a conditioned stimulus.

conditioned stimulus: A neutral stimulus that becomes associated with an unconditioned stimulus and thereby comes to elicit a similar response.

conditioning: Laboratory techniques or methods used to study learning processes in organisms. Two broad commonly used methods are the Pavlovian or classical method, and the instrumental or operant method. The term conditioning may also be applied to the learning processes taking place in the organism.

delayed conditioning: In classical conditioning, a variety of procedures where the conditioned stimulus comes on before the unconditioned stimulus and goes off at various other times.

distribute normally: When the frequencies of things or events form a normal distribution.

extinction: The ending of certain members of a species or of a species. Also, the ending or decrease in certain responses following the removal of reinforcement.

fixed-interval schedule: A reward schedule in which a fixed amount of time must pass before a reinforcer becomes available to the organism.

fixed-ratio schedule: A reward schedule in which a fixed number of responses must occur before the organism receives a reinforcer.

heterogeneous models: Observed models who differ in the ways they accomplish a particular task.

higher-order classical conditioning: Once conditioning has taken place, additional neutral stimuli are presented in the absence of the unconditioned stimulus. The additional neutral stimuli come to elicit responses similar to those of the original conditioned stimulus.

homogeneous trends: Social trends that engage many people in the same activities or thinking.

instrumental conditioning: A laboratory procedure for the study of learning that is based upon freely emitted behavior (operants). The consequences determine its degree of recurrence in the original or similar situations. Equivalent term: operant conditioning.

Law of Effect: A generalized statement about the relationship between the consequences of behavior and the reoccurrence of that behavior. Behavior followed by satisfaction will likely be repeated; behavior followed by dissatisfaction will less likely be repeated.

learned helplessness: An expectancy that develops in an organism after it has been subjected to a punishing, inescapable stimulus, disrupting later conditioning aimed at teaching the organism to escape the punishing situation.

learning: Relatively permanent change in behavior potentiality, that occurs as the result of reinforced practice or experience with the environment.

natural selection: In the Theory of Evolution, since organism characteristics form somewhat of a normal distribution, their individual fitnesses to survive and reproduce in the pressures of the environment will vary. Those individuals that are "fit" to the point of reproducing are thus "selected" to become a part of the distribution of the ongoing species.

negative reinforcement: The strengthening of a response by the removal of a thing or event. The thing or event that, when removed, strengthens a response (negative reinforcer).

neutral stimulus: The conditioned stimulus before it has become associated with an unconditioned stimulus.

normal distribution: Many things and events distribute themselves in such a way that extremes are few in frequency. When the frequencies are graphically presented for these distributions they take on a standard bell-shaped appearance.

phobia: An unwarranted anxiety or fear that disrupts a person's normal pattern of behavior in certain situations.

primary reinforcer: A stimulus that will strengthen behavior prior to conditioning or learning.

programmed textbooks: Textbooks which have been organized in such a way that the learner is able to move through the material at his or her own pace. This type of text is prepared so that learning and motivation are enhanced and success virtually ensured.

punishment: The delivery of an unpleasant stimulus upon the occurrence of some particular behavior. The behavior in question decreases in strength.

reflex: An inborn stereotypical response to a particular type of stimulus that occurs in all members of a species.

reinforcement: Any strengthening of a response. The thing or event that strengthens a response (reinforcer).

scalloping: Curves appearing in graphic response records that indicate different rates of responding depending upon the schedule of reinforcement.

scheduled reward: A schedule that indicates when the organism is to be reinforced. The schedule may be in terms of either the passage of time or a required number of responses.

schedules of reinforcement: See scheduled reward.

secondary reinforcement: A stimulus that will strengthen behavior only after it has been associated with a primary reinforcer or unconditioned stimulus.

second-order conditioning: A higher-order conditioning procedure wherein only a second neutral stimulus is added to an established conditioned stimulus.

self-fulfilling prophecy: Behavior that increases the likelihood that an expected behavior will come true. If a student expects he or she will fail an exam, this may result in not attending class or not studying, increasing the likelihood of failure.

serendipity: Discovering one thing while studying another.

shaping (through successive approximations): The guiding of an organism's behavior to perform some final task.

social learning: Learning that occurs through the observation of other organisms.

sociobiology: Theory, methods, and findings concerned with the biological (genetic) basis of social behavior.

spontaneous recovery: The reappearance of a response that has undergone extinction.

stimulus generalization: Once a stimulus elicits a response, similar stimuli will also elicit the response but with less magnitude.

successive approximations: A series of behaviors which are reinforced as an organism is conditioned to perform some final task.

superstitious behavior: Conditioned responses that do not lead to the goal to which the organism is being conditioned.

theory of evolution: The theory that all presently living things developed through a process of selection from other pre-existing species.

unconditioned response: A response that is elicited by a particular stimulus before any conditioning or learning.

unconditioned stimulus: A stimulus that will act as a reinforcement or punishment prior to any conditioning or learning. Usually used in classical conditioning; however, it applies as well to stimuli that reinforce or punish in other conditioning methods.

variable-interval schedule: A reward schedule in which a varying amount of time must pass before a reinforcer becomes available to the organism.

variable-ratio schedule: A reward schedule in which a varying number of responses must occur before the organism receives a reinforcer.

Learning: Doing Psychology on Your Own

LOIS McDERMOTT

Basic Concept #5—Two Types of Learning

Learning is a relatively permanent change in an organism's behavior that results from experience with the environment. Psychologists have described at least four distinct types of learning—habituation, respondent conditioning, operant conditioning and higher order process. Each of these types of learning has been elucidated in terms of how the environment must be structured so that each type of learning takes place. It is currently believed that the evolution of the nervous system of animals has resulted in a capacity for increasingly more complex ways of learning. Species very low on the phylogenetic scale are only capable of habituation learning (the simplest type of learning) whereas the most highly evolved species (human and non-human primates) are capable of all four types of learning.

In this unit we will look at two very interesting types of learning—respondent and operant conditioning. These two types of learning, discovered early in the 20th century have dominated psychological research on learning for most of the 20th century—and have proven to be two of the "biggest ideas" in the psychology of learning. From this **behavioral** research on learning has developed a powerful and entirely new approach to the study of psychology—this approach is known as **Behaviorism.** Prior to the emergence of behaviorism, the study of psychology was dominated by biological and psychodynamic explanations for human behavior. This was all soon to change—the central tenet of behaviorism being that we are what we do and, do what we do because of our environment.

Nobel Laureate. It was some time **after** Ivan Pavlov won a Nobel Prize in Physiology that he discovered the phenomenon that was to make him famous around the world. He had been studying and describing the mammalian digestive system for some years when he grasped the significance of a troubling "side-effect" of his experimental studies with salivating dogs. What he noticed defied one of the central tenets of what physiologists believed to be true of the autonomic nervous system—namely, it was a system that was supposedly innately determined by genetics, inheritance, and evolution. Could it be true that dogs were **learning** to alter the function of this system, a system that was supposed to be **automatic, instinctive and determined?** Pavlov proved it to be so and went on to elucidate the environmental conditions that must be present for such learning to occur.

With the realization that he was witnessing a type of learning which had not previously been recognized, he abandoned his study of digestion and focused his attention, for the remainder of his career, on this intriguing new phenomena, now called **classical conditioning.** It was the widespread application of his basic research to the understanding of a host of human experiences that elevated Pavlov from virtual obscurity in Russia, to the status of icon in Western psychology. His study of **drooling** led to the understanding of phenomena such as phobias, psychosomatic illness, the acquisition of emotions and the ability to control the body's response to stress and disease (e.g., via conditioning of the immune system).

The Idea of the Century. In the year of its first centenary, the American Psychological Association awarded B. F. Skinner the Psychologist of the Century Award. Skinner was not the first behaviorist, nor the last; but the intensity and brilliance of his research, as well as the far flung effects it had on the science of psychology was second to none in the first century of psychology. The research of no single theorist has had the depth and breadth of impact on psychology since Freud. Skinner forced psychology to consider the role of the minute to minute environment in the causation of the behavior of humans.

The theory and research of Skinner threatened the stranglehold that the biological and psychodynamic theorists had on psychology. Rather than humans being ruled by their inheritance or unconscious drives, Skinner held environmental factors to be necessary and sufficient to explain all human behavior. The image of human-as-puppet—having no essential qualities—was forced to the foreground in psychology. Skinner's impact on the social sciences in the 20th century was of the same magnitude as Darwin's on the natural sciences in the 19th. Like Darwin, Skinner was heralded by most as a genius without peer and also reviled by some as the would-be destroyer of human free will.

As the 21st century approaches, the heyday of behaviorism seems on the wane, but like Darwin and Freud, Skinner's legacy has become indelible in our concept of the human psyche. The widespread use of **operant conditioning** in child-rearing (e.g., time-out), the training of new skills (e.g., computer assisted learning), treatment of behavior disorders (e.g., weight reduction) and managerial policies in the workplace (e.g., incentive programs) assures a place for Skinner in history on a par with Darwin and Freud. He has changed our way of thinking about ourselves in a very fundamental way—as products of our ***experience*** and environment.

Unit Focus. This unit will focus on the groundbreaking discoveries of learning by association and learning by consequences. We will go into this material in somewhat more detail than some of the other topics for two reasons. Firstly, the laws of Pavlovian and Skinnerian conditioning are so powerful that they are found throughout most domains of psychology. Virtually every course that focuses on the content of psychology (rather than methods) will make use of these concepts. They are found in such diverse subfields as the study of child development, personality, clinical psychology, abnormal psychology, social behavior, motivation, and industrial psychology. These principles are so fundamental they are somewhat akin to the periodic table in chemistry or the phylogenetic scale in biology.

Secondly, the laws of conditioning arise from an excruciatingly exacting study of behavior—definitions are precisely specified. This precision is central to this science of behavior and gives it its power and elegance. A brief view of these principles usually leads to confusion and misinterpretation of its tenets. Much of the terminology of this field has entered common parlance—unfortunately in imprecise ways. At first pass, because the terminology feels familiar a beginning student is likely to think that it will be easy to learn this material. However, only careful and thorough study, result in sensible interpretations of conditioned behavior.

Study Objectives

1. Distinguish between association, consequence and concept learning.
2. Understand the relation of the elements (CS, UCS, CR, and UCR) of classical conditioning during acquisition, maintenance and extinction.
3. Be able to label the Ss and Rs in an example of classical conditioning.
4. Understand the relation of the elements (Sd, R, S+, S–) of operant conditioning during acquisition, maintenance and extinction.
5. Be able to label the Ss and Rs in examples of operant conditioning.
6. Be able to distinguish among positive punishment, negative punishment, positive reinforcement, negative reinforcement, extinction training.
7. Diagram how classical and operant conditioning and concept learning occur simultaneously in particular situations.

Key Terms

backward conditioning
classical conditioning
computer-assisted instruction
conditioned response
conditioned stimulus
conditioning
delayed conditioning
distribute normally
extinction
fixed-interval schedule
fixed-ratio schedule
heterogeneous models
higher-order classical conditioning
homogeneous trends
instrumental conditioning
Law of Effect
learned helplessness
learning
natural selection
negative reinforcement
neutral stimulus
normal distribution
phobia
primary reinforcer
programmed textbooks
punishment
reflex
reinforcement
scalloping
scheduled reward
schedules of reinforcement
secondary reinforcement
second-order conditioning
self-fulfilling prophecy
serendipity
sociobiology
shaping
social learning
spontaneous recovery
stimulus generalization
successive approximations
superstitious behavior
theory of evolution
unconditioned response
unconditioned stimulus
variable-interval schedule
variable-ratio schedule

Problem Set #5: Learning

A. *Classical Conditioning Examples*

1. The first time your lover kissed you an ad for toilet paper was being broadcast on the TV. Now you find yourself automatically grinning every time you see a roll of toilet paper. Why?

   UCS: UCR: good feeling

   CS: toilet paper CR:

2. A week ago, you witnessed a serious car accident on the Montlake Bridge. Seeing all the blood and gore made you feel nauseous. Today, you feel nauseous as you approach the Montlake Bridge. Why?

   UCS: UCR:

   CS: CR:

3. As a young child, Karms was playing in the yard when the neighbor's dog wandered over to smell the flowers. His mother (who is a nervous, overprotective type) screamed, snatched him abruptly into her arms and ran inside with him. Her behavior scared Karms and he cried out in fear (ANS startle response). Now 20 years later Karms is very uneasy around dogs. Why?

   UCS: UCR:

   CS: CR:

4. Karms decides to seek treatment for his dog phobia from a behavioral psychologist. There are two related treatments that the psychologist could use. The first involves presenting the CS to Karms repeatedly, without the UCS. If over time the strength of the CR diminishes the treatment has been a success.
   a. What is the process called:
   b. Describe the treatment in operational terms
5. Karms is no longer feeling fearful of dogs. However the psychologist wants to continue treatment because she is concerned that the occasional, chance presentation of the CS could result in a return of the symptoms. The second treatment the psychologist uses is designed to associate dogs with calm, pleasant, pleasurable feelings rather than fear or even neutral feelings.
   a. This process is called ______.
   b. Diagram and explain how the psychologist might do this.

B. *Operant Conditioning Paradigms*

Identify the Schedules of Reinforcement

Ask yourself:

Is reinforcement linked to the passage of time (interval) or the amount of performance (effort of the learner)? (ratio)
Is the interval or ratio determined by a number which is constant (fixed) or a number which varies around some average? (variable)

1. Occasionally glancing at the television hoping to observe the beginning of the 6:00 news is likely to be reinforced on a ______ schedule.

   (Does the effort of the learner have any effect on the appearance of the reinforcement?)
2. Periodically checking for the arrival of the evening paper will be reinforced on a ______ schedule.

   (Does the effort of the learner have any effect on the appearance of reinforcement?)
3. Phillip sells magazine subscriptions on the telephone. He is paid $5 for every subscription he sells. His calling is reinforced on a ______ schedule.

   (Does the effort of the learner have any effect on the appearance of reinforcement?)
4. Bill sells subscriptions on the phone also. He is paid $1.00 for every five calls he makes. His calling is being reinforced on a ______ schedule.

   (Does the effort of the learner have any effect on the appearance of reinforcement?)
5. Shihfen is learning to play tennis. At first her coach praises her each time she hits the ball; then he praises her each time she returns the serve over the net; finally he praises her only when the return is within bounds.
   a. This process is called ______.
   b. If the coach praises her every time the ball is hit correctly, he would be using ______ reinforcement.
   c. The schedule of reinforcement is called ______.

d. If the coach praises her more or less after every 10th correct hit, the coach is using _______ reinforcement and the schedule is called _______.

e. If the coach praises her about 10 times during the course of an hour's lesson, the schedule of reinforcement is called _______.

Identify the Type of Operant Conditioning

An organism performs a target behavior. This behavior is followed by a consequence (a stimulus with the potential to change (increase or decrease) the occurrence of the behavior in the future). Answer each of the four questions about each of the following scenarios (#1–16) (use the chart in the lecture outline as an aid).

a. Identify the *target behavior:* (i.e., the behavior which changed.)

b. Identify the *direction of change:* increased (or maintained)? or decreased?

c. Identify the *agent of change* (i.e., the consequence): the presentation of a positive stimulus; the presentation of a negative stimulus; removal or termination of a negative stimulus; prevention of loss of positive stimulus; loss of a positive stimulus

d. Identify the *process of operant conditioning* which has influenced the learner's behavior: pos. Rf? neg. Rf? pos. Pun? neg. Pun?

1. The more often Matthew is scolded following a temper tantrum, the more frequently he loses his temper. In this case, the scolding serves as a _______ for Matthew's temper tantrums.

   a.

   b.

   c.

   d.

2. Matthew's father has stopped taking his son to the playground because he feels embarrassed by Matthew's temper tantrums. In this case the tantrums served as a _______ for Matthew's dad.
3. Judge Hays reviews the parole file of a 21-year-old drug dealer, Jim, whose record already includes seven prior convictions and incarcerations as a juvenile and one prior jail sentence as an adult. This record of offenses which has been increasing in frequency and severity convinces the judge, who took Psych 101, that jail time serves to _______ Jim's drug offenses.
4. Julie finds that drinking alcohol in the early evening relieves her stress of the work day. Her drinking is increasing in frequency and quantity.
5. I turn a book in late to the library. They charge me $5.00. If my tardiness with books decreases in the future and I never turn a book in late again, the fine is serving as _______ for being late. If I always turn books in on time in the future, preventing the fine is serving as a _______ for being on time.
6. An electric bill arrives in the mail. I pay the bill promptly. Paying the bill on time prevents a "late charge"—this process is called _______. Paying the bill guarantees continuation of my electric service—this process is called _______.
7. I noticed that attendance at class decreases following a difficult exam and increases after an easy exam. It would seem that difficult exams are a form of _______ with regard to class attendance.
8. Jan and Jay are newlyweds. Jan is a mediocre cook while Jay is a great cook. Every time it is Jan's turn to cook Jay comes to the kitchen to "help." Jan's cooking is steadily getting worse. Jay's "helpfulness" is serving as a _______ for Jan's cooking.
9. Jay notices he is spending increasingly more time in the kitchen in order to avoid having to eat Jan's poor cooking. Jan's poor cooking is serving as a _______ for Jay's cooking.
10. June and Joe are special friends but they notice that they seem to be having more and more arguments about seemingly senseless stuff. After taking Psych 101 it occurs to them that perhaps this increase in fights is due to the fact that every time they have an argument they kiss and make up(out). What operant process would explain this increase in fights?

11. Hank is with a bunch of friends in the cafeteria. He is eating his salad and spaghetti with his hands and wiping his face on his sleeve. His friend Joe says, "Yuck, you geek, you are disgusting"; his friend Ralph leaves the table. Hank stops eating with his hands. What different but related processes are Joe and Ralph using to shape Hank's behavior?
12. Ralph returns with a fork and napkin and gives them to Hank and says kindly, "Here at the UW we are proud of our good table manners." Henceforth Hank eats with his fork while enjoying the company of Ralph and Joe. What process is involved in this change in etiquette?
13. Sue and Linda are roommates. Sue is a real slob; Linda is nagging and uptight. Typically, Linda arrives home around 5:00 P.M. As soon as Sue hears the sound of the elevator signaling Linda's arrival, Sue begins racing around the living room collecting cigarette butts, apple cores, dirty Kleenex, and empty soda cans. Linda arrives home to a reasonably tidy apartment and does not nag. Sue's frantic cleaning is being maintained by:
14. Occasionally Sue fails to hear the elevator and doesn't bulldoze the mess soon enough. Linda comes in and begins her diatribe about "godliness and cleanliness." The next day the living room is as neat as a pin when Linda arrives home. Linda's nagging is being maintained by:
15. Sue ditches Linda and moves in with Frank who is a more easygoing type who notices and compliments every little attempt that Sue makes to be orderly—no matter how small. Soon Sue has become a neatness freak and Frank looks like the slob. What process has changed Sue's behavior?
16. Jack wants to quit smoking. He decides to take up knitting as a way to calm his nerves as well as to keep his hands busy. Jack decides to use his cigarette money to buy yarn. Every time Jack has the urge to smoke he picks up his knitting. Jack asks his friends to compliment him every time they see him knitting. Jack knits 12 scarves and quits smoking. What operant principle is illustrated in this story?

C. Classical or Operant Conditioning

Questions 1–14: (see Tables 5.4 through 5.9 and Figures 5.5 through 5.10) indicate whether the statement pertains to classical or operant conditioning.

1. Behavior is an ANS response.
2. Behavior operates on the environment to produce a consequence.
3. Extinction: the association between stimuli is broken.
4. Extinction: the contingency between an R and S is broken.
5. Behavior is an overt action involving skeletal muscles.
6. Playing the piano.
7. Feeling frightened.
8. Discriminative stimulus alerts the learner to perform the behavior.
9. CS is a warning of the occurrence of the UCS.
10. Skinner.
11. Post Traumatic Stress Disorder.
12. Respondent conditioning
13. Counter-conditioning
14. DRO training

See Appendix C for answers to problem set.

6

Cognition: Memory, Human Development, Creativity, Intelligence

Mnemonic Techniques

At the beginning of the last chapter, techniques were described that could help you improve your learning. Now, in this chapter on cognition we will describe techniques that will help you improve your memory. Just as most traditional subjects in school are not developed with ease of learning in mind, they are not developed with ease of remembering them in mind either. In addition, you have probably never been shown how to use your memory properly. Your memory, just like any other ability you have—artistic, musical, mathematical, athletic, etc.—can be trained to improve. One basic method is the mnemonic technique.

Mnemonic techniques have actually been used for thousands of years. Frances Yates (1966) tells us that the Greeks and Romans had developed seemingly amazing memory strategies. The following is a quote from her book on the history of mnemonics, *The Art of Memory.*

> The Elder Pliny, whose son attended Quintilian's school of rhetoric, brings together a little anthology of memory stories in his *Natural History.* Cyrus knew the names of all of the men in his army; Lusius Scipio, the names of all the Roman people; Cineas repeated the names of all the senators; Mithridates of Pontus knew the languages of all the twenty-two peoples of his domains; the Greek Charmadas knew the contents of all the volumes of a library. (p. 41)

Finally Pliny states that the art of memory "was invented by Simonides Melicus and perfected (consummata) by Metrodorus of Scepsis who could repeat what he had heard in the very same words."

These feats may sound outrageously amazing but the point is that mnemonic techniques are not a fad, and with them a great deal is possible.

The way in which most people, including most college students, try to remember things is by the *rote memory technique.* The rote technique is just a matter of going over and over information to be remembered until it just sort of "clicks in" and you say, "I think I've got it memorized." In Table 6.1 rote techniques are compared with mnemonic techniques.

Eight Mnemonic Principles of Memory

Principles of good memory techniques can be used to get you from the rote techniques to the mnemonic techniques. If you understand and follow these principles, you will become a better student.

The following principles have been derived from many sources. Some are psychologists like Laird Cermack (1975) and Douglas Griffith (1979), others are memory experts like Harry Lorayne (1957) and Arthur Bornstein (1979), and others historians like Frances Yates (1966).

1. In order to remember well you must imagine how the information you are trying to remember will be later recalled. That is, you must use preplanned retrieval cues.
2. Rehearsing of information alone is not necessarily related to your later ability to recall it.
3. Long-term remembering (perhaps for a lifetime) is best accomplished through your visual imagination.
4. The recoding of meaningless or abstract information into meaningful concrete networks greatly improves the memory of that information.
5. Elaboration of information, so that visual imagination can link the information to retrieval cues (coding), helps long-term remembering best when you use your personal imagination.
6. Moderate emotional arousal helps your memory best.
7. Memory strategies themselves must be learned. The roles of reward, immediate feedback, and the breaking of materials down into meaningful steps apply to learning memory strategies, just as they apply to learning anything else.
8. Good mnemonic techniques are not magic any more or any less than is art, music, or athletic skills, although they all may seem to be magic once accomplished.

Now, let's apply these principles to some concrete examples so that you can begin to use them on this chapter. You will find that you can apply them to virtually anything for which your memory can be used.

Table 6.1 Comparison of Memory Techniques

ROTE TECHNIQUE	*MNEMONIC TECHNIQUES*
A	
Typical approach used by most college students.	Memory strategies used by top students (they read a memory improvement book, took a memory course, or simply stumbled onto some good strategies).
B	
When used to prepare for exams, student is never sure what has been learned and remembered until after the exam.	When used to prepare for exams, the student "knows" what he knows, and knows what he does not know.
C	
Instructors expect students to use this method and load exams with difficult factual material that will separate student scores.	Mnemonic techniques make short work of factual information. If everyone used mnemonic techniques, exams would contain much more conceptual challenges.
D	
Most of the factual information material is forgotten shortly after the exam. In fact, students often don't remember what they "put" on the exam.	Material may be remembered for the rest of the student's life. Students walk out of an exam knowing exactly how they did.

Principle 1: Imagining How the Information Will Be Reviewed Ahead of Time. My wife is constantly amazed that I go to the grocery store, purchase as many things as we need (often 30 or 40 items) with no list at all. What's my secret? Principle 1. Rather than try to remember the long list at random, I simply notice where the desired item is needed—refrigerator, bathroom cupboard, the kitchen table, a plate (of food) because I know what we are having for dinner. These are my cues for later retrieval. This technique is called the *method of loci.* In this method a series of locations is used to form visual images for the items to be remembered.

If, for example, you wanted to remember the parts of a speech, you could use the rooms of your own home, or parts of the campus, or even parts of the human body (whichever makes the most sense to you) as visual retrieval cues for each part of the speech. Just put them into some sort of reasonable order ahead of time. This way you will not find yourself suddenly puzzled by what is supposed to come next or by inadvertently leaving out an important part of your speech.

A commonly used method of loci (places) is called the *pegword technique.* In this preplanned strategy pegwords replace rooms, refrigerators, etc. This strategy allows you to peg new information onto a series of visually imaginative words you have already taken a little trouble to memorize. In Table 6.2 Griffith (1979) provides an example of the pegword strategy. Now, let's say you wished to remember the list of five items at the right of the numerical pegwords. All you need do is form a visual image that links the loci to the new list. In Table 6.3 are Griffith's examples.

You may find that the method of loci is "clicking" very well with Griffith's example above. The biggest reason for this is that you are probably attempting to "see" them. If you "see" in your mind the examples, you will be amazed at what will happen to your memory.

Table 6.2 Pegword Technique

PEGWORD	*THINGS TO BE REMEMBERED*
1. is a bun	1. helicopter
2. is a shoe	2. rifle
3. is a tree	3. jeep
4. is a door	4. desk
5. is a hive	5. house

Table 6.3 Visual Images of Items to be Remembered

One might imagine:

1. a helicopter wrapped in a bun
2. a rifle stuck in a shoe
3. a jeep up in a tree
4. a desk blocking a door
5. a house underneath a beehive

Principle 2: Rehearsing (the Rote Technique) May Not Help Memory Much. How many times have you gone over and over something, trying to remember it? It doesn't make any sense, but after a while things seem to get hammered into memory. For example, you may want to remember telephone numbers, addresses, dates, etc. It's often like slowly stamping these numbers into wax. Finally, the impression is clear and you can "see" it in your mind. But this method is terribly hit-and-miss, especially miss! Try not to use this technique.

Principle 3: Visual Imagination Helps You Remember Things for Years. Names, not faces, are forgotten over the years. Faces are meaningful visual images by their very nature. This illustrates the long-term memory power of good visual imagery. And, think of how helpful it would be if you could get all information to be as visually meaningful as are faces! Don't worry about overloading your visual memory capacity. It seems to be able to take whatever you wish to give it.

Principle 4: If Something Doesn't Seem to Want to Go into Memory as It Is, Recode It so that It Takes on Meaning to You. The principles we have discussed so far have all involved *recoding.* Recoding, put simply, is turning information into something visually meaningful. Put your hand over the far right column in Figure 6.1. How would you code the Chinese ideographs into your memory? Rote memorization of the meanings of these symbols would be difficult. But now remove your hand and see how recoding immediately helps.

	Meanings	Mnemonic Cues
日	Sun	Visualize the sun coming through the window
月	Moon	Visualize a ladder to the moon
火	Fire	Visualize a man running from fire
水	Water	Visualize a cockeyed spider thirsty for water

Figure 6.1 Recoding of Information

Principle 5: Coding or the Elaboration of Information Is Best When You Use Your Own Visual Examples. In the example of recoding Chinese ideographs coding images were supplied for you. This will work fairly well, but if you want the information to stay with you for a long time, it is best to make up your own coding. I make it a point to learn all of my students' names. The first time I tried I could think of only a couple of coding techniques. I'd ask myself, does the student "look" like their name, or is there some unusual feature about the student's face or hair? With experience, I soon invented all sorts of images. For example, a student named Doug Boteler (boat a leer) comes to mind. He looked very French to me. So, I simply imagined him filling thousands of wine bottles (a wine boataleer). It's been three years now, I can still see him filling wine bottles! Learn to rely on your own personal visual imagination.

Principle 6: Moderate Emotional Arousal Helps Remembering Best. I am sure you have seen people get up to give a well-prepared speech, get a good case of stage fright, and make shambles of it. Another example is the problem of not being able to use your storehouse of wit, information, or ideas in an argumentative discussion. Afterwards, when you have calmed down, you find yourself saying "Why didn't I say that?" It is hard to find the student who doesn't become a little too apprehensive at exam times. The use of mnemonic techniques will help lower your apprehension.

Principle 7: Memory Techniques Must Be Learned—You Can't Do Them Just by Knowing About Them. As I have said of my own experiences with learning mnemonic techniques, they require effort and they develop over time. I can recall my own amazement at how my learning was going after struggling with 180 student names each term for a year, and then walking into a summer-session class of only 21 students. As usual, I told the students I was working on learning mnemonics and to bear with me while I took a few minutes to learn each of their names. I read through the list of names, briefly looking at each face and conjuring up an appropriate image. I then stopped and looked over the whole class to see if I had any weak spots. I could not believe what I saw! Each person's name was like my own. A year before, learning 21 names, for me, in less than five minutes would have been impossible!

As time has gone by I have noticed that I remember things in general much better than ever before—even though I don't intentionally try to use a mnemonic at the time. Perhaps for me the coding of information has become, to some degree, unconscious—as do other learned skills like riding a bicycle, playing a piano, or reading.

Principle 8: Mnemonic Techniques Are Not "Magic." People who see performances of great *mnemonists* often get the idea that a few memory "tricks" might allow them to do the same thing. This is not true. It is unfortunate that the phrase "memory tricks" is used at all. Mnemonic techniques are not tricks any more than artistic, musical, or even magic performances are tricks. Mnemonics are skills that enhance memory just as the learning of tunes enhances musical ability.

Toward a Philosophy of Memory

There are at least two distinct parts of the philosophy of memory: (1) How should we think about the relationship between learning and memory?, and (2) How should we think about the fact that memories don't seem to be perfect?

The Relationship Between Learning and Memory

Learning and memory are very much interrelated. When we ask a child to learn the alphabet, he essentially memorizes it. So, did he learn it or did he memorize it? We could think about the child applying learning principles from the beginning of Chapter 5, or we could equally think about him applying some of the memory principles from the beginning of this chapter. The definition of learning involves relatively permanent changes in behavior, the definition of memory involves relatively permanent changes in your storehouse of experience. So learning of the alphabet and memory of the alphabet have a lot in common. The relationship grows even closer when we realize that the only way we can tell if anything has been learned is through some sort of memory system. In other words, if we took your memory away, we also would be taking away any possibility of knowing if you ever did learn anything. At this point it almost sounds as if learning and memory are the same thing.

A Matter of Emphasis. What is the relationship between learning and memory inside the brain? If we watch the activities at the synapses, the sprouting of dendrites, and the patterns of neuronal activity, what would learning and memory look like? While they would not appear the same, whenever one is going on, the other is also occurring. While learning is taking place, there would be more neural activity in dialogue with the external world. While memory is occurring, there would be more internal dialogue within the brain. In learning, the processing emphasis is upon interacting with the environment in the acquisition of behavior. In memory, on the other hand, the emphasis is upon the processes of retention of behavior capacities. Learning and memory are totally interrelated processes.

Evolution has provided the nervous systems of all animals with the capacities to acquire, store, and retrieve an ongoing relationship with the environment. For the psychologist, it is a matter of emphasizing either the more external dialogue with the environment (learning), or the more internal dialogue (memory) related to retention of and retrieval of information (the study of memory). Figure 6.2 compares learning and memory to a videotape recorder system. Learning is like taping the information, memory like storage and retrieval.

Are Memories Perfect?

The seeming permanence sometimes and impermanence at other times of memory is an interesting phenomenon. There is a great deal of controversy about the very nature of memory. Are all memories really perfectly recorded in the brain forever? Is that the basis for our storehouse of experience? Or, is memory a constant processing and updating of past experience, and is that the basis for our storehouse of experience?

There is some evidence that memories are permanently recorded in the brain in detail. Wilder Penfield, in his *The Permanent Record of the Stream of Consciousness* (1955), has reported that he has been able to elicit totally

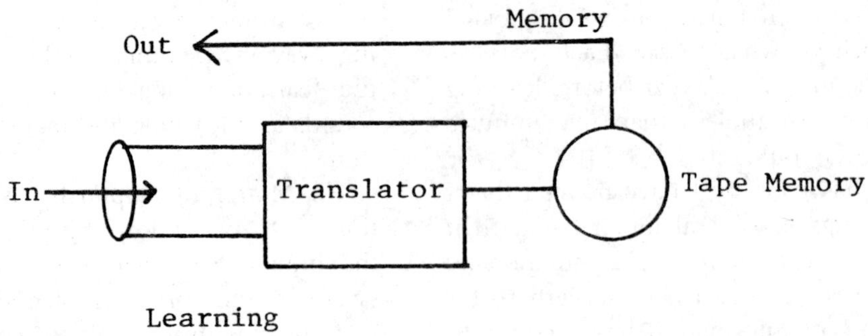

Figure 6.2 Comparison of Memory and Learning

intact memories from patients via direct electrical stimulation of the exposed brain. Patients would recall experiences that seemed to be from earlier times in their lives.

On the other hand, Elizabeth Loftus (1980) has critically evaluated Penfield's reports. First, she points out that a *permanent record* occurred in only a small portion of the patients. Second, there seems to be no way to be sure whether the reported experiences were actually memories or simply elicited experiences. In her studies Loftus has emphasized the *reconstruction processes* of memory, just as when passing on a rumor you reconstruct the parts you can't really remember. In other words, according to Loftus, vague memories seem to be strongly influenced by a make-it-up-as-you-go-along principle.

Loftus's criticisms of Penfield's reports, of course, do not deny the possibility of permanent memories. Reconstruction processes may occur simply as the result of retrieval difficulties (see *control processes*), and not because a permanent record does not exist. Penfield's approach may have bypassed any possible retrieval difficulties by directly stimulating the permanent record in memory. The idea of permanent memories has some support from everyday experience. How is it that we sometimes dream of past experiences in very complete detail—things which we have totally forgotten about? How is it that we can recognize faces after not seeing them for 50 years—just from a photograph?

For the time being we should probably accept both the idea of a permanent record and the reality of reconstructive processes. The two ways of thinking about memory can live side-by-side. The fading of memories from immediate awareness when not needed is an efficient balancing of what is and what is not important to survival from moment to moment. Aleksandr R. Luria (1976) described a man who had phenomenal memory for great strings of numbers and letters and so on, but the poor man could not keep it in the background. It intruded in his conversation so badly that he was often incoherent.

Theories of Memory: Theories of Remembering and Theories of Forgetting

Theories of memory really need two types of explanation: remembering and forgetting. What are some of the explanations for this phenomenon?

Remembering: Information Theory of Memory

In information theory, the flow of cognitively controlled processes of memory attempts to show how memories are acquired, stored, and retrieved. The cognitively controlled processes are essentially what you do about the retention of information. The flow diagram shown in Figure 6.3 is a modified version of one proposed by Shiffrin and Atkinson (1969). It best illustrates a general version of how information might be processed in memory.

Without the influence of control processes (you), it is impossible to say what would end up in memory—if anything. Here the computer analogy to information flow is especially pertinent. What would end up in a computer's memory without control processes? You will see shortly that the control processes include the use of mnemonic techniques.

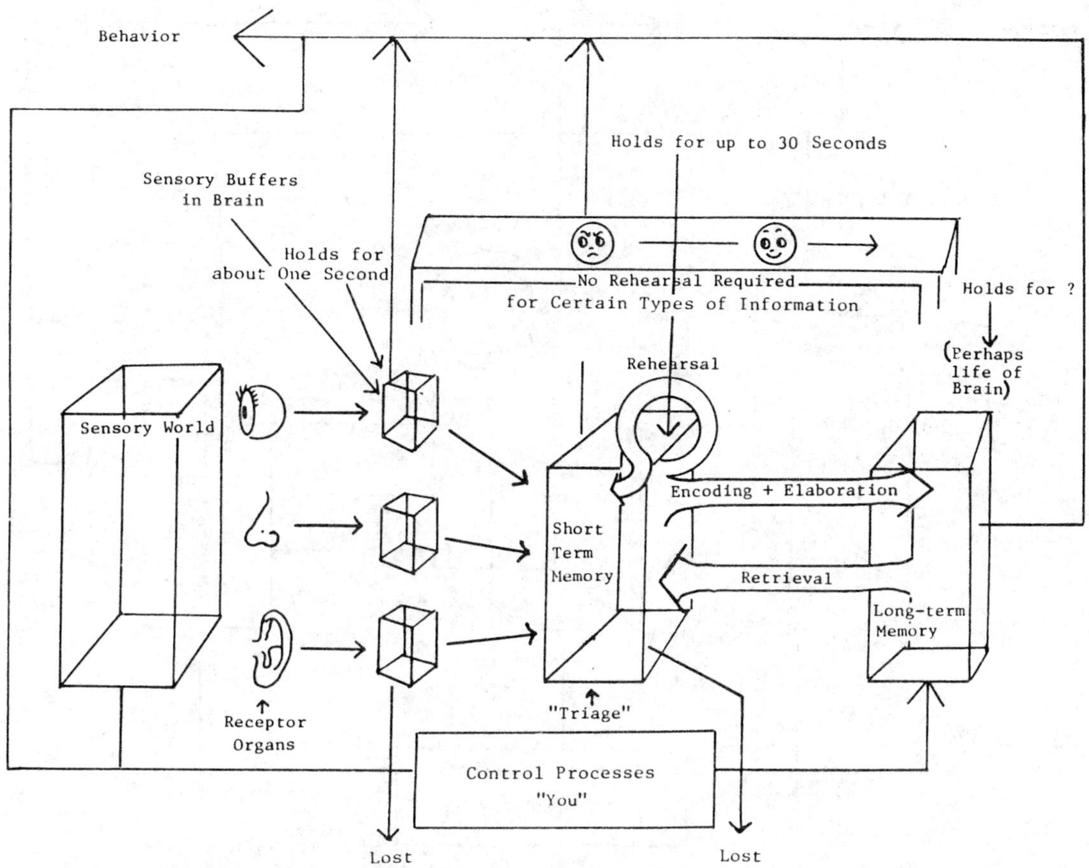

Figure 6.3 Processing of Information in Memory

Stimuli entering the sensory channels in the diagram would actually consist of all of the sensory channels listed in the summary Table 3.8 in Chapter 3. In the *sensory brain buffers,* information seems to hold just long enough to get the focus of your attention. If it does not get immediate attention, it is permanently lost. If it gets our attention, arousal processes will keep holding the information in *short-term memory* automatically for up to about 30 seconds. If further rehearsal of the information, encoding, or elaboration of the information occurs, it is held longer in short-term memory or transferred to *long-term memory,* or both. At the same time information is flowing out of long-term memory status back to short-term working memory. This retrieval process involves information about what's in long-term storage. At any point in this process, behavior using any of these forms of information can be expressed. The control processes (you) determine the extent, contents, and details of the flow of information.

Let me take you through a living example of the flow of information described in Figure 6.3. Right now as you read this page, your central nervous system is processing information depicted in Figure 6.4 continuously. As the individual words reach the sensory buffers in the brain, they are held only a fraction of a second. You're probably reading at a rate of about five words a second. Depending on your reading style (part of control processes), not all of the "a's," "the's," "that's," will make it to short-term memory. They are not that important. Although depending on the context, this information is likely to go via the direct line to long-term memory. Why? Some "a's" are very important to control processes. For example, a horse can mean something very different from the horse, depending on the context.

Though some information might be lost at the sensory buffer level, when you get to the next sentence there must be some information still in the flow that will help make it logical. So certain words, because you focused upon them, continue

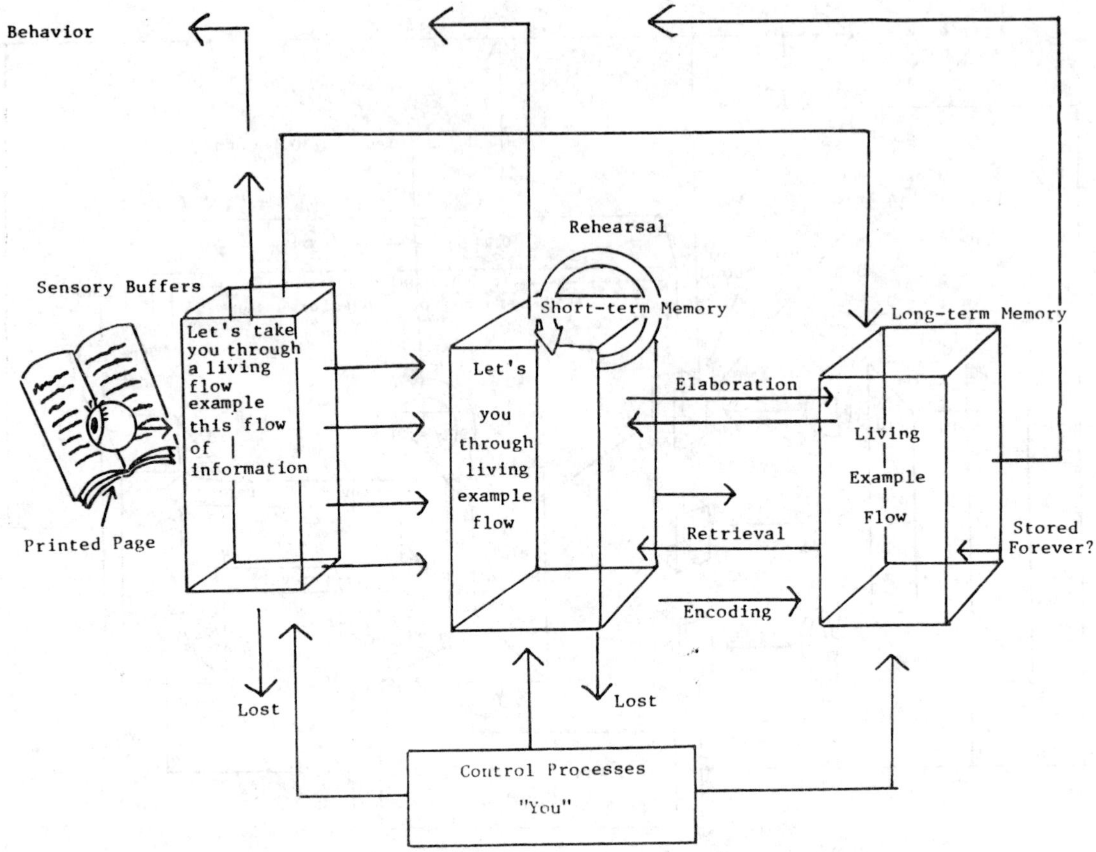

Figure 6.4 A Living Example of the Information Theory of Memory Processing

on to short-term storage. Now some of the information left in the system from the original sentence will hold for about one to about 30 seconds (see the short-term storage box above). This will help you piece together the overall meaning of this paragraph. Notice that the various control processes are responsible for what's lost at the sensory buffers, how long any bit of information stays in short-term memory, what must be pulled out of long-term storage and into short-term working to help in your understanding.

As you read, and look back and forth at the diagrams, control processes are controlling the encoding and elaboration processes—putting the meaning of the living example of memory into your long-term memory. If you go back over this sequence of memory events or any part of them, that is rehearsing. Rehearsing keeps the short-term memory information alive until it gets property encoded or elaborated into long-term storage. How long this goes on is up to the control processes.

Now, let's see how much of the above example was lost or poorly encoded in your system under the guidance of your control processes. Keep your eyes on these sentences. What page are you on (probably lost at your sensory buffers, control processes didn't focus on it)? Can you recall any of the foregoing sentences? Or were they lost at the sensory buffers and short-term memory? What do you recall of the living example described above? Whatever you can recall is new long-term memory. Is it permanent? That's a matter for the control processes quality of retrieval strategies—my mnemonic techniques that directly assist in the encoding and elaboration processes.

Mnemonic Techniques and the Structuring of Long-Term Memory

Our understanding of how information might be structured in long-term memory can help us understand why mnemonic techniques are so powerful in the hands of controlled processing (you).

Endel Tulving (1972, 1985) has proposed that long-term memory is organized or structured in three different ways. First, think about what you did on your first date. The memory for this type of personal experience or episode is coded in space and time in your long-term memory. It is called *episodic memory*. Figure 6.5 illustrates how the memory of an episode might be structured in long-term memory.

But not everything you have in long-term memory started as a personal episode. Think about all of the information you have about the world in general. For example, you know about nature with its animals and plants, and about arithmetic with its numbers and operations. This part of your memory is not structured in terms of episodes (space/time), but in terms of what things mean, and is called *semantic memory*. Figure 6.5 shows how episodic and semantic memory structures differ and how they might be related. Tulving's third type of memory is called *procedural memory*. Procedural memory refers to an organism's (or a machine's) ability to retain stimulus/response information that allows it to interact in complex ways with the environment. The P2 autonomous robot described at the beginning of Chapter 2 has the procedural form of memory.

The organization of long-term memory and mnemonic techniques are notable for their prestructuring of retrieval strategies. Both episodic and semantic structures help in the encoding and elaboration on new long-term memory information. Mnemonic techniques seem to provide artificial structures for long-term memory which are partially "empty." That is, control processes can use these artificial structures for any purpose at hand. It doesn't have to be related to the rest of long-term memory. And these structures can be used over and over again for hundreds of different purposes. Figure 6.6 is a speculative drawing of what the pegword mnemonic technique structure might look like. Such structure could contain both semantic and episodic elements.

Are mnemonic technique structures more episodic or semantic? Tulving has described the three systems of memory as forming a single hierarchy. Procedural memory is the most simple, with the more complex semantic memory developing out of it. Finally the most complex episodic memory develops out of the semantic memory. Tulving feels that episodic memory includes personal awareness and the highest degrees of personal knowledge and control. Therefore, episodic memory would seem most important in the development of mnemonic techniques. (Also see control processes, p. 295, and metamemory, p. 305.)

The Limiting Short-Term Memory

Do we really have short-term and long-term memories rather than just a single overall memory with varying degrees of retrieval difficulty? It does appear that your short-term working memory is distinct from your long-term memory.

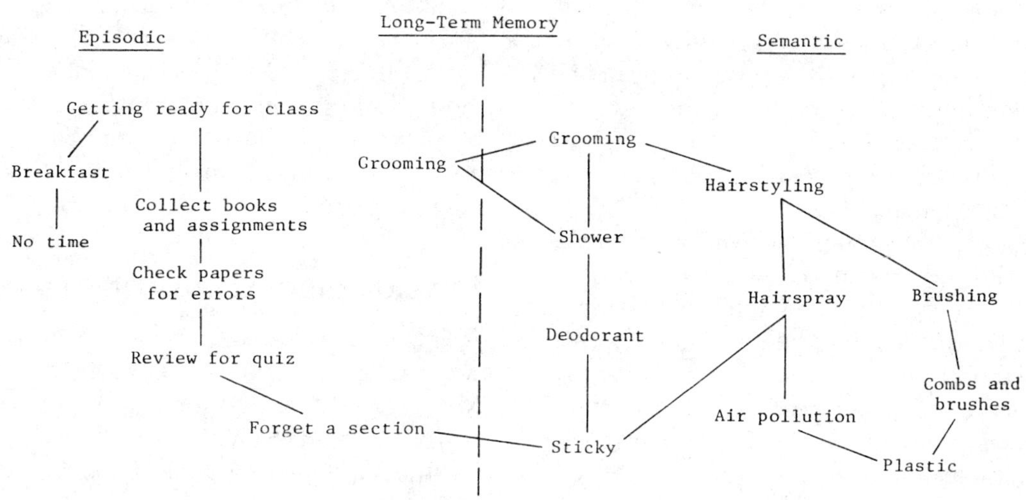

Figure 6.5 Comparison of Semantic and Episodic Memories

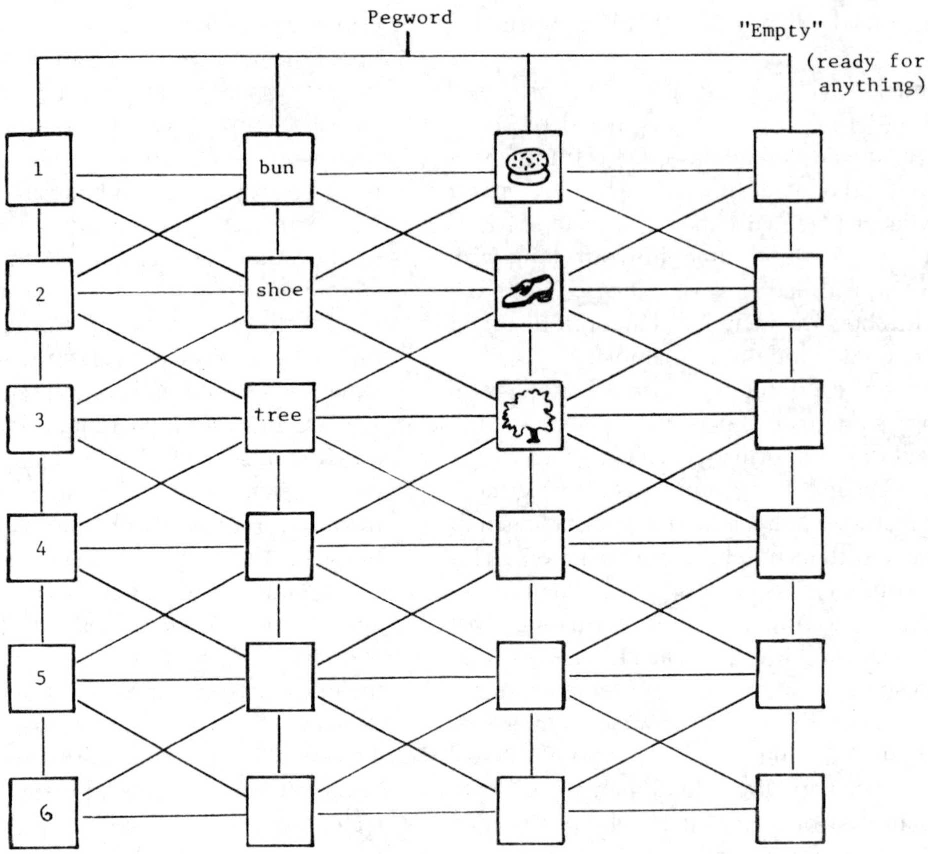

Figure 6.6 Structure of a Pegword Mnemonic Technique

Patients who have suffered certain damage to the brain may lose the ability to form or retrieve new long-term memory, but have excellent short-term memory. For example, when talking to one of these people in the present (short-term memory) everything seems fine. But, if you leave the room for a short time, he or she will not recognize you upon your return! Whether this is actually a cognitive control problem or a long-term memory problem is not known. However, it does illustrate that short-term and long-term memory are not simply a matter of difficulty of retrieval.

The capacity of short-term memory can easily be shown by having you attempt to remember a string of meaningless numbers because, if you're typical, you have little chance to encode and elaborate them. Of course, if you have had memory training, the encoding and elaboration processes would quickly put the numbers into long-term memory.

But there is an important aspect of the limiting short-term memory. Two common expressions we all hear during discussions are: (1) "Let me say this, before I forget it" and (2) after being disrupted by a waiter taking your order, several people at the table may say, "Now what were we talking about?" (and often nobody does remember what was being said, which leads to the conclusion, "Oh well, it mustn't have been important").

The important point is that unless your day is structured somehow, the limits of short-term memory can guide you through a day of pretty much doing nothing. How might mnemonic techniques help you with this common problem?

Physiological Theory of Memory

A little earlier we discussed the question of whether or not memories might be permanent. Recall Penfield's (1955) point of view of a permanent record. This proposed permanent record illustrates a physiological theory of memory and suggests that memories are somehow fixed in the biochemistry of the nervous system.

Penfield also found that a part of physiological memory has to do with how we interpret present experiences. This means that not only do memory processes deal with past experiences and past feelings, but they tell us that a memory is a memory rather than a present experience, and whether a memory is an older one or a relatively new one!

Have you ever had a sense of déjà vu (the feeling that you've already experienced what you see unfolding in the present)? Is this a mysterious phenomenon? No. It's just a memory processing error. Penfield elaborates:

> As an example of interpretive responses, take again the case of M. M. When the electrode was applied to another area of the temporal lobe it produced a sudden sense of familiarity which she referred at once to her present experience. She felt the operation had happened before and that she even knew what the surgeon was about to do. This occurred independently of any recollection of the past.
>
> When such interpretations have been described by temporal lobe epileptics, clinicians have long called them déjà vu phenomena. They are disturbances of the present process of interpretation. (Penfield, p. 60)

Since Penfield has doubtlessly shown some sort of memory is recorded in the physiology of the brain, do we know what might be the bases of these traces or *engrams* of memory? How does the brain record whatever it does record?

Essentially there are three theories of storage of information in the brain. First, the chemical holding of species genetic memory is known to be coded in *deoxyribonucleic acid (DNA)*. Notice that we can refer to a genetic memory as carried by alleles, genes, and chromosomes, because it is a long-term holding of information concerning the designs of an organism (see Chapter 9). The control processes required for this memory to be brought into a working state are beginning to be understood.

Second, the control processes related to DNA are capable of directing the manufacture of *ribonucleic acid (RNA)*. RNA itself is capable of control processes related to the development of cell functions—a holding of information. RNA is then thought by many to be at the bottom of memory processes in the individual (Davis & Squire, 1994). This situation gives rise to the idea that RNA can help memory form, and even more importantly, the idea that once the coding is formed it might be transferred in some instances from one organism to another (McConnell & Shelby, 1970). Information is regularly transferred from one organism to another via DNA—from any parent organism to its offspring. It directs the overall growth processes in the new organism, including a new brain that comes equipped with all sorts of reflexes and extremely subtle equilibration processes.

But is there really any evidence that RNA coding can transfer directly from one organism to another carrying information? There are very strong proponents of the idea that RNA is vitally involved in memory, and these in certain cases are transferable. In experiments, McConnell and Shelby (1970) attempted in a number of ways to discover whether RNA structurally coded in simple flat worms. While nothing final could be concluded from these particular studies, they have led to investigations that will eventually likely determine the actual chemical coding of memory in the brain. Recently, Georges Chapouthier (1983) has reviewed the status of these studies. He concludes that while RNA is a constant correlate of memory and learning activities in the brain, the exact coding relationship remains unknown.

Third, Penfield's permanent memory record may also be coded in synaptic (between neurons) patterns of operation that come about through learning. You will recall from Chapter 2 that recent studies have shown that learning produces changes in the synaptic organization of the brain. Nakaakira Tsukahara (1981) has provided a sweeping description of how the brain might learn and remember.

> Axonal sprouting and formation of new synapses, including changes with much longer duration, are now accepted as widespread phenomena in the central nervous system. . . . These phenomena may provide a morphological basis for recovery of function after brain damage, and more generally, of learning and memory in normal animals. Network plasticity, such as reverberatory activities of populations of neurons, may constitute a neuronal basis for short-term memory storage. (p. 372)

Metamemory Theory

Metamemory concerns the cognitive control processes of the information theory approach. This is essentially how you as a controller enter into the memory processes. Metamemory is a very broad idea of conscious aspects of these control processes.

John H. Flavell and H. M. Wellman (1977) have described three general sources of knowledge which lead to control processes that are unique to you: (1) When you say something like "I'd better write your address down, or I'll forget it," it means you know something about the practical capacity of your own short-term memory; (2) If you say, "Gee, it's strange, I can remember all of the state capitals, and all of the U.S. presidents, but I have trouble with the names of people I meet," it means that you know about the fact that some memory tasks are harder for you than are others; (3) If you have developed or learned little strategies that help you remember, like "Every other month, starting with January, has 31 days—except that the long, hot months of July and August both have 31," it means you know about memory strategies. Together, these types of knowledge about memory constitute metamemory. Metamemory has much in common with episodic memory discussed earlier.

The more metamemory knowledge a person has, the better will be his control processing of memory. While most metamemory operates in a more or less automatic and implicit fashion, it doesn't have to. Metamemory strategies of control can be explicit, like mnemonic techniques and their principles.

Flavell and Wellman's idea of metamemory is a part of a larger concept they call *metacognition*. Metacognition concerns the monitoring and regulation of all cognitive functions. The development of the control of control processes can include both learning and memory. The eight principles of learning that were described at the beginning of Chapter 5 are now a part of your own control of your learning processes—your metacognition. Flavell and Wellman see in the future the possibility of the meta activities of teaching general universal learning and memory approaches that would apply to all sorts of situations.

Theories of Forgetting

In the information processing and the physiological theories of memory there is an emphasis on the durability of memories. Once information has been coded into long-term memory, it might be there for good. And, metamemory processes might help ensure a very high capability of retrieval. But, still, we do forget information.

Decay Theory. When you look at a bright light, then look away, the image of the light persists in your eye for a few moments. This image, or eye memory, decays from existence very quickly—and it is gone forever as chemicals in the eye quickly reestablish themselves. *Decay theory* is the view that a similar thing happens throughout memory.

In the sensory buffers of the brain information from the outside world holds only for a fraction of a second or so and if not focused upon by control processes disappears forever. It decays out of the system. Like the eye, the brain sensory buffers experience a great turnover of information and, therefore, must use their chemical energies for more immediate information and must chemically release the unimportant.

Information that was focused upon goes on to short-term memory. Processing determines whether rehearsal or coding elaboration will occur. If either of them do, the information will likely go on to long-term memory; if not, it disappears or decays out of the system. Figure 6.7 is a diagram of the now familiar information theory flow. Notice in this diagram I have only included the memory decay or forgetting possibilities as were just described. The decay idea is a function of time alone in its effect on biochemical states in the brain.

Decay seems to be a rather common information-related phenomenon in the nervous system. We can certainly see the necessity of decay processes in the pre-long-term aspects of holding information. The whole process reminds us of a small version of the survival of the fittest—the fittest information. But what happens after control processes have put information into long-term memory? Does it decay over time? The idea of decay is an inviting explanation for forgetting—of even long-term memory. However, decay alone certainly does not explain how some very old memories can seem permanent to

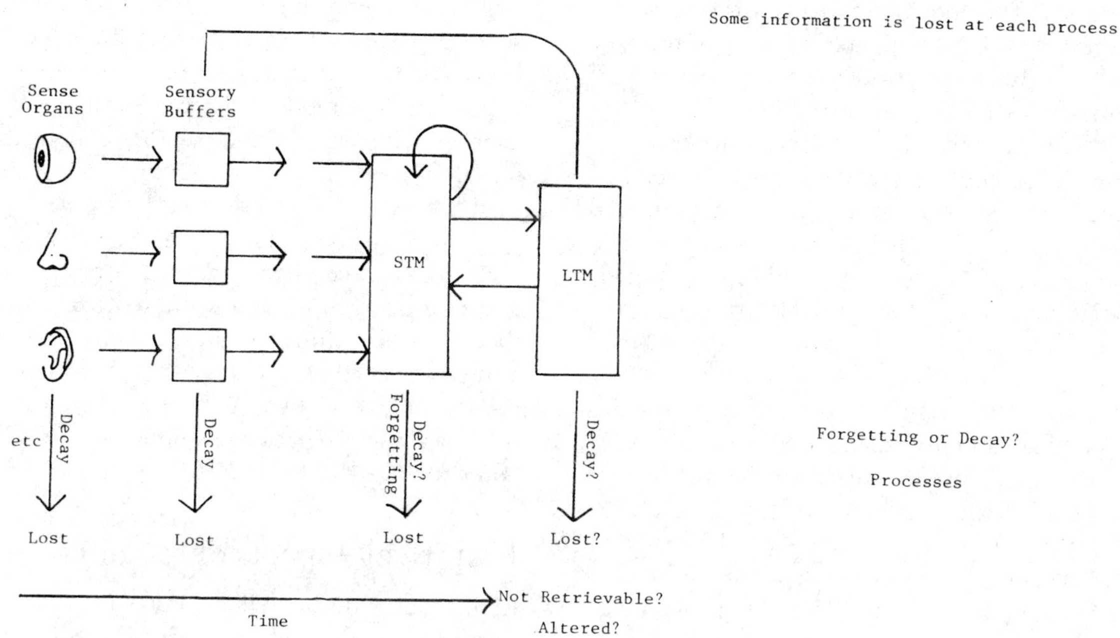

Figure 6.7 Information Theory Flow

us. It remains an open question as to how decay processes are involved in forgetting of long-term memory—if at all.

Reverse Decay Problem—Consolidation Theory. In the decay explanation of forgetting, a decay of existing biochemical impressions or synaptic patterns is suggested. It appears that a reverse of this storage problem actually does occur. It seems to take time for the long-term biochemical impressions to "fix" or consolidate in long-term storage. I like to think about this as being analogous to the time required for a camera film to be exposed. Photos can be made in a camera obscura made from a shoe box. To expose standard film with such a crude camera, the exposure time for a clear photo must last about 8 seconds! Less exposure times (consolidation of image time) result in fuzzier and fuzzier and finally meaningless photos. This is the essential idea in the *consolidation theory* of memory.

How do we know that it takes time for memories to consolidate in long-term memory? It seems that any sudden disruption while information is in short-term memory will cause an immediate loss of that information. *Retrograde amnesia* is a prime example of what happens when the consolidation process is stopped. A good bump on the head might cause total amnesia for experiences just preceding the injury. The bump on the head is a little like putting your hand over the pinhole opening (a sudden disruption) of the shoe box camera after only 2 or 3 seconds—not enough time for the image to consolidate on the film.

Consolidation theory is a very sound explanation of how we forget and of retrograde amnesia in certain situations. However, it doesn't necessarily support the reverse process of decaying of long-term memory. We might say that while exposure time is important for the memory to consolidate, once the picture does form properly, it could be quite resistant to decay.

Interference Theory of Forgetting. *Interference theory* of forgetting is based upon observations that certain experiences can interfere with the memory of others. Recently, I lived in England for a year while teaching psychology at Leeds Polytechnic. Early in the year I had to learn and remember how to drive on the left hand side of the road with the steering wheel on the right hand side of the car. In other words, the driving situation in England was just the reverse of the situation in the United States. I had a hard time of it! What I had learned in the U.S. about driving, interfered with what I was having to remember in

England. The prior U. S. driving was blocking or inhibiting the learning and memory of the new way of driving. Psychologists call this sort of interference *proactive inhibition* (blocking).

Another type of interference can occur, not prior to something new you want to remember, but afterwards. I am sure you have experienced the problem of studying for an exam and then hoping it gets started before other things interfere with your memory of what you studied. It seems like the best thing to do is study, and then go directly to your exam—don't let anything interfere. The kind of interference you fear in this type of situation is called *retroactive inhibition* or blocking because the effects of the interference go back in time to inhibit things learned earlier.

When I was in graduate school I had to take comprehensive exams three days in a row, starting at 8 A.M. each day. To avoid any effects of retroactive interference with my memory, I would study my outlines from about 5 to 10 P.M. each night, go to sleep, get up and go take the exams for the day. The sleep period should have stopped most interference from retroactively blocking my memory.

Does sleeping before an exam really work? Yes it does! John G. Jenkins and Karl M. Dallenbach (1924) studied the effects of sleep on forgetting. They found, indeed, recall of information after sleep was far superior to recall after wakefulness. And the difference was not just a little! In Figure 6.8 the amounts of recall after sleep and after wakefulness are shown. Please note that recall within 1 hour of wakefulness was worse than after eight hours of sleep!

This study by Jenkins and Dallenbach show that interference theory goes a long way in explaining forgetting. It also shows that a decay theory of forgetting might be fairly limited. Tonight, study this psychology chapter on memory for an hour or two. As soon as you awaken, use your metacognition to note exactly what you remember having studied.

Empirical Aspects of Memory

In the light of the great flexibility of the power of control processes of memory, much of the empirical findings concerning memory might be looked upon as tentative. It is difficult to predict, for example, what the empirical findings of memory studies would show if all subjects were highly in mnemonic techniques (mnemonists) rather than leaving the whole matter of metamemory uncontrolled. With this

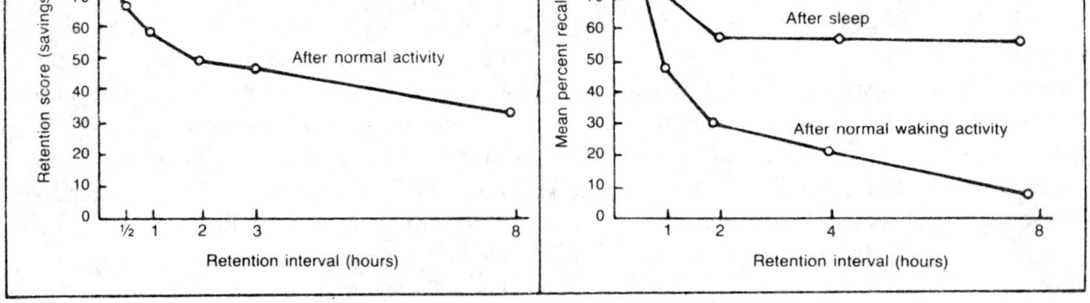

The interference theory of forgetting. Left-hand panel (A) shows data taken from *Minimi and Dallenbach (1946)* who compared retention of an avoidance task over an 8-hour period for cockroaches either allowed normal activity or physically immobilized for similar retention intervals. Right-hand panel (B) shows data based on *Jenkins and Dallenbach (1924)* who measured retention of CVCs for college students over an 8-hour period of either sleep or noral waking activity.

Figure 6.8 Interference Theory of Forgetting

qualification in mind, let's look at some of the characteristics of the "natural" memory.

The problem of the effects of one's control processes on the performance of memory was clearly recognized in the first important scientific studies of memory. Hermann Ebbinghaus, who published his now classic forgetting curve in 1885, knew that meaningfulness for whatever materials he used for his studies would influence how the information was handled by control processes although he did not know of this terminology. His own control processes were those in question—he studied his own memory. So, he devised meaningless words to be used in the study of memory. These were generally three-letter, consonant-vowel-consonant arrangements like TAZ, MUN, WOK, etc. The empirical forgetting curve shown in Figure 6.9 is the result of his work with these "nonsense syllables."

Does forgetting actually occur this fast? According to this curve, after just 19 minutes 42 percent of what was learned is forgotten. I suppose if you go through life memorizing nonsense, forgetting would occur this fast. But, you don't. Ebbinghaus' forgetting curve does not (by design) take into account any flexibility of control processes. And these, including metamemory and mnemonic techniques, are integral parts of your memory system. The steep forgetting curve does not represent a true picture of forgetting (except with nonsense). However, we probably can say that if you're going to forget, even when using mnemonic techniques, it is most likely to occur very soon after being committed to memory.

An example of both of these points is demonstrated in the findings of a study by Bahrick, Bahrick, and Willinger (1975). They examined the process of forgetting of meaningful material over a period of as long as 48 years! Subjects who had graduated from high school between 3 months and 48 years earlier had their memories studied. Their ages ranged from 17 to 74. They were to identify the names and faces of people with whom they had graduated. The results are shown in Figure 6.10. None of these curves looks like Ebbinghaus' overall curve, nor is anyone near 80 percent of the information forgotten within 48 hours, as is the case in the Ebbinghaus curve. One similarity is the sudden drop in the curve, but the percentages lost to forgetting are extremely small.

What are we to make of this disparity between the curves? Is one right and the other wrong? No, we simply must realize that memory consists of many systems (Tulving, 1985). This is the whole point of mnemonic technique training. Standing, Conezio, and Haber (1970) pro-

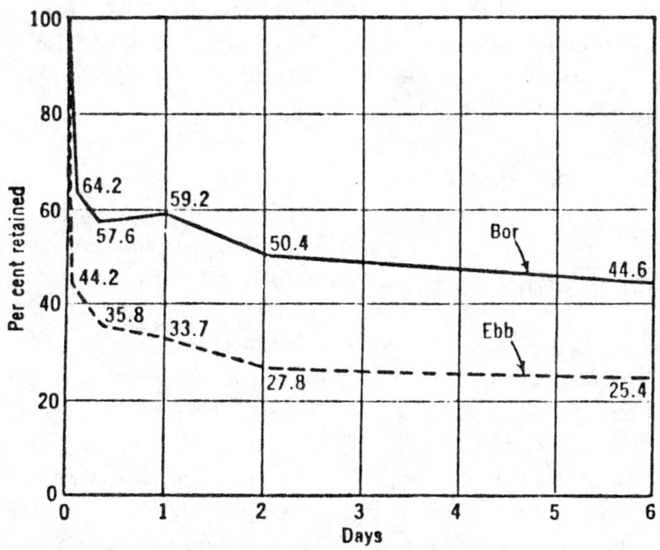

The dotted line represents Ebbinghaus' (1885) classic forgetting curve. This curve was based upon the performance of one subject, 40 years of age. The solid curve (Boreas, 1930) is based upon 20 college students, and is of the same general form as the Ebbinghaus curve.

Figure 6.9 Ebbinghaus Forgetting Curve

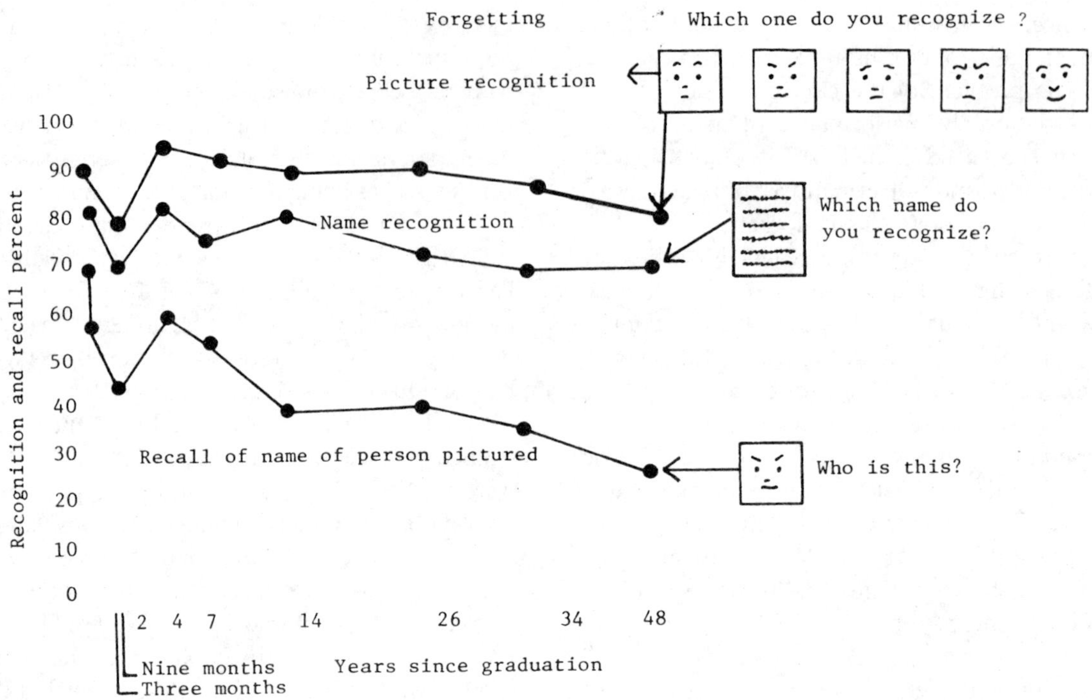

Memory for classmates after retention intervals ranging from three months to forty-eight years. As usual, recognition is better than recall. (Data from Bahrick, Bahrick, and Willinger, 1975)

Figure 6.10 Forgetting Curves After a Long Period of Time

duced a forgetting curve using 2,560 magazine picture recognitions that looks very little like Ebbinghaus' curve. They showed the pictures at 5 and 10 second intervals and found that subjects would then recognize about 95 percent of them on a later test. Recognition memory for pictures is obviously extremely powerful! This is why so many memory training experts tell their students to use visual techniques and to see what it is they are trying to commit to memory.

Forgetting Curves When Using Mnemonic Techniques

The method of loci technique requires you to use visual imagery to help reduce forgetting. Lowell D. Groninger (1971) has experimentally shown the power of this technique after only a few minutes of training. Groninger asked subjects to memorize 25 high imagery words in order. High imagery words are easy to picture like "banana" or "skeleton." Paivio, Yuille, and Madigan (1968) have rated 925 nouns along these lines. The experimental group was very briefly instructed to think up a series of 25 locations (loci) that suited them and could easily be ordered in the subjects' minds. They were then instructed in the method of loci, and told to use their 25 places to remember the 25 word list. The control subjects on the other hand were simply told to memorize the 25 word list in order in whatever way they wished.

Groninger then measured forgetting of the list after one week, and then after five weeks. Figure 6.11 shows what was found. The use of the method of loci dramatically changed the forgetting rate. Also, the students who used the method of loci took less time to memorize the list in the first place.

Some might argue that at least Ebbingbaus studied memory objectively and in its pure form by using syllables. But, this is not actually true. Meaningfulness and the power of imagery are integral parts of memory processing. The evolution of memory processes in the human brain has put visual memory and learned control processes in important and fundamental memory roles.

The Serial Position Effect. If I asked you to write down what you remember about the first day of your psychology class, and then a day or so

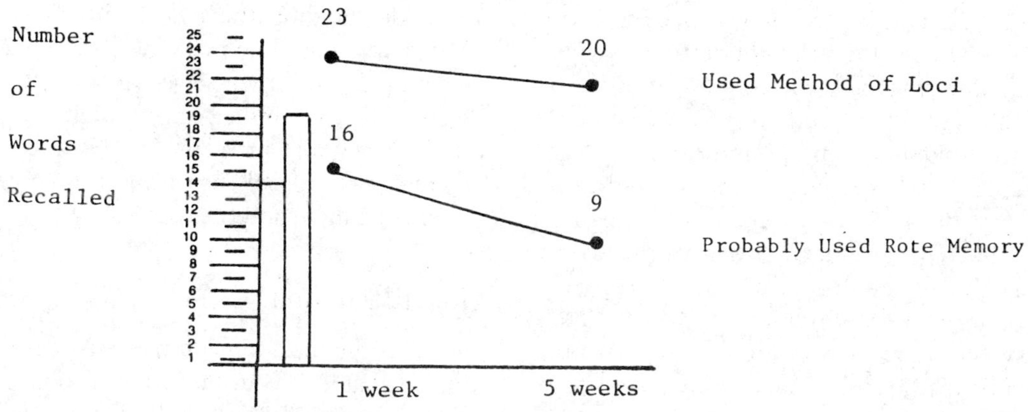

Figure 6.11 Groninger Forgetting Curve

Table 6.4 Serial Position Effect on College Lecture

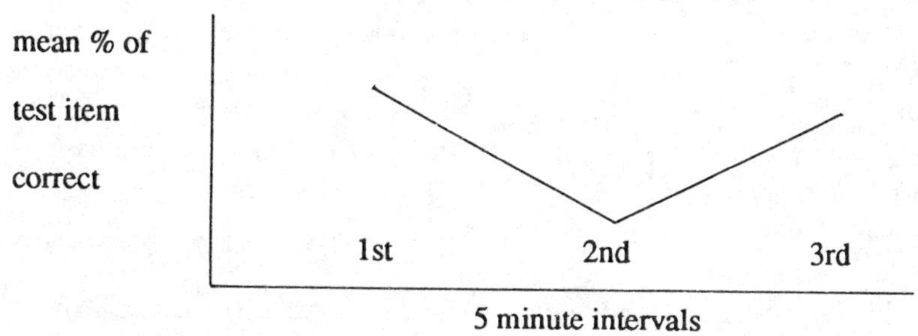

1st 5 minutes = 67%

2nd 5 minutes = 56%

3rd 5 minutes = 64%

ago in class, you could probably write down all sorts of things for both occasions. But, what if I asked you to recall what you were doing in this class, say, two or three weeks ago? You'd probably go blank for any particular day in between the earliest days of class and the most recent ones.

This effect of an experience's position on memory occurs in almost any situation. If you meet five people at a party, all things being equal, you'll remember the first person's name and the last person's name best. Everything in between gets rather fuzzy. This phenomenon is called the *serial position effect*.

Important to you is the fact that the serial position effect on memory is at work in every college lecture you attend. Michael Holen and Thomas R. Oaster (1967) have found that even memories of lectures are greatly affected by the serial position of information in the lectures. Forgetting of information is greatest during the middle of the lecture. You might think that the reason for this is that by the middle of the lecture you might be getting bored, and that's why so much is forgotten. This is not the case. The lecture used in this study, with highly attentive students, lasted only 15 minutes!

Serial position forgetting of things in the middle of anything is a phenomenon of memory. However, mnemonic techniques can help reduce the serial position effect. Next time you go to the grocery store, work on those things that you thought of in the middle of your mental list. They're the ones you're likely to forget.

The Yerkes-Dodson Law. There are two times when you are likely to fail—when you are not trying very hard, and when you try too hard.

Let's say you have a speech to give in class. If you don't prepare well, you might embarrass yourself by confusing the sections or forgetting some of it. On the other hand, you might be really well prepared, but your "A" in the course might be riding on this speech—this also could cause you to perform poorly. It certainly seems that you're likely to produce a low performance by being either under- or over-motivated. Thus, the best performance will result when you are moderately motivated. Psychologists call this phenomenon the *Yerkes-Dodson Law* (Winton 1987). Figure 6.12 illustrates this commonly found relationship between level of performance and level of motivation/emotion.

Methods of Studying Memory

General Methods

Earlier we examined the results of the study by Bahrick and his colleagues that involved memory for high school classmates for up to 48 years. Three different forgetting curves resulted from using three different methods of recalling what is in memory. This illustrated that different methods of studying memory can produce greatly different results. Therefore, choice of retrieval method when studying memory, *recall, recognition,* or *re-learning,* is extremely important in understanding the true nature of memory. The point should be made here that mnemonic techniques are themselves memory retrieval methods that produce a very high measure of what is actually in memory. The three fundamental methods of measuring the contents of memory can be described as follows.

Recall Method

Recall is the most difficult method of remembering at what is in your memory because you must produce an item from your memory itself. The power of your own elaboration and uncoding is what is measured here. If you were asked to make a list of everything your psychology instructor discussed in class yesterday, normally you couldn't until you searched your memory for something familiar. You might start by saying, "What *did* we do in class yesterday?" and hope that something pops into mind. This is the reason that recall of names in Figure 6.10 were poorest.

Recognition Method

Recognition is the easiest method of tapping what is in memory. In recognition, most of the work of retrieval is done for you. You only have to determine whether or not a match occurs between something outside your

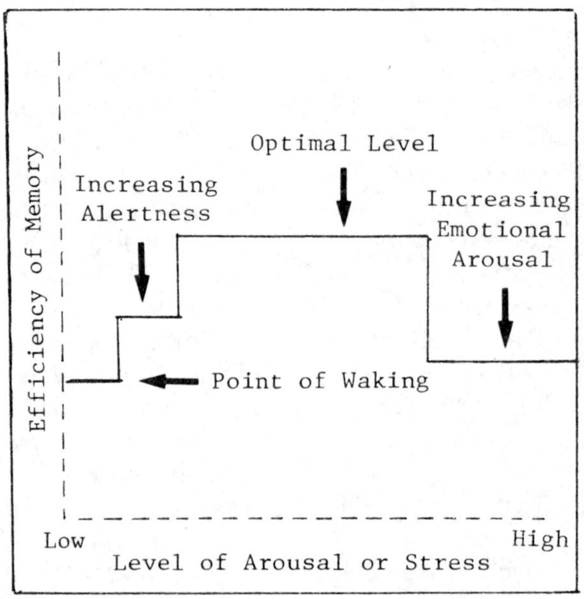

Figure 6.12 Yerkes-Dodson Law

brain and something already in it. Psychologists don't yet know the exact nature of this matching process. However, it might have something to do with the automatic interpretive aspects of memory. We discussed these earlier in regard to Penfield's notion of a permanent record. In Figure 6.10 you can see that recognition of pictures was very high even after 48 years.

Relearning or Savings Method

The method of savings is a measure of just how much time you save in relearning a task. It is therefore a method of measuring what is in your memory. Suppose your friend took 10 hours to learn a list of, say, 100 French vocabulary words, and later, thought he had forgotten them. If it took him 5 hours to relearn them, the measure of retention would indicate a 50 percent savings. There is a formula we can use for determining a savings score. For our example it would appear as in Figure 6.13.

The savings method gets at what is in memory better than recall, but not as well as recognition. C.W. Luh (1922) has illustrated how these three methods compare in getting at the memory of the same task. Figure 6.14 shows that when you think you have forgotten something, the relearning method will show that you really have not forgotten it.

$$\text{SAVINGS} = \frac{\text{(Original learning time (or trials)} - \text{Relearning)}}{\text{Original Learning Time}} \times 100$$

$$\text{SAVINGS} = \frac{\text{10hrs} - \text{5hrs}}{\text{10 hrs}} \times 100 \quad \text{SAVINGS} = 50\%$$

Figure 6.13 Formula for Time Saved in Relearning

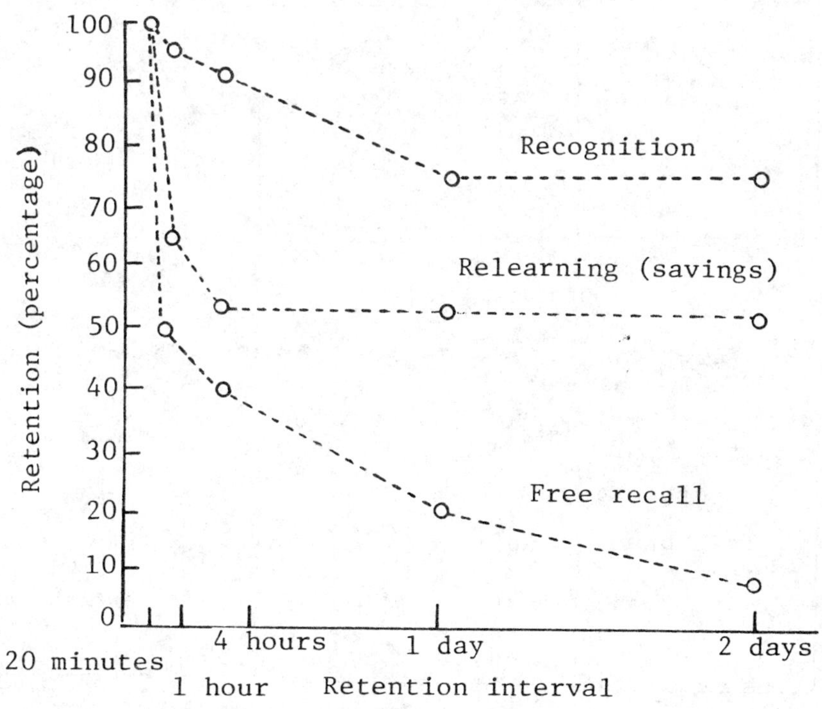

Figure 6.14 Luh's Comparison of Methods of Retention

Methods of Studying Interference

In the theoretical section we discussed the interference theory of forgetting. Recall the ideas of proactive inhibition or blocking (driving in U.S. interfered with driving in England), and of retroactive inhibition or blocking (I slept after studying to prevent interference from inhibiting my memory after study). In this section we will describe the methods by which these kinds of interference can be experimentally studied.

Proactive Inhibition

My experience with driving in England was really half of the method used to study proactive inhibiting effects on memory. In Figure 6.15a are illustrated the stages of the half of this experiment which actually took place with me as an experimental group subject. To make this into the classic design for an actual proactive inhibition study, we need only add a control group (Figure 6.15b).

Obviously, we would expect the control group subjects to make fewer errors in remembering how to drive, which side of the road to stay on, which way to look for the rear-view mirror, etc. And they would make fewer errors. There would be no prior reversed driving experience to proactively interfere with driving in England.

Although this method is usually confined to a laboratory setting, there is no reason why we could not use the above example to scientifically show proactive interference effects. Tests for recall could be traffic sign meanings or recognition of traffic signs. They would all likely show proactive blocking effects for the experimental group subjects.

Retroactive Inhibition

While Jenkins and Dallenbach (1924) have demonstrated the value of sleeping after studying to prevent retroactive interfering with memory of what you have studied, there are more direct methods of showing these effects.

In the case of retroactive inhibition, my personal example of studying and then sleeping put me in the *control group* for this experimental

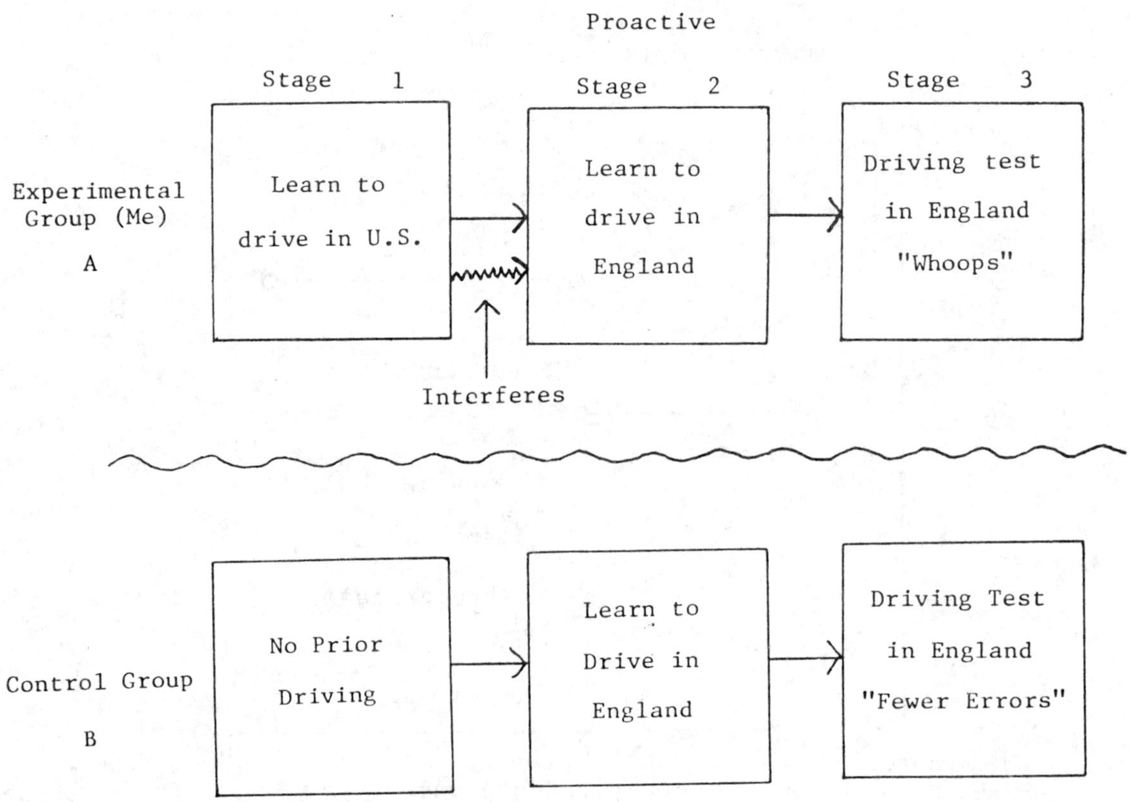

Figure 6.15 Proactive Inhibition

design. That is, where I did actually suffer from the effects of proactive interference in England, I did not suffer from retroactive inhibition in taking my exams. Now, we would need only add an experimental group who would experience the retroactive blocking. Obviously, again, the control group will do less forgetting—this time on the exam.

This experiment could actually be carried out in a laboratory setting, but as with the proactive inhibition method example, that's not really necessary. As I have illustrated these interference effects take place in or out of the researcher's laboratory.

Human Development: Levels of Developmental Thought

By the time you reach early adulthood your cognitive intellectual development has reached an advanced level. Jean Piaget (1952), has referred to this level, or stage of intellectual development as *formal thought* because people at this level tend to use formal or abstract rules to explain things. Unlike younger children, you are able to go beyond what is actually present and to think about and to understand what is possible. For example, Barbel Inhelder and Jean Piaget (1958) conducted one experiment in which children of different ages were asked to balance a scale (see Figure 6.16). Weights could be hooked at various places on the scale arms. Most very young children could not do this at all. For example, one four-year-old simply put two weights on one side of the fulcrum, but didn't seem to notice that the distance from the center was critically important in balancing the scale. By the age of 10 the children could move the weight around to produce a number of combinations that balanced. But this could only be done on a trial-and-error basis. Finally, around the age of 14, some of the children grasped a formal law or rule which would tell them in advance whether or not certain weights would balance. That is, given certain weights at various distances from the fulcrum, they could predict whether or not a balance would be achieved without actually trying it. They had gone beyond what is present to what is possible. This formal level of thinking develops to some degree between the ages of 14 and 21 in most people. When it develops in a particular person depends upon the quality of his or her education (Inhelder & Piaget, 1958).

Formal Thought

Patricia Arlin (1984) has developed diagnostic descriptions and exercises which measure eight different formal reasoning capacities suggested by Inhelder and Piaget. The Arlin Test of Formal Reasoning (1984) can help determine a person's level of formal reasoning development. So that you can see what is involved in the eight formal reasoning capacities, I have provided examples directly from your introductory course in psychology. Examples could be provided for the natural sciences, mathematics, or other areas of college work.

1. MULTIPLICATIVE COMPENSATIONS—understanding the idea of a steady state even though conditions might be changed.

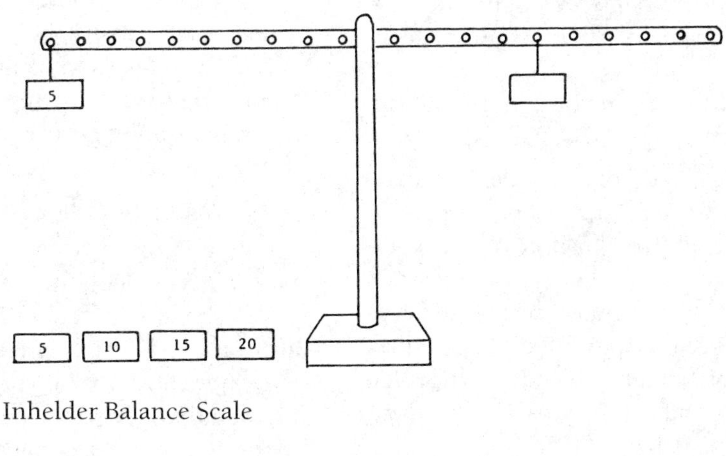

Figure 6.16 Piaget, Inhelder Balance Scale

Biofeedback loops, the regulation of body temperature by the hypothalamus, and the course of the General Adaptation Syndrome.

2. PROBABILITY—understanding and figuring the odds.

   Different levels of probability associated with the normal curve, natural selection, and extinction (Chapter 5).

3. CORRELATIONS—understanding the relationship between certain variables.

   Learning and hereditary factors related to intelligence and other variables. The details of the correlational methods are discussed in Chapter 1 and in the Statistical Appendix.

4. COMBINATORIAL REASONING

   Computation of the number of possible brain states that exist given a brain of about 50 billion neurons. Later in this chapter, you will learn about possible combinations in understanding genetic outcomes.

5. PROPORTIONAL REASONING—understanding transformations and analogies.

   Conversions of energy in the nervous system. In a similar way, the general systems approach directs our attention to parallelisms across disciplines and theoretical approaches within psychology.

6. FORMS OF CONSERVATION BEYOND DIRECT VERIFICATION—inferring the existence of systems not directly observable.

   Inferring the nature(s) of the principle of "mind"—the unseen animating principle from behavior. The processes we infer are thought of as being in a "black box."

7. MECHANICAL EQUILIBRIUM—equilibrium through complementary and contradictory systems.

   The dynamic Freudian systems (id, ego, and superego) of personality theory.

8. THE COORDINATION OF TWO OR MORE SYSTEMS OF FRAMES OF REFERENCE—interacting systems.

   The overall coordination of the combined functions of the nervous system (Chapter 2), of integrated sensory-perceptual experience (Chapter 3), of the complex diagnosis of mental disorders (DSM-IV, Chapter 12), and complex psychotherapeutic approaches (Chapter 10).

Measurement of Formal Thought. Psychologists and educators (applied psychology) have developed ways of measuring your *cognitive development*. The higher levels of the behavioral model are related to the formal level of thought.

Benjamin Bloom (1956) and his colleagues have organized levels of cognitive capacity into a behavioral hierarchy. Following are the main categories of this hierarchy and examples of related behavior.

Evaluation:	Judgments are made on the basis of specified criteria.
Synthesis:	Ideas are rearranged or combined into a new perspective.
Analysis:	Interrelationships are identified and inconsistencies detected.
Application:	Principles are applied in new situations.
Comprehension:	Facts and principles are restated or interpreted in another form.
Knowledge:	Facts and principles are recognized and recalled.

Richard C. and Norman A. Sprinthall (1981), leading educational psychologists, have pointed out:

> Although Bloom and his associates did not directly connect their objectives to developmental and Piagetian cognitive stages, there is an implicit relationship. Bloom's levels one, two, and three—basic knowledge and facts, comprehension and application—are all clearly within the grasp of elementary-age concrete thinkers. When we reach levels four, five, and six, we are moving toward the need for symbolic and logical thinking on Piaget's formal operations sense. (1981, p. 376)

Table 6.5 shows this relationship. Concrete thinking is the type of thinking typical of elementary schoolchildren (non-formal).

The nice thing about Bloom's work is that it also provides sample multiple choice test items that show how we can assess each of the levels of cognitive development. We can apply these model items to any college subject. The test

Table 6.5 Developmental Stages of Thinking

Approximate Chronological Age	*Bloom*	*Piaget*
Elementary-school ages, grades K–5	Rote memory Concrete understanding Application	Concrete operations
Early adolescence, grades 6–9	Analysis	Formal operations
Late adolescence, early adult, grades 10–adult	Synthesis Evaluation	

items you have had on your psychology exams we probably taken from a variety of these levels.

Toward a Philosophy of Human Development

Human development is especially concerned with the whole person. The interest of developmental psychology includes not only the development of the whole of personality, abilities, motives, feelings, etc., but also during the whole life span itself. From conception to death we are undergoing growth and change. So when we study, for example, the development of thinking capacity, we are not only interested in thinking capacity as a topic, but also its growth and change.

The idea of human development is captured in everyday life. People who haven't seen you for some time will say, "My how you've grown or changed!" When you take out old picture albums, you may find photos of your parents—or yourself—as infants, as children, and then as adults. There you see human development.

The Ideas of Nature and Nurture

There are several important philosophical questions for human development. Photos of people can tell us a great deal about both their genetic (*nature*) backgrounds and about their learning experiences (*nurture*). Ronald Reagan in a swim suit shows a strong young man. Ronald Reagan as a radio announcer, movie star, and political leader illustrates a series of learning experiences. Some psychologists emphasize the role of maturation (genetic unfolding), and others emphasize the role of learning (experience) in growth and development. We will attempt to understand the interaction of genetic and learning influences.

Stages of Development or Continuous Growth

A second philosophical question concerns whether or not growth and change take place in actual *stages* or simply occur more or less smoothly. Bloom (1956) described a cognitive scheme in terms of a hierarchy. Even family photos and photos of the president seem to follow the idea of important stages of development. For example, here is Johnny taking his first step, here he is graduating from high school, etc. In primitive societies, there are puberty rites for both boys and girls. From these particular examples, it does seem that growth and change occur in stages where some sort of equilibrium is reached. The idea of stages of development is usually based upon biological examples.

On the other hand, the smooth continuity of growth and change is proposed by other psychologists. When you are with people day in and day out, they don't seem to grow and change in stages, although the rate of smooth change does seem to speed up and slow down from time to time. The analogy might be to look at the growth and development of people, not in a brief series of photos as we did earlier, but in billions of frames in a 72-year-long movie. We could reduce this 72-year-long movie to a rather interesting 72 minutes by shooting one frame every six hours during the person's lifetime. This idea of continuous growth parallels instrumental and Pavlovian learning explanations of how behavior changes and grows—not by leaps and bounds, but by reinforcer after reinforcer.

I think that both positions represent useful ideas. Both stages and smooth continuous development can be understood, not by emphasizing either plateaus or continuous smooth changes, but by emphasizing the constant processes of equilibration which are common to them both. Equilibration is constantly taking place in both sequences of growth. The biological changes (nature) always open new possibilities for learning (nurture). Development is the result of this interaction. In terms of the general systems perspective, the various areas of human development (intellectual, personality, moral, and physical) are examples of coordinated systems or frames of reference.

Theories of Human Development

It is especially important that you first understand some conceptual schemes concerning the course of growth and change. Your thinking here will involve formal reasoning. This is like Piaget's formal thinking scheme that involves the coordination of two or more systems or frames of reference.

Jean Piaget's Theory of Cognitive Development

While there have been many modifications to his original findings, Jean Piaget (1952) was responsible for the most widely accepted theory of cognitive development. Later in Chapter 11, you will learn about J.P. Guilford's (1967, 1979) structure-of-intellect model. I bring this to your attention now because it offers a comparison between a development theory of intellect and a non-developmental theory of the structure of intellect. These theories do not contradict one another, they attempt to explain the structure of intellectual phenomena in different ways.

Piaget saw cognitive development occurring as the person interacts with his environment. A child, for example, can be potentially ready for cognitive development to take place (maturation), but it will not if the child does not experience the environment in the appropriate ways. For example, recall that quality of educational experience helps determine when a person enters the stage of formal operations.

Piaget's study of the growth of intellect stemmed from his studies with Alfred Binet (below) on intelligence. Binet was interested in what children of certain ages knew; Piaget became interested in the process of knowing. The purposes of Binet's work and those of Piaget were different. Because Piaget emphasized the role of the interaction between maturation and experience with the environment, his work has been of extreme value to educational planning.

Sensorimotor Stage (Birth to about 2 Years). The interplay between maturation and experience is clearly seen in the *sensorimotor stage* or sequence of cognitive development. Sensory and motor behavior interacting with the environment slowly begin to organize the world into some very fundamental *activity schemes,* which are totally grounded in the infant's sensorimotor interaction with the environment.

During this stage of cognitive development, a fundamental organization scheme does begin to emerge—*object permanence.* Before the age of four months, infants behave as if objects do not exist as objects. Piaget describes this sensorimotor "state of mind":

> The universe of the young baby is a world without objects, consisting only of shifting and insubstantial "tableaux" which appear and then are totally reabsorbed, either without returning, or reappearing in a modified or analogous form. At about five to seven months, . . . when the child is about to seize an object and you cover it with a cloth or move it behind a screen, the child simply withdraws his already extended hand or, in the case of an object of special interest (his bottle, for example), begins to cry or scream with disappointment. He reacts, therefore, as if the object had been reabsorbed. (1969, p. 14)

In the months to come, object permanence slowly becomes more and more refined. By the end of the sensorimotor stage, the child should be able to follow a slow-moving shell game.

There are many things the parent could do to help the full development of the infant's capacity for object permanence. But, most of it comes about quite naturally. Games such as peek-a-boo supply the infant with experiences that lead to the belief that objects have permanence. So, routine experiences like the parent simply leaving the room (being reabsorbed), and then returning naturally, lead to a child's awareness of the permanence of objects.

The Preoperational Stage (about 2 to 7 years): The Transition to Symbolic Schemes. During the *preoperational stage,* with the acquisition of language, children can begin to think about things before they act. They can be imaginative in their play. Being able to begin to manipulate words and symbols in thinking allows the beginnings of higher-level abstract processes. For example, knowing that a dog is a dog whether it's a poodle or Great Dane indicates the beginning of understanding a concept.

However, the accurate use of this new capacity with symbols takes time and interaction with the environment to blend object permanence into the emerging symbol system. Piaget and Inhelder say of this time:

> Children of four and five often go by themselves from home to school and back every day even though the walk may be ten minutes or so in length. Yet if you ask them to represent their path by means of little three-dimensional cardboard objects (houses, church, streets, river, squares, etc.) or to indicate the plan of the school as it is seen from the main entrance or from the side facing the river, they are unable to reconstruct the topological relationship, even though they constantly utilize them in action. Young children's memories are in some sense motor-memories and cannot necessarily be represented in simultaneous unified construction. The first obstacle to operations, then, is the problem of mentally representing (transferring into symbols) what has already been absorbed on the level of action. (1969, p. 94)

The slow transition to symbolic representation during this period can also be seen in the child's egocentric application of symbols. In the sensorimotor stage, the infant progressed toward object permanence and setting itself apart from the environment as an object. Now, with symbols, the same sort of thing must be accomplished. For example, the child in this stage may have difficulty appreciating another person's point of view. The child's early symbolic schemes puts his own view of the world at the center of attention. Often if you take a child of this age to help buy a gift for someone, she will suggest something she would like to have. However, it has more recently been found that children at these ages are less egocentric than Piaget originally thought (Flavell, Eaverett, Croft & Flavell 1981).

The Concrete Operations Stage (about ages 7 to 11 years). As the use of symbols becomes more and more refined in the child's mind, he becomes more and more capable of making transformations of reality. These transformations are what is meant by operations. The key to this refined symbol manipulation in thinking is the capacity to reverse operations in thinking. As an example of *concrete operations,* if I asked you to pour a short, wide glass of water into a tall, narrow one, and then asked you which of the glasses had more water, you would say they had the same. One of the reasons you know this is that you can reverse the operation in your head—you can imagine pouring the water back into the short glass. Similarly, you know that the operation of addition is the reverse of subtraction, and you can easily make these transformations.

Piaget would say that in making these transformations you *conserve* the original amount of water (or number values, etc.) as they take on different formations. You recognize that simply changing the shape of something, for example, doesn't change the original amount of substance. This is a level of abstraction that preoperational children do not understand. Figure 6.17 illustrates various types of conservation among preoperational children.

The Formal Operations Stage (about 12 to 15 Years of Age and Older). The *formal operations stage* of intellectual development involves conservations, but here we must go beyond the pieces clay and string. In Table 6.6 is one of Patricia Arlin's diagnostic items from her test of formal reasoning (1984). In attempting to understand the answers to these questions, you must develop a rule, law or scheme which is not dependent on any particular situation, but would apply to any like it.

Not everyone gets a chance to develop his full capacity for formal reasoning. I have found in my own classes that only about 50 percent of college students reach what Arlin calls the high formal level of cognitive development. Appropriate educational experiences can help students develop their full capacities.

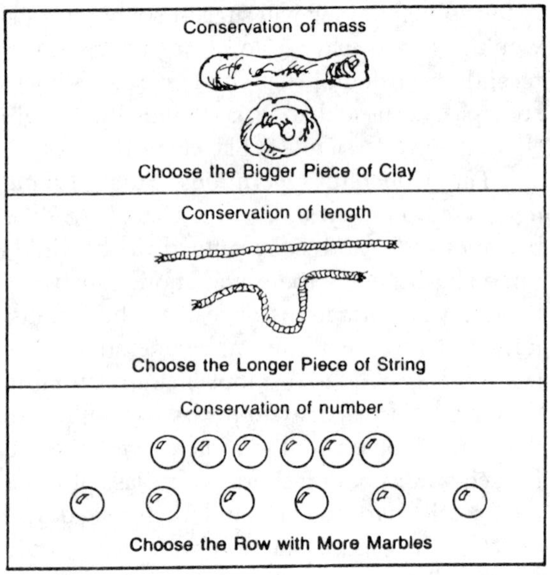

Figure 6.17 Conservation

Intellectual Development After Adolescence and After Formal Reasoning. What happens to intellectual development after adolescence and after formal reasoning has been achieved? Patricia Arlin (1975) has proposed that if we see formal reasoning as essentially a problem-solving capacity, then a new capacity, *problem finding,* might develop. Problem finding is seen in the student who asks those "pointed questions" for which the instructor doesn't always have an answer. This is a part of creativity.

A Theory of Personality Development: Erik Erikson's Life-Span, Psychosocial Crises

Sigmund Freud's psychoanalytic theory of personality development influenced Erik Erikson. Freud saw psychological processes related to a person's personality arising out of *psychosexual stages of development* (see Table 6.7). If the child learns gratification of these erogenous forces, he will move smoothly on to the higher sequences of personality development.

In Erikson's (1963) theory of *psychosocial development,* the stages of personality development have been extended to include the entire life span—not just up to full sexual development. Erikson's approach extends Freud's in two fundamental ways. First, he goes beyond sexual gratification at each of Freud's stages. Second, he goes beyond sexual maturity at puberty and extends personality development to the entire life span. Erikson believes that movement through all of the stages throughout life depends upon social influences. At each stage, according to Erikson's theory, there is a turning point that is influenced by social facilitations or by social pressures.

Table 6.6 Test of Formal Reasoning

Two people are sitting on a train as it passes through a long tunnel in the side of a mountain. Mr. Red (R) is sitting at the front of the train and Mr. Blue (B) is sitting at the back of the train. For the following two situations, decide whether Mr. R and Mr. B will stay in the tunnel for the same time.

SITUATION 1: After the train enters the tunnel Mr. R gets up from his seat in the front, and walks back to sit with Mr. B. How much time altogether will Mr. R spend in the tunnel?

A. Less time in the tunnel than Mr. B.
B. Twice the time in the tunnel as Mr. B.
C. The same amount of time.
D. More time in the tunnel than Mr. B.

SITUATION 2: After the train has entered the tunnel, Mr. B gets up from his seat in the back. He walks forward to sit with Mr. R. Halfway on his trip forward, he decides to go back to his seat for his paper. He gets his paper and then goes forward again and joins Mr. R while the train is still in the tunnel. How much time did Mr. B spend in the tunnel?

A. Less time in the tunnel than Mr. R.
B. More time in the tunnel than Mr. R.
C. One-and-one-half as much time in the tunnel as Mr. R.
D. The same amount of time in the tunnel as Mr. R.

Table 6.7 Schema for Various Developmental Stages

Ages	*Psychosexual Stages (Freud)*	*Psychosocial Stages (Erikson)*	*Cognitive Stages (Piaget)*
0–18 months	Oral	Basic trust vs. mistrust	Sensorimotor
18 months–3 years	Anal	Autonomy vs. doubt, shame	Sensorimotor/preoperational
3–5 years	Phallic	Initiative vs. guilt	Preoperational
6–11 years	Latency	Industry vs. inferiority	Concrete operational
12–17 years	Genital	Identity vs. role confusion	Formal operational (beginning to develop for some)
Young adult	**	Intimacy vs. isolation	**
Maturity	**	Generativity vs. stagnation	**
Old Age	**	Ego integrity vs. despair	**

**No additional stages described for these stages.

Basic Trust vs. Mistrust: Toward Hope

> The basic psychosocial attitude to be learned at this stage is that you can trust the world in the form of your mother, that she will be back to feed you, that she will feed you the right thing in the right quantity at the right time, and that when you're uncomfortable she will come and make you comfortable, and so on. That there is some correspondence between your needs and your world, this is what I mean by basic trust. (Erik Erikson in Evans 1967, pp. 14–15)

You can see from Erikson's own description of this first stage of psychosocial development that the trust versus mistrust outcome is not an either/or situation. It is a crisis. The child learns both trust and mistrust and one will tend to dominate. If this need for trust/mistrust is gratified in a healthy way, a basic attitude or feeling of trust will dominate. In the case of the first stage, the fundamental human strength of hope can emerge.

> You see, hope is a very basic human strength without which we wouldn't stay alive, and not something invented by theologians or philosophers . . . children who give up hope because they do not get enough loving and not enough stimulation may literally die. (Spitz, 1945, p. 17)

So, if a child comes through the first crisis with a positive feeling he will have the strength of hope. He trusts the world.

Autonomy vs. Shame/Doubt—Toward Will Power. The social environment determines how the child will come through a crisis. If the environment is too permissive, the child may encounter too many difficulties; if too restrictive, the child cannot obtain autonomy—to be successful on his own.

> He puts his will against the will of others—even that of his protectors. Cultures have different ways of cultivating or breaking this will. Some are shame, which can be a terrible form of self-estrangement for the human. On the other hand, one cannot imagine a human who is not afraid of being embarrassed—afraid of being in a situation in which other people will find him shameful. This is the age when the child begins to blush, which is a symptom of knowing one is being watched and is found wanting. (p. 19)

Out of this crisis comes the strength of will power. If a child learns autonomy in the control of his general musculature at this stage, he will experience the emergence of reasonable will power. This strength clearly illustrates the idea of how a balance between autonomy and doubt (not one or the other) is struck in most of us. You do not either have a will or not have one, but rather you have degrees of will power depending upon the situation.

Initiative vs. Guilt—Toward Purpose. In this stage the child faces the crisis of redirecting his energies away from fantasy and toward the concrete world. If creative play activities are encouraged rather than restricted, the child develops more initiative than guilt.

> The child begins to envisage goals for which his locomotion and cognition have prepared him. The child also begins to think of being big and to identify with people whose work and or whose personality he can understand and appreciate. "Purpose" involves this whole complex of elements. For example, when the child plays, it's not just a matter of practicing his ability to manipulate. He begins to have projects, as it were. . . . (p. 25)

Industry vs. Inferiority—Toward Competence. The child is now somewhere between six and eleven years of age. Just as personality development has involved psychosexual development along with psychosocial development, cognitive development too, has been an important influence.

> There is an enormous curiosity during this stage of life—a wish to learn, a wish to know. Piaget's work permits us to bring the cognitive elements together with the psychosocial ones, for obviously learning is not just suppressed or displaced sexual curiosity; learning contains an energy of its own. . . . (p. 27)

During this time the child either tends to be successful in the achievements of competencies or does not. The key here is guiding the child through appropriate tasks at the right time. If the child succeeds at learning, he will tend to become industrious; if not, he will tend to feel inferior. His attempts toward mastery during the crisis stage have failed.

Identity vs. Role Confusion—Toward Fidelity. Here, too, Erikson's interest in the cognitive determinants of behavior can be clearly seen. The crisis is partly sexual, partly social, and partly cognitive in origin. Adult developmental stages (Levenson, Darrow, Klein, McKee, 1978) are organized on the continuum of identity and role confusion.

> . . . we have almost an instinct for fidelity—meaning that when you reach a certain age you can and must learn to be faithful to some ideological view. Speaking psychiatrically, without the development of a capacity for fidelity, the individual will either have what we call a weak ego, or look for a deviant group to be faithful to. (p. 30)

The critical points here are that, first, you must have an identity, and second, ideologies are the ultimate bases for them and include elements such as who you are, what you want to achieve in life, what kind of work you want to do, etc. The more structured society is, the less likely role diffusion will occur. American culture allows a great deal of identity flexibility. This opens possibilities of what one can become, but it can also lead to role confusion.

Why particular ideologies appeal to particular people is socially complex. However, Erikson emphasizes that each new stage of development rests upon how all previous stage crises were worked out:

> Identity develops through all earlier stages; it begins way back when the child first recognizes his mother and feels recognized by her, when her voice tells him he is somebody with a name, and he's good. . . . Mixed in with the positive identity, there is a negative identity which is composed of what he has been shamed for, what he has been punished for, and what he feels guilty about: his failures in competency and goodness. Identity means an integration of all previous identification and self-images, including the negative ones. (p. 35–36)

Again, as with the other stages, it can be seen that identity and role diffusion are a matter of balance. One hopes that the balance is in favor of the positive identity.

Intimacy vs. Isolation—Toward Love. The establishment of the balance toward intimacy or toward isolation is based upon the previous stages. The establishment of identity is extremely important to any establishment of intimacy.

> I mean intimate relationships, such as friendships, love, sexual intimacy, even intimacy with oneself, one's inner resources, the range of one's excitements and commitments. Intimacy is really the ability

> to fuse your own identity with somebody else's without fear that you're going to lose something yourself. It is this development of intimacy which makes marriage possible as a chosen bond. (p. 49)

Generativity vs. Stagnation—Toward Caring. At this stage one begins to take one's place in society, and to take the responsibility for the development and perfection of whatever it produces. (p. 50)

Many students get the idea that generativity means being highly creative or making a great contribution. Actually, Erikson's idea of generativity during mature adulthood has little to do with outstanding works:

> I use the word "generativity" because I mean everything that is generated from generation to generation: children, products, ideas, and works of art. . . . It is possible for a person to fulfill his generativity by working with other people's children or helping to create a better world for them—it is important for us to support the idea that a person can be generative by helping to create a world which can promise a minimum to every child born. (p. 51)

The strength of personality that comes with the balancing toward generativity is care. In general this means a caring society—a little like becoming a caretaker for society. When we care for starving children in Ethiopia, this is an expression of generativity.

Integrity vs. Despair—Toward Wisdom. In old age, a person is in a position of summing up the meaning of his life. If the person is, on the whole, satisfied with the life he has managed to live, then there is emotional integration of a completed and accepted life. If the person's life experiences balance in favor of this integrity, then there can be wisdom—or perhaps just the feeling of wisdom:

> And in old age, some wisdom must mature, if only in the sense that the old person comes to appreciate and to represent something of the "wisdom of the ages," or plain folk "wit." (p. 54)

This final stage of personality development represents the embodiment of all of the stages of development. The person is satisfied, at least to some degree, that her total life balances on the positive side.

Erikson's eight stages are summarized in Table 6.8. Do we really go through these eight sequences of development during our lifetimes? While there is not clear empirical evidence, the theory does two very important things for us. First, it is a way of conceptualizing the course of the entire life span. Second, it sensitizes us toward the entire life span. All too often we tend to look upon the later years as simply living out one's life. Erikson's model dramatizes the fact that psychosocial, psychosexual, and cognitive equilibration, like physiological equilibration, continue until the moment of death.

Erikson's theory should be looked upon in much the same way we thought about Abraham Maslow's need hierarchy (Chapter 4). It offers a great overall perspective that helps to put many

Table 6.8 Erikson's Eight Stages of Psychosocial Development

Stage	*Age*	*Results of Successful Resolution*	*Results of Unsuccessful Resolution*
1. Trust vs. Mistrust	Birth–1	Hope	Fear
2. Autonomy vs. Shame and Doubt	1–3	Willpower	Self-doubt
3. Initiative vs. Guilt	4–5	Purpose	Unworthiness
4. Industry vs. Inferiority	6–11	Competency	Incompetency
5. Ego Identity vs. Role Confusion	12–20	Fidelity	Uncertainty
6. Intimacy vs. Isolation	20–24	Love	Promiscuity
7. Generativity vs. Stagnation	25–65	Caring	Selfishness
8. Ego Integrity vs. Despair	65–Death	Wisdom	Meaninglessness and despair

things into place. Thus we can begin to see how processes are interrelated.

Kohlberg's Stages of Moral Development

Moral behavior has to do with knowing the difference between what is right and wrong. What you might not know is that moral judgment grows and changes much like the cognitive and personality stages we have been examining. At each stage of this *moral development,* we change our reasons for our moral decisions.

Six Stages of Moral Growth Plus One. Kohlberg (1969) has proposed that we grow and change in moral judgment from early childhood through adulthood. Our capacity to understand right from wrong—what is justice and what is not, he feels, develops directly with our cognitive capacity to reason. In this regard, Kohlberg's moral stages closely parallel Piaget's stages of cognitive development—the idea of coordinated systems. Table 6.9 illustrates the relationship between Piaget's stages of cognitive development and Kohlberg's stages of moral development.

The easiest way to understand Kohlberg's stages is to start with some idea of what conventional means. Conventional simply refers to what is generally accepted as right or wrong by society (or by a group). These include particular laws, codes, and practices which are widely accepted. Conventions can range from laws governing automobile traffic to practices like wearing a shirt when you go to a restaurant for dinner. Kohlberg's ideas of preconventional, conventional, and postconventional stages of moral development are shown in Table 6.10.

Table 6.10 contains a complete description of Kohlberg's stages. You are already familiar with the idea of conventional morality (stages 3 and 4). As you can see, the child progressively makes moral judgments on the basis of a widening cognitive perspective—first himself, then a limited social context (society as he finds it), and, finally, an unlimited social context (society as it could or ought to be). In this widening perspective, the parallel sensorimotor, then concrete, and finally the formal Piagetian elements can be seen. This progressive moral detachment can be illustrated in one of Kohlberg's long-term subjects. It should be noted that Kohlberg may be in error as to the ages of onset for this sequence (Damon 1984). The subject, "Joe," was asked, "Why shouldn't you steal from a store?" Here are recorded his answers at ages 10, 17, and finally 24:

> Joe at age 10: Why shouldn't you steal from a store?
>
> "It is not good to steal from the store. It's against the law. Somebody could see you and call the police."
>
> Joe at age 17: Why shouldn't you steal from a store?
>
> "It is a matter of law. It's one of our rules that we're trying to help protect everyone, protect property, not just to protect a store. It's something that's needed in our society. If we didn't have these laws, people would steal, they wouldn't have to

Table 6.9 Comparison of Piaget and Kohlberg

Piaget (Cognitive Stage)		*Kohlberg (Moral Stage)*	
Age	*Stage*	*Age*	*Stage*
0–2	Sensorimotor	0–9	Preconventional (Stages I and II)
2–7	Intuitive/Preoperational		
7–11	Operational concrete	9–15	Conventional (Stages III and IV)
11 and up	Formal/abstract thinking	16 and up	Postconventional (Stages V and VI)

(adapted from Walker, 1980)

Table 6.10 Kohlberg's Stages of the Development of Moral Reasoning

Level 1:	***preconventional morality***	
Stage 1:	Punishment and obedience orientation	Control of behavior is external, based on commands, punishments, and rewards. What is punished is bad, what is rewarded is good. The child obeys because adults have superior power.
Stage 2:	Individualism, instrumental purpose, and exchange	Also described as "naive hedonism." Things that satisfy the self are right. Right is also what is fair, what is an equal exchange. Agreements and deals are valued.
Level 2:	***conventional morality***	
Stage 3:	Good boy/nice girl orientation: interpersonal conformity	What is good is what pleases others, especially those to whom one is attached (e.g., family and friends). More broadly, moral actions are those that match what is expected of you.
Stage 4:	Law and order orientation; social system and conscience	Reference group broadens to include the larger society. Good is defined as fulfilling duties you've agreed to, obeying the law, and respecting authority. Virtue should be rewarded.
Level 3:	***post-conventional or principled morality***	
Stage 5:	Social contracts; legalistic orientation	Laws are seen as important, but changeable. Alternative sets of principles are recognized. Existing laws and customs should be upheld to maintain the social order. The general rule is to act so as to achieve the "greatest good for the greatest number." Contracts and agreements are seen as binding.
Stage 6:	Universally ethical principles	Self-chosen ethical principles dominate moral decisions. Since laws are usually consistent with such ethical principles, obeying the law is usually morally right, but when there is a conflict, the personal conscience is dominant.
Stage 7:	Religious morality	A recent proposed final stage, involving religious "transcendence." Moral choices are based on universal principles, such as love; the individual—perhaps someone in Erikson's stage of ego integrity versus despair—seeks to find some ultimate order to experience. Such reasoning is found only rarely. Some examples: Teilhard de Chardin and Martin Luther King.

work for a living and our whole society would get out of kilter."

Joe at age 24: Why shouldn't you steal from a store?

"It's violating another person's rights, in this case to property."

Does the law enter in?

"Well, the law in most cases is based on what is morally right, so it's not a separate subject, it's a consideration."

What does "morality" or "morally right" mean to you?

"Recognizing the rights of other individuals, first to life, and then to do as he

> pleases as long as it doesn't interfere with someone else's rights."

Joe progresses here from stage 2 all the way to stage 6. At age 10 there is still a hint of the idea that if you get away with it, it might not be so wrong. By the age of 17 Joe sees the world in a wider perspective. He is now in stage 4. He states the law not simply as a local convention, but as a generalized one; he even tells why we have to have laws, which puts him partially into stage 5. Finally, at age 24, Joe has moved beyond conventions of right and wrong and a little beyond "laws" themselves. He sees the relevance of universal ethical principles from which laws are ultimately created. This is stage 6 of moral development. We don't know if Joe ever reached stage 7, but we do know of people who have.

Erik Erikson has carefully studied and described the development of Mohendas Gandhi as a person in his book *Gandhi's Truth.* Gandhi seems to have reached stage 7 in his moral development. Erikson described this moral transcendence:

> (Gandhi) now seemed to me to exemplify in word and deed what I had come to perceive as a modern version of the Golden Rule. To put it briefly, this version suggests that whenever one has a choice, one should choose to act so as to enhance the potentials of one's counterplayer's development as well as one's own. I know of no other example in world history where a man made such a principle so completely his own by always extending it to his opponent (Evans, p. 72)

Kohlberg's theory of moral development, just as Piaget and Erikson's theories, has important implications for education. It has been found that presenting a child with moral dilemmas and then working through the reasoning of a higher stage than that at which the child is, will facilitate the development of moral reasoning. (This is not teaching particular morals, but moral reasoning.) How would you decide the rights and wrongs of some of the pressing moral dilemmas of our times? At which of Kohlberg's stages should we look for moral judgments on these issues? As world society becomes more and more complex, these and other moral questions will have to be resolved.

Creativity, Intelligence, Aptitudes

Putting Together the "Wrong" Pieces—Creativity

Traditionally, introductory psychology textbooks place the importance of the study of intelligence before creativity—if creativity is discussed at all. We have taken the step of placing creativity first because it appears that a shift is rapidly occurring in the relative importance of these two areas of intellectual ability. Whereas genius used to be thought of pretty much as a matter of high intelligence, John Briggs (1994) now tells us ". . . most researchers agree that the and important variable in genius is not IQ but creativity."

The Discovery of the Stress Syndrome. Canadian physician Hans Selye is noted for his creation and work on the general concept of stress. Chapter 4, *Motivation,* introduced you to the highlights of Selye's ideas and contributions concerning the concept of stress. According to his work, environmental stress causes the release of adrenal gland hormones that helps a person meet the demands at hand—to adapt. Recall from Chapter 2 that the autonomic nervous system functions to meet stress through its fight or flight responses. Selye's contributions postulate that diseases of adaptation usually occur when stress is prolonged, causing anything from headaches to emotional disturbances, or diseases of the kidney.

Selye is introduced in this chapter not because of his work on stress, but because of his creative contributions. In his book *From Dream to Discovery* (1964), Selye coaches young medical researchers on the role of intuition in their work. After recounting the creative insights of several other famous people, Selye tells his own story of the creation of the stress concept. This first example of the role of intuition in creative work sets the stage for a more detailed description of his own intuitions about stress.

The Discovery of the Ring Structure of Benzene. The German chemist Kekule was trying to put order into his thoughts about the structure of benzene. These ideas would eventually revolutionize chemistry:

> But it did not go well; my spirit was with other things. I turned the chair to the fire-

place and sank into a half sleep. The atoms flitted before my eyes. Long rows, variously, more closely untied; all in movement wriggling and turning like snakes. And see, what was that? One of the snakes seized its own tail and the image whirled scornfully before my eyes. As though from a flash of lightning I awoke; I occupied the rest of the night in working out the consequences of the hypothesis . . . Let us learn to dream, gentlemen. (p. 50)

Now, let's see how Selye put together "wrong" pieces. He describes how he saw things a little differently from the rest and was thereby led to the stress concept:

> . . . I first hit upon the concept of stress and the general adaptation syndrome (GAS) in 1925 when I studied medicine at the University of Prague. I had just completed my courses in anatomy, physiology, biochemistry, and the other pre-clinical subjects which were required as a preparation before we saw a patient. . . . Then came the great day, which I shall never forget, when we were to hear our first lecture on internal medicine and see how one examines a patient.
>
> It so happened that, on that day, by way of an introduction, we were shown several instances of the earliest stages of various infectious diseases. As each patient was brought into the lecture room, the professor carefully questioned and examined him. It turned out that each of these patients felt and looked ill, had a coated tongue, complained of more or less diffuse aches and pains in the joints, and of intestinal disturbances with loss of appetite. Most of them also had fever (sometimes with mental confusion), an enlarged spleen or liver, inflamed tonsils, and so forth. All this was quite evident, but the professor gave very little significance to any of it.
>
> Then he enumerated a few "characteristics" which might help in the diagnosis of the disease. These I could not see. They were absent or, at least, so inconspicuous that my untrained eye could not distinguish them; yet these we were told, were the important changes to which we would have to give all our attention. At present, our teacher said, most of the characteristic signs were still absent, and, until they appeared not much could be done. Without them it was impossible to know precisely what the patient suffered from, and hence it was obviously not feasible to recommend any efficient treatment. It was clear that the many features of disease which were already manifest did not interest our teacher very much because they were "nonspecific" (not characteristic of any one disease), and, hence, of no use to the physician. . . .
>
> I could not understand why, ever since the dawn of medical history, physicians should have attempted to concentrate all their efforts upon the recognition of individual diseases and the discovery of specific remedies for them, without giving any attention to the much more obvious "syndrome of just being sick." I knew that a syndrome is "a group of signs and symptoms that occur together and characterize a disease." Well, the patients we had just seen had a syndrome, but this seemed to be the syndrome that characterized disease as such, not any one disease. Would it be possible to analyze the mechanism of this "general syndrome of sickness" and perhaps even to find drugs which act against the nonspecific factor in disease? It was not until a decade later, however, that I managed to put all this into the precise language of experimentally established scientific description. . . .
>
> [After testing a new hormone] I suddenly remembered my classroom impression of the "syndrome of just being sick." In a flash I realized that what I had produced with my impure extracts and toxic drugs was an experimental replica of this condition. This model was then employed in the analysis of the stress syndrome using the adrenal enlargement, gastrointestinal ulcers and thymicolymphatic involution as objective indices of stress. This simple hunch of a connection between the almost forgotten, purely speculative, clinical concept of student days and the reproducible and objectively measurable changes in the animal experiments at hand

was the basis for the development of the entire stress concept.

Toward a Philosophy of Human Ability: Creativity, Intelligence, and Aptitudes

In both the stories of Friedrich Kekule and of Hans Selye, we find a point where *intelligence* as we have traditionally understood it leaves off and an almost mysterious putting together of "wrong" pieces of a puzzle occurs. Metaphorically, I like to think of cognition as a great puzzle of the universe. In our intelligence, we attempt to see how well we might be able to put together the puzzle. In *creativity* we have a curious (but related) interest: How do we find and then fit seemingly wrong pieces together which then make new and better puzzle pictures?

Broader Conceptions of Intelligence and a Shift Toward Creativity. When robot computer intelligence can put puzzle pieces together as well as we can, it appears we might be left with finding and fitting "wrong" pieces—we might be left with creativity. It is very doubtful that in the foreseeable future intelligent robots will be able to find and fit wrong pieces for us. The reason is simply that we must, of course, first tell robots how to do whatever they do. And, currently we have very little, if any, idea how we actually go about finding and fitting "wrong" pieces (see Chapter 7). Therefore, we can't teach them how. How little do we know about the interworkings of the creative processes? Some time ago the poet Amy Lowell (1930), speaking about the mystery of her own creativity, came very close to the reality of the situation:

> In answering the question, How are poems made? my instinctive answer is a flat, "I don't know." It makes not the slightest difference that the question as asked me refers solely to my own poems, for I know as little about how they are made as I do of anyone else's. What I do know about them is only a millionth part of what there must be to know. I meet them where they touch consciousness, and that is already a considerable distance along the road of evolution. (p. 24)

While we don't know much about the processes underlying creativity and how it is related to our cognitive activities such as intelligence, psychologists have developed a number of approaches and methods that are helping us to at least address this intriguing topic.

The movement toward attention to creativity also coincides with the movement toward the importance of general systems theory. That these two trends in thinking in psychology are converging is more than a simple coincidence. Ronald Levy (1979) has compared the goals of creative problem solving and of general systems theory:

> General systems and creativity relate in the way that each deals with seeing the totality of a situation. Creative problem-solving processes develop new ways of gaining new insights or perspectives as to how seemingly unassociated factors are relevantly related to a problem. Similarly, the general system approach attempts to gain the most comprehensive view of a set of circumstances by interrelating them in new and meaningful ways. (abstract, p. 181)

It is very reasonable to think about young Hans Selye being a general systems theorist (although he didn't know it at the time) as he sat thinking not about how each disease was different from the rest, but how all diseases were interrelated. This divergence from his fellow students and his professors was the basis of his later insight—the creation of the stress concept.

How should we think about the interrelationship between creativity and intelligence? Although we emphasize a shift or trend toward the importance of creativity, intelligence is not dead. We should think of different aspects of overall intellectual functioning as they are organizationally interrelated to one another. So, rather than tying to clearly differentiate intelligence(s) from creativity, we should see how all of the intellectual abilities might be organized in relationship to one another.

Theories of Abilities: Creativity and Intelligence(s)

A Working Definition of Intellectual Ability. How should we define *intellectual ability*? At the theoretical level, a description was offered recently by Howard Gardner in his *Frames of Mind: The Theory of Multiple Intelligences* (1983). He says:

> To my mind, a human intellectual competence must entail a set of skills of problem solving—enabling the individual to resolve genuine problems or difficulties that he or she encounters and when appropriate, to create an effective product—and must also entail the potential for finding or creating problems—thereby laying the groundwork for the acquisition of new knowledge. (pp. 60–61)

This is a broad conception of intellectual ability that embraces both the ideas of intelligence and of creativity, and more.

Guilford's Structure of the Intellect Model. The easiest way to illustrate how all of the abilities of our intellect might be interrelated has been provided by the work of J.P. Guilford and R. Heopfner (1971). Guilford's structure-of-intellect model provides the best understanding of the intellect to systems engineers who are developing plans for NASA's space station. For example, in their recent survey of "human capability" models, researchers at McDonnell Douglas Astronautics Company concluded:

> While considerable quantitative data were [have been] found in the literature defining sensory discrimination abilities and the fine and gross motor responses that humans are capable of making, the higher level cognitive functions are not as precisely defined in terms that can be used directly by systems engineers. To address this problem of defining the "intelligent" operations of the human element in *man-machine* [emphasis added] systems, we have borrowed the terminology proposed by the eminent psychologist, J.P. Guilford, in his "Structure-of-intellect" model, (1984, p. 60–61)

Guilford's overall structure-of-intellect model includes abilities related to intelligence, *aptitudes, problem solving,* and creativity. Figure 6.18 is Guilford's (1977) version of your entire intellect. The model contains 150 (5 × 5 × 6) organizationally interrelated little boxes. Each box represents an ability. In Figure 6.19, I have slid the *operation* of *divergent thinking* slice out of the model for you. According to Guilford and a great many other investigators, this slice of intellect is highly related to creativity or is perhaps

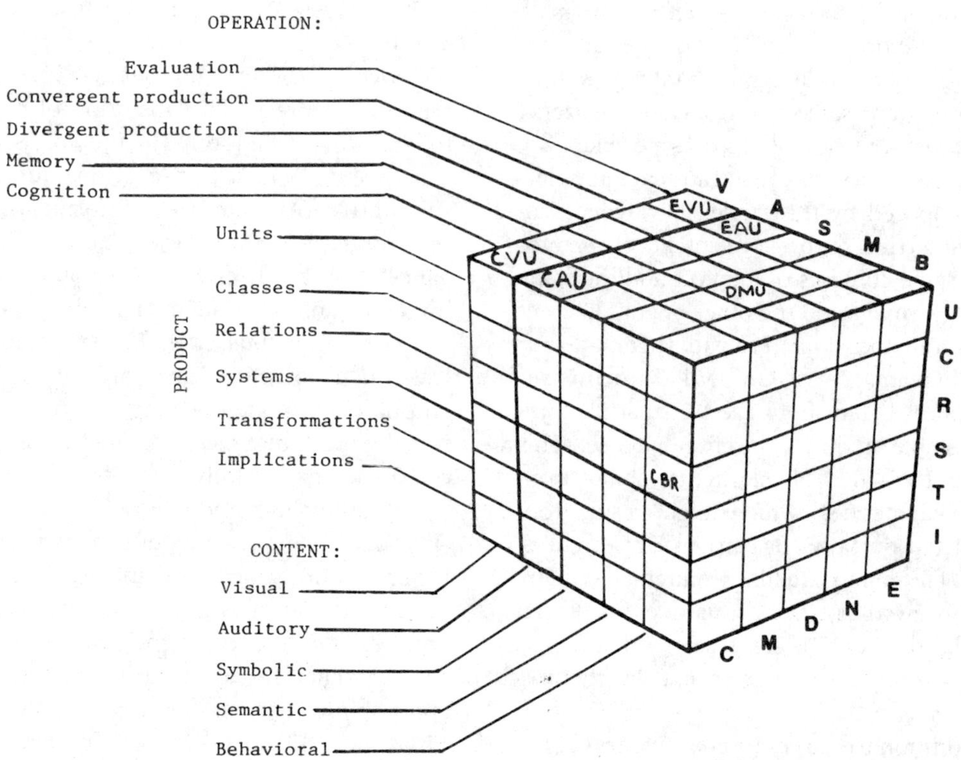

Figure 6.18 Guilford's Structure-of-Intellect Model

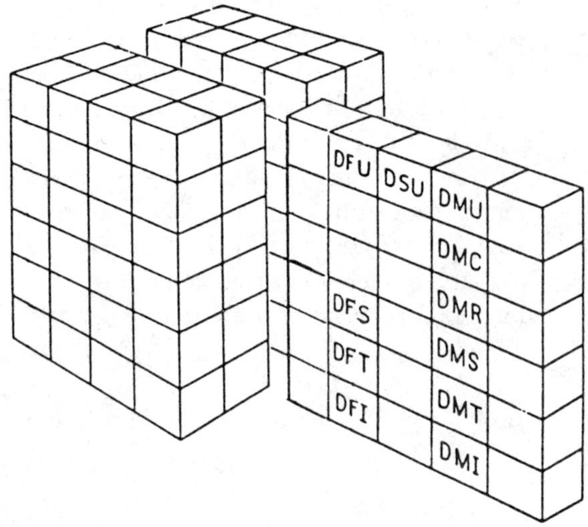

CODE SYMBOLS

Operation	Products
D - Divergent Production	U - Units
	C - Classes
Contents	R - Relations
F - Figural	S - Systems
S - Symbolic	T - Transformations
M - Semantic	I - Implications
B - Behavioral	

Figure 6.19 Operation of Divergent Thinking

the basis of it. It is important to notice that divergent thinking is organizationally interrelated to other abilities in the model through the *content* and *product* categories.

Divergent thinking occurs whenever you are allowed to (or just do) go off in different directions in your thinking. The goal of divergent thought is to explore, and to find as many solutions to a situation as might be reasonable—not just a single "correct" solution. Obviously, both Kekule and Selye were "guilty" of divergent thinking (Kekule that snakes were somehow related to benzene, and Selye that somehow all diseases are alike).

Once again, see the organizational interrelatedness proposed by the model. Divergence, an operation carried on by your intellect, operates with the same contents of intellect and the same products (forms) as do the other operations, but just does something different with them.

The advantages of Guilford's structure-of-intellect model stem from the fact that it represents a testable model for the entire intellect. This helps free the study of intellectual ability from any short-sightedness which might result from the restricted purposes of particular researchers. The fact of testability is a first requirement for any scientific view of intellect. This does not mean that Guilford's theory is correct, only that he has supplied us with a way to determine whether it is or not.

In addition to the comprehensiveness of the structure-of-intellect model, it is also organized so that each of the 150 proposed abilities involves three dimensions of intellect. The following is a brief description of the entire model.

Operations. Major kinds of intellectual activities or processes; the processing of information, information being defined as "that which the organism discriminates."

Cognition (C) Immediate discovery, awareness, rediscovery, or recognition of information in its various forms; comprehension or understanding.

Memory (M) Fixation of newly-gained information in storage. The operation of memory is to be distinguished from the memory store.

Divergent production (D) Generation of logical alternatives from given information, where the emphasis is upon variety, quantity, and relevance of output from the same source. Likely to involve transfer recall instigated by new cues.

Convergent production (N) Generation of logical conclusions from given information, where emphasis is upon achieving unique or conventionally best outcomes. It is likely that the given (cue) information fully determines the outcome, as in mathematics and logic.

Evaluation (E) Comparison of items of information in terms of variables and making judgments concerning criterion satisfaction (correctness, identity, consistency, etc.).

Contents Broad, substantive, basic kinds or areas of information.

Visual and Auditory—Figural (F) Pertaining to information in concrete form, as perceived or as recalled in the form of images. The term "figural" minimally implies figure-ground perceptual organization. Different sense modalities may be involved—visual, auditory, kinesthetic, and perhaps others.

Symbolic (S) Pertaining to information in the form of denotative signs having no significance in and of themselves, such as letters, numbers, musical notations, codes, and words (as ordered letter combinations).

Semantic (M) Pertaining to information in the form of conceptions or mental constructs to which words are often applied, hence most notable in verbal thinking and communication, but not necessarily dependent upon words. Meaningful pictures also convey semantic information.

Behavioral (B) Pertaining to information, essentially nonfigural and nonverbal, involved in human interactions, where the attitudes, needs, desires, moods, intentions, perceptions, thoughts, etc., of others and of ourselves are involved.

Products. Basic forms that information takes in the organism's processing of it.

Units (U) Relatively segregated or circumscribed items or "chunks" of information having "thing" character. May be close to Gestalt psychology's "figures on a ground."

Classes (C) Conceptions underlying sets of items of information grouped by virtue of their common properties.

Relations (R) Connections between items of information based upon variables or points of contact that apply to them. Relational connections are more definable than implicational connections.

Systems (S) Organized or structured aggregates of items of information; complexes of interrelated or interacting parts.

Transformations (T) Changes of various kinds (redefinitions, shifts, transitions, or modifications) in existing information.

Implications (I) Circumstantial connections between items of information, as by virtue of contiguity, or any condition that promotes "belongingness."

Each of the abilities (little boxes) is coded first by operation, then by content, then by product (form).

DMU: This box represents an ability involving the mental process of divergence, with semantic (meaning) content and in the form of units of information. A likely test item type for this ability is shown below.

Utility Test (fluency) The subject lists uses he can think of for a common brick, a wooden pencil, or a wire coat hanger, the total number of relevant responses being counted.

The entire slice of divergent processing abilities, of which DMU above is but one of thirty potential, represents a theory of what underlies creativity.

Not all of the 150 abilities suggested in the structure-of-intellect model have been demonstrated to exist—about 100 of them have. Most standard intelligence tests measure only a small portion of Guilford's entire model. For example, the *Wechsler Adult Intelligence Scale* (WAIS), the most widely used intelligence test, includes only 11 subtests. None of these scales involve divergent thinking. In the empirical section, we discuss a new abilities test, the Structure of Intellect Learning Abilities Test, (based on the Guilford model) which does measure divergent thinking and contains twice as many subtests as the WAIS.

Bringing It All Together

Cognition or thinking may be the most complex topic in psychology. Cognition is made up of memory processes, the growth of thinking capacities starting in early childhood, and thought processes that can be broken down into at least 180 different kinds of intelligence.

People spend a great deal of their thinking time in metamemory, that is, thinking about how their own memory processes work. They also spend a lot of time thinking about things in their memories. Many things we remember were first learned at an earlier stage of cognitive development—a time when our thinking was "different."

In looking toward the future of cognition we can wonder how human thinking will change as robots reach human equivalence as suggested in Chapter 2. Perhaps we'll move more toward divergent thinking that is described in Guilford's model of intelligence.

Glossary

activity schemes: Early repeatable cognitive and behavioral units that allow the infant to begin to relate to the world.

aptitude(s): The ability or capacity to acquire knowledge or proficiency of performance. Usually the term is applied to more specific tasks and areas of future performance, however, intelligence may be thought of as a general aptitude.

cognitive development: The stages of developing thinking skills and abilities in problem solving and creativity.

concrete operations stage: In Piagetian theory, cognitive development between about ages 7 to 11. The child can manipulate symbol systems in orderly ways, but must perceive things in a present, concrete reality.

conserve: In Piagetian theory, to understand that properties of things (numbers, matter, length, volume, etc.) remain the same even though their appearances may change.

consolidation theory: The view that the psychological and physiological processes that result in memory and learning continue on for a period of time after an experience.

content(s): In Guilford's theory, the various classes or types of information that are used in intellectual abilities.

control processes: In the formation of memory, the active thought processes of the person that help determine what is acquired, stored, and later retrieved.

creativity: A type of problem-solving ability where the precise sequence of steps is not totally known. It involves an ability to restructure the meaning of problems or to find/discover problems that had not before been known.

decay theory: The view that forgetting is based upon the decay of physiological processes related to retention. See engrams.

deoxyribonucleic acid: The double helix chemical code in genes and chromosomes that contains each person's genetic inheritance.

divergent thinking: Thinking or mental processes that lead to a broad variety of solutions to problems rather than a single "pat answer."

DNA: See deoxyribonucleic acid.

engrams: A hypothetical state or circuit of living brain tissue that is inferred to be the physiological basis for retention.

episodic memory: The highest form of a three-system view of memory that retains information related to self-awareness and self-identity through time.

formal operations stage: In Piagetian theory, cognitive development from about age 12 and beyond. The child can manipulate symbol systems in totally logical and abstract ways in dealing with realities that are beyond the present, concrete reality.

human development: A branch of psychology that studies changes in behavior from conception to death. All aspects of the changing person are included, for example, learning, inheritance, perception, etc.

intellectual ability: A general term for all aptitude, intelligence, creative, and problem-solving abilities.

intelligence: A general term for the ability to learn and to profit from experience (see learning).

interference theory: A view that forgetting is the result of either past or future conflicting experiences.

long-term memory: The portion of memory that retains information for a considerable length of time.

metacognition: Several types of knowledge and regulation one has concerning all forms of his or her own cognition. Metacognition includes learning, memory, motivation, creativity, and certain aspects of personality regulation.

metamemory: Several types of knowledge and regulation one has concerning his own memory abilities and strategies.

method of loci: A mnemonic technique that uses the visualization of a series of places or things with which is associated a less meaningful series of information.

mnemonic techniques: Any of a broad variety of techniques that aid in the recall of information, the key aid being the use of visual imagery.

mnemonist: An expert in the use of mnemonic techniques.

moral development: The stages of developing a sense of right and wrong as it is seen by society.

nature: The genetic inheritance that contributes to the behavior of an organism (compare with nurture).

nurture: Conditions or experiences of the environment that contribute to the behavior of an organism (compare with nature).

object permanence: The ability to know that objects continue to exist even though they are not present or observable. Infants attain this ability at about four to six months of age.

operation(s): In Guilford's theory, the various kinds of mental processes or kinds of thinking involved in intellectual abilities.

pegword technique: A mnemonic technique that uses a rhyme scheme or other known scheme (for example, the alphabet) for a series of visualized places or things with which is associated a less meaningful series of information.

permanent record: The view that all memories are permanently stored in the brain.

preoperational stage: In Piagetian theory, cognitive development between 2 and 7 years. Even though the child learns symbolic systems such as language during this period, it cannot fully perform orderly manipulations (operations) upon them.

proactive inhibition: Memory interference stemming from a person's past experience that leads to forgetting.

problem finding: A proposed level of cognitive development beyond Piaget's formal operations level. Here the person can not only solve problems in a formal way, but can discover or invent new problems to solve.

problem solving: Behavior and cognitive processes that an organism directs toward some end or goal for which the means or steps are not readily apparent. The behavior and cognitive processes may involve either/both verbal and nonverbal communication systems.

procedural memory: The most fundamental form of a three-system view of memory. This form of memory is of a nonknowing consciousness like that of simple animal organisms, plants, and machines. It retains stimulus response information that allows the organism or machine to relate to its environment.

product(s): In Guilford's theory, the forms information takes, or the way in which it is organized.

psychosexual stages of development: In Freudian theory, the idea that the psyche or mind (especially its personality aspects) develops because of the way a person experiences various sexual stages of development.

psychosocial development: In Erikson's theory, the idea that the psyche or mind (especially its personality aspects) develops because of the way a person experiences various stages of social development.

recall (method): Producing an item directly from one's own memory.

recoding: A mnemonic technique that involves the transformation of less meaningful information into something visual and more meaningful.

recognition (method): The recognition that one has experienced a particular stimulus in the past.

reconstructive processes: Some memory theorists believe that little, if anything, of entire experiences are permanently stored in the brain; most of what is remembered is the result of active reconstruction of what likely occurred in earlier experiences.

relearning (method): A measure of retention that is based upon the relative amount of time it takes to relearn a task a second time.

retroactive inhibition: Memory interference that stems from activities occurring after learning has taken place.

retrograde amnesia: Loss of memory for experiences that preceded some event. The loss thus goes back in time from the point of the event.

ribonucleic acid: Nucleic acids found in cells that are related to the control of chemical activities in cells. Since RNA is formed from DNA and carries out many DNA transfer and messenger functions, it has been hypothesized that it is involved in the formation of memory. Research evidence supports this hypothesis.

RNA: See ribonucleic acid.

rote memory technique: A technique used to improve the recall of information that involves the repeated rehearsal of the information.

semantic memory: The second or middle form of a three-system view of memory that includes knowledge of the organism's world. Lower animals and very young children may have this form of memory with or without some degree of episodic memory.

sensorimotor stage: In Piagetian theory, the first two years of cognitive development during which perceptions are coordinated with behavior.

sensory brain buffers: The portion of memory that retains sensory information, unless continued attention is given to it for very brief periods of time (about 1 second).

serial position effect: The finding that the recall of items or events is related to the sequence in which they occur. Items or events that occur in the middle of the sequence are more difficult to recall than either those occurring near the beginning or the end.

short-term memory: The portion of memory that retains information, unless continued attention is given to it, for up to about 30 seconds.

stage(s): Natural levels or divisions that occur in a changing process.

Yerkes-Dodson Law: A generalized relationship between a person's level of motivation and performance. Low and high levels of motivation are related to lower performance, and moderate levels to higher performance.

Cognition: Doing Psychology on Your Own

LOIS MCDERMOTT

Basic Concept #6—I "Think," Therefore I "Am"

How often have you heard reference to the *information age*, the information explosion? The study of cognition and the development of computers that "think" have gone hand-in-glove since the 1960's. Developments in one field have fueled developments in the other, producing a revolution in the way we live our lives and understand the workings of the mind. No longer do we live in the "Age of Aquarius," but now in the "age of information processing." Emerging from this revolution is a cognitive science, a science of information processing, that marries what we know about the mind, the brain and the workings of computers. Psychology, once defined as the study of behavior, is now defined as the study of behavior and mental processes of sentient (i.e., thinking, knowing, remembering, planning, deciding, problem solving, and intelligent) beings. No longer are psychologists content with focusing only on observable behavior and ignoring the mind because it is not tangible. They want to get in to the black box to elucidate the workings of the intangible mind—the ultimate information processor. "I think, therefore I am" is the new motto. Within the field, two long-standing areas of interest are memory and intelligence.

Memory. The lay public has been swept up in the cognitive revolution by stories of amazing and/or unusual examples of human memory. For example, a grown woman begins in adulthood to have memories of her father murdering a playmate some 30+ years previously. A man, in hypnotic trance, recalls the letters and digits of the license plate of the truck of the driver who killed his child—leading to successful prosecution and conviction. A man suffers an injury and loses his ability to form new memories—living each day as if it where the only day of his life. An elderly man can remember minute details of baseball games from the 1930's, 40's and 50's but can't remember to take his heart medication regularly. We also hear the reports of psychological pain from the loss of sense of self and loved ones, as dementia from Alzheimer's or other disease sets in.

Intelligence. Smart computers, smart people. Do computers have intelligence? What is intelligence anyway and where does it come from? Questions about the nature and origin of intelligence have always existed. Research in this field has often been fueled by some social prejudice and/or some pressing social need. This domain of psychology has been fraught with some of the most fraudulent data ever published in psychology. Early studies of intelligence attempted to measure intelligence by measuring the size (circumference) of the head. The researcher eventually abandoned this approach because his data failed to support his hypothesis that white, upper-class males of European descent (and presumably of superior intellectual powers) would have larger heads than women of all races and classes and larger than those of males of "inferior breed." Later examination of the *volume* of skulls from various racial groups and genders seemed to support the superiority of white, upper-class males of European descent. However, it was latter shown that the data were fraudulent. Then came the famous British studies of monozygotic (MZ) (i.e., identical) and dizygotic (DZ) (i.e., fraternal) twins who had been reared apart and reared together. Concordance rates of intelligence as measured by newly invented intelligence tests established as fact that intelligence was highly heritable and that racial differences were to be expected. It took many years to discover that the twins on whom the conclusions were based did not exist, nor did the collaborators who were listed on many of the papers. It was a hoax of massive proportion. Back to the drawing board.

In the meantime, immigration to the US from Europe and Asia was in full swing; wars were being fought and cannon fodder was needed for the war machine. What could be more useful than "intelligence" tests to decide—fair and square—who should be let into the country, who should be admitted to school and who should have the privilege to serve as infantry in the trenches and foxholes of Europe? The tests themselves, while rather naive, were the least of the problem. The assumptions about their results were devastating for many. Could it be true that the rate of mental retardation among eastern and southern European immigrants and recruits was double or triple the rate among immigrants and recruits from northern and western Europe and that that of Asians was five to ten times the base rate?

It was accepted as fact, it seems, because of the social values of the time. A troubling positive correlation between number of years and/or number of generations in the US and IQ scores was ignored as irrelevant. The data clearly showed that the longer a person or his family had been in the US the more intelligent he was. What does this say about these revolutionary, new, objective measures of intelligence? Obviously, that they are culturally bound and dependent on the degree of assimilation in the culture and not true, objective measures of "natural intelligence."

Unit Focus. Psychologists' understanding of mental processes and intelligence has been transformed in the last couple of decades. The

information-processing model of memory has been refined and expanded to encompass the revolution in cognitive science. Study of this model will help you test the validity of claims of recovered repressed memories and memories obtained during hypnosis and/or "age regression." It will help you make sense of the loss of some types of memory while others remain miraculously intact. Until introduced to this research, many assume that memory functions like a video camera which reliably records whatever events it is aimed at and will play them back if we only can find the replay button. This idea ignores the fact that our brain is a living organ and that memory is a living process—it is subject to many types of disruption, injury and reconstruction. Memory is not etched in granite; it is preserved in the millions of living neuronal connections which are constantly being activated and destroyed. What passes for an accurate description of one's life is actually a constantly evolving description.

Although we use the analogy of the computer to think about the processes of memory we must keep in mind that memory is a living process. Unlike a library or computer, memories are growing and changing moment by moment as the brain grows and changes and as we reprocess memories again and again. It is not a static process but a dynamic one. The most important concept to grasp is that memory does not produce an accurate picture of historical fact—but a personal view of the experience. Memories are constructed and reconstructed. The lecture will use the concepts reviewed in the text to address the questions of accuracy and contamination in the phenomenon of "recovery of repressed memories" of childhood abuse.

The new **theories of intelligences,** which we will be studying, have developed because the old ones could not hold up to the test of rigorous scrutiny that is now commonplace in this science. It is an entirely a new ballgame. Our understanding of inheritance and gene expression makes the simple-minded claims of the early 20th century laughable, at best, fraudulent, at worst. The past focus on crude measures of the verbal skills of humans can no longer be passed off as valid measures of the numerous complex cognitive skills exhibited by humans and other primates. Too much is known about the workings of the mind to tolerate such simplicity. We must now speak of *intelligences*—not intelligence. How else can we understand savants who can barely talk or read who can calculate pi to 36 places in their head or produce an accurate drawing of a cathedral after only a brief glance? How else can we understand brilliant musicians who retain their entire musical repertoire but cannot distinguish a toothbrush from a hairbrush?

The big idea in this unit is the discovery that intelligence is not a unitary phenomena but is of several types. It is more accurate to speak of human intelligences. The lecture will introduce these ideas and will talk about how fraudulent data have been used from the very beginning of research on this topic to further the myth that intelligence is essentially innate and to justify (even promote) the social inequities seen between groups in American society. It is now appreciated in psychology that all tests of cognition or intelligence measure learned behaviors—no matter what the tests are called. It is also well understood that genetic expression requires environmental input at every level. Psychologists no longer ask "nature or nurture?" or even "in what proportion?" Questions such as these belie a poor understanding of the interactive processes of genes and environment.

A word of warning is appropriate. As long as we insist that this society is a meritocracy and assume that intelligence is the main path to success and that failure to succeed is a sign of intellectual inferiority, simple-minded, prejudicial debates about the nature and cause of intelligence will continue to occur regularly. Unfortunately the past tells us that when investment in a particular outcome (of research) is large, science becomes fraud.

Study Objectives

1. Learn in some detail the information-processing model of memory.
2. Compare and contrast the different types of memory—e.g., declarative, non-declarative, semantic, episodic, procedural and dispositions.
3. Learn the various explanation of forgetting.

4. Learn common causes of memory contamination.
5. Compare and contrast the various theories of intelligences.
6. Learn the development of cognition during childhood and the aging process.
7. Compare and contrast the different types of current measures used to assess cognitive abilities.

Key Terms

activity schemes
aptitude(s)
cognitive development
concrete operations stage
conserve
consolidation theory
content(s)
control processes
creativity
decay theory
deoxyribonucleic acid
divergent thinking
DNA
engrams
episodic memory
formal operations stage
human development
intellectual ability
intelligence
interference theory
long-term memory
metacognition
metamemory
method of loci
mnemonic techniques
mnemonist
moral development
nature
nurture
object permanence
operation(s)
pegword technique
permanent record
preoperational stage
proactive inhibition
problem finding
problem solving
procedural memory
product(s)
psychosexual stages of development
psychosocial development
recall (method)
recoding
recognition (method)
reconstructive processes
relearning (method)
retroactive inhibition
retrograde amnesia
ribonucleic acid
RNA
rote memory technique
semantic memory
sensorimotor stage
sensory brain buffers
serial position effect
short-term memory
stage(s)
Yerkes-Dodson Law

Problem Set #6: Memory and Intelligence

A. *Match the following terms with the correct definition.*

working memory
automatic processing
g factor
object permanence
mnemonic
retrograde amnesia
context-dependent memory
echoic memory
proactive interference
practical intelligence
preoperational stage
declarative memory
repression
sodium amytal
kinesthetic intelligence
chunking
long-term memory
WAIS
fluid intelligence
episodic memory
recency effect
confabulation
implicit memory
recall task
aptitude test
interperson intelligence
spacing effect
crystallized memory
recognition task

1. knowing to use flour to smother a cooking fire on the stove rather than water
2. storage maintained by active rehearsal; capacity about 7 units of information
3. a drug which has no efficacy in accurate memory retrieval
4. rehearsal approach that is superior for the long-term storage of memories
5. memories of facts or experiences which can be described in words
6. a memory assessment technique
7. tendency to remember the material studied at the end of a list
8. memory of your favorite birthday party

9. intelligence which is inherent in the performance of all tasks (common to all tasks)
10. abstract reasoning
11. psychological amnesia
12. short-term memory
13. intelligence which does not decline with age
14. Jesus Christ Made Seattle Under Protest (names of streets in business district)
15. assessment measure of adult intelligence
16. example of sensory memory register
17. inability to remember events occurring prior to the trauma
18. memory without conscious recall
19. disruption of prior learning on the storage of new information
20. using language but not concrete logic
21. the type of memory which declines with age
22. the ability to identify Harrison as a president of the United States when given the following names and asked to pick the one which does not belong: Lincoln, Reagan, Adams, Harrison, King, Carter, Jefferson.
23. ability to talk your way out of an impending physical assault or rape
24. intelligence involved in being an Olympic athlete

B. *Short Answer*

1. What are two differences between long-term and short-term memory according to the Information Processing Model of Memory?
2. Give an example of an encoding strategy which involves using a hierarchy.
3. Give two fundamentally different examples of non-declarative memory.
4. What is the fundamental difference between the amnesia observed with Alzheimer's Disease and Dissociative Disorders?
5. What are the pros and cons on using hypnosis as a memory retrieval strategy in eyewitness recall?
6. What is the current controversy about using "derepression" techniques to uncover memories of chidhood abuse?
7. What generally can we conclude about the contribution of genetics in the development of intelligence from the study of twins (MZ and DZ, reared together and reared apart).
8. What does this statement mean? The heritability of intelligence seems to be about .55 (accounts for 55 percent of the variance)?
9. Is the Sternberg-Wagner theory of intelligence closer to the Spearman or the Gardner theory of intelligence? Explain why.
10. How would each theory of intelligence explain a person's ability to build beautiful, functional, durable furniture?
11. Which theory has the best explanation for a person who can compute pi to 3,000 places "in his head" but is unable to read the *Reader's Digest*?
12. What is the most significant cognitive capacity which distinguishes a 1 year old from a 5 year old from a 10 year old from a 20 year old?

See Appendix C for answers to problem set.

7

Social Influences Upon Behavior: Social Psychology

Imagine yourself at a two-week workshop in a remote jungle in some small foreign country. You are a member of a *guerrilla army.* The workshop has been secretly set up to help you use psychology to influence the speedy development of a full-scale revolution among the common people toward democracy. You have been selected to participate because you have shown ability to express yourself. You and your fellow guerrillas each have been given a copy of a manual prepared by the United States Central Intelligence Agency (CIA). The title of the manual is *Psychological Operations in Guerrilla Warfare** (Tayacan, 1984). Let us see how this manual suggests you might influence the inhabitants to help overthrow their government.

Psychological Operations in Guerrilla Warfare: The Purposeful Management of an Entire Society

You have opened the manual and are reading the preface.

> Guerrilla warfare is essentially a political war. Therefore, its area of operations exceeds the territorial limits of conventional warfare, to penetrate the political entity itself: the *"political animal"* that Aristotle defined.
>
> In effect, the human being should be considered the priority objective of a political war. And conceived as the military target of guerrilla war, the human being has his most critical point in his mind. Once his mind has been reached, the "political animal" has been defeated, without necessarily receiving bullets. . . .
>
> This conception of guerrilla warfare as political war turns *Psychological Operations* into the decisive factor of the results. The target, then, is the minds of the population, all the population: our troops, the enemy troops and the civilian population.
>
> This book is a manual for the training of guerrillas in the psychological and democratic crusade being waged in Nicaragua by the Freedom Commandos.
>
> Welcome!

*The portions of this manual that appear here are from the actual CIA manual which was made available by the Library of Congress, October, 1984. This secret manual was brought to light as a result of an airplane crash that took the lives of three CIA agents.

This and the following excerpts from the 41-page manual will provide you with an overview of what the guerrillas would learn. First you are to think of yourself as a *Combatant-Propagandist* Guerrilla.

Combatant-Propagandist

> The objective of this section is to familiarize the guerrilla with the techniques of psychological operations, which maximizes the *social psychological* effect of a guerrilla movement, converting the guerrilla into a propagandist, in addition to being a combatant. The nature of the environment in guerrilla warfare does not permit sophisticated facilities for psychological operations (like newspaper and television campaigns), so that use should be made of the effective face-to-face persuasion of each guerrilla.

Face to Face Social Influence. So, you are going to have to influence the minds of others on a face-to-face basis.

> The individual political awareness of the guerrilla, the reason for his struggle, will be as important as his ability in combat. This political awareness and motivation will be achieved: . . . by developing in each guerrilla the ability of persuasion face-to-face, at the local level, to win the support of the population, which is essential for success in guerrilla warfare.

Group Dynamics. You are also taught the essentials of group dynamics.

> This political awareness-building and motivation are attained by the use of group dynamics at the level of small units. The group discussion method and self-criticism are a general guerrilla training and operations technique.
>
> Group discussions raise the spirit and increase the unity of thought in small guerrilla groups and exercise social pressure on the weakest members to better carry out their mission in training and future combat actions. These group discussions will give special emphasis to: . . . showing each guerrilla the need for good behavior to win the support of the population. Discussion guides should convince the guerrillas that the attitude and opinion of the population play a decisive role, because victory is impossible without popular support. . . .
>
> It is appropriate for the *cadre* (or the leader) to guide the discussion of a group to cover a number of points and to reach a correct conclusion. The guerrillas should feel that it was their free and own decision. The cadre should serve as a private teacher. The cadre or leader will not act as a lecturer, but will help the members of the group to study and express their own opinions. . . .
>
> This means that every guerrilla will come to have effective face-to-face persuasion as a combatant-propagandist in his contact with the people, to the point of giving 5–10 logical reasons why, e.g., a peasant should give him a piece of cloth, or a needle and thread to mend his clothes. When a guerrilla behaves in this manner, no type of propaganda of the enemy will be able to make a "terrorist" of him in the eyes of the people.

You, then, are being trained through this manual to become a group leader or cadre. You must help make the guerrillas feel that they are coming to their own conclusions about what they are doing as a part of the democratic struggle. And you must help them develop persuasive ways to win over the common people. Next you are taught how to propagandize about the frightening guns you and the other guerrillas are carrying and using.

Armed Propaganda

> Frequently a misunderstanding exists on *"armed propaganda,"* that this tactic is a compulsion of the people with arms. In reality, it does not include compulsion, but the guerrilla should know well the principles and methods of this tactic. The objective of this section is to give the guerrilla student an understanding of the armed propaganda that should be used, and that will be able to be applied in guerrilla warfare.

Becoming a Reliable Source—Influencing the Attitudes of Others.

> Close Identification with the People
>
> Armed propaganda includes all acts carried out by an armed force, whose results improve the attitude of the people toward

this force, and it does not include forced indoctrination. This is carried out by a close identification with the people at any occasion. For example:

How to Present the Message— Its Form and Content

—Putting aside weapons and working side by side with the peasants in the countryside: building, fishing, repairing roofs, transporting water, etc.
—When working with the people, the guerrillas can use slogans such as "many hands doing small things, but doing them together."
—Participating in the task of the people, they can establish a strong tie between them and the guerrillas and at the same time a popular support for our movement is generated . . .

In places and situations wherever possible, e.g., when they are resting during the march, the guerrillas can explain the operation of weapons to the youths and young men. They can show them an unloaded rifle so that they will learn to load it and unload it; their use, and aiming at imaginary targets since they are potential recruits for our forces.

The guerrillas should always be prepared with simple slogans in order to explain to the people, whether in an intentional form or by chance, the reason for the weapons.

"The weapons will be for winning freedom; they are for you."

"With weapons we can impose demands such as hospitals, schools, better roads, and social services for people, for you."

"Our weapons are, in truth, the weapons of the people; yours."

The Creation of the In-Group

. . . All of this should be designed to create an identification of the people with the weapons and the guerrillas who carry them. Finally, we should make the people feel that we are thinking of them and that the weapons are the people's in order to help them and protect them from a Communist, totalitarian, imperialist regime, indifferent to the needs of the population. . . .
—*Interior Group/Exterior Group.* It is a principle of psychology that we humans have the tendency to form personal associations from "we" and "the others," or "we" and "they," "friends" and "enemies," "fellow countrymen" and "foreigners," "mestizos" and "gringos."
—The Armed Propaganda Team can use this principle in its activities, so that it is obvious that the "exterior"/outside/groups ("false" groups) are those of the Sandinista regime, and that the "interior"/ inside/groups ("true" groups) that fight for the people, are the Freedom Commandos.
—We should inculcate this in the people in a subtle manner so that these feelings seem to be born of themselves, spontaneously. . . .

Influencing the Attitudes of Various Target Groups

In the motivation of the target groups by the Armed Propaganda Teams, the cadre should apply themes of "true" groups and themes of "false" groups. The true group will correspond to the target group and the false one to the Sandinista regime.
—For the economic interest groups, such as small businessmen and farmers, it should be emphasized that their potential progress is "limited" by the *Sandinista government,* that resources are scarcer and scarcer, the earnings/profits minimal, taxes high, etc. This can be applied to entrepreneurs of transportation and others.
—For elements ambitious for power and social positions, it will be emphasized that they will never be able to belong to the governmental social class, since they are hermetic in their circle of command. Example, the nine Sandinista leaders do not allow other persons to participate in the government, and they hinder the development of the economic and social potential of those like him, who have desires of overcoming this, which is unjust and arbitrary.
—Social and intellectual criticisms. They should be directed at the professionals, professors, teachers, priests, missionaries, students and others. Make them see that

their writings, commentaries or conversations are censored, which does not make it possible to correct these problems.
—Once the needs and frustrations of the target groups have been determined, the hostility of the people to the "false" groups will become more direct, against the current regime and its system of repression.

The plan for the guerrilla Armed Propaganda Teams is clear and simple. The people must be brought to identify with the guerrilla movement. But this must be done subtly so that the identification seems spontaneous. The formation of an *in-group* and *out-group* in the minds of the people is a very powerful social psychological principle. We will now skip over a section of the CIA manual that deals with a refinement of the development of "front groups" of businessmen, teachers, etc., to the final stages of the revolution—the control of mass meetings.

Control of Mass Concentrations of People and Meetings

In the last stages of a guerrilla war, mass concentrations and meetings are a powerful psychological tool for carrying out the mission. This section has as its objective giving the guerrilla student training on techniques for controlling mass concentrations and meetings in guerrilla warfare. . . .

Creating Prejudice and Stereotypes

—Our psychological war team should prepare in advance a hostile mental attitude among the target groups, so that at the decisive moment they can turn their furor into violence, demanding their rights that have been trampled upon by the regime.
—The basic objective of a preconditioning campaign is to create a negative "image" of the common enemy, e.g.:
—Describe the managers of collective government entities as trying to treat the staff the way "slave foremen" do.
—The police mistreat the people like the Communist "gestapo" does.
—The government officials of National Reconstruction are puppets of Russian-Cuban imperialism.

Selection of Appropriate Slogans

The leaders of the guerrilla warfare classify their slogans in accordance with the circumstances with the aim of mobilizing the masses in a wide scale of activities and at the highest emotional level.

When the mass uprising is being developed, our covert cadres should make partial demands, initially demanding, e.g. "We want food. We want freedom of worship. We want union freedom," steps that will lead us toward the realization of the goals of our movement, which are: GOD, HOMELAND AND DEMOCRACY. . . .

An example of the need to give simple slogans is that few people think in terms of millions of cordobas, but any citizen, however humble he may be, understands that a pair of shoes is necessary. The goals of the movement are of an ideological nature, but our agitators must realize that food, "bread and butter," "the tortilla and red beans," pull along the people, and it should be understood that this is their main mission.

Helping Create the Behavioral Components of Prejudice Creation of Guerrilla Agitator Groups

This involves the mobilization of a specific number of agitators of the guerrilla organization of the place. This group will inevitably attract an equal number of curious persons who seek adventures and emotions, as well as those unhappy with the system of government. The guerrillas will attract sympathizers, discontent citizens as a consequence of the repression of the system.

Way to Lead an Uprising at Mass Meetings

It can be carried out by means of a small group of guerrillas infiltrated within the masses, who will have the mission of agitating, giving the impression that there are many of them and that they have popular backing. Using the tactics of a force of 200–300 agitators, a demonstration can

> be created in which 10,000–20,000 persons take part. . . .
>
> Agitators of rallying cries and applause. They will be trained with specific instructions to use tried rallying cries. They will be able to use phrases such as "WE ARE HUNGRY. WE WANT BREAD." "WE DON'T WANT COMMUNISM." Their work and their technique for agitating the masses is quite similar to those of the leaders of applause and slogans at the high school football or baseball games. The objective is to become more adept and not just to shout rallying cries.

The revolution you have helped to create is now in final stages. Soon, if things go well, thousands of people will be running in the streets, the present regime will become disorganized. Then your leaders will be back in power! You have participated in the purposeful psychological management of a society.

The Value of the CIA Manual

This CIA manual caused quite a stir when its existence was accidentally discovered in 1984. To many, it seemed that the CIA was going against the very democratic ideals the manual was intended to rescue by proposing such a purposeful manipulation of a foreign country. However, no matter what your political persuasion happens to be, or how you personally react to portions of the manual, it does bring the power of social influences abruptly before us. The manual helps us bring together a great many applications of what *social psychology* has learned about how people influence the behavior of other people. As you study this chapter you will learn how social psychology has provided us—and the CIA—with enough knowledge to actually manage a society. I will discuss all of these topics which appear in the CIA manual and more in this chapter. It should strike you that this same information concerning social influences upon behavior can be and is used by politicians, advertisers and organizers from within and from without any country. While you can never be free from social influences, knowing more about how they operate can help you become more intelligent consumers of them.

Toward a Philosophy of Social Influences in Psychology: What Is the Subject Matter of Social Psychology?

Students of social psychology have designed the CIA manual. Social psychology can tell us precisely why and how its various recommendations would be effective. Going back to the subject matter question in psychology, we see in social psychology how minds influence minds (and therefore behavior) in the CIA example in a political/guerrilla setting. You already know what psychology is—the scientific study of human and animal behavior. Social psychology adds the social ingredient to the understanding of human behavior. Actually, you have already seen the effects of social influences described in other chapters. For example, Mohandas K. Gandhi was certainly influenced by both others and settings. I will draw your attention to more on the relationship of social psychology to other chapters in this book in a moment.

So, what is this social element? There are two ideas that must be addressed if we are to understand what social psychology is all about: (1) how the psychological part is pertinent in social psychology, and (2) how the social part is pertinent in social psychology.

The Psychological Part of Social Psychology. The first idea separates social psychology from its cousin, sociology (although there is a good deal of overlap between social psychology and sociology). The separation comes from social psychology's focus upon the behavior of the individual. Here's how Gordon Allport described this psychological part which is pertinent in social psychology: Social psychology is an attempt to understand how the thought, feeling, and behavior of the individual are influenced by the actual, imagined, or implied presence of others" (1968, p. 3). Exactly what this description means can be clarified through some examples of how people are actually influenced by others. Elliot Aronson (1984) suggests that this is the best way of getting a feel for social psychology. In the following examples, I have included two of Aronson's and one of my own. You can decide in each example whether the presence of others is actual, imagined, or implied.

> A four-year-old girl is given a toy drum for her birthday. After pounding on it for a few minutes, she casts it aside and studiously ignores it for the next several weeks. One day, a friend comes to visit, picks up the drum, and is about to play with it. Suddenly the young "owner" tears the drum from her friend's grasp and proceeds to play with it as if it had always been her favorite toy. (1984, p. 2)

> A ten-year-old boy avidly consumes two bowls of Wheaties daily because an Olympic decathlon champion endorses the product and implies that he owes his athletic prowess, in part, to the consumption of that particular brand of cereal. (p. 2)

> When the Reverend Jim Jones sounded the alert, over 900 members of the People's Temple settlement in Guyana gathered before him. He knew that some of the members of the congressional investigation party had been murdered and that the sanctity and isolation of Jonestown would soon be violated. Jones proclaimed that it was time for them to die. Vats of poison were prepared, and amidst only scattered shouts of protest or acts of resistance, mothers and fathers administered the fatal mixture to their infants and children, drank it themselves, and lay down, arm in arm, waiting to die. (p. 3)

The example I would like to add is the one I presented of myself in Chapter 8. It is 2 A.M. in the morning, and I am driving home from a late meeting in another city. I come to a stop light at a deserted intersection. I wait. The light doesn't change. I continue to wait, but I begin to question whether to just carefully look for traffic, and then go through the red light.

The Social Part of Social Psychology. The second idea that is important to understand social psychology is the fact that these thoughts, feelings and behavior are influenced within some setting. A *social setting* or context can be seen in each of the above examples of how people might be influenced by real, imagined, or implied others. Carolyn Wood Sherif has recently described the role of the social context or setting in relation to social influences. The current injunction (reminder as to how to go about social psychology), which is not new, is to study individual experience and behavior in social context. But what is a social context?

> In introductory psychology texts, a common definition of a social context is the presence, even the imagined presence, of other individuals. Others say that the social context is composed of interactions among individuals. As environmental psychologists remind us, however, individuals are located in some place, frequently in human-made locations with human-made objects, facilities, equipment, tools, books, and televisions, all of which are social. In those places, individuals engage by themselves, in pairs, in dyads, in quartets, or in larger groups in activities. Such activities are seldom random affairs without pattern. Individuals' encounters occur also within socially defined time frames and for varying periods.
>
> There is more to a social situation than can be seen with a glance or even with careful measurement of its physical character and count of its participants, as important as these are. Certain locations go with some activities but not with others, as one will quickly find if one has the impulse to turn handsprings in a lecture hall. (1982, p. 13)

The importance of considering context in social influences can be clearly seen in the example of the tragedy of Jonestown, and in my waiting for the traffic light to change. The emphasis on how the individual is affected by others and by the social settings created by others completes the essential picture of social psychology. You have seen how fundamentals from social psychology have been applied in a guerrilla warfare setting. These same fundamentals are applied quite differently in designing, for example, a space station habitat. There the social settings are studied not in terms of guerrilla disruption, for example, but for cooperation and productivity. But, in either case, the thoughts, feelings, and behavior of individuals are affected by others—or their real, imagined, or implied context.

Social Psychology Is Related to All of the Topics in Psychology. A final, helpful, way for you to understand social psychology is to think of it as a psychology within psychology. Social psychology can easily be related to the contents of the other chapters of this book. While these interrelationships are not the main concern of this chapter—that can await a later course devoted to social psychology—social influences upon individuals should be thought of in this very broad way. Figure 7.1 will help you understand what I mean by this idea. Perhaps you can think of a few more interrelating examples; there are a great many.

Theories in Social Psychology

Because social psychology has social influence concerns that are to a degree unique to itself, theories of social influence are likewise to a degree unique derivations of the traditional views in psychology. This may sound a little complicated, but it really isn't. Before discussing these "special" derivations it will be helpful to place them in relation to what you already know of the traditional theories. Table 7.1 contains a list of some of the major explanations of social influences, their focus in terms of causes, and the topics where commonly applied.

Since you are already familiar with the traditional views in psychology (from especially Chapters 1, 5, 6 & 8), I will discuss only the features of the derivatives. However, the overall frameworks of the traditional views are relevant to social psychology.

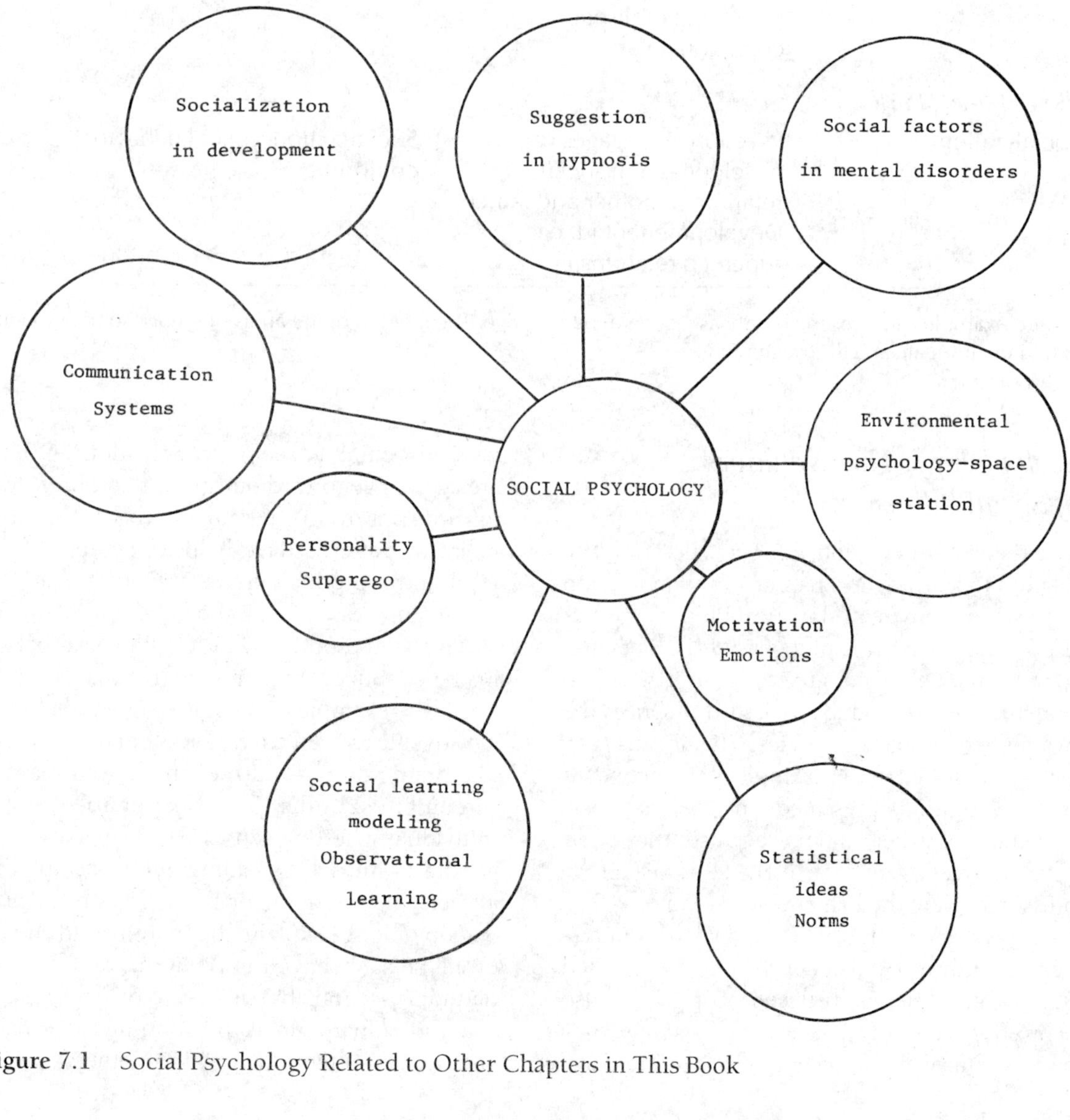

Figure 7.1 Social Psychology Related to Other Chapters in This Book

Table 7.1 Derivative Theories in Relation to the Traditional Views in Psychology

Theory	*Focus*	*Examples of Application in Social Psychology*
BIOLOGICAL		
Sociobiology	Social behavior traits subject to natural selection	In-group/out-group behavior, sexual behavior, territorial influences
LEARNING		
Social Learning	Imitation/modeling	Socialization, attitudes, attraction, in-group/out-group aggression and mutual protection
COGNITIVE		
Attribution Consistency Cognitive Dissonance	Interpretation and meaning of events involving others and contexts Balancing of disparate cognitions	Attitudes, attraction, conformity in-group/out-group perceptions
PSYCHOANALYTIC		
Socialization	Psychosexual stages of development in social relation to mother and father Development of id, ego, superego relationships	Socialization, sexual behavior, conformity

*These examples are presented only as a general perspective. The overlap of the areas of theory application are extremely intricate and thoroughgoing.

Sociobiology: The Evolution of Social Influences

The theory of evolution has been described in relation to learning in Chapter 5, and in relation to the development of statistical ideas in the statistical appendix. It is quite easy to understand how individuals who survive natural selection pressures to reproduce would influence the overall gene pool of a species. This idea is very clearly described in the example of the peppered moth evolution presented in the statistical appendix. Darker moths against the soot-covered trees were less likely to be eaten by birds than were the lighter colored moths.

Edward Wilson (1978), and Charles Lumsden and Edward Wilson (1981) have suggested that social influences between people have also evolved because of the adaptive advantage they bestow. This view is called *sociobiology*. Humans, baboons, chimpanzee troops, etc., form groups, are aggressive toward out-groups and protective toward in-group members, because these behavior patterns have helped ensure the survival and reproducibility of offspring. If evolutionary processes favor those who individually survive to reproduce, why would social behavior be adaptive? An often cited explanation for this is the example of the *"altruistic" social behavior* advantage seen in various rodent species—like prairie dogs—and broken-wing displays of certain birds. In the case of the prairie dog, the individual who first senses danger makes a target out of himself by calling out a warning that attracts the attention of the predators to him. Sociobiologists explain the adaptive advantage of this social behavior not in terms of individual natural selection, but in terms of *kin selection*. The individual animal, by sounding the alarm and drawing attention away from others, is actually more fit because its behavior allows more of his type genes (those of his related kin), including those related to altruistic behavior, to survive. This example is similar to the situation where a soldier leaps onto a live grenade, losing his life, but saving the lives of many humans who are his comrades. The point of these examples is that kin selection processes translate into a basis for social influences—the soldier would doubtlessly dive away from a live grenade if he were alone.

In the case of social influences among humans, Lamsden and Wilson argue that they evolved during the tens of thousands of generations of *hunter/gatherer groups* of the Ice Age epochs. Selection pressures over these generations of human groups resulted in what social influences we now see among modern human beings: altruism, in-group/out-group tendency, conformity, sexuality, love, attitudes (including religion and religious susceptibility to suggestion)—in short, the stuff of this chapter.

How would bigotry, racism, group aggression, etc., be adaptive social behavior that would increase kin survival, and therefore become a part of the genetic makeup of man? Wilson (1978) feels that these behavior tendencies stemmed from the most formidable of selection pressures, those of competing hunting and gathering groups. Thus, a strong fear of strangers would have led to a greater likelihood of survival, and to the successful survival of offspring, especially to an age at which they themselves could reproduce. As Lumsden and Wilson (1981) amplify on this:

> It may well be that bigotry and group aggression stem from the interaction of several quite distinct behaviors, including the fear of others' response, the proneness to associate with groups in the early stages of social play, and the intellectual tendency to dichotomize . . . other human beings into in-groups and out-groups. (p. 358)

This sort of social behavior may seem somewhat harmless, and somewhat protective, but in the modern world of billions of people competing for territory and resources, these genetically determined tendencies may be "outdated." Coming out of our Ice Age era of survival are some social tendencies Wilson refers to as the "single most dangerous force in the world today"—overly dogmatic religions.

> The highest forms of religious practice . . . can be seen to confer biological advantage. Above all they congeal identity. In the midst of the chaotic and potentially disorienting experiences each person undergoes daily, religion classifies him, provides him with an unquestioned membership in a group claiming great powers, and by this means gives him a driving purpose in life compatible with his self-interest. (1978, p. 188)

In the CIA manual, great advantage was taken of man's tendency to see others as belonging to either an in-group or an out-group. Lumsden and Wilson are suggesting that this tendency is now an outdated holdover from Ice Age survival.

Genes obviously play a great role in the social behavior of many species of animals—including insects—Wilson is an *entomologist* by training. Whether or not "social gene" effects will be isolated for human social behavior is presently unknown. On this we must keep an open mind. Language is, of course, social behavior. Lumsden and Wilson likewise see genes and *epigenetic rules* producing social deep structures in the brain that predispose humans to certain social behaviors and not others.

At any rate, while we wait for the resolution of this question, the sociobiological point of view is a helpful social systems view of social influences. It provides this systems perspective on two levels. First, the selection of social behavior among hunter/gatherer groups during the Ice Age offers a way to put the topics of social psychology into meaningful interrelationships. A simplified illustration of this idea is presented in Figure 7.2. Second, Lumsden and Wilson have placed *Genes, Mind, and Culture* (the title of their book) into a *coevolution* of mutual interactions. In this model, mind and social mind have become the prominent systems for analysis. This puts social psychology right in the middle of sociobiology and vice versa. Figure 7.3 illustrates this coevolutionary interrelationship. Genes and experience structure the human brain in a way that biases the brain to adopt certain types of culturally-related behaviors (e.g., in-group versus out-group), and, in turn, this affects the gene pool for the species

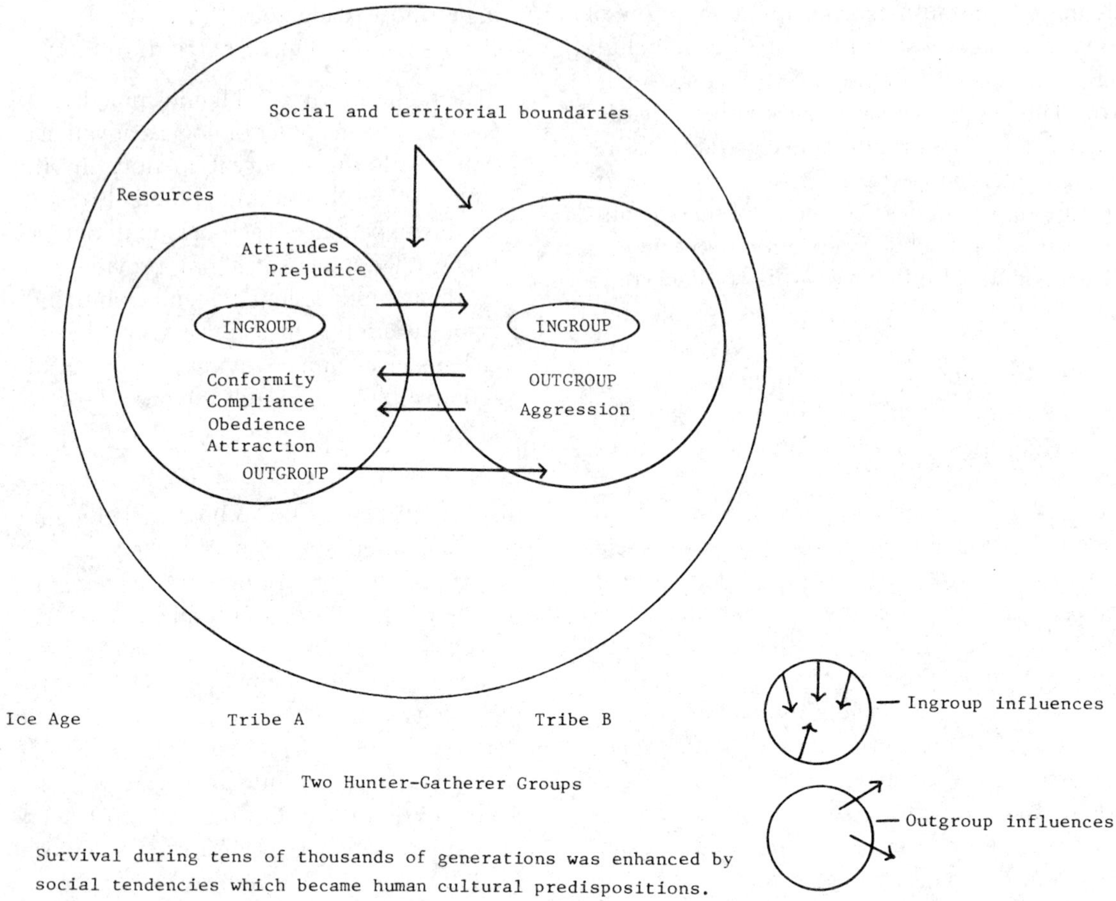

Figure 7.2 Sociobiological Perspective on Topics in Social Psychology

(for example, if in-group/out-group behavior is adaptive, it will become more dominant in the gene pool).

Sociobiology offers a broad perspective on social psychology. However, the details which explain the effectiveness of the CIA psychological warfare can be made more apparent by examining additional theories in social psychology.

Attribution Theory: Explaining the Behavior of Others

In Chapter 4, we discussed the attribution process in terms of how people explain the behavior of others to themselves. *Attribution theory* can also help explain a great deal about social influences.

Let's try to use this theory to explain why propagandist guerrillas would, for example, talk of true groups (us) and false groups (them), and create slogans which go hand-in-hand with the idea of "us" versus "them." Is this technique actually helpful, or is it so much wishful thinking? If it does help, why does it? There is no doubt that in-groups and out-groups form. And as Marilynn Brewer (1979), who has reviewed studies on this process, concluded: "Although groups may function in the absence of any other groups, the mere presence of an out-group is sufficient to significantly alter in-group processes (toward in-group favoritism)" (p. 322). So it appears that if you can get people to believe or realize that there is an out-group, they will become more favorable to members of the in-group with which they identify.

Once the idea that an out-group exists has been accepted (an attribution itself), aggressive attributions about the members of that out-group can easily be based upon their supposed *dispositional nature*. Simple slogans can help form and solidify *stereotypes* concerning the out-group. Now, any event that occurs such as scarcity of food

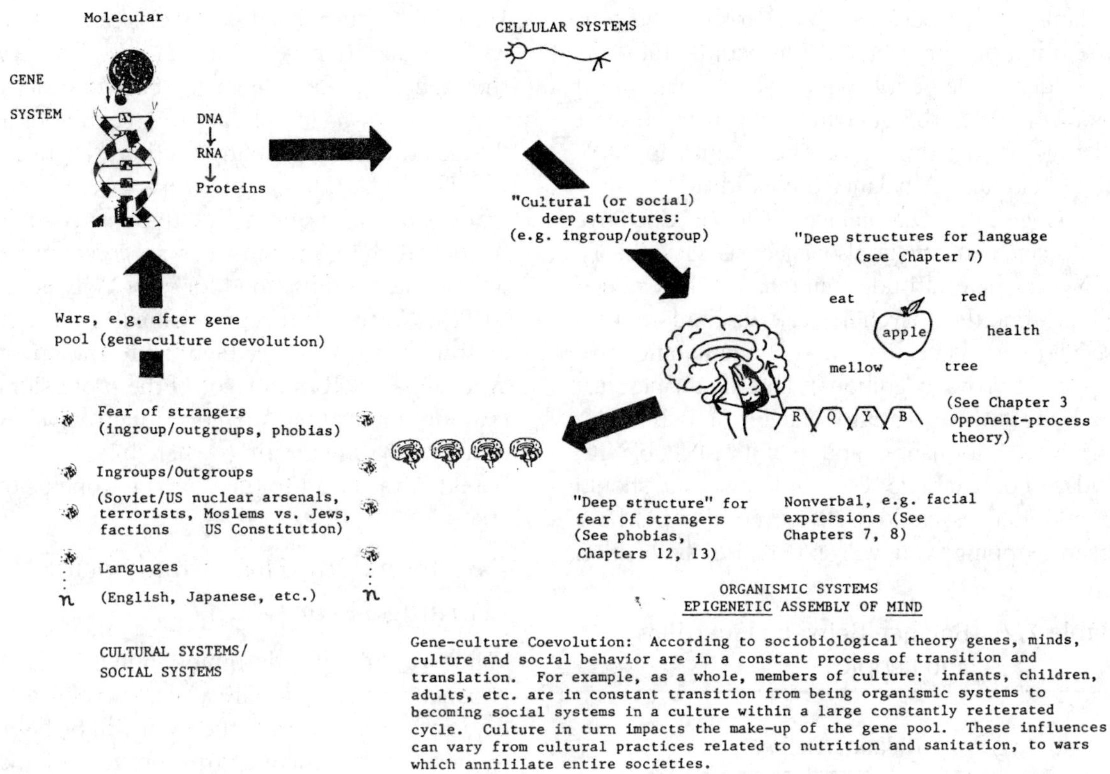

Figure 7.3 Gene-Mind-Culture Systems

or increased unemployment can be attributed to the stereotypical characteristics of the out-group. "They" are greedy, don't really care about the people, etc. These attributions satisfy the people's need to know why the events are occurring. According to attribution theory, every person, no matter how well educated, or what society he or she lives in, attributes events to something—right or wrong. Out-group stereotypes perform this function as long as the persons simply "spontaneously arrive at these conclusions themselves." Recall that the CIA manual emphasized that the combatant-propagandist must take this approach.

Attributions of why other people, groups, and even we ourselves do things are involved in one way or another in all areas of social influence—including attitudes, attraction, group aggression, etc. Attribution theory is an especially important explanatory model in social psychology.

Consistency Theories of Social Influence

The attribution process is fundamental in terms of explaining social influences. However, a person's *attitudes* about groups and stereotypes, for example, also are somehow maintained, and undergo change. Can we explain how the guerrillas mold, change, and maintain attitudes? *Consistency theory* helps answer these questions.

The guerrilla combatant-propagandists were very carefully taught to portray consistent pictures of what they stood for and were fighting for. They spoke of democracy, of being with the people, they had answers which all fit together concerning the why of their causes, they worked alongside the people, and they were honest with them. While these would be very nice attributes to find in anyone, the consistency of ideas, behavior, and feelings can very powerfully change and maintain attitudes.

There are several ways to look at the reason consistency influences attitudes. I will illustrate two of these consistency theories—balance theory and cognitive dissonance theory.

Balance Theory. Fritz Heider (1946) suggested that people balance their feelings and beliefs about other people against their feelings about aspects of the environment—an idea, object, or situation. This idea is called *balance theory*. If in the minds of the people there is a balance struck between the guerrillas and, say, the traditions or needs of the people, then the attitudes of the people will either be maintained as favorable to the guerrillas and their cause or change in that direction. The balance in Table 7.2 illustrates the balance theory idea.

Cognitive Dissonance Theory. Cognitive dissonance theory is also a consistency theory. However, here, attitude maintenance and changes hinge on the psychological discomfort (*dissonance*) that occurs when entertaining two opposing views (cognitions). This dissonance, just as hunger drives eating behavior, it is thought, drives the formation and maintenance of attitudes. For example, if you know you should attend your psychology class every day, but have been skipping, you will experience dissonance.

Table 7.2 Balance Between Guerrillas and People

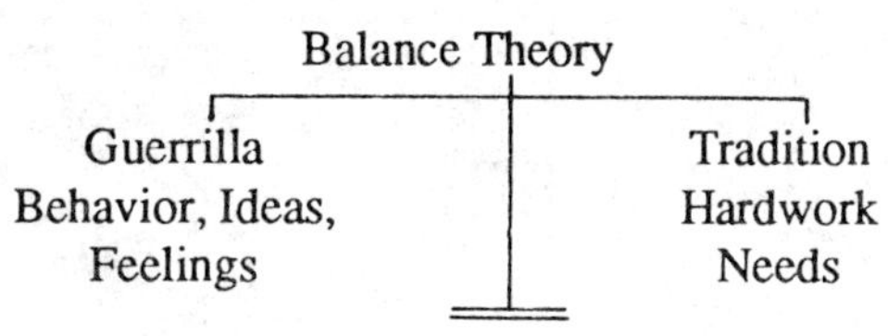

You could reduce this dissonance in any way you wish. It doesn't have to be sensible. Figure 7.4 shows how dissonance might be reduced by a variety of consonant, or balanced, cognitions and this determines the amount of attitude change.

The CIA-trained guerrillas were taught many ways to bring about dissonance in the people. If the government is so good for you, why is there so little food for you? Why is there so little work? In the professional groups, the existing dissonance (see Figure 7.5) was encouraged to be resolved in favor of the professional's training, rather than the government. This was done by holding meetings where free discussion would always lead to the "correct" conclusions.

Psychoanalytic Theory and Social Learning Theory

While you are already quite familiar with psychoanalytic theory (really a sociobiological theory) and social-learning theory, it will be helpful to closely relate them to the concerns of social psychology and to social influences. Both of the views rely heavily upon the role of social influences in the development of personality.

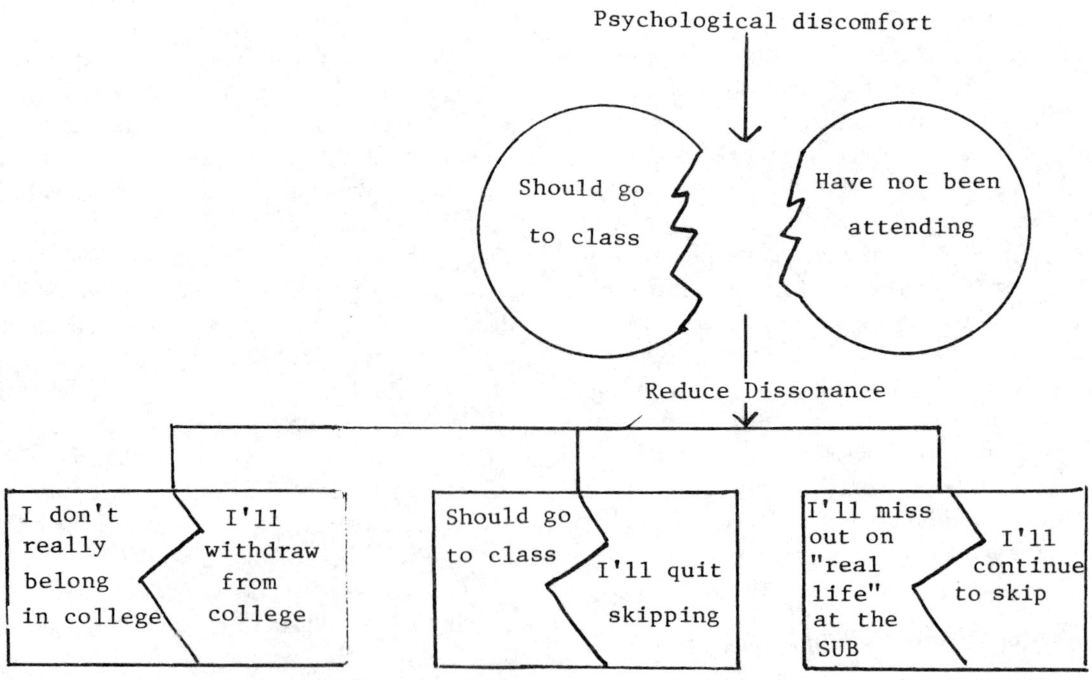

Figure 7.4 Consonant Alternatives That Reduce Psychological Discomfort

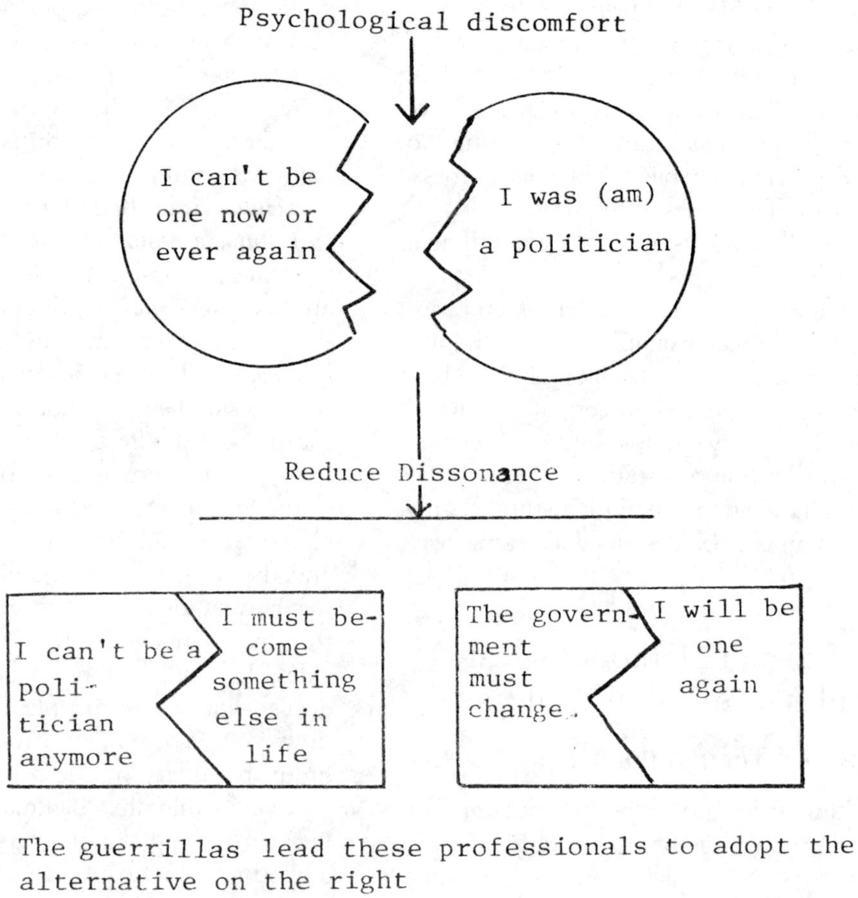

Figure 7.5 Resolution of Consonant Alternatives

Psychoanalytic Theory. In Chapter 6 and especially in Chapter 8, *Personality,* psychoanalytic theory viewed the development of the person as a social process. This process included the development of the id, ego, and superego relationships, and in turn in relation to what Freud termed the psychosexual stages of development. These developments are seen as powerfully influenced by the social interaction between the child and its mother and father. And the superego is essentially the internalized social influencing of behavior. In Chapter 10, *Treatment of Mental Disorders,* psychoanalytic therapy is described as a social influence process between the patient and the therapist. This relationship between the patient and therapist has a great deal to do with attribution and consistency theory. Finally, psychoanalytic theory takes the position that aggression and sexual behavior are innate (sociobiology).

Social Learning Theory. Social learning theory was discussed in some detail in Chapter 5, *Learning,* and Chapter 8, *Personality.* Social learning theory emphasizes the idea that skills, personality, attitudes, and aggression are learned through the observation and imitation of others. For example, attitudes can be socially learned simply through the observation of a model. In the case of the CIA manual recommendations, the combatant-propagandist was not only to serve as a model for the people (by knowing exactly why he was doing what he was doing), but of course for the children. Children naturally identify with and imitate the behavior of available models.

A Note on Social Influence Theories

It should be apparent that the various explanations of social influences on behavior pop up in a great variety of overlapping ways in everyday experience and application. The CIA examples illustrate this very well. For example, as one sees a combatant-propagandist guerrilla chatting and working side-by-side with the people he is trying to influence, one can see the formation of in-group/out-group boundaries, attributions taking place, consistencies and inconsistencies being experienced, and social learning occurring. So, as in the previous chapters, our goal is to see how the various theories of social psychology fit together in helping us to understand human social behavior.

We will now examine a variety of empirical and methodological examples of social influences that researchers in social psychology have provided for us. These examples will provide us with details of how groups, attitudes, persuasion, and attraction are studied. These studies take place in laboratories, in the natural setting, and some can only be described as taking place somewhere in between.

Empirical and Methodological Examples of Social Influences

Groups and Their Influence

If you think about groups of our ancestors surviving by pulling together in hunting and gathering parties, it is easy to get an initial perspective on groups. And the idea of in-groups and out-groups further broadens our understanding. But just what is a *group*? Some groups like a close-knit family or an army unit have very cohesive identity boundaries. Other groups, like the group that meets for your psychology class, may vary from being a minimal group with minimal boundaries to one that is very cohesive. You have likely been in classes of each kind. Finally, some groups are no more than an *aggregation* of people at a bus stop or waiting to board an airplane. In these aggregations of people, the group boundary is the most open. The essential feature in all of these examples of groups is the idea that there exists some degree of social influence boundary. All the way from the close-knit family to the aggregation waiting for the bus, a boundary exists that separates to some degree the members of the group from others who are not members. Another way to understand the idea of a group is to recognize that you and the other people who are milling about at a carnival do not constitute a group. There is no actual, imagined, or implied boundary that makes you members of a group. The people waiting for the bus, on the other hand, have such a boundary—both in their minds and in the minds of others. Or as McGrath and Kravitz (1982) put it, that the members take one another into account and that their relationship has some continuity of time or purpose

How Group Boundaries Have Been Found to Influence Behavior. Group boundaries tend to influence those inside to act similarly. If you are in an aggregation riding in an elevator, how do you act? Do you stand backwards staring everyone in the face? Do you crack jokes? Probably you stand silently, not moving much, facing the door. The effects of being a member of a group certainly involve conforming to the *norms* of the group. You conform to the norms of the elevator, the norms of your psychology class, and the norms of your family. It is interesting just how subtle the conformity can be in relation to group boundaries. You are walking down a sidewalk alone—with no actual group influences—you see five people looking up at a window, you also look up. You have broken the group boundary by the act of conforming! By the way, Milgram, Bickman, and Berkowitz (1969), found that if one person is looking up at a window, your chance of being influenced into conformity is about 40 percent. If five people are looking up, the chance goes to 75 percent. This greater influence of a larger number of people is important to note. We will return to it shortly.

Conformity. The classic experiment of the influence of groups on conformity to norms was conducted by Asch (1951). A group of subjects was asked to examine the standard line in Figure 7.6. Then they were asked which of the comparison lines corresponded in length to the standard line. This is obviously an easy judgment task. However, within the group of subjects only one subject (a *naive subject*) was actually being tested.

The rest of the subjects really consisted of a group of *confederate subjects* who, on certain trials, would unanimously choose the wrong comparison line. Even though this was a very easy task, approximately 33 percent of the naive subjects altered their responses to fit in with, or to conform to, the group norm (the wrong comparison line).

In Figure 7.7, you can see that the more confederates that were involved, the greater was the percentage of conformity. This finding is

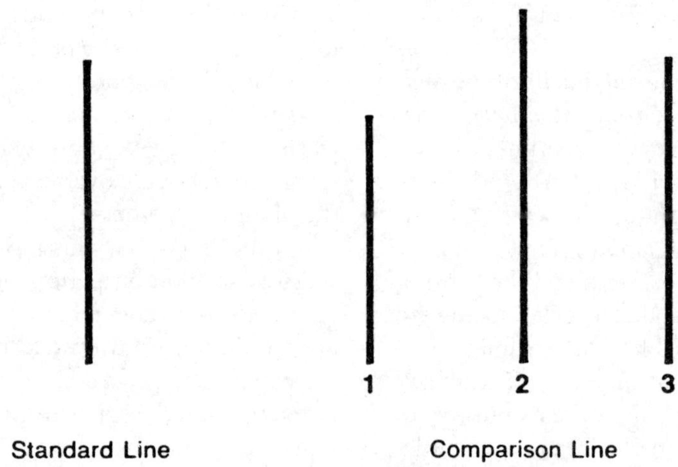

Figure 7.6 Conformity Study

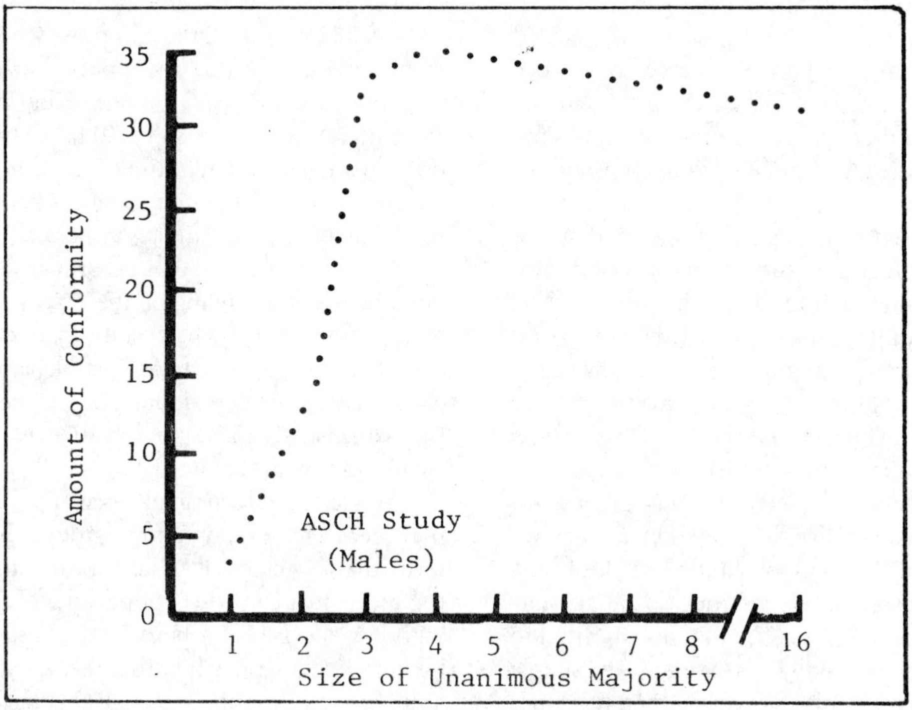

Figure 7.7 Three Studies of Conformity

similar to the situation where various numbers of research confederates were looking up at a window. You should also notice that the effect of the number of confederates reaches a plateau with three or four confederates.

This very pronounced tendency for persons to conform under group influence was used in the training of combatant-propagandists. While there were a number of reasons given by the naive subjects as to why they altered their judgments to conform to the group norm, they still did alter their responses. Whether they actually saw the wrong comparison line as the correct one, or just went along not to appear different, their conforming behavior was influenced by the group. How this type of conformity is influenced by guerrilla ideological discussion groups is complex. However, recall that discussion group pressure was recommended, especially in the case of members who did not seem to be so strongly committed to the causes of the revolutionary movement.

Why Conformity? Social Facilitation and Improved Efficiency of Group Members. The earliest social psychology experiment was designed by Triplett in 1898. This study is a classic in that it gets right at the heart of what social psychology is all about. First, Triplett compared the speeds of racing cyclists from their records. He found that cyclists racing in competition with cyclists had faster times than when racing alone against the clock. The social influence of other competing cyclists improved performance. Triplett then designed a little experiment involving the speed at which children could turn fishing reels (somewhat analogous to cranking the pedals on a bicycle). He found the same *social facilitation* effect. When in competition, many of the children could exceed the maximum they had been able to achieve when alone. In both of these examples, you can think of the other cyclists or other reelers as the actual, imagined, or implied group (presence of others who are taken into account).

The Triplett studies make it appear that one reason to form groups and to conform under in-group pressures would be to increase performances of group members, and thereby the group performance. This certainly happens under many circumstances, for example, in games or on the battlefield. However, the presence of others, it has been found, can also reduce the performances of group members under certain circumstances—a facilitation in a negative direction. Often when we are learning a new skill, we find ourselves asking others not to watch lest we foul up our performance. My own son is constantly disconcerted to find that some new skill he is learning, like simple juggling, always seems to go awry when he comes to show me. While we could explain this negative social influence by pointing out that the Yerkes-Dodson principle (Chapter 6) predicts such a negative outcome, the social influence remains the phenomenon of interest to social psychology.

Robert B. Zajonc (1965) has put both the positive and negative types of social facilitation into a social influences perspective. Zajonc has suggested that the presence of others, either as co-actors or spectators, facilitates or increases the dominant response (behavior) tendencies of the individual. Therefore, if the performance involves correct response tendencies such as simple reeling or pedaling behaviors, social influence will push the performance in a positive direction. If, on the other hand, the dominant response tendencies are incorrect (my son just learning to juggle), those will be facilitated, or increased, reducing overall performance when in the presence of others (his father in this case).

It may seem that this mixed bag of effects of social facilitation on performance might *not* be a reason to form and maintain group boundaries and to conform. However, it should be noted that the net effects of social facilitation, while at times negative, would be positive. The real effects of reduced performance during the learning of a new skill just gets the person to work harder. These are the effects of negative reinforcement. The person works harder to avoid the aversive disappointment expressed by real or imagined others.

Social Loafing. If the group as a whole, rather than individuals within the group, has some task to perform, *social loafing* occurs. Bibb Latané, K. Williams, and S. Harkins (1979) have studied this phenomenon in many settings. Each member of the group in these situations reduces his effort and productivity. For example, a person will pull harder on a rope when alone than when there are other people also pulling on the rope; people clap their hands louder when alone than when in a crowd (see Figure 7.8). As a student in college classrooms, you have doubtlessly noticed that in very large classes there is less participation than in small classes—academic loafing.

While social loafing, like negative facilitation, may seem a reason not to form groups and to conform, the net effect is just the opposite. In a group, the individual can reap the benefits of the group with less effort. His or her physical resources can be conserved. And while this "Let George do it" attitude, as Kerr and Brunn (1983) have characterized this phenomenon, may be looked upon as "loafing," loafing has other values to the individual. It allows participation in many groups—in some of which the individual's performances may be being positively facilitated. In other words, it is important for us not to evaluate the social influences in relation to one group only. Each person participates in a larger system of groups. It is unlikely that he or she "loafs" in all of them.

The Group's Effect on the Formation of Conforming Cognitions and Cognitive Performance. We have seen how group pressures lead to conformity in perceptual reports (Asch), and

Figure 7.8 Social Loafing

to facilitating motor performances (Triplett, Latané, Williams & Harkins). Group pressures to conform also alter the formation of cognitions and cognitive performance. So, the alterations in performance we have been discussing are probably not a simple matter of subjects purposely conforming just to be polite, or loafing to get out of work. Rather, the way things are thought to be is actually being influenced by the presence of a group. You may recall that I suggested something very much akin to this at the beginning of the hypnosis section in Chapter 4—your entire belief in what is taking place at a public event may be greatly influenced by a crowd.

Groupthink. Irving Janis (1971, 1972, 1973) has studied the performance of very high-ranking and talented groups and found that they, as a group, often came to some rather stupid decisions. Janis was puzzled by the United States military and political fiascoes like the disastrous decision by John F. Kennedy to invade Cuba's Bay of Pigs, and Franklin D. Roosevelt's failure to have the nation prepared for Pearl Harbor. It seemed that if any rational person had been in possession of the same information these men had they would not have acted so foolishly! But therein lies the problem. Small, cohesive groups, such as the president and his advisors, do not come to their decisions on a purely rational basis. Rather, in-group pressures to maintain group cohesion and its comforts of a pleasant consensual atmosphere—". . . the lazy, we-feeling atmosphere"—are at work. Because group members do not want to spoil this atmosphere of belonging and consensus, critical evaluations and misgivings are bypassed for fear of "rocking the boat." But, an important thing to realize here is that group members don't deliberately let things go on in this irrational manner. The members actually rationalize a set of unconsciously shared illusions—"*groupthink.*" You might wish to compare this idea with the idea of ego defensive mechanisms, Chapter 8.

Janis has proposed a number of techniques which can help prevent the solidification of a cohesive group's mind-set (groupthink). While you may think in terms of the president and his advisors, these groupthink-busting techniques can be applied to any group which has a tough decision to make. Remember, the family is usually an example of a small cohesive group.

Breaking Up Groupthink(ing)

1. Discuss the dangers of groupthink with the group members.
2. The group leader should remain impartial.
3. Everyone should be instructed to express any objections and/or doubts.

4. At any meetings, assign at least one group member to play the role of devil's advocate by taking an opposing viewpoint.
5. Occasionally subdivide the group into small groups that meet separately.
6. Pay attention to all warning signals from a possible rival nation, business, group, etc.
7. Relax; change your thoughts (see below, second-chance meeting).
8. Invite outside experts to come in to challenge the group's views.
9. Encourage group members to sound out group thoughts with trusted associates.
10. Have several independent groups work on the same question or problem at the same time.
11. Call a "second-chance" meeting to reevaluate the preliminary decision.

> ***Second-Chance Meeting***
>
> It might not be a bad idea for the second-chance meeting to take place in a relaxed atmosphere far from the executive suite, perhaps over drinks. According to a report by Herodotus dating from about 450 B.C., whenever the ancient Persians made a decision following sober deliberations, they would always reconsider the matter under the influence of wine. Tacitus claimed that during Roman times, the Germans also had a custom of arriving at each decision twice—once sober, once drunk. (Janis, 1973, p. 16)

It should be pointed out that representatives of the CIA were intensively consulted on what was to become known as the Bay of Pigs fiasco. CIA representatives were also involved in the writing of the guerrilla training manual. While many portions of this manual represent sound social psychology applications, and certainly represent an enlightened way of winning the people of a society to your cause, some portions were outrageous distortions of the way the United States would have peoples come to embrace the principles of a free democracy. This point is not necessarily a failing on the part of the CIA, but an illustration of the tremendous power of some social influences—like groupthink!

Brainstorming. You have probably heard the term "brainstorming." *Brainstorming* is a group technique which was developed with the aim of getting groups to produce creative ideas. Initially, the technique was developed by Alex Osborn with the goal of producing advertising campaigns. Keep this original purpose in mind when you read the details of the technique. Brainstorming can be used for any group purpose (actually an individual can apply it to situations in his own life—more on this in a moment). The technique is especially useful in two types of situations: (1) in determining how a certain goal might be achieved, and (2) discovering the possible consequences of certain actions. An example of the first situation might be, "How could we eradicate terrorism from the world?" An example of the second situation might be, "What would be the effects of desalinizing vast quantities of ocean water to irrigate all of the available land in the world?" The following are Osborn's rules for a group brainstorming session (1957):

1. All criticism or analysis of suggestions is withheld until the end of the session.
2. "The wilder the idea the better."
3. A great number of suggestions is desired.
4. Building on previous suggestions, in the form of combinations of improvements, is welcome.

Typically, the group is presented with the question or problem, and a session leader or monitor records the suggestions of the "brainstormers" on a chalkboard or a flipchart. Once a large number of suggestions have been recorded, a judgment process reduces the list to the more useful ones. For example, considering the desalinization problem, the suggestion "The price of salt would go down" might be eliminated; and the suggestion, "Certain sea animals/plants might lose their tenuous hold in sea ecosystems, leading to a domino effect," might be further considered.

The need for brainstorming techniques is not unrelated to the problem of groupthink. Both brainstorming and Janis's recommendations on how to avoid groupthink involve the central idea of preventing a group mental-set by allowing group members to be "devil's advocates" without threatening their secure place in the group. In this way, brainstorming can be looked upon as a technique which works against conformity pressures when the situation requires it. In other words, neither Janis' nor Osborn's techniques would be necessary if it were not for the presence of in-group pressures to conform. Further, it is of interest to note along this line that the group setting itself in typical brainstorming practices tends to contain an element of pressure to conform. H. Lamm and G. Trommsdorf (1973) have found that an equal number of individuals brainstorming alone produce more ideas than those brainstorming in-groups. This means that you, working alone, can achieve some benefits from applying the technique to your own decision making.

Obedience: An Illustration of the Power of a Group's Influence on the Individual

In all of the examples of conformity we have examined, the distortion of line lengths in Asch's experiments, the effects of groupthink, etc., can be thought of as *obedience* to group pressures. Within the framework of social influences, obedience is a conforming to real, imagined, or implied group norms. The importance of noting this full spectrum of social influences will be clear in a moment.

It is difficult for you, sitting there reading this textbook, to understand how well-educated Nazi German officers could obediently commit atrocities. It is equally difficult for you to understand how nearly 900 members of Jim Jones's People's Temple could obediently commit mass suicide. But it is important for you as a student of social psychology to realize that most of us would do the same thing if under the same group pressures to conform!

The Milgram Experiments on Obedience. You do not have to be in an actual group to respond to group pressure. Institutionalized group symbols, like uniforms, social positions, and roles imply broad group participation and norms. If you are a religious person, certain members of the church and what they wear represent enormous pressures for you to conform. If you are a law-abiding citizen, the appearance of a police officer in uniform is a strong pressure for you to conform; you may respect the uniform, if not the person wearing it.

During the Nazi war criminal trials held at Nuremburg, soldiers who had committed great atrocities on their fellow humans were asked how they could possibly have committed such acts. A common excuse came down to, "I was just following orders." Is it possible that these people really had no other rational explanation for their behavior? Stanley Milgram (1963) has very carefully studied this possibility with some rather shocking findings. I am going to put you right into one of Milgram's experiments—into a social context.

The Experiment. Imagine yourself and one other subject being brought into a Yale University laboratory. You are here because you have responded to a newspaper advertisement appealing for subjects to participate in a study of learning and memory. The university has paid you $4.50 (it's 1961) just for coming into the laboratory about the study. The study is explained to you. "After a general introduction on the presumed relation between punishment and learning," you are told:

> But actually, we know very little about the effect of the punishment on learning, because almost no truly scientific studies have been made of it in human beings.
>
> For instance, we don't know how much punishment is best for learning and we don't know how much difference it makes as to who is giving the punishment, whether an adult learns best from a younger or an older person than himself—or many things of that sort.
>
> So in this study we are bringing together a number of adults of different occupations and ages. And we're asking some of them to be teachers and some of them to be learners.
>
> We want to find out just what effect different people have on each other as teachers and learners, and also what effect punishment will have on learning in this situation.
>
> Therefore, I'm going to ask one of you to be the teacher here tonight and the other one to be the learner.
>
> Does either of you have a preference?

Neither of you has a preference. So, you are asked to draw slips of paper from a hat for assignment. One slip of paper says "teacher," the other "learner." You get the slip that says "teacher." You and the other subject who is the learner are taken to an adjacent room, and the learner is strapped into an "electric chair"-appearing apparatus. The experimenter tells you both that the straps are necessary to prevent excess movement when the learner is being shocked (punished). You can also see that it would be nearly impossible for the learner to escape on his own. The experimenter attaches an electrode to the learner's wrist. An electrode paste was applied between the electrode and the learner's skin. The experimenter explains that this is necessary to avoid blisters and burns. You are both told that the electrode is attached to a shock generator in the next room. The learner asks about the severity of the shock he will receive. The experimenter replies, "Although the shocks can be extremely painful, they cause no permanent tissue damage."

The learning task is explained to you and the learner. You, the teacher, are to read pairs of words to the learner, then you read the first word only along with four terms. The learner is to indicate which of the four terms was originally paired with the first word. This is like an oral multiple-choice exam.

You are then taken to the next room and seated before the shock generator. You notice that the generator instrument panel is marked off with voltages from 15 to 450 volts. The voltage switches for administering the shocks are marked off in 15-volt increments. In addition, each set of four switches is labeled as the voltages increase as follows: Slight Shock, Moderate Shock, Strong Shock, Very Strong Shock, Intense Shock, Extreme Intensity Shock, Danger: Severe Shock, and the last two switches are simply marked "XXX."

You are now told to use the shock punishment as follows: Each time the learner makes an error, shock him. And, each time, move one switch higher on the shock generator. Each time before you administer the shock, announce the voltage level. Before you begin you are given a sample shock of 45 volts so that you have an idea of the amount of punishment you are delivering—the 45 volts gives you a good sting.

You begin. As the experiment progresses, the learner makes errors, and you find yourself steadily increasing the amount of shock you administer to him. Soon, at 75 volts, the learner moans a little, at 150 volts, he demands to be released from the chair, at 180, he says he can no longer stand the pain; at 300 volts the man screams and says he has a heart problem! You look to the experimenter. He prods you on, finally saying, "You have no other choice, you must go on." After the 300-volt level, you continue on, but the learner no longer responds to your word pair questions. And, he no longer says anything as the experimenter prods you on to higher and higher voltages.

Startling Results of the Experiment. Would you go on if you were really the "teacher" in this situation? Would you have gone up to 450 volts? You are probably saying, "No, of course not!" Milgram found, much to everybody's amazement, that in such a situation all teachers went at least to the 300 volt level, and 65 percent of the teachers (26 out of 40 subjects) went all the way to 450 volts—most of the teachers!

Actually, no one was really shocked in this experiment. You, the teacher, were deluded into thinking it was the behavior of the learner that was being studied. In fact, it was your behavior that was under study. The learner was a research confederate. Both pieces of paper in the hat you drew from said "teacher" on them. You were found to be very obedient to authority—65 percent chance that you would go all the way to 450 "deadly" volts. What would you say after taking the poor learner up to 300 very painful volts, "I was just following orders?" It is interesting to note that many of the teachers suffered a great deal of emotional strain during their supposed delivery of shocks. Here's one observer's account of the effect on one teacher:

> I observed a mature and initially poised businessman enter the laboratory smiling and confident. Within 20 minutes he was reduced to a twitching, stuttering wreck, who was rapidly approaching a point of nervous collapse. He constantly pulled on his earlobe, and twisted his hands. At one point he pushed his fist into his forehead and muttered: "Oh God, let's stop it." And yet he continued to respond to every word of the experimenter, and obeyed to the end.

This sort of hardship under the false pretenses of the experiment led university officials to question the experimenters as to why they allowed the duped subjects to suffer such stress. Their answer? "Milgram told us to!"

This example of obedience (and those of Nazi soldiers) may leave you wondering why such a tendency to conform is so powerful. It seems stronger than gravity! And why is it that not only is the tendency so powerful, but why is the aggression? Why would we allow ourselves to hurt other people? Actually, the situation is not totally bleak. If we consider this behavior from the sociobiological point of view, our social behavior is that of survival among hunter/gatherer parties. We can see that the powerful tendency to conform is not only behind aggressive behavior, but also behind *prosocial behavior*—the tendency to protect, defend, and help those we perceive to be a part of our hunting/gathering group, if you will. In other words, we tend to be aggressive toward the members of other groups (outgroups), but just as powerfully protective of members of our own group. You will recall from Chapter 8, *Personality,* that psychoanalytic theory saw the harnessing of the powerful sexual and aggressive drives (id) toward socially acceptable and prosocial works as sublimations of this energy.

The often-cited closest relative of humans, the chimpanzee, survives in the wild in prehuman-like food hunting and gathering groups (troops). Making the sociobiological argument, David Hamburg (1983) describes these in-group/out-group parallels:

> Monkeys and apes are particularly likely to engage in aggression in the following situations:
>
> 1. When competing for scarce and/or valuable resources that promote survival and reproductive success (for example, food, and for males, access to fertile females).
> 2. In competition for high status within the group; severe aggression is particularly likely during periods of unstable dominance relationships.
> 3. When protecting close friends or relatives, and particularly infants, from threat or attack by other group members.
> 4. In response to threat or attack by higher-ranking animals; in this case, redirection of aggression toward subordinates is common.
> 5. Toward strangers trying to enter the group and toward members of other groups, particularly when the groups are in competition for access to mates,

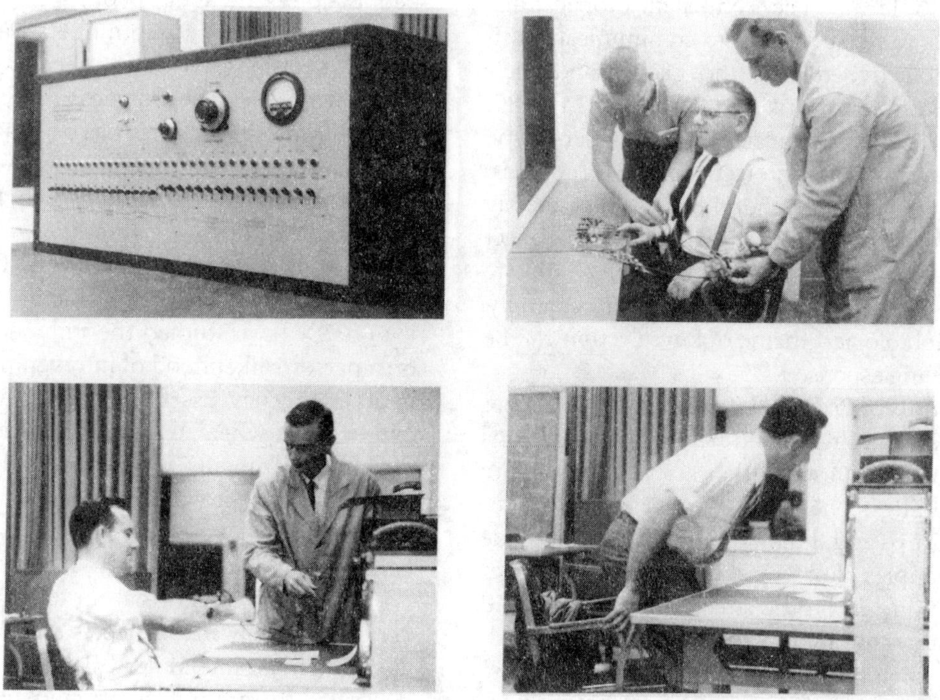

Figure 7.9 Milgram Obedience

territory, or high-quality, clumped foods.

6. In at least some species, lower-ranking individuals are sometimes attacked when they refuse to cooperate with the goals of higher-ranking animals; for example, female chimpanzees who resist a male's attempts to mate, or female and infant baboons who refuse to serve as "buffers" for a male engaged in aggressive interactions with another male. (p. 59)

It is true that aggressions seems to be emphasized here, but the prosocial behavior toward members of one's own group and kin is also very apparent (see especially Hamburg's examples 3 and 5). So it can be seen that the very pressure you saw pushing Milgram's teachers to be obedient also drives us to use our abilities to protect.

Prosocial Behavior

The results of Milgram's experiments then may seem to reveal a side of human nature that is antisocial. However, we see around us in the world people giving, sharing, helping, doing volunteer work, and risking their lives to save others. And, while you may see armies as merchants of death, the purpose of your own army is to protect you—the soldier risks his life to protect his group, and is a hero for it. The combatant-propagandist guerrillas were taught how to communicate both their protective role to the people and their aggressive role toward the out-group. In 1985, great collections of musicians and singers came together to save and protect starving Ethiopians. This group conceived the whole world as one big in-group. They used their special skills to collect millions of dollars writing and singing "We Are the World." If one listens to the lyrics carefully, the sociobiological theme of kin selection can be heard being espoused.

Details of Prosocial Behavior. The number of volunteer workers and helping organizations in the world attests to the fact that people are very willing to help others. The United States Peace Corps and the International Red Cross are fine examples of prosocial behavior. If a stranger comes up to us on the street (and he is dressed reasonably) asking directions, we are very willing to take the responsibility to help. These examples, however, generally constitute non-emergency situations. It might seem that people would be even more willing to help in emergency situations. However, as you will see, emergency situations contain a number of factors which may retard or complicate the behavior of potential helpers or prevent bystanders from intervening.

Bystander Intervention Studies. On occasion, you will read or hear of situations where someone badly needed help, but no one gave it. The case of Kitty Genovese's murder has become a classic example of this, and it spurred much research into the complexities of bystander intervention in emergency situations. Kitty was attacked at night on a street in Queens, New York, in 1964. The killer stabbed her as she fought and screamed. At least 38 residents of a nearby apartment building were awakened. They turned on their lights and looked out of their windows to see Kitty being stabbed to death. The lights from the apartments scared off the killer. Kitty was left lying in the street. The apartment dwellers turned off their lights and offered no help. The killer returned. Again Kitty's screams brought on the lights. The killer again fled. The apartment lights again went out—still no help—not even a phone call to the police. The killer returned a third time and killed Kitty. Only after it was too late did anyone call the police.

This story should not suggest to you that people don't care about people. This is not true any more than that groupthinkers want to make stupid decisions, or that obedient shockers shock with glee. The slowness of bystanders to help in some emergencies has been attributed to what has been called a *diffusion of responsibility*. This phenomenon is akin to the mechanism described earlier in social loafing—"Let George do it," or, in this case, "George will do it." Latané (whose work I cited on social loafing) and Darley (1970) have studied the influence of others on a person's likelihood of intervening with help in an emergency. Essentially, across a number of experiments where sham emergencies came up during experiments purported to be studying something else, it was found that if the subjects thought others were also witnessing the emergency, they were less likely to intervene.

It must be noted that an emergency by its very nature may involve costs and confusion to any potential interveners. Latané and Darley described the general situation in an emergency in this way:

> Faced with a situation in which he can gain no benefit, unable to rely on past experience, on the experience of others, or on forethought and planning, denied the opportunity to consider carefully his course of action, the bystander to an emergency is in an unenviable position. It is perhaps surprising that anyone should intervene at all. (p. 31)

Whether or not a person or a group of people do intervene in an emergency, then, depends not just on a ready willingness to be helpful—like giving directions—but on some cognitive considerations first. Figure 7.10 illustrates the process that a person must complete before intervention occurs.

A police officer is highly trained for emergency circumstances, and you can easily trace the components of his training in this model. In the case of starving people in Ethiopia, the massive response that was needed was rather slow. It was a little like Kitty's situation. People in the United States and Europe were very slow to even notice that something was happening in Ethiopia. Then, it was some time before it was interpreted as an emergency (surely, they thought, the government will do something). The decision about whose responsibility it was took time. After a time, it was found that help was not forthcoming as fast as was necessary—it was a more complex problem (emergency) than had been thought. The "How can I help?" part left many people paralyzed—if the government can't help, how can I? Some people began to conceptualize the "emergency" as a crest in an ongoing problem. Finally, some people, like Harry Belafonte, realized that the great power of the media would be a way to intervene. The "We Are the World" campaign was one way of addressing the question in the "What Should I Do?" box. Unfortunately, many people have died in Ethiopia partly because of this sort of global bystander apathy, and the bystander apathy of their own government. On the other hand, of course, we eventually got through the decision process, and many people are alive in Ethiopia today because of bystander intervention.

You should not get the idea from this that if you are in trouble when many people are around, you are a "goner." In real-life situations it has been found that bystanders usually do help—it depends on the circumstances. Piliavin, Robin, and Pitiavin (1969) and other researchers have noted that people in emergencies are very seldom left to flounder. They have concluded that the presence of other bystanders actually increases the chances that someone will help. People apparently assume that other bystanders will help them in their efforts to go to the distressed person's aid. Does this mean that Latané and Darley were wrong? No, it means we must modify the nature of the diffusion of responsibility in their model above. We must add the bystander's cognitive analysis of costs and benefits of intervening. Morgan (1978) has found that when perceived costs to the intervener are high, and the benefits of not intervening are also high, people tend not to intervene so rapidly. But when perceived costs of intervening are low, and the benefits of not intervening are also low, diffusion of responsibility did not occur. Figure 7.11 is a modified version of Latané and Darley's taking into account the bystander's analysis of cost and benefits of intervening. Perhaps we can now understand why there was no intervention for Kitty Genovese.

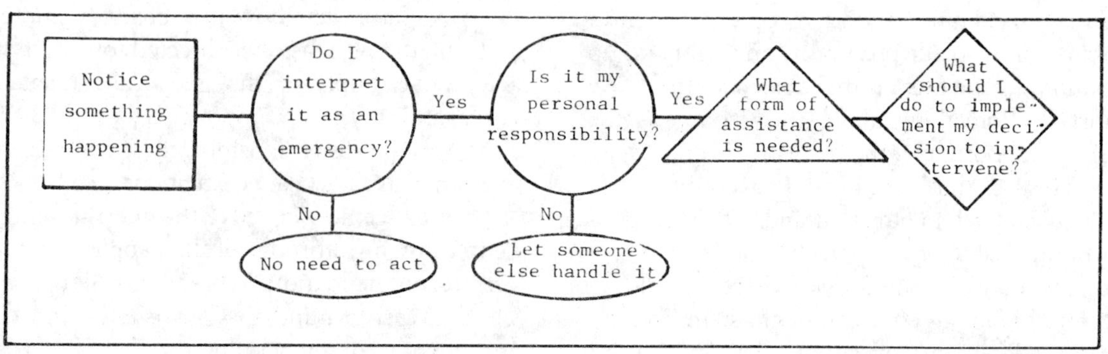

Figure 7.10 Intervention Model of Latané and Darley

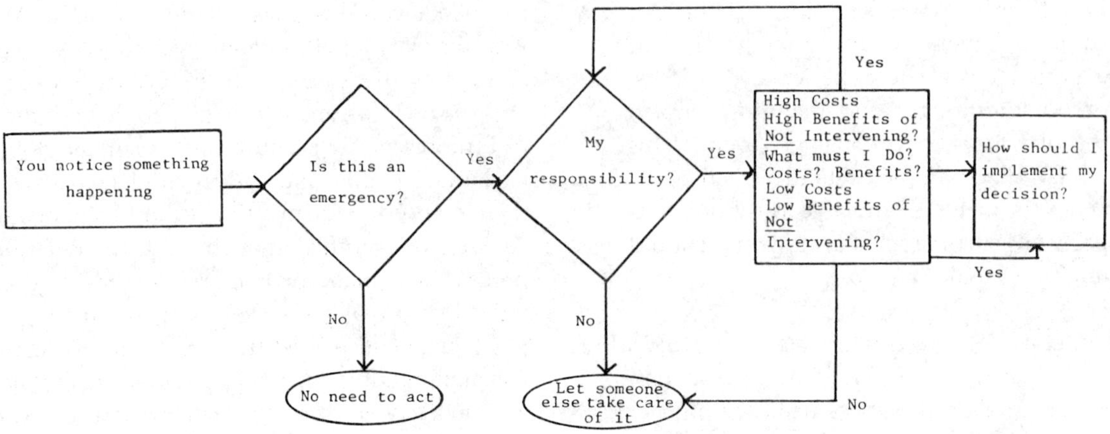

The Costs of Intervening are Usually Weighed. If the answer is NO anywhere along the way toward a decision, there is no intervention. If YES occurs *twice* after "Is it my responsibility?" the person takes on a high cost intervention. The diagram shows that responsibility is determined partly on the basis of costs involved. For example, a person may say YES, it is my responsibility, but the costs *to me* are too high. I'd better let someone else (stronger, more skilled, etc.) handle it.

Figure 7.11 Modified Intervention Model

Attitudes and Changing Attitudes

The influence of the presence of others on behavior is readily seen in all of the foregoing examples of group influences. However, we now come to social influences which affect entire ways in which we relate to the world. Attitudes are usually defined as a "predisposition to respond in a certain way to a particular object, event, or experience." It is important for you to understand that while the cognitive components of attitudes are the largest components, attitudes simultaneously carry behavioral and affective predispositions with them. For example, if I were to ask you about your attitudes concerning terrorism, you might feel outraged at some of the innocent victim of terrorism (the affective part of the predisposition); you might be of the opinion that terrorists must be crazy people (a cognitive portion of the predisposition); and might end up pounding your fists on the table, shouting, "We must do something about this scourge!" (the behavioral portion of the predisposition).

The fact that we humans have attitudes at all may go back to our thousands of generations in hunter/gatherer existence. Recall earlier that Lumsden and Wilson suggested that racial bigotry and religious cohesion might stem from in-group adaptation for survival. This idea fits quite well with nonsociobiological explanations of why we form attitudes. For example, Katz (1960) sees the function of attitudes as providing a framework within which we can make sense of the world in ways that will meet our needs.

Changing Attitudes: Persuasion. Particular attitudes that we come to hold are largely learned through socialization. Attitudes are therefore always open to change. The entire purpose of the guerrilla psychological warfare program was the changing of attitudes (all three components) of an entire society.

Usually, the process of persuasion, whether it be by political candidates, advertising campaigns, or guerrilla combatant-propagandists, is broken down into the interacting components in Figure 7.12. This allows us to study attitude modifiability from the standpoint of who is attempting to change attitudes, how it is being attempted, and who the persuasion is directed toward. If we take the example of the guerrilla combatant-propagandist, these components become quite clear. You can easily transform these components into other attitude change situations.

Let us see how effective the guerrillas might be in changing attitudes of the people using the CIA recommendations. As we go along, you should keep in mind the consistency and balance theories of social influence.

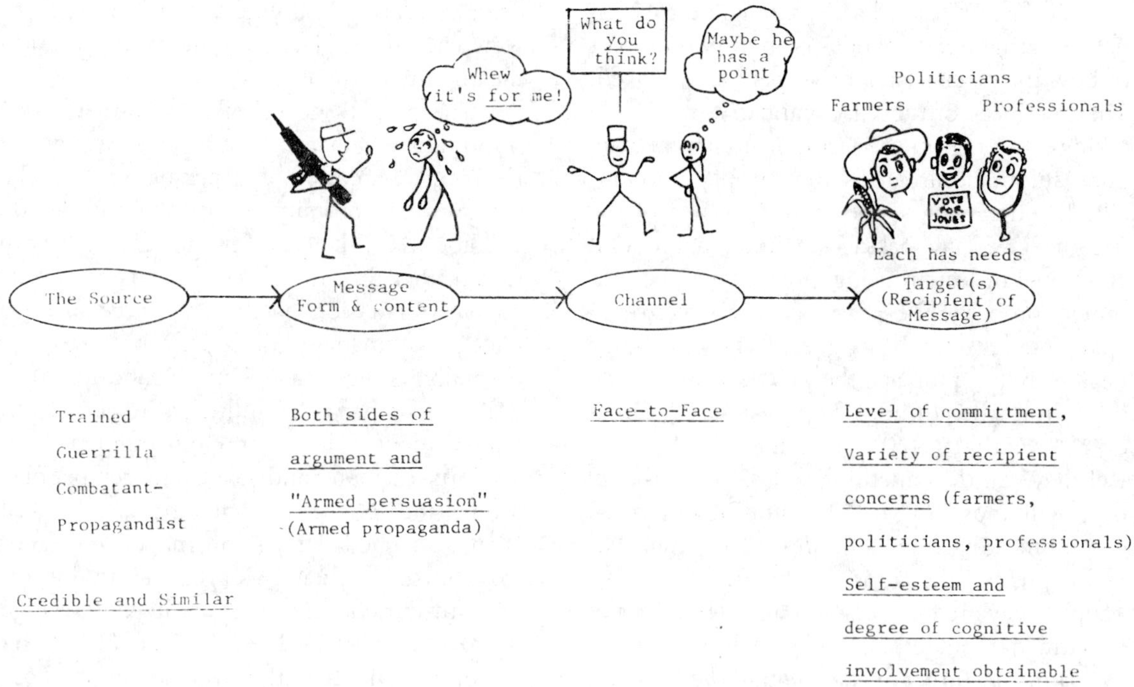

Figure 7.12 Attempting to Cause Attitude Change

How the Source Can Influence Attitude Change. The reason the guerrillas were carefully trained in clearly understanding and being able to communicate what their fight was all about was to help ensure that they had credibility. Hovland and Weiss (1951) have found that high credibility sources of messages are much more effective in changing people's attitudes. To help fix this attitude change over time, the high credibility message simply needs to be repeated many times. The guerrillas were trained to be both expert in what they were talking about and trustworthy. These traits are automatically perceived as a high credibility source. Recall that the guerrillas were taught to work and live with the people whenever possible. This of course made them appear to be trustworthy, but this also led the people to like the guerrillas, and find them similar to themselves. Brock (1965) has pointed out that when people see the source of the communication as similar to themselves, they will more likely be persuaded by them. For example, we tend to identify with certain people we see on TV commercials who seem to be like us, and we are influenced by them.

Finally, the guerrillas were taught to allow a free exchange of ideas to lead the people to come to the "correct" conclusion seemingly spontaneously. Robert B. Cialdini, R.E. Petty, and T.T. Casioppo (1981) have concluded that this sort of self-persuasion is more powerful than information provided by others.

How the Message Content Can Influence Attitude Change. The form and content of attempts at attitude change are simply a matter of how you "package" your information for delivery. How you approach your target requires that you first know something about him. Hovland, Lumsdaine, and Sheffield (1949) have found that it is helpful to know whether the target initially opposes or initially agrees with the attitude you are trying to influence in him. If the guerrilla decides the people he is dealing with oppose what he stands for, he will be more successful if he presents a two-sided argument (both the guerrilla point of view and the opposing government's point of view). This makes the guerrilla appear to be fair-minded and knowledgeable (credible). It also facilitates the people coming to their own conclusions (self-persuasion). On the other hand, if he knows that the people are already leaning strongly toward the guerrilla cause, a one-sided argument will tend to be more effective.

The fact the guerrillas were taught the essentials of "armed propaganda" is an important part of how their persuasive messages are packaged. The designers of the CIA manual were simply taking advantage of the fact that troops carrying guns automatically arouse the people emotionally. In other words, the mere presence of the firearms gives any message an emotional tone. If emotional or fear-arousing messages can be presented properly, they can be very effective in changing attitudes. If the guerrillas use the guns negatively (as a threat), the people would move away from the attitudes being espoused. However, Leventhal (1970) has found that if people feel they can do something to lessen the threat, they will move toward the attitudes of those communicating the attitudes. The guerrillas really present the guns as the friends of the people, they are for you—for "us." They are not to harm you, but to help you get what you want.

How the Target or Recipient of the Message Influences Attitude Change. An easy way to think about the importance of the characteristics of the target is to consider how TV advertising that is directed toward persuading children differs from that which is directed toward persuading adults. The adult target is somewhat more discerning about what is relevant and what is irrelevant about the product.

The guerrillas were taught to carefully take the characteristics of the recipient of the messages into account in a variety of ways. For example, farmers, politicians and professionals were each to be given arguments that would be meaningful to them.

The target's level of commitment is an important characteristic. If you can get the recipient of an attempt at persuasion to make a some small commitment to an attitude, they become more likely to commit themselves further in that direction. This fact has been put to use in persuasion as the *foot-in-the-door technique*. Freedman and Fraser (1966) have experimentally studied this technique and found that it is a very powerful influence toward further commitment. Sales promotions often give away all sorts of merchandise just to get people to "come and look," or "come and hear" with no strings attached. They know that once you commit yourself to their message, even in this small way, further commitments are likely (see Figure 7.13). Pliner, Hart, Kohl & Saari (1974) have hypothesized that this phenomenon occurs because those who make a commitment see themselves "as the kind of person who does this sort of thing." The guerrillas, while helping the people, also were taught to ask for food, shelter, small uniform repairs, etc., and given several good reasons why the people should give them these things. Once the people have made a commitment to help the guerrillas, the guerrillas' feet are in the door.

Figure 7.13 Compliance

The degree of cognitive involvement in the recipient's mind has also been found to be related to the degree of attitude change which occurs. Petty and Cacioppo (1979) have described two levels of cognitive processing during which attitude change occurs—*central route processing* and *peripheral route processing*. In central route processing, the targeted person is motivated and thinks carefully about the issues of the message. In peripheral route processing, the target is not motivated, or perhaps not able because of the situation, to think much about the message. In a face-to-face situation of persuasion, the higher cognitive involvement of central route processing that is nearly always produced usually has an enduring effect on attitude changes that occur. This, of course, is especially true if the target recipients of the persuasion believes they are making up their own mind. On the other hand, in watching TV commercials which are not face-to-face, the target, or recipient, may only peripherally process important aspects of the message. For example, you may notice that the TV commercial is very funny, but be oblivious to what product is being advertised. Because of the low or nonexistent cognitive involvement, your attitude changes about this product would likely be nil.

The Target's Self-Esteem. Hovland and Janis (1959) long ago found that people who are easily persuaded under one set of circumstances are often easily persuaded under other circumstances. This essentially means that there is probably some personality factor that is related to persuasibility. (In general, intelligence is not reliably related to persuasibility in any simple fashion.) McGuire (1969) has found a relationship between a person's *self-esteem* and his persuasibility. Apparently, people with low self-esteem do not consider their own opinions as being very sound. Therefore, they more easily give them up in the face of forceful messages. However, as Zellner (1970) and Gollob and Dittes (1965) have found, there is more to this self-esteem and persuasibility relationship. Feelings of self-esteem have both short-term and long-term components. If you get a low grade on an English paper assignment that you put your "all" into, your short-term self-esteem could be quite low! But these feelings pass. Soon you are back to your normal level of self-esteem. The interesting part of this is that these researchers have found that you are most vulnerable to persuasive messages during these periods of short-term low self-esteem—even more vulnerable than people with long-term low self-esteem! Why is this the case? Researchers really are not sure. However, we might speculate that short-term low self-esteem more greatly disturbs the balance of beliefs and feelings of the person. As you seek to restore balance, available messages are more likely to be incorporated. In other words, you are looking for information just as are the unfortunate people who happened to find themselves as an out-group in another country where guerrillas are attempting to propagandize. The people are likely to be suffering short-term low self esteem. They, like you in the example above, have temporarily "lost out." They are looking for messages that will help put things back into a balanced perspective. Recall what Lumsden and Wilson and Katz said was the purpose of attitudes in the first place. The guerrillas offer such messages, especially to the special interest groups—the farmers, professionals, and politicians.

Prejudice and Stereotypes. The idea of *prejudice* is familiar to everyone. This negative attitude toward a specific group is an example of the in-group/out-group phenomenon. Prejudice is a very fine example of all three of the components of attitudes we discussed earlier—cognitive, affective, and behavioral. The affective portion is basically the negative feelings about the perceived out-group members; the behavioral component in the context of prejudice can lead to *discrimination*. An approach to the cognitive portion of prejudice can been seen in the studies of social stereotypes among college students by Katz and Braley (1960) and by Karlins, Caffman, and Walters (1969). These three studies, conducted in 1933, 1951, and 1967, used identical research methods. Each study provided 100 Princeton University undergraduate students with a list of 84 adjectives and asked the students to use them to label Americans, Germans, Chinese, English, Italians, Japanese, blacks, and Jews. The cognitive components (images) of these students' attitudes about Americans included the labels "sportsmanlike" and "industrious." Italians were labeled as "artistic" and "impulsive." (It is important to note that stereotypes are not necessarily associated with prejudice. For example, what is your stereotype of astronauts? There is no negative attitude in this case. Stereotypes, as attitudes, are simply ways of conceptually organizing all of our experiences about certain collections of people.) While many students who participated in the 1967 survey protested at having to make ethnic judgments at all (a seeming fading of stereotypes), this may have been the result of the particular ethnic groups they were asked to label. If, for example, the more controversial ethnic groups of the time were included, they might have happily labeled them. To informally check this speculation, I polled 100 of my students, but included such groups as Moslems, Soviets, Palestinians, Israelis, etc. The results appear in Table 7.2.

As you can see from the responses of my own students, they have different ideas about the particular groups they were asked to describe. And equally important here, not one of my students protested that it was unsound to make such ethnic generalizations.

Why certain stereotypes turn out to also be prejudicial ones may have its roots in our social evolution. Recall Lumsden and Wilson's remarks on the origins of racial bigotry. Their idea was based upon the notion of fear of the strangers' adaptation for survival discussed earlier. Beyond this, and likely related, is the possibility that certain high-fearing personality patterns are responsible for high degrees of prejudice. Adorno, Frenkel-Brunswick, Levinson, and Sanford (1950) have linked prejudicial attitudes to what they have referred to as *authoritarian personalities*. The authoritarian personality puts strong demands on obedience and conformity, with a great deal of hostility toward outgroups. An example of this would be the model of the authoritarian personality of members of the Nazi party with their anti-Semitic prejudice: fear of strangers gone wild.

What we have seen in the "fading of social stereotypes," as Karlins and his colleagues put it, has been the result of a progressive exposure to these ethnic groups (at least on the part of Princeton undergraduates). Exposure to "other groups" can reduce stereotyping and prejudice. Through television, travel, forced desegregation, etc., people are seeing themselves more and more similar to these ethnic groups (all one large in-group). Recall how the guerrillas made themselves appear to be similar to the people in order to reduce the "guerrilla stereotype." On the other hand, attitude-altering media can be packaged in such a way that it emphasizes dissimilarities between ethnic groups.

Table 7.2 Cultural Stereotypes

SFCC 1985	
JAPANESE	*PERCENT*
Scientifically-minded	34
Intelligent	32
Industrious	32
Quiet	22
Loyal to family ties	20
SOVIETS	*PERCENT*
Industrious	26
Intelligent	24
Aggressive	24
Arrogant	24
Scientifically-minded	16
ISRAELIS	*PERCENT*
Very religious	28
Aggressive	22
Extremely nationalistic	22
Shrewd	20
Revengeful	20
GERMANS	*PERCENT*
Intelligent	42
Scientifically-minded	22
Stubborn	20
Industrious	16
Quick-tempered	14
MOSLEMS	*PERCENT*
Very religious	64
Faithful	20
Meditative	18
Aggressive	16
Extremely nationalistic	14
PALESTINIANS	*PERCENT*
Radical	32
Aggressive	22
Revengeful	20
Cruel	16
Quick-tempered	14

Interpersonal Attraction

At the beginning of Chapter 1, we described the story of Psyche and Eros. This story tells how the ancient Greeks understood beauty, love, mind, and immortality to be interrelated. In Chapter 3, we examined more closely the mind part of the story—consciousness. In this section, we will discuss the attraction portion of the social mind—Aristotle would have put it. It is significant that the Greek concept of the immortal Psyche was framed in a story of love. Attraction, liking, love, and social interaction, as Aristotle thought, remain fundamental to mind. In this light we will discuss what social psychologists have discovered about this category of social influences.

Contextual and Cognitive Aspects of Attraction. It is helpful to organize the various determinants of attraction more or less loosely into those that are more context related and those that are more related to ongoing cognitive influences. Context-related determinants of attraction include such things as physical attractiveness of faces, bodies, clothing, frequency of contact, and proximity. These determinants involve less active cognitive evaluation. The more cognitive aspects of attraction include the more active and complex attributions, comparisons, and balancings (discussed in the theory section), which people make in regard to others.

Frequency of Contact as an Influence. You may have noticed that many of your friends and people to whom you are attracted are simply people you have been around a lot. People who you work with, or sit next to in class just seem to become better and better friends as frequent contacts continue. Robert Zajonc (1968) has found that this frequency of contact is a social influence in and of itself. That is, it isn't that you find that you like people you come into contact with on the basis of their merits—it's just the contact. Let me explain. Zajonc found that simply by increasing the number of exposures subjects received to a person's photo increased the favorableness of their response to the person in the photograph. It seems true that people do seem to just "grow on you."

Proximity as an Influence. The fact that you live near someone will increase the likelihood that some attraction between you will occur. This may seem to be just a variation on the idea of exposure during frequent contacts, but takes us beyond the idea of just seeing someone's face frequently. For example, when you live near to someone or work closely with him or her, you learn more about his or her habits, and have an opportunity to exchange ideas. In part, you are attracted because you find yourself in the same place as the other person. In an interesting illustration of the proximity-attraction relationship, M.W. Segal (1974) found that a group of police academy cadets tended to have cadet friends with last names alphabetically close to their own. As you have probably guessed, the cadets had been assigned living quarters and classroom seats alphabetically. You anticipate this phenomenon each time you are about to enter a new life situation—"I wonder who I will meet at this new job, in this new class, etc." The effect of proximity occurs on a plane ride. You may be attracted and strike up a good friendship with another passenger only because you are sitting together.

Physical Attractiveness as an Influence. It does not take a lot of cognitive decision-making ability or analysis to determine if another human being is physically attractive! Exactly why certain people are seen by others to be physically attractive is unknown. However, as sociobiologists point out, an attraction toward strength (fitness), and symmetry (as opposed to irregularities of features) would increase chances for evolutionary survival (see Brown & Brown 1985). But our question here is, does physical attractiveness result in the actual formation of relationships, as was the case with frequency and proximity? Are physically attractive people just revered, or are they actually sought after?

There are two ways to approach this question. First, it has been found by Karen Dion, E. Berscheid, and E. Walster (1972) that physically attractive people are perceived as better in additional ways. The title of her report says it all, "What Is Beautiful Is Good." They found that attractive men and women are seen as more poised, strong, interesting, sociable, modest, kind, sensitive, intelligent, successful, happy, and make better husbands and wives. Of course, whether they really are or not is a completely different question. The second approach involves the actual selection of friends on the basis of attractiveness. Elaine Walster, Vera Aronson, Darey Abrahams, and L. Rottman (1966) found that a random selection of university students on blind dates liked each other and repeated the date on the basis of one determinant—physical attractiveness. It appears that physical attractiveness is not only revered, it is sought after in the formation of relationships.

The More Cognitive Aspects of Attraction

Similarity and Complementarity—Cognitive Aspects which Help Determine Staying Power. Ellen Berscheid (1984) has pointed out that people who are similar in height, weight, wealth, attractiveness, education, religious preference, and intelligence tend to stay together in enduring relationships. Many of these similarities involve a great deal of cognitive recognition and decision making. However, it is also true that under certain circumstances *complementarity* of people leads to attraction and lasting relationships. This is the idea that opposites attract. The above similarities of height, weight, etc., did not include the personality characteristics of couples or friends. In some personality characteristics, opposites may attract because of their mutually supportive effect. For example, Elliot Aronson has pointed out in his witty style:

> A man who is very nurturant might be miserable if he found himself in a relationship with a highly independent woman—and vice versa. By the same token, what could be better for a dependent man than to live out his life on the bosom of someone who really enjoyed being nurturant? The same holds true for masculinity-femininity, assertiveness-passivity, and dominance-submissiveness. And, in the somewhat more facetious vein, what union could be happier than that of a sadist and masochist? (1984, pp. 306–307)

Love—The Ultimate In-Group? In Chapter 1, we examined the way in which Zick Rubin has operationally defined love. To help compare love with the more run-of-the-mill idea of liking, we can also look at some of Rubin's findings (1970). College students were asked to select statements that reflected liking and loving feelings for their current boy or girlfriends. The liking statements included the following.

> I think that my (girl or boyfriend) is usually well-adjusted.
> I have great confidence in (girl or boyfriend's) good judgment.
> I think that (boy or girlfriend) and I are quite similar.

The loving statements included:

> If I could never be with (boy or girlfriend), I would feel miserable.
> I would do almost anything for (boy or girlfriend).
> I feel that I can confide in (boy or girlfriend) about almost anything.

Loving seems to define the ultimate in-group. It is possible that this in-group is necessary in humans for very simple survival reasons. By staying "magically bound together" the offspring of humans would be given the chance to themselves reproduce—they must live an average of 13 to 15 years to do so! The idea that the human brain is an organ destined to love is supported by findings of Liebowitz and Klein (1979) that a high level of the chemical phenylethylamine in the brain might be associated with being in love. Interestingly, this chemical is found in chocolate. One can only speculate on the connection between our fascination with chocolate, its importance on Valentine's Day, and being in love!

Bringing It All Together

We began this chapter with psychological warfare aimed at getting at Aristotle's "political animal." In everyday affairs, as Aristotle pointed out, we cannot separate humans from social influences; if we do we are left with either a god or a beast, he tells us. This notion leads us to the highly applied nature of social psychology. At the beginning of this chapter, I described the tactics of guerrilla propagandists; this is applied social psychology. All of this comprises an especially important theme of social psychology and the interrelatedness of social psychology to other areas within psychology.

Finally, the relatively new sociobiology, especially in the form of Lumsden and Wilson's *Genes, Mind and Culture* (1981), provides an appropriate evolutionary frame of reference for social psychology. Lumsden and Wilson put mind right in the middle of the action. This puts psychology and the development of mind and brain in the critical position in the development and evolution of social being. The sociobiological perspectives allow us to begin conceptually with hunter/gatherer groups and to tie them and all of the interrelated topics of this chapter together.

Glossary

aggregation: A collection of individuals.

altruistic social behavior: Social behavior that concerns the protection of the interests of others. In sociobiology, inherited social behavior that increases the likelihood of survival (fitness) of the gene type of the organism exhibiting the behavior.

armed propaganda: Anything that an army does to encourage positive attitudes toward it and its cause among those not directly involved in warfare.

attitudes: A fairly stable predisposition to respond to people, ideas, or things in a particular way.

attribution theory: A view that concerns how an individual explains behavior. This explanation may come about by the individual relating the behavior to luck, the situation, or some characteristic of the person.

authoritarian personality: A pattern of personality characteristics in which the person demands unquestioning subordination, obedience, and allegiance from others, and is extremely critical of perceived out-groups.

balance theory: A view of attitude formation that people compare their feelings and beliefs about people, ideas, or things and attempt to strike a balance across or among them.

brainstorming: A technique used to promote the free expression of ideas among group members.

cadre: A core group of highly trained people within an organization. The individuals of this group are capable of assuming leadership if necessary, and of indoctrinating future members of an organization or the cadre itself.

central route processing: In attitude formation, the careful consideration of issues and facts.

coevolution: The mutual influencing of different but related evolving systems.

cognitive dissonance theory: A view of attitude formation based upon psychological discomfort arising out of perceived contradictions. Attitudes are formed to reduce the discomfort.

combatant-propagandist: A soldier who uses the equipment and occasion of warfare to defeat the enemy and promote positive attitudes about his cause among those not directly involved in warfare.

complementarity: The mutual completion of a whole by different parts or persons.

confederate subjects (confederates): Subjects in experiments in social psychology who are working with the experimenter so that a naive subject is put in an artificial social situation which the naive subject perceives as real.

consistency theory: A view of attitude formation that holds that people strive to achieve a state of cognitive equilibrium.

diffusion of responsibility: The tendency for people in groups to distribute the felt responsibility for action in emergencies so that action becomes less likely.

discrimination: Actual action toward a member of a group or the group itself which is based upon prejudice.

dispositional nature: The perceived characteristics of a person or group.

dissonance: The psychological discomfort that arises out of perceived incongruity.

entomologist: A scientist who specializes in the study of insects.

epigenetic rules: Rules that govern the processes of development or evolution other than genetic instructions.

foot-in-the-door technique: A technique of persuasion based upon the tendency of people who have made a small commitment or compliance to make larger ones.

group: A collection of individuals in which there is mutual social influence.

groupthink: The tendency toward diminished rationality among members of cohesive groups caused by conscious and unconscious needs to maintain group cohesion and stability.

guerrilla army: An army that carries out warfare in an irregular way in hostile territory.

hunter/gatherer groups: During several hundred thousand years of Ice Age epochs, groups of prehumans evolved in terms of hunting and gathering skill fitness. In sociobiology, it is thought that in-group and out-group social tendencies were selected for during this tune.

in-group: A group with which an individual feels a strong loyalty and pledges allegiance.

interior group/exterior group: See in-group and out-group.

kin selection: Within the theory of evolution, the selection processes that favor the survival of related organisms and their common gene types.

naive subject: A subject in an experiment is ignorant of what the experiment is attempting to determine.

norms: Standards of conduct or values.

obedience: The tendency to behave in accord with authority figures or symbols.

out-group: A group that is different from one's own and usually looked down upon.

peripheral route processing: In attitude formation, a meager amount of consideration of issues and facts.

political animal: A description of human behavior, originating with Aristotle, stating that human beings are most essentially social animals.

prejudice: A generally negative and biased attitude toward an individual because of his group membership, or this same attitude toward the group itself.

prosocial behavior: Actions that benefit others, often at a cost to the person taking the action.

psychological operations: In military operations, the application of psychological and social psychological principles in warfare tactics.

Sandinista government: The current government of Nicaragua.

self-esteem: The degree to which one values or feels good about oneself.

social facilitation: The tendency to increase/decrease performance levels in the presence of others beyond what an individual would achieve alone.

social loafing: The tendency when a person is a part of a group to decrease effort below that which it would be if the person were alone or in a smaller group.

social psychological: See social psychology.

social psychology: A subdiscipline of psychology that studies how the behavior, feelings, and thoughts (psyche) of individuals are influenced by the actual, imagined, or implied presence of other people. Human social settings contribute significantly to the interpretation of actual, imagined, or implied presence of other people.

social setting: Particular places or times that influence social behavior, thoughts, and feelings.

sociobiology: The study of and view that much social behavior has a genetic (biological) basis. This view is based upon Darwin's theory of evolution through natural selection. In this view, social behavior such as altruism, love, aggression, and morality increase the likelihood that an organism's genetic type will survive and continue in the gene pool of the species; through this process these social behaviors are selected for and become a part of the inherited behavior of the species.

stereotypes: A rigid, oversimplified, and biased perception of the characteristics of persons or groups; this perception may be either positive or negative.

Social Behavior: Doing Psychology on Your Own

LOIS MCDERMOTT

Basic Concept #7—The Imagined Minds of Others

Attribution of cause. *"While attending a funeral, a young man approached the bier where the deceased lay and smashed open the dead man's skull with a wooden mallet."* What prompted this behavior—some flaw in his personality, some deep-seated unconscious hatred of the deceased, some psychotic illness? Or was it some aspect of the social situation or the cultural context that prompted the behavior? Is it something **dispositional** or

situational that led to this act? Does it change your view of this protagonist's actions to know that it was his duty as the eldest son to release his father's spirit to join the ancestors prior to the cremation of the deceased's body? Social psychology is devoted (a) to the description of the laws of social behavior; (b) to uncovering how being a member of a group or in opposition to a group alters our behavior and mental processes. Social psychology is about the power of the social situation to control our behavior, to cause us to act and feel differently than we would if free of the pressure of social norms and sanctions.

Cultural Styles. Psychology has finally begun to extend its understanding of the importance of social dynamics, to the understanding of cultural dynamics. For most of the hundred years of psychological research, psychologists have presented the research findings collected on middle-class college sophomores of European descent, living in the last half of the 20th century on the North American continent, as if *they* embodied human psychology. This is so obviously absurd, one wonders how psychologists got away with it for so long. The vast majority of the earth's people do not fit that description. The first breakthrough of this hegemony was the discovery that females and various ethnic minorities did not present the same picture as white males.

Many developments in the social fabric of the US have occurred (e.g., more openness to other cultures, more indigenous psychology in various areas of the world, and more diversity within American culture) in the past few decades. These ultimately lead to an interest in the effect of cultural style in determining sense of self, parenting styles, definition of mental illness and wellness, and social behavior. A first approximation of these differences has been described with reference to **collectivist** and **individualist** cultures.

A Most (In)famous Experiment. We often hear of heinous crimes committed by groups of "good kids." We marvel in disbelief at the lunacy of the acts—feeling positive that we would have had the moral fortitude to overcome whatever peer pressure was at work at the moment of free choice. We hear of widespread genocide instigated by demagogues, in distant places in the world and feel confident that our democratic society would never obey any of the butchers of the world. Can we be so sure?

In the early 1960's a young psychologist, Stanley Milgram, became fascinated with emerging information about the magnitude and sophistication of the carefully coordinated genocide of 6 million human beings (e.g., Jews, homosexuals, gypsies, Seventh Day Adventists and others who protested the barbarism of the Third Reich). Milgram couldn't fathom how such an atrocity could occur in a society that at that time was considered to be at the pinnacle of Western civilization—a society of philosophy, science, and high culture. Many lay the cause at the feet of the "Germanic, authoritarian personality style." Milgram, a social psychologist, was not convinced. He devised the most famous of social science studies—involving 1000 male and female subjects from all walks of life. With the many replications and variants of this study, he brilliantly made the point that *situational* factors in social situations are powerful determinants of behavior. He convincingly argued that is was not the German character, but the manipulation of social variables that made the genocide possible.

Many recoil at the idea that given the right circumstances, we too, could be induced to participate in dreadful acts of inhumanity. We cling to the belief that our moral fortitude would stand us in good stead—that we would be truth tellers and loyal human beings—no matter what. As worrisome as the results may be, research such as this and that on conformity holds a welcome promise. If it is the situation, then, we are in luck—we have some basis for optimism about human nature. It is easier to work on changing the situation than trying to change someone's character (e.g., long-standing personality traits or genetic predispositions). Those who prefer to blame the victim or excuse the status quo, loath the idea that the social situation is the powerful causative agent in much of human altruism and evil. It takes a real sense of humility to acknowledge this power and work to harness it for the collective good.

Unit Focus. Hate crimes are prominent in the news—whether it is gay bashing, sexual assault of women, harassment of the homeless, burning down immigrant housing, or burning crosses on the lawns of racial minorities. Hate crimes are about the stuff of social psychology—the laws of group dynamics. For hate to produce a crime people must perceive themselves as a member of a group that is different, usually superior, from the target group or its proxy. The "in-group" must define the "out-group" and then take action against it. The structure of hate crime will be used to help you understand common group dynamics. You will be introduced to the dynamics that (1) aid in creating a sense of group cohesiveness, (2) define a target for the hate and (3) motivate members of a group to take hateful action.

Study Objectives

1. Distinguish the *macro* differences in *collectivist* and *individualist* cultures with regard to social dynamics, sense of self, social judgment and parent-child relations.
2. Distinguish the *micro* differences in *dyadic, intragroup* and *intergroup* dynamics. Give examples.
3. Know the defining characteristics of hate crimes—i.e., explain how group dynamics function in hate crimes.
4. Learn the dynamics that facilitate or arise from group cohesiveness (membership).
5. Describe the research on altruism, the *bystander effect* and the factors that alter the effect.
6. Define and illustrate the *fundamental attribution error.* Explain the role of positive versus negative events and the role of empathy in the occurrence of this error.
7. Give examples of the *just-world* and *blaming-the-victim* phenomena and the self-fulfilling prophecy.
8. Develop a thorough understanding of the Milgram Studies of Obedience—the method, findings, interpretation, variables affecting the outcome, and follow-up studies.
9. Compare and illustrate two types of *conformity,* and the factors affecting its strength.

Key Terms

aggregation
altruistic social behavior
armed propaganda
attitudes
attribution theory
authoritarian personality
balance theory
brainstorming
cadre
central route processing
coevolution
cognitive dissonance theory
combatant-propagandist
complementarity
confederate subjects (confederates)
consistency theory
diffusion of responsibility
discrimination
dispositional nature
dissonance
entomologist
epigenetic rules
foot-in-the-door technique
group
groupthink
guerrilla army
hunter/gatherer groups
in-group
interior group/exterior group
kin selection
naive subject
norms
obedience
out-group
peripheral route processing
political animal
prejudice
prosocial behavior
psychological operations
Sandinista government
self-esteem
social facilitation
social loafing
social psychological
social psychology
social setting
sociobiology
stereotypes

Problem Set #7: Social Behavior

1a. One Saturday afternoon, little Susie is rowdy and noisy, while little Janice is quiet. You might think that Susie is a rowdy kind of girl, while Janice is more of the quiet type. If so, you would be explaining the girls' behavior according to _______ factors.

1b. It turned out that Susie was at the park, while Janice was at the library. Now you are more likely to explain the girls' behavior as being due to a _______ factor, such as _______.

2a. Charlie is looking out of the window and sees a stranger stumble as he crosses Red Square. According to social psychology, Charlie will most likely explain the stranger's stumble as being due to a _______ factor, such as _______. On the other hand, the stranger will most likely explain his stumble as being due to a _______ factor, such as_______.

2b. What principle do social psychologists use to explain the difference between Charlie's and the stranger's explanation?

3. When surveyed last July, Annie indicated that she was in favor of a woman's right to decide whether or not to carry her pregnancy to term (in other words, Annie was "pro-choice"). In

August, Annie's priest told all of the church members to join an anti-abortion protest march. Suppose that Annie joined two protest marches in August and September.

a. If you were to contact Annie in October and ask her opinion about abortion, what is she most likely to say?

b. What social psychological principle or concept explains Annie's opinion about abortion, as measured in October?

Assign the correct social psychological principle to each of the following stories in Questions 4–18: (obedience to authority, fundamental attribution error, just-world phenomenon, social loafing, social facilitation, cognitive dissonance, group polarization, de individuation, groupthink, bystander intervention, normative social influence, informational social influence, in-group bias).

4. You don't really believe in the "death with dignity" initiative, but you have been assigned to be the project manager on the pre-election ad campaign that your agency is running for the supporters of the initiative. By the day of the election, you have decided to vote in favor of the initiative.
5. As you drive along icy streets you notice the "unusual" driving of the car ahead. You feel angry that this "ignorant, careless, reckless, and irresponsible" person is on the road without chains on his "boat."
6. A group of soldiers opens fire upon a group of civilians, killing five children. When asked why, the soldiers replied "We were just following orders."
7. You have noticed that you are more likely to throw your trash under your seat when you are at Husky Stadium than when you are sitting with a friend at a restaurant.
8. You are asked to make a hiring decision between two applicants who have equal education and experience. One of the applicants is a UW graduate, while the other is a WSU graduate. You just have this gut feeling that the UW graduate will make a better employee, so you hire her.
9. It's Saturday night on the Ave. You see two young "Hispanic-looking dudes" exchanging little white packages in the doorway of an apartment building where a big party is taking place. Although you can't see the packages clearly, you conclude that you are watching a drug deal. You are wrong—they are checking out their condom supply in anticipation of events later in the evening.
10. At a recent Busy Bagel Company meeting, the president, vice-president, and several other executives spoke out enthusiastically about a new proposed vanilla-flavored bagel. Since the president seemed so enthusiastic about the proposal, Mr. Quinn kept quiet about his observation that vanilla seemed to be only a passing flavor fad. The Busy Bagel Company decided to invest 1 million dollars into an ad campaign to launch the new vanilla flavor. Six months later, the Company was bankrupt. Vanilla bagels turned out to be only a fleeting fad. The Busy Bagel Company's poor decision-making is an example of ______.
11. If a teenager moved from an isolated village in a Third World country to a middle or upper-class area in Seattle, within a year or so he or she would probably be wearing the same clothes that the popular kids were wearing. In addition, this teenager would also be listening to all of the popular rock songs on the popular radio station. These behavioral changes were probably motivated by the teenager's desires to fit in with his or her peers, and to be accepted and approved of by them. In other words, the changes would be due to ______.
12. You read a Daily article aloud to your roommate. According to the article, a male student was stabbed on campus at 7:30 PM on a dark January night, as he was leaving the bank machine in the HUB. Your roommate responds: "What did he expect? He probably did something to deserve it."
13. A contractor hired 10 strong men to help dig a drainage ditch. Since each man could dig out 1 cubic yard per hour, the contractor expected that the job, which consisted of 10 cubic feet total, could be finished in one hour. However, the job took one and one-half hours to complete.

14. You are a video game junkie. You notice that your score is usually better on weekend nights when you are playing with your friends than it is on week nights when you are playing alone.
15. You drive by the scene of an accident. There are two cars smashed in an intersection, and two people on the sidewalk having a fist fight surrounded by a small crowd of observers. One of the two people fighting has blood gushing from a head wound. You drive on, feeling confident that the police have already been called.
16. You overhear this conversation at a dinner at your church/temple: "I'm so glad he won the raffle. He is such a good person, he devotes so much time to the food drive every year. See, good deeds don't go unrewarded."
17. A social psychologist has been studying the attitudes and opinions of UW students. He notices that students in Dorm L tend to be "Somewhat Liberal" as freshmen, and "Very Liberal" by the time that they are seniors. Other students in Dorm C tend to be "Somewhat Conservative" as freshmen, and "Very Conservative" by the time that they are seniors. Over their 4 year college careers, the development of the students' attitudes from "Somewhat Liberal/Conservative" to "Very Liberal/Conservative" in the two separate dorms is due to ___.
18. Milgram's obedience studies, rate of compliance with the instructions of the "experimenter" was a function of several situational (rather than dispositional) factors. For each of the following situations, indicate whether compliance was high (greater than 50 percent) or low (less than 50 percent).
    a. the teacher had no visual or auditory contact with the learner
    b. the teacher received tape-recorded instructions from the experimenter
    c. the teacher had to put the learner's hand on the shock plate
    d. the teacher was a member of a group of co-workers who were eager to continue the experiment
    e. another co-experimenter was present to support the teacher when he decided to quit the experiment
    f. the teacher knew that the learner had a heart condition
    g. the teacher was allowed to choose the level of shock
    h. the teacher read the instructions and a co-worker delivered them
    i. Which situation produced the highest level of compliance'?
    j. Which situation produced the lowest level of compliance?
19. Give examples from "The Wave" which illustrate each of the following:
    a. cognitive dissonance
    b. groupthink
    c. normative social conformity
    d. interpersonal dynamics
20. In your text there is a brief description of a social psychological experiment that took place some years ago. The psychologists were interested in the typical behaviors of guards and prisoners, and wondered how much of these behaviors might be determined by situational factors (such as being "assigned" by society to be a "guard"). They decided to find out by setting up a mock prison on a college campus, and recruited some volunteers. In order to control for the effects of any dispositional factors, the male college students who volunteered for the experiment were randomly assigned to the roles of "prisoner" or "guard." The experiment was supposed to run for 14 days. However, because the "guards" became TOO "guard-like" (and the prisoners became TOO "prisoner-like"), the experiment was called off after six days. Describe how each of the following concepts or principles may have affected the "guards."

a. scapegoat theory
b. just-world hypothesis
c. de individuation
d. normative social influence
e. attitudes follow behavior
f. in-group bias
g. cognitive dissonance

21. Given what you know about bystander intervention, what should you do if you are in a busy public place and need help?
22. Give examples of each of the social dynamics
    a. individualism
    b. collectivism
    c. dyadic
    d. intragroup
    e. intergroup

See Appendix C for answers to problem set.

8

Personality

Gandhi: A Search for Perfection

By now everyone knows something of the story of Mohandas K. Gandhi—The *Mahatma*. The great soul and spirit of this man was key in the liberation of India from British colonial rule. One might think that a man like Gandhi must have a powerful, outgoing personality. He deliberately went against all odds, suffered abuse and imprisonment for ideals—he could not be stopped!

Yet, as *psychohistorians* Hyman Muslin and Prakash Desai (1984) and others have pointed out, "The mystery of Mohandas K. Gandhi resided in his transformation from a painfully shy boy saddled with innumerable fears and intensely attached to his mother to the man who was universally regarded as the great liberator of India."

Gandhi's personality is a mystery. In order to help understand him and some of the problems of studying personality, we should know more about him—his childhood, how he saw himself in the world, and his environment. Somewhere in these "parts" of Gandhi is an explanation of how a person can be at once shy and fearful, and invincible. Later, in the theory section we will relate each of these three parts of Gandhi to the traditional views of psychology.

Gandhi's Childhood

There seem to be at least two very important things about Gandhi's childhood to understand. First, both his mother and father were extremely confident, capable and busy people. Gandhi's mother, Putaliba, was extremely faithful to the rituals of her religion. At the same time Gandhi's father, Kaba, was a prime minister in the family's hometown. The following will give you a feel for what life was like in the Gandhi home.

> Kaba Gandhi's house, where Mohandas was raised, amounted to a miniature court and the number of guests who sat down to dinner was seldom less than 20 including the family, secretaries, and officials. In Mohandas' eyes Kaba, the head of the clan, was an important presence. He arranged marriages, secured jobs, and was called to intercede in all domestic matters concerning members of the clan. From early in life, then, Gandhi's notion of acceptable interaction with his father pertained to service; he had to serve his father in order to receive parental approbation. (Gandhi, p. 8)

The second outstanding thing about Mohandas as a young child was his fearfulnesses—about almost anything. He was even afraid of school recess when he would often ran home to avoid the possibility of being hurt. And after school he would hurry home to the safety of his family. He was unreasonably fearful of thieves, ghosts, and serpents. His general fearfulness also affected his school work. He was driven to perfection in school work to offset his fears of failure. Young Mohandas was clearly in awe of his father and mother, and frightened of his own ability to perform.

Gandhi's Perception of Himself in the World

In his early childhood, Gandhi's home environment promoted a sense that service to Kaba was necessary for approval. When Mohandas was thirteen years of age, his father was severely injured in an accident. For three years, until his father's death, Gandhi cared for him daily. During this period Gandhi was able to carry out his strong desires to be of service, and at the same time be constantly with his revered father. However, this wonderful association with his father ended in a manner which must have had a critical impact upon the way Gandhi would view his place in the world.

Figure 8.1 Mohandas Gandhi

On the night of his father's death, Gandhi left his father briefly to make love to his wife. While Gandhi was gone his father died in the arms of Gandhi's uncle. This experience had a profound effect on him. For Hindus it is an extremely important tradition for both the father and the son to be together at a father's death so as to allow for the transfusion of the person of the father to the son in order to ensure a spiritual generational continuity. Gandhi later wrote of his feelings upon the situation and death of his father.

> So, all was over! I had but to wring my hands, I felt deeply ashamed and miserable. I ran to my father's room. I saw that if animal passions had not blinded me, I should have been spared the torture of separation from my father during his last moments. I should have been massaging him, and he would have died in my arms. But now it was my uncle who had this privilege. He was so deeply devoted to his elder brother that he had earned the honor of doing him the last services! (Gandhi, 1957, p. 30)

This shattering experience must have only reinforced the idea of fearful ineptitude in the way Gandhi viewed himself. Mohandas spent the rest of his life pursuing a merger with perfection in Gurus and in God. Gandhi was sixteen years of age when his father died. Forty years later he said: "My search (for a perfect Guru—an ideal parent) still continues," and, at age 57, speaking of this search he says, ". . . the throne remains vacant."

Gandhi's Environments: An Interesting Interplay

After the death of Gandhi's father, it was decided that he would go to London to study to become a barrister. In his new environment Gandhi began slowly to emerge, at least outwardly, as a more secure person. In the course of completing his legal studies and gaining admittance to the Bar, he became a confident student. He also branched out to start a local vegetarian society that held meetings to discuss nutrition. His revered mother was devout in her religious adherence to vegetarianism. Perhaps Gandhi saw this as service to his mother. And this helped him to curb his shyness.

Upon return to India, Gandhi attempted to become a barrister in Bombay. However, now back in the Indian environment the overwhelming feelings of ineptitude within him overwhelmed him. He was unable to conduct cases because of his shyness. After two years of unhappy work he left India to try again as a barrister in Pretoria, South Africa.

This new environment was immediately hostile to Gandhi—because he was Indian. This situation forced Mohandas to once again work through his shyness in service to his fellow Indians. The importance of service in Gandhi's mind can be seen in a later recounting of his feelings of being abused in South Africa:

> I began to think of my duty. Should I fight for my rights or go back to India, or should I go on to Pretoria without minding the insults, and return to India after finishing the case? It would be cowardice to run back to India without fulfilling my obligation. The hardship to which I was subjected was superficial—only a symptom of the deep disease of color prejudice. I should try if possible to root out this disease and suffer hardships in the process. (Gandhi, p. 112)

Over the next several years Gandhi worked out the ideals which would allow him to "root out the disease." He developed an invincible (in his mind) set of ideas which would allow a shy boy to be of service. It was this person who eventually returned to India—to become the Mahatma.

Toward a Philosophy of Personality

What you have just read is a brief psychohistorical account of the possible development of Mohandas K. Gandhi's personality. The psychohistorical approach represents one of many good approaches to understanding one of the most complex of topics in psychology—human personality. Psychohistories have been conducted on an enormous number of well-known individuals. For example, psychohistorical studies of American presidents offer valuable insights into the interworkings of those personalities. William Gilmore (1984) has provided over 4,000 psychohistorical references for a variety of people from Leonardo da Vinci to Adolf Hitler. And, Peter Loewenberg (1985) has provided an overview of the psychohistorical method with many examples. On the other hand, there is no reason to think of *psychohistory* as being only for famous personalities. Your own personality is probably just as complex and just as interesting. In fact, later in the empirical section we will discuss Henry Murray's (1938; and see White, 1952, 1975) approach to personality, *personology*—a historical approach stemming from Freud's work to the study of themes which appear in a person's lifetime.

Throughout the brief historical account of the development of Gandhi's personality, we were attempting to illustrate the consistencies and inconsistencies of Gandhi's characteristic ways of behaving. This is the philosophical quest of the study of personality. This idea in turn can be used to define broadly what we are after in the study of personality. While there are slight variations in definitions, I like best Lawrence A. Pervin's way of stating it (1984): *Personality* refers to "Those characteristics of the person, or of people generally, that account for consistent patterns of response to situations." Gandhi had two inconsistencies, shyness and desire to be of service in his personality.

Another important idea concerns the intuitive validity of the whole idea of people having "personalities." It certainly seems on the surface that people are consistent and predictable, or possess personalities. Think about some of the people you know well. It seems fairly certain that you can characterize them as to what they are like in various situations. We all know people who are forever bubbling with enthusiasm and others who never are, or the student who is the assertive, outspoken captain of the football team and is also mortified to get up in front of his speech class, or to ask a girl for a date.

There has been considerable attention by psychologists to the philosophical nature of personality. At one end of the extreme, the philosophical behaviorist might emphasize the overriding importance of situations (the environment) to the point of denying the existence of "personalities." Behaviorism dismisses the role of internal determinants of behavior, or inner persons. At the other end, humanistic psychologists might emphasize the person's conscious control to become whatever he wishes. Overall, the most recent trends favor the original and common sense idea that people do have consistent personalities. Stanton Peele (1984), among many others, has convincingly argued that methods used to study personality can often get in the way of recognizing the consistent core characteristics and temperament of people.

The Self

An idea closely related to the assumption that people have these consistent, predictable personalities is the one of self. Certainly, each of us is at least intuitively aware of a self within. It is the "thing" that organizes everything else in our minds. "I think I should work hard, go to college, always attend classes, get good grades, be somebody useful," and so on. Who is this "I" that is doing all of this planning, valuing and decision making? Again, you will find that different theories put different degrees of emphasis on the idea of self. Some see self as an illusion. After all, a complex robot could carry out most of the above functions. On the other hand, others see self as the highest human condition, and the most determinate of what personality becomes.

Personality and Self as Interrelated Processes: Autopoiesis

A general systems model called *autopoiesis* (literally, self-production) is a helpful way to think about a philosophy of personality. My favorite example of how we might think about the idea of autopoiesis was provided by Milan Zeleny (1981):

> We observe self-production phenomena intuitively in living systems. The cell, for example, is a complex production system, producing and synthesizing macromolecules of proteins, lipids, and enzymes, among others; it consists of about 100,000 macromolecules on the average. The entire macromolecular population of a given cell is renewed about 10,000 times during its lifetime. Throughout this staggering turnover of matter, the cell maintains its distinctiveness, cohesiveness, and relative autonomy. It produces myriads of components, yet it does not produce something else—it produces itself. A cell maintains its identity and distinctiveness even though it incorporates at least 1,000,000,000 different constitutive molecules during its life span. This maintenance of unity and wholeness, while the components themselves are being continuously or periodically disassembled and rebuilt, created and decimated, produced and consumed, is called "autopoiesis." (pp. 4–5)

By analogy, the autopoiesis in the cell is a lot like the fact that you go through many experiences and situations, but to paraphrase Zeleny, throughout this staggering turnover of events, the person maintains its distinctiveness, cohesiveness, and relative autonomy. A consistency is maintained. Although I like to think that the cell Zeleny is talking about is a neuron, it seems to me that cells, bodies, brains, and personalities represent analogies of the autopoiesis idea. Read again Milan Zeleny's last sentence, "The maintenance of unity and wholeness. . . ." Think about how you go through the changes in your life: home, school, work, visit other cities, watch movies, and age. Through it all you may change a bit (cells and neurons grow and develop too), but you are always you, and you know it.

Theories of Personality

Personality is one of the most complex topics within psychology. As you study each of the approaches toward understanding personality, keep in mind the idea of autopoiesis. Think about how the cell continues to produce itself, how it adapts, and how it can change.

Sigmund Freud's Psychoanalytic Theory of Personality

Through his *psychoanalytic theory*, Sigmund Freud (1953–55) has doubtless made the single most significant contribution to understanding human personality. In a very clear sense, Freud's approach to understanding personality represents a restricted general systems theory of personality. It brings together biological, social and self systems in attempting to understand personality. For a fascinating discussion of the parallels between Freud's views and sociobiology, see the synthesis work by Leak and Christopher (1982). All of the ideas that help understand the person according to Freud are organized around an energy system model.

The idea of an energy system underlying the workings of your personality might sound a bit abstract or complicated, but it doesn't need to be. An automobile is a physical energy system. It was just the idea of the operation of such physical energy systems that gave rise in Freud's mind to his *psychodynamics* or psychological forces. Think for a moment about the uses of energy by a car. For example, the car has access to just so much energy it can organize. But it has different types of energy: electrical, mechanical, etc. If energy is used one way in a car's overall system, it will take away from the release or use of another. When the car is going up a steep hill, it will not accelerate quickly. Energy in the car's system will make it move (the motor), and energy in the system will stop it (the driver and the brakes). Complex relations between these two energy systems can result in interesting behavior on the part of the car. It can run wild with the accelerator stuck to the floor, or it can stop cold. If the brakes and the accelerator are both applied fully, both systems will burn out. Normal healthy driving consists of carefully metered release of the forces of the systems. According to psychodynamics, human personality is a similar sort of constant balancing of opposing forces. As you read through the dynamics of the psyche, according to Freud, keep this idea in mind.

The Structure of the Psychodynamic Energy System: Id-Ego-Superego

The Id. The *id* is instinctual and is the source of all driving energy in the psychodynamic system. It is kind of like the motor in a car. All it seems to want to do, in order to function, is burn up all the gas in the gas tank. In terms of the personality, Freud would say it operates in accordance with the *pleasure principle*. The id, by itself, is much like the energy expression in young children, young animals, or perhaps even terrorists. In all of these examples, the id structure predominates in the control of energy. The id wants only what it wants, and it wants it now! Where is the id in your brain? Even though the id is thought by Freud to be a structural part of your personality, the emphasis is on dynamics or forces and not upon things. We can use the engine of the car as its id only in a metaphorical sense. We know that there is an engine in a car, and we know where to look for it. However, Freud never had the opportunity to "look under the hood" of personality, he just felt something had to power it, and he called it "id." So keep the hood closed on our car, just noting that somewhere in the car's system is something that makes it go. This problem of where the id (and the other structures) is in the brain is best understood as a "black box" problem. You may wish to review that discussion in Chapter 1.

The pleasure principle, seeks two goals—sexual expression and aggression. To get a feel for what Freud had in mind, imagine the total uninhibited expression of all of your *life instincts* (sex), and all of your *death instincts* (aggression). If you didn't just imagine them in society you wouldn't last long—no longer than a car with the accelerator stuck. But, if you look around you in society, you can see the almost direct expression of id forces. No matter what they might say, they are by definition in Freud's scheme under the control of the instinctual biological processes. Terrorists seem to be irrational, demanding, impulsive, selfish, pleasure loving, and very willing to destroy humans or anything else—even themselves (death instinct at its totality). But one might say they are driven not by the id, but by ideals. Perhaps they are.

The Superego. The *superego* modulates the use of energy in accordance with the rules of society you have learned to accept. Whereas the id would have the car's engine racing all over the countryside, running people down, running through stop signs, etc., the superego would bring energy to obey all traffic signs and rules of the road. Whereas the terrorist seems controlled somewhat by id energy primarily, the members of parliaments are more strongly influenced by their adherence to the rules of government to accomplish goals for the system.

The superego structures are committed to what has been learned about following the rules.

Based upon rewards and punishments for id expressions, the superego forces may come to impose a very restrictive set of rules on a particular individual. In this case, if circumstances lead such a person to "breaking a rule," he may feel the great fear and anxiety originally associated with the punishment of "being bad." This feeling is guilt

The Ego. People neither race all over the countryside in a car until they are out of gas nor run into a surprisingly solid tree, nor do they obey perfectly all of the rules of the road. There is a reasonable reality which is neither of these. We are not totally governed by the pleasure principle, nor by the rules of society. On an icy road our car may crawl along. On a hot summer day we may find our car zooming above the speed limit along an isolated highway. The *ego* modulates the expressions of the id and the superego by taking reality into account. The ego, operating in accordance with a *reality principle,* supports an optimum expression of the id but is not dominated by it. The ego has us going slowly on ice, not so much because of a law to do so (superego), but because the reality of the situation is that we might slide off the road and be hurt (avoidance of pain). Finally, when we go over the speed limit on a hot day, the id is being served by the pleasure principle and the reality that a traffic ticket is unlikely—especially if the ego keeps an eye on the rear-view minor.

The id, ego, and superego represent forces, not things. We tend to think of these aspects of the energy system as either being in control or not being in control. Virtually everything we do is a constant balancing of the energy forces of these systems. From moment to moment the forces are shifting in relationship to meet the subtle changes in demands in the environment. I often contemplate what Freud had in mind in the following sort of situation. I have occasionally found myself alone at night at a deserted stop light with no one in sight. I sit obediently waiting for the light to change. I am wondering, "What am I doing?" Should I go ahead through the light? It doesn't make any difference at this time of night. The law is for safety. There's no question of safety here. Maybe the light is stuck? I am getting uneasy. Finally, I get up the courage and cautiously go through the red light (looking each way about 10 times in rapid succession). For the next mile, I look in the rear-view mirror occasionally. In this little story you can probably see the three dynamic forces at work.

The Psychodynamics of Consciousness

Freudian psychodynamics depend heavily upon the idea that much of what leads to our behavior is *unconscious.* We are unaware of most of the dynamics behind our behavior. It is one thing for me to relate my story about the traffic light; it is quite another thing to understand why that is my story.

The standard model used to illustrate the relationship between the id, ego, superego, and consciousness is that of an iceberg. We often use the expression "That's only the tip of the iceberg," referring to the fact that most of it lies hidden below the surface. Figure 8.2 takes the iceberg model, the split-brain model we examined in Chapter 2, and the duality of consciousness model we examined in Chapter 3 into account (see, for example, Galin 1974, 1977; Joseph 1983; Miller 1986). It shows the larger portions of the preconscious, ego, and superego that are attributed to the left hemisphere's more verbal consciousness. The larger portions of the id and superego are attributed to the right hemisphere's more nonverbal consciousness (see Chapter 3).

The ego somehow optimizes the expression of the instinctual drives of sex and aggression in the face of society's rules. Freud postulated a number of details on how this is accomplished. A portion of emergent ego functioning is unconscious (see Figure 8.3). In the unconscious, imaginative processes can make of the world whatever is expedient. This appears in creativity, imagination, dreams, and beliefs. At the same time, conflict between the id-ego-superego can make life very uncomfortable. The feeling arising from conflict is anxiety which drives the ego to use its imagination to reduce the anxiety to acceptable limits. It accomplishes this through various unconscious perceptual, intellectual, emotional, and memory-distorting strategies or mechanisms called *ego defense mechanisms.*

Ego Defending (Conflict Reducing) Mechanisms

Unconscious Distortion through Repression. Several years ago when I was a college student I

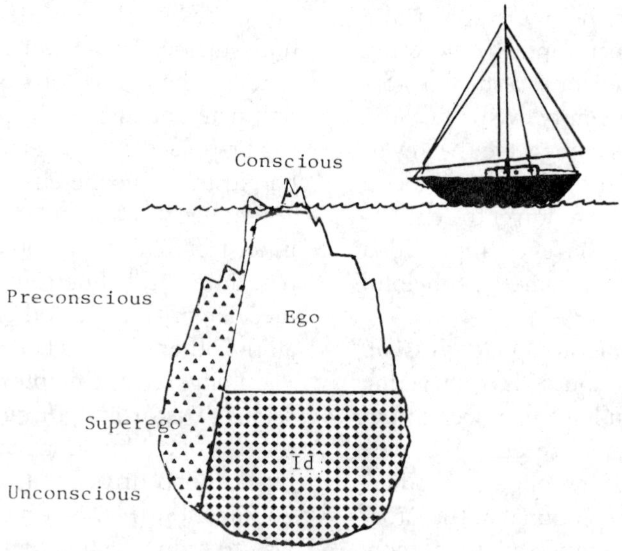

Figure 8.2 Freud's Personality Structures

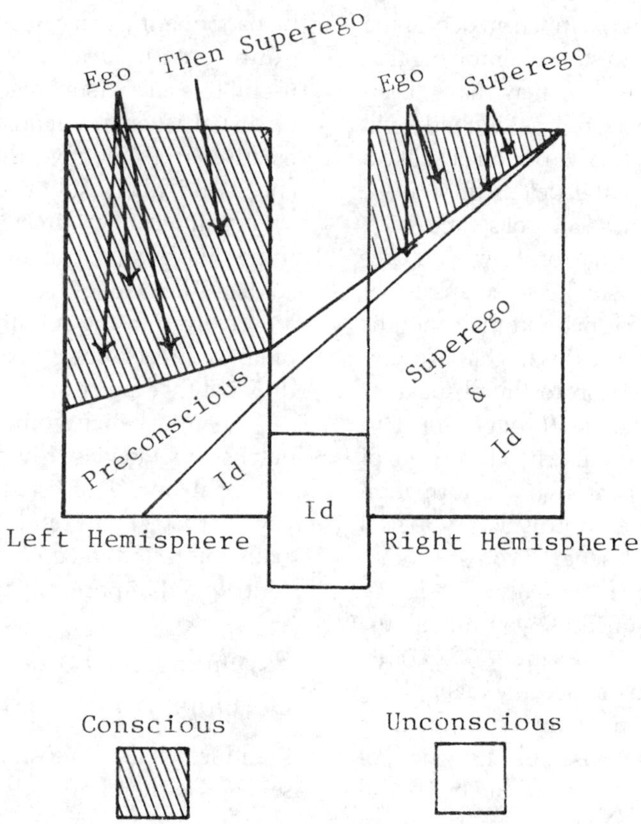

Figure 8.3 Consciousness and Unconsciousness Related to the Cerebral Hemispheres

can remember getting in an argument with one of my instructors about whether roads made cities or cities made roads. Because he badly embarrassed me in front of the class, I will never forget that situation—except for one thing! I cannot remember his name. I can easily remember the names of other instructors I had, but never his. The reason is probably an unconscious distortion of memory to help me forget the source of the embarrassment and therefore the embarrassment. This repression is a small distortion of my retrievable memory. Why just the name? The person and his name were the key to the embarrassment. Forgetting that much goes a long way toward helping me to forget the embarrassment. We might say the ego employed a strategy that was least troublesome/most helpful to help reduce anxiety.

Unconscious Distortion through Regression. Has anyone ever said to you "Oh, quit acting like a child"? Perhaps you have had occasion to have also said this to someone else. You may have been pouting, stamping about, or otherwise being unnecessarily emotional in the situation and have probably regressed to a more comfortable (less complicated) approach to the problem at hand. After all, no one expects a child to deal with adult problems.

If the ego experiences too much anxiety at the complicated adult level, a distortion implying that a childlike approach, which may have been acceptable when the person was a child, will reduce the ensuing anxiety. The person acts like a child, totally unaware of the defensive strategy, although afterwards he may feel foolish and wonder what prompted his behavior. Have you ever noticed that when some smokers get upset that they can't seem to get a cigarette in their mouths fast enough? Do you suppose this might have anything to do with a regression to thumbsucking?

Unconscious Distortion through an Opposing Reaction Formation. The distortion of anxiety-causing feelings through the formation of a believed opposite reaction is a very logical way to reduce anxiety. Whenever you see someone exhibiting extreme *compulsive behavior* toward people, things, or ideas, you might suspect reaction formation. For example, very often people who crusade against homosexuality have anxiety about their own id drives concerning sexuality. This is an unconscious distortion of belief and if the anxiety is strong, the belief will have great force. One must be careful about ascribing reaction formation to all strong compulsive behavior. Certainly, a strong anti-terrorist position would not represent an underlying anxiety about wanting to be a terrorist, would it? Think about this for a moment.

Unconscious Distortion through Projection. The anxiety-reducing strategy of projection simply places what is inside the person bothering him outside. This distortion, too, is very logical because the source of superego-related anxiety originated outside in the parents, society, etc., in the first place. Often when a person has a strong hatred for someone else, it causes guilt anxiety. To reduce this anxiety a person projects this inner feeling onto the other. Instead of saying "I hate him" and thus causing anxiety, "He hates me," is projected. In other words, the anxiety is all the other person's fault

Long-Term Complex Systems of Unconscious Distortion through Sublimation. The process of sublimation is used by the ego not to block the id drives, but rather to redirect them. Sublimation then is a more long-term, efficient way to reduce conflict anxiety. Whereas the ego defenses described above pretty much develop in relation to an individual's own life, sublimations have more of a social origin. For example, by participating in a career of any kind, id energy can be used to create or to destroy in a manner useful to society (superego). Likely sublimations of sexual id energy tend to be directed toward creative or productive things—art, music, science. And likely sublimations of aggressive id energy might be directed toward destructive things like boxing, driving a bulldozer, or being a soldier. All societies have patterns of humor that are involved in the sublimation process. Humor often redirects both sexual and aggressive id drives at the same time.

There are many other subcategories of ego defensive strategies. I have included only those principal ones suggested by Freud's daughter, psychiatrist Anna Freud (1946), who was especially interested in ego defense mechanisms and contributed importantly in this area.

Psychological Forces in the Early Development of Personality

Freud felt that the most powerful id forces were sexual. He therefore used sexual stages of development as a model for early personality development—*psychosexual stages of development.* In this model, the early core of personality that will influence all later personality development is laid down in a dynamic pattern of id, superego, and ego relationships by about age six.

We might ask why Freud did not also develop a model of personality development around aggression—a sort of psychoaggression model along with the psychosexual one? There are probably two reasons for this. First, Freud felt the sexual id energy was the more powerful in organizing the personality. Second, it is difficult to relate aggression to any organized pattern of biological development. This is not so for sexual development!

Sexual development can be organized into a series of stages. In each of these stages sexual id drives either might be facilitated toward mature, optimum expression of sexual energy, or to various degrees of thwarted energy. The sexuality of the id contains biological stages of potential development toward mature sexuality. In the Freudian view, sexuality is hierarchically arranged and is represented in four different drives to satisfy the pleasure principle (see Table 6.7).

Freud felt that if a person experienced either too much comfort or too much discomfort during the stages of sexual growth he would become psychologically fixed in these stages. These possible fixations could form rather reliable relationships between the id, superego, and ego—your core personality. Earlier we discussed the ego defense strategy of regression. If fixations are developed during the early stages of sexual development, ego defensive regressions to these stages are more likely. The person will exhibit behavior like that originally related to that particular stage. In Freud's theory there are five stages of early sexual development including three thought to be related to basic personality dynamics—the oral, anal, and phallic stages.

Oral Sexuality—Stage 1. Sexuality in the Freudian scheme is very broadly related to species reproductive processes. Often, we tend to think of sexuality in a narrow sense involving only the genitals. The *oral stage* of sexuality concerns the first necessity of survival for the species—feeding. This gratification (pleasure principle) involves first the lips and mouth structure (sucking), and then biting (eating). While this activity is concerned with species survival, is it really sexual? We can only say that kissing is an oral activity that is related to both friendship and romantic love.

Fixations that occur during this stage of development are thought to be metaphorically related to later personality characteristics described as the oral personality. These people seem to be interested only in themselves. They tend to see others for only what they can provide (feed) them. It is better to receive than to give. Regressions to these tendencies will be most evident when the person is under stress.

Anal Sexuality—Stage 2. In the *anal stage* the focus of the pleasure principle has shifted to the accumulation and release aspects of elimination. Here the child has the opportunity to become a "partner" in the gratification of anal pleasure drives. He becomes an active participant in the conditions relating to toilet training. Society has great demands and expectations concerning toilet training. But the child soon learns that he, too, has some control over the situation. He, or she, must attempt to reduce conflict anxiety arising from social pressures on the one hand and sexual id drives on the other.

Fixations in the anal sexuality stage may be either retentive (holding back) or expulsive (releasing) if toilet training is harsh. The anal personality may at times show both the retentive and expulsive fixations depending on the situation at hand. Retentive strategies form a core of obstinacy and stinginess. The expulsive strategies form a core of explosiveness when under stress—tantrums, destructiveness, and disorderliness. Expect these tendencies when the person is under stress.

Phallic Sexuality—Stage 3. Up to this point the psychosexual development of male and female personality has been essentially the same because the *erogenous zones* have been the same. The male and female genitals now become the actual and symbolic focus of psychosexual development, the *phallic stage*. In fantasy, the boy becomes attracted to his mother, the girl to her father. In reality, these attractions represent conflicts. Freud called these the *Oedipus complexes* (the female conflict is called the Electra complex). Ego and superego development in the child attempt to reduce the conflict anxiety so that the boy can identify with his father (use him as the appropriate role model) and the girl with her mother. The female conflict does not have the pressure on it for quick ego resolution as does the boy's, who fears castration for his affections. According to Freud, this is a fundamental point of difference between male and female personality.

Fixation in the phallic conflicts may result in extreme attempts at appearing strongly male or female. The male whose ego has not resolved this conflict must always let people know how strong and masculine he is. The female may carry her unresolved conflict into adulthood as a seductive flirt who acts naive about any sexual intentions.

Mature Sexual Development. Freud postulated two more periods of development that had little to do with the development of core personality. The period following the phallic stage was called a latent period of time. Psychosexual conflicts during this period of age 6 or 7 to puberty are relatively free of the necessity of ego to square reality with the sexual instincts. (This does not mean children of this age group are not involved in sexual thinking or behavior, there is simply not a pressing conflict to resolve the issues.)

Finally, puberty signals the onset of the genital stage. During this time, heterosexual activity, including intercourse, will take place. At puberty, the general states of Oedipal conflict resolution returns. For one teenager this "reawakening" is a trying time; for another it is a happy growth into a mature, heterosexual relation with another person.

Overall, the stages of psychosexual development are not abrupt in any sense; they are completely overlapping. The stage should be understood as only the focus of *libidinal energy* within the system. In all stages the other forms of sexuality are present, but to lesser degree, than the one in focus. Oral, anal, phallic, and genital sexuality come together in adult life with genital sexuality usually the focus. Kissing, caressing, etc., are a normal part of mature heterosexual and homosexual behavior. Freud felt that every person is by nature bisexual. We are attracted to members of both sexes to varying degrees. This inherent degree of attraction and our development through the psychosexual personality results in our individual sexuality.

Freud's Followers: A Dynamic Reorganization

There is no doubt that Freud's psychodynamic approach stands as a great contribution to our understanding of personality. Psychoanalysis, an application of the psychodynamics to psychotherapy, is used throughout the world. There is an emphasis upon the importance of early experiences, the fact that the reasons people do things are very often unknown to them, and that these reasons can be brought to light.

But there have also been countless adjustments to Freudian psychodynamics and psychoanalysis. Probably every professional who adopts or partially adopts the approach makes subtle adjustments. However, there are four reorganizations of the dynamics that have had the greatest influence. These include the modifications of Alfred Adler, Carl Jung, Karen Horney, and Anna Freud.

Alfred Adler: Feelings of Inferiority

Alfred Adler (1927) broke away from Freud because of several theoretical disagreements, but primarily because of Freud's strong emphasis on sexual drives as the framework, for personality development. Adler proposed a shift in dynamics that gives us the concept of the *inferiority complex* and *superiority complex*. We are all constantly driven by our feelings of inability and imperfection (Gandhi). Our entire psyche is pervaded by the motivation to win, to achieve, dominate, and be the best. The condition of childhood we all must go through puts us in a position of smallness, weakness, neglect, etc. These early experiences form feelings of inferiority in all of us, that drive us to feel good about ourselves. The situation can be distorted by the illusion of superiority—the superiority complex.

Each person has his, or her, own way of striving to compensate or make up for his, or her, feeling of inferiority. This is referred to as that person's *style of life*. The deep-rooted inferiority complex might help explain why we are all constantly attracted to winners and attractive people, and why we continue to feel we were "just lucky" even though we continue to succeed. At any rate, Adler felt that people have inferiority-related goals, and strive to reduce the related anxiety.

Carl G. Jung: The Unconscious and the Emergence of Self

Carl Jung was probably the most brilliant of Freud's followers. Freud had said of him, "When the empire I have founded is orphaned, no one but Jung must inherit the whole thing." But this same brilliance led Jung to found his own conception of mind. Jung's work is fascinating and far ranging.

Jung felt that everyone has a personal unconscious related to his own individual life.

The ego normally makes free use of this unconscious. In addition to the personal unconscious, Jung postulated a *collective unconscious* that contains the experiences, not of a specific person, but of all humans who preceded her. Experiences repeated over and over through countless generations become primordial images in man's unconscious. These unconscious images are usually called *archetypes* and provide the fundamental base for man's personality. Archetypical images were thought to include such things as fear of the dark, the creation of deities, the idea of life after death, the idea of the world coming to an end, hero and villain polarity, and others. That these archetypical representations appear in so many legends and mysteries in so many different cultures gave rise to the idea for Jung.

Do we actually have a collective unconscious? Perhaps we do. If the repeated meanings of the images over generations were related to survival selection situations (evolution), then a neurological basis for them might be inherited. We could certainly see the idea of the end of the world archetype being selected in this way. For example, those who have survived periodic calamities may have been those who had a tendency to be prepared, have reserves on hand, etc., because of feelings of impending disaster (see the idea of gene-culture coevolution, Chapter 7). However, Jung's theory of simple repetition of the experience over generations, which is not natural selection, would not lead to the formation of a collective storehouse of primordial imagery.

Below the collective unconscious, Jung suggested still a deeper collection of images concerning our animal past. This he calls the shadow. In the shadow is the savage animalistic part of man. The shadow is a collection of images of our animal existence that were repeated over and over again. Whether any symbolic meaning accompanies the shadow is an important question.

Synchronicity All of these ideas about primordial images and symbolism transcending time might help us appreciate another interesting creation of Jung's—*synchronicity*. Have you ever noticed how things occasionally seem to happen together in strange ways? Perhaps you have been thinking of someone you have not seen for years and the next day you bump into him on the street. Or you have a dream about something, and the next day parts of the dream seem to come true. This represents the idea of synchronicity. Jung felt very strongly that relationships between things and events might exist in a way other than the causal relationships to which we normally restrict our thinking and our brains can tune into this noncausal synchronous plane of relationships. For example, Jung saw synchronicity behind the more or less common emergence of the idea of sun worship in two different parts of the world at the same time. Jung was also interested in the study of parapsychology and felt that synchronicity explained parapsychological events.

Finally, Jung differed from Freud by putting a great deal of emphasis upon the self as the equilibrator of the psyche. Jung's idea of autopoiesis would be one which finally achieves a perfect balance of all opposing forces within us; within us is a symbolic archetypical striving for perfection.

As more and more of us approach this self-actualization, the more this becomes, itself, a symbolic archetypical image for all humans. Ultimately, Jung felt that humans would become this ideal man through the symbolic image of his actualized self, each of us contributing along the way. The collective self-symbol appears throughout the world as the balanced magic circle, a mandala.

Karen Horney: Social and Cultural Influences

Karen Horney (1939) did not so much break away from Freud as she shifted dynamics within the scheme. For this reason she is referred to as a neo-Freudian. Today neo-Freudian ideas have generally replaced strictly Freudian ones.

It is important to understanding Karen Horney's contribution to note that she was trained as an analyst in Germany. Upon immigration to the United States, she could readily see the effects of cultural influences upon her American patients. For example, she found that in American culture her patient's problems were more related to the Great Depression than to psychosexual problems. Along this same line, she came to feel that women's development was greatly influenced by culture. Women, she thought, were really living in a different culture from men. Even though Karen Horney died in 1952, her ideas are very much in vogue today.

The move toward social and cultural influences on personality led Horney to postulate that interpersonal relationships, and not instincts, are at the core of personality. Starting with the idea of a child's basic anxiety about acceptance and nurturance from others, she suggested three ways we might go about reducing it. These are fairly straightforward strategies that you see in operation every day. The strategies include moving toward, moving against, and moving away.

In moving toward, the person reduces basic anxiety by taking a dependent role in relation to others. He gives himself to others to be accepted. In moving against, anxiety is reduced by the person excessively denying that he needs others. He becomes tough and hostile. Finally, one can move away to reduce basic anxiety. The person excessively avoids attachment with others.

You might see some distant relationship between these three ways of reducing anxiety and the Freudian ego defense strategies. Just as with the defense strategies of Freud, the question is not whether a person uses them; it is the degree to which he uses a particular strategy over the others.

Anna Freud: The Extension of Psychoanalysis to Children

Sigmund Freud died in 1939 in London, England. There his daughter, Dr. Anna Freud, continued the development of psychoanalytic techniques. She was director of the Hampstead Child Therapy Clinic until her death in 1982.

Of special interest is Anna Freud's (1974) development of techniques that have helped in understanding children. Due largely to her work, now a great deal of therapy for children in both the United States and the United Kingdom is based upon Freudian psychoanalytic theory.

The Emergence of Self in Personality Theory

Carl Rogers: How Can the Self "Actualize"?

Carl Rogers put self-organization more in control of what is happening. According to Rogers, it is the development of the self that is directed at taking the person through true human existence.

In this model of personality, human beings are seen as capable of creating a complex system of experiences and their meanings—a *phenomenal field.* Your phenomenal field is different from that of anyone who has ever lived—or ever will. But, in addition, we are capable of organizing a part of this phenomenal field to represent the self—a condition of being human.

Animals do have phenomenal fields of experiences and meanings, but there is not a differentiation of a "self-field" within it. You have probably noticed that when animals encounter a mirror they seem either puzzled or oblivious about their own image. This leads us to conclude that their part of the phenomenal field referring to themselves is either very small or nonexistent.

Self-Actualization. Rogers, in a different way from Jung, would also appreciate the self-production phenomenon of autopoiesis. The idea of *self-actualization* replaces the Freudian idea of instincts with the idea of a striving to cause and maintain constant growth in experiencing. Growth is such an important part of the phenomenal self, that it contains experiences and meanings that the person would most like to become. Rogers likened the whole system's actualization of self to a striving plant that can encroach on even a hostile environment and grow and prosper to "hold its own, . . . to adapt, develop, become itself" (Rogers, 1963, p. 2). Carl Rogers believed that many people in society achieve full potential or self-actualization in a broad variety of pursuits. Gandhi, Eleanor Roosevelt, Martin Luther King, Jr., and Albert Einstein might be considered examples of people who achieved self-actualization.

As the self and the ideal self continue to emerge, we tend to behave consistently with the self-concept. However, there are occasions when inconsistency with the self-concept appear. Most men, for example, have a concept that sees themselves as someone who does not cry at the movies. What happens if one of these men finds himself crying while watching a movie? Rogers would say he is in state of incongruence with the self-concept. This, of course goes against the whole idea of an equilibration process toward an ideal self. However, the self-organization will attempt to maintain its conceptual integrity by

Figure 8.4 Albert Einstein, Eleanor Roosevelt and Martin Luther King, Jr., might be examples of people who achieved self-actualization.

distorting or denying the incongruent experience (crying in this case).

But, where do the labels that get in the way of self-actualization come from in the first place? Underlying the problem of congruence Rogers suggested was our need for positive regard. We all need to be loved and accepted. You can really be you when you are with people you think like you—hold you in positive regard. If you are loved, you remain open to new experiences and you will find little incongruence between your flexible self-concept and your ideal self. However, whenever love and acceptance are made conditional, the self-concept labels become more rigid and incongruencies become more common. These incongruencies cause more distortion and denial between your self-concept and your ideal self—and self-actualization.

So, next time you see that big macho man crying while watching a tear-jerker, don't laugh at him. Show him some positive regard; compliment him on his great sensitivity, or his great insight into the feelings of others. You'll be helping both of you along toward self-actualization.

If Rogers is right in his fundamental idea of self, then in expanding the number of labels for the phenomenal self, he has increased our possibilities. The more we know about ourselves, the more we can then become. Freud did this too with his idea of the unconscious. He just didn't tell us that knowing about the possibility of an unconscious alone, would expand our phenomenal selves and help lead to self-actualization.

George Kelly: Personal Constructions of the World

In Carl Rogers's theory of personality, the self-organization was the important dynamic in personality. In George Kelly's (1955, 1980) *personal construct theory* each person is seen as a scientist trying to predict and control events. We go through life constantly hypothesizing about everything that is going on around us. Every person, according to Kelly, is free to construe the world in any way he wishes. Then as predicted events do or do not come about, the personal constructs of the world are modified. There are no true maps of future events, only continuing hypothetical ones construed by each individual person. After all, Kelly would say, why are there theories of religion, science, art, and human affairs in the first place? They exist because that is the way all human beings organize themselves in relation to the world. Each person's system of personal constructs is unique, and his personality is a reflection of them.

Just as a scientist hypothesizes about how an experiment will turn out to help validate his picture of the world, so does each of us constantly. For example, we often find ourselves trying things out to see how people will react. We try new clothes, new thoughts, new words, new humor. We carefully note the results of these little experiments and adjust our personal construction of the world accordingly. Very young children constantly experiment with the environment in trying to develop some personal construction of how the world might be predictable and controllable, or they are trying out new modifications of personal constructs. Either the personal construct is validated or if not, the person simply and naturally reconstrues the world a little by loosening or by abandoning the construct altogether. The scientist does the same thing.

The Personality as Make-Believe. Kelly felt that all personal constructs are make-believe, that allow a lot of subjective thinking. This can provide what Kelly called an invitational mood to open the personality to virtually any hypothesis. Have you ever wanted to try something totally outrageous (but harmless) just to see what happens or how people react? If so, your personal constructs are probably good make-believe, and you are probably going to succeed. We all love the daring who succeed, and appreciate the efforts of those who failed.

The perfect personal construct is not obtainable according to Kelly, though some may work exceedingly well. Just as all scientific theories are eventually either replaced or modified, so are all personal constructs. Information in the world is constantly changing. There are alternative ways of construing the same information. Sciences (including Einstein's $E = mc^2$) and personalities do not discover truth, but only attempt to construct systems that help anticipate events.

> To me the truth is precious . . . I should rather be right and stand alone than to run with the multitude and be wrong. . . . The holding of views herein set forth has already won me the scorn and contempt and ridicule of some of my fellow men. I am looked upon as being odd, strange, peculiar. . . . But Truth is truth and though all the world reject it and turn against me, I will cling to truth still. (Gardner, 1957, p. 12)

Here the view (construct) being discussed was that of Charles deFord, who was convinced he had proved the world to be flat! Just as there are poor scientific theories, people, too, construe invalid constructs. The problem occurs when they stay with the invalid personal construct in the face of invalidating evidence. Sometimes it is helpful to hold on to a slightly invalid personal construct. For example, we can't all be physically beautiful—but it is nice to construe that we are. However, if a person has so much anxiety that his personal constructs prohibit the personality from growing and achieving happiness, that is not good—as in deFord's case.

To help people who have faulty constructs, Kelly would suggest they need retraining as a scientist—at forming new constructs. There are three parts to helping people become better personal scientists. First, there must be an atmosphere of experimentation—let people try new things. Second, new situations must be provided for the person so he can try new things. Third, the person must know the results of his new experimentations to validate or invalidate his new personal construings. If you stop to think about it, this is pretty much the way good friends relate to one another.

You might guess that Kelly's personal construct theory of personality is of more than passing interest to me as a scientist. My personal construct of Kelly's system is that if people are really like scientists construing theories about the world, they are probably general systems theorists. Kelly said that personal construing was based upon observing repeated patterns. This is exactly what produces general systems ideas across the sciences. Second, evidence concerning the development of personal constructs supports a hierarchical organization and integration across constructs. This implies that at some point the personal constructs would anticipate events as would a general systems theorist. As the personality matures it is construing constructs that apply to as many situations as possible.

Summary

Some of the ideas you have encountered concerning the emergence of self in theories of personality, ideal self, self-actualization, and the personality as a scientist, can be related to Gandhi's story. Did you know that Gandhi titled his autobiography *The Story of My Experiments With Truth?* There are many other psychologists who emphasize the role of the self in personality. But now it is time to discuss another general source of personality theory—the effects of the environment.

Albert Bandura and Walter Mischel: The Social Learning of Personality

The study of learning and conditioning is essentially the study of influence of the environment upon behavior patterns. And our definition of personality asks us to account for its characteristics that in turn account for consistent patterns of response to situations. What we are really doing here is applying what we know about environmental influences on behavior to the understanding of how complex aspects of personality might be learned.

The behavioral learning theorist would propose that personality simply amounts to a unique pattern of learned response in each of us. For the learning theorist there is no reason to postulate ids, egos, superegos, selves, personal constructs, etc. Behaviorist John B. Watson said, "Give me a dozen healthy infants . . . , and I'll guarantee to take any one at random and train him to become . . . doctor, lawyer, artist, merchant-chief, and yes, beggar-man and thief. . . ." In exactly the same way, Watson could have put different personalities in this famous paragraph—all due to the influence of the environment.

There are few psychologists who would accept this view of personality in total. And there is a growing realization among those of the behaviorist view that something must be added to explain a concept as complex as personality—something cognitive—something that, to put it simply, thinks. Can this be done while staying within the context of the environment? Albert Bandura (1977a, 1977b) and Walter Mischel (1973, 1977) propose that a "thinking" element in the social learning theory of personality involves the self-regulation of a person in relationship to his environment, and once learned, it becomes a partner in controlling behavior.

In a manner a little similar to Kelly's personal construct idea, self, regulation includes expectancies or anticipations concerning environmental consequences of behavior. In self-regulation, the person becomes capable of self-reward and self-punishment. The environment can become internalized within a system of standards that allows learned self-regulation concerning goals and plans. Overall conceptions of *self-efficacy,* what you think you can and can't do, are established in the person. With learned standards and self-efficacy established, anticipatory judgments about what can be

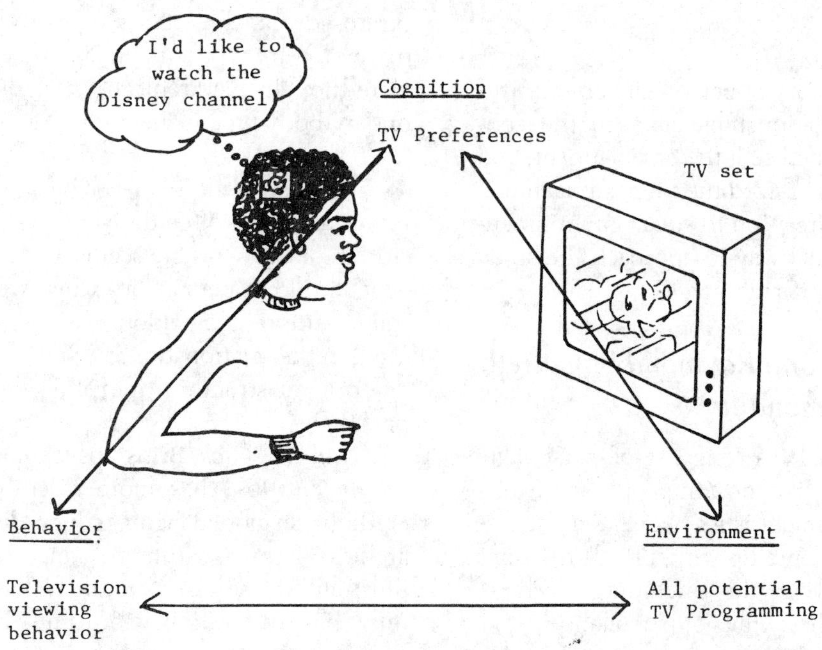

The illustration shows the interaction of cognition, behavior, and the environment constituting a "self." In this way the self is a dependent system. The TV preferences result in TV programming and vice-versa. The viewing behavior results in TV preferences and vice-versa. Viewing behavior results in programming and vice-versa. (Adapted from Bandura, 1978)

Figure 8.5 Bandura's Reciprocal Self-System

accomplished occur in the person. The difference between Kelly on the one hand, and Bandura and Mischel on the other, is really a matter of how this sort of thinking comes about in the first place. Bandura and Mischel conclude that it is learned; Kelly feels that construing is simply the way the system works.

The Self-System. Bandura (1978) has proposed the idea of a three-part self-system that sees self as a reciprocal interaction of environmental, behavioral, and cognitive influences originating through social learning. Figure 8.5 illustrates how this interlocking system might function.

If social learning theory is on the right track, then we are offered a great hope. Perhaps great talent can be a matter not only of social learning, but also of "great personality." In Chapter 5, we have listed Benjamin Bloom's factors that seem to produce great talent. It seems possible that if these were internalized as standards for self-reinforcement and self-efficacy, one might well turn out to be a great personality. The great value of social learning theory is that it offers not just a way to think about personality, but also an objective way to study its development.

Summary

Social learning theory of personality emphasizes the reciprocal relationships between the constantly being learned self, the environment, and behavior. We emphasized the idea that Gandhi's story emerged in relation to social environmental extremes. A final way to approach the study of personality is *personality traits.*

Hans Eysenck and Raymond B. Cattell: Describing Personality

If we were to make a long list of personality characteristics we like most in people and a long list of those characteristics we like least, we would probably come up with a lot of the same ones everyone else would—including psychologists who study these traits of personality.

Traits. According to one tally, there are 17,953 terms descriptive of how people are predisposed to behave in situations. This is the fundamental theoretical idea behind trait theory—that people have certain predispositions to behave in fairly consistent ways and that these are the basis of personality. This trait idea fits in with the definition of personality itself. So in a very real sense, we are all trait theorists just by virtue of the way we go about classifying people on how we expect and predict they will typically behave.

But trait theory doesn't stop here. It suggests that we go on to analyze the 17,953 or so trait possibilities looking for two things. First, trait explanations attempt to reduce as much unnecessary overlap or redundancy among the thousands of factors as possible. For example, the descriptive trait factors of dull, boring, uninteresting, etc., might well be reduced to one descriptive term. This you could do using your own correlational logic (you decide the three are essentially the same and call them collectively the "nerd factor"). Second, trait explanations of personality attempt to show which of these reduced traits are related to one another, and which are more important in describing a person's personality. In other words, it is important in trait theory, to show some sort of hierarchy or ranking of traits in a personality structure.

Both of these principles can be seen in what is an interesting and well worked out, but discredited, trait approach. William Sheldon (1954) proposed that three body types were related to three primary types of personality. These in turn were thought hierarchically related to four secondary body types. The outline is shown in Figure 8.6.

This trait model also illustrates another important point often derived in factor-reducing studies of traits—there seems to appear a strong genetic role in personality when viewed from a trait standpoint. Sheldon was essentially interested in the relationship of a person's genetically determined structure (morphogenotype) to his personality.

Hans Eysenck. British psychologist Hans H. Eysenck (1969) has more recently and more credibly developed factor-reduced lists and hierarchies of traits within personality. Figure 8.7 illustrates the sort of structure he has found. Not only has the number of traits been greatly reduced, but the hierarchical structure is very clear.

Eysenck has also devoted a great deal of time attempting to explain how his personality factors are related to genetic and neurological ones. His correlational studies indicate that genetic factors account for about two-thirds of what is behind

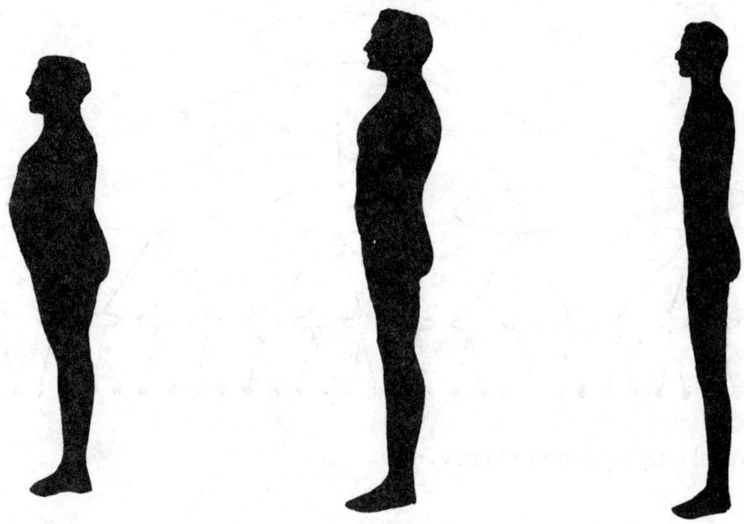

Endomorphy	Mesomorphy	Ectomorphy
Viscerotonia	Somatotonia	Cerebrotonia
Types		
Relaxed posture	Assertive posture	Restrained posture
Slow reactions	Energetic reactions	Staccato reactions
Love of polite ceremony	Bold directness of manner	Self-conscious motility of eyes and face
Complacency	Spartan indifference to pain	Hypersensitivity to pain
Appears to be his own age	Appears older	Appears younger
Relaxed under the influence of alcohol	Assertive under the influence of alcohol	Resistant to alcohol and other depressant drugs
Personality characteristics		
Need of people when troubled	Need of action when troubled	Need of solitude when troubled
Oriented toward childhood and family relationship	Oriented toward goals and activities	Oriented toward the later periods of life

Figure 8.6 Body Types

personality. While these are interesting findings, they are not generally agreed upon. Most theorists see traits as largely genetically determined and neurologically based.

Raymond B. Cattell. Raymond B. Cattell (1950) has also worked with the trait theory of personality using the analysis of correlated factors to reduce redundancy across the thousands of likely factors. Cattell is a very important trait theorist for at least two reasons. First, his approach squarely addresses the problem of just what reduced traits there really are. While we might assume that the list of 17,953 traits are all of the possibilities for personality, how do we check to see that we are reducing the redundancy properly? It would be valuable to have other sources of trait descriptions to get at the dynamic aspects of traits across situations. This is the whole point of personality theory.

Cattell feels that information about a person's personality should converge from three types of assessment. First, there is real life situations information. This source includes information about what you are like at school, on the job, in the courts. Second, the person can be given a questionnaire on which he can rate himself, or herself, on traits. Third, he or she can be objectively tested in situations especially set up to measure traits.

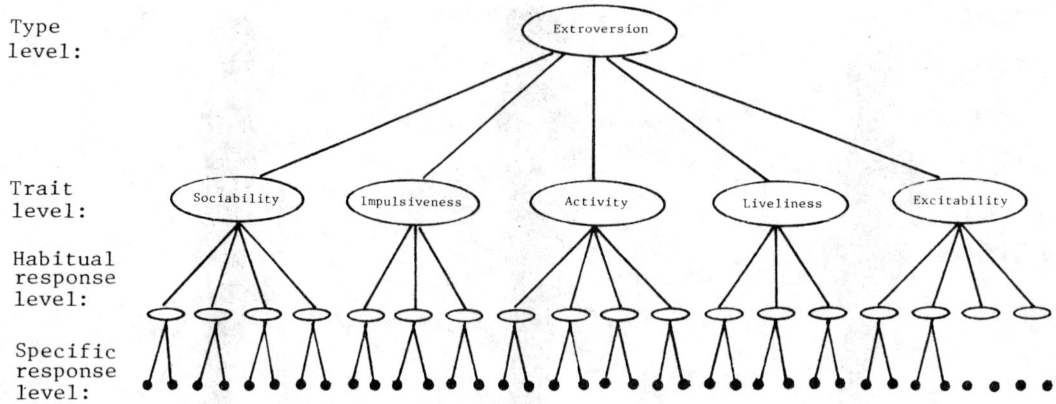

Figure 8.7 Hierarchical Organization of Personality

The second feature of Cattell's approach is that he does not force an oversimplification of the complexity of personality into just a few types—as does Eysenck. Recall that Sheldon's few body types also seemed a little too restrictive. Cattell has developed a system of surface traits and source traits. Surface traits are like the symptoms of a cold that appear only on the surface. Source traits are more like the underlying cause of the cold—the virus and the predisposing conditions of the body.

In the same way that a cold is the result of both constitutional factors of a person's body and environmental factors (the virus), the underlying source traits are thought to be either constitutional or environmental (learned) in origin. Cattell would agree with Hans Eysenck that about 65 percent of your personality traits have a genetic origin.

There is little doubt that investigators like Hans Eysenck and Raymond Cattell have conducted fine *nomological* work toward the discovery of the structural "bricks" of personality—traits. But, we must ask, "Is human personality, possibly the most complex phenomenon in the universe, fully understandable from a scientific point of view?" And, a related question, "Is each person to some degree totally unique?"

Gordon W. Allport devised the 17,953 descriptive terms for personality in the first place. He felt that each person must be the focus of trait theory studies. This *idiographic* approach allows, at least in theory, the complete study of personality. Rather than only comparing people with others, we must compare them with themselves on different factors. This can be done only by intensive study of the individual.

Summary

Can all of the individual be captured by scientific forms of analysis? What about Gandhi's traits? Was he like everyone else to varying degrees? Or was there something totally unique about him and out of the reach of science?

We have only briefly presented the ideas behind theories related to the five broad traditional views of personality. While the philosophical question about whether or not each of us really has an enduring and consistent pattern of responding to the world is still open, the evidence suggests that we do. We do seem to have unique personalities, and each of the five approaches, including trait theory, helps in our understanding.

At the same time we must keep in mind the systems concept of autopoiesis. This model recognizes the interrelatedness of all that is involved in theorizing about personality—consistent patterns of response, the self, other internal processes, external influences, growth, uniqueness, and self-production over time.

Empirical and Methodological Aspects of Personality

Personality Test Scales and Outcomes

The empirical aspects of personality must all ultimately be based upon behavior. Recall Cattell's three sources of information concerning personality: observation by others in life situations, your own behavior on questionnaires, and in objective test situations. An easy way to think about this is to represent all personality and personalities as comprising a universe of behaviors and behavior patterns. These will include all of those 17,953 outward indications of personality that we have agreed apply. In reality this approach would obviously get out of hand. For the sake of simplicity and clarity, and to illustrate the point, let's use Anne Anastasi's description of what should be included in this universe (1982). She includes the measurement of ". . . emotional states, interpersonal relations, motivation, interests, and attitudes." So, within this universe of behaviors we could measure these overlapping subparts.

When personality tests are devised, samples are taken from our conception of the universe of behaviors for personality. This is really no different in theory from taking a sample of blood in order to determine its state, condition, or type. Just as blood tests do, some personality tests sample the entire universe of possible behaviors, others only a well defined subpart. How large a sample do you need to get to know a personality? If you are skillful at sampling the behavior related to personality, you can get to know a lot about personality very quickly.

In the theory section we discussed many theoretical ideas that help us understand personality. Now, in the empirical section we could find measurable factors in tests that would help us assess them. There are tests of ego, superego, and even id factors. There are tests of self-concept, ideal self, and personal constructs. And there are tests that measure all of the traits of the theorists. In most actual personality tests, there is a great overlap in the representation of theoretical ideas.

Though there are over 500 personality tests available, we will limit our description to a few important ones—those most widely used and studied. We will start with examples of personality tests that get at unconscious determinants of personality.

Projective Tests

Projective tests attempt to measure the projected motivations, emotional states, interpersonal relations, interests, and attitudes in a person's personality. You are familiar with the idea of *projection* from our discussion of Freud's ego defense mechanisms. In addition to this theoretical basis as an unconscious process, projective tests are thought to measure unconscious processes because the person taking the test is not aware of the relationship between the test materials and the aspects of personality being measured. None of this proves that unconscious processes are actually being tapped by projective tests (see Figure 8.8).

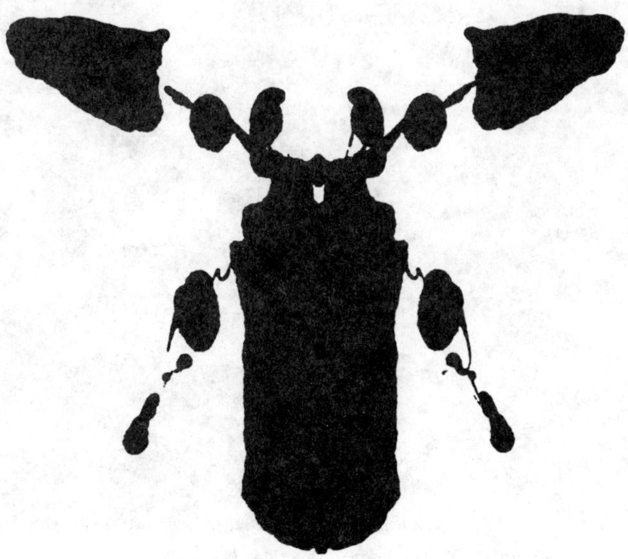

Figure 8.8 Rorschach Inkblot Test

Leonardo da Vinci noticed something interesting about the paint on his walls.

> I cannot forbear to mention a new device which, although it may seem trivial and almost ludicrous, is nevertheless extremely useful in arousing the mind to various inventions. And this is, when you look at a wall spotted with stains, or with a mixture of stones, and you have to devise some scene, you may discover a resemblance to various landscapes, beautified with mountains, rivers, rocks, trees, plains, wide valleys and hills in varied arrangements; or again, you may see battles and figures in endless action; or strange faces and costumes, and an endless variety of objects . . . and these appear on such walls confusedly, like the sound of bells in whose jangle you may find any name or word you choose to imagine.

Although he did not use the term, da Vinci's new device, while we can never specifically determine that it was so, involved projection. The process might even have been used by cave dwellers. About 15,000 B.C., they drew accurate and skillful images of bison, antelope and other animals on their cave walls and perhaps used the projections and recessions of the walls to provide contours for their art.

The Rorschach. The idea behind the *Rorschach Inkblot Test* is very simple. Inkblots, like the walls of da Vinci, provide convenient sources of ambiguous stimulus patterns. The person taking the test simply projects aspects of his personality into the ambiguous blots. An advantage of using standardized inkblots is that people can be compared with one another, and with themselves on different occasions. In Figure 8.8, what do you see? Compare your interpretation of the blot with someone else's. The projecting that you are doing is really what happens whenever "personality" is at work in processing information. Whenever ambiguous stimuli are present, the individual's unique pattern of response can be revealed.

The Thematic Apperception Test. Examine the picture in Figure 8.9. Do you see two people

Figure 8.9 A Picture Similar to Those of the Thematic Apperception Test
What has been happening to this person? What is she feeling? How will things come out for her?

having a conversation? If you are not absolutely sure, then you are confronted with another type of ambiguous situation. In this item from Henry Murray's (1943) *Thematic Apperception Test (TAT)*, what do you think is occurring? Write a paragraph about this picture, and then compare it with a paragraph written by someone else. The *TAT* was originally developed to get at dominant themes in a person's personality. It was a part of the psychoanalytic assessment in Murray's (1938) study of 50 young men's lives. Later Robert White (1952, 1975) studied three *Lives in Progress* using the *TAT* and other methods. This approach to personality was termed personology by Murray.

The *Rorschach Inkblot Test* can be scored in many ways. The individually scored test is quite complicated and takes a good deal of training. One standardized form, which nicely illustrates many of the commonly scored attributes, has been developed by Joics Stone (1958). These attributes, which are measured by Stone's test, the *Structured-Objective Rorschach Test (SORT)* are easily scored. Different aspects of the blots have standard implications for the scoring of attributes.

The *TAT* measures personality much more in relation to social responses. Each of twenty cards like the one shown contains at least one person with whom the person taking the test can identify. In scoring, it is determined who the person identifies with, what human needs are projected, and what environmental conditions are projected. How many human needs are expressed in personality? A list of the needs scored on the *TAT* card appears in Table 8.1 (Murray, 1938). If you have written a paragraph on this *TAT* card, you might see some of these needs revealed in your response.

You might be a little uneasy as to whether or not these types of tests constitute reliable and valid measures of personality. Compared to questionnaire-type tests of personality, projective tests do not fare as well on validity. However, projective tests are presently extremely popular among clinicians. According to Bernard Lubin and his coworkers (1984), the Rorschach is the fourth and the *TAT* the sixth in current use of all tests. If the validity of these tests is suspect, why is it so widely used? It is likely that these projective tests give impressions to clinicians that might not fit scientific validating procedures well, but still offer helpful insights. The clinician, besides being scientifically knowledgeable, takes impressions, synthesizes, and thinks about the person as a whole person. This describing of total personality is an important aspect of the idea behind projective tests.

Table 8.1 Psychogenic Needs

1. Abasement: to surrender, to comply and accept punishment.
2. Achievement: to overcome obstacles.
3. Affiliation: to form friendships and associations.
4. Aggression: to assault or injure; to belittle a person.
5. Autonomy: to resist influence; to strive for independence.
6. Counteraction: proudly to overcome defeat by restriving.
7. Deference: to admire and willingly follow a leader.
8. Defendance: to defend oneself against blame or belittlement.
9. Dominance: to influence or control others.
10. Exhibition: to attract attention to one's person.
11. Harm avoidance: to avoid pain, physical injury, illness, death.
12. Infavoidance: to avoid failure, shame, humiliation, ridicule.
13. Nurturance: to nourish, aid or protect a helpless other.
14. Order: to arrange, organize, put away objects; to be tidy.
15. Play: to relax; amuse oneself; seek diversion and entertainment.
16. Rejection: to snub, ignore or exclude another.
17. Sentience: to seek and enjoy sensuous impressions.
18. Sex: to form and further an erotic relationship; to have sex.
19. Succorance: to seek aid, protection or sympathy.
20. Understanding: to analyze experience; to synthesize ideas.

Self-Report Tests

In self-report tests, the test-taker has the opportunity to report on her own personality by responding to statements about herself. In the projective tests we have little control over what we might be saying about ourselves; in self-report tests we have a good deal of control. This, of course, opens the opportunity for us to misrepresent what our personality is like on these tests. However, good self-report tests have questions built into them that can help detect how honestly we are responding.

The MMPI. The most widely used and studied personality test of any kind is the *Minnesota Multiphasic Personality Inventory MMPI* (Hathaway & McKinley 1942–67). According to Lubin (1984) it has become increasingly popular over the last four decades and has been the source of many studies that are forever extending its use to more groups of people and to other nations.

The *MMPI* consists of 566 true/false items that provide a pretty good sample or picture of what a person is like. (The Rorschach or *TAT* procedures can also involve hundreds of questions depending upon the responsiveness of the person taking the test.)

You may be surprised to find that the dimensions of personality measured by the *MMPI* are those of what we would usually call abnormal tendencies in people. This information would then be used in clinical practice and research. However, the *MMPI* has been found extremely useful when applied to normal people as well. New scales have been derived from new sub-groupings that measure such things as ego-strength, dependency, dominance, prejudice, and social status. Drake and Oetting (1959) have prepared a handbook for the use of the *MMPI* in counseling normal young adults.

After a person completes the *MMPI,* a personality profile like the one appearing in Figure 8.10 is prepared. The profile shows that a person, normal or abnormal, is high on some dimensions and low on others. This is a typical outcome. In order for a person to be considered abnormal, he must usually score above 70 or below 30 on the profile. It is absolutely essential for us to understand abnormal here only means abnormal in comparison to other people's scores. Outside of the norming sample of other people, there can be no objective sense of either normal or abnormal. This is also true of all psychological tests, including those of intelligence, creativity, etc. The selection of the scores 70 and 30 for being abnormal is also somewhat arbitrary. These scores would put you in the top 2½ percent or the bottom 2½ percent of the norming sample.

But, what does the profile tell us? There are many sources that can help the doctor, psychologist, or counselor interpret the profile. For example, Starke R. Hathaway (one of the men who created the *MMPI*) and Paul E. Meehl have prepared *An Atlas for the Clinical Use of the MMPI* (1951). It contains over 900 short case histories along with their profiles of scores. This book is organized so that you can locate cases with profiles that are shaped like the one you wish to interpret. A computer printout of this same sort of information is also available.

Does the *MMPI* really reveal the abnormal personality? Starke R. Hathaway and Dr. Elio Monachesi (1953) have plotted the scores for delinquent versus nondelinquent adolescents (9th graders). What they found is presented In Figure 8.11. Notice the scale name where the delinquents go above 70 (abnormal). Also, note the scales where the delinquents were normal. How might the normal scale information be helpful to counselors?

Personality at the Methodological Level

Methods used in the study of personality consists of clinical, experimental, and correlational approaches. Freud and Rogers have been strongly clinical in their methods, and social learning theorists strongly experimental. A third approach, like that of Eysenck and Cattell, relies neither on clinical or experimental techniques, but rather on correlational methods.

Tests of personality themselves are methods of understanding and studying personality. We have used the term "test outcomes" to help you put the emphasis there rather than upon the test itself. Tests, as methods, can be looked upon as extensions of both the clinical and research methods. For example, the *MMPI* is really an objective version of what a clinician might sample in a very lengthy interview method. But, at the same time, items of a test can also be used as variables in correlational research studies.

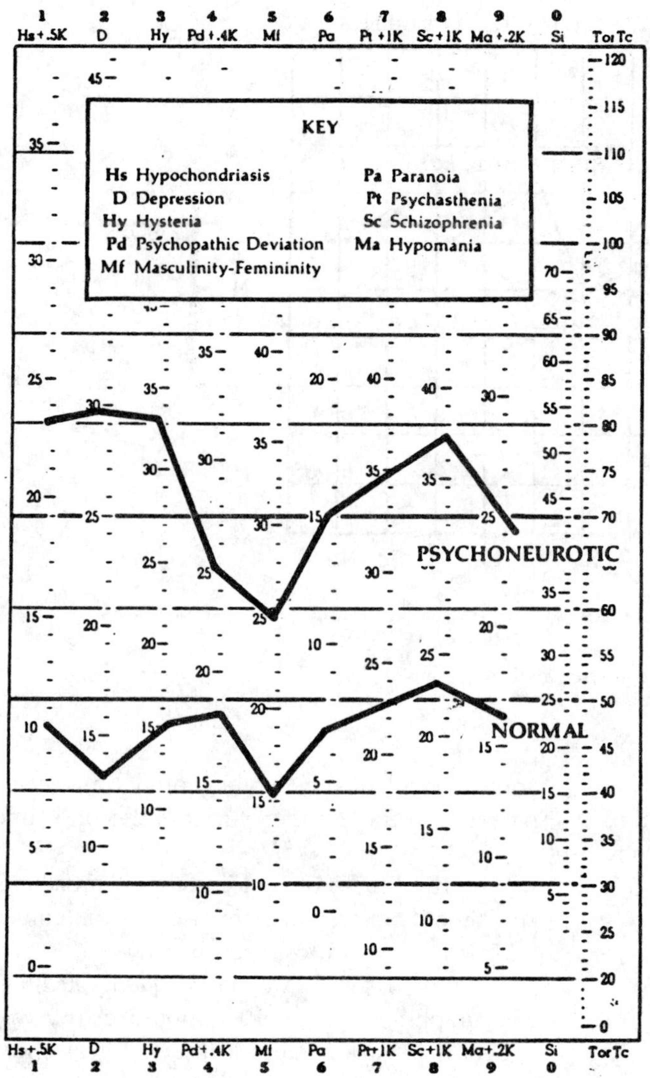

Figure 8.10 *MMPI* Profiles

Methods of testing personality do not have to consist of only paper and pencil tests or interviews. Personality can be measured through direct behavioral assessment. Recall that Raymond Cattell felt that objective test information, along with life and questionnaire information was important in the search for the factors of personality. In these objective test methods, the person is observed in a situation set up to elicit specific aspects of his personality. Sometimes in James Bond movies, we will see spy agents being put through life-like ambiguous test situations. In this way personality can be directly observed and assessed. Agents can then be given assignments based upon these "tests of personality." This method can also be used to help agents learn to take the ambiguity out of threatening situations that might arise and leads to a more predictable performance.

Methods of Establishing Reliability and Validity

None of the methods of personality assessment would be of any value if we did not have reasonable methods for determining their *reliability* and their *validity*, which are critical to tests and to all methodologies. In this section we will illustrate simple reliability and validity methods that apply to tests. Reliability simply refers to

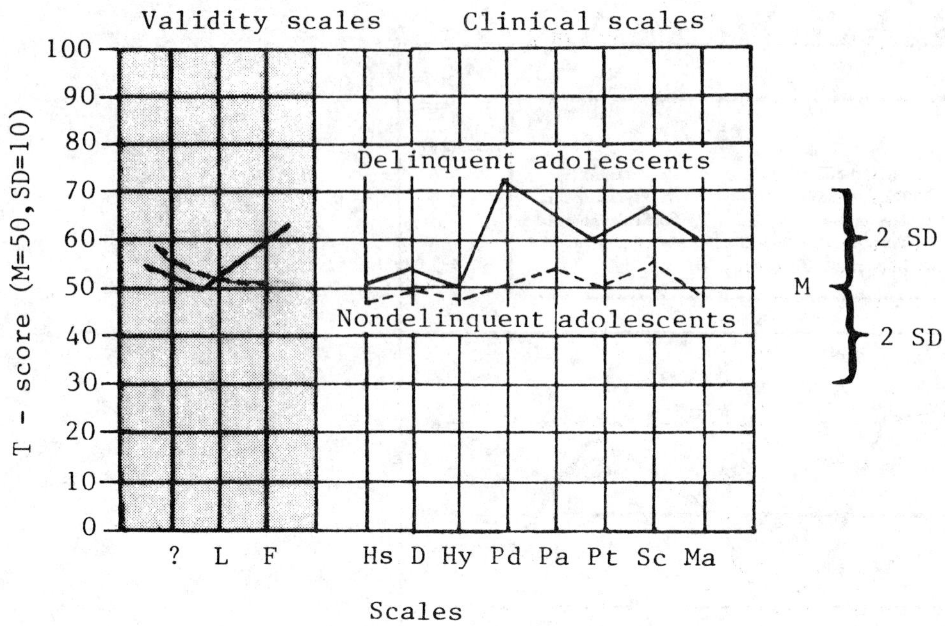

Figure 8.11 Plotting the Profile of Scores from the *MMPI*

how likely you are to get a similar score if you take the test on different occasions. Test validity simply refers to whether or not the test actually measures what it is expected to measure. Think about these four questions:

1. Can a test be both reliable and valid?
2. Can a test be neither reliable nor valid?
3. Can a test be reliable but not valid?
4. Can a test be valid but not reliable?

If you can answer all four of the questions correctly, you understand the ideas of reliability and validity perfectly. The answers to the first three questions would be yes. The answer to the last one is no. If we were trying to measure your height, and got a different result each time we tried (no reliability), then whatever method I was using would not be a valid measure of height.

Degrees of Reliability and Validity. Degrees of reliability and validity can be determined very simply. We can illustrate these graphically. In reliability, we can simply examine the repeated outcomes of several people (see Figure 8.12). The first graph shows high reliability, the second moderate, and the third no reliability at all. If you wished to turn to the section on correlation in the statistical appendix, you could calculate reliability correlations (coefficients) on these sets of first time/second time scores.

In the study of validity the approach is similar, only instead of comparing test outcomes with themselves, test performance must be compared to some *external validating measure*. The graphs in Figure 8.13 should clarify this situation for you. Suppose the test scale here is social status from the *MMPI*. The judgments of the psychologists or instructors, counselors, etc., serve as the external sources of validation for the test. In the first case, the test would agree well with the psychologist(s) (high validity), the second moderately, and the third would indicate the test was totally invalid. Again, you could use the correlational procedure to find a validity correlation (coefficient) if you wished.

The importances of the reliability and validity questions cannot be overestimated. All tests are required to meet certain standards of reliability and validity just as good laboratory research must meet high standards of reliability of results, and validity as to what is being investigated. The *Mental Measurements Yearbooks* (1985) edited by James V. Mitchell, Jr., addresses the continuing analysis of reliability and validity of tests.

scores

	1st tested X	2nd tested Y	1st tested X	2nd tested Y	1st tested X	2nd tested Y
Bob	10	10	10	10	10	10
Mary	20	20	20	30	20	20
Alice	30	30	30	20	30	10

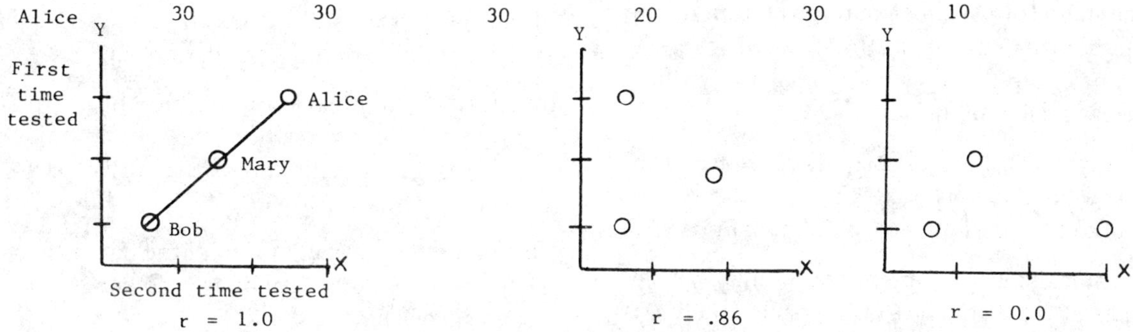

Figure 8.12 Reliability

scores

	test result	psychologists judgement	test	psychologist	test	psychologist
Bob	10	10	10	10	10	10
Mary	20	20	20	30	20	20
Alice	30	30	30	20	30	10

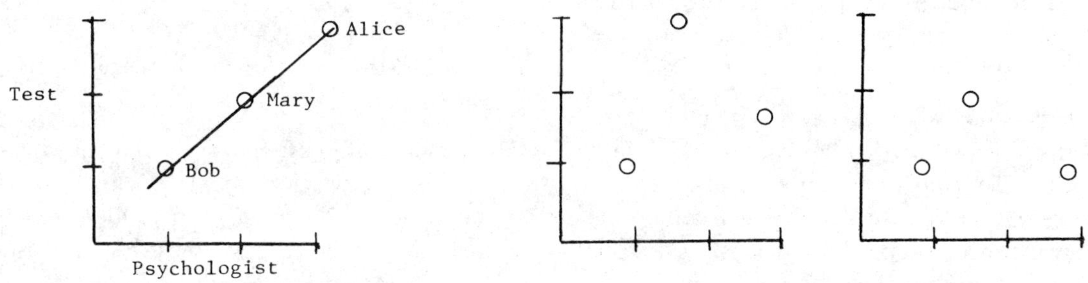

Figure 8.13 Validity

Bringing It All Together

The whole point of theories, tests, and research on personality is to help us understand the more or less consistent patterns of behavior we see in people. Each of the approaches and methods we have examined is helpful in understanding personality. You will have to decide the relative importance of each contribution.

Do we understand Gandhi any better, having studied some of the factors that are involved in personality? I think we do. If nothing more, we can see how events in his childhood, his own self-development, and his environments played a role.

Now, you can begin to think about your own psychohistory in these same terms. One of the things that impresses us about Gandhi is that as he grew, he continued to search for constant improvement. He never felt he had arrived. Perhaps, while we should take satisfaction in our accomplishments, we should always consider our potential for improvement. I think this is the message that Gandhi gave to the people of India—and to us.

Glossary

anal stage (of psychosexual development): In psychoanalytic theory, the structuring of personality on the basis of early sexual gratifications related to the anus.

archetypes: in Jung's theory, the collective primitive unconscious images that are fundamental to the development of the human psyche.

autopoiesis: The maintenance of unity, wholeness, and uniqueness in a system, such as a cell, an organ, or a person, even though its constituent parts and/or environments may change.

collective unconscious: In Jung's theory, a part of the unconscious that is inherited and shared by all members of a species.

compulsive behavior: Behavior that is repeated even though it is inappropriate to the situation at hand.

death instincts: In psychoanalytic theory, all instincts that lead the organism away from pleasure and full expression and toward denial, rejection, constriction and death (see also id).

ego: In psychoanalytic theory, a system of forces within the psyche that has conscious contact with and memory of reality. Its task is self-preservation. It determines when, where, if, how instincts will be allowed satisfaction (see also id). The ego is a portion of the self.

ego defense mechanism: In psychoanalytic theory, the ego has many capacities (mechanisms) by which it can reduce felt anxiety arising from id and reality relationships. It does this by distorting memories, perceptions, and feelings.

erogenous zones: Any of the body openings where the internal world of the body meets the external environment giving rise to sexual feelings or behavior.

external validating measure: In the study of test validity, an external criterion of whatever is being measured that is compared to the new test outcomes.

id: In psychoanalytic theory, the instinctual reservoir of primitive drives. These drives represent forces that are thought to be involved in the structuring of the psyche.

idiographic: Having to do with characterizing the individual event, person, or group.

inferiority complexes: In Adler's theory, repressed (unconscious) feelings of ineptitude stemming from childhood that drive us to become better.

libidinal energy: The portion of the life instinct drives related to sexual or erotic feelings, fantasies, or behavior.

life instincts: In psychoanalytic theory, all instincts that drive the organism toward the preservation of life, for example, sex and hunger (see also id).

Mahatma: Literally means *great soul.* A person of great wisdom and selflessness.

Minnesota Multiphasic Personality Inventory (MMPI): A series of questions that reveals normality or abnormality on a variety of aspects of personality.

MMPI: (see *Minnesota Multiphasic Personality Inventory*).

nomological: Having to do with laws or their establishment.

Oedipus complexes: In psychoanalytic theory, residual unconscious sexual feelings toward the same-sexed parent, and residual unconscious aggressive feelings toward the opposite-sexed parent.

oral stage (of psychosexual development): In psychoanalytic theory, the structuring of personality on the basis of early sexual gratifications related to the mouth.

personal construct theory: Kelly's view of how the personality develops and is maintained much in the way scientists construct theories about how the world works and then constantly test their accuracies.

personality: The characteristics of a person that account for the consistent patterns of response to various situations.

personality traits: Enduring characteristics, either inherited or acquired, that consistently appear in a person's behavior.

personology: An approach to the study of personality development where the major themes in the person's unique life experience are determined.

phallic stage (of psychosexual development): In psychoanalytic theory, the structuring of personality of the basis of early sexual gratifications related to the male and female genitals.

phenomenal field: The experienced world of the individual that may or may not coincide with objective reality.

pleasure principle: In psychoanalytic theory, the principle that all organisms are driven to avoid pain and to seek pleasure. These drives arise from the id or instincts.

projection: The process of perceiving objective ambiguous stimuli in terms of unconscious needs, fears, expectations, or meanings.

psychoanalytic theory: Sigmund Freud's view that interacting psychological forces dating from early childhood structure the psyche, especially the personality.

psychodynamics: In psychoanalytic theory, the psychological forces such as the id, ego, and superego that structure the personality.

psychohistorian: A psychologist who studies the history of a person (usually a prominent person) to help determine how his/her personality formed and what led to his/her prominence.

psychohistory: The study of a person's history that accounts for the development of her unique personality. While most psychohistories gather information from a psychoanalytic viewpoint, other views of personality are often included in the analysis.

psychosexual stages of development: In psychoanalytic theory, the structuring of the psyche, especially the personality, on the basis of early sexual gratifications.

reality principle: In psychoanalytic theory, the tendency for an organism to be aware of the demands of the environment, and to behave in such a way that instinctual drives can ultimately be satisfied in the face of these demands. It is an ego function that modifies the pleasure principle.

reliability: The degree to which test outcomes are the same for a person upon repeated measurement.

Rorschach Inkblot Test: A series of ten ambiguous inkblots that reveals, through projection, unconscious needs, fears, and expectations. Devised by Hermann Rorschach.

self-actualization: The making of the potential self, actual. Becoming or being all that the self can become.

self-efficacy: The abilities or effectiveness of a person in different situations, including self-knowledge.

style of life: In Adler's theory, a style inclusive of one's behavior for dealing with one's inadequacies and for getting ahead in life.

superego: In psychoanalytic theory, a system of forces within the psyche consisting of parental and societal standards as they are seen by the ego.

superiority complexes: In Adler's theory, an unconscious defensive reaction to the inferiority complexes.

synchronicity: Postulated by C.G. Jung, the more or less simultaneous occurrence of meaningfully related events. This is a noncausal explanation of mind/body, daily experience, and cultural development parallelisms.

TAT: (see *Thematic Apperception Test*).

Thematic Apperception Test (TAT): A series of twenty ambiguous pictures that reveals, through projection, unconscious and dominant drives and emotions of the person.

unconscious: In psychoanalytic theory, the portion of the psyche containing impressions, idea, memories, etc., either not easily brought to conscious awareness, or not capable of being brought to conscious awareness, yet influences behavior.

validity: The degree to which a test actually measures what it is intended to measure.

Personality: Doing Psychology on Your Own

Lois McDermott

Basic Concept #8—Who Am I?

Being Uniquely You. I love Halloween parties, or any parties that allow me to alter my persona. I feel especially successful when close friends fail to recognize me when I'm in disguise—one year I managed to fool my own parents. Do clothes make the man (or in this case the woman)? Surely not, but my experiences of many a Halloween make me wonder. What is it then that makes you, you, and me, me? If we traded brains, or parents, or genes, or cognitive styles, or life history, would you be me and me you? Would we need to swap all of that? or just some? or much more? Now that I think of it—exactly what makes you, you and not me or anyone else? How could we describe those qualities? Should the qualities be evident no matter what situation we are in? Would we be recognizable no matter what role we played? I also love repertoire theater, where the same collection of actors plays different roles in a series of plays. It is so intriguing to see who is who in a particular role. Of course, there is typecasting, but generally a really good actor can play a whole range of parts. Does a person with such a gift, lose track of his/her unique self? The recent books, *I Am Not Spock* and *I Am Spock*, written by Leonard Nimoy, make one wonder.

The earliest theories of personality were based on the idea that an imbalance of humors (fluids) in the body produced different personality styles—sanguine, choleric, etc. In this century we have data from very young infants and MZ twins which make the case that basic temperament is evident very early in life and may well be innate. But is this the whole story? A truly interesting finding is how dissimilar personalities can be within the same family. Shouldn't all that genetic inheritance and similarity of rearing produce near clones in a family? Clearly the development of personality is multifaceted. So enter our "elephant"—our logo of diversity of causality. All the theoretical approaches introduced in the first unit (and others besides) have offered explanations for the diversity of personality within and between families and cultures.

Unit Focus. This unit begins recapping all that we have learned this quarter about the various theoretical approaches to understanding the human psyche. In actuality there are multiple psychodynamic, humanist, biological, sociocultural, behavioral, and cognitive theories about human personality. In the interest of simplicity and time we will lump similar theories together. (A full course in theories of personality which reviews more variants of these six theories and others beside, might be a good next course if you wish to continue your study of psychology.)

The *psychodynamic* theories of personality are the oldest, the most highly developed, the most explanatory and currently, the least respected in mainstream psychology. The *biologists, behaviorists* and *cognitivists* have effectively sidelined the psychodynamic theorists out of the discipline. There are currently no psychodynamic researchers or theorists in the department of psychology at the UW. It is a hotbed of cognitive-behaviorists. However, psychodynamic theory seems to have a tenacity all its own, unlike humanistic theory, which essentially died with Carl Rogers.

Psychodynamic theory (in the form of object relations theory) has out-lived Freud by a long shot and is proving useful in the understanding of the development of different character styles and the treatment of personality disorders.

Study Objectives

1. Compare and contrast the six theories of personality and give examples of each.
2. Learn the meaning of the key terms of psychodynamic theory—e.g., structure of consciousness, *id, ego,* and *superego* and various *defense mechanisms.*
3. Distinguish the psychosexual and psychosocial theories of personality development.
4. Know the characteristics of the actualized self.
5. Learn how the cognitive behaviorists explain the emergence of personality.
6. Learn the sociocultural theory of personality development and the involvement of social role and the impact of social role strain.
7. Compare and contrast the common assessment tools used to assess personality

Key Terms

anal stage (of psychosexual development)
archetypes
autopoiesis
collective unconscious
compulsive behavior
death instincts
ego
ego defense mechanisms
erogenous zones
external validating measure
id
idiographic
inferiority complexes
libidinal energy
life instincts
Mahatma
Minnesota Multiphasic Personality Inventory (MMPI)
MMPI
nomological
Oedipus complexes
oral stage (of psychosexual development)
personal construct theory
personality
personality traits
personology
phallic stage (of psychosexual development)
phenomenal field
pleasure principle
projection
psychoanalytic theory
psychodynamics
psychohistorian
psychohistory
psychosexual stages of development
reality principle
reliability
Rorschach Inkblot Test
self-actualization
self-efficacy
style of life
superego
superiority complexes
synchronicity
TAT
Thematic Apperception Test (TAT)
unconscious
validity

Problem Set #8: Personality

A. *Identify the concept*

1. Part of personality which is concerned with what one "should" do
2. Set of mental processes which search for realistic ways of gratifying drives and impulse
3. Personality style associated with continuing to work at difficult tasks
4. Psychodynamic theorist who emphasized the social rather than sexual dynamics at each stage of development
5. Belief that chance or luck, rather than individual effort, plays a role in determining a person's fate
6. Personality stage in which a person develops basic sense of trust
7. Thoughts which are immediately available to awareness
8. Personality style characterized by being easily overwhelmed and drained by stimulation—especially from other people
9. Personality stage in which a person focuses on productivity at home and at work
10. Being valued in spite of personal failings
11. Process of fulfilling our fullest potential as human beings
12. Mechanism used by our ego to protect us from the anxiety of unconscious conflicts
13. Readiness to perceive ourselves favorably
14. Passive resignation stemming from repeated uncontrollable traumatic events
15. A personality feature which provides a global, stable interpretation of events
16. Personality stage in which children grapple with sense of bodily control
17. Process by which our world view influences the experience we have which in turn influences our world view
18. Personality component present at birth
19. One's own unacceptable impulses are attributed to other people
20. One's own unacceptable impulses are expressed as their opposite
21. One's own unacceptable impulses are directed at safer substitute targets

22. One's own unacceptable impulses are expressed in social appropriate ways
23. One's own unacceptable impulses are expressed through behavior associated with an earlier stage of life
24. An example of an assessment technique arising from the behavioral perspective
25. An example of an assessment technique arising from the psychodynamic perspective
26. An example of an assessment technique arising from the trait (biological) perspective
27. The most important feature of the growth promoting environment of humanist psychology
28. Basic, psychological, and growth needs
29. Social rules and laws which shape our personalities

B. *Indicate which defense mechanism is operating in each vignette.*

a. repression—amnesia for the forbidden emotion, impulse
b. regression—retreat to earlier stage
c. reaction formation—do/feel/express opposite
d. rationalization—attempt to justify the forbidden, feared
f. displacement—divert forbidden, feared emotion elsewhere
g. sublimation—socially acceptable expression of forbidden
h. projection—see the forbidden emotion/behavior in others

1. Even a top baseball player will sometimes strike out on an easy pitch. When this happens, his next action may be to throw his bat or kick the water cooler with all his might.
2. Soldiers exposed to traumatic experiences in concentration camps during wartime sometimes had amnesia and were unable to recall any part of their ordeal.
3. The mother of an unwanted child may feel guilty about not welcoming her child. As a result, she may try to prove her love by becoming overindulgent and overprotective of the child.
4. Mrs. Brown often accuses other women of talking too much and spreading rumors. It is obvious to those who know Mrs. Brown that she is revealing her own inclination in that area.
5. Paul, an aggressive child, had problems in elementary school, as he would frequently fight with other children. Paul found when he entered high school he could channel this hostility into sports such as football and soccer.
6. The habitual drinker insists he really doesn't care much for the effects of alcohol but feels he must drink with his friends "just to be sociable."
7. Parents might be reassured to know that children who pull wings off of flies and jab pins in the dog may eventually find their niche in the areas of dentistry or surgery.
8. Mike is always trying to impress his pals with how strong and independent he has become. However, when Mike faces social or emotional problems, he still wants his dad to figure out the solution.
9. A student failed to show up for her dreaded final in psychology (for which she had not studied). She claimed she had "just totally spaced out about it." This seemed unusual since she had it marked on her calendar for weeks.
10. A male will sometimes react against his own unconscious sexual attraction for males by becoming very hostile to gay males.
11. The majority group of a culture may blame all the ills of society on a small minority group. This process is called scapegoating in social psychology and is factor in hate crimes. Freud called this phenomena _______.
12. Joan Rily has suffered heavy financial losses while playing the stock market. Upon trading her big luxury car for a used small car Joan informed her associates that she bought the cheaper car to do her part in the battle against air pollution.

13. Marianne lost her executive position in a large corporation. Rather than seek a new job, she finds comfort and escape through drinking alcohol and overeating.

C. *Psychological Disorders: Causal Explanations*

Tim feels "dead inside." He feels he does not deserve to live. He feels that "nobody would want him." These symptoms are consistent with depression. Which theory would place special emphasis on the following details of Tim's background as an "explanation" for Tim's symptoms?

1. Tim's father committed suicide when Tim was age 3 (early loss of love object)
2. Tim's grandfather was hospitalized for depression (family history of depression)
3. Tim feels somehow responsible for his father's death (self-defeating beliefs and self-attributions of blame)
4. Tim only received love and attention when he was feeling sad (reinforcement history)
5. Tim, coming from a single parent family, was financially deprived and had to tolerate all sorts of overt and covert harassment and stigmatization as a child at school from both teachers and peers (product of disturbed social system)
6. Tim has been stuck in dead-end jobs since high school. He is frustrated that he was not able to complete his education and become an oceanographer—a dream he has had since his early teens (failure to self-actualize)

D. *List two key assumptions for each of the following theories; give an example of an assessment technique associated with this theory*

1. trait /biological
2. psychodynamic
3. social-cognitive, cognitive-behavioral

See Appendix C for answers to problem set.

9

Abnormal Behavior—Mental Disorders

A Philosophy of Abnormal Behavior

What is abnormal must to a great degree always be considered to be a *relative judgment* as was illustrated in the discussion of personality test outcomes (Chapter 8). The personal profile on the *MMPI* (Chapter 8) showed that relative to other people, the person varied a great deal. Sometimes the person was "very normal" (in the middle of the norming sample), and sometimes almost two standard deviations away—abnormal. Without such norming reference points, it would be impossible to even think about what's normal and abnormal.

The Meaning of Abnormal

The criteria for what is normal and what is not are to some extent a little arbitrary; however, psychologists and psychiatrists agree that the abnormal *mental disorders* involve difficulty of functioning in society as we define it. (For our purposes here, this does not include people who are simply at odds with society.) The American Psychiatric Association (APA) has developed and refined a classification system for what it considers to be mental disorders that are abnormal. This classification system is incorporated in what the APA calls its *Diagnostic and Statistical Manual of Mental Disorders,* 4th edition (*DSM-IV*). Notice in the following definition of mental disorder (the philosophical heart of the classification system) that the ideas of distress and disability are central to what is thought to be abnormal:

> . . . each of the mental disorders is conceptualized as a clinically significant or psychological syndrome or pattern that occurs in an individual and that is typically associated with either a painful symptom (distress) or impairment in one or more important areas of functioning (disability). In addition there is an inference that there is a behavioral, psychological, or biological dysfunction, and that the disturbance is not only in the relationship between the individual and society. (When the disturbance is limited to a conflict between an individual and society, this may represent social deviance which may or may not be commendable, but is not by itself a mental disorder.)

The last sentence of this definition of mental disorder needs some clarification. There are three prime areas the APA wishes to exclude from its list of mental disorders. First, homosexuality is excluded by the three sentences. In and of themselves homosexuality and bisexuality are not considered mental disorders. Second, criminal law-breaking behavior and, finally, political dissidents are excluded. This third situation may not seem critically important, but peaceful protests against nuclear bombs, abortion, etc., could be extremely critical. The Soviet Union, for example, has developed criteria in its psychiatric community for classifying people in such a way that virtually any dissident can be locked up in a mental institution. The APA is at odds with Soviet psychiatry over this issue.

So, while judgment about what is normal and what is abnormal is necessarily relative, it is essentially a means of attempting to help people who are hurting (distressed) or are not functioning well (disabled). This definition of mental disorder leads to a philosophy and to classification procedures in which each person must be studied as a case of interacting systems of symptoms and life conditions. As DSM-IV experts Webb, DiClemente, Johnstone, Sanders, and Perley (1981) have pointed out concerning the philosophy of the definition, "It classifies disorders, not individuals."

The Application of Theory to Mental Disorders

In previous chapters, we have had the job of explaining how a normal system (for example, the nervous system—Chapter 2) or a normal person (Chapters 6, 8), operates. These are theories of normal functioning. Now we must attempt to extend these theories to include explanations of abnormal functioning. You may have recognized in the DSM-IV definition of mental disorder that, ". . . there is an inference that there is a behavioral, psychological, or biological dysfunction." The writers are suggesting that these three traditional views are the explanatory bases of mental disorders. These are the fundamental explanatory sources we have been using and even though we are familiar with them, it will be helpful if we apply them in an attempt to understand them as component explanations of overall behavior. The DSM-IV suggests that all three of these views be systematically taken into account in diagnosing any mental disorder.

Savants and the Enigma of Abnormal Behavior

A fascinating mystery in the literature of psychology and psychiatry has been the phenomena of the so-called *"idiot savant"* (hereafter referred to as *retarded savant*), and the *autistic savant*. These strange, incongruous two-part terms refer to individuals who possess some very extraordinary abilities, usually far beyond the capabilities of normal people, but are overall intellectually or developmentally abnormal. Retarded savants, and autistic savants are only abnormal because either (1) their IQ was dramatically low in comparison with other people (70 or less), or (2) the person was greatly unresponsive to others and they performed phenomenal feats.

A. Lewis Hill (1974), Bernard Rimland (1984), and others have provided intriguing descriptive case reports of some of the types of special abilities or savant-like capacities that have been observed. These phenomenal reports include the following:

Phenomenal Computational Abilities. Bernard Rimland opened his paper, *The Autistic Savant* (1978), with this more or less characteristic example of phenomenal computational ability.

> "Arthur, how much is 6,427 times 4,234?" Arthur turned his head in my direction and said, slowly but without hesitation, "27,211,918." His voice was stilted but precise. His eyes never lost their blank stare, and now he returned to gazing into space, without seeing anything, a handsome, impassive eight-year-old. (p. 69)

And A. Lewis Hill, citing a report by D.C. Rife and H. Snyder provides a similar example of a retarded savant—a blind man who:

> . . . could give the square root of any number running in to four figures in an average of four seconds, and the cube root of any number running in to six figures in six seconds. When he was asked how many grains of corn there would be in any one of sixty-four boxes, with one in the first, two in the second, four in the third, eight in the fourth, and so on, he gave the answers for the fourteenth (8,192), for the eighteenth (131,072), and the twenty-fourth (8,388,628) instantaneously, and he gave the figures for the forty-eighth box (140,737,488,355,328) in six seconds. He also gave the total in all sixty-four boxes correctly in 45 seconds. (1974, p. 12)

Just thinking about this last feat staggers most of our imaginations—even with pocket calculator in hand! In both of these examples, there were nearly instantaneous solutions. Such lightning performances do not seem to fit the idea of the way we go about solving such problems. This idea of simultaneous operations will appear again in other examples to follow. We will discuss some of the implications of this later.

Lightning Calendar Calculators. Horwitz, Denning, Edwards and Winter studied a set of identical twin retarded savants, Charles and George. These twins have been extensively studied, and you will read of some of the other amazing abilities shortly. Charles and George are best known for their almost instantaneous calendar calculations: what day of the week a certain day fell upon or would fall upon in the future. Horwitz reported, "With equal facility, George can identify instantaneously the 15th of February 2002 as a Friday, or August 28th, 1591 as a Wednesday" (1965, p. 1075).

Oliver Sacks, who has also studied the twins, has more recently reported that the number of years they can deal with is truly phenomenal. "The twins say, 'Give us a date—any time in the last or next forty thousand years.' You give them a date, and, almost instantly, they tell you what day of the week it would be" (1985, p. 16). In addition, George and Charles, in strange similarity to Harriet G., (Chapter 1) can give you detailed weather accounts of any day in their experience!

It is important for you to note that George and Charles can do these lightning calculations even though they cannot manage addition, subtraction, multiplication, or division of simple single digit numbers—the product of 3×6 might be given as being 8!

Special Musical Abilities. Musical ability, in the normal person usually learned over years of arduous practice (mostly through successive approximations and social learning, Chapter 5), comes upon retarded and autistic savants rather suddenly or, at least, rather mysteriously. And the performances, like the above calculations, are often flawless.

The most amazing case story of phenomenal musical ability in either a retarded or autistic savant is that of Leslie Lemke. Leslie was born mentally retarded, without eyes, and with cerebral palsy. He seemed totally lifeless in the normal sense and without hope to even live. In spite of all of this, May Lemke adopted Leslie and gave him all the loving care she could. After 19 years Leslie still seemed hopeless; he was still a baby in every way but size. Noticing by accident that Leslie seemed to be trying to pluck a string on a package, May decided, maybe, just maybe, Leslie would finally begin to respond in some way to music. A piano was put in Leslie's room, his fingers pressed against the keys in hopes that he would get the idea—nothing! Time passed. Then *suddenly,* as writer Joseph Blank (1982) reported, something amazing happened:

> It happened in the winter of 1971. May was awakened by the sound of music. It was 3 A.M. Someone was playing Tchaikovsky's Piano Concerto No. 1. She shook Joe (her husband), "Did you leave the radio on?" she asked.
>
> "No," he said.
>
> "Then where's the music coming from?" She swung out of bed and turned on a living-room light. It dimly illuminated Leslie's room. Leslie was at the piano. May saw a smile glowing on his face.
>
> He had never before gotten out of his bed on his own. He had never seated himself at the piano. He had never voluntarily or deliberately struck the keys with his fingers. Now he was actually playing a concerto—and with deftness and confidence. (p. 84)

Leslie could not only play Tchaikovsky, but had a broad repertoire which included all types of music to which he had been exposed. He had never practiced nor played before! Leslie can also play virtually any new tune upon first hearing it and without error.

Super-Expanded Span of Attention. In his classic paper, *The Magical Number Seven, Plus or Minus Two: Some Limits on Our Capacity for Processing Information,* George Miller (1956) has noted that both immediate attention span and short-term memory (see Chapter 6) seem to be limited to about 7 items. Glance quickly at the items in Figure 9.1 then quickly away. How many objects are in the figure? You will have difficulty discriminating the number of items present if it is much over seven. And if I read a number of random numbers or words to you,

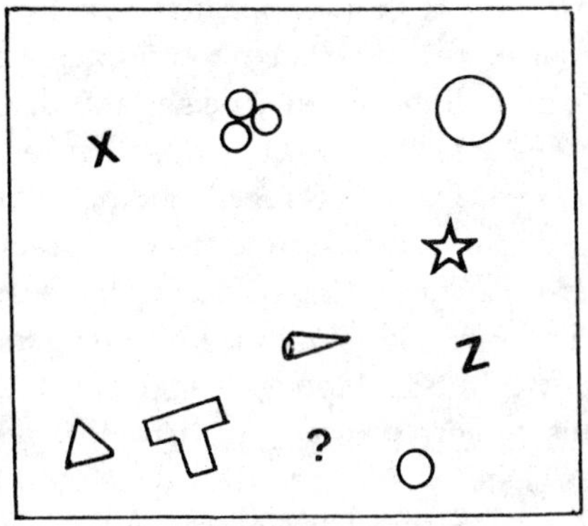

Figure 9.1 Short-term Memory

you will also have difficulty with short-term memory if the number of items is more than seven.

But even this general rule concerning span of attention gives way to some retarded and autistic savants. It seems to appear in those with high speed (almost instantaneous) calculating ability—but seems not to be the result of any specific, known, calculation. Oliver Sacks (1985) reported this ability in the twin retarded savants and in another 19th century high-speed calculator:

> A box of matches on their table fell, and discharged its contents on the floor. "111," they both cried simultaneously; . . . I counted the matches—it took me some time—and there were 111. "How could you count the matches so quickly?" I asked. "We didn't count," they said. "We *saw* the 111."
>
> Similar tales are told of Zacharias Dase, the number prodigy, who would instantly call out "183" or "79" if a pile of peas was poured out, and indicate as best he could—he also was a dullard—that he did not count the peas, but just "saw" their number, as a whole, in a flash. (p. 17)

There are two curious things here which I will return to later. First, this expanded span of attention accompanies the lightning calculation ability. Second, the dozens of items (peas, match sticks) are said not to have been counted, but rather seen as a *whole*.

Clearly, savant behavior is abnormal behavior. And we do not yet understand how such behavior comes about. William Horwitz and his colleagues concluded:

> The importance, then, of the Idiot Savant lies in our inability to explain him; he stands as a landmark of our own ignorance and the phenomenon of the Idiot Savant exists as a challenge to our capabilities. (1965, p.1078)

Of course, Horwitz's statement applies equally well to the autistic savant. •

Psychological Explanations of Savant Behavior

Psychological explanations for both retarded and autistic savant abilities include the cognitive, psychoanalytic, and humanistic ones we have referred to several times earlier. When we try to explain how a savant can execute all of his phenomenal performances, super psychological functioning is an inviting approach. Bernard Rimland (1978a) has proposed that autistic savants (and autistic people in general) have an attentional disorder. This results in super attention being focused upon whatever proves of interest or is rewarding to the savant. The first case report (phenomenal computational ability) might illustrate this idea. Rimland also feels that this attention disorder has a biological basis. Psychoanalytic explanations of savant behavior have included unconscious *compensatory dynamics*. For example, Steven B. Smith (1983) cites the many examples of how people compensated for their isolated lives by developing some very special calculational abilities. He reported a quote from psychologist Frank D. Mitchell who himself also happened to be a great mental calculator (but a normal one):

> Several of the calculators . . . were shepherd boys, an occupation which, since it requires an ability to count and affords ample leisure, is peculiarly favorable for practicing calculation; several, [Savants] again, Grandmange (born without arms or legs), Safford, Pierini, the present writer,—were sick or otherwise incapacitated for active play to a greater or less extent, and thus enjoyed an equally good opportunity to practice calculation. Fuller and Buxton, on the other hand, whether precocious or

> not, were men of such limited intelligence that they could comprehend scarcely anything, either theoretical or practical, more complex than counting; and their purely manual occupations left their minds free to carry on almost without limit their slow and laborious calculations. (pp. 98–99)

Similarly, David Viscott concluded that Harriet G. used music to compensate for abnormal relationships with others:

> If music became a wedge which separated Harriet from the other children and kept her from developing normally, it also became the only modality she was to develop which allowed her to communicate her feelings to other people. Music became a special language and it remained a language of an endless infancy. (p. 509)

The role of unconscious processes in savant capacities is suggested by the fact that the savants themselves are totally unaware of how they perform their amazing feats. The savant twins Charles and George, for example, when asked how they instantly calculated the calendar can say only they don't know, they just "see" the answer. And Alexander Aitken, a brilliant mathematics professor and great mental calculator, said this of his own calculations:

> I have noticed also at times that the mind has anticipated the will; I have had an answer before I even wished to do the calculation; I have checked it, and am always surprised that it is correct. This, I suppose (but the terminology may not be right), is the subconscious in action; I think it can be action at several levels; and I believe that each of these levels has its own velocity, different from that of our ordinary waking time, in which our processes of thought are rather tardy. (Smith, 1983, p. 27)

The unconscious certainly does seem to influence our behavior in a variety of ways. Unconscious processes in the savant may, like the high attentional focus mentioned earlier, be harnessed in special routine problem-solving strategies. Psychological processes including attention, social learning, compensation, and those of the unconscious doubtlessly play some role in all mental disorders.

Behavioral Explanations of Savant Behavior

Just as much normal behavior is learned through trial and error, reflex conditioning, and imitation, so is much abnormal behavior. Learning occurs along with any cognitive or biologically-based activity. In the cases of both retarded and autistic savants, learning appears not to be the sole determinant of the special patterns of behavior. George and Charles, the twin retarded savants, both went through periods of time when learning and social learning contributed greatly to their talents:

> The development of George's special talent was observed at age 6—it had been noted that he would spend hours poring over an almanac which contained a perpetual calendar. From what has gone before [retarded and unmanageable] it comes as a distinct surprise that George *could* or would pore over the almanac at 6 years, but the fact is George could decipher an almanac. The parents felt this talent was a compensation from God, and the father later got a silver perpetual calendar that George played with for hours and hours. He made no errors from the beginning. A parental aunt, a legal secretary, used to call to check dates of documents with him. The father praised George—calling him a smart boy. This pleased George, who frequently asked why he was different from the sisters [his normal sisters]. Charles, who was always slower in both physical and mental development, did not play with the almanac and initially showed no interest in dates. He and George had no close relationship until they were institutionalized at Letchworth Village at age 9. At that time George and Charles became inseparable. Charles became interested in telling dates but was noted to go through a period in which he made many mistakes. (p. 1076)

While the effects of biological abnormality are readily apparent by observing these savant twins, and that compensatory adjustments can be seen in the above report (for example, when their relationship changed dramatically upon institutionalization), learning also obviously played a role. George had to learn the perpetual calendar over a period of time. The other twin, Charles, came to calendar calculation more through social learning in imitation of George. Learning clearly plays some role in the development of nearly all savants. And, likewise, learning likely plays some role in the development of all mental disorders.

Biological Explanations of Savant Behavior

Biochemistry and physiology are the basis of normal functioning of the nervous system (Chapter 2), just as they are the basis, both directly and indirectly, of many mental disorders. For example, the neurotransmitter dopamine (Chapter 2) is directly implicated as a basis of schizophrenia. Both mental retardation and autism are either known, or thought, to have biological bases. The more we learn about our 100,000 which contribute to both body and behavior, the more clearly we begin to see how certain mental disorders have a biological component that starts with the *genetic code.*

Many of the savant's super abilities seem to have something in common with the functions of the right cerebral hemisphere. Musical, artistic, intuitive talents, keen spatial orientation, and instantaneous calculation all suggest a good deal of involvement with simultaneous *interregional processing* (see Goldberg & Costa model, Chapter 2). Bernard Rimland (1978a) has proposed an interesting explanation of savant ability which concerns the functions of the right cerebral hemisphere. In an attempt to see if a normal person could learn to calculate dates as fast as the twins, George and Charles, researchers Barnett Addis and Oscar Parsons (Rimland, 1978a) had a psychology graduate student see if he could learn a method of calculation that would allow him to equal the twins' lightning performances (see Smith, pp. 163–165). The graduate student, Benj Langdon, got pretty good at calendar calculating:

> But despite an enormous amount of practice, he could not match the speed of the twins for quite a long time.
>
> Then suddenly, he discovered he could match their speed. Quite to Langdon's surprise, his brain had somehow automated the complex calculations; it had absorbed the table to be memorized so efficiently that now calendar-calculating was second nature to him; he no longer had to consciously go through the various operations.
>
> My hunch is that when this dramatic, quantum change took place in Langdon's capacity, the site of processing had migrated from the left hemisphere of the brain—which specializes in logical, sequential, step-at-a-time processes—to some other area, quite possibly in his right hemisphere—which grasps patterns of information all at once. Whether my hunch is correct or not, it does become clear that a very complex set of calculations can become automated if repeated often enough, and can then be done in what is, apparently, a simultaneous rather than a sequential fashion. (Rimland, 1978a, p. 74)

Rimland may be right about the switch to the right hemisphere. After all, the two hemispheres are in constant communication with one another, and share the same world of environmental problems and events. We might want to add, however, that, as Smith has pointed out, the left hemisphere also automates its performances quite well—like those involved in the complexities of our rapid-fire language capacities. Here, we can recall Goldberg and Costa's routinized descriptive systems of the left hemisphere (Chapter 2). It may be that Rimland and Smith are both right. Mental calculators may involve the routinized left hemisphere capacities, other spatially related savant abilities—like 19 year-old Michael Hickey who on his first try unscrambled a Rubik's cube in 40 seconds—may draw upon automated right hemisphere capacities. In addition to all of this, the cerebellum must be developed which is known to control automated sensory-motor activity (Chapter 2).

Rimland's hypothesis illustrates an interplay of psychological, biological, and learning processes. Langdon's abnormal calendar calculating feat (matching the twins' speed) involved learning, unconscious processes, and automated patterns of response likely somewhere in specialized brain structures.

Empirical and Methodological Aspects of Mental Disorders

Earlier, the distribution of personality (Chapter 8) helped us to arrive at some standard for what might be considered normal performance and what is not. On the other hand, the definition of mental disorder in the DSM-IV allows for more people with a mental disorder than not! Because the definition relies on the presence of distress and/or disability it is theoretically possible that everyone in society, including the psychologists and psychiatrists, could have a mental disorder As a comparison, Table 9.1 estimates the prevalence of major maladjustments in the United States in 1987 and Table 9.2 indicates the incidence rates of retarded and autistic savants.

It can be seen in Table 9.2 that even though there are many times more retarded persons in the population than there are autistic ones, the number of autistic savants estimated is much greater than retarded savants. It is further interesting to note the frequencies of the different kinds of savant ability that show up in the autistic savant group. In Table 9.3 you can see that musical and memory savantism are the most common expressions. Note also that boys develop savant abilities far more often than do girls.

Table 9.1 Estimate of Prevalence[1] of Psychiatric Disorders in the United States in 1987[2]

Schizophrenia	1,824,000
Affective Psychosis	1,032,000
Neurosis	14,280,000
Personality Disorder	10,056,000
Overall "Functional" Disorders	34,200,000
"Demoralization"[3]	66,000,000

1. *Prevalence* refers to the number of active cases that can be identified at a given time. It is to be distinguished from incidence, the rate at which a given disorder manifests itself (even if only briefly) in a given population. *Incidence rates* are normally reported as the "lifetime risk" of an individual from a given population contracting the disorder in question (Coleman, Butcher, & Carson, 1984).
2. The estimates are based upon a U.S. population of 240 million (Statistical Abstract of the United States).
3. "Demoralization" includes such disorders as low self-esteem, feelings of helplessness/hopelessness, dread, anxiety, sadness, and confused thinking (in Frank, Jerome (1973), *Persuasion and Healing.* Baltimore, MD: Johns Hopkins U. Press).

Figures for this entire table are based upon Dohrenwend & Dohrenwend, 1982

Table 9.2 Estimated Incidence Rates of Autistic and Retarded Savants*

7,200,000	cases of mental retardation
× .06%	savant rate
4,320	retarded savants
120,000	cases of autism
× 9.8%	savant rate
11,760	autistic savants
16,000	total savants

*Based upon a population of 240 million (1987)
Cases of retardation based upon Edgerton, 1979
Cases of autism and savant rates based upon Rimland and Hill, 1984
Note: The savant rate among autistic population is greater than that among normals.

Table 9.3 Frequency of Savant Abilities in Autistic Individuals

Skill	*Boys (N = 91)*	*Girls (N = 28)*	*Total (N = 119)*	*Percent Girls*
Music	43	20	63	31.7
Memory	41	7	48	14.7
Art	16	7	23	30.4
Pseudo-Verbal	16	3	19	15.7
Mathematics	12	5	17	29.4
Mechanical	14	0	14	0
Coordination	11	5	16	31.2
Directions, Paths, etc.	13	0	13	0
Calendar Calculation	10	3	13	23.0
"Extrasensory Perception"	3	1	4	25.0

An Empirically-Based Method for the Classification and Diagnosis of Mental Disorders: The DSM-IV

Now that we know the general extent of mental disorders in the United States, let's look at the modern classification system for them. Most mental disorders do not have a known biological basis. Recall in the DSM-IV's definition of mental disorder, ". . . there is an inference that there is a behavioral, psychological, or biological dysfunction . . ." Whether or not a person is actually said to have a mental disorder depends upon both who is doing the classifying and upon what classification scheme is being used. There have been other classification systems in the past, for example, a DSM-I, DSM-II, and DSM-III. Widely used throughout the rest of the world, the ninth edition of the International Classification of Diseases (ICD-9) contains a section for the classification of mental disorders. Because the DSM-IV is not perfect and we are learning more about mental disorders, no doubt there will one day be a DSM-V.

Improved Diagnostic Accuracy: The DSM-IV

There are four broad reasons the DSM-IV has such great and improved accuracy: it uses an objective approach; takes a holistic approach; uses diagnostic decision trees; and has a complete empirical and theoretical description of each disorder.

Objective Approach. First, the DSM-IV asks that raters begin diagnosis not with the classification system itself, but with careful objective study of the observable aspects of each case. Only when the clinician is familiar with the observable patient or client symptoms that confront him should he go on with the proper use of the classification system—the labeling part of diagnosis.

Holistic Approach. Second, the DSM-IV takes a *holistic approach* to diagnosing each person. Realizing that a person is much more than a set of symptoms that the rater sees in his office or in the ward, the DSM-IV developers have each person rated in five different ways—along five different *diagnostic axes*. These five axes or ways of observing and understanding the person include those listed in Table 9.4.

Altogether, these five axes can give the rater a good picture of the forces and conditions acting on the person—from within and from without. The holistic intention of the DSM-IV multiaxial approach is captured in the logo of the *DSM-IV Training Guide* illustrated in Figure 9.2. The five axes represent diagnostic subsystems in a holistic or systems approach to diagnosis.

The DSM-IV can be looked upon as a systems analysis applied to the diagnosis and understanding of abnormal behavior. What this means is that each case of disorder can be viewed from the perspective of five subsystems of interrelated causes. This systems analysis will be seen in action when we discuss diagnostic decision trees of the DSM-IV.

Table 9.4 Multiaxial Classification System

Official Diagnostic Axes	
Axis I:	More severe mental disorders that are observed in the person
Axis II:	Personality disorders that are observed in the person
Axis III:	Any physical disorders or conditions that are observed in the person
Supplemental Diagnostic Axes (to help document and understand the person's overall life situation)	
Axis IV:	Consideration of any stresses in the person's life that may have a role in contributing to the person's current mental disorder
Axis V:	Consideration of how well the person has been functioning in relation to family and friends; as a co-worker, student, or homemaker, and in recreations.

In Table 9.5 are outlines of mental disorders of Axes I and II. We will discuss these disorders later with case examples. Axis III (Physical Disorders) sometimes will have a direct bearing on the diagnosis, sometimes indirect, and often must be left as "None Known" by the clinician.

Axis IV (life stresses) applies to children, adolescents and adults. The types of *psychosocial stresses* that may contribute to mental disorders include things like: divorce, friction with child, illness of friend, retirement, job change, change in residence, bank loan, bankruptcy, lawsuit, jail, puberty, menopause, accident, rape, etc.

Psychosocial stressors can be rated on a scale from 1 (none) to 7 (catastrophic). When determining the rating, the psychiatrist looks at only the stressors that have exacerbated or contributed to the onset of the mental disorder. A mild stress event might be a change in residence, while an extreme stress might be a divorce or death of a spouse. There may be one or more stressors that are judged to be etiologically significant. The rating should reflect the summed effect of all the psychosocial stressors.

Areas of Adaptive Functioning

The Holmes and Rahe *Social Readjustment Scale* discussed in Chapter 4 has the same idea with the same implications. Among the levels of *adaptive functioning* in Axis V, social relations are given the greatest stress weight as a possible key to understanding a mental disorder because functioning with family and friends is of great diagnostic significance. These areas include the following: **Social relations**—all interpersonal relations but with particular emphasis placed on friend and family. The breadth and quality of relationships are also taken into consideration; **Occupational functioning**—the amount, complexity, and the quality of the work accomplished as a worker, student, or homemaker; **Leisure time**—range and depth of involvement in recreational activities or hobbies.

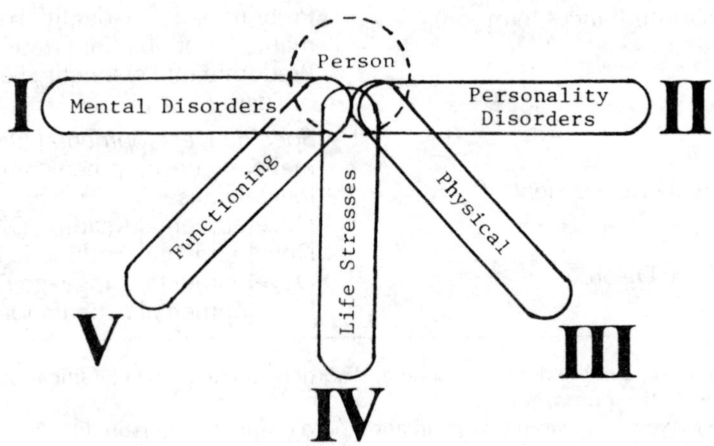

Figure 9.2 The Five Axes of the DSM-IV

Table 9.5 Mental Disorders Described in the DSM-IV (Axes I & II)*

Axis I Mental Disorders

1. *Disorders Usually First Evident in Infancy, Childhood, or Adolescence*
   - Intellectual
     - Mental Retardation (includes all of the retarded, and the retarded savant)
   - Behavioral
     - Attention Deficit Disorder
     - Conduct Disorder
   - Emotional
     - Anxiety Disorders of Childhood and Adolescence
     - Other Disorders of Infancy, Childhood, or Adolescence
   - Physical
     - Eating Disorders
     - Stereotyped Movement Disorders
     - Other Disorders with Physical Manifestations
   - Developmental
     - Pervasive Developmental Disorders (includes autism, and the autistic savant)
2. *Substance Abuse Disorders* (alcohol, cocaine, etc.)
3. *Organic Mental Disorders* (temporary or permanent alterations in brain physiology)
4. *Schizophrenic Disorders* (hallucinations, delusions, severely deranged behavior, and disrupted thinking)
   - Disorganized Type
   - Catatonic Type
   - Paranoid Type
   - Undifferentiated Type
   - Residual Type
5. *Paranoid Disorders* (non-schizophrenic—yet, psychotic)
   - Paranoia
   - Shared Paranoid Disorder
   - Acute Paranoid Disorder
6. *Affective Disorders* (disturbances in mood)
   - Bipolar Disorder
     - Manic
     - Depressed
     - Mixed
   - Major Depression
7. *Anxiety Disorders* (experienced fearful distress)
   - Phobic Disorders
   - Obsessive Compulsive Disorder
   - Panic Disorder
     - Panic Disorder (panic)
     - Generalized Anxiety Disorder (persistent anxiety)
8. *Somatoform Disorders* (complaint of physical stress or disability with no known physical cause)
   - Somatization Disorder
   - Conversion Disorder
   - Psychogenic Pain Disorder
   - Hypochondriasis
9. *Dissociative Disorders* (breakdown of normal psychological integration)
   - Psychogenic Amnesia
   - Psychogenic Fugue
   - Multiple Personality
   - Depersonalized Disorder
10. *Psychosexual Disorders* (psychological sexuality deviations)
    - Gender Identity Disorders
    - Paraphilias
    - Psychosexual Dysfunctions
11. *Factitious Disorders* (desire to be a patient)
12. *Disorders of Impulse Control Not Elsewhere Classified* (uncontrollable impulses)
    - Pathological Gambling
    - Kleptomania
    - Pyromania
    - Intermittent Explosive Disorder
    - Isolated Explosive Disorder
    - Atypical Impulse Control Disorder
13. Adjustment Disorders (overreaction and maladaptation to psychosocial stress)

*Axis II Mental Disorders***

1. *Personality Disorders* (disruptive personality features)
   - Predominant Personality Feature: "Odd" or Eccentric
   - Predominant Personality Feature: Dramatic, Emotional, or Erratic
   - Predominant Personality Feature: Anxious or Fearful
2. *Specific Developmental Disorders* (abnormal early development—no known biological cause)
   - Developmental Reading Disorder
   - Developmental Arithmetic Disorder
   - Developmental Language Disorder
   - Developmental Articulation Disorder

*This table does not include some of the derivative mental disorders. Some of the classifications are more detailed than others for illustrative purposes only.

**The separation of the two axes, ". . . was made in an attempt to ensure that personality Disorders and Specific Developmental Disorders are not overlooked when attention is focused on the more florid symptoms of the Axis I disorders."

Careful Diagnosis through Decision Trees. The third reason the DSM-IV has great and improved accuracy of diagnosis is that once the clinician has applied a tentative label to the case confronting him, the DSM-IV provides him help in deciding on other possible explanations for the abnormal behavior. This is done through eight *differential diagnosis decision trees.* From the DSM-IV:

> The purpose of these decision trees is to aid the clinician in understanding the organization and hierarchical structure of the classification. Each decision tree starts with a set of clinical features. When one of these features is a prominent part of the presenting clinical picture, the clinician can follow the series of questions to rule in or out various diagnostic categories. The questions are only approximations of the actual diagnostic criteria. The decision trees are not meant to replace the specific diagnostic criteria. (p. 339)

The decision tree contains a list of questions for the clinician. With its yes/no branchings, it may remind us of the way in which a computer might reach a decision. Essentially, the decision trees ask the clinician to check all other relevant possibilities for diagnosis—thus helping to avoid diagnostic error. The following *case vignette* has been evaluated using the series of questions on the decision tree.

Case Vignette. George is a fourth-grader who is having difficulty in school. He gets along well with other children but has poor academic performance. George is flunking reading and spelling and having difficulty in science. He is passing math, art, and physical education. On the *Wechsler Intelligence Scale for Children,* he obtained a full scale I.Q. score of 100 with a verbal score of 95 and a performance score of 103. On an individual achievement test, George's reading comprehension score was at grade level 1.6, his spelling score was at grade level 2.0, and his math score was at grade level 3.2. There were no notable problems at home with the exception of the parents' difficulty in getting George to do his homework.

This case can be reviewed using the Decision Tree for Differential Diagnosis of Academic or Learning Difficulties, DSM-IV.

This individual is having school difficulties in areas that depend on reading for adaptive functioning. He is performing two years below expected grade level although he has normal intelligence. Arithmetic skills are basically intact and only mildly affected by the reading disorder; minor problems in arithmetic are probably due to difficulty with mathematical word problems.

Axis II—Developmental Reading Disorder Note that even though a diagnosis of specific developmental disorder was made early in the tree, the diagnostic process continued to allow for the ruling in and out of other diagnostic possibilities.

A Complete Empirical Picture for Each Disorder. Finally, the DSM-IV has great and improved accuracy because it contains a complete empirical and *atheoretical* description of each disorder. This information permits firm establishment of a diagnosis.

All disorders are presented in a uniform format. The manual presents a concise discussion of each class of disorders that includes:

- essential features and a clinical sketch
- features usually associated with the disorder
- typical onset, clinical course, impairment and complications
- specific predisposing factors (if known), prevalence, sex ratio, and familial pattern
- differential diagnostic criteria for the class and all of the disorders in it.

The following is an actual example of the description of a mental disorder—*Simple Phobia:* The essential feature is a persistent, irrational fear of, and compelling desire to avoid, an object or a situation other than being alone or in public places away from home (Agoraphobia), or of humiliation or embarrassment in certain social situations (Social Phobia). Thus, this is a residual category of Phobic Disorder. This disturbance is a significant source of distress, and the individual recognizes that his or her fear is excessive or unreasonable. The disturbance is not due to another mental disorder.

Simple Phobias are sometimes referred to as "specific" phobias. The most common Simple Phobias in the general population, though not necessarily among those seeking treatment, involve animals, particularly dogs, snakes, insects, and mice. Other Simple Phobias are claustrophobia (fear of closed spaces) and acrophobia (fear of heights).

Associated Features. When suddenly exposed to the phobic stimulus, the individual becomes overwhelmingly fearful and may experience symptoms identical with those of a panic attack. Because of anticipatory anxiety, the individual will often try to gain considerable information before entering situations in which the phobic stimulus may be encountered.

Age at Onset. Age at onset varies, but animal phobias nearly always begin in childhood.

Course. Most simple phobias that start in childhood disappear without treatment. However, those that persist into adulthood rarely remit without treatment.

Impairment. Impairment may be minimal if the phobic object is rare and easily avoided, such as fear of snakes in someone living in the city. Impairment may be considerable if the phobic object is common and cannot be avoided, such as a fear of elevators in someone living in a large city who must use elevators at work.

Complications and Predisposing Factors. No information.

Prevalence. Simple Phobias may be common; but since they rarely result in marked impairment, individuals with Simple Phobia rarely seek treatment.

Sex Ratio. The disorder is more often diagnosed in women.

Differential Diagnosis. In Schizophrenia certain activities may be avoided in response to delusions. Similarly, in Obsessive Compulsive Disorder phobic avoidance of certain situations that are associated with anxiety about dirt or contamination is frequent. The diagnosis of Simple Phobia should not be made in either case.

Diagnostic Criteria for Simple Phobia.

A. A persistent, irrational fear of, and compelling desire to avoid, an object or a situation other than being alone, or in public places away from home (Agoraphobia), or of humiliation or embarrassment in certain social situations (Social Phobia). Phobic objects are often animals, and phobic situations frequently involve heights or closed spaces.

B. Significant distress from the disturbance and recognition by the individual that his or her fear is excessive or unreasonable.

C. Not due to another mental disorder, such as Schizophrenia or Obsessive Compulsive Disorder.

Descriptions for the more than 200 mental disorders which appear in the DSM-IV follow this same outline—often the descriptions are much more detailed than the one above.

A good deal of information is provided for diagnosis of mental disorders. No theoretical explanations are presented—just the facts that might apply to the case that confronts the clinician. The DSM-IV includes a decision tree of *anxiety disorders* that includes the phobias. The decision tree helps clinicians relate what they observe to the other axes that might be involved—Axes II, and III in the case of the simple phobia.

Empirical Examples of the Mental Disorders—Case Vignettes

As we describe the following observable characteristics of the mental disorders you may feel at times you have some of the symptoms yourself. This is quite normal for introductory psychology students. We all rely a great deal on external sources of information in our attempts to understand ourselves. And sometimes we tend to internalize some of the disorders simply because we seem to "understand" them from personal experience. This is true of everyone. If we could not understand and appreciate the mental disorders to some small extent, we would be unable to understand abnormal behavior at all. The key to understanding the disorders is to think of people with varying degrees of distress and/or disability.

As we examine the following disorder descriptions, remember that the case vignette (report) or vignette is only an example, and each actual case remains unique. The cases provide the bases for the classification system—the classification system does not provide the bases for the cases. In presenting case vignettes, we will follow the organization of Table 9.5.

Axis I

Disorders Usually First Evident in Infancy, Childhood, or Adolescence

In this classification of disorder we will take a closer look at *mental retardation* (Table 9.6).

Case Vignette. "Harriet's psychological tests showed her to be at a severe disadvantage." On the Wechsler Adult Intelligence Scale (WAIS), she

Table 9.6 The Five Subtypes of Mental Retardation

Subtype	*IQ*	*Typical Performance Level*	*Portion of Retarded*
Mild	50–70	Sixth grade level by late teens	80%
Moderate	35–49	Not likely to go beyond second grade level	12%
Severe	20–34	Little speech ability	7%
Profound	Below 20	Limited training in self-care	1%

had a verbal scale IQ of 65 and a performance IQ of 87 with a full-scale score of 73. Outside her special area (music/memory), her fund of general knowledge was limited. She believed that there were 48 weeks in a year. Harriet's capacity for abstract reasoning was remarkably impaired; when asked how two things were alike, regardless of how obvious the relationship was, she was unable to answer. No matter how much the instructions were clarified, how much coaxing she was given, or how many illustrations and corrections were made, she was unable to give evidence of a capacity to think abstractly. When asked how a nickel was like a dime she could not even say that they were both round or made of metal, let alone that they were forms of money. No amount of pressure would make her say anything except, "A nickel is a nickel and a dime is a dime. They are not alike at all" (Viscott, p. 504).

We may wonder if Harriet is really retarded with an overall IQ of 73. Two important points here are that (1) the DSM-IV suggests that an IQ of 70 be considered a flexible band of 65 to 75, and (2) this flexibility allows other clinical judgments—like Harriet's lack of abstract thinking ability—to enter into the diagnosis.

Since we have seen a case vignette of a retarded savant, let us also examine a case vignette for an autistic savant which also falls into this category of the DSM-IV.

Pervasive Developmental Disorders

One of these pervasive disorders is *infantile autism*. The essential feature of this disorder is a pervasive unresponsiveness to other people, poor language development, and bizarre response patterns to certain aspects of the environment. This infantile form of the disorder begins sometime before 30 months of age.

Case Vignette. Nadia was 6½ years old when her mother, an emigree from the Ukraine, brought her to the Child Development Research Unit at Nottingham University. Nadia had almost no speech and was making almost no progress at a local school for severely subnormal children. A teacher of autistic children suggested that Nadia's mother take her to the university clinic.

During the interview, the mother mentioned that Nadia liked to draw, and pulled a small bundle of Nadia's drawings from her handbag. Life was never again the same for that psychologist. She was stunned by what she saw. Few of us would not have been stunned, for Nadia's untutored drawings provide us with a totally unexpected and tantalizing glimpse of extraordinary artistic genius. Any normal 6-year-old would have been hailed as a creative prodigy for producing these pictures. But Nadia? Nadia, a clumsy, lethargic, impassive child who hardly knew her own name? There are 146 of Nadia's drawings in this book (Lorna Selfe, 1978). Some are better than others. Some are not very good. But those that are good are extraordinary by any standards, including the standard of the highly gifted adult. Nadia had started drawing at about 3½ years of age. She reportedly didn't scribble, just began drawing recognizable objects from the "moment she put pen to paper" (Rimland & Hill, 1984).

Substance Use Disorders

Many drugs such as alcohol, coffee, Valium, etc., if used in moderation, can be helpful to a person. Alcohol can help relax us in a social situation, coffee can give us a "bright" start in the morning, and Valium can ease us when we have become distressed. Substance use disorders only apply when the use of some drug, chemical, or alcohol has been abnormal to the point where the substance itself begins to cause stress or disability. Within substance use, there are different degrees of disorder. A *substance abuse* label is applied if the substance causes distress/disability for at least one month. *Substance dependence* is a greater degree of disorder, where signs of *substance tolerance* to the drug and withdrawal problems become apparent. You might wish to reexamine the opponent-process explanation of how substance use disorders might come about (Chapter 8).

Case Vignette. A 25-year-old housewife with insomnia obtained a prescription for 10 mg of Valium from her family physician, who also prescribed the medication for the patient's mother. The patient found that two pills at bedtime brought satisfying sleep, but she raised the dose to three just to be sure she had enough. Then she started taking the medicine during the day for relaxation. For about three months, two pills during the day were sufficient, but for the last four months the drug seemed to lose its effectiveness. Consequently, she was taking four and then five pills through the daytime. She had to consume her mother's supply as well as her own, and to pretend that she'd lost a prescription or two in order to secure a sufficient supply. The mother raised objections, but the patient declared that she couldn't cope without the Valium, and that she only craved it more when she tried to cut down. Despite her claim of coping, the patient's husband declared that she was "zonked out" all day and didn't keep up with the housework.

Organic Mental Disorders

The normal biochemistry and physiology of the brain can be temporarily put into disorder by several means. Fever, coffee, alcohol, amphetamines, cannabis, etc., can temporarily upset brain chemistry and brain functioning in an abnormal way. These are not classified as *organic mental disorders*. For the label of Organic Mental Disorder to be applied, problems at work or in social relationships must result as in the following case vignette.

Case Vignette. A 43-year-old divorced housepainter is examined in the hospital emergency observation ward. His sister is available to provide some information. The sister indicates that the patient has consumed large quantities of cheap wine, daily, for five years. Evidently, he had a reasonably stable home life and job record until his wife left him for another man five years ago. The sister indicates that the patient drinks more than a fifth a day, and that this has been a pattern since the divorce. He has often had blackouts from drinking, missed work, and consequently has been fired from several jobs. Fortunately, painters are in great demand and he has been able to provide marginally for himself during these years. However, three days ago he ran out of money and has had to beg on the street to buy a meal. He has been very poorly nourished, eating perhaps one meal a day and evidently relying on the wine as his primary source of nourishment.

The morning after his last day of drinking he felt increasingly tremulous, with his hands shaking so grossly that it was difficult for him to light a cigarette. Accompanying this was an increasing sense of inner panic which has made him virtually unable to sleep. A neighbor became concerned about the patient when he seemed not to be making sense and was clearly unable to take care of himself. The neighbor contacted the sister who brought the patient to the hospital.

On examination, he alternates between apprehension and chatty superficial warmth. He is quite keyed up and talks constantly. At times he recognizes the doctor, but sometimes he thinks that the doctor is the patient's older brother. Twice during the examination the patient called the doctor by his older brother's name and asked when he had arrived, evidently having lost track of the interview up to that point. There is a gross hand tremor at rest and there are periods of picking at bugs he sees on the bedsheets. The patient is disoriented regarding time and thinks that he is in a supermarket parking lot rather than in a hospital. He indicates that he feels he is fighting against a terrifying sense that the world is ending in a holocaust. He is startled every few minutes by sounds and scenes of fiery car crashes (based on the sound of rolling carts in the hall). Efforts at testing memory and calculation fail because his attention shifts too quickly to sustain the effort.

How many of the axes can you see involved in the above case?

Schizophrenic Disorders

Schizophrenic disorders are extremely serious and extremely pervasive in their effects on mental functioning, The schizophrenic is *psychotic* (he lives in a detached world of his own), and his communication, both written and spoken, mirrors this. When the schizophrenic is in an active phase of his illness, he doesn't make sense when he talks. In order to be classified as schizophrenic, the person had to have once been functioning normally. The label of schizophrenia is not used unless there is some period of time where the psychosis is florid. This means there must be at some time full-blown hallucinations, delusions, *catatonia,* or pervasive derangement of thought processes. The symptoms also must persist over at least six months (not necessarily in a continual florid state). Finally, if a specific organic brain disorder can be detected, the label of schizophrenia is not used. The diagnosis would then be that of Organic Mental Disorder.

The reason the schizophrenia classification is not used when a known organic disorder is present is because for many patients the schizophrenic symptoms are present, but no definite organic disorder can be found. Do we know anything about the causes of those cases that are labeled as schizophrenia? Schizophrenia does seem to have a hereditary component. Some alteration in the DNA (see Chapter 9) produces a brain chemistry, physiology, or anatomy that predisposes the person to schizophrenia. Rosenthal and Guinn (1977) have reported on four identical quadruplets (all shared the same zygote, therefore the same DNA genes) who all developed schizophrenia by the time they were in late adolescence. The chance of four identical quads developing schizophrenia by chance alone (no genetic involvement) would be about one in two billion. In addition, this dramatic case supports earlier concordance rate studies for schizophrenia.

In addition to this clue of genetic transmission, positron emission tomography of brains of the four identical quads show abnormality, as do computer-enhanced EEG patterns.

Researchers studying the dopamine hypothesis have been steadily closing in on the specific cause of schizophrenia. A recent international effort by P. Seeman and his colleagues (1984) has shown that about one half of schizophrenics have excess dopamine receptors in their brains. It now appears, for the moment, that there may be at least two separate schizophrenia disorders, one of which involves too much dopamine-related neural transmission—via too many receptors.

Case Vignette A 16-year-old boy moved from a small rural school to a large urban high school for his junior year. Without voicing any lack of confidence about handling this new situation, he became increasingly less communicative over the course of that school year. His grades, which had been all B's and C's, fell to D's and D–'s. Through the following summer, his family noticed that he seemed to have changed, to have become withdrawn. He tended to give laconic responses and sometimes had an inscrutable expression on his face. Two weeks after the senior year began, the boy became so disturbed in the classroom that school authorities contacted his parents, who brought him to the hospital the next week. He appeared rather stunned and perplexed, and his tone of voice was flat and mechanical. Occasionally he contorted his face into a grimace and twirled the hair of his right temple between his thumb and fingers. He moved easily about and complied with instructions. He was verbal, but his speech was like "word salad," just an incoherent jumble. He seemed to try to listen to questions, but his answers were a stream of incoherent speech. He seemed at times to be hearing voices or other sounds.

Paranoid Disorders

Paranoid Disorders involve psychosis, detachment from reality, but are not pervasive. The person, except for the paranoia, leads a well-integrated, normal life. The essential features in paranoia include delusions of persecution (someone's out to get me), or of jealousy (something's going on behind my back). The delusions of a true Paranoid Disorder are delusions about things that are in reality possible, but simply are not true. The totally bizarre and impossible imaginings associated with schizophrenia are not included in symptoms classifiable as Paranoid Disorders.

Case Vignette. A beautiful, successful, 34-year-old interior designer is brought to the clinic by her 37-year-old husband, a rather prominent attorney. The husband laments that for the past three years his wife has made increasingly shrill accusations that he is unfaithful to her. He declares that he has done everything in his power to convince her of his innocence, but there is no shaking her conviction. A careful examination of the facts reveals that there is actually no evidence that the man has been unfaithful. When asked what her evidence is, she becomes somewhat vague and mysterious, declaring that she can tell by such things as a faraway look in his eyes.

She is absolutely sure that she is right and considers herself highly insulted to be told that she is imagining the disloyalty. The husband reports that for the last year she has been increasingly bitter, creating a kind of "cold war" atmosphere in the household. Militantly entrenched against the husband and refusing to show him any affection except at social gatherings, she seems intent on giving the impression socially that they have a good relationship. However, after they are alone, the coldness reenters the picture. She has actually physically assaulted the husband on occasion, but her account obscures the fact that she initiated the assault. Her description of the tussles actually begin with the point where the husband attempted to interrupt her assault by holding her arms. She declares that she will never forgive him for holding her down and squeezing her arms, and her accounts make it appear that she was unfairly pinned down by the husband.

The patient experiences no hallucinations; her speech is well organized; she interprets proverbs with no difficulty; she seems to have a good command of current events; and generally she displays no difficulty with thinking, aside from her conviction of the disloyalty. She describes herself as having a generally full and effective life, with a few close friends and no problems except those centering on her experiences of unhappiness in the marriage. The husband reports that his wife is respected for her skills but that she has had difficulties for most of her life in close relationships with friends. She has lost a number of friends because she seems always to be intolerant of differences in opinion. The woman reports that she does not want to leave the marriage, nor does she want to have her husband leave her; instead she is furious about the injustice and she demands that it be confessed and redeemed.

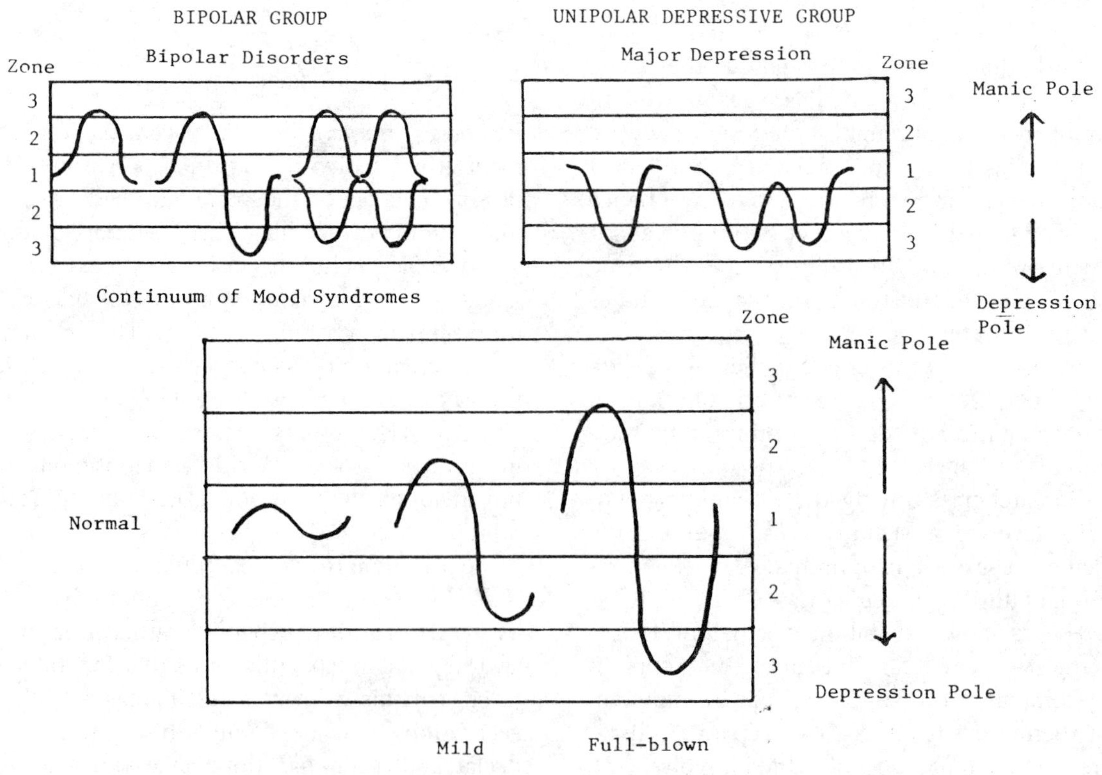

Figure 9.3 Bipolar and Unipolar Affective Disorders

Affective Disorders

Moods are powerful sources of emotional states that guide the entirety of our thought processes. When mood disturbances become so great that the person is working under prolonged distress and/or disability, he or she would be classified as having an *affective disorder.* Moods can range from highs, *mania,* or lows, *depression.* In Figure 9.3 are outlines of the sort of states mania and depression involve. Some people with affective disorders may experience *bipolar mood shifts,* which involve both mania and depression, others *unipolar mood shifts,* which involve only bouts of depression.

The manic syndrome is at the other end of the continuum—perhaps more enjoyable but just as deranged. The features of mania can be grouped in four areas: mood, vitality, agitation, and pleasure-seeking behavior (Table 9.7).

The scales in Figure 9.3 (c) represent normal (1), and abnormal degrees of mood shift (2, 3). While it may seem that the characteristics of mania (Table 9.7) may be kind of fun, you will see in the case vignette that in the disorder stage it leads to both stress and disability. You might wish to reexamine the discussion on the opponent-process theory of emotion in relation to Affective Disorders.

Case Vignette. Harold, a 27-year-old Coca-Cola truck driver, functioned in a routine manner until three weeks ago when his wife suffered a miscarriage. He was found shortly afterward to be in surprisingly and increasingly high spirits—talking loudly and animatedly, clowning around, and cracking jokes that became increasingly crude and coarse. Co-workers, who found this amusing at first, found it exhausting after a while, and they complained that he was racing through his work in a reckless fashion. Warned that his job was in jeopardy, he declared that he didn't need it anymore since he had just invented a new drink that would outsell Coca-Cola and make him a billionaire. A friend from the lab analyzed the drink and found it to be no more than club soda with vanilla flavoring. Undaunted, Harold claimed that this wonder drink would also be a cancer cure that would bring him the Nobel Prize.

Somehow, Harold talked the neighborhood bank into a $10,000 loan for his venture, but

Table 9.7 Features of Mania

Mood

Elation—cheerfulness, high spirits.

Humor—joking, clowning, irrepressible infectious quality.

Schemes—into everything, flighty, distractable.

Expansiveness—feeling unusually gifted, superior, talented.

Vitality

Well-being—feeling robust, exuberant, on top of the world.

Stamina—tireless, refreshed with minimum sleep.

Appetite—zest for eating, tendency to excess.

Libido—enhanced, interest expressed readily, possibly promiscuous.

Agitation

Turmoil—may have urgent sense of restlessness.

Irritability—may be demanding, pushy, especially when curbed.

Behavior—restless, constant motion, loud speech, possibly somewhat physically aggressive.

Pleasure-Seeking Behavior

Relationships—unnatural warmth, engages strangers, may show undue generosity, may be on the phone into the middle of the night.

Food, Drugs, Alcohol—indiscretion and excesses.

the family soon found that he had given considerable amounts to strangers, whom he referred to as "business associates," after meeting them in bars. He had been spending most of the nights in bars, since he was tireless despite only two or three hours of sleep a night. The family finally persuaded him to go into the hospital.

When the doctor arrived, Harold bounded over and greeted him in an effusive warm manner, as if they were old buddies, and made several grand, cavalier-like gestures in a ceremonial fashion, as if this were a gala occasion. Harold's voice and manner were irrepressively humorous; on hearing the doctor's name, he spun off seven puns in rapid succession associated with the name.

Anxiety Disorders

Anxiety disorders are very easy for most of us to identify with. We all have experienced fear or anxiety of one kind or another, and exaggerations of these felt anxieties are the key elements of anxiety disorder. There are three classes of anxiety disorder: *phobias, panic attacks,* and *obsessive compulsive disorders.*

The phobias involve an irrational fear of some object, activity, or situation. The person knows the fear is unwarranted but still avoids the phobic stimulus(i) out of fear. This can be very disruptive to the person's life. There are three classes of phobia. *Agoraphobia* (agora means meeting place, or, in ancient Greece, a market place) is the most pervasive of the phobias. With agoraphobia, the person fears being alone or being in public places. Trains, buses, busy streets, crowded stores, elevators (because of the crowd) might cause him severe panic (see Figure 9.4). This phobia greatly restricts what he is free to do unless he requests that a friend or relative accompany him whenever he leaves home. *Social phobia* involves the irrational fear of

Figure 9.4 Agoraphobia is the fear of being alone or in crowded places.

being scrutinized by others. Many people have experienced mild social phobia in relation to public speaking or performing. Social phobia extends to irrational fears of being scrutinized in public lavatories, eating in public, etc. Social phobias can be very debilitating for anyone who would like to have a career where public displays of behavior are a required part of the job. The final class of phobias, simple phobia includes the general layman's idea of phobia—more specific fears. Simple phobias can include virtually anything not included in agoraphobia or social phobia. An exhaustive list of simple phobias could be quite lengthy. However, common simple phobias include fears of animals like dogs, snakes, spiders, mice, and heights (acrophobia), closed spaces (claustrophobia), and riding in airplanes or elevators (this time because they are closed or might fall).

Panic attacks differ from the phobias in that there is not always a common object, situation, or activity that produces them. Sometimes the panic attack comes "out of the blue." The person experiences a sudden feeling of impending doom. There is usually fear of going crazy, dying, or doing something "out of control" while the attack persists—usually a matter of several minutes. The criteria for classification as a panic attack include: (A) At least three panic attacks within a three-week period in circumstances other than during marked physical exertion or in a life-threatening situation; (B) Discrete periods of apprehension or fear, and at least four of the following symptoms appearing during each attack:

1. dyspnea (labored breathing)
2. palpitations
3. chest pain or discomfort
4. choking or smothering sensations
5. dizziness, vertigo, or unsteady feelings
6. feelings of unreality
7. parethesias (tingling in hands or feet)
8. hot and cold flashes
9. sweating
10. faintness
11. trembling or shaking

Obsessive compulsive disorders involve recurrent involuntary obsessions and/or compulsions. Anxiety occurs in this disorder when the person attempts to resist the recurrent pattern. Recurrent obsessions are a little like the times when a tune enters your head and just keeps running through for some time. This example, of course, does not constitute a disorder, but if the tune were instead a senseless thought, a repugnant image or idea, it easily could be. The compulsive expression of this disorder is a matter of carrying repetitious behavior too far. For example, most of us wash our hands several times a day, often unconsciously, without thinking much about it. But, when a person washes her hands 50 times a day for no practical reason, that's a compulsion. It may disrupt that person's life. The compulsive hand washing may be driven by an obsession that germs are all over everything touched and will lead to disease. In this situation, if the person resists hand washing (which she knows is irrational), she will experience great anxiety or may panic.

Case Vignette. Harry is a 40-year-old white male who comes to intake (e.g., initial interview procedures at hospital or clinic to determine whether a person should be admitted) because he is feeling very nervous. During the past month he has been overwhelmed by anxiety on at least eight to ten different occasions. These "fits" come on suddenly and happen at work, at home, and sometimes while he is driving. He gets dizzy, begins to sweat, and becomes very tense. The attacks scare him because he feels he is going to lose all control. He has no history of mental problems and this is the first time he has come to a clinic for help. He has been to his medical doctors but they could not find anything physically wrong. At first, he thought he might be having a heart attack. Harry does not know why these attacks occur and wants to get rid of them.

Somatoform Disorders

Very often when we don't want to do something that is causing a lot of anxiety or fear, we take the day off and later explain that we were ill. Sometimes we may even wish that we were ill. But we remain healthy as ever and must go on to face the frightening situation. *Somatoform disorders* occur when a person has a physical complaint, but no physical disorder is actually present. In somatoform disorders, the wishing or faking is not voluntary. The person is unaware (at least consciously) of the source of his "physical" complaint.

The physical complaints of somatoform disorders take various forms: *conversion disorder, psychogenic pain,* and *hypochondriasis* (literally under the breastbone—originally thought the location of hypochondria). Conversion disorders simply mean that the person has involuntarily converted his psychological anxiety into a physical means of avoiding whatever is causing the anxiety. The involuntary regions of the brain, in subtle relationships with the cortex, can manipulate the sensory-motor functions of the body in any way to fit and meet the threatening situation. If the person does not want to be able to see something, he may go "blind"; if a soldier does not want to face having to kill another person, his arm or hands may become "paralyzed," and so on. Conversion disorders are extremely interesting examples of the complex ways the brain can function. While the person who becomes blind, for example, may not be able to see, he is not usually too upset about it, and curiously may not stumble about. Of course, there is absolutely nothing wrong with his visual system. Yet, he is not consciously faking—he is in fact functionally blind.

Psychogenic pain refers to the complaint of pain with no detectable physical reason for pain. Usually the felt pain is located in the back, lower limbs, or vital organs. Pain has complicated neurological bases. Hypochondriasis consists of an unrealistic fear and/or belief that a person has a disease. Of course, no basis for any disease can be found. In both psychogenic pain disorders and hypochondriasis, the person's life is disrupted by frequent trips to doctors and days missed at work or school. People with somatoform disorders are in no way faking or malingering. And, while they may be able to avoid situations (as in conversion disorders), or get needed medical attention (as in psychogenic pain or hypochondriasis), their disorder is completely out of their own voluntary control, and they are distressed and disabled.

Case Vignette. Aretha is a 37-year-old secretary who is separated from her husband. Five months ago she discovered that her husband was having an affair and he then asked for a divorce. Six weeks ago she began coughing and having a difficult time breathing. She went to her doctor but he could find nothing wrong. However, she was not convinced of his findings. She believes that she has lung cancer. Her father died of lung cancer five years ago and Aretha has smoked cigarettes since she was 14. She is also losing weight, which she feels confirms her belief. She has gone to cancer specialists and had X rays which were negative. However, no one has been able to explain her persistent coughing and she remains convinced that she has lung cancer. Recently she lost her job because she has taken off so many sick days for doctor's visits and because she stays home in bed.

Dissociative Disorders

Sometimes we all "forget" things that we don't want to remember. We may want to run away from what we are doing and sit on a beach for a week or two. Or, we may argue with ourselves. A part of us wants to go to the party, another part wants to stay home and study. And sometimes we may suddenly, quite unexpectedly, ask ourselves, "What am I doing here?" These are normal everyday dissociative feelings and are helpful in relieving stress and in making decisions.

However, *dissociative disorders* are such involuntary exaggerations of dissociation that they cause great distress and/or disability. Dissociative disorders include *psychogenic amnesia, psychogenic fugue* (flight), *multiple personality,* and *depersonalization disorder.* In psychogenic amnesia, the person simply can't recall important personal information. The amount of information forgotten may involve a certain period of time, certain events during a period of time, the entire lifetime, or everything since a certain time. In psychogenic fugue, the person suddenly travels to a new location, takes up a new identity, and is unable to recall his previous identity. Multiple personality is probably the most fascinating of the dissociative disorders, if not of all mental disorders. In multiple personality, the dissociation results in the creation of two or more distinct personalities, each with its own memories, perceptions, values, etc. Sometimes the various personalities that emerge are aware of one another, sometimes not. Multiple personality disorders have been the subject of many popular books and films. For a very readable and up-to-date summary and bibliography on this subject consult, the Harvard Medical School Mental Health Letter, April 1985. Finally, depersonalization disorder involves a sense of estrangement or detachment from the normal sense of self to the point of causing the disruption of normal social or occupational functioning.

Case Vignette. Burt Tate is a 42-year-old white male. He was brought to the emergency room by the police. He had been in a fight in the diner where he worked. When the police began to question him, they discovered that he had no identification, that he had drifted into town last week and begun working as a short-order cook at the diner. He did not know where he had come from before this time and could not recall any details of his past life. When the police ran a description check on him, they found that he fit the description of Gene Smith, a missing person who disappeared one month ago from a town 200 miles away. A physical exam did not uncover any head trauma and there was no evidence of drug abuse. A visit by his wife confirmed the real identity of the man as Gene Smith. His wife explained that he had been having a lot of problems with his job and had been under a considerable amount of stress. There was no history of any previous psychiatric disorder or serious medical problem.

Psychosexual Disorders

Psychosexual disorders refer only to disorders of sexual arousal which, for the most part, have psychological origins. Since there are so many subclasses of psychosexual disorders, we have placed their descriptions in Table 9.8 to avoid confusion.

Table 9.8 Psychosexual Disorders

Gender Identity Disorders

Gender identity is the sense of knowing to which sex one belongs, that is, the awareness that "I am a male," or "I am a female."

Individuals with this disorder usually complain that they are uncomfortable wearing the clothes of their own anatomical sex; frequently this discomfort leads to cross-dressing (dressing in clothes of the other sex). Often they choose to engage in activities that in our culture tend to be associated with the other sex.

Paraphilias (deviant sexual attractions)

The essential feature of disorders in this subclass is that unusual or bizarre imagery or acts are necessary for sexual excitement.

- *Fetishism*

  The essential feature is the use of nonliving objects (fetishes) as a repeatedly preferred or exclusive method of achieving sexual excitement. Fetishes tend to be articles of clothing, such as female undergarments, shoes, boots, etc.

- *Transvestism*

  The essential feature is recurrent and persistent crossdressing by a heterosexual male that during at least the initial phase of the illness is for the purpose of sexual excitement. Transvestite phenomena range from occasional solitary wearing of female clothes to extensive involvement in a transvestite subculture.

- *Zoophilia*

  The essential feature is the use of animals as a repeatedly preferred or exclusive method of achieving sexual excitement.

- *Pedophilia*

  The essential feature is the act or fantasy of engaging in sexual activity with prepubertal children as a repeatedly preferred or exclusive method of achieving sexual excitement. Adults

(continued)

Table 9.8 *(continued)*

with this disorder are oriented toward children of the other sex twice as often as toward children of the same sex.

- *Exhibitionism*

The essential feature is repetitive acts of exposing the genitals to an unsuspecting stranger for the purpose of achieving sexual excitement with no attempt of further sexual activity with the stranger.

- *Voyeurism*

The essential feature is repetitive looking at unsuspecting people, usually strangers, who are either naked, in the act of disrobing, or engaging in sexual activity, as the repeatedly preferred or exclusive method of achieving sexual excitement.

- *Sexual Masochism*

The essential feature is sexual excitement produced in an individual by his or her own suffering. The diagnosis of sexual masochism is warranted under either of two conditions:

1. A preferred or exclusive mode of producing sexual excitement is to be humiliated, bound, beaten, or otherwise made to suffer.
2. The individual has intentionally participated in an activity in which he or she was physically harmed or his or her life was threatened in order to produce sexual excitement, which did occur.

- *Sexual Sadism*

The essential feature is the infliction of physical or psychological suffering on another person in order to achieve sexual excitement. The diagnosis of sexual sadism is warranted under any of three different conditions:

1. On a nonconsenting partner, the individual has repeatedly and intentionally inflicted psychological or physical suffering in order to achieve sexual excitement.
2. With a consenting partner, a repeatedly preferred or exclusive mode of achieving sexual excitement combines humiliation with simulated or mildly injurious bodily suffering.
3. On a consenting partner, bodily injury that is extensive, permanent, or possibly mortal is inflicted in order to achieve sexual excitement.

- *Atypical Paraphilia*

This is a residual category for individuals with Paraphilias that cannot be classified in any of the other categories. Such conditions include: Coprophilia (feces); Frotteurism (rubbing); Klismaphilia (enema); Mysophilia (filth); Necrophilia (corpse); Telephone Scatologia (lewdness); and Urophilia (urine).

- *Psychosexual Dysfunctions*

The essential feature is inhibition in the appetitive or psychophysiological changes that characterize the complete sexual response cycle.

An essential feature of each disorder is that it must be the repeatedly preferred or exclusive mode of achieving sexual excitement. The only exceptions to this are Sexual Sadism and Sexual Masochism—in their more extreme forms one incidence of the behavior is enough for the diagnosis. Second, the psychosexual disorders occur almost exclusively in males. With Gender Identity Disorders the ratio of male to female occurrence is between 2 : 1 to 8 : 1. With Paraphilias, occurrences in females are virtually unheard of with the exception of Sexual Masochism and Sexual Sadism. You might speculate as to the reason Sexual Masochism and Sexual Sadism are exceptions to both of the above points.

Factitious Disorders (Artificial or Sham Disorder)

In the *factitious disorders,* the person voluntarily goes to great lengths to put himself in a position of becoming a patient. He will often risk health or even life through self-inflicted injury, drugs, etc., solely to become a patient.

Case Vignette. A 29-year-old laboratory technician was admitted to the medical service via the emergency room for gross hematuria. The patient said that she was being treated for lupus by a physician in a different city. She also mentioned that she had Von Willebrand's Disease as a child.

On the third day of her hospitalization, a medical student mentioned to the resident that he had seen this patient several weeks prior at a different hospital in the area. A search of the patient's belongings revealed a cache of anticoagulant medication. When confronted with this information, she hurriedly signed out of the hospital against medical advice.

That evening she was admitted to another hospital in the area with similar complaints (adapted from Spitzer, et al., 1981).

Disorders of Impulse Control Not Elsewhere Classified

We have already described disorders where lack of impulse control was an essential feature in the illness. For example, the Substance Abuse Disorders and the Paraphilias involve lack of impulse control. This class of disorders is interesting because it emphasizes the idea that mental disorders involve any mental illness where distress or disability occur. There are six subcategories within this disorder

1. *Pathological Gambling*—can't resist impulse to gamble
2. *Kleptomania*—can't resist impulse to steal
3. *Pyromania*—can't resist impulse to set fires
4. *Intermittent Explosive Disorder*—can't resist aggressive impulses
5. *Isolated Explosive Disorder*—can't resist aggressive impulses on a one time basis but has violent and disastrous effects
6. *Atypical Impulse Control Disorder*—any other situational inability to resist impulses

Case Vignette. A pregnant 27-year-old mother of six seen at the community mental health center confided that she was subject to "spells," which went away as quickly as they came. During the "spells" she struck her children and threw things at her husband with little or no provocation. She confessed that she loved her family and didn't know why she did those things. She expressed feelings of deep regret and shame and a release of tension after the incidents.

Adjustment Disorders

Usually when a person suffers greatly from some psychosocial stress such as breaking up with a girlfriend or boyfriend, divorce, being laid off at work, getting married, or going to college for the first time, we normally expect some small problems with adjustment. However, sometimes people overreact to those stresses and do not adapt well—to the point where the person functions poorly socially or at work. These are classified as *adjustment disorders.* The person may become overly anxious, moody (usually depressed), withdrawn, or simply not able to perform at school or work.

Case Vignette. A 24-year-old single dental technician terminated brief psychotherapy after 10 sessions. She entered treatment two weeks after she discovered that the man she had been involved with for four months was married and wanted to stop seeing her. She reacted with bouts of crying, unaccustomed absences on three occasions from her job, and vague thoughts that the future was so pessimistic that life might not be worth the effort. She responded to mixed supportive-insight psychotherapy and toward the end of the treatment had begun dating a law student whom she met at a local cafe (adapted from Spitzer, et al., 1981).

Axis II

Personality Disorders

Everyone has a personality, and we often think of people we know in terms of types of personality (see Chapter 8). For example, some people are "outgoing, friendly," some "a little aloof, quiet" etc. All of these variations in personality are quite normal and acceptable. However, sometimes personality variations become so inflexible or maladaptive that they cause a great deal of distress and/or disability for the person. *Personality disorders* can be classified in terms of their prominent features. To avoid confusion, we have placed these categories of disorder in Table 9.9.

Case Vignette. Susan is a 26-year-old teacher's aide who came to the center for counseling. For six months she had been feeling increasingly lonely and "lost" since her sister, who is two years older, was married and moved out of town. This sister had been Susan's only real social contact; otherwise she had no girl-

Table 9.9 Personality Disorders

Paranoid Personality Disorder

The essential feature is a Personality Disorder in which there is a pervasive and unwarranted suspiciousness and mistrust of people, hypersensitivity, and restricted affectivity not due to another mental disorder, such as Schizophrenia, or a Paranoid Disorder.

Schizoid Personality Disorder

The essential feature is a Personality Disorder in which there is a defect in the capacity to form social relationships, evidenced by the absence of warm, tender feelings for others and indifference to praise, criticism, and the feelings of others. Individuals with this disorder show little or no desire for social involvement, usually prefer to be "loners," and have few, if any, close friends.

Schizotypal Personality Disorder

The essential feature is a Personality Disorder in which there are various oddities of thought, perception, speech, and behavior that are not severe enough to meet the criteria for Schizophrenia. The disturbance in the content of thought may include magical thinking (or in children, bizarre fantasies or preoccupations), ideas of reference, or paranoid ideation. Prominent Personality Feature: Dramatic, Emotional, or Erratic.

Histrionic Personality Disorder

The essential feature is a Personality Disorder in which there are overly dramatic, reactive, and intensely expressed behavior and characteristic disturbances in interpersonal relationships.

Narcissistic Personality Disorder

The essential feature is a Personality Disorder in which there is a grandiose sense of self-importance or uniqueness; preoccupation with fantasies of unlimited success; exhibitionistic need for constant attention and admiration; characteristic responses to threats of self-esteem; and characteristic disturbances in interpersonal relationships, such as feelings of entitlement, interpersonal exploitativeness, relationships that alternate between the extremes of overidealization and devaluation, and lack of empathy.

Antisocial Personality Disorder

The essential feature is a Personality Disorder in which there is a history of continuous and chronic antisocial behavior in which the rights of others are violated, persistence into adult life of a pattern of antisocial behavior that began before the age of 15, and failure to sustain good job performance over a period of several years.

Borderline Personality Disorder

The essential feature is a Personality Disorder in which there is instability in a variety of areas, including interpersonal behavior, mood, and self-image. A profound identity disturbance may be manifested by uncertainty about several issues relating to identity, such as self-image, gender identity, or long-term goals or values. There may be problems tolerating being alone, and chronic feelings of emptiness or boredom. Prominent Personality Feature: Anxious or Fearful.

(continued)

Table 9.9 *(continued)*

Avoidant Personality Disorder

The essential feature is a Personality Disorder in which there is hypersensitivity to potential rejection, humiliation, or shame; an unwillingness to enter into relationships unless given unusually strong guarantees of uncritical acceptance; social withdrawal in spite of a desire for affection and acceptance; and low self-esteem.

Dependent Personality Disorder

The essential feature is a Personality Disorder in which the individual passively allows others to assume responsibility for major areas of his or her life because of a lack of self-confidence and an inability to function independently; the individual subordinates his or her own needs to those of others on whom he or she is dependent in order to avoid any possibility of having to be self-reliant.

Compulsive Personality Disorder

The essential feature is a Personality Disorder in which there generally are restricted abilities to express warm and tender emotions; perfectionism that interferes with the ability to grasp "the big picture," insistence that others submit to his or her way of doing things; excessive devotion to work and productivity to the exclusion of pleasure; and indecisiveness.

---

friends to speak of and was extremely afraid of men. Because she felt that she had very little to offer, she had always anticipated that men, even if attracted, would quickly find fault with her and she would be "dropped." Although she wanted to get married, she never dated a man beyond three dates. This was her first attempt to get professional help.

Specific Developmental Disorders

This last classification of disorders is reserved for specific disorders that do not result from any of the earlier discussed disorder categories. For example, a child who was significantly slow in reading or language development might simply be mentally retarded (the first classification on Axis I). However, if an individually administered IQ test for this child results in a finding of normal intellectual functioning, then he or she would be classified as having a Specific Developmental Disorder.

The categories of Specific Developmental Disorders follow:

Reading	significant delay in development of reading skills (previously referred to as "dyslexia")
Arithmetic	significant impairment in development of arithmetic skills
Language	significant problem in either (1) expressing language verbally or (2) comprehending oral language
Articulation	significant problem with the articulation of the later learned speech sounds (such as r, sh, th, f, z, l, or ch); omission or substitutions for these sounds gives the impression of "baby talk"

Bringing It All Together

The DSM-IV classification system, which structures and defines mental disorders, is based upon the idea of deviations in terms of distress and disability—not simply behavior that is bizarre or different from cultural norms.

What is normal and what is abnormal lies on a continuum. While we talk about mental disorders being maladaptive, much of the time we must remember that the disorder is adaptive in the person's terms of experience. The savant has adapted within the capacity he does have. And in the depressed, the impulsive, the hypochondriac, and the many others who don't wish to have their disorders—their behavior represents the best they have been able to do on their own and under the circumstances.

Where possible, the DSM-IV attempts to list the predisposing factors that might lead to a mental disorder. Often this is "unknown." In some cases, as we saw with schizophrenia, we are beginning to understand the predisposing biochemistry, physiology, and anatomy of specific mental disorders. With new techniques such as positron emission tomography and rapidly increasing understanding of behavior genetics and DNA, the future looks bright for clearer explanations.

Finally, the savants represent a double, at-odds puzzle for abnormal psychology. They attest to the potential of the abnormal human brain in two opposing directions. There are many researchers presently attempting to understand the cognitive, behavioral, and physiological bases of savant behavior. It is likely that both the technical and popular psychology literature will be grappling with these special people for many years to come.

Glossary

adaptive functioning: In the diagnostic strategies of the DSM-IV, the degree to which a person functions well in social situations, occupation, and leisure activities.

adjustment disorders: A class of mental disorders wherein the person overreacts to stressful events, for example, to loss of job, divorce, etc.

affective disorders: Mental disorders that involve excessively high or low mood swings.

agoraphobia: An irrational fear of being either alone or in public places.

anxiety disorders: A broad category of mental disorders that are based upon an excessive and unwarranted fear.

atheoretical: Not theoretical in basis or nature.

autistic savant: A person (usually a child) who is generally autistic, but who has a very high degree of skill in special areas of cognitive function and behavior (see also *infantile autism*).

bipolar mood shifts: Mood swings that include some sequence of high and low feelings.

case vignette: A short, descriptive sketch that describes a patient, her behavior, her life situations(s), and any other data that might be significantly related to her disorder.

catatonia: Rigidity of thought, movement, or posturing.

compensatory dynamics: Forces that help a person or system make up for some loss so that he or she can maintain an equilibrium of function.

conversion disorder: A specific loss of sensory or motor control that removes the person from potentially painful circumstances.

depersonalization disorder: An uncontrollable flight or estrangement from the normally perceived self. This disorder has no known physical basis.

depression: Low mood swings.

Diagnostic and Statistical Manual of Mental Disorders: See DSM-IV.

diagnostic axes: In the diagnostic strategies of the DSM-IV, different lines (axes) of approach used in understanding and treating mental disorders. The axes may also be thought of as dimensions of the person being diagnosed.

differential diagnosis decision trees: In the diagnostic strategies of the DSM-IV, eight suggested decision paths that help mental health professionals rule in or rule out the many mental disorders a client might have. Each decision path (or "tree") is a structured flow of yes/no questioning concerning the client. Usually only one or two decision paths (along with much other information) allows the professional to make a diagnosis.

dissociative disorders: A class of mental disorders with an alteration or loss of the normal integration of consciousness (see also normal dissociation, and neodissociative).

DSM-IV: The *Diagnostic and Statistical Manual of Mental Disorders,* fourth edition, of the American Psychiatric Association. This manual aids mental health professionals in the diagnosis of mental disorders.

DSM-IV Training Guide: A 158-page training guide which helps mental health care professionals learn to use the DSM-IV.

factitious disorders: A class of mental disorders wherein the person voluntarily fakes illness or the incidence of injury in order to become a patient. While the behavior is voluntary, it is compulsive in nature.

genetic code: The chemical information in DNA that contains the instructions for processes that constitute the gene-directed making of an organism.

holistic approach: Any view or practice that takes into account all known aspects or subparts of a system in order to understand or modify it.

hypochondriasis: A mental disorder in which there is an irrational fear and belief that one has a disease for which there is no actual basis in fact.

idiot savant: Outdated term, see retarded savant.

incidence rates: Calculated "lifetime risks" of contracting a particular disorder.

infantile autism: A general unresponsiveness to others, often with atypical responses to the environment. Due to, or concomitant with, an onset prior to 2½ years of age, there is impairment of language development.

interrater agreement: The degree to which different raters agree in the diagnosis of mental disorders or other ratings or rankings of individuals.

interregional processing: Processing of information between different regions of the brain.

mania: Excessively high mood swings.

mental disorder: A mental or behavioral pattern that causes a person disabling pain or impairment of daily functions.

mental retardation: Significant below-average intellectual functioning at a general level.

multiple personality: The development of two more distinct personalities in the same person. Each is a separate integrated personality. Often the different personalities are not aware of one another. It has no known physical basis.

obsessive compulsive disorders: A class of disorders in which a person has uncontrollable repetitive thoughts, ideas, images, or impulses (obsessions); and/or uncontrollable repetitive behavior (compulsions).

organic mental disorders: Any mental disorder that has as a basis the derangement of the physical brain. These disorders include, for example, intoxication, some memory disorders, and delirium.

panic attack: The sudden occurrence of extreme apprehension or terror, often with feelings of impending doom.

paranoid disorders: Psychotic disorders based upon delusions about everyday experiences. Usually the person with this type of disorder will have misconceptions that someone is out to get them or that things are secretly going on behind their backs.

personality disorders: A broad class of mental disorders wherein extreme and inflexible characteristics of personality impair a person's functioning in everyday activities.

phobias: A broad class of irrational fears of things, events, and situations. The victim recognizes that the fear is unwarranted, but can do little about its effect. The phobias include simple phobias, agoraphobia, and social phobia.

prevalence: The number of active cases of a mental disorder that can be identified at any given time for a geographical region or a population.

psychogenic amnesia: A rather pronounced sudden loss of memory for which there is no known physical basis.

psychogenic fugue: A sudden, unexpected and unexplainable flight (fugue) from a person's normal home or work to a new location with the assumption of a new identity. This disorder has no known physical basis.

psychogenic pain: The feeling and complaint of pain that has no known physical explanation.

psychosexual disorders: A broad class of mental disorders in which sexual arousal and satisfaction are regularly obtained in ways that are ultimately painful or impairing to the person's everyday life.

psychosocial stressors: Stresses or hardships in a person's personal and social life that may contribute to a mental disorder.

psychotic: Loss of contact with reality.

relative judgment: Human characteristics such as personality, intelligence, and normality versus abnormality do not exist in any absolute sense of measurement. Therefore judgment about these characteristics must always be done through comparison with other individuals or groups.

retarded savant: A person who is generally retarded, but who has a very high degree of skill in special areas of cognitive function and behavior. (See also mental retardation).

schizophrenic disorders: Severe pervasive mental derangements that impair functioning in all aspects of everyday behavior and thought. Impairment includes that of communication with others, thought, perception, feelings, self-experience, motivation, social relations, movement, and inappropriate anguish.

simple phobia: An unwarranted fear of some object or situation that does not fit the criteria for other specific phobias. Simple phobias include the fears with which the layman is familiar, for example, fear of snakes, elevators, the number "13," etc.

social phobia: An irrational fear of being looked at by others.

somatoform disorders: A class of mental disorders wherein the person has a bodily (somato) complaint with no actual physical basis. However, the person has no control over the symptoms.

substance abuse: An atypical overuse of a substance for more than one month that leads to impairment of everyday activities.

substance dependence: Substance abuse that includes substance tolerance and/or painful withdrawal if the substance is not used.

substance tolerance: In substance abuse, where the person must increase the level of substance dosage in order to maintain the effect.

unipolar mood shifts: Mood swings that include some sequence of low (depressed) and normal feelings.

Psychological Disorders: Doing Psychology on Your Own

Lois McDermott

Basic Concept #9—The DSM-IV

The Origin. Down through history various explanations of psychological disorders (mental illness, psychopathology) have held sway. Most notable and interesting are explanations such as devil-possession, imbalance of the body's humors, moral turpitude, "bad seed" (genes), punishment for the sins of the parents, the self or other family members, and criminal personality. More recently, attention shifted to the traumas and/or unconscious conflicts arising from disturbed childhood experiences.

The Catalogue. Regardless of the cause, the cataloguing of the various types of psychological disorders has an interesting history in and of itself. Sometimes disorders have had more political significance than medical significance. For example there was a mental disorder which was prominent in slaves during the 19th century—namely the "urge to flee captivity." Many sexual practices that are commonplace today and then, were defined as symptoms/causes of mental illness until well into the 20th century—e.g., masturbation, nocturnal emission, homosexuality, oral sex and female orgasm.

The Diagnostic and Statistical Manual, Fourth Edition (DSM-IV) is the bible of emotional and mental disorders. This compendium cuts such a wide swath across human experience that there is a diagnosis waiting for all of us—and many of us have already earned one. The multitude of diagnoses described today in the DSM-IV essentially guarantees that all of us will earn the diagnoses of some psychological distress at some point in our life—just as we all have suffered physical illness and dental problems. The range includes very rare disorders and extremely common ones; those that are severely debilitating and those that are simply annoying; those that have a good prognosis and those for which we have no treatment or cure. The trend in conceptualizing mental illness is to de-stigmatize it and treat it no differently than any other malady. However, many find they suffer terrible stigma, shame, self-blame and pessimism around emotional problems and wish to avoid and deny their reality.

This humanizing approach to mental illness is not always the case. Defining certain patterns of emotions, behaviors or cognitions as abnormal is a tricky business. Who decides? Diagnosing mental illness has long been used for politically repressive purposes—in our society, as well as others around the world. Diagnoses have been used to deny citizens their freedom, custody of their children, control of their finances, and have been used to punish those who have behaviors and/or lifestyles of which the dominant group disapproves. We don't have to look far to document these abuses. In every era constant vigilance is required to prevent the misuse of diagnosis. A most recent example is the inclusion of "late luteal phase dysphoria" in the DSM-IV. In short, the experience of unpleasant physical and/or emotional symptoms prior to menstruation is now defined as a type of mental illness—one that only half of the population could experience.

Carrying the diagnosis of mental illness does not inevitably predict a dysfunctional life. I have struggled intermittently for 30+ years with episodes of depression. In spite of this malady, I have been able to complete three educational degrees and post doctoral training, rear a family, do research, publish, hold down a demanding teaching job and maintain a psychologist's license and help others heal from their disorders. Mental illness need not be a death knell. Those who suffer mental illness need not be defined by their symptoms—I am not a depressive person; I am a parent, spouse, teacher, psychotherapist, voter, church-goer, friend, and sibling who episodically experiences depressive symptoms.

Unit Focus. What feature(s) define(s) a behavioral, emotional, or cognitive pattern as "disordered?" Is it determined by how rare the pattern occurs in society in general? If so then alcoholism, which occurs in 30 percent of the population, would not be included in the DSM-IV. Is the degree of suffering of the individual the defining characteristic? If so then mania and dementia, and other disorders that "sufferers" deny or are unaware of would be omitted. Is degree of discomfort or annoyance caused by the pattern to "normal" members of society the defining characteristic? If so then we would need to have diagnoses for those who wear stripes with plaids, who pick their nose, who chew with their mouths open, and who play their music systems too loud.

Psychological symptoms are collected into general categories and then subdivided further by outstanding features. The main categories of interest in this unit are disorders marked by (1) maladaptive responses to stress, (2) anxiety and fear of loss of control, (3) atypical physical deficits, (4) dissociation of thought, affects and behavior, (5) changes in mood, and (6) disturbed cognitive states.

Study Objectives

1. Understand the basic organization and use of the DSM-IV.
2. Distinguish feature(s) of each of the six general categories of psychological disorders.
3. Learn the components of the diathesis stress model of psychological disorders.
4. Know the somatic, cognitive, emotional and behavioral aspects of depression.
5. Know the core features of psychotic disorders.
6. Distinguish among the subtypes of disorders marked by physical symptoms.
7. Define the main subtypes of anxiety and dissociative disorders.
8. Understand how various personality theories are used to explain the causes of mental disorders.

Key Terms

adaptive functioning
adjustment disorders
affective disorders
agoraphobia
anxiety disorders
atheoretical
autistic savant
bipolar mood shifts
case vignette
catatonia
compensatory dynamics
conversion disorder
depersonalization disorder
depression
Diagnostic and Statistical Manual of Mental Disorders
diagnostic axes
differential diagnosis decision trees
dissociative disorders
DSM-IV
DSM-III Training Guide
factitious disorders
genetic code
holistic approach
hypochondriasis
idiot savant
incidence rates
infantile autism
interrater agreement
interregional processing
mania
mental disorder
mental retardation
multiple personality
obsessive compulsive disorders
organic mental disorders
panic attack
paranoid disorders
personality disorders
phobias
prevalence
psychogenic amnesia
psychogenic fugue
psychogenic pain
psychosexual disorders
psychosocial stressors
psychotic
relative judgment
retarded savant
schizophrenic disorders
simple phobia
social phobia
somatoform disorders
substance abuse
substance dependence
substance tolerance
unipolar mood shifts

Problem Set #9: Psychological Disorders

A. *Classification of Psychological Disorders*

Identify each of the disorders illustrated below.

1. Mark was a paramedic in Vietnam who now works as a nurse in the local hospital. He's been doing fine for years working on the pediatric unit. Recently he was transferred to the emergency room and has had a great deal of absenteeism. His memory is flooded with terrible images of mangled bodies every time he hears the code for incoming ambulances.
2. Whenever Ben gets a new job he has to be sure that his office is large with doors and windows which open. It must also be below the 4th floor because he cannot ride on elevators. Ben feels very anxious and uncomfortable in enclosed spaces.
3. Jan hates her job as an assembly-line worker in a microchip factory. She wants to quit but her father would be extremely angry if she quit since he pulled some strings to get her the job. One morning she woke up and her hand was paralyzed. She could not work and was laid off. Medical examination ruled out any known physiological cause for the paralysis.
4. Mark is an emergency room jockey. Every time he has a headache, stomachache or muscle ache he goes to the emergency room. His medical chart is a mile thick. The doctors reassure him that he has no brain tumors, cancers or other rare disease. But Mark insists that he is seriously ill and seeks further consultation and numerous diagnostic tests.
5. Jim recently moved away from his family, friends and lover to start a new job in a distant city. His job requires a lot of overtime and he hasn't been able to meet new people. He feels really down and lonely a great deal of the time and his work is beginning to suffer.
6. When Mr. and Mrs. Cameron met their son Harry at the airport at the beginning of Spring break, they were somewhat confused by his behavior. He spoke rapidly and excitedly about his classes, his girlfriend, world religions, new advancements in molecular biology, similarities between various Afro pop groups and the Mayan calendar, among other topics. Over the next few days, Mr. and Mrs. Cameron found it increasingly difficult to get a word in edgewise. Meanwhile Harry hasn't slept since he came home and claims he feels fine.

7. Ali had eight panic attacks in the last couple of weeks—on the bus, during class, in the grocery store, at home while watching TV. She feels restless and nervous much of the time.
8. Barry suffers from asthma which seems to get worse when he argues with his wife, or is under stress at work.
9. As Amy was leaving work late one evening she witnessed a murder. The murderer looked her right in the eye and threatened to harm her. When the police arrived, Amy was in a state of shock and could not be questioned. Amy could not remember anything about the event, or what she had been doing for the past few days.
10. Matt and his wife were having severe marital problems after the accidental drowning of their 4 year old daughter. One day Matt's wife disappeared without a trace. Three years later a private detective found her living in the town where she had gone to college. She had taken on the name and occupation of her old college roommate—a kindergarten teacher. When Matt arrived to bring her home she did not recognize him and claimed she had never been married. However, she had no explanation for her whereabouts in the preceding period of her life.
11. A month after Cynthia was raped she discovered she was pregnant. Feeling confident her husband was the true father she decided against abortion. A few months after the baby was born she became preoccupied with the thought the baby might become ill and die. She became very concerned about keeping herself and the house free of germs. After changing the baby's diaper she would wash her hands five times. Within a few weeks she was washing her hands ten times each time she changed the baby, picked up the baby, touched the baby's toys, bottle, food or even thought about the baby.
12. A college student is describing her new roommate, Beth. "Beth is really weird. Sometimes she's really sweet, too sweet, like saccharin. When she's like that she insists her name is not Beth but Beverly. Most of the time she's a really athletic, outgoing type. Then it's okay to call her Beth. Still other times she's gone for a couple of days and then returns but with no memory of where she's been. She gets phone calls for Betty but has no idea who is calling. If I call her Betty she tells me to go to hell."
13. Simon is experiencing slurred speech, memory loss and periods of confusion after his motorcycle accident.
14. Mary says she never feels really happy anymore and never feels really sad. Mary has been beaten numerous times by her husband during their 15-year marriage. When asked why she doesn't leave she says it wouldn't make any difference, he would just find her and beat her again anyway.
15. Hank has been crying a lot lately for no apparent reason. He has insomnia and has no appetite and lost a great deal of weight. He lies in bed most of the day because nothing seems worth getting up for. He quit the lacrosse team and broke up with his girlfriend. He sees no reason to live and thinks a great deal about killing himself. He can't seem to forgive himself for not spending more time with his twin brother who suffers from cerebral palsy. He feels terribly guilty that he is healthy but his brother is confined to a wheelchair.

See Appendix C for answers to problem set.

10

Treatment of Mental Disorders

What Is Psychology Able to Do About Mental Disorders?

In Chapter 9 we discussed mental disorders. In this chapter, we will see how psychology can be applied to the treatment of mental disorders. To introduce you to the ideas of treatment and therapy, we shall take a close look at an area of mental disorder where psychology has been especially successful: the treatment of *phobias* and *panic disorders*.

Phobias

Somewhere in your neighborhood, there may be a person like Ann, who didn't leave her home for years. Her behavior wasn't caused by physical illness, advanced age or psychosis (loss of contact with reality). Instead, she suffered from *agoraphobia* (see Figure 10.1), a debilitating condition due to marked fear of being alone, or paradoxically, in public places, that restricts a person's lifestyle.

For 25 years, Ann had been afflicted with an intense, irrational fear of dying if she left her parents' home. It first occurred when she was 17 years old, safe in her bedroom doing homework, with a mysterious *panic attack* (a brief but powerful episode of chest pain, palpitations, rapid breathing, sweating and terror). As a result, she became phobic—unreasonably afraid of having more panic attacks and losing control. Because she was so terrified of what might happen, Ann began to avoid certain situations for no apparent reason (*avoidance behavior*).

As her worry about having more panic attacks grew worse, Ann shunned more and more activities. Eventually, she stopped going out altogether. She dropped out of school and gave up plans for a nursing career. Marriage and children were out of the question. Ann was completely unable to function without the constant companionship of one of her parents (*pathologic dependency*). Agoraphobia dominated her life, leaving her a virtual prisoner in her own house.

Some 20 years of traditional psychiatric treatment—insight-oriented psychotherapy, major tranquilizers and psychiatric hospitalization—were of no avail. There seemed to be no help for what was diagnosed as "anxiety neurosis." Ann's syndrome persisted until she began a course of medication and behaviorally-oriented treatment that worked.

After two years of relaxation exercises, practice exposures to feared situations (for Ann, anything outside her parents' home) and intensive supportive work, she is living on her own and functioning almost normally. She now works in a phobia clinic, where she encourages others along the road to recovery. And she hasn't had a panic attack in about three years. Advancements in the

Figure 10.1 Agoraphobia

diagnosis, treatment, and general understanding of phobia cases such as Ann's are very recent. Simply stated, a phobia is "an irrational, involuntary fear that is inappropriate to the situation."

The American Psychiatric Association's current edition of its *Diagnostic and Statistical Manual of Mental Disorders* (DSM-IV) describes three types of phobic disorders: agoraphobia, social phobia, and simple phobia. Theoretically, each can exist with or without panic attacks. In actuality, agoraphobia without panic attacks is quite rare. Many experts now view agoraphobia as a complication of panic disorder. The relationship between other phobias and panic attacks is uncertain.

Agoraphobia is not related to other serious psychiatric disorders such as major depression, schizophrenia, or paranoid disorders which you studied in Chapter 9. In essence, this condition involves multiple ("mixed") phobias, because many objects and situations are irrationally feared. However, the core fear is of having panic attacks and losing control.

Who Is Afflicted. Worldwide statistics are presently lacking on the prevalence of phobias. The Phobia Society of America, the largest organization in the world devoted to the study and treatment of phobias, estimates there are 20 million people with phobias in the United States. Agoraphobia itself was formerly believed to affect roughly one million individuals, or about one-half percent of the nation's people. Precise data on social and simple phobias are not known, but simple phobia is regarded as the most common in the general population, whereas agoraphobia is most prevalent among those actually seeking treatment.

Robert L. Dupont, Jr., (1983) clinical professor of psychiatry at Georgetown University Medical School in Washington, D.C., and founding president of the Phobia Society of America, believes that social phobia affects males and females more or less equally. Overall, women seem to be afflicted with agoraphobia and simple phobia more often than men. Dr. Dupont estimates that approximately 80 percent of phobics in treatment are female. Among the explanations advanced are the possible influences of learned sex-role behaviors, the action of female hormones on the nervous system and the demands of earning a living.

"Men are generally less able to miss work, so they keep on functioning even with panic attacks," says Michael Liebowitz, director of the anxiety disorders clinic at New York State Psychiatric Institute and assistant professor of psychiatry at Columbia University College of Physicians and Surgeons in New York City. "Given the same anxiety attacks, I've found that women more readily tend to become house-bound, whereas men may instead turn to alcohol" (Dupont, 1983).

Children are commonly afflicted with phobias, especially phobias that are related to normal developmental fears (for example, phobias regarding animals, doctors, darkness). The disorder peaks in children between the ages of two and four. As with adults, phobias are more frequent among female children than males. Interestingly, most phobic adults were not phobic children.

Phobias usually begin between the ages of 15 and 30, with the average age of onset at 24 years. Most phobics seem to be people who function well in work, school, and interpersonal relationships. However, as you might guess, social phobics may be more isolated than most individuals. Phobics tend to be perfectionists, and especially sensitive, although they may hide their feelings and show a calm outward appearance to those around them.

Phobias usually begin when the person is experiencing a physical or psychological stress that is out of the ordinary for him or her. For example, surgery, childbirth, marriage or loss of a loved one may precipitate the initial phobic experience, which often takes the form of a panic attack.

Fears. Joseph Wolpe and Peter Lang (1969, 1977) have developed a widely used survey that helps identify and quantify people's fears. It is called the *Fear Survey Schedule,* and contains the measurement of 108 different fears. Table 10.1 contains a sample of the stimulus objects and situations which are included in the survey. Along with the items, I have included the responses of 46 of my own students so that you can get an idea of what fears college students might have. Note that some of my students are "very much" disturbed by the items reported.

If you have rated some of the items as fearing them very much, do you need treatment? If your fear(s) are working against you to the point that you are making career decisions around them, or find yourself not functioning well because of them, treatment is in order.

Treatments. Until about 10 years ago, *insight-oriented psychotherapy* was customarily employed in the treatment of phobias. Results were generally poor. Although the patient often gained in terms of general personal growth and self-knowledge, the actual phobic symptoms usually resisted treatment.

Today, two modes of treatment or therapy are most commonly used, often in combination. The first is a relearning method that requires actual exposure to the phobic stimulus. This is done gradually, repeatedly and with intensive support. Variously called *supported exposure, contextual therapy,* or *in vivo treatment* (real life), this type of therapy is relatively short-term, usually lasting 10 to 20 weeks.

The support element may consist of a group or individual who accompanies the phobic patient into the feared situation. Family members, psychiatrists, clinical psychologists, various trained therapists, and former phobics themselves, like Ann, provide support during the exposure phase of the treatment. Relaxation exercises are usually included.

A treatment session with an agoraphobic might involve the therapist going to the patient's home and escorting him or her, literally step by step, to the bus for a brief ride. Some of the techniques employed include counting exercises or the repetition of reassuring phrases such as: When the fear appears, wait and let it pass!

The second type of therapy involves prescribing medications currently approved to treat other medical and psychiatric conditions. Usually,

Table 10.1 Fear Schedule

On the following scale, how much are you disturbed by the items?

	0	1	2	3	4
0. Not at all	| |	| |	| |	| |	| |
1. A little	| |	| |	| |	| |	| |
2. A fair amount	| |	| |	| |	| |	| |
3. Much	| |	| |	| |	| |	| |
4. Very much	| |	| |	| |	| |	| |

Items	*Distribution of student responses*				
	0	1	2	3	4
Open wounds	9	15	10	8	4
Being alone	23	10	10	2	1
Speaking in public	4	14	12	10	6
People who seem insane	5	15	17	6	3
Falling	10	21	9	6	0
Dentists	16	14	9	4	3
Failure	3	11	14	10	8
Looking down from high buildings	6	14	9	14	3
Journeys by airplane	32	6	4	2	2
Darkness	27	9	7	3	0
Fire	13	15	11	5	2
Sick people	13	21	9	3	0
Being touched by others	25	16	4	1	0
Flying insects	17	14	10	4	1
Crowds	29	13	2	2	0
Mice or rats	16	18	7	2	3
Human blood	22	15	6	0	3
Feeling rejected by others	5	11	14	9	7
Feeling disapproved of	5	13	16	9	3
Harmless snakes	18	11	6	8	3
Taking written tests	12	15	12	6	1
Germs	18	23	3	1	1
Being punished by God	14	12	8	3	9
Hurting the feelings of others	3	7	18	12	6
Marriage	18	10	13	1	4
Hospitals	14	13	13	3	3

according to the experts, medication is helpful when there is a history of panic attacks and when the phobia is not a specific (single) type. However, a single public speaking or flying phobia may respond well to one drug traditionally used in the treatment of high blood pressure. Certain antidepressant and antianxiety agents are being investigated for treating panic symptoms, allowing the practice of supported (in vivo) exposure to take place. We will discuss these drugs in more detail a little later. A great deal of research in this area is presently underway.

In a two-year follow-up study of 100 phobia patients who received a variety of treatments, 78 percent reported improved coping skills and 51 percent reported a significant reduction or complete elimination of phobic feelings—impressive figures that represent potential relief for millions of phobics.

Toward a Philosophy of Treatment

The title of this chapter is treatment of mental disorders. The mental disorders, of course, were discussed in some detail in Chapter 9. Mental disorders have to do not with "crazy people," but with presenting psychological and/or behavioral syndromes (cases) of ". . . either a painful symptom (distress) or impairment in one or more important areas of functioning (distress) or impairment in one or more important areas of functioning (disability)." Treatment is a matter of improving or removing the distress or disability which a person suffers. Treatment involves the application of much of what you have studied earlier in this book. This chapter on treatment should be thought of as an *applied psychology* chapter devoted to the potential mental disorders a person might encounter in life—psychology at work in the world. Psychology is applied in treatments in education, *engineering psychology, environmental psychology, industrial-organizational psychology,* and other areas. The relationship between these applied domains of psychology is an interesting one. If a manager in an industrial plant changes the work environment to remove stress and disability in his workers, it might be referred to as the application of industrial-organizational psychology. If a therapist would happen to recommend the same course of treatment for one of his clients, it might be referred to as *psychotherapy*. A similar application of psychology results in a similar outcome. The special interest of this chapter is the application of psychology to mental disorders.

Theories of Change and Treatment: A Perspective

The traditional explanatory models of human behavior have been discussed within several contexts in Chapters 1, 4, 5, 6, 8, and 9. These explanatory models include those you are familiar with—cognitive, behavioral, and physiological.

We should not think that psychologically-based therapies are somehow separate from the rest of psychology because they attempt to cause change in people. Changes are occurring in everyone, all of the time. Personality psychologist Lawrence Pervin (1984) has pointed this out in regard to change and therapies, "Change, of course, is not limited to psychotherapy—it occurs at all levels and to varying degrees."

The Professionals Involved in the Treatment of Mental Disorders

From a theoretical point of view, we are seeing a slightly different application of the various theories. Just as each of the traditional approaches contributes to our understanding of normal behavior, they all contribute to an integrated understanding of mental disorders. In the traditional areas of applied psychology, professionals such as teachers, managers, and workplace consultants are involved. In psychologically based treatment, a different set of equally trained professionals are involved. Table 10.2 briefly describes the training of these professionals.

Methodological and Empirical Aspects of Treatment

It is through applications to case studies that treatment can be best understood. In the final portion of this section, we will describe how all of the approaches have been integrated in the modern treatment of phobias.

Psychoanalysis

In Chapter 8, we studied the basic ideas that are involved in psychoanalysis. The actual clinical application of this point of view will be clearly related to what you have learned about it in Chapter 8. You may wish to review the ideas of the unconscious, the psychosexual stages of development, and the importance of early experiences.

Probing the Unconscious: Dreams. Because Sigmund Freud and his followers felt that the unconscious had a great deal to do with everyday

Table 10.2 Personnel in Psychotherapy

PROFESSIONAL

Clinical psychologist

Ph.D. in psychology with both research and clinical skill specialization. One-year internship in a psychiatric hospital or mental health center. *Or,* Psy.D. in psychology (a professional degree with more clinical than research specialization) plus one-year internship in a psychiatric hospital or mental health center.

Counseling psychologist

Ph.D. in psychology plus internship in a marital or student counseling setting; normally, the counseling psychologist deals with adjustment problems not involving mental disorder.

Psychiatrist

M.D. degree with internship plus residency training (usually three years) in a psychiatric hospital or mental health facility.

Psychoanalyst

M.D. or Ph.D. degree plus intensive training in theory and practice of psychoanalysis.

Clinical pastoral counselor

M. Divinity/D. Min./Th.D. plus internship and residency which includes personal involvement in psychotherapy or analysis.

Psychiatric social worker

B.A., M.S.W., or Ph.D. degree with specialized clinical training in mental health settings.

Psychiatric nurse

R.N. in nursing plus specialized training in care and treatment of psychiatric patients. M.A. and Ph.D. in psychiatric nursing is possible.

Occupational therapist

B.S. in occupational therapy plus internship training with physically or psychologically handicapped, helping them make the most of their resources.

PARAPROFESSIONAL

Community mental health worker

Capable person with limited professional training who works under professional direction (especially crisis intervention).

Alchohol or drug-abuse counselor

Limited professional training but trained in the evaluation and management of alcohol- and drug-addicted persons.

Pastoral counselor

Ministerial background plus training in psychology. Internship in mental health facility as a chaplain.

In both mental health clinics and hospitals, personnel from several fields may function as an interdisciplinary team in therapy—for example, a psychiatrist, a clinical psychologist, a social worker, a psychiatric nurse, and an occupational therapist may work together.

behavior, including abnormal behavior, they developed methods that allowed them to get at unconscious material. Freud's most important work in this area, according to Freud himself, was his volume on the *Interpretation of Dreams* (1953). Dreams, Freud felt, were the "royal road" to the unconscious. In psychoanalysis, dreams are thought to consist of both *manifest contents* and *latent contents.* In the manifest content, the dream is simply what it is thought to be by the dreamer. In the latent content is the hidden or unconscious meaning. Why are there two types of content? Many sexual or hostile wishes we have can be expressed safely if disguised by the manifest content of the dream. For example, according to psychoanalysis, a dream about flying (its manifest content), is a disguise for sexual desires (the latent wish). Calvin Hall's book, *The Meaning of Dreams* (1966) can be consulted for more on this (see also Chapter 3, *Dreams*). Since it is true that the meaning of our dreams often escapes us, the psychoanalytic view of dreams and fantasy is attractive.

Free Association. To help the analyst get closer to unconscious material and to discover what patient dream reports mean to that individual, Freud developed *free association* techniques. In free association, the client assumes a relaxed position. He, or she, is asked to talk about anything that comes to mind with no censoring. A person normally does this only with his, or her, innermost thoughts. Eventually, of course, the psychoanalyst becomes more and more familiar with the client's full tapestry of conscious and unconscious activity.

Therapists knowing what their dreams and past experiences really mean might give the clients a few helpful insights into themselves. However, for these people to get past the problem *fixation* (see Chapter 8) that is causing inadequate personality development, they must reexperience the emotional trauma and deal with it. The tapestry shows the clients themselves, at an earlier age being not gratified, not able, and anxious in the face of certain life events—the source of their present distress or disability. Now, he, or she, is reexposed to these situations. But they (their ego) can succeed this time because they are (1) older, (2) the situation is not all-consuming to them, and (3) the therapist does not act like the original persons in the client's earlier life situation (usually parents). The therapist has a warm, helping, supportive attitude (which the parent, for example, may not have had through ignorance). The therapist essentially plays a role in the tapestry of the client's earlier life. The clients transfer the feeling they had for earlier mother and father figures to the therapist. This development of *transference* is not unique to psychoanalytic therapy. Each one of us regularly transfers our deep feelings onto significant people in our lives. Whenever you "see" your mother, father, sister, or brother in someone, you are developing a transference. The emotional transference can variously be loving, sexual, hostile, admiring, etc. Now, with the therapist replacing the original figures that were related to the source of the maladaptive fixation, the therapist and the client can work together through the fixation.

Finally, probing of the unconscious can be guided through the use of *projective assessment techniques.* You studied these methods briefly in Chapter 8. It might be helpful for you to think about the relationship between transference and projection. The development of transference involves a full, complex, holistic projection which can be understood by the client and the therapist.

Case Vignette: Little Hans. "Little Hans" was the five-year-old young son of a friend of Freud's, Max Graf. While Freud did not work directly with little Hans, he corresponded regularly with Hans' father. Hans had a very strong phobia concerning horses. He was terrified they would bite him. This was a great problem because the fear virtually kept Hans indoors. In Vienna, shortly after the turn of the century, horses, of course, were in the streets everywhere! Hans, from the age of three to age five had an intense interest in his penis, his "widdler," as he referred to it. He was also very interested in the widdlers of everyone and every animal, including horses. During this time, Hans was very affectionate toward his mother (see *Oedipus complex,* Chapter 8). Hans reported a rather involved fantasy (not a dream): he imagined a big giraffe and a crumpled one, "In the night there was a big giraffe in the room and a crumpled one; and the big one called out because I took the crumpled one away from it. Then it stopped calling out; and then I sat down on top of the crumpled one." In this Oedipal fantasy, the giraffe's neck would be interpreted to be a manifest disguise of the father's penis. The crumpled giraffe symbolically represents the mother. The fear of horses biting him symbolized Hans' fear of his father for his Oedipal fantasies about his mother. Hans' father, who was quite knowledgeable of Freudian analysis, explained to Hans that his fear of horses was really coming from his fondness for his mother, his interest in widdlers, and that women do not have widdlers. Thanks to his father's open, therapist-like attitude, and the making of what was unconscious conscious, Hans made it through this temporary Oedipal fixation and his fear of horses. (This case vignette interpretation is essentially Freudian. Other interpretations are, of course, possible. From Freud, 1909, 1959, pp. 3–149.)

Client-Centered Therapy

Actualizing the Organizational Power of the Self. In Chapter 8, we discussed the personality theory of Carl Rogers. Now, we can put some of the assumptions of that theory to work. For the treatment methods of client-centered therapy, it will be important for you to recall the ideas of self-actualization and the need for positive regard.

The client-centered method is a matter of the therapist, or counselor, fully taking on the frame of reference of the client. The therapist tries to understand how his client sees the world, and how he sees himself in it. Then, with this orientation in mind, the therapist creates a climate of experiences and growth for the client. This climate includes these conditions for the relationship between the therapist and client: *congruence* or genuineness, *unconditional positive regard,* and *empathetic understanding.* If the therapist is to be genuine (and thereby bring the client to a genuineness of his or her own), he must be "himself" with the client. This is necessary even if, at times, the therapist must share with the client some negative feelings toward him. Unconditional positive regard means that the therapist lets the client know that he or she is respected as an important human being. The client is made to feel prized; that he is being regarded as a total human being; and that he is a good human being. This gives the client the confidence to explore his inner feelings completely. Finally, empathetic understanding means that the therapist is "with" the feelings and experiences of the client, and not simply reflecting them.

Centering attention upon the client can be described as friendship. You have noticed how when you are with a good friend you are yourself, and you can discuss anything without worrying about revealing something you shouldn't. You seem to be "with" the feelings and experiences of one another. Rogers feels these are the conditions for self-growth.

Case Vignette: Mrs. Oak. The case of Mrs. Oak (not her real name) has been presented in full detail by Rogers (Rogers & Dymond, 1954). The following vignette and description represents a very small portion of the case report.

> Mrs. Oak was a housewife in her late thirties who was in a deeply discordant relationship with her husband and also much disturbed in her relationship with her adolescent daughter, who had recently been through a serious illness which had been diagnosed as psychosomatic. Mrs. Oak felt that she must be to blame for this illness. She herself was a sensitive person, eager to be honest with herself and to search out the causes of her problems. She was a person with little formal education, though intelligent and widely read. (p. 262)
>
> By the third interview Mrs. Oak described a feeling in a way that is almost a forecast of what therapy was to mean for her. This is the way the interview started.
>
> ***Mrs. Oak:*** I feel very glad to get back today. (Both laugh.) A couple of things just came to my mind, say in passing so to speak. The fact that once I get into this thing, as I start talking, I'm not the least bit conscious of you. And I, of course, I know ideally I shouldn't (word lost) . . . but I'll simply have to go on as it's been. And, secondly, the realization that last time I was here I experienced a-an emotion I had never felt before—which surprised me and sort of shocked me a bit. And yet I thought, I think it has sort of a . . . the only word I can find to

describe it, the only verbalization is a kind of cleansing. I-I really felt terribly sorry for something, a kind of grief. And found myself comparing with, with things I had felt before, I-I . . . when Peggy was ill and I had felt this terrible anxiety and what I thought was a terrible kind of grief, I realize now it wasn't. It was a kind of hysterical feeling.

Therapist: You mean there, that this last was sort of somehow a pseudo-feeling. This that you felt here last time was a real, genuine emotion of deep regret.

Mrs. Oak: That's right. And I-I've never experienced it before. It sort of makes me wonder how many things I probably am sincerely sorry for, but just have never felt, covered up. (pp. 311–312)

[Mrs. Oak] was unusually sensitive to the process she was experiencing in herself. To use some of her expressions, she was feeling the pieces of a jigsaw puzzle, she was singing a song without words, she was creating a poem, she was learning a new way of experiencing herself which was like learning to read Braille. Therapy was an experiencing of herself, in all its aspects, in a safe relationship . . . along with these went the experiencing of self as having a capacity for wholeness, a self which was not possessively loving toward others but was "without hate," a self that cared about others. This last followed what was, for her, one of the deepest experiences in therapy (between interviews Nos. 29 and 30)—the realization that the therapist cared, that it really mattered to him how therapy turned out for her, that he really valued her. She experienced the soundness of her own basic directions. She gradually became aware of the fact that, though she had searched in every corner of herself, there was nothing fundamentally bad but, rather, at heart she was positive and sound. (pp. 262–263)

Mrs. Oak later referred to [this] as the most meaningful point in therapy for her.

When she left therapy (after 48 interviews), it was with the feeling that a process was going on in her that would continue to operate. She felt that the relationship with the therapist had been very meaningful and in a psychological sense would never stop, even though she walked out of the office for good. She felt ready, she thought, to cope with her life, though she realized it would not be easy. (p. 263)

While I have emphasized the portions of the interviews where Mrs. Oak developed a better understanding of her self, and not the specific problems with which she came to therapy, it was the more genuine experiencing of self that allowed her to deal with those problems.

Direct Behavior Modification

More direct approaches to behavioral change in therapy can be accomplished by applying what we know about behavior change from studies on classical, operant and social learning. You have studied these approaches in some detail in Chapter 5, *Learning and Conditioning,* and in Chapter 8, *Personality.*

Behavior therapies rest upon an attitude that constitutes helpful behavioral change just as do psychoanalysis and client-centered therapy. The behavior therapist looks at the whole person and attempts to identify that part of the behavior repertoire that is maladaptive. While the actual behavioral applications may seem fragmented, they are nonetheless applied within the context of the entire behavioral person. According to this view, a mental disorder always has a component that is a behavioral disorder. In Chapter 5, you studied behaviorist John B. Watson's (1970) ideas of how important learning is in the development of the whole person. Watson felt that he could effect any behavior change desired using the direct behavior change methods you studied in Chapter 5. Watson (1970) also clearly believed that this idea applied to the development and treatment of mental disorders.

> Without taking anyone into my counsel suppose I once trained a dog (Figure 10.2)

so that he would walk away from nicely-ground, fresh hamburg steak and would eat only decayed fish. I trained him by use of the electric shock to avoid smelling the female dog in the usual canine way—he would circle around her but would come no closer than ten feet (J.B. Morgan has done something very close to this on the rat). Again, by letting him play only with male puppies and dogs and punishing him when he tried to mount a female, I made a homosexual of him.

Instead of licking my hands and becoming lively and playful when I go to him in the morning, he hides or cowers, whines and shows his teeth. Instead of going after rats and other small animals in the way of hunting, he runs away from them and shows the most pronounced fears. He sleeps in the ash can—he fouls his own bed, he urinates every half hour and anywhere. Instead of smelling every tree trunk, he growls and fights and paws the earth but will not come within two feet of the tree. He sleeps only two hours per day and sleeps these two hours leaning up against a wall rather than lying down with head and rump touching. He is thin and emaciated because he will eat no fats. He salivates constantly (because I have conditioned him to salivate to hundreds of objects). This interferes with his digestion. Then I take him to the dog psychopathologist. His physiological reflexes are normal. No organic lesions are to be found anywhere. The dog, so the psychopathologist claims, is mentally sick, actually insane; his mental condition has led to the various organic difficulties such as lack of digestion; it has "caused" his poor physical condition. Everything that a dog should do—as compared with what dogs of his type usually do—he does not do. And everything that seems foreign for a dog to do he does. The psychopathologist says I must commit the dog to an institution for the care of insane dogs; that if he is not restrained he will jump from a ten-story building, or walk into a fire without hesitation [Figure 10.3].

I tell the dog psychopathologist that he doesn't know anything about my dog; that, from a standpoint of the environment in which the dog has been brought up (the way I have trained him), he is the most normal dog in the world; that the reason he calls the dog "insane" or mentally sick is because of his own absurd system of classification.

I then take the psychopathologist into my confidence. He becomes extremely angry. "Since you've brought this on, go cure him." I attempt then to correct my dog's behavior difficulties, at least up to the point where he can begin to associate with the nice dogs in the neighborhood. If he is very old or if things have gone too far, I just keep him confined; but if he is fairly young and he learns easily, I undertake to retrain him. I use behavioristic methods. I uncondition him and then condition him. Soon I get him to eating fresh meat by getting him hungry, closing up his nose and feeding him in the dark. This gives me a good start. I have something basal to use in my further work. I keep him hungry and feed him only when I open his cage in the morning; the whip is thrown away; soon he jumps for joy when he hears my step. In a few months' time I not only have cleared out the old but also have built in the new. The next time there is a dog show I proudly exhibit him, and his general behavior is such an asset to his sleek, perfect body that he walks off with the blue ribbon [Figure 10.4].

Figure 10.2 Normal Dog

Figure 10.3 Conditioned to be Mentally Ill

Figure 10.4 Unconditioning and Counterconditioning

> All this is an exaggeration. . . . Surely there is no connection between this and the poor sick souls we see in the psychopathic wards in every hospital! Yes, I admit the exaggeration, but I am after elementals here. I am pleading for simplicity and ruggedness in the building stones of our science of behavior. I am trying to show . . . that you can by conditioning not only build up the behavior complications, patterns and conflicts in diseased personalities, but also by the same process lay the foundations for the onset of actual organic changes which result finally in infections and lesions—all without introducing the concepts of the mind-body relation ("influence of mind over the body") or even without leaving the realm of natural science. In other words, as behaviorists, even in "mental diseases" we deal with the same material and the same laws that the neurologists and physiologists deal with. (pp. 297–300)

This clearly illustrates the idea that mental disorders can be viewed as having a behavioral component. This component can be approached directly using behavior modification methods. As we discuss some of these methods, keep Watson's psychopathological dog in mind.

Unconditioning and Counterconditioning

You are familiar with conditioning methods from Chapter 5. It would be especially helpful for you to recall the case of "Little Albert." *Unconditioning* and *counterconditioning* involve the removal of unwanted behavior by reversing the conditioning process.

Case Vignette: Peter. For example, Mary Cover Jones (1924), writing at about the same time Watson wrote the above story about the psychopathological dog, and in consultation with him, attempted to uncondition a young boy's (Peter) great fear of white rats, rabbits, etc. (Recall the generalization phenomena associated with little Albert's fears, Chapter 5.) Peter was seen by Jones and Watson as an older version of Albert and they eagerly sought to study the possibility of unconditioning the generalized fear.

Jones started by simply having the boy progress through stages of unconditioning the fear by systematically moving the boy closer and closer to the feared object (rabbit) while nothing threatening happened. Peter proceeded through the first nine steps nicely. But then he became ill with scarlet fever and could not continue the unconditioning for two months. When he returned to Jones's Laboratory for a continuation of the unconditioning, Peter had reverted to the original level of fear. At this point Jones changed her strategy a little. This time she not only brought the rabbit closer and closer to Peter, but rewarded him with pleasant food at each occurrence. Now, the fear response was actually being displaced by a countering response for the food reward. This is counterconditioning. Watson used both unconditioning and counterconditioning to get his dog to the blue ribbon.

Extinction and Systematic Desensitization

In the case of Peter, the unconditioning procedure (used before he became ill) amounted to *extinction*. A negative reinforcer was gradually losing its effect. The extinction method can also be applied to both positive and negative reinforcers in counterconditioning. This was taking place in Jones' second approach to Peter's fear. The fear response was extinguished by the displacing feelings of pleasure whenever the rabbit was brought closer. Joseph Wolpe (1969) has further developed this idea in a method of therapy he calls *systematic desensitization*. Wolpe's method involves a similar stepwise desensitizing (literally, so they are not so sensitive to the stimuli causing the problem) of people to fear arousing stimuli. In this version, of the method relaxation, which is incompatible with anxiety, is learned step-by-step, in the presence of the fear-arousing stimulus objects or situations. Since relaxation responses are to displace fear responses, the person being desensitized must learn to control his ability to relax, and to learn to completely relax. Many *progressive relaxation training* methods have been developed, for example, those by Jacobson (1938).

Just as Jones's young boy Peter was counter-conditioned through a stepwise hierarchy of threatening distances from the rabbit, systematic desensitization also relies on the development of reasonable hierarchy of steps of anxiety-arousing threat which can be slowly mastered. These steps, as in Peter's case, would be arranged from the least fearful to the most fearful situations. For example, if a client feared riding in airplanes (as millions of people do), the therapist and client together might work out a hierarchy starting with just reading about airplane travel (how much fun and safe it is), then to thinking about taking an airplane ride, then to going to the airport, then to boarding a plane (but not actually going up), then to an actual plane ride. Once the hierarchy seemed right, the person would be helped to relax systematically (rather than become anxious) at each step in the hierarchy.

Aversive Conditioning

If every time you do something, you get hurt, you soon learn to quit doing it. This idea can be applied in helping people learn to quit anything which is causing them problems. For example, if a person would like to quit smoking, or drinking alcohol, the behavior therapist might administer *aversive stimuli* following each encounter with the smell, taste, or indulgence in these habits. *Aversive conditioning* is not widely used.

Operant Positive Reinforcement

You will recall from Chapter 5 that pigeons could learn to perform circles by the method of successive approximations or shaping. If desired behavior is of such a low incidence that it only rarely, or partly, occurs, shaping can be used by the therapist to bring it to a desired level. In the biofeedback example in Chapter 5, every small EEG, body temperature, and EEG operants could all be shaped by simply letting the person know that he was successful in producing some very minute level of behavior. This shaping idea can be very helpful in teaching people how to profoundly relax. Full relaxation is critical to the systematic desensitization method described earlier.

Economic Systems of Secondary Reinforcers as Direct Behavioral Therapy. The everyday normal behavior of people is to a large extent maintained by systems of secondary reinforcers (see Chapter 5). You get up in the morning, dress, groom, and get to work on time for the secondary reinforcer of money. Your behavior is similarly maintained with respect to attending classes, taking exams, etc., by grades. Each exam score is a token that will lead to grades, which leads to credits, which lead to degrees. In all of the cases, your behavior is maintained at a very high rate by something you can later turn in or "trade" for primary reinforcers to more directly satisfy your needs. Both at work and in school your behavior is operantly maintained by a complex system of secondary reinforcers—a *token economy*. (Although, we generally, of course, refer to the money token economy as simply "the economy.")

Especially designed token economy systems have been developed by psychologists such as T. Ayllon and N.H. Azrin (1968) to help bring the behavior of abnormal individuals under operant influence. For example, Ayllon and Azrin found that the behavior of institutionalized psychotics (see *Schizophrenia and Paranoia,* Chapter 9) could be shaped to more productive levels by issuing special tokens (not money) for appropriate behavior. Then, like in a monetary system, these tokens within this economy could be traded in for primary reinforcers and other things by the patients. Table 10.3 contains a list of these reinforcers (and their relative token values) that were found to be important to these patients in their particular hospital situation. How did Ayllon and Azrin develop this list? They simply and carefully observed what the patients liked to do, and how intensely they liked to do it. They then put a token price on each item or activity. Other economies come to be in pretty much the same way. What do you suppose the list of reinforcers would look like for students on your college campus? What would cost more tokens, an hour in the library during final exam week, or an hour in the student center?

Cognitive-Behavioral Treatment

In the direct behavioral treatment methods we have discussed so far, we have not mentioned

Table 10-3 List of Reinforcers Available for Tokens

Reinforcers	*Number of Tokens Daily*	*Reinforcers*	*Number of Tokens Daily*
I. Privacy		Private audience with social worker	100
Selection of Room 1	0		
Selection of Room 2	4	IV. Devotional Opportunities	
Selection of Room 3	8	Extra religious services on ward	1
Selection of Room 4	15	Extra religious services off ward	10
Selection of Room 5	30		
Personal chair	1	V. Recreational Opportunities	
Choice of eating group	1	Move on ward	1
Screen (room divider)	1	Opportunity to listen to a live band	1
Choice of bedspreads	1	Exclusive use of radio	1
Coat rack	1	Television (choice of program)	3
Personal cabinet	2		
Placebo	1–2	VI. Commissary Items	
II. Leave from the Ward		Consumable items such as candy, milk, cigarettes, coffee, and sandwich	1–5
20-min. walk on hospital grounds (with escort)	2	Toilet articles such as Kleenex, toothpaste, comb, lipstick and talcum powder	1–10
30-min. grounds pass (3 tokens for each additional 30 min.)	10	Clothing and accessories such as gloves, headscarf, house slippers, handbag, and skirt	12–400
Trip to town (with escort)	100	Reading and writing materials such as stationery, pen, greeting card, newspaper, and magazine	2–5
III. Social Interaction with Staff		Miscellaneous items such as ashtray, throw rug, potted plant, picture holder, and stuffed animal	1–50
Private audience with chaplain, nurse	5 min. free		
Private audience with ward staff, ward physician (for additional time—1 token per min.)	5 min. free		
Private audience with ward psychologist	20		

Above is a list of reinforcers (and their relative token values) which were found to be important to patients in a particular hospital situation. How did Ayllon and Azrin develop this list? They simply and carefully observed what the patients liked to do, and how intensely they liked to do it.

anything about what the client might be thinking during therapy (their cognitive involvement). In psychoanalysis and in client-centered therapy, what the client was thinking was extremely important. In our earlier discussion of systematic desensitization, we came close to discussing cognitive processes when we described the construction of fear hierarchies, imagery of the hierarchies, and voluntary relaxation. These are really cognitive components of the method. Now we will examine direct behavioral approaches where the role of thinking and the dialogue one carries on with one's self play the leading role in behavior management.

We might want to think of cognitive activity as being shaped and maintained much in the same way operant behavior is. While Watson didn't allow it, more recent behaviorists have suggested links between behavior and mind, and have given us a way to think about them. For example, Lloyd E. Homme (1965) has proposed that thoughts, just like publicly observable behavior (operants), are emitted responses, only they are internal behavior or *coverants.* In terms of behavior change, including therapy, the same principles of operant learning and shaping (Chapter 5) apply to them. A thought that is reinforced by a pleasant state of affairs will become a more likely thought, or a more likely approximation of some thought. Homme more or less seriously referred to these emitted coverants as "operants of the mind."

Rational-Emotive Therapy. *Rational-emotive therapy (RET)* developed by Albert Ellis (1977) is a clear example of how thoughts might be manipulated to cause behavior change. Ellis puts beliefs and thoughts at the center of therapeutic attention. Using Ellis's terminology, let's examine a situation where distress or disability might occur in a person and see how beliefs and thoughts relate to this emotional situation. Normally, if a person sees a snake in a zoo setting, we might expect the rational behavior depicted in Table 10.4.

However, Ellis believes that the real reason for what happens at C (consequences) is not A (the activating experience of the snake), but a third factor B, the person's belief and thoughts about snakes. In the rational situation depicted in Table 10.4, B is not considered important because the person is not unduly distressed or disabled by the presence of the snake. B is there all right, it is just that the beliefs or thoughts in this person are rational in terms of the reality of the situation. But if the person were phobic about snakes, we would have great distress in the person, and the B part becomes clinically significant. This situation is depicted in Table 10.5.

So, according to Ellis, it is the irrational thoughts and beliefs that are causing the emotional problem—the distress and disability. The job of the therapist in RET is to restructure the rational—emotional relationship so that it is rational as in the first person above, and riot irrational as in the second person with the snake phobia. It is important to realize that B is always there; the question is, is it rational or irrational? With successful RET, the new B will be rational. Systematic desensitization could alternatively be used to help deal with the snake phobia, but here the emphasis is not on counterconditioning of behavior alone directly, but on helping the person restructure his beliefs more realistically—on the cognitive patterning of coverant activity.

A RET therapist might use any means of very directive restructuring of the client's beliefs. Some of the more generalized irrational beliefs that cause people distress appear in Table 10.6.

Preoccupation, number 6 in the list, is probably at the core of the snake phobia described above. Below is a case therapy session using RET which also involves preoccupation. Avoidance and victim of the past are also irrational beliefs involved in distressing this college student who is being counseled by a fellow student "therapist."

Case Vignette: Distressed College Student

DISTRESSED STUDENT: I am not taking the psychology quiz tomorrow. I'll be sick.

STUDENT RET THERAPIST: Why? Are you afraid of the quiz?

Table 10.4 Normal Reaction to Snakes at a Zoo

A—(SNAKE) ⟶	C—(Person examines snake, perhaps keeps an eye on it)
Activating experience	Consequences in behavior, including emotions

Table 10.5 Phobic Reaction to Snakes at a Zoo

A—(SNAKE) ⟶	B—(irrational concentration) ⟶	C—(Person is paralyzed, faints)
Activating Experience	on "what if" phobic thoughts: What if the glass breaks? What if I fall into the class cage? What if it bites me? What if it crushes me, and slithers all over me, etc.? irrational beliefs	

Table 10.6 Irrational Beliefs (B's) Which Cause People Distress

1. *Need for Approval.* I must have love or approval from all of the people I find significant.
2. *Perfectionism and Fear of Failure.* I must prove that I am thoroughly competent, adequate, and achieving. I must have great competence or talent in some important area.
3. *Blame.* When people act obnoxiously and unfairly, I should blame and damn them, and see them as bad, wicked, or rotten individuals.
4. *Frustration-Catastrophe.* I have to view things as awful, terrible, horrible, and catastrophic when I get seriously frustrated, treated unfairly, or rejected.
5. *Helplessness.* Emotional misery comes from external pressures, and I have little ability to control or change my feelings.
6. *Preoccupation.* If something seems dangerous or fearsome, I must preoccupy myself with it and make myself anxious about it.
7. *Avoidance.* I can more easily avoid facing many life difficulties and self-responsibilities than undertake more rewarding forms of self-discipline.
8. *Victim of the Past.* My past remains all-important, and because something once strongly influenced my life it must keep determining my feelings and behavior.
9. *Chasing Nirvana.* People and things should turn out better than they do and I must view it as awful and horrible if I don't find good solutions to life's grim realities.
10. *Passivity and Boredom—Avoiding Risks.* I can achieve maximum human happiness by inertia and inaction or by passively and uncommittedly enjoying myself.

DISTRESSED STUDENT: I have never been good at quizzes. They always ask the wrong questions.

STUDENT RET THERAPIST: They always ask the wrong questions? Boy, "they" must have the CIA following you!

DISTRESSED STUDENT: I just can't bear to get another low grade.

STUDENT RET THERAPIST: Yes, but do you know what the purpose of having quizzes is?

DISTRESSED STUDENT: Yes, to find out who's stupid, not studying, and to weed us out!

STUDENT RET THERAPIST: Actually, the purpose of the quizzes is to let you know how you are doing in class. You know the instructor even told us that! If you don't take the quiz, the next quiz will be even worse. If you take the quiz and fail it, you can talk to the instructor about it, or to me! But, if you do a good job, you'll know everything is okay.

DISTRESSED STUDENT: Yes, this is the first psychology course I have ever taken.

STUDENT RET THERAPIST: Right. Study the material. Are you using the SQ3R method as the instructor suggested?

DISTRESSED STUDENT: No.

STUDENT RET THERAPIST: Well, let's get with it!

DISTRESSED STUDENT: You're right. I guess the worst thing that can happen is that I'll have a reason to go to the instructor for help.

STUDENT RET THERAPIST: Right. Study hard, and give it your best shot tomorrow.

The student therapist has attempted to help his friend rationally analyze the situation involving the quiz. At the beginning of their discussion, the distressed student may have held the irrational belief of being a victim of his past. "I have never been good at quizzes. They always ask the wrong questions," etc. Some parts of the discussion may have seemed a little rough on the poor distressed student. Sometimes it takes a jolt to let go of irrational beliefs.

Changing Perceived Self-Efficacy: Modeling. Recall the ideas of learned self-efficacy, and learned self-reward (Chapter 8). A person's self-efficacy influences his ability to deal with various kinds of situations. Social learning theorist Albert Bandura (1982) describes how these cognitive factors of self-percepts of efficacy can lead to distress and disability.

> People's judgments of their capabilities additionally influence their thought patterns

> and emotional reactions during anticipatory and actual transactions with the environment. Those who judge themselves inefficacious in coping with environmental demands dwell in their personal deficiencies and imagine potential difficulties as more formidable than they really are. Such self-referent misgivings create stress and impair performance by diverting attention from how best to proceed with the undertaking to concerns over failings and mishaps. In contrast, persons who have a strong sense of efficacy deploy their attention and effort to the demands of the situation and are spurred to greater effort by obstacles. (p. 123)

In order to help people improve their self-perception of inefficaciousness, Bandura suggests *modeling* and *guided participation.* In this sort of therapeutic situation, people who are distressed from, for example, low efficacy phobic "what if" thoughts can learn through imitation to judge themselves as more efficacious.

Table 10.7 Trends in Psychotherapy

a. Theoretical Views of Psychotherapists	
Psychoanalytic	11%
Behavioral	7%
Cognitive Behavioral	10%
Person-centered	9%
Rational-emotive	2%
Eclectic	41%
b. Trends Seen by Psychotherapists Toward:	
Multimodalism	19%
Creative Synthesis	19%
Systems Theory	9%
Emerging Eclecticism	17%
c. Most Influential Psychotherapists (in rank order)*	
1. Carl Rogers	
2. Albert Ellis	
3. Sigmund Freud	
4. Joseph Wolpe	

*adapted from Smith (1982)

Trends in Psychotherapy and Behavioral Therapy

Trends in the use of treatment methods are becoming more and more eclectic in approach. Each of the approaches, in the hands of qualified professionals and used in treatment of the salient disorders, has its firm place. It seems likely that psychotherapies are pretty much equivalent (Stiles, Shapiro & Elliot, 1986). You will also see this same argument made for biological approaches to adjunctive therapy—including electroconvulsive shock therapy (ECT).

Table 10.7 combines the recent findings of Darrell Smith (1982) in *Trends in Counseling and Psychotherapy* (including the behavior therapies). The *eclectic approach* is overwhelmingly the most common therapeutic approach. Carl Rogers is the overwhelming influence upon professionals. In Smith's 1982 report, only 2 percent of the professionals questioned suggested exclusive approaches as future trends.

While systems theory, as a theory, was mentioned only a respectable 9 percent of the time Table 10.7(b), it was the only theory, per se, mentioned to any significant degree. Also, all of the more popular trends suggested are compatible with and in keeping with a general systems view of the client. The idea of treating the client holistically, using a variety of interrelated approaches (a central systems concept), is apparent in Smith's conclusion.

> Eclecticism is clearly the preference of the largest number of psychologists. Yet there seems to be a dissatisfaction with the term eclecticism per se. Concepts such as multimodal, creative synthesis, emerging eclecticism, integration, and systems theory appear to be most descriptive of the current trend toward broad spectrum approaches to counseling and psychotherapy. (1982, p. 808)

Let's examine more closely the various elements of this integrative approach that very effectively treats the disorder of agoraphobia, and the whole person.

Behavior Therapy Aspects. In the beginning of therapy, in vivo systematic desensitization therapy is used to get the patient successfully moving out into his, or her, environment.

> Early in treatment, specific areas and parameters of limitations are established so

> as to begin to design with the client a hierarchy of in vivo tasks which will gradually expose the individual to the phobic settings. Graduated levels of accomplishment, made up of in vivo goals and steps, become an ongoing process and are an intrinsic part of the group work These steps progress from easily attainable (with some expected discomfort) to relatively more difficult tasks associated with higher fear levels.
>
> Weekly in vivo homework assignments, progressively structured, are planned with the client, along with the individualized and group in vivo field practice accompanied by the therapist. The sense of increased physical autonomy and independence enhances the individual's self-esteem and establishes a pattern of new responses. Our observation has been that, for optimal desensitization and integration of the in vivo experience, exposure must be gradual and each goal must be manageable and yet stimulate a moderately high arousal level in the individual. (p. 45)

You can also see how self-efficacy would be increasing in this early part of the therapy. To maximize the effects of the systematic desensitization, the program places the therapy in a group setting so that a number of cognitive-behavior goals can be achieved.

> The in vivo tasks are established by the client with staff and group input. Group in vivo field trips are significant because of the modeling and supportive group behavior, which has a very positive effect in directly influencing the individual member's attempt to confront extremely phobic situations. Group exposure in outings also tends to increase group cohesiveness and intimacy through the mutual sharing of one's vulnerable self. (p. 45)

The use of groups can be applied in any therapy. Groups allow more people to be treated, and have unique benefits.

Cognitive Restructuring Aspects. Earlier, we discussed how psychoanalysis, client-centered approach, and rational-emotive therapy help to restructure cognitively the person's beliefs and perception of experience. Such restructuring is a part of an integrated approach.

> In order to aid the individual in confronting his fears in the real setting, coping strategies, that are mainly centered in cognitive restructuring and relaxation methods, are introduced to the client. These techniques, which vary in effectiveness, include educating the individual in recognizing secondary thought processes which generate multiple arousal stimulation, helping the person to alter thought to a positive and calming imagery, and diverting attention to positive cues in the immediate environment. (p. 46)

A very valuable and appropriate part of the cognitive aspects of the program is to have patients tape record their thoughts while actually having a phobic attack! This technique was developed by Manuel Zane.

> These tapes are subsequently evaluated with the client to identify patterns of phobic thought and frightening imagery that tend to increase tension. Methods designed to help maintain thought in the manageable present and distract catastrophic imagery can then be discussed with the client.
>
> I have observed that the tape recorder not only is a means of feeding information back to the therapist and group, but also effectively acts as an instrument of communication representing a connection with a comforting and empathetic figure. This tends to help the individual feel less isolated when being exposed alone to the phobic setting, and it helps neutralize anxiety through the incorporation of positive imagery. In effect, the tape recorder acts as a transitional object imbued with a magic-like security function. The tape recorder becomes an extension of the safe and protective person or group. (pp. 46–47)

Psychoanalytic Aspects. Finally, the eclectic approach includes psychoanalytic consideration of the patient. Cohen feels that the roots of the agoraphobic syndrome begin within the first three years of life—particularly the period between the 15th and 24th months of age.

> There is evidence to indicate that the adult agoraphobic experienced trauma in early childhood interfering with the process of development, such as the loss of

> a significant person, a sudden emotional [loss of support] by the mother, an entrapment by mother's overly dependent or possessive needs and ensuing fears of being alone, or the presence of severe ambivalence on the part of one or both parents. The phobic-depersonalization syndrome in adulthood, characterized by the phobic's fear-panic response when venturing away from a safe place or securing person, can be viewed a paradigmatic of the disturbance in the child-parting relationship and of the child's ensuing feelings of disconnection and disruption during the critical *individuation stage* of psychological growth. (p. 49)

Of course, the longer-term integrated approach provides the opportunity for the patient to come to grips with these unconscious origins of his disorder.

> Treatment in the therapy group must also deal with these underlying issues of primary ego integrity involving conflicted emotions pertaining to loss, separateness and self-esteem. Helping the individual to identify and express these emotions is important because it goes to the heart of the interpersonal conflict, the avoidance of feelings which, if acknowledged and communicated, would provoke [old, unconscious] fears of abandonment and annihilation. (p. 50)

It is obvious that the eclectic approach involves many aspects of the whole person in relation to his phobic distress. Likewise, several of the behavioral and psychological therapies find an appropriate role to play in treatment. This is why such eclectic approaches are the trend in treatment programs

Treatments That Alter Biological Makeup

All mental disorders can be thought of in terms of possible biological counterparts in the nervous system. For example, in schizophrenia there seems to be involvement of dopamine receptors at synapses in the brain, and in the case of phobias there is clear involvement of the autonomic nervous system activity associated with panic attacks (see Chapter 2, and the symptoms of panic attacks present at the beginning of this chapter). This does not mean that mental disorders always have biological origins. The biological bases of mental disorders is relatively obscure—as is the biological basis of cognition in general. However, biologically-based treatments of various mental disorders have had a great deal of success.

Alteration of the Brain: Surgery. Direct surgical tampering with the various areas of brain function would obviously result in changes in behavior. In fact, much of what we know about brain function has come about in just this way (see methods section, Chapter 2). *Psychosurgical methods* as treatment have come to involve a number of brain areas. In the 1930s, the *frontal lobotomy* was developed as a means of altering the brain structure of certain psychotic patients. It had been observed that destruction of the prefrontal areas of the brains of monkeys resulted in a calming effect on the more agitated ones. In human treatment, the procedure was a matter of piercing the frontal portion of the brain (through the eye orbits behind the eyeballs) with an ice-pick-like instrument, and stirring about. Thousands of frontal lobotomies were performed over the next decades. This procedure may sound gruesome. It is. However, given the alternatives available at the time, it seemed justifiable. This process destroys the interconnectedness of the frontal area of the brain. Why the calming effect occurs is uncertain.

Fortunately, psychosurgical treatment has diminished in recent years. Much of the reason for this has been the discovery of effective drug treatments. Elliot Valenstein (1980) has provided a view of more recent applications of psychosurgical treatments. Treatment and research on psychosurgical techniques continue. And Suzanne Corkin (1980) has reported that, at least in the case of one operation related to a broad variety of mental disorders, refinements are being made.

Electroconvulsive Shock Therapy (ECT). Another way to alter the brain physically and its activity has been to apply an electric current. This procedure, *electroconvulsive shock therapy (ECT),* amounts to passing an electrical surge through the brain for up to 1½ seconds. The surge of electric current is typically about 150 volts with 200–500 milliamperes, and results in convulsions which are necessary to the achieve the therapeutic value of ECT.

The ECT surge of current can be applied to either the whole brain or to only one hemisphere. It has been found that applying the surge of current to only one hemisphere in very short bursts results in less adverse side-effects—such as permanent loss of some memory (Daniel & Crovitz 1983). Usually the right, nondominant, hemisphere is given the treatment to help protect the verbal memory. ECT treatments cause violent seizures. These seizures, at the behavioral level, are reduced nearly to zero by administering muscle relaxant to the patient prior to treatment. Upon the surge of current, the patient immediately loses consciousness. Several minutes later, the patient regains consciousness, but is somewhat dazed and confused. After this passes, the patient usually has some difficulty with memory. Even though it is not understood why ECT helps, there are several theories about how it reduces depression and there has recently been new interest in its use in treating a variety of deep depressions (U.S. Department of Health and Human Services, 1985).

Altering Chemical Balances in the CNS. As you learned in Chapter 2, the brain functions most essentially as a chemical system. Motor-sensory relationships, thought, sleep, temperature regulation, etc., all have a basis in neurotransmitter chemicals.

Since the mid-1950s the *pharmacological treatment* of mental disorders has made so much progress that the entire concept of mental disorder has changed from notions of "madness" to recognition of the chemical subtleties of the brain. As a result, the number of patients in mental hospitals has drastically declined.

Figure 10.5 shows this dramatic decrease or *deinstitutionalization* of mental patients. The effects of one class of *psychotropic drugs* (the antipsychotic compounds) were even more dramatic than the figure would lead us to believe. Here is the eyewitness report of one psychologist who was there when these drugs became available.

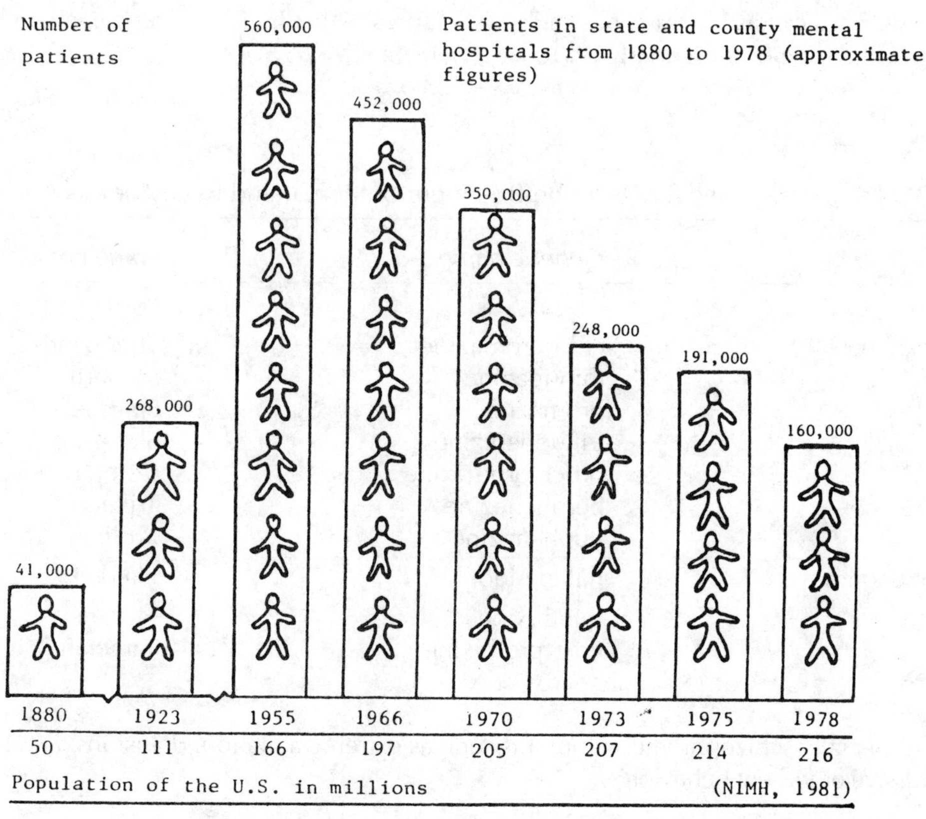

Figure 10.5 Deinstitutionalization of Mental Patients

Although the benefits of the antipsychotic compounds have often been exaggerated, it is difficult to convey the truly enormous influence they have had in altering the environment of the mental hospital. One of the authors, as part of his training, worked several months in the maximum security ward of one such hospital immediately prior to the introduction of this type of medication in 1955. The ward patients fulfilled the oft-heard stereotypes of individuals "gone mad." Bizarreness, nudity, wild screaming, and an ever present threat of violence pervaded the atmosphere. Fearfulness and near-total preoccupation with the maintenance of control characterized the attitudes of staff. Such staff attitudes were not unrealistic in terms of the frequency of occurrence of serious physical assaults by patients, but they were hardly conducive to the development or maintenance of an effective therapeutic program.

Then, quite suddenly—within a period of perhaps a month—all of this dramatically changed. The patients were receiving antipsychotic medication. The ward became a place in which one could seriously get to know one's patients on a personal level and perhaps even initiate programs of *"milieu therapy"* and the like, promising reports of which had begun to appear in the professional literature. A new era in hospital treatment had arrived, aided enormously and in many instances actually made possible by the development of these extraordinary drugs. (Coleman, Butcher, & Carson, 1984, p. 15)

More recently, Zitrin, Klein and Woerner (1978) have shown that certain antidepressant drugs are effective in the treatment of phobias. For example, imipramine, phenelzine, and alprazolam, are being used as pharmacological adjuncts to other psychotherapeutic treatment. The integrative program at the Centrum Phobia Clinic uses such drugs as adjuncts. Table 10.8 provides an overview of psychotropic drugs, what disorders are treated by them, and their general effects.

These drugs do not "cure" mental disorders. They reduce symptoms to manageable levels for the patient and/or the ward staff. These drugs often have serious side effects. In some cases symptoms persist at high levels in spite of the drugs so that ECT, for example, might be recommended.

Table 10.8 Frequently Used Drugs in the Treatment of Mental and Behavior Disorders

Class	*Generic name*	*Trade name*
Antipsychotic		
a) phenothiazines	chlorpromazine	Thorazine
	thioridazine	Mellaril
	promazine	Sparine
	trifluoperazine	Stelazine
	prochlorperazine	Compazine
	perphenazine	Trilafon
	fluphenazine	Prolixin
b) butyrophenones	halaperidol	Haldol
c) thioxanthenes	thiothixine	Navane
	chlorprothixine	Taractan

Used to treat:

Psychotic (especially schizophrenic) symptoms such as extreme agitation, delusions, and hallucinations; aggressive or violent behavior.

(continued)

Table 10.8 *(continued)*

Effects:

Somewhat variable in achieving intended purpose of suppression of psychotic symptoms. Side effects, such as dry mouth, are often uncomfortable. In long-term use, may produce motor disturbances such as Parkinsonism and tardive dyskinesia.

Class	*Generic name*	*Trade name*
Antidepressant		
a) tricyclics	imipramine	Tofranil
	amitriptyline	Elavil
	nortriptyline	Aventyl
	protriptyline	Vivactil
	doxepin	Sinequan
b) monoamine oxidase (MAO) inhibitors	isocarboxazid	Marplan
	phenelzine	Nardil
	tranylcypromine	Parnate

Used to treat:

Relatively severe depressive symptoms, especially of psychotic severity and unipolar in type; phobias (except simple phobias).

Effects:

Somewhat variable in alleviating depressive symptoms, and noticeable effects may be delayed up to three weeks. Multiple side effects—some of them dangerous. Use of MAO inhibitors requires dietary restrictions.

Class	*Generic name*	*Trade name*
Antimanic (bipolar)	lithium carbonate	Eskalith
		Lithane
		Lithonate
		Lithotabs
		Phi-Lithium

Used to treat:

Manic episodes and some severe depressions, particularly recurrent ones or those alternating with mania.

Effects:

Usually effective in resolving manic episodes, but highly variable in effects on depression, probably because the latter is a less homogeneous grouping. Multiple side effects unless carefully monitored; high toxicity potential.

Class	*Generic name*	*Trade name*
Antianxiety (minor tranquilizers)		
a) propanediols	meprobamate	Equanil
		Miltown
b) benzodiazepines	diazepam	Valium
	chlordiazepoxide	Librium
	flurazepam	Dalmane

(continued)

Table 10.8 *(continued)*

	oxazepam	Serax
	clorazepate	Tranxene
	alprazolam	Xanax

Used to treat:

Nonpsychotic personality problems in which anxiety and tension are prominent features; also used as anticonvulsants and as sleep-inducers (especially flurazepam); panic disorder.

Effects:

Somewhat variable in achieving intended purpose of tension reduction. Side effects include drowsiness and lethargy. Dependence and toxicity are dangers.

Class	*Generic name*	*Trade name*
Stimulant	dextroamphetamine	Dexedrine
	amphetamine	Benzedrine
	methylphenidate	Ritalin

Used to treat:

Hyperactivity, distractibility, specific learning disabilities, and, occasionally, extreme hypoactivity.

Effects:

Rather unpredictable. When maximally effective, can enable otherwise uneducable children to attend regular schools. Side effects often troublesome, including recently discovered retardation of growth.

Bringing It All Together

The most important idea in this chapter is the answer to the question, "What can psychology do about mental disorders?" Psychology has developed many methods of systematic behavior change that lead away from the distress and disability of mental disorders.

The trend set by the DSM-IV (Chapter 9) is clearly a holistic approach to the diagnosis of mental disorders—recall the five axes. The eclectic trends in the treatment of mental disorders parallels this idea. If mental disorders have a variety of origins and features, then treatment will naturally follow with a variety of approaches. The whole person is understood as a composite of interacting and interrelated parts.

Glossary

agoraphobia: An irrational fear of being either alone or in public places.

applied psychology: The application of psychological theories and/or principles to everyday human problems such as those in a business and industrial setting, in human engineering work, in advertising, in education, and in the treatment of mental disorders.

aversive conditioning: The control and shaping of behavior through the application of unpleasant or painful stimuli upon the occurrence of the behavior.

aversive stimuli: Unpleasant or pain-producing stimuli.

avoidance behavior: Behavior that prevents the onset or occurrence of certain potentially fear- or pain-inducing situations.

congruence: Agreement between what a person really feels or thinks and that which is presented to others.

contextual therapy: See supported exposure.

counterconditioning: Decreasing a certain behavior by removing the reward, or punishment for it, and reinforcing incompatible behavior (see unconditioning).

coverants: Elements of thoughts or mental images which, if rewarded, will become more likely in the future; if not rewarded, they will become less likely.

deinstitutionalization: The process by which great numbers of mental patients were removed of mental institutions upon the discovery of pharmacological treatments.

eclectic approach: Treatment approaches that draw upon diverse sources of theory and techniques to provide an integrated and harmonious approach to the patient.

ECT: See electroconvulsive shock treatment.

electroconvulsive shock therapy (ECT): A treatment technique in which an electrical current is passed through the brain thereby momentarily disrupting a broad variety of brain processes. Although this treatment markedly relieves severe depression in most patients, researchers are not sure how it works.

empathetic understanding: Understanding of another that comes about by fully placing one's self in another's situation.

engineering psychology: A branch of applied psychology involved in the design of machine systems so that they am suited to human behavioral, sensory, and perceptual characteristics and capacities.

environmental psychology: A branch of social psychology involved in both pure and applied study (see pure and applied psychology). Environmental psychologists study the influence of environmental settings on behavior that include the city, industrial and space station settings.

extinction: The ending of certain members of a species or of a species. Also, the ending or decrease in certain responses following the ch as vocal tone.

fixation: Development which remains for a long time at a given level, or a habitual wave of responding to certain situations; dynamically related in psychoanalytic theory and therapy.

free association techniques: In psychoanalysis, a technique used by the analyst to probe the material and organization of the patient's unconscious. The patient is encouraged to freely report whatever comes to mind. He may be prompted with a word or by his own free flow of thoughts.

frontal lobotomy: A psychosurgical method in which nerve connections within the frontal lobes of the brain are severed. This procedure, rarely used now, has a calming effect on certain agitated psychotic patients.

guided participation: see supported exposure.

individuation stage: The stage of development within which a person perceives herself as an individual.

industrial-organizational psychology: A branch of applied psychology involved in solving problems related to organizations, especially business and industrial ones. This includes, for example, the selection and training of personnel, the design of the workplace, and maximizing human organizational performance.

insight-oriented therapy: Treatments that attempt to get the patient to see the basis and nature of their own mental disorder and thereby gain self-control over it.

in vivo treatment: See supported exposure.

latent content (of dreams): In psychoanalytic theory and therapy, the unreportable repressed or unconscious meaning of a dream (see manifest content).

manifest content (of dreams): In psychoanalytic theory and therapy for the dreamer, the reportable description of a dream (see latent content).

milieu therapy: Treatment which takes place in and via the living and working environment of the patients(s) and the team of professional mental health care staff.

modeling: In cognitive-behavioral treatments, a technique wherein the therapist acts as a model of appropriate behavior in regard, for example, to some object or situation feared by the patient.

Oedipus complex: In psychoanalytic theory, residual unconscious sexual feelings toward the same sexed parent, and residual unconscious aggressive feelings toward the opposite-sexed-parent.

panic attack: The sudden occurrence of extreme apprehension or terror, often with feelings of impending doom.

panic disorder: See panic attack.

pathologic dependency: An excess reliance on another person or persons that has its origins in a mental disorder.

pharmacological treatment: A broad variety of drug treatments that alter the chemistry of the brain and thereby relieve certain mental disorders.

phobias: A broad class of irrational fears of things, events, and situations. The victim recognizes that the fear is unwarranted, but can do little about its effect. The phobias include simple phobias, agoraphobia, and social phobia.

progressive relaxation training: Training exercises which begin by having the person focus on relaxation of his own breathing and then systematically to other and greater numbers of muscle groups.

projective assessment techniques: Methods which measure unconscious needs, fears, expectations, and meanings of a person. See also projection, *Rorschach Inkblot Blot Test,* and *TAT.*

psychosurgical methods: The alteration of psychological process by direct surgical intervention in the brain.

psychotherapy: The treatment of mental disorders through techniques involving close communication and interaction between a therapist knowledgeable about psychological and behavioral problems and a patient or group of patients.

psychotropic drugs: Drugs that influence psychological processes.

rational emotive therapy (RET): A treatment technique in which the therapist actively encourages the patient to restructure beliefs held about certain things or events that are causing impairment.

RET: See rational emotive therapy.

supported exposure: A treatment technique, especially in the treatment of phobia, where the person slowly learns to confront the feared or pain causing situation in real life, and with the understanding aid of others.

systematic desensitization: A reduction in fear or anxiety (desensitization) that proceeds by having the person completely relax while being confronted by closer and closer approximations of that which is feared.

token economy: A form of treatment that modifies behavior through a formal system of secondary reinforcers. Tokens (secondary reinforcers) are given to patients for appropriate behavior (reinforcement), and removed (punishment) or not available for inappropriate behavior.

transference: The process in which a patient shifts feelings applicable to another person onto the therapist. These may include either positive or negative feelings.

unconditional positive regard: An attitude toward another that he or she is valued in and of themselves, and not because of some conditions that have been met.

unconditioning: Decreasing a certain behavior by removing the reward, or punishment for it. (See counterconditioning.)

Treatment of Psychological Disorders: Doing Psychology on Your Own

LOIS MCDERMOTT

Basic Concept #10—Moving Beyond Freud

The historical assumptions of the causes of mental illness (described in the previous unit) gave rise to amazingly diverse strategies for restoring mental health. Among the most notable/memorable were (1) boring holes in the skull to release spirits or devils, (2) bleeding, purging, starvation and cold baths to restore balance to the humors, (3) restraints, isolations and confinements of various types to calm the senses, (4) beatings, public exposure, hard labor to punish sin and moral turpitude, (5) castration to prevent the passing on of "bad seed," (6) hypnosis to uncover unconscious conflicts, and repressed childhood traumas and (7) psychosurgery to remove diseased brain areas. Essentially all of these have fallen into disrepute and are no longer used as valid treatments by mainstream clinicians.

The advent of the modern treatment of mental illness began with the advent of Freud's talking therapy in the early 20th century. By the end of this century no less than 50 brands of psychotherapy have been explored. In the middle of the 20th century the discovery of medications which calmed the hallucinations and delusion of psychosis, was quickly followed by the development of medications to elevate mood, quiet mania and soothe anxiety. Mental hospital stays shortened and the bed counts plummeted.

By the 1980s the future looked bright for the effective treatment of mental illness with the combination of medications to relieve symptoms and psychotherapy to effect long-term behavior change. With the increasing acceptance of mental illness as a medical illness rather than a mark of sin, moral turpitude or weakness of character, people increasingly sought help from therapists of various stripes. Unfortunately some folk suffer from disorders for which no effective cure or treatment is currently available. However most suffer or will suffer from disorders for which help is available.

Although I have struggled with depression since my teen years it is because of access to unlimited, high quality treatment that the trajectory of my life has had an upward course. With sufficient effective care the prognosis for those who struggle with mental illness is good-to-excellent in most cases. However as fate would have it, this success and new optimism about healing from mental illness has proved to be a threat to the profits of the mental health insurance industry. As the century draws to a close all the strides made in the development of (a) diagnosis, (b) a wide range of effective treatments, and (c) the acceptability of openly acknowledging the need and desire for treatment may ultimately be for naught. The health industry has decided to ration these treatments and erect psychological and financial barriers to obtaining care. In the same decade that many are gaining comfort with the idea of utilizing mental health care others are prevented by their embarrassment, ignorance or financial status from getting the effective treatment they need.

Unit Focus. The vast majority of college educated folks will seek or have sought treatment for some psychological distress (e.g., family, marital, individual). This probably results from the fact that college-educated people have (a) high expectations for their own functioning and that of their loved ones, (b) are aware and accepting of treatment as a social good and (c) have financial access to care. This unit is designed to help you be an informed consumer when your turn comes to be a "client or patient"; to help you make intelligent decisions about your treatment. Mental health treatment, like other health procedures, will be effective to the extent you are committed and involved. These treatments can also be harmful under certain conditions and in certain situations. By understanding your range of choices and the pitfalls of incompetent, unethical care, you can go a long way to ensuring a good outcome for yourself. I wish you great success.

Study Objectives

1. Learn the uses of voluntary and involuntary hospitalization in the treatment of mental illness.
2. Distinguish among the various general types of medication used to treat mental illness and the potential side effect and problems associated with such use.
3. Compare and contrast the past and present use of ECT in the treatment of mental illness.
4. Compare and contrast the broad types of psychotherapy developed in response to the major theoretical perspectives in psychology.
5. Learn the types of psychotherapy that are characteristic of each of the theoretical approaches.
6. Learn the stages of psychotherapy common to approaches and the uses of eclectic psychotherapy.
7. Learn your basic rights as a consumer of psychotherapy and the important therapeutic qualities you should seek.
8. Learn the common and distinguishing characteristics of the various types of mental health providers.

Key Terms

agoraphobia
applied psychology
aversive conditioning
aversive stimuli
avoidance behavior
congruence
contextual therapy
counterconditioning
coverants
deinstitutionalization
eclectic approach
ECT
electroconvulsive shock therapy (ECT)
empathetic understanding
engineering psychology

environmental psychology
extinction
fixation
free association techniques
frontal lobotomy
guided participation
individuation stage
industrial-organizational psychology
insight-oriented therapy
in vivo treatment
latent content (of dreams)
manifest content (of dreams)
milieu therapy
modeling
Oedipus complex
panic attack
panic disorder
pathologic dependency
pharmacological treatment
phobias
progressive relaxation training
projective assessment techniques
psychosurgical methods
psychotherapy
psychotropic drugs
rational emotive therapy (RET)
RET
supported exposure
systematic desensitization
token economy
transference
unconditional positive regard
unconditioning

Therapeutic Approaches: A Case Study

Ralph, a shy, talented, 20-year-old upper-class Caucasian male, has been feeling quite depressed and anxious (e.g., acid stomach, insomnia) recently. He has been doing poorly in school; in particular he is failing his Chem 101 class. In addition, his roommate is threatening to move out because Ralph is constantly losing his temper over trivial matters. Ralph generally feels fed up with everyone—viewing the world as full of self-centered people who are too busy to care about him or anybody else. For example, Ralph wants to approach his Chem professor for help but is sure that she will be too busy with other important matters and will have no time for his "trivial" problems. He feels overwhelmed by anxiety at the thought of talking with her. In therapy Ralph begins to realize that this fear of approaching others for help is a life-long pattern. His therapist has been helping him explore various types of factors involved in this problem.

BIOLOGICAL: Genetically inherited, organic predisposition
Ralph inherited a shy, sensitive temperament. He is easily overwhelmed by SNS discharge during periods of crises. His own temperament serves to exacerbate most stressful situations. Since infancy even minor stresses resulted in excessive physical symptoms, and difficulty becoming calm again. Ralph has always been somewhat introverted and feels most comfortable when alone. Ralph is undertaking a stress management program which reduces caffeine in his diet, includes more exercise and increases his vitamin B level.

PSYCHODYNAMIC: Unconscious conflict
Ralph's mother was alcoholic during his childhood and was available to nurture him only sporadically. Ralph developed a sense that "helpers" are unpredictable and overwhelmed by their own needs. Ralph developed feelings of helpless rage at his mother's inability to nurture him. His fear of further abandonment forced this rage in unconsciousness. It surfaces now as unconscious/conscious rage directed toward "unhelpful" others (e.g., friends, professors, his therapist). Ralph feels certain his professor and therapist won't be able to be helpful to him (i.e., they will prove to be inadequate "mothers").

COGNITIVE: Schemas, beliefs, attributions
In therapy, Ralph is examining the "automatic tapes" which play in his head. The pressure (shaming) which was put on Ralph to "parent" himself led to feelings which surface now as "irrational beliefs" e.g., "I'm sooo ashamed that I'm such a no good, horrible, lousy student" and "It is so unbearably embarrassing to have to get down on my knees and grovel in front of my professors to get help." His view that the world is full of "selfish bastards" anyway makes it easy to not ask for help and thus he can protect himself from these feelings of shame. He is learning to use "thought-stopping" when these unhelpful tapes keep him from taking needed action.

BEHAVIORAL: Learning history, rewards and punishers
Ralph's parents used to criticize (punish) him if he didn't know things and asked too many questions. However, they heaped compliments on him for figuring things out without any help from them. Some

teachers in the past made him feel real dumb for asking "obvious" questions in class. He now avoids asking for help as a way of reducing his anxiety and avoid getting further possible negative responses. This "avoidance" behavior prevents him from getting the help he needs. His therapist is putting him through extinction training and counter-conditioning to deal with this "phobia;" and behavior modification to train up a new strategy.

BEHAVIORAL THERAPY

PROBLEM:	Phobic response to "helpers" (CER)				
	History of being punished for "asking for help"				
	Learned to avoid "helpers" (neg. reinforcement)				
	OPERANT:	Sd	R	S	
	Punishment	helpers	ask for help	criti-cism	unwell being
	CLASSICAL			USC–	UCR–
		CS			CR–
TREATMENT:	Change emotional response to helpers to positive tone (via systematic desensitization and counter-conditioning)				
	Positively reinforce asking for help				
	OPERANT:	Sd	R	S+	
	Pos. ref.	helpers	ask for help	gain help	well-being
	CLASSICAL			USC+	UCR+
		CS			CR+

HUMANISTIC: Inherent tendency for growth; satisfaction of basic needs
Ralph's current fear of asking for help makes perfect sense ("it is valid") in light of his life circumstances. He is striving for psychological safety by avoiding possible future disappointment and rejection. However he is also a talented student whose self-actualization is threatened by continuing this strategy for meeting psychological safety needs. With unconditional positive regard (the growth promoting environment of therapy) his self-esteem will grow and safety needs will be handled more productively—thus allowing him to continue toward self-actualization.

SOCIOCULTURAL: Role dysphoria
Ralph's father, an exceedingly successful business man, models, forcefully, the ideal that white, upper-class males, aren't supposed to need any help; they've got it made. Ralph is having a difficult time fulfilling these role expectations. In therapy Ralph is examining his internalized sense of the masculine role and working to expand it to include "the need for help."

Problem Set #10: Treatment of Disorders

Match the treatment approach (cognitive, behavioral, humanistic, sociological, psychodynamic, biomedical) with each of the following.

1. learned helplessness would be an important issue
2. utilized most by psychiatrists
3. examining a person's automatic "tapes" plays a central role
4. assumes client's problems are illnesses

5. assumes client's problems will be cured through "insight" into unconscious motives
6. assumes client's problems are conditioned emotional responses
7. assumes client's problems are a meaningful, valid reaction to current life circumstances
8. assumes client's problems stem from dysfunctional roles
9. Freud
10. Erikson
11. Carl Rogers
12. interpretation of dreams
13. use of bright lights
14. use of the empty chair technique
15. psychoanalysis
16. therapist runs for legislative office
17. systematic desensitization
18. examining the effects of discrimination and racism
19. pharmacotherapy
20. transference is a central aspect of therapy
21. building a congruent sense of self
22. use of unconditional positive regard
23. electroconvulsive shock therapy
24. relapse prevention therapy
25. family therapy, feminist therapy

Match the treatment or professional with the criterion, classification or description listed below. Treatments/professionals may be used more than once. Not all need be used.

hospitalization	involuntary treatment	pharmacotherapy
ECT	civil commitment	light therapy
antipsychotics	anxiolytics	antidepressants
psychoanalysis	insight-oriented therapy	person-centered
Gestalt, psychodrama	support group	behavior modification
systematic desensit.	aversive condition	RET
cognitive therapy	eclectic	family therapy
couples therapy	parent training	social activist
lobbyist	educator, bureaucrat	psychologist
psychiatric nurse	counselor	MHPs
relapse-prevention	psychoanalyst	

1. trained as an MD, or Ph.D. in psychology and has a special focus in the psychodynamic perspective
2. an example of therapy from the humanistic perspective
3. used to treat only severe, acute depression which does not respond to other treatments
4. "face-to-face" version of psychodynamic therapy
5. are licensed to prescribe medications
6. is used to help coordinate the consultation with many professionals
7. appointed by the State to assess the need for civil commitment and protect the civil liberties of clients
8. used to change undesirable emotional responses such as sexual arousal to kiddie porn

9. major side effects are movement disorders (e.g., tardive dyskinesia)
10. used for the treatment of seasonal affective disorder
11. relies on the manipulation of rewards and punishers to change behavior
12. have very extensive training in both psychological theory and research and the practice of psychotherapy
13. only professionals who are licensed to administer psychological tests
14. have no license or training requirements
15. clinicians who are extremely concerned about social justice might have roles as ______
16. therapy is designed to *confront* irrational beliefs
17. examples of the humanistic therapies
18. involves the clarification of true inner feelings by acting out some situation
19. would be the best therapy strategy for someone who wants to lose weight or quit smoking
20. would be the best strategy for helping someone deal with "fear of flying" or some other phobia
21. therapy attempts to provide an in depth analysis of all significant childhood traumas and conflicts
22. types of systems or sociological therapy
23. can be justified if the person meets a DSM-IV diagnosis and is gravely disabled
24. common side effect of treatment is memory loss
25. must have seven years of post-degree mental health experience before assuming their professional role
26. treatments which rely heavily on the "transference" relationship
27. two common side effects are dry mouth and sexual dysfunction
28. typically prescribed to treat hallucinations
29. treatment as high addictive potential
30. may use several different techniques at different stages of the treatment
31. What are the four stages of therapy? How would each theoretical approach be used?
32. What are four rights you have as a client in therapy in Washington State?
33. What clues would suggest that a particular therapist is not going to be able to help you or may even harm you in therapy?
34. What can you do if a therapist is unethical in your treatment?

See Appendix C for answers to problem set.

Appendix A

Operational Definitions Made Simple, Lasting and Useful

One of the most difficult things to get across to beginning psychology students is a reasonable understanding of the usefulness and limitations of *operational definitions.* To be sure, there are always students who quickly grasp these ideas and see their significance, but those students always seem to be in the minority. Should we go to a lot of trouble for operational definitions? I believe we should. One of the deeper appreciations for modern psychology, in my estimation, comes from the way psychologists have dealt with "mind" while attempting to maintain a scientific framework of activity. This is a perspective on psychology that students cannot afford to miss, and psychology probably cannot afford to have them miss it.

My goal, when dealing with difficult concepts, is to find something that is in the background of all of my students that will help them recognize the new as something already understood. One way has been to use analogy. I have used the household kitchen and kitchen recipes as analogies to the scientific laboratory and the operational definition. The analogy becomes so thoroughgoing, and the students' understanding so great, that many students become able to write fairly good definitions for certain psychological concepts. Some students, perhaps the more creative ones, are even able to originate fictitious psychological concepts and write operational definitions for them. I will give an example of these student efforts later. (Vandervert, L.R., Operational Definitions Made Simple, Lasting and Useful. *Teaching of Psychology,* Volume 7 (1), Feb., 1980, 57–59.)

Kitchen Analogy

The purpose of the *kitchen analogy* is to show students that they are already familiar with the important ideas related to operational definitions of psychological concepts. The main ideas covered are: Constructs, Empirical Referents, Quantification, Conditions of Control, and Scientific Agreement.

Most Americans grow up in homes that contain highly sophisticated scientific laboratories—the household kitchen:

- Hot and cold running water—into a temperature- and corrosive-resistant basin
- An adjustable cooling chamber
- An adjustable heating chamber

- A motorized, variable-speed mixing device
- A high-speed blending device
- A long list of measuring devices and containers
- Containers for use in the heating and cooling chambers
- A collection of substances that may be combined in accordance with empirically established (often internationally) methods and rules
- Handling and cutting tools
- Specialized texts, handbooks, and manuals of methods

Most of the things we prepare in the kitchen require several activities in the combining of ingredients. Therefore, we might easily refer to the things we prepare as things we construct—or simply refer to them as *constructs.* For example, we might refer to a cake prepared in our scientific kitchen as a physical construction. More simply, we may refer to a cake (or a building) as a *physical construct.* We usually follow a precise recipe in constructing a cake. The recipe lists specific activities or *operations* we must perform to obtain the desired physical cake. The recipe can be referred to as a definition of the cake in terms of operations. More simply, the recipe is an operational definition of the cake. Now, we have two ways of saying the same thing: "recipe for a cake," or "operational definition for a physical construct."

The operational definition (recipe) for a cake consists of written instructions including specification of the substances to be mixed in relation to one another, *empirical referents,* the apparatus to be used, conditions of control, the various amounts of substances and apparatuses used, quantification, and the operations we must perform to mix things in the proper relationship. If the operational definition is followed carefully, the result will be the specific desired cake. Perhaps the operations have defined a chocolate cake with vanilla frosting—first defined by that team of French experts in 1938.

The perfect cake obtained by sticking closely to the operational definition for the physical construct, "cake," should be identical to the one the French creators had in mind in 1938. We might conclude that the motive behind writing operational definitions for cakes is to ensure that anyone, anywhere who wished to follow the operations could produce and observe the same cake. This result is a type of scientific agreement. One may not like this particular cake, or think anyone ought to eat it, but he certainly could produce what the French experts had in mind.

These ideas about converting the making of a cake into a set of operations to be carried out in a scientific laboratory are:

- Physical Construct—"Cake"
- Operational Definition—Recipe
- Empirical Referents—Ingredients, aspects of apparatus
- Quantifications of Control Conditions—Cups, teaspoons, ounces, etc.; Specification of apparatus conditions, e.g., 350° for 45 minutes
- Scientific Agreement—Identical cakes produced in France and United States 39 years apart

At this point in the analogy two very important points should be made. Both of them refer to the limitations of operational definitions, and the limitations apply to both the constructing of cakes and to the construction of psychological concepts. First, cakes never occur naturally—they must be constructed. The same may be said of psychological constructs. At least three ideas (in analogy form) are important here:

- Cakes can only be constructed by following the appropriate operational definition (recipe).
- In reality, then, the recipe cannot be separated from the cake—the operational definition cannot be separated from the construct.
- It would be a mistake to assume that the recipe carried some "real" meaning beyond the cake it produced.

Second, the writing of recipes for the constructing of cakes may tend to fix the way cakes are generally constructed, as well as the way we think about them, but it certainly does not fix the way they can be made in the future. Actually, if one realizes that the set of operations is always open to alteration, it can be seen that the operational definition can serve as a basis for the continual refinement of the construct in question. We can always attempt to produce a better cake by adding a little extra of this or that. It sometimes happens that we follow the recipe perfectly, except for one mistake or accident, and we stumble onto a new treat. A new construct has come into being, and if we are smart, we'll immediately write a set of operations that will reproduce it.

Psychological Concepts (Ideational Constructs)

In the same way we talk about a cake as a physical construct, we can talk about certain psychological concepts such as "fear" or "intelligence" as *ideational constructions.* With the appropriate operational definition, a particular version of the psychological concept can be produced for observation.

Through the kitchen analogy we have been brought very close to what P.W. Bridgeman was expressing in his *The Logic of Modern Physics* (1927), "We mean by any concept nothing more than a set of operations: the concept is synonymous with the corresponding set of physical operations." Students do not find it too difficult to interpret Bridgemen's statement in terms of cakes and recipes.

A summary which matches the ideas presented in the physical construction of a cake with the identical construction of a psychological concept of "fear" is as follows:

- Ideational Construct—"fear"
- Operational Definition—written statement of operations to perform to observe
- Empirical Referents—stimuli, responses, and organismic variables; apparatus (one may wish to equate S, R, and O with matching versions of them)
- Quantifications of Control Conditions—amplitude, frequency, duration, latency, type; specification of apparatus conditions
- Scientific Agreement—identical observations of "fear," and possible identical notions of fear in observers

In a scientific psychology, ideational constructs such as "fear" are constructed from such empirical "ingredients" as stimulus, response, and organismic variables. These variables are expressed in a particular relationship to one another (mixed and baked) to stand for, for example, "fear." Notice that the S, O, and R variables serve as the building blocks in the derivation of the construct of fear.

Classroom Exercise

I have found that students enjoy this classroom exercise on operational definitions tremendously. The exercise illustrates in a simple way the necessity of reaching agreement as to what set of operations will be used to define the psychological concept in question.

Having been exposed to the kitchen analogy, students are asked to write an operational definition for the construct "fear" (since they have not yet been given a complete definition of it). If they are cautioned to think through the analogy and to carefully restrict themselves to statements about stimuli, responses, and organismic variables, they will find that they can do quite well. They might even find that they have improved upon the definition of "fear" provided by William S. Verplanck in his "A Glossary of Some Terms Used in the Objective Science of Behavior" (1957):

> FEAR: 1. (empirical, behavior theory) the behavior produced either by sudden and intense stimulation or by specific classes of stimuli that must be identified empirically for each species studied. Responses include alterations of sphincter control, flight behavior, respiratory changes, and the suppression of behavior occurring at the onset of stimulation. (p. 15)

The fear definition has been used because it illustrates the S-O-R construct so well. Also, students can identify in a humorous way with alterations of sphincter control, and suppression of behavior occurring at the onset of stimulation (just say, BOO!). Students become particularly fascinated when given a chance to try their hand at writing operational definitions for such concepts as love or religion, etc. They also now have a clear mental set to ask critical questions about what sub-sets of S's are mixed with what sub-sets of R's and O's to produce what psychologists are talking about.

The most exciting things the kitchen analogy has produced for me have been occasions when students have gone beyond the classroom activity of writing operational definitions for already defined "pieces of mind," and have attempted to produce new operational expressions of "mind" that have never before been written (as far as they know). For example, one student decided (after a discussion about how intelligence might be operationalized) that belief was an ability, and, further, was normally distributed. He suggested that some people had a greater ability to believe than others, and variations in the ability to believe accounted for a number of everyday observations on human behavior. He felt he could eventually define belief as an ability and develop a test for it. I don't know whether or not he ever did. But I have the satisfaction of knowing that his belief about belief was originally cultured into existence by a discussion of intelligence within the context of the kitchen analogy. I also know that the student came to grips with one of the deeper appreciations of modern scientific psychology.

Glossary

constructs: Any things or events which come about by carrying out operational descriptions.

empirical referent: The basis to which reference is made.

ideational construct: Any complex idea which is capable of becoming observable, or assuming an observable form, through specified operations.

kitchen analogy: The description of the similarities between the activities and tools of the household kitchen, and those of the scientific laboratory.

operational definition: A statement of the operations necessary to objectively observe what is meant by a term. This procedure permits the scientific study of the term.

operations: The activities and tools which are specified in operational descriptions, including recipes.

physical construct: Any complex observable thing or event which comes about through specified operations.

Appendix B

Practice Exam Questions

Lois McDermott

Answers are not provided to these questions because we want you to study the material until YOU know the answers.

Exam 1: Methods and Biopsychology

1. A hypothesis is a(n):
   a. statement of actual results.
   b. organizing principle.
   c. testable prediction.
   d. operational definition.

2. In psychology, we study sentient organisms. Sentient organisms are those that:
   a. are capable of higher order mental processes.
   b. possess a nervous system.
   c. are capable of locomotion.
   d. are mammals.

3. A researcher did a predictive study to look at the relationship between variables x and y. He obtained a coefficient of .85. What kind of relationship does this correlation suggest?
   a. strongly positive
   b. weakly positive
   c. strongly negative
   d. weakly negative

4. In an explanative study, the group you want to generalize FROM is called the ______; the group you want to generalize TO is called the ______.
   a. control group; experimental group
   b. random sample; representative sample
   c. sample; population
   d. population; sample

5. You want to determine the effect of various amounts of caffeine on anxiety as measured by galvanic skin response (GSR). You select a sample of 150 Psych 101 students to participate in the study. You want to understand how caffeine affects people in general, not just college students. By using only Psych 101 students as subjects, which of the following may be jeopardized?
   a. reliability
   b. generalizability
   c. significance
   d. validity

6. In the caffeine study above, you find that caffeine does indeed increase anxiety as measured by GSR. You decide to do a follow-up study in which you measure the effect of caffeine on anxiety as measured by the scores on the McDermott Anxiety Index. You administer the caffeine exactly the same way you did in the first study. How is the second study DIFFERENT from the first study?
   a. It uses a different independent variable.
   b. It uses a different dependent variable.
   c. It uses a different operationalization of the independent variable.
   d. It uses a different operationalization of the dependent variable.

7. Dr. Tseng is conducting research on human decision making in a business setting. He studies actual decision making in the workplace. His research focuses on how people process and retrieve information in order to make business decisions. What is Dr. Tseng's research perspective?
   a. humanistic
   b. behavioral
   c. biological
   d. cognitive

8. Which of the following is true of balanced assignment as a method for placing subjects in groups for an experiment?
   a. it is inexpensive
   b. it ensures that all the groups are equal with regard to the variable balanced for
   c. it is relatively easy to do
   d. it is particularly well-suited for large samples

9. Dean Fred Campbell wants to know what students who participate in the U.W. Freshman Interest Group program think of this program. To find out, he prepares and distributes opinion surveys to all students in the program. What kind of research is Dr. Campbell conducting?
   a. descriptive
   b. predictive
   c. explanative
   d. archival

10. Dr. Lundy, an IBM researcher, wants to develop an easy-to-use keyboard for IBM computer systems. She designs four different keyboards and randomly assigns subjects to use one of the keyboards to type for one minute. She assesses the number of typing errors made in order to see which keyboard is easiest to use. Which scientific value has been addressed in the methods used to conduct the experiment?
    a. power
    b. reliability
    c. significance
    d. generalizability

11. In the keyboard study above, the independent variable (IV) is ______ and the independent variable (DV) is ______.
    a. keyboard design, typing accuracy
    b. typing accuracy, typing speed
    c. typing speed, keyboard design
    d. there is no IV or DV because this is a correlational study
12. Which of the following statements about explanative research is FALSE? Explanative research:
    a. has two or more quantifiable variables
    b. requires that the dependent variable can be manipulated
    c. is used to assess cause-and-effect relationships
    d. tests a hypothesis
13. Which of the following factors is NOT an appropriate goal in correlational research? Correlational research is used to:
    a. determine the direction of the correlation
    b. determine the strength of the correlation
    c. establish whether there is a relationship between the variables
    d. determine which of the variables causes changes in the other variable
14. In the "kitten study" film shown in class, kittens were raised either in normal light or in total darkness. Kittens in both groups received the same amount of food and lived in the same-sized cages. After a few months, their visual acuity was assessed by having them navigate a visually-confusing maze. Which of the following was a control variable?
    a. number of errors made navigating the maze
    b. light deprivation during early development
    c. cage size
    d. time required to navigate the maze
15. The type of statistics we use to analyze scientific results depends upon the goal of our study. Which of the following is a correct pairing of goals and statistics?
    a. description—correlation coefficients
    b. prediction—averages
    c. prediction—inferential statistics
    d. cause/effect—inferential statistics
16. The text mentions a predictive study which showed that low self-esteem tends to be associated with a high level of depression. If this finding is true, how would we best describe the correlation between self-esteem and depression?
    a. causal
    b. random
    c. negative
    d. positive
17. Dr. Sorenson is a psychologist who encourages his psychotherapy clients to focus on the here and now, to accept themselves, and to take personal responsibility for their own actions. Which of the following best characterizes his perspective?
    a. behavioral
    b. psychoanalytic
    c. biological
    d. humanistic

18. A student was asked to design a study for a research methods class. She proposes a study to look at the relationship between head circumference (head size) and IQ. What kind of research is she proposing?
    a. descriptive
    b. correlational
    c. experimental
    d. inferential
19. Which of the following describes a difference between dendrites and axons?
    a. dendrites are typically longer in length than axons are
    b. dendrites inhibit action potentials; axons transmit action potentials
    c. dendrites are not myelinated; axons are myelinated (have a myelin sheath)
    d. dendrites receive sensory information; axons transmit motor information
20. If you are being chased by a bear, which of the following systems would **NOT** be helpful in making your escape?
    a. sympathetic nervous system
    b. somatic nervous system
    c. central nervous system
    d. parasympathetic nervous system
21. What is a likely result of stimulating the amygdala?
    a. spontaneous reoccurrence of memories
    b. clenching your fists and standing aggressively
    c. eating more
    d. apathy; lack of emotion
22. Joan works in an architecture firm. She was in a car accident that damaged the right side of her brain. When Joan was able to return to work, she had trouble with:
    a. telling her coworkers about her ideas
    b. designing the layout of buildings
    c. writing a letter to a client
    d. reading her coworker's evaluation report
23. Sarah had her corpus callosum severed because she suffered from severe epilepsy. As part of a study, she is shown an apple. What result occurs when she is asked to identify the object?
    a. If shown in her right visual field, she can tell the experimenter that the object is an apple.
    b. If shown in her right visual field, her left hand can pick out the apple.
    c. If shown in her left visual field, she can tell the experimenter that the object is an apple.
    d. If shown in her left visual field, her right hand picks out an apple.
24. You are testing subjects to find out which hemisphere is dominant for language. After anesthetizing the left hemisphere in your subjects, you find that:
    a. right handed subjects have more language difficulty than left handed subjects
    b. right handed subjects have less language difficulty than left handed subjects
    c. right handed and left handed subjects have the same amount of language difficulty
    d. none of the subjects have language difficulty
25. Andy is a two-year-old who fell from a swing and hit his head on a rock. Dr. Jones determined that Andy has permanent damage in Wernicke's area. What does Dr. Jones tell Andy's mother? Andy will:
    a. initially have difficulty comprehending speech, but will probably recover his ability to comprehend speech.
    b. initially have difficulty producing speech, and will probably not recover his speaking ability.
    c. initially have difficulty producing speech, and will probably recover his speaking ability.
    d. have no discernible problems as a result of the damage.

26. Which of the following would be used to show the brain's consumption of glucose?
    a. magnetic resonance imaging (MRI)
    b. positron emission tomograph scan (PET)
    c. computerized axial tomograph scan (CAT)
    d. Electroencephalogram (EEG)

27. Janet has no awareness of the left side of her body. When she looks at her left arm, she doesn't recognize it as her own. When she eats food, she ignores the left side of her plate. When asked to draw a star, she only draws the right half of the figure. What area of Janet's brain has probably been damaged?
    a. right visual association area
    b. left visual association area
    c. left somatosensory association area
    d. right somatosensory association area

28. Dr. Smith asks Tom to select an object that MATCHES the image of a frying pan. Which of the following correctly pairs the visual field with the response that would be made?
    a. right visual field—left hand selects racquetball racquet
    b. right visual field—right hand selects toaster
    c. left visual field—left hand selects toaster
    d. left visual field—right hand selects racquetball racquet

29. When experimenters damage the reticular formation, the organism:
    a. cannot fall asleep
    b. cannot wake up
    c. has little control over voluntary coordinated movement
    d. cannot spatially orient itself

30. Which of the following pairs correctly matches the brain area with its function?
    a. Wernicke's area—speech production
    b. angular gyrus—pattern recognition
    c. somatosensory cortex—word comprehension
    d. visual cortex—visual pattern extraction

31. When someone lightly taps you on the arm, the sensory neurons in your arm:
    a. will fire as often as they would if you were punched in the arm
    b. fire an electrical impulse with less intensity than they would if you were punched in the arm
    c. fire at a rate of about 2 miles per hour, as opposed to up to 200 miles per hour if you are punched in the arm
    d. fire less often than they would if you were punched in the arm

32. Motivation, emotion, and simple memory are controlled by the:
    a. brainstem
    b. cerebellum
    c. cerebrum
    d. limbic system

33. Which of the following describes your brain?
    a. the larger a body part is, the greater the area of sensory cortex devoted to it
    b. your brain has more association areas than the brains of less intelligent organisms
    c. it is divided into six lobes
    d. we use less than 10 percent of our brain

34. Which pair correctly matches the cortical lobe with a function associated with that lobe?
    a. frontal lobe—hearing
    b. parietal lobe—motor
    c. temporal lobe—smell
    d. occipital lobe—vision

Exam 2: Consciousness and Motivation

1. Dexter always seemed to be trying to develop new inventions. Dexter's thinking is probably energized and directed by which of Maslow's needs?
    a. safety
    b. physiological
    c. love
    d. self-actualization
2. Nancy always seems to be terribly hurt if she doesn't receive an occasional pat-on-the-back for doing everyday things. Nancy is probably feeling this way due to which of Maslow's needs?
    a. esteem
    b. self-actualization
    c. love
    d. physiological
3. Which of Maslow's needs probably does NOT influence a dog's behavior?
    a. safety
    b. love
    c. esteem
    d. physiological
4. Which of the following is NOT a part of achievement motivation?
    a. accomplish something unique
    b. overcome obstacles
    c. high standards
    d. intelligence
5. Which of the following is the James-Lange theory of emotion?
    a. perception; sadness; tears
    b. perception; hypothalamic activity; tears
    c. perception; tears and ANS activity; sadness
    d. tears; sadness; perception
6. Anna was at a Huskies football game. When the Huskies scored a touchdown, Anna immediately fell asleep, and fell out of her chair. Anna suffers from:
    a. sleep apnea
    b. narcolepsy
    c. epilepsy
    d. somnambulism
7. Which of the following is a characteristic of stages 2–4 sleep?
    a. restorative sleep
    b. muscle paralysis
    c. increased sensory awareness
    d. SNS tone

8. Joe has been asleep for about one hour. Kelly has been asleep for about one and a half hours. Which statement is TRUE?
   a. Joe's EEG shows LVF waves; Kelly's EEG shows HVS waves.
   b. Kelly will be harder to awaken and get moving around than Joe.
   c. Kelly is less likely to show signs of sexual arousal than Joe is.
   d. If Joe and Kelly are awakened, both may report they were dreaming.
9. When you wake up in the morning, you remember dreaming about an abandoned old house. According to the psychodynamic theory of dreaming:
   a. The house is the manifest content of the dream.
   b. If the abandoned house represents feelings of loneliness, the feelings of loneliness are the manifest content of the dream.
   c. The latent content of the dream consists of experiences and preoccupations from the day's events.
   d. A house is just a house.
10. Research on hypnosis has shown that when hypnotized people are exposed to an acute pain, they:
    a. have no physiological response to the stimulus
    b. report less pain than unhypnotized people
    c. if asked to do so, indicate nonverbally that no part of them feels pain
    d. experience the same level of pain as unhypnotized people
11. Which statement about sleep apnea is FALSE?
    a. Most people who suffer from sleep apnea are overweight men.
    b. People with sleep apnea "snore."
    c. People with sleep apnea have cardiovascular (heart) trouble which wakes them up throughout the night.
12. Which of the following pairings of drug and effect on consciousness is INCORRECT?
    a. LSD—hallucinations
    b. nicotine—arousal
    c. opiates—relief of pain
    d. barbiturates—alertness
13. According to the BIOLOGICAL model of dreaming:
    a. REM decreases with age, as the rate of new learning decreases
    b. PGO spikes cause NREM activity
    c. REM decreases as the CNS matures and external stimuli increase
    d. REM increases during periods of emotional stress
14. What is the PRIMARY reason most research psychologists do not believe in extrasensory perceptions (ESP)?
    a. Psychologists know people are easily deceived.
    b. Near-death experiences can be explained as hallucinogenic effects.
    c. Findings of extrasensory perceptions have not been reproducible.
    d. Although a few individuals have shown clear-cut extrasensory abilities, they are too few to conclude that extrasensory perception is possible.
15. When a person has night terror, s/he:
    a. is in paradoxical sleep
    b. may sit up, experience a doubling of heart rate, and appear terrified
    c. is usually in Stage 5 sleep
    d. is probably in the last hour of sleep

16. Dr. Yang is conducting research on dreaming. In order to measure subject's eye movements, she uses a(n):
    a. electrooculargram (EOG)
    b. electromyogram (EMG)
    c. electroencephalogram (EEG)
    d. electrocardiogram (EKG)
17. The COGNITIVE model of dreaming is supported by the fact that:
    a. PGO spikes disrupt thoughts and memories
    b. REM increases during periods of emotional stress
    c. REM deprivation decreases learning and memory
    d. Studying the dreamer's view of the dream brings insight into the personality of the dreamer
18. John is a high school senior who gets high grades and excels in team sports. His friends say he is very competitive. He has applied to highly-ranked colleges such as Harvard and Yale. Maslow would say that John spends much of his time satisfying his:
    a. physiological needs
    b. esteem needs
    c. belongingness and love needs
    d. safety needs
19. In animal studies, when the lateral hypothalamus (LH) is DESTROYED:
    a. well-fed animals want to eat
    b. starving animals do not want to eat
    c. adult animals want to copulate
    d. adult animals do not want to copulate
20. When nine-year-old Suzie was shown a plate of chocolate chip cookies after she had eaten a full meal, she could not resist munching on a cookie, even though she was full. In this case, Suzie is:
    a. responding to the incentive value of food
    b. responding to an internal food cue
    c. trying to achieve homeostasis
    d. exhibiting free feeding
21. From lowest to highest, what is the correct order of Maslow's hierarchy of needs?
    a. physiological, safety, esteem, belongingness, self-actualization
    b. safety, physiological, belongingness, esteem, self-actualization
    c. physiological, safety, belongingness, esteem, self-actualization
    d. belongingness, safety, physiological, esteem, self-actualization
22. An incentive is:
    a. the physiological aim of drive reduction
    b. a type of instinct
    c. any cyclic behavior
    d. an external stimulus whose power to energize behavior is learned

Exam 3: Learning and Cognition

1. Joe studies hard at the university to keep his scholarship, to avoid his parents' disapproval, and to get into graduate school. What type of operant schedule is Joe on?
    a. continuous reinforcement
    b. multiple reinforcement
    c. concurrent reinforcement and punishment
    d. primary reinforcement

2. In classical conditioning, behavior is MAINTAINED when:
   a. the conditioned stimulus is introduced after the conditioned response reoccurs spontaneously.
   b. the unconditioned stimulus is periodically presented with the conditioned stimulus.
   c. a stimulus similar to the original conditioned stimulus is presented.
   d. the conditioned stimulus is presented without the unconditioned stimulus.
3. In a famous experiment, Little Albert played with a white rat. Then experimenters introduced a scary noise while Albert was playing with the rat. Albert became fearful not only when he saw rats, but when he saw anything that reminded him of a rat, such as a blanket or his mother's fur coat. Albert's fear in response to his blanket is an example of:
   a. extinction
   b. generalization
   c. acquisition
   d. spontaneous recovery
4. To DECREASE the incidence of an unwanted behavior, which two operant techniques would you use?
   a. positive punishment and negative punishment
   b. negative punishment and negative reinforcement
   c. negative reinforcement and DRO
   d. extinction training and negative reinforcement
5. Which of the following does NOT belong to this set of synonyms (i.e., all refer to the same thing)?
   a. operant conditioning
   b. instrumental conditioning
   c. classical conditioning
   d. Skinnerian conditioning
6. You work full-time as an accounting manager at Games-Are-Us Software. If your employer pays you every two weeks, your employer is using a(n) ______ reinforcement schedule; if you are paid on commission (a percentage of each batch of items you sell) your employer is using a ______ reinforcement schedule.
   a. fixed ratio; variable ratio
   b. fixed interval; variable ratio
   c. fixed interval; variable interval
   d. variable interval; fixed ratio
7. In operant conditioning, if you want to MAXIMIZE a behavior's resistance to extinction, you would use ______ reinforcement during shaping and ______ reinforcement during the maintenance phase.
   a. continuous; intermittent
   b. primary; reinforcement
   c. intermittent; partial
   d. multiple; concurrent
8. John is afraid of flying on airplanes after he had a bad experience in a plane when he was a child. John's therapist treats John's phobia by having him imagine being in a plane while breathing deeply and listening to soothing music. What technique is the therapist using to treat John's phobia?
   a. aversion training
   b. DRO
   c. relaxation training
   d. consequential learning

9. In operant conditioning, when the reinforcement for a particular response is removed, the incidence of that response will:
   a. gradually decrease at a steady pace
   b. initially increase, then gradually decrease
   c. initially decrease slightly, then rapidly decrease
   d. be maintained until a positive punishment is administered; then it will decrease gradually

10. In operant conditioning, a response cost results when:
    a. a positive stimulus (S+) is added
    b. a positive stimulus (S+) is removed
    c. a negative stimulus (S–) is added
    d. the loss of a positive stimulus (S+) is prevented

11. Cigarette ads in magazines often show young, attractive people smoking cigarettes. What behavioral technique are these ads using to sell cigarettes?
    a. relaxation training
    b. consequence learning
    c. operant conditioning
    d. associative learning

12. Which of the following is NOT an example of a classically conditioned response?
    a. playing the piano
    b. disliking smoking after receiving aversion training
    c. feeling terrific after winning the Washington State lottery
    d. feeling angry after someone ridicules you

13. When you turn the ignition in your new car, an annoying buzz appears until you buckle on your seat belt. According to operant conditioning principles, the buzz is a ______.
    a. positive reinforcer
    b. negative reinforcer
    c. positive punisher
    d. negative punisher

14. When we teach a pigeon to turn counter-clockwise in a 360 degree circle by rewarding him every time he turns a little further around the circle in the correct direction, we are employing:
    a. counter-conditioning
    b. maintenance training
    c. DRO
    d. shaping

15. A secondary reinforcer is the same thing as a(n):
    a. positive conditioned stimulus (CS+)
    b. positive unconditioned stimulus (UCS+)
    c. negative reinforcer (S–)
    d. non-contingent reinforcer (S–)

16. Mary was awakened by her smoke detector. Her pulse raced; she felt fear. She jumped out of bed and fled her smoky apartment. In Pavlovian terms, the blaring alarm is a(n) ______; in Skinnerian terms, her fleeing the apartment is being ______.
    a. discriminative stimulus (Sd); negatively punished
    b. discriminative stimulus (Sd); positively reinforced
    c. unconditioned response; negatively punished
    d. unconditioned stimulus; negatively reinforced

17. In ESCAPE training, the response serves to ______ the negative stimulus; in AVOIDANCE training, the response serves to ______ the onset of the negative stimulus or the loss of the positive stimulus.
    a. terminate; prevent
    b. prevent; increase
    c. prevent; terminate
    d. increase; decrease

18. Little Jerry throws a tantrum at nursery school, so the teacher tells him to take a "time out" (to go sit in the corner without anything to play with) until he can behave more appropriately. What behavioral technique is the teacher using?
    a. extinction
    b. negative reinforcement
    c. positive punishment
    d. negative punishment

19. If I pay my electric bill (1) to avoid a late charge and (2) to get continuing electric service, which of the following is FALSE?
    a. The late charge is serving as a negative reinforcer and the electric service is serving as a positive reinforcer.
    b. The late charge is a S– and the electric service is a S+.
    c. The arrival of the electric bill is the Sd.
    d. The late charge and electric service are unconditioned reinforcers.

20. Following removal of his temporal lobes, H.M., who no longer could no longer form new memories for facts and experiences, lost his ______ memory system but not his ______ memory system.
    a. nondeclarative; declarative
    b. declarative; nondeclarative
    c. semantic; episodic
    d. episodic; semantic

21. Which of the following types of memory retrieval is involved when a student is asked to take an essay type of examination?
    a. recognition
    b. relearning
    c. rehearsal
    d. recall

22. Sarah is describing what her summer camp was like to a friend who is considering going there. Which type of memory is she using?
    a. semantic
    b. episodic
    c. nondeclarative
    d. declarative

23. If you cannot correctly draw an exact replica of the "tails" side of a quarter, what type of memory problem are you MOST LIKELY to be experiencing?
    a. encoding failure
    b. retrieval failure
    c. storage problem
    d. repression

24. The echoic storage of memory requires ______ input whereas the iconic storage processes ______ memory.

    a. semantic; episodic
    b. episodic; semantic
    c. visual; auditory
    d. auditory; visual

25. Subjects hear a list of 15 words. Following a one-minute delay where subjects are asked to count backwards in threes, they are asked to recall as many of the words from the list as they can. They will be most likely to remember words at the ______ of the list.

    a. beginning
    b. middle
    c. end
    d. beginning and end

26. If people are given a long list of words to remember, they will recall more words if:

    a. they repeat each word over and over until they hear the next word
    b. they concentrate on rehearsing the first and last few words on the list
    c. they organize the list into semantic categories
    d. a line drawing accompanies the word

27. According to the "levels of processing" model of memory, you will remember something better if you:

    a. store it in LTM
    b. process it deeply
    c. store it with related concepts
    d. repeat it over and over

28. What is the effect of aging on memory?

    a. Recall decreases more rapidly than recognition.
    b. Recognition decreases more rapidly than recall.
    c. Recall and recognition decrease by the same amount.
    d. Recognition increases, but recall decreases.

29. If you study in the same room in which you later take an exam, you may do better on the exam than if you had studied in a different room. This finding is best explained by:

    a. context-dependent memory
    b. state-dependent memory
    c. memory construction
    d. flashbulb memories

30. When a student learns the colors of the visual spectrum by using the term ROY G, BIV, the student is using:

    a. an acronym
    b. the peg word system
    c. the method of loci
    d. mental imagery

31. Consider the experiment presented in class about the two-car accident at an intersection. Half of the subjects were asked to estimate the probable speed the cars were going when they "smashed," the other half were asked the speed the cars were going when they "hit." The "hit" group will estimate the speeds of the cars to be ______ than the "smashed" group will, because of ______.

    a. faster; context-dependent memory
    b. slower; memory construction
    c. faster; memory construction
    d. slower; context-dependent memory

32. You have an exam in eight hours. You plan to study for four hours and relax for four hours. You would be better off first ____, because it would minimize ___ interference.
    a. studying; retroactive
    b. relaxing; retroactive
    c. relaxing; proactive
    d. studying; proactive

33. Patients with anterograde amnesia:
    a. cannot remember events before their injuries
    b. cannot remember their names
    c. cannot hold anything in short-term memory
    d. cannot learn anything new after their injuries

34. Lesions of the hippocampus lead to an impairment in the ability to:
    a. transfer information from the sensory register to STM
    b. retrieve information from STM
    c. retrieve information from LTM
    d. transfer information from STM to LTM

Exam 4: Social and Personality

1. Joe Smith, a businessman, comes from an individualistic culture. He flies to Jan Sodal's country, which has a collectivist culture. When Joe has a business meeting with Jan, he will probably get along with her best if he:
    a. is candid and open about any criticisms he has
    b. gets right to the point of the meeting, with few introductions
    c. speaks highly of his own skills and accomplishments
    d. avoids confrontation

2. Harold listens to the evening news and hears about a plane crash in Europe in which all 200 people died, including two Americans. Harold is most upset about the death of the two Americans. This is an example of:
    a. prejudice
    b. in-group bias
    c. just-world phenomenon
    d. attribution theory

3. Ken knows that the number of salmon in the Skagit River has been declining in recent years, but he continues to fish anyway. Ken later cancels his membership in an environmental group, saying he doesn't believe in the group's ideas. What psychological process is at work here?
    a. self-serving bias
    b. fundamental attribution error
    c. cognitive dissonance
    d. superordinate goals

4. In the 1994 Olympics, the United States ski team and the Norwegian team are fierce competitors. What would be the best way to encourage them to get along?
    a. When they compete, stage the results so that the teams vie for first place.
    b. Have both teams eat their meals in the same cafeteria.
    c. Organize a second ski event in which the U.S. and Norway team up against Canada and Russia.
    d. Hold a meeting in which you explain the benefits of superordinate goals to both teams and encourage them to interact.

5. Hate crimes are acts of violence which:
   a. are motivated by hatred of a particular person
   b. only happen after a bad experience with a group or victim
   c. are rarely seen on college campuses
   d. are directed towards a particular group or an individual as its proxy.

6. While visiting France, Lisa met a couple of very loud, rude, and obnoxious Frenchmen. Lisa returned home and told her friends that French people are loud, rude, and obnoxious. Her thoughts about the French can best be described as:
   a. categorization
   b. overgeneralization
   c. deindividuation
   d. in-group bias

7. Jill sees on the news that Mr. Smith was robbed. According to the just-world phenomenon, she is most likely to think that Mr. Smith was robbed because:
   a. Mr. Smith lives in a bad neighborhood
   b. the robber was clever
   c. the robber got lucky
   d. Mr. Smith was careless

8. In the Milgram studies of obedience to authority, Milgram found that subjects are LEAST likely to give the maximum shock when they:
   a. have more aggressive personalities
   b. are put in a position of authority
   c. never see the victim
   d. think no one would know they were the ones giving the shocks

9. Fred is led into a room with 10 other people. Fred and the others are shown a slide of two lines. Line A is clearly shorter than Line B. But when the experimenter asks everyone which line is shorter, all the other people say Line B is shorter. Then Fred must give his response. Based on Asch's experiments, we would expect Fred to say that:
   a. the lines are the same length
   b. Line A is shorter
   c. Line B is shorter
   d. he doesn't know which line is shorter

10. Based on the Milgram studies, you design an experiment in which you have a doctor order a nurse to give 20 mg of a drug. You also have another doctor say, "No, I think that's a bad idea." The nurse knows that 5 mg is the recommended dose and that 10 mg is the maximum dose allowed. Based on what you know about Milgram's studies, what percentage of nurses do you predict will comply with the 20 mg order?
    a. 95 percent
    b. 65 percent
    c. 50 percent
    d. 1 percent

11. Larry works in a shoe factory and rides the bus to work to save money. A stranger gets on the bus and drops a lot of coins on the floor. Under what circumstances will Larry be MOST likely to help the person pick up the coins?
    a. There are 20 other people on the bus.
    b. Larry found a ten-dollar bill just before he got on the bus.
    c. Larry lives in a large city.
    d. The stranger is a well-dressed, confident male.

12. Dr. Levins trained confederates to act as interviewers and told subjects that they would be interviewed for a job. Dr. Levins made sure that all of the subjects were equally qualified for the job and had similar verbal skills. Then the interviewers either gave cold, guarded interviews or friendly interactive interviews. Dr. Levins found that subjects performed well in the warm interview and performed poorly in the cold interview. This illustrates which of the following?
    a. racial bias
    b. self-fulfilling prophecy
    c. deindividuation
    d. informational social influence
13. Karen works at a bank in which Fred was just fired. She thinks that he was fired because he's a lazy worker. Karen's explanation reflects all of the following principles EXCEPT:
    a. just-world phenomenon
    b. blaming the victim
    c. individualism
    d. fundamental attribution error
14. You've just aced an exam. You think you did well because you studied hard and are an intelligent person. This is an example of:
    a. self-serving bias
    b. low empathy
    c. situational factors
    d. categorization
15. In the Zimbardo study involving Stanford students acting as prisoners or guards, the "guards" treated the "prisoners" poorly, and the prisoners also fell into their roles as prisoners very quickly. All of the following can help explain the behavior of the guards EXCEPT:
    a. group polarization
    b. in-group bias
    c. social facilitation
    d. deindividuation
16. If Dr. Wen describes Elmira as being extroverted, anxious, soft-hearted, imaginative and impulsive, he is describing Elmira's personality from a ___ perspective.
    a. psychodynamic
    b. trait
    c. humanistic
    d. social-cognitive
17. ___ are devices for assessing personality that ask subjects to respond in some way to ambiguous stimuli.
    a. Personality inventories
    b. Objective psychological tests
    c. Projective tests
    d. Structured interviews
18. Eysenck believes that all personality traits can be explained in terms of combinations of:
    a. introversion-extroversion and stability-instability
    b. introversion-extroversion and agreeableness-disagreeableness
    c. stability-instability and agreeableness-disagreeableness
    d. agreeableness-disagreeableness and optimistic-pessimistic

19. According to Freud, children in the ___ psychosexual stage of development are very interested in their sexual organs and must resolve conflicts with their parents.
    a. genital
    b. phallic
    c. anal
    d. oral
20. Ron is a typical extrovert. This suggests that he will _______, and is _______.
    a. seek out stimulating situations; insensitive to punishment
    b. avoid stimulating situations; insensitive to punishment
    c. seek out stimulating situations; sensitive to punishment
    d. avoid stimulating situations; sensitive to punishment
21. Freud uses several techniques to study a person's unconscious. Which technique did he NOT use?
    a. dream analysis
    b. handwriting analysis
    c. free association
    d. slips of the tongue
22. The id is:
    a. entirely unconscious
    b. entirely conscious
    c. largely conscious
    d. half unconscious and half conscious
23. Tom really dislikes his boss Joe, but represses his feelings so that he can do his job. One day, Joe has been particularly difficult. As Joe gets ready to leave for a meeting, Tom intends to say, "Have a nice day." However, what he actually says is, "Have a nice death." Tom's error is called a ________, and is a product of his ______ mind.
    a. displacement; unconscious
    b. slip of the tongue; unconscious
    c. displacement; conscious
    d. slip of the tongue; conscious
24. Which of the following ego defense mechanisms involves the use of false, but plausible, explanations or excuses for anxiety-arousing behavior?
    a. sublimation
    b. reaction formation
    c. rationalization
    d. projection
25. The superego differs from the ego in that:
    a. the ego is realistic and the superego is moralistic
    b. the ego tries to control the id, while the superego controls the ego
    c. the ego is conscious and the superego is unconscious
    d. the ego is realistic and the superego is impulsive
26. As a child, whenever Victoria got angry, she was severely punished. As a result, whenever something happens in her adult life to anger Victoria, she feels anxious and guilty instead. Victoria's behavior is being governed by the:
    a. ego
    b. alterego
    c. id
    d. superego

27. The self-concept, according to Carl Rogers:
    a. is an organized, consistent set of perceptions and beliefs about oneself
    b. is a seething cauldron of basic instincts
    c. seeks immediate gratification
    d. avoids contact with reality

28. David accepts the person whom he is. He is independent, funny, spontaneous, and has several extremely intimate friends. Maslow would describe David as:
    a. extraverted
    b. self-actualizing
    c. well-socialized
    d. stable and well-adjusted

29. Daniel's older brother Jackson is always teasing him, picking on him, and making him feel inadequate. Daniel has a great deal of anger towards Jackson which he cannot acknowledge. One day, when Jackson makes him especially angry, Daniel kicks Jackson's dog very hard. Daniel is using the defense mechanism of:
    a. reaction formation
    b. displacement
    c. sublimation
    d. projection

30. One example of an objective psychological test is the ______; one example of a projective test is the ______.
    a. Cattell 16 PF; MMPI
    b. MMPI; Thematic Apperception Test (TAT)
    c. Thematic Apperception Test (TAT); Rorschach Inkblot test
    d. Rorschach Inkblot test; Thematic Apperception Test (TAT)

31. Research suggests that the validity of the Rorschach test is:
    a. extremely high
    b. high
    c. moderate
    d. low

32. Fifteen-year-old Karen believes that she can't really control her own life or influence the lives of others. She gets mediocre grades in school. She is dependent, easily stressed, and frequently depressed. She also tends to think that all her problems are someone else's fault. According to Julian Rotter, Karen probably has ______.
    a. an external locus of control
    b. an internal locus of control
    c. both an external and internal locus of control
    d. neither an external nor an internal locus of control

33. If a personality test actually measures what it is supposed to measure, it is ______; if the measures of the test repeatedly results in the same answers, the test is ______.
    a. generalizable; reliable
    b. valid; reliable
    c. reliable; valid
    d. valid; generalizable

34. A dog is repeatedly given an electric shock that he can't escape from. Then he is given an electric shock that he could easily escape from by jumping a barrier. What is the dog most likely to do?

   a. immediately jump the barrier
   b. hesitate briefly before jumping the barrier
   c. excitedly run around in circles without jumping the barrier
   d. cower in place

Exam 5: Disorders and Treatment

1. Marianna is agitated, unfocused, and euphoric. She seldom sleeps more than four hours a night. She goes on buying sprees where she buys thousands of dollars' worth of clothes at a time. Using these symptoms as a guide, a psychologist would probably diagnose Marianna's problem as ______.

   a. a bipolar disorder
   b. mania
   c. hypochondriasis
   d. a somatoform disorder

2. Joanne has been recently diagnosed with schizophrenia. Based on what you know about schizophrenia, which of the following statements is probably FALSE?

   a. Joanne is a young adult.
   b. Joanne has a 2/3 chance of recovering completely.
   c. Joanne has had episodes of disordered thinking.
   d. Joanne has a relative with schizophrenia.

3. Munchausen syndrome is a type of ______ which is characterized by ______.

   a. factitious disorder; a desire for the "patient" role."
   b. anxiety disorder; fear of a specific place or object
   c. somatoform disorder; low self-esteem
   d. organic disorder; an actual physical disorder

4. Which of the following is NOT a suicide risk factor?

   a. being single
   b. making overt suicide threats
   c. recent history of severe depression
   d. being female

5. When someone has a conversion disorder, he/she:

   a. has a physical symptom that has no organic cause
   b. has converted a physical ailment into a psychological symptom
   c. usually has a brain tumor
   d. consciously creates the symptoms he/she exhibits

6. DSM-IV decision trees are used primarily to ______.

   a. help psychologists to classify a patient's psychological problem
   b. determine how a patient's personal history has contributed to his/her psychological symptoms
   c. determine which drug treatment should be used for a patient's symptoms
   d. develop computerized treatment plans

7. Mr. Barker washes his hands at least 30 times a day because he is preoccupied with the thought that he may contract a disease by touching a dirty person or object. A psychotherapist diagnosing Mr. Barker's problem would state that Mr. Barker's thinking is ______ and his behavior is ______.
   a. obsessive-compulsive; conditioned
   b. obsessive; compulsive
   c. compulsive; obsessive
   d. disassociative; obsessive-compulsive
8. Which of the following statements about antisocial personality disorder is FALSE?
   a. Persons diagnosed with this disorder are sometimes termed sociopathic psychopathic.
   b. Males are more likely than females to have this disorder.
   c. Most criminals suffer from some form of this disorder.
   d. Persons diagnosed with this disorder tend to have little regard for the rights of other people.
9. John is in the military reserves but he doesn't want to risk fighting if the U.S. declares war on Serbia. So he fakes a back injury to avoid being eligible for active service. This behavior reflects what kind of psychological disorder?
   a. hypochondriasis
   b. Munchausen syndrome
   c. malingering
   d. psycho-physiological disorder
10. Which of the following statements about psychological disorders is FALSE?
    a. Psychological disorders are characterized by impaired psychological functioning.
    b. Psychological disorders tend to be distressing.
    c. Psychological disorders are pretty much the same in different cultures.
    d. Psychological disorders reflect behavior that is atypical.
11. A year ago, Sara was in a serious car accident in which she was uninjured but one of her best friends died. She has recently been diagnosed with post-traumatic stress disorder (PTSD). Which of the following symptom clusters would Sara most likely exhibit?
    a. amnesia, mood swings, and inappropriate affect
    b. SNS distress, emotional numbing, and hypervigilance
    c. organic loss of function, major depression, and substance abuse
    d. euphoric feeling, frantic activity, and insomnia
12. Which of the following is NOT a dissociative disorder?
    a. amnesia
    b. fugue
    c. multiple personality
    d. obsessive-compulsive disorder
13. Which of the following is NOT an assumption of the diathesis-stress model?
    a. Current life events and personal history both contribute to psychopathology.
    b. Psychological assessment includes the evaluation of symptoms, current stressors, and risk factors.
    c. Positive life changes, such as job promotions or sudden financial gain, are rarely stressors.
    d. Interventions can take the form of formal therapies and/or social and economic consequences.
14. Approximately what percentage of people in the U.S. will have some kind of psychological disorder in their lives?
    a. less than 1 percent
    b. 30 percent
    c. 70 percent
    d. 99.9 percent

15. Which of the following is NOT a symptom of schizophrenia?
    a. disorganized thinking
    b. inappropriate emotions and actions
    c. exhibiting two or more distinct personalities
    d. disturbed perceptions

16. Mr. Soames has not been able to sleep well for weeks. He feels edgy all the time for no particular reason. He has had no big life changes in recent months. Last week he had a panic attack that he thought was a heart attack. What kind of problem does Mr. Soames most likely have?
    a. obsessive-compulsive disorder
    b. phobic disorder
    c. generalized anxiety disorder
    d. adjustment disorder

17. A thorough psychological evaluation of William Kurelek would describe six categories of risk factors. Which of the following risk factors is NOT correctly labeled?
    a. feelings of abandonment by mother: psychodynamic risk factor
    b. criticism and lack of praise: behavioral risk factor
    c. need to be perfect: cognitive risk factor
    d. introversion and shyness: sociological risk factor

18. Dissociative disorders:
    a. usually have organic causes
    b. include schizophrenia, multiple personality, and fugue
    c. are relatively common, especially among young adults
    d. occur when current awareness becomes separated from previous thoughts and feelings

19. Which mental health provider must have 7 years of post-degree (M.D. or Ph.D.) psychodynamic training before assuming his/her professional role?
    a. psychiatric social worker
    b. psychiatrist
    c. psychoanalyst
    d. psychotherapist

20. In her therapy session, Brenda talks to her mother, who is symbolized as an empty chair, in an effort to better understand her feelings toward her mother. This technique comes from the _______ perspective.
    a. humanistic
    b. psychodynamic
    c. behavioral
    d. cognitive

21. "Working through" is the stage of therapy characterized by:
    a. building trust with the therapist
    b. uncovering the patient's issues which are out of awareness
    c. learning more adaptive strategies
    d. evaluation and integration of the therapy process

22. According to the sociological perspective, a client's problems _______.
    a. are caused by unconscious motives
    b. are conditioned emotional responses
    c. are a meaningful, valid reaction to current life circumstances

23. George was so afraid of snakes that he decided to see a therapist. The therapist first showed George a photograph of a snake. When George was no longer afraid of the photograph, the therapist had George watch someone else touch a real snake. Then the therapist gradually had George approach and touch the snake himself. The technique used by this therapist is called ______.

    a. behavior modification
    b. aversive conditioning
    c. systematic desensitization
    d. rational-emotive therapy (RET)

24. In the film, "Psychotherapy," Sarah exhibited marked anger at her therapist. Which statement about this outburst of anger is FALSE?

    a. It is an example of transference.
    b. It is typical of interactions in psychodynamic therapy.
    c. It demonstrated the failure of the "therapeutic alliance."
    d. It illustrates a defense mechanism at work.

25. Which of the following is NOT an example of therapy from the humanistic perspective?

    a. gestalt therapy
    b. person-centered therapy
    c. encounter groups
    d. family therapy

26. Electroconvulsive therapy (as it has been and AFTER 1980):

    a. has no therapeutic effects in the vast majority of cases when it is administered.
    b. is the recommended treatment of last resort in cases of severe acute depression.
    c. is administered to a patient who is fully conscious.
    d. causes massive memory loss in most cases.

27. Johnny is in treatment for depression. He is asked by his therapist to recall a childhood memory and then say whatever comes into his mind. This technique is the cornerstone of:

    a. cognitive therapy
    b. pharmacotherapy
    c. person-centered therapy
    d. psychoanalysis

28. Movement disorders such as tardive dyskinesia are a major side effect of using ______ as a drug treatment.

    a. antidepressants
    b. Vitamin B
    c. antipsychotics
    d. anxiolytics

29. Which of the following approaches emphasizes the erasing of destructive "automatic tapes" that can play inside our heads?

    a. cognitive
    b. sociological
    c. humanistic
    d. behavioral

30. Andre is autistic and hits himself whenever he is upset. In order to change Andre's behavior, Dr. Young sprays water in Andre's face anytime Andre starts to hit himself. Which of the following terms does NOT apply to what Dr. Young is doing?
    a. behavioral therapy
    b. aversive conditioning
    c. self-control strategy
    d. behavior modification

31. Civil commitment can be ordered if a person:
    a. has been evaluated by a licensed psychiatrist or psychologist
    b. is a danger to him(her)self, to others, or to property
    c. is living on the street and is mentally ill
    d. has a DSM-IV-R diagnosis and is gravely disabled

32. Lisa tells her therapist, Dr. Brewin, that it upsets her when someone doesn't like her. Dr. Brewin gently points out that it is illogical for Lisa to think that everybody must love her. Dr. Brewin shows Lisa that it is more logical to expect that not everyone will love her. Dr. Brewin also tells Lisa to interact with people with the expectation that not everyone will love her. This approach can best be described as ______ therapy.
    a. psychodynamic
    b. cognitive
    c. person-centered
    d. sociological

33. After several therapy sessions, Terry begins to have feelings of dependence and love toward the therapist. The therapist, a psychoanalyst, sees this as an example of:
    a. a conditioned emotional response
    b. transference
    c. free association
    d. unconditional positive regard

34. Dr. Stein tells Ken that his identity is defined by the roles he plays as a father, husband, a teacher. Dr. Stein also says that Ken's psychological troubles are likely a result of role dysphoria, among other things. Dr. Stein suggests parent training and marital therapy to help Ken with his troubles. Dr. Stein is taking which approach?
    a. cognitive
    b. sociological
    c. humanistic
    d. behavioral

35. Tony lives in a home for juvenile delinquents. Every time he cleans his room, plays cooperatively, or does any other appropriate behavior, he receives a token. These tokens can be exchanged for candy, watching television, or taking trips to town. This is an example of:
    a. counterconditioning
    b. a self-control strategy
    c. behavior modification
    d. a client-centered approach

APPENDIX C

Answers to Problem Sets

LOIS MCDERMOTT

Solutions to Problem Set #1

1. Ethnic backgrounds of students
   a. descriptive method (survey)
2. Relationship between weather and latte sales
   a. correlations (positive, negative, zero)
3. Expected correlations
   a. family income and number of bathrooms: positive
   b. time watching TV and time reading books: negative
   c. number of umbrellas and inches of rainfall: positive
   d. anxiety level and desire to give a speech: negative
   e. age (to age 40) and hours of sleep: negative
   f. favorite color and years of education: zero
4. Relationship between depressed relatives and depressed individuals
   a. predictive method
   b. No IV or DV
   c. biological perspective
5. Depression as a learned behavior
   a. descriptive method (case study)
   b. no IV or DV
   c. depression is a learned and reinforced behavior
   d. behavioral perspective
6. Contribution of early trauma to depression
   a. descriptive method
   b. no IV or DV
   c. neglect and trauma during infancy tend to cause depression
   d. psychoanalytic/psychodynamic

7. Relationship between thinking habits and depression
   a. explanative method
   b. IV = thinking habits, operationalized as exposure to informational lecture (self-blame focus, neutral focus, no lecture)
      DV = depression level as measured by 1–10 scale
   c. habitually blaming oneself for failure increase depression
   d. cognitive/sociocultural
   e. Group 2 (the one receiving a neutral lecture) was used as a control group to see whether simply receiving a lecture (and hence increased attention) affect depression level (NOTE: Studies have shown that simply giving subjects increased attention can affect mood and behavior.)
   f. confounding variable
   g. Groups 2 and 3 are examples of control groups (designed to account for potential alternative hypotheses)

8. Effect of light on depression
   a. biological perspective
   b. amount of full spectrum light affects depression level
   c. experimental
   d. inferential statistics (used for generalizing to the population that the sample represents)
   e. IV = exposure to light (full-spectrum, non full-spectrum, no exposure but instructions to sit, no exposure with no instructions)
   f. DV = depression level
   g. groups 2, 3, 4 = control groups
   h. purpose of group 2: to rule out the possibility that light in general (as opposed to full spectrum light)
   i. purpose of group 3: to rule out the possibility that sitting still for 30 minutes may affect depression
   j. purpose of group 4: to rule out the possibility that simply participating in a study (i.e., getting attention) may affect depression level
   k. confounding variables
   l. flaws: subjects were not randomly assigned to group (decreases generalizability)

9. Weaknesses in study on exercise on depression
   a. Subjects were not randomly selected but self-selected (volunteers). They may be atypical in some way, which may restrict the generalizability of the results.
   b. Experimental group and control group were not drawn from the same population (experimental group subjects drawn from health club members; control group subjects drawn for psychology class). Maybe other differences between these groups account for the results, rather than the experimental manipulation. Thus, the validity of the study is questionable.
   c. Control group subjects were in experimenter's own course (she could potentially bias their moods).
   d. Experimental groups varied not only in type of exercise done (aerobic vs. non-aerobic) but in setting for exercise (posh health clubs vs UW gym). Setting is a potential confounding variable because it might affect mood.
   e. Post-test DV not operationalized very objectively (interviews by psych grad students were used to assess depression instead of a standardized test). Different interviewers may vary in their interpretations of subject depression. Also, it may be difficult to compare BDI pre-test scores with interviewer ratings of depression.

Solutions to Problem Set #2

1. a. synapse
   b. soma
   c. vesicles, (presynaptic) terminal
   d. receptors
   e. axon
   f. axon

2. a. occipital cortex: allows you to see
   b. hypothalamus: suppresses any digestive or sexual behavior
   c. precentral cortex: allows you to move
   d. frontal cortex: allows you to plan an escape
   e. parietal cortex: allows you to receive sensory input
   f. amygdala: makes you feel aggressive or fearful
   g. limbic system: makes you feel aggressive or fearful, suppresses any digestive or sexual behavior
   h. Broca's area: allows you to form words (like "help")
   i. ANS: increases pulse and respiration, to sweat and release adrenaline
   j. somatic NS: allows voluntary movement (like running)
   k. temporal lobes: allows you to hear the dog barking
   l. adrenal glands: produces adrenaline to give that extra "oomph" to your body to allow escape
   m. reticular activating system: makes sure important sensory input gets sent to the correct place; also makes sure that the brain is aroused
   n. endorphins: allows you to tolerate pain better

3. a. somatic nervous system
   b. central nervous system
   c. somatic nervous system
   d. sympathetic nervous system
   e. parasympathetic nervous system
   f. sympathetic nervous system
   g. autonomic nervous system

4. a. parietal cortex
   b. precentral cortex
   c. occipital cortex
   d. somatosensory cortex
   e. reticular activating system
   f. angular gyrus

5. a. temporal lobe
   b. R somatosensory association areas
   c. medulla
   d. R motor cortex
   e. somatosensory cortex
   f. visual cortex
   g. Broca's area and/or motor cortex
   h. L somatosensory cortex
   i. pituitary
   j. hypothalamus
   k. frontal cortex

6. LVF: toy car, because he was able to use his sensory input to detect the car. RVF: bench, because he was able to verbalize what he saw. He must use his left hand, since that is the hand which receives commands from the right half of the brain.
7. left hand: right hemisphere matches to appearance
   right hand: left hemisphere matches to function
8. a. snowman and house covered with snow
   b. right hand—L brain matches to function
   c. The left hemisphere, which has language capabilities, will attempt to explain why the left hand picked what it did (confabulation).

Solutions to Problem Set #3

1. a. 5
   b. bizarre nature, sensory incorporation (air raid signal, pencil)
   c. frequency (speed)
   d. rapid eye movement, heart beat increase, etc.
   e. 90 minutes (unless narcoleptic!)
2. a. 5
   b. 1–4
   c. 5
   d. 1–4
   e. 5
   f. 5
   g. 1–4
   h. 5
   i. 5
   j. 5 (spontaneous awakenings)
   k. 1–4
3. a. narcolepsy
   b. sleepwalking
   c. night terrors
   d. insomnia
   e. bizarre mentation
   f. pseudo-insomnia
   g. narcolepsy
   h. natural short sleep
   i. sleep apnea
   j. insomnia
4. a. improvement of task performance regarding precision; control of certain disease states
   b. hypnotist has special powers; trance is sleep; only emotionally weak can be hypnotized; it is a unique physiological state
5. perceptions occurring apart from sensory input
6. telepathy (mind-to-mind communications); clairvoyance (perceiving remote events); precognition (predicating future events)
7. The results have not been replicated.
8 a. cocaine, amphetamines, caffeine (increase EEG, body activity)
   b. opiates, barbiturates, alcohol (decrease EEG, body activity)
   c. marijuana, LSD (distort perceptions and evoke images)

9. Misconceptions:
   a. addictions can't be overcome voluntarily
   b. there are many more "crazed" users than controlled occasional users; alcohol and tobacco kill more people than all illegal drugs; alcohol disrupts the processing of recent experiences into long-term memory; nicotine mimics the action of acetylcholine.

Solutions to Problem Set #4

1. a. b
   b. p
   c. a
   d. b
   e. p
   f. a
   g. p
   h. a
   i. p
   j. p
2. Check your own solution using the scoring method at the beginning of Chapter 4.
3. drives: sex, thirst, sleep, pain avoidance
4. incentives: chaotic, overweight, anorexia, acquired, ideal weight, dieting
5. a. high
   b. LH, motivate
   c. destroyed
   d. destroyed
   e. seek, increase
6. a. After her first diet, metabolism returns to normal. Then, it slows to subnormal, and finally it is permanently lowered. When the brain realizes there are fewer calories, it reduces metabolism.
   b. normal weight +7 percent increment with each diet cycle
   c. metabolism lowered, weight increased
   d. metabolism will become closer to normal, weight more stabilized
   e. do not diet, use mild exercise such as aerobics, adopt healthy eating habits
7. a. drop quickly and then stabilize
   b. decrease
   c. decrease
   d. increase
   e. increase
   f. decrease
8. a. CD
   b. N
   c. A
   d. A
   e. A, B, CD
   f. CD
   g. B
   h. N
   i. CD
   j. N

k. CD
l. A, B, CD
m. N
n. B
o. A
p. A, B, CD

9. anorexia: denial, severe health problem, perfectionism (straight A's), hyperactivity (over exercise), age of onset (high school), distorted image

Solutions to Problem Set #5

1. UCS: kiss
   CS: toilet paper
   UCR: good feeling
   CF: grin
2. UCS: blood gore
   CS: bridge
   UCR: nausea
   CR: nausea
3. UCS: mom's scream
   CS: dogs
   UCR: Karm's startle response
   CR: uneasiness
4. a. extinction training
   b. expose to CS (dogs) without UCS (mom's anxiety or his own startle response); the CR (feelings of uneasiness) will gradually diminish as the CS is dissociated from the UCS and becomes a neutral stimulus:
      UCS: <nothing>
      CS: dogs
      UCR: <nothing>
      CR: <nothing>
5. a. relaxation training
   b. A psychologist and Karms determine Karms' "hierarchy of generalization," a list of stimuli involving dogs (e.g., dog photos, small dogs, large dogs), in the order of how much anxiety each stimuli causes. Next, the psychologist has Karms relax by using a pleasurable, relaxing UCS (music, deep breathing exercises, etc.) to engender a pleasant UCR, a feeling of relaxation. Then the psychologist exposes Karms to a relatively non-threatening situation involving dogs while Karms is in a relaxed state, so that Karms will begin to associate dogs (the CS) with a relaxed state (a new CR). This is done for each item on the list, moving slowly up the hierarchy, until Karms is able to maintain a relaxed mental state while being exposed to what were once maximally-threatening "dog stimuli."
      UCS: music, deep breathing
      CS: dogs
      UCR: relaxation
      CR: relaxation

Operant Conditioning Paradigms

1. fixed interval
2. variable interval
3. variable ratio
4. fixed ratio
5. a. shaping
   b. positive reinforcement
   c. continuous (fixed ratio)
   d. positive reinforcement, variable ratio
   e. variable interval

Identify the Type of Operant Conditioning

#	*Fill in the Blank*	*Target Behavior*	*Inc/Dec*	*Agent of Change*	*Process*
1	positive reinforcer	loss of temper	increased	presentation of s+ (scolding)	pos. Rf
2.	positive punishment	going to park	decreased	presentation of s– (tantrums)	pos. Pun
3.	positively reinforced	dealing drugs	increased	presentation of s+ (jail time)	pos. Rf
4.		drinking alcohol	increased	removal of s– (stress)	neg. RF (escape training)
5.	pos. Pun	returning books late	decreased	presentation of s– (fine)	pos. Pun
	neg. Rf	returning books on time	maintained	avoidance of an s– (fine)	pos. Pun
6.	avoidance training	prompt payment	maintained	avoidance of s– (late charge)	neg. Rf
		prompt payment	maintained	presentation of s+ (electrical service)	neg. Rf
7.	pos. Pun	class attendance	decreased	presentation of s– (hard exams)	pos. Pun
8.	pos. Pun	quality of Jan's cooking	decreased	presentation of s– (Jay's helping)	pos. Pun
9.	pos. Rf	Jay's helping	increased	avoidance of s– (Jan's poor cooking)	neg. Rf
10.	pos. Rf	fighting	increased	presentation of s+ (kiss and make up)	pos. Rf
11.	pos. Pun	poor table manners	decreased	Joe: presentation of s– (ridicule)	pos. Pun
	neg. Pun			Ralph: removal of s+ (company)	neg. Pun
12.	pos. Rf	good table manners	increased	presentation of s+ (praise)	pos. Rf
13.	desire to avoid getting nagged	frantic cleaning	maintained	avoidance of s– (nagging)	neg. Rf
14.	Sue's cleaning	nagging	maintained	presentation of s+ (cleaning)	pos. Rf
15.	pos. Rf	routine cleaning	increased	presentation of s+ (praise)	pos. Rf
16.	differential	smoking	decreased	competing response (knitting)	DRO
	reinforcement of other behavior (DRO)	knitting	increased	presentation of s+ (praise)	pos. Rf

Classical or Operant Conditioning

1. c
2. o
3. c
4. o
5. o
6. o
7. c
8. o

9. c
10. o
11. c
12. c
13. c
14. o

Solutions to Problem Set #6

Match

1. practical intelligence
2. working memory
3. sodium amytal
4. mnemonic chunking
5. declarative memory
6. recall task
7. recency effect
8. episodic memory
9. g-factor
10. fluid intelligence
11. repression
12. working memory
13. crystallized intelligence
14. mnemonic
15. WAIS
16. echoic memory
17. retrograde amnesia
18. implicit memory
19. proactive interference
20. preoperational
21. fluid intelligence
22. recognition task
23. interpersonal intelligence
24. kinesthetic intelligence

Short Answers

1. The capacity and duration are different between STM and LTM. In STM, the capacity is 7+–2 and duration lasts about 12 seconds. In LTM, the capacity is unlimited and the duration is relatively permanent.
2. When you want to remember the various types of long-term memory, you put the most wide category on the very top of the hierarchy (long-term memory), and you divide the long term memory into two parts which are explicit and implicit memory, then you divide these two types of memory into more specific types of memory under the appropriate categories.

3. a. procedural memory: memory involves motor and cognitive skills
   b. conditioned disposition memory: memory as a result of classical or operant conditioning
4. The amnesia caused by Alzheimer's Disease has a physiological basis, while the amnesia found in dissociative disorders is caused by psychological factors.
5. Pros: may be able to get at a bit of information the subject knew, but is too distressed to recall.

   Cons: we can't be sure whether subject recalls the events accurately and whether subject put own meaning into recall.
6. Are the memories real or could they "become" real through the suggestions of the therapist?
7. The most genetically similar people have the most similar intelligence score; however, environment does have an effect on the development of intelligence.
8. Genetics accounts for 55 percent of the differences we see within a certain specific group of people.
9. Gardner, because both Gardner and Sternberg-Wagner believe that environment plays an important role in determining one's intelligence. Also, Spearman argues that one "score" measures general intelligence, whereas Sternberg & Wagner agree with Gardner there are at least three types of intelligence.
10. Spearman will propose that people with the specific ability of building furniture have greater tendency to score higher on other factors such as verbal and reasoning ability, thus evidence for general intelligence.

    Gardner believes that intelligence comes in different packages. People who have the ability to build beautiful furniture may have virtually no language ability.
11. Howard Gardner
12. According to Piaget, specific developmental milestones can be achieved before the end of each cognitive development stage. So, those cognitive achievements can give us a cue to distinguish the age of individuals.

    1 year old object permanence

    2 year old conservation

    10 year old think logically

    20 year old abstract reasoning

Solutions to Problem Set #7

1. a. dispositional
   b. situational; environmental location
2. a. dispositional-clumsiness, situational-water puddles
   b. fundamental attribution error
3. a. right to life
   b. cognitive dissonance
4. cognitive dissonance
5. fundamental attribution error
6. obedience to authority
7. deindividuation
8. in-group bias
9. fundamental attribution error
10. groupthink

11. normative social influence
12. just-world phenomenon
13. social loafing
14. social facilitation
15. bystander intervention
16. just-world phenomenon
17. group polarization
18. a. high
    b. low
    c. low
    d. high
    e. low
    f. high
    g. low
    h. high
    i. peer gives shock while teacher just gives orders
    j. when teacher gets to pick the shock level
19. a. First, some students thought the wave principles were stupid. Then, after they played their roles in class, they favored the wave (their attitude changed).
    b. They became carried away with the principles of the wave and they assumed everyone thought it was a perfect system.
    c. The students stuck with the wave, to a large extent because they all felt accepted in their group.
    d. The stressful interactions between David and Laurie and the teacher and his wife.
20. a. Degrading prisoners boosted guards' self-esteem.
    b. Guards thought prisoners deserved bad treatment.
    c. "We are just a group of guards acting like guards."
    d. Guards felt acceptance in their group.
    e. After a few days of playing the guard role, the guards devised cruel punishments and did harsh things.
    f. guards felt that they were better than the prisoners
    g. at first students were not harsh, then they played their roles, then looked down upon prisoners
21. make yourself noticeable; say you really need help; ask people specifically for their help
22. a. a person focusing on self-actualization and trying not to be influenced by what his family tells him/her to do
    b. an athlete who care a lot more about his/her team's goals than personal accomplishments
    c. a brother and sister talking to each other
    d. a family argument
    e. two sports teams in conflict with each other.

Solutions to Problem Set #8

A.

1. superego
2. ego
3. self-efficacy

4. Erikson
5. external locus of control
6. attachment (Erikson); oral (Freud)
7. preconscious
8. introversion
9. relationships (Erikson)
10. unconditional positive regard
11. self-actualization
12. repression
13. conscious awareness of emotional states
14. learned helplessness
15. tape
16. anal (Freud); individuation (Erikson)
17. reciprocal determinism
18. temperament
19. projection
20. reaction formation
21. displacement
22. sublimation
23. regression
24. checklists, interviews, surveys, observations
25. research, tai, free association
26. MMPI, introversion/extroversion, 16PF, big 5
27. unconditional positive regard
28. hierarchy of needs
29. social norms

B.

1. displacement
2. repression
3. reaction formation
4. projection
5. sublimation
6. rationalization
7. sublimation
8. regression
9. rationalization
10. reaction formation
11. projection
12. rationalization
13. displacement

C.

1. psychodynamic
2. biological
3. cognitive-behavioral
4. cognitive-behavioral
5. sociocultural
6. humanistic

D.

1. a. personality = temperament and traits; traits are biologically based; personality is controlled/expressed by nervous system
   b. MMPI, Big 5, 16PF, etc.
2. a. personality is the interplay of conscious and unconscious conflicts/motives; developmental stages, traumas; sexual impulses, object relations, defense mechanisms
   b. Rorschach, TAI, free association
3. a. rewards and punishers shape behavior; we extract and project schemas on the environment
   b. checklists, interviews, surveys, etc.

Solutions to Problems Set #9

A. Classification of Psychological Disorders

	Disorder	*Type of Disorder*
1.	post traumatic stress disorder (PTSD)	anxiety
2.	claustrophobia	anxiety
3.	conversion disorder	somatoform
4.	hypochondriasis	somatoform
5.	adjustment disorder	current stress
6.	mania	mood
7.	generalized anxiety	anxiety
8.	psychophysiological disorder	disorder w/physical symptoms
9.	psychogenic amnesia	dissociative
10.	fugue	dissociative
11.	obsessive-compulsive disorder	anxiety
12.	multiple personality	dissociative
13.	organic mental disorder	disorder w/physical symptoms
14.	abuse/oppression artifact disorder	current stress disorder

NOTE: THIS WAS NOT COVERED IN CLASS; WON'T BE ON EXAM 5

15.	depressed mood	mood

Solutions to Problem Set #10

1. psychoanalyst
2. person-centered
3. ECT
4. insight-oriented
5. psychiatrist, psychoanalyst, psychiatric nurse practitioners
6. hospitalization
7. MHP
8. counterconditioning—aversive training
9. antipsychotic medications
10. light (chrono) therapy
11. behavior modification
12. psychologists
13. psychologists
14. counselors
15. social activists, social workers
16. RET
17. Gestalt, psychodrama
18. psychodrama
19. behavior modification, relapse prevention training
20. counterconditioning, systematic desensitization and relaxation training
21. psychoanalysis
22. parent training, couples and family therapy
23. civil commitment
24. ECT
25. MHP
26. psychodynamic, insight-oriented, psychoanalysis
27. antidepressants
28. antipsychotics
29. anxiolytics
30. eclectic
31. therapeutic alliance, working through, changing patterns, termination
32. confidentiality, written contract, discontinue therapy, chose the therapist and treatment mode, etc.
33. dual relationship with therapist, therapist lacked training in your type of problem, therapist is not involved in consultation, therapist is too worried about whether you are “happy”
34. call the state licensing board and complain

REFERENCES

Adler, A. (1927). *Practice and theory of individual psychology.* New York: Harcourt, Brace & World.

Adorno, T.W., Frenkel-Brunswick, E., Levinson, D.J., & Sanford, R.N. (1950). *The authoritarian personality.* New York: Harper.

Ainsworth, M.D.S., Blegar, M., Waters, E., & Wall, S. (1978). *Patterns of attachment: A psychological study of the strange situation.* Hillsdale, NJ: Lawrence Erlbaum.

Alderfer, C.P. (1972). *Existence, relatedness, and growth.* New York: Free Press.

Alexander, F. (1946). Individual psychotherapy. *Psychosomatic Medicine, 8,* 110–115.

Allison, T., & Van Twyver, H. (1970). The evolution of sleep. *Natural History, 79,* 57–65.

Allport, G. (1968). The historical background of modern social psychology. In G. Lindzey & E. Aronson (Eds.), *The handbook of social psychology* (Vol. 1). Reading, MA: Addison-Wesley.

Allport, G.W., & Odbert, H.S. (1936). Trait names, a psycholexical study. *Psychological Monographs,47,* 1–171.

Alluisi, E.A., Muller, P.F., & Fitts, P.M. (1957). An information analysis of verbal and motor responses in a forced-pace serial task. *Journal of Experimental Psychology, 53,* 153–158.

Amabile, T.M. (1983). *The social psychology of creativity.* New York: Springer-Verlag.

American Psychological Association Polygraphs. (1987, March). *American Psychological Association Legislative Briefing Sheet,* p. 1.

Amoore, J.E. (1970). *Molecular basis of odor.* Springfield, IL: C.C. Thomas.

Anastasi, A. (1982). *Psychological testing* (5th ed.). New York: Macmillan.

Anrep, G.V. (1920). Pitch discrimination in the dog. *Journal of Physiology,* 367–385.

Apgar, V., & Beck, J. (1973). *Is my baby all right?* New York: Trident Press.

Apple, W., Streeter, L.A., & Krauss, R.B. (1979). Effects of pitch and speech rate on personal attributions. *Journal of Personality and Social Psychology, 37,* 715–727.

Argyle, M., & Engham, R. (1972). Gaze, mutual gaze, and proximity. *Semiotica,* 6(2), 32–50.

Arlin, P. (1984). *Arlin test of formal reasoning: Test manual.* East Aurora, NY: Slosson Educational Publications.

Arlin, P.K. (1975). Cognitive development in adulthood: A fifth stage? *Developmental Psychology 11,* 602–606.

Aronson, E. (1984). *The social animal* (4th ed.) New York: W.H. Freeman.

Asch, S.E. (1951). Effects of group pressure upon the modification and distortion of judgments. In H. Guetzkow (Ed.), *Group, leadership, and men.* Pittsburgh: Carnegie Press.

Asch, S.E. (1956). Studies of independence and conformity. A minority of one against a unanimous majority. *Psychological Monographs, 70* (9, Whole No. 416).

Atkinson, J.W. (1958). *Thematic apperceptive measurement of motives within the context of a theory of motivation.* In J.W. Atkinson (Ed.), Motives in fantasy, action, and society. New York: D. Van Nostrand.

Ayllon, T., & Azrin, N.H. (1965). The measurement and reinforcement of behavior of psychotics. *Journal of the Experimental Analysis of Behavior, 8,* 357–383.

Ayllon, T., & Azrin, N.H. (1968). *The token economy: A motivational system for therapy and rehabilitation.* New York: Appleton-Century-Crofts.

Bahrick, H.P., Bahrick, P.Q., & Willinger, R.P. (1975). Fifty years of memory for names and faces: A cross-sectional approach. *Journal of Experimental Psychology: General, 104,* 54–75.

Bailey, R.W. (1982). *Human performance engineering: A guide for systems designer.* Englewood Cliffs, NJ: Prentice-Hall.

Bandura, A. (1977). *Social learning theory.* Englewood Cliffs, NJ: Prentice-Hall.

Bandura, A. (1977a). *Social learning theory.* Englewood Cliffs, NJ: Prentice-Hall.

Bandura, A. (1977b). Self-efficacy: Toward a unified theory of behavioral change. *Psychological Review, 84,* 191–215.

Bandura, A. (1978). The self system in reciprocal determinism. *American Psychologist, 33*(4), 344–358.

Bandura, A. (1982). Self-efficacy mechanism in human agency. *American Psychologist, 37*(2), 122–137.

Bandura, A., & Adams, N.E. (1977). Analysis of self-efficacy theory of behavioral change. *Cognitive Therapy and Research, 1,* 287–310.

Barber, T.X. (1969). *Hypnosis: A scientific approach.* New York: Van Nostrand Reinhold.

Barker, R.G. (1968). *Ecological psychology: Concepts and methods for studying the environment of human behavior.* Stanford, CA: Stanford University Press.

Barron, F., & Harrington, D.M. (1981). Creativity, intelligence and personality. *Annual Review of Psychology, 32,* 439–476.

Bartley, S.H. (1969, 1981). *Principles of perception.* New York: Harper & Row.

Bayer, R., & Spitzer, R.L. (1985). Neurosis, psychodynamics and DSM-III: A history of the controversy. *Archives of General Psychiatry, 42,* 187–196.

Beek, A.T., Ward, C.H., Mendelson, M., Mock, J.E., & Erbaugh, J.K. (1962). Reliability of psychiatric diagnoses II: A study of consistency of clinical judgments and ratings. *American Journal of Psychiatry, 119,* 351, 357.

Beck, R.C. (1983). *Motivation: Theories and principles* (2nd ed.). Englewood Cliffs, NJ: Prentice-Hall.

Bekesy, G. von. (1960). *Experiments in hearing.* New York: McGraw-Hill.

Berger, K. Stassen. (1986). *The developing person* (2nd ed.). New York: Worth Publishers.

Berscheid, E. (1984) Interpersonal attraction. In G. Lindzey & Aronson (Eds.), *Handbook of social psychology* (3rd Ed.) Reading, MA: Addison-Wesley.

Bertalanffy, L. von. (1969). *General systems theory.* New York: Holt.

Binet, A., & Simon, T. (1905). The methodes nouvelles pour le diagnostic du niveau intellectuel des anormaux, *Annee Psychol. 11,* 191–244.

Birmingham, H.P., & Taylor, F.V. (1961). A design philosophy for man-machine control systems. In H. Wallace Sinaiko (Ed.), *Selected papers on human factors in the design and use of control systems.* New York: Dover.

Blank, J.P. (1982, October). The miracle of May Lemke's love. *Reader's Digest,* pp. 81–86.

Block, N. (Ed.). (1980). *Readings in the philosophy of psychology: Volume 1.* Cambridge, MA: Harvard University Press.

Bloom, B.S. (Ed.). (1956). *Taxonomy of educational objectives. Handbook 1: Cognitive domain.* New York: David McKay.

Bloom, B.S. (Ed.). (1985). *Developing talent in young people.* New York: Balantine.

Bluth, B.J. (1982). The psychology and safety of weightlessness. *International Astronautical Federation, 15th Symposium on Space Safety and Rescue, IAA-82–252,* (pp. 1–8). Paris.

Bluth, B.J. (1984, June). Human systems interfaces for space stations. *AIAA/NASA Space Systems Technology Conference,* (pp. 84–115, 40–49).

Bluth, B.J., & McNeal, S.R. (Eds). (1981). *Update on space* (Vol. 1). Granada Hills, CA: National Behavior Systems.

Bogen, J.E., & Vogel, P.J. (1962). Cerebral commissurotomy: A case report. *Bulletin of the Los Angeles Neurological Society, 27,* 169.

Boll, F. (1977). On the anatomy and physiology of the retina. (Trans. by R. Hubbard) *Vision Research. 17,* 1253–1265.

Boring, E.G. (1942). *Sensation and perception in the history of experimental psychology.* New York: Appleton-Century-Crofts.

Boring, E.G. (1950). *A history of experimental psychology.* (2nd ed.). New York: Appleton-Century-Crofts.

Bornstein, A. (1979). *Memory: Arthor Bornstein's memory training course.* Los Angeles, CA: Bornstein's Memory Schools.

Bouchard, T.J., Jr., & McGue, M. (1981, May 29). Familial Studies of Intelligence: A review. *Science, 212,* 1055–1059.

Bowlby, J. (1969). *Attachment and loss. Vol.1, Attachment.* New York: Basic Books.

Bowler, T.D. (1981). *General systems theory: Its scope and applicability.* New York: North Holland.

Bowles, N., & Hynds, F. (1978). *Psi search.* San Francisco: Harper & Row.

Boycott, B.B., & Dowling, J.E. (1969). Organization of the primate retina: light microscopy. *Philosophical Transactions of the Royal Society of London. 255B,* 109–176.

Boynton, R.M. (1979). *Human color vision.* New York: Holt, Rhinehart & Winston.

Brady, J.V. (Ed.). (1980). *Human behavior in space environments: A research agenda.* Baltimore: The Johns Hopkins School of Medicine.

Brewer, M.B. (1979). In-group bias in the minimal intergroup situation: A cognitive-motivational analysis. *Psychological Bulletin, 86*(2), 307–324.

Briggs, J. (1984). The Genius Mind. *Science Digest, 92*(12), 75–77, 102–103.

Brislin, R.W. (1983). Cross-cultural research in psychology. In M.R. Rosenzweig & L.W. Porter (Eds.), *Annual review of psychology* (pp. 363–400). Palo Alto, CA: Annual Reviews.

Brock, T.C. (1965). Communicator-recipient similarity and decision change. *Journal of Personality and Social Psychology, 1,* 650–654.

Broughton, R. (1986). Human consciousness and sleep/waking rhythms. In B.J. Wolman and M. Ullman (Eds.), *Handbook of states of consciousness* (pp. 461–486). New York: Van Nostrand Reinhold.

Brown, A. Kodic-, & Brown, J.H. (1985). Why the fittest are the prettiest. The *Sciences, 25,* 26–33.

Buchwald, J.S., & Shipley, C.A. (1985). A comparative model of infant cry. In B.M. Lester & C.F. Zachariach Boukydis (Eds.), *Infant crying* (pp. 279–305). New York: Plenum.

Buckalew, L.W. (1973). Relationship between physiological and personality index of excitability. *Physiological Psychology, 1,* 158–160.

Bulfinch, T. (1970). *Bulfinch's mythology.* New York: T.Y. Crowell. pp. 80–91.

Buscaglia, L. (1972). *Love.* New York: Fawcett.

Calhoun, G., & Herrson, S. (1981). Computer generated cockpit engine displays. *Proceedings of the Human Factors Society, 25th Annual Meeting,* (pp. 127–131).

The camera. (1970). New York: Time-Life.

Campbell, D.E. (1982). Lunar-lunacy research: When enough is enough. *Environment and Behavior, 14*(4), 418–424.

Cannon, W.B. (1927). The James-Lange theory of emotions: A critical examination and an alternative. *American Journal of Psychology, 39,* 106–124.

Cannon, W.B. (1934). *Hunger and thirst.* In C. Murchinson (Ed.), Handbook of general experimental psychology. Worcester, MA: Clark University Press.

Carlson, N.R. (1981). *Physiology of behavior.* (2nd ed.). Boston: Allyn & Bacon.

Carterette, E.C., & Friedman, M.P. (1978). *Handbook of perception* (Vols. 2–6b). New York: Academic Press.

Cattell, R.B. (1950). *Personality: A systematic theoretical and factual study.* New York: MacGraw-Hill.

Cattell, R.B. (1965). *The scientific analysis of personality.* Chicago: Aldine.

Cattell, R.B. (1973). *Measuring intelligence with culture fair tests: Manual for scales 2 & 3; Test, scale 3.* Munster, IN: Psychometric Affiliates (IPAT).

Caulfield, H. John. (1984, March). The wonder of holography. *National Geographic, 165*(3), 364–377.

Cermak, L.S. (1975). *Improving your memory.* New York: W.W. Norton.

Chapouthier, G. (1983). The physiological bases of memory. In J.A. Deutsch (Ed.), *Protein synthesis and memory* (pp. 1–47). New York: Academic Press.

Chase, M. (1979, November). Every 90 minutes a brainstorm. *Psychology Today, 172.*

Chase, M.H., & Weitzman, E. (1983). *Sleep disorders: Basic and clinical research* (Vol.8). New York: Spectrum.

Cheers, D.M. (1983, December 12). World's most unusual twins: One is black, the other is white. *Jet, 65*(14), 21–24.

Cheers, D.M. (1984, April). Britain's most amazing twins. *Ebony, 39,* 42, 46, 48.

Cheston, S.T. (1984). Orbital human factors. In T.S. Cheston, C.M. Shafer, & S.B. Chafer (Eds.), *Social Sciences and Space Exploration* (pp. 65–71). Washington, DC: NASA, EP-192.

Cheston, S.T., & Winter, D.L. (1980). *Human Factors of Outer Space Production.* Washington, DC: American Association for the Advancement of Science, AAAS Selected Symposium 50.

Cheston, S.T., Chafer, C.M., & Chafer, S.B. (1984, November). *Social Sciences in Space Exploration.* NASA, EP-192.

Chomsky, N. (1972). *Language and mind.* New York: Harcourt Brace Jovanovich.

Chomsky, N. (1975). *Reflections on language.* New York: Pantheon Books.

Cialdini, R.B., Petty, R.E., & Cacioppo, J.T. (1981). Attitude and attitude change. *Annual review of psychology, 32,* 257–404. Palo Alto, CA: Annual Reviews.

Cohen, J. (1969). Personality assessment. *Eyewitness Series* in *Psychology, 18.* Chicago: Rand McNally.

Cohen, J. (1969). Personality dynamics. *Eyewitness Series* in *Psychology, 17.* Chicago: Rand McNally.

Cohen, M.R. (1982). An integrative approach to agoraphobia: Centrum—a model program. In R.L. Dupont (Ed.), *Phobia: A comprehensive summary of modern treatments* (pp. 44–53). New York: Brumer/Mazel.

Coleman, J.C., Butcher, J.N., & Carson, R. (1984). *Abnormal psychology and modern life* (7th ed.). Glenview, IL: Scott, Foresman & Company.

Collins, A., & Quillian, M.R. (1969). Retrieval time from semantic memory. *Journal of Verbal Learning and Verbal Behavior, 8,* 240–247.

Corkin, S. (1980). A prospective study of cingulotomy. In E.S. Valenstein (Ed.), *The Psychosurgery Debate.* San Francisco, CA: W.H. Freeman.

Cornsweet, T.N. (1970). *Visual perception.* New York: Academic Press.

Cowan, W.M. (1979, September). The development of the brain. *Scientific American, 241*(3), 112–113.

Cowan, W.M. (1985). In C. Cordes (Ed.). Development: Early life a saga of fierce rivalry, lengthy migration. *APA Monitor, 16*(9), pp. 20, 22–23.

Curtis, H., & Barnes, S.N. (1981). *Invitation to biology.* New York: Worth.

Cuzzort, R.P. (1969). *Humanity and modern sociological thought.* New York: Holt, Rinehart, & Winston.

Cytowic, R. (1984, October 22). Unpublished study concerning brain blood flow and synesthesia. *Brain-Mind Bulletin, 9*(17).

Damon, W. (1994). Self understanding and moral development from childhood to adolescence. In W.M. Kurtines & J.L. Gewirtz (Eds.), *Morality, moral behavior and moral development.* New York: Wiley.

Daniel, W.F., & Crovitz, H.F. (1983). Acute memory impairment following electroconvulsive therapy 1. Effects of electrical stimulus and number of treatments. *Acta Psychiatrica Scandinavia, 67,* 1–7.

Darwin, C. (1872). *The expression of emotions in man and animals.* London: Murray. Reprinted by University of Chicago Press, 1965.

Darwin, C. (1968). *The origin of species.* New York: Penguin Books.

Davis, H.P., & Squire, L.R. (1984). Protein synthesis and memory: A review. *Psychological Bulletin, 96,* 518–559.

de Waal, F. (1982). *Chimpanzee politics: Power & sex among apes.* New York: Harper & Row.

DeBold, R.C. (1968). *Manual of contemporary experiments in psychology* (pp. 173–181). Englewood Cliffs, NJ: Prentice-Hall.

Defries, J.C., & Plomin, R. Behavioral genetics. In M.R. Rosenzweig & L.W. Porter (Eds.), *Annual Review of Psychology,* 29. Palo Alto, CA: Annual Reviews.

Deininger, R.L. (1960, July). Human factors studies of push-button characteristics and information processing in keyset operation. *Bell System Technical Journal, 39*(4), 995–1012.

Dement, W.C. (1972). *Some must watch while some sleep.* San Francisco: W.H. Freeman.

Dement, W.C., & Kleitman, N. (1957). The relation of eye movements during sleep to dream activity: An objective method for the study of dreaming. *Journal of Experimental Psychology, 53,* 339–346.

Denes, P.B., & Pinson, E.N. (1963). *The speech chain.* Murray Hill, NJ: Bell Laboratories.

Denning Mobile Robotics, Inc. (1983). *Annual Report.* Woburn, MA.

DeValois, R.L., & DeValois, K. (1975). In Carterette & Friedman (Eds.). Neural coding of color. *Handbook of perception.* (Vol. 5). New York: Academic Press.

DeValois, R.L., Abramov, I., & Jacobs, G.H. (1966). Analysis of response patterns of LGN cells. *Journal of the Optical Society of America, 56,* 966–977.

Diagnostic and statistical manual of mental disorders (DSM-IV). (1980). Washington, DC: American Psychiatric Association.

Dion, K., Berschied, E., & Walster, E. (1972). What is beautiful is good. *Journal of Personality and Social Psychology, 34,* 285–290.

Dobelle, W.H., Mladejovsky, M.G., & Girvin, J.P. (1974). Artificial vision for the blind: Electrical stimulation of the visual cortex offers a hope for a functional prosthesis. *Science, 183,* 440–444.

Dohrenwend, B.P., & Dohrenwend, B.S. (1982). Perspectives on the past and future of psychiainc epidemiology: The 1981 Rema Lapouse lecture. *American Journal of Public Health, 72,* 1271–1279.

Dowling, J.E., & Boycott, B.B. (1966). Organization of the primate retina: Electron microscopy. *Proceeding of the Royal Society of London, 166B,* 80–111.

Drake, L.E., & Oetting, E.R. (1959). *An MMPI codebook for counselors.*

Dreikurs-Ferguson, E. (1976). *Motivation: An experimental approach.* New York: Holt, Rinehart & Winston.

Dunker, K. (1945). On problem solving. *Psychological Monographs, 58,* Whole No. 270.

Dunn, A.J. (1980). Neurochemistry of learning and memory: An evaluation of recent data. In M.R. Rosenzweig & L.W. Porter (Eds.), *Annual Review of Psychology, 31,* 343ff. Palo Alto, CA: Annual Reviews Inc.

Dupont, R.L. (1983). Diagnosis and treatment of phobias. *Directions in Psychiatry,* Vol. 3, Lesson 4. New York: Hatherleight.

Dupont, R.L. (Ed). (1982). *Phobia: A comprehensive summary of modern treatments.* New York: Brunner/Mazel.

Dutton, D.G., & Aron, A.P. (1974). Some evidence for heightened sexual attraction under conditions of high anxiety. *Journal of Personality and Social Psychology, 30,* 510–517.

Ebbinghaus, K. (1913). *Memory: A contribution to experimental psychology.* (H.A. Ruger & C.E. Bussenius, Trans.). New York: Columbia University Press. (Original publication, 1885).

Eccles, J.C. (1970). *Facing reality.* New York: Springer-Verlag.

Edelman, G.M., & Mountcastle, V.B. (1978). *The Mindful Brain.* Cambridge, MA: MIT Press.

Edgerton, R.B. (1979). *Mental retardation.* Cambridge, MA: Harvard University Press.

Eibl-Eibesfeldt, I. (1971). *Love and hate.* New York: Holt, Rinehart & Winston.

Eibl-Eibesfeldt, I. (1975). *Ethology: The biology of behavior* (2nd ed.). New York: Holt, Rinehart & Winston.

Eibl-Eibesfeldt, I. (1980). Strategies of social interaction. In R. Plutchik and H. Kellerman (Eds.), *Emotion: Theory, research, and experience: Vol 1. Theories of Emotion.* New York: Academic Press.

Ekman, P. (1971). *Universals and cultural differences in facial expressions of emotion* (pp. 207–83). Nebraska Symposium on Motivation.

Ekman, P. (1982). *Emotions in the human face* (2nd ed.). Cambridge: Cambridge University Press.

Ekman, P., & Friesen, W.V. (1969). Nonverbal leakage and clues to deception. *Psychiatry, 32,* 88–106.

Ekman, P., & Friesen, W.V. (1975). *Unmasking the face.* Englewood Cliffs, NJ: Prentice-Hall.

Ekman, P., & Oster, H. (1979). Facial expressions of emotion (527–554). In *Annual Review of Psychology, 30.*

Ekman, P., Levenson, R.W., & Friesen, W.V. (1983). Autonomic nervous system activity distinguishes among emotions. *Science, 221,* 1208–1210.

Ellis, A. (1962). *Reason and emotion in psychotherapy.* New York: Lyle Stuart.

Ellis, A. (1977). The basic clinical theory of rational-emotive therapy. In A. Ellis & R. Grieger (Eds.), *Handbook of rational-emotive therapy.* New York: Springer.

Ellis, A., & Harber, R.A. (1975). *A new guide to rational living.* North Hollywood, CA: Wilshier.

Ellsworth, P.C., Carlsmith, J.M., & Henson, A. (1972). The stare as a stimulus to flight in human subjects: A series of field experiments. *Journal of Personality and Social Psychology, 21,* 302–311.

Encyclopedic dictionary of psychology. (1986). Guilford, CT: Dushkin Publishing Group, Inc.

Epstein, S.M. (1967). Toward a Unified Theory of Anxiety. In B.A. Maher (Ed.), *Progress in experimental personality research* (Vol. 4). New York: Academic Press.

Erikson, E. (1963). *Childhood and society.* New York: W.W. Norton & Company.

Erikson, E.H. (1969). *Gandhi's Truth.* New York: W.W. Norton & Company.

Ertl, J., & Schafer, E. (1969). Brain response correlates of psychometric intelligence. *Nature, 223,* 421–422.

Estes, W.K. (1976). Intelligence and cognitive psychology. In L.B. Resnick (Ed.), *The nature of intelligence.* New York: Lawrence Erlbaum Associates.

Evans, R.I. (1967). *Dialogue with Erik Erikson.* New York: Harper & Row.

Evarts, E.V. (1979, September). Brain mechanisms of movement. *Scientific American, 241*(3),164–179.

Exline, R.V. (1971). Visual interaction: The glances of power and preference. In J.K. Cole (Ed.), *Nebraska symposium on motivation,* (Vol. 19, p. 163–206). Lincoln: University of Nebraska Press.

Exline, R.V., & Winters, L. (1965). Affective relations and mutual glances. In S.S. Tomkins & C.E. Izard (Eds.), *Affect, cognition, and personality.* New York: Springer Publishing.

Eylon, Bat-Sheva. (1979). Effects of knowledge organization on task performance. *Dissertation Abstracts International, 40,* 3923A. (University Microfilms No. 80–00, 336).

Eylon, Bat-Sheva, & Reif, F. (1984). Effects of knowledge organization on task performance. *Cognition and Instruction, 1,* 5–44.

Eysenck, H.J. (1970). *The structure of human personality.* London: Methuen.

Eysenck, H.J., & Kamin, L. (1981). *The intelligence controversy: H.J. Eysenck vs. Leon Kamin.* New York: John Wiley & Sons. (Published in Great Britain as *Intelligence: The Battle for the Mind.*)

Eysenck, H.J., & Prell, D.B. (1951). The inheritance of neuroticism: An experimental study. *Journal of Mental Science, 97,* 441–446.

Faraone, S. (1982). Psychiatry and political repression in the Soviet Union. *American Psychologist, 37*(10), 1105–1112.

Farber, S. (1981). Telltale behavior twins. *Psychology Today, 15*(1),60ff.

Festinger, L.A. (1957). *A theory of cognitive dissonance.* Stanford, CA: Stanford University Press.

Fireside, H. (1982). *Soviet psychoprisons.* New York: W.W. Norton.

Fisher, D., & Byrne, D. (1975). Too close for comfort: Sex differences in response of invasions of personal space. *Journal of Personality and Social Psychology, 32,* 15–20.

Fisher, J.D., Rytting, M., & Henslin, J. (1976). Hands touching hands: Affective and evaluative effects of an interpersonal touch. *Sociometry,* 33, 178–183.

Flavell, J., Eaverett, B.A., Croft, K., & Flavell, E.R. (1981). Young children's knowledge about visual perception: Further evidence for the Level 1-Level 2 distinction. *Developmental Psychology, 17,* 99–103.

Flavell, J.H. (1979). Metacognition and cognitive monitoring: A new area of cognitive-developmental inquiry. *American Psychologist, 34,* 906–9 11.

Flavell, J.H., & Wellman, H.M. (1977). Perspectives on the development of memory and cognition. In R.V. Kail & J.H. Hagen (Eds.), *MetaMemory.* Hillsdale, NJ: Lawrence Erlbaum Associates.

Fleming, J.D. (1974). Field report: The state of the apes. *Psychology Today, 7,* 31–46.

Fletcher, J.M. (1942). Homeostasis as an explanatory principle in psychology. *Psychological Review, 49,* 80–87.

Flight management system: Boeing 757–767. (1982, October). Seattle, WA: The Boeing Company, D6-49385R2.

Foulkes, D. (1966). *The psychology of sleep.* New York: Scribner's.

Foulkes, W.D. (1962). Dream reports from different stages of sleep. *Journal of Abnormal Social Psychology, 65* (14), 14–25.

Fouts, R.S., & Fouts, D.H. (1985). Signs of conversations in chimpanzees. In B.T. Gardner, R.A. Gardner, & T. Van Cantfort (Eds.), *Sign language of the great apes.* New York: State University of New York Press.

Frederiksen, N. (1986). Toward a broader conception of human intelligence. *American Psychologist, 41* (4), 445–452.

Freedman, J.L., & Fraser, S.C. (1966). Compliance without pressure: The-foot-in-the-door technique. *Journal of Personality and Social Psychology, 4,* 195–202.

Freud, A. (1946). *The ego and the mechanisms of defense.* New York: International Universities Press.

Freud, A. (1974). *Introduction to psychoanalysis: Lectures for child analysts and teachers.* New York: International Universities Press.

Freud, S. (1905). Three essays on sexuality. In J. Strachey (Trans.), Standard edition. (Vol. 7, pp. 219–220). London: Hogarth Press. (Quoted by Mitchell, J., On Freud and the distinction between the sexes. In J. Stroude (Ed.), *Women and analysis,* p. 31.)

Freud, S. (1933). *New introductory lectures on psychoanalysis.* New York: W.W. Norton & Co.

Freud, S. (1953). *A general introduction to psychoanalysis.* New York: Permabooks. (Boni & Liveright edition, 1924).

Freud, S. (1953). *The interpretation of dreams.* In the standard edition. (Vols. 4, 5). London: Hogarth Press. (First German edition, 1900).

Freud, S. (1953–1955). *The standard edition of the complete psychological works.* James Strachey (Trans.). 24 volumes. London: Hogarth.

Freud, S. (1959). *Analysis of a phobia in a five year old boy.* In standard edition. Vol. 10. (First German edition, 1909).

Gagnon, J.H. (1977). *Human sexualities.* Glenview, IL: Scott, Foresman & Co.

Galanter, E. (1962). Contemporary psychophysics. In *New directions in psychology* (Vol. 1, pp. 87–156). New York: Holt.

Galin, D. (1974). Implications for psychiatry of left and right cerebral specialization: A neurophysiological context for unconscious processes. *Archives of General Psychiatry, 31,* 572–583.

Galin, D. (1977). Lateral specialization and psychiatric issues: Speculations on the development and evolution of consciousness. In S.J. Dimond & D.S. Blizzard (Eds.), *Evolution and laterization of the brain* (pp. 397–411). New York: New York Academy of Sciences.

Galin, D., & Ornstein, R. (1972). Lateral specialization of cognitive mode: An EEG study. *Psychophysiology, 9,* 412–418.

Gallup, G.G. (1974). Animal hypnosis: Factual status of the fictional concept. *Psychological Bulletin, 31,* 836–853.

Gandhi, Mohandas K. (1957). *An autobiography: The story of my experiments with truth.* Boston: Beacon Press.

Gardner, A.R., & Gardner, B.T. (1969). Teaching sign language to a chimp. *Science, 165,* 664–672.

Gardner, H. (1983). *Frames of mind: The theory of multiple intelligences.* New York: Basic Books.

Gardner, M. (1957). *Fads and fallacies in the name of science.* New York: Dover.

Garzino, S.J. (1982). Lunar effects on mental behavior: A defense of the empirical research. *Environment and Behavior, 14*(4), 395–4 17.

Gazzaniga, M. (1967). The split brain in man. *Scientific American, 217,* 24–29.

Gazzaniga, M.S. (1983). Right hemisphere language following brain bisection: A 20-year perspective. *American Psychologist, 38* (5), 525–537.

Gazzaniga, M.S., & LeDoux, J.E. (1978). *The integrated mind.* New York: Plenum Press.

Geen, R.G., Beatty, W.W., & Arkin, R.M. (1984). *Human motivation: Physiological, behavioral, and social approaches.* Boston: Allyn & Bacon.

Geschwind, N. (1979, September). Specializations of the human brain. *Scientific American, 241*(3), 180–201.

Gibson, H.B. (1977). *Hypnosis: Its nature and therapeutic uses.* New York: Taplinger.

Gillam, B. (1980). Geometrical illusions. *Scientific American, 242*(1), 102–111.

Gilmore, W.J. (1984). *Psychohistorical inquiry: A comprehensive research bibliography.* New York: Garland.

Glass, A., Holyoak. K.J., & Santa, J.L. (1979). *Cognition.* Reading, MA: Addison-Wesley.

Gnitecki, J. (1982). Efficiency of structural teaching at university. *Neodidagmata, 15,* 121–138.

Goldberg, E., & Costa, L. (1981). Hemisphere differences in the acquisition and use of descriptive systems. *Brain and Language, 14,* 144–173.

Gollob, H.F., & Dittes, J.E. (1965). Effects of manipulated self-esteem on persuasibility depending on threat and complexity of communication. *Journal of Personality and Social Psychology, 2,* 195–201.

Goodall, J. van Lawick-. (1971). *In the shadow of man.* Boston: Houghton Mifflin.

Gottesman, I.I. (1962). Differential inheritance of the psychoneurosis. *Eugenics Quarterly, 9,* 223–227.

Gottesman, I.I. (1963). Heritability of personality: A demonstration. *Psychological Monographs, 77*(9), Whole Number 572.

Gottesman, I.I., & Shields, J. (1966). Schizophrenia in twins: 16 years consecutive admission to a psychiatric clinic. *British Journal of Psychiatry, 72,* 112, 809–818.

Gould, J.L. (1986). The locale map of honey bees: Do insects have cognitive maps? *Science, 232,* 861–863.

Gould, R.L. (1972). The phases of adult life: A study in developmental psychology. *American Journal of Psychiatry, 129*(5), 521–531.

Graves, R. (Ed.). (1959). *La Rousse encyclopedia of mythology.* New York: Prometheus.

Griffin, D.R. (1978). Prospects for a cognitive ethology. *The Behavioral and Brain Sciences, 1*(4), 527–538.

Griffin, D.R. (1994). *Animal thinking.* Cambridge, MA: Harvard University Press.

Griffin, D.R. (Ed.). (1985). The cognitive dimensions of animal communication. In B. Holldobler and M. Lindauer (Eds.), *Experimental behavioral ecology and sociobiology* (pp. 471–482). Sunderland, MA: Sinauer Associates.

Griffith, D. (1979). A review of the literature on memory enhancement: The potential and relevance of mnemonic techniques for military training. U.S. *Army Research Institute for the Behavioral and Social Sciences, Technical Report #436.*

Groninger, L.D. (1971). Mnemonic imagery and forgetting. *Psychonomic Science, 23*(2), 161–162.

Gruber, B.L., School, P.J., & Taub, E. (1981). Thermal and EEG biofeedback training in nonhuman primates. *Proceedings of the Biofeedback Society of America,* 12th Annual Meeting, 19–20.

Gruber, H.E. (1980). The evolving systems approach to creativity. In S. Modgil & C. Modgil (Eds.), *Toward a theory of psychological development.* Windsor, England: NFER.

Gruber, H.E. (1982, September). On the hypothesized relation between giftedness and creativity. *New Directions for Child Development,* No. 17, 7–29.

Grunebaum, H. (1985). Helpful and harmful psychotherapy. *The Harvard Medical School Mental Health Letter, 1*(10), 5–6.

Guilford, J.P. (1967). *The nature of human intelligence.* New York: McGraw-Hill.

Guilford, J.P. (1971). *Creativity tests for children: A manual of interpretation.* Beverly Hills, CA: Sheridan Psychological Services.

Guilford, J.P. (1977). *Way beyond the IQ.* Buffalo, New York: Creative Education Foundation.

Guilford, J.P. (1979). *Cognitive psychology with a frame of reference.* San Diego, CA: EdITS.

Guilford, J.P., & Heopfner, R. (1971). *The analysis of intelligence.* New York: McGraw-Hill.

Haley, R.I., Richardson, J., & Baldwin, B.M. (1984). The effects of nonverbal communication in television advertising. *Journal of Advertising Research, 24*(4), 11–18.

Hall, C. (1966). *The meaning of dreams.* New York: McGraw-Hill.

Hall, C.S., & Gardner, L. (1978). *Theories of personality* (3rd ed.). New York: John Wiley & Sons.

Hall, E.T. (1966). *The hidden dimension.* New York: Doubleday.

Hall, E.T. (1977). *Beyond culture.* New York: Anchor Books.

Hamblin, D.J. (1966, March 16). They are "idiot savants"—wizards of the calendar. *Life, 60,* 106–108.

Hamburg, D.A. (1983, May). The ultimate peril of our species. *Across The Board,* pp. 55–61.

Harding, S.R., Mogford, B., Melching, W.H., & Showel, M. (1980). *The development of four job oriented skills (JOBS) programs.* San Diego, California: U.S. Navy Research and Development Center.

Harlow, H.F. & Harlow, M. (1962). Social deprivation in monkeys. *Scientific American, 207*(5), 136–147.

Harlow, H.F., & Harlow, M. (1966). Learning to love. *American Scientist, 54,* 244–272.

Harlow, H.F., & Woolsey, C.N. (Eds.). (1958). *Biological and biochemical bases of behavior.* Madison: University of Wisconsin Press.

Harre, R., & Lamb, R. (Eds.). (1984). *The encyclopedic dictionary of psychology.* Cambridge, MA: MIT Press.

Hathaway, S.R., & McKinley, J.C. (1942–67). *MMPI: Group form, form R, individual form.* New York: The Psychological Corporation.

Hathaway, S.R., & Meehl, P.E. (1951). *An atlas for the clinical use of the MMPI.*

Hathaway, S.R., & Monachesi, E.D. (1953). *Analyzing and predicting juvenile delinquency with the MMPI.* Minneapolis: University of Minnesota Press.

Hathaway, S.R., & Monachesi, E.D. (1963). *Adolescent personality and behavior.* Minneapolis: University of Minnesota Press.

Hecht S., & Schlaer, S. (1938). An adaptometer for measuring human dark adaptation. *Journal of the Optical Society of America, 28,* 269–275.

Heider, E.R., & Olivier, D.C. (1972). The structure of the color space in naming and memory in two languages. *Cognitive Psychology, 3,* 337–354.

Heider, F. (1946). Attitudes and cognitive organization. *Journal of Psychology, 21,* 107–112.

Heider, F. (1958). *The psychology of interpersonal relations.* New York: Wiley.

Helmholtz, H.L.F. (1924). *Physiological optics.* (Trans., J.P.C. Southall). Vol. 2, Rochester, New York: Optical Society of America.

Hendrickson, D.E. (1982). The biological basis of intelligence. In H.J. Eysenck (Ed.), *A model for intelligence.* New York: Springer-Verlag.

Henning, H. (1916). Die qualitatsreibe des geschmacks. *Zeitschrift fiur Psychologie, 74,* 203–209.

Henning, H. (1927). Psychologische Studien am Geschmacksinn. In E. Abderhalden (Ed.), *Handbuch der biologischen arbeitsmethoden.* Berlin: Urban & Schwarzenberg.

Hetherington, A.N., & Ranson, S.W. (1942). The spontaneous activity and food intake of rats with hypothalamic lesions. *American Journal of Physiology, 136,* 609–617.

Hilgard, E. (1965). *Hypnotic susceptibility.* New York: Harcourt Brace Jovanovich.

Hilgard, E. Consciousness in contemporary psychology. In M.R. Rosenzweig & L.W. Porter (Eds.), (1980). *Annual Review of Psychology, 31,* 1–26. Palo Alto, CA: Annual.

Hilgard, E.R. (1976). Neodissociation theory of multiple cognitive control systems. In G.E. Schwartz & D. Shapiro (Eds.). *Consciousness and self regulation: Advances in Research, 1,* 137–171. New York: Plenum.

Hill, A.L. (1974, December). Idiot savants: A categorization of abilities. *Mental Retardation,* 12–13.

Ho, M., Saunders, P., & Fox, S. (1986, March 27). A new paradigm for evolution. *New Scientist, 109*(1501), 41–43.

Hobson, J.A., & McCarley, R.W. (1977). The brain as a dream state generator: An activation-synthesis hypothesis of the dream process. *The American Journal of Psychiatry, 134,* 1335–1348.

Hoffman, E. (1971). The idiot-savant: A case report and a review of explanations. *Mental Retardation, 9*(4), 18–21.

Hogan, W. (1978). A theoretical reconciliation of competing views of time perception. *American Journal of Psychology, 91*(3), 417–428.

Holen, M.C., & Oaster, T.R. (1976). Serial position and isolation effects in a classroom lecture simulation. *Journal of Educational Psychology, 63*(3), 293–296.

Holmes, D.S. (1984). Meditation and somatic arousal reduction: A review of the experimental evidence. *American Psychologist, 39*(1), 1–10.

Holmes, T.H., & Rahe, R.H. (1967). The social readjustment rating scale. *Journal of Psychosomatic Research, 11,* 213–218.

Homme, L.E. (1965). Perspectives in psychology: Control of coverants, the operants of the mind. *Psychological Record, 15,* 501–511.

Horney, K. (1930). *New ways in psychoanalysis.* New York: Norton.

Horwitz, W.A., Deming, W.E., & Winter, R.F. (1969). A further account of the idiot savants, experts with the calculator. *American Journal of Psychiatry, 126*(3), 160–163.

Horwitz, W.A., Kestenbaum, C., Person, E., & Jarvik, L. (1965). Identical twin—"idiot savants"—calendar calculators. *American Journal of Psychiatry, 121*(11), 1075–1079.

Hoskovec, J., & Svorad, D. (1969). The relationship between human and animal hypnosis. *American Journal of Clinical Hypnosis, 11,* 180–182.

House, W. (1984, November 30). FDA approval of cochlear implant. *Spokesman-Review,* p. 6.

Hovland, C.I., & Janis I.L. (Eds.), (1959). *Personality and persuasibility.* New Haven, CT: Yale University Press.

Hovland, C.I., Lumsdaine, A.A., & Sheffield, F.D. (1949). *Experiments on mass communication.* Princeton, NJ: Princeton University Press.

Hovland, C.I., & Weiss, W. (1951). The influence of source credibility on communication effectiveness. *Public Opinion Quarterly, 15,* 635–650.

Howe, M.J.A. (1980). *The psychology of human learning.* New York: Harper & Row.

Hubel, D.H. (1979, September). The brain. *Scientific American, 241*(3), 44–53.

Hubel, D.H., & Wiesel, T.N. (1979, September). Brain mechanisms of vision. *Scientific American, 241*(3), 150–163.

Hulse, S.J., Egeth, H., & Deese, J. (1980). *The psychology of learning.* New York: McGraw-Hill.

Hunt, M. (1982). *The universe within.* New York: Simon & Schuster.

Huttonlocker, J. (1968). Construction spatial images: A strategy in reasoning. *Psychological Review, 75,* 550–560.

Inhelder, B., & Piaget, J. (1958). *The growth of logical thinking from childhood to adolescence.* New York: Basic Books.

Inouye, E. (1965). Similar and dissimilar manifestations of obsessive-compulsive neuroses in monozygotic twins. *American Journal of Psychology, 121,* 1171–1175.

Iversen, L.L. (1979, September). The chemistry of the brain. *Scientific American, 241*(3), 134–149.

Izard, C.E. (1971). *Face of emotion.* New York: Appleton-Century-Crofts.

Izard, C.E. (1978). *Emotions as motivations: An evolutionary-developmental perspective.* In H.E. Howe, Jr. (Ed.). Nebraska Symposium on Motivation. Lincoln: University of Nebraska Press, 1979.

Jacobson, E. (1938). *Progressive Relaxation.* Chicago: University of Chicago Press.

James, W. (1890). *The principles of psychology.* New York: Holt, Rinehart & Winston.

James, W. (1970). *The principles of psychology:* Vols. 1 & 2. New York: Dover. (Originally published in 1890.)

Janis, I.L. (1971). Groupthink. *Psychology Today, 5,* 43ff.

Janis, I.L. (1972). *Victims of groupthink: A psychological study of foreign-policy decisions and fiascos.* Boston: Houghton-Mifflin.

Janis, I.L. (1973, January). Groupthink. *Yale Alumni Magazine.*

Janis, I.L. (1982). Counteracting the adverse effects of concurrence-seeking in policy planning groups: Theory and research perspectives. In I.H. Brandstatter, J.H. Davis, & G. Stocker-Kreichguer (Eds.), *Group decision making.* New York: Academic Press.

Janis, I.L., & Mann, L. (1977). *Decision-making: A psychological analysis of conflict, choice and commitment.* New York: Free Press.

Janowitz, H.D., & Grossman, M.I. (1949). Effects of variations in nutritive density on intake of food on dogs and cats. *American Journal of Physiology,* 158, 184–193.

Jenkins, J.G., & Dallenbach, K.M. (1924). Oblivesence during sleep and waking. *American Journal of Psychology, 35,* 605–612.

Jersild, A.T. (1952). *In search of self.* New York: Teachers College, Columbia University.

Jolly, A. (1985, March). A new science that sees animals as conscious beings. *Smithsonian,* pp. 67–75.

Jones, B., & Huang, Y.L. (1982). Space-Time dependencies in psychological judgment of extent and duration: Algebraic models of the Tau and Kappa effects. *Psychological Bulletin, 91*(1), 128–142.

Jones, M.C. (1924). A laboratory study of fear: The case of Peter. *Journal of Genetic Psychology: Developmental and Clinical Psychology, 31,* 308–315.

Joseph, R. (1982). The neuropsychology of development: Hemispheric laterality limbic language and the origin of thought. *Journal of Clinical Psychology.*

Jouvet, M. (1975). The function of dreaming: A neurophysiologist's point of view. In M.S. Gazzaniga & C. Blakemore (Eds.), *Handbook of Psychobiology.* New York: Academic Press.

Jouvet, M. (1979). What does a cat dream about? *Trends in Neurosciences, 2,* 280–282.

Jouvet, M. Neurophysiology of the states of sleep. *Physiological Reviews, 47,* 117–177.

Jouvet-Mounier, D., Astic, L., & Lacote, D. (1970). Ontogenesis of the states of sleep in rat, cat and guinea pig during the first post-natal month. *Developmental Psychology, 2,* 216–239.

Jung, C.G. (1959). The concept of the collective unconscious. In *Collected works* (Vol. 9, Part 1). Princeton: Princeton University Press.

Kandel, E.R. (1979, September). Small systems of neurons. *Scientific American, 241*(3),66–87.

Kandel, E.R., & Schwartz, J.H. (1981). *Principles of neural science.* New York: North Holland.

Kandel, E.R., & Schwartz, J.H. (1982, October, 29). Molecular biology of learning. *Science, 281*(4571), 433–443.

Karlins, M., Coffman, T.L., & Walters, G. (1969). On the fading of social stereotypes: Studies in three generations of college students. *Journal of Personality and Social Psychology, 13,* 1–16.

Katz, D. (1960). The functional approach to the study of attitude. *The Public Opinion Quarterly, 24,* 163–204.

Katz, D., & Braley, K.W. (1932). Racial stereotypes of 100 college students. *Journal of Abnormal and Social Psychology, 28,* 280–290.

Katzell, R.A., & Guzzo, R.A. Psychological approaches to productivity improvement. *American Psychologist, 38*(4), 468–472.

Kaufman, A.S. (1984). K-ABC and controversy, *The Journal of Special Education, 18*(3), 409–444.

Kaufman, A.S., & Kaufman, N.L. (1983). *Kaufman assessment battery for children: Sampler manual.* Circle Pines, MN: American Guidance Service.

Kaufman, L., & Rock, I. (1962). The moon illusion, I. *Science, 136,* 953–961.

Kaufmann, E.L., Lord, M.W., Reese, T.W., & Volkman, T. (1949). The discrimination of visual numbers. *American Journal of Psychology, 62,* 498–525.

Kearsley, G., Hunter, B., & Seidel, R.J. (1983). Two decades of CBI research: What have we learned? *HumRRO Professional Paper,* pp. 3–83.

Kelley, H.H., & Michela, J.L. (1980). Attribution theory and research. *Annual Review of Psychology, 31,* 457–501.

Kelly, C.R. (1968). *Manual and automatic control.* New York: John Wiley & Sons.

Kelly, D.D. (1981). Physiology of sleep and dreaming. In E.R. Kandel & J.H. Schwartz (Eds.), *Principles of neural science.* New York: Elsevier/North-Holland.

Kelly, G.A. (1955). *The psychology of personal constructs.* New York: W.W. Norton & Co.

Kelly, G.A. (1980). A psychology of the optimal man. In A.W. Landfield & L.M. Leitner (Eds.), *Personal construct psychology: Psychotherapy and personality* (pp. 18–35).

Kennedy, S., Scheirer, J., & Rogers, A. (1984). The price of success: Our monocultural science. *American Psychologist, 39*(9), 996–997.

Kerr, N., & Brunn, S.E. (1983). Dispersibility of member effort and group motivation losses: Free-rider effects. *Journal of Personality and Social Psychology, 44,* 78–94.

Kessey, R.E., & Powley, T.L. (1975). Hypothalamic regulation of body weight. *American Scientist, 63,* 558–565.

Kettlewell, H.B.D. (1965). Insect survival and selection for pattern. *Science, 148*(3675), 1290–1296.

Kety, S.S. (1979, September). Disorders of the human brain. *Scientific American, 241*(3), 202–218.

Key, M.R. (1990). Language and nonverbal behavior as organizers of social systems. In M.R. Key (Ed.), *The relationship of verbal and nonverbal communication* (p. 1–33). New York: Mouton.

Khatena, J. (1978). *The creatively gifted child: Suggestions for parents and teachers.* New York: Vantage.

Kimble, G.A. (1961). *Hilgard and Marques: Conditioning and learning.* New York: Appleton-Century-Crofts.

Kleinmuntz, B., & Szucko, J.J. (1984). Lie detection in ancient and modern times: A call for a contemporary scientific study. *American Psychologist, 39*(7), 766–776.

Kliegel, R., Smith, J., & Baltes, P.B. (1986). Testing-the-limits, expertise, and memory in adulthood and old age. In F. Klix and H. Hagendorf (Eds.), *Proceedings of symposium in memoriam Herman Ebbinghaus, Vol. 2.* Amsterdam: North Holland.

Koestler, A. (1964). *The act of creation.* New York: Dell.

Kohlberg, L. (1969). Stage and sequence: The cognitive-developmental approach to socialization. In D. Goslin (Ed.), *Handbook of socialization theory and research.* New York: Rand McNally.

Kohlberg, L. (1981). *The philosophy of moral development, essays on moral development series,* Vol 1. New York: Harper & Row.

Kohlberg, L., & Hewer, H. (1983). *Moral stages: A current formulation and a response to critics.* New York: S. Karger.

Kohlberg, L., & Ullman, D.Z. (1974). Stages in the development of psychosexual concepts and attitudes. In Friedman, et al., *Sex differences in Behavior* (pp. 209–222).

Konner, M. (1987, March). The enigmatic smile. *Psychology Today, 21,* 42–44, 46.

Kornilov, K.N. (1930). Psychology in the light of dialectical materialism. In C. Murchison (Ed.), *Psychologists of 1930* (pp. 243–280). Worcester Clark University Press.

Kornilov, K.N. (Ed.). (1925). *Psychology and Marxism.* Moscow: Gosudarstvennoe Izd.

Kosslyn, S.M. (1985). Stalking the mental image. *Psychology Today, 19*(5), 22–28.

Kosslyn, S.M. (1985). Mental imagery ability. In R.J. Sternberg (Ed.), *Human abilities: An information processing approach* (pp. 151–172). New York: W.H. Freeman.

Kovalev, A.S., Stepanov, A.A., & Shabalin, S.N. (Eds.). (1966). *Psychology: A textbook for pedogogical institutes.* Moscow: Proveshchenie Izd.

Kozulin, A. (1986). The concept of activity in Soviet psychology. *American Psychologist, 41*(3), 264–274.

Krathwohl, D.R., Bloom, B.S., & Masia, B.B. (1964). *Taxonomy of educational objectives, handbook II: Affective domain.* New York: David McKay.

Kripke, D.F., & Sonnenschein, D. (1978). A biologic rhythm in waking fantasy. In K. Pope & J. Stinger (Eds.), *The stream of consciousness* (pp. 321–332). New York: Plenum.

Krippner, S., Ruttenber, J.A., Engelman, S.R., & Granger, D.L. (1985). Toward the application of general systems theory in humanistic psychology. *Systems Research, 2*(2), 105–115.

Kübler-Ross, E. (1969). *On death and dying.* New York: Macmillan.

Kübler-Ross, E. (1975). *Death: The final stage of growth.* Englewood Cliffs, NJ: Prentice-Hall.

LaBerge, S. (1985). *Lucid Dreaming.* New York: J.P. Tarcher.

Lamm, H., Trommsdorf, G. (1973). Group versus individual performance on tasks requiring ideational proficiency (brainstorming): A review. *European Journal of Social Psychology, 3,* 361–388.

Lange, C.J. (1967). The emotions (trans. of Lange's 1885 monograph). In C.J. Lange & W. James (Eds.), *The emotions.* New York: Hafner Publishing Co.

Larkin, J. & Reif, F. (1979). Understanding teaching and problem solving in physics. *European Journal of Science Education, 1,* 191–203.

Laszlo, E. (1972). *The system view of the world.* New York: Braziller.

Latané, B., & Darley, J.M. (1970). *The unresponsive bystander: Why doesn't he help?* New York: Appleton-Century-Crofts.

Latané, B., Williams, K., & Harkins, S. (1979). Many hands make light work: The causes and consequences of social loafing. *Journal of Personality and Social Psychology, 37,* 822–832.

Lazarus, R.S. (1980). The stress and coping paradigm. In L. Bond & J. Rosen (Eds.), *Competence and coping during adulthood,* pp. 28–74. Hanover, NH: University Press of New England.

Leahey, T.H. (1980). *A history of psychology.* Englewood Cliffs: Prentice-Hall.

Leak, G.K., & Christopher, S.B. (1982). Freudian psychoanalysis and sociabiology: A synthesis. *American Psychologist, 37*(3), 313–322.

LeDoux, J.E., Wilson, D.H., & Gazzaniga, M.S. (1977). A divided mind: Observation on the conscious properties of the separated hemispheres. *Annals of Neurology, 2,* 417–421.

Lenneberg, E.H. (1967). *The biological foundations of language.* New York: John Wiley.

Lerner, E.J. (1985, July). Robotics: The birth of vision. *Science Digest,* pp. 29–33.

Leventhal, H. (1970). Findings and theory in the study of fear communication. In L. Berkowitz (Ed.), *Advances in experimental social psychology* (Vol. 5). New York: Academic Press.

Levinson, D.J. (1986). A conception of adult development. *American Psychologist, 41*(1), 3–13.

Levinson, D.J., Darrow, C., Klein, E., & McKee, B. (1978). *The seasons of a man's life.* New York: Knopf.

Levinson, H.N. (1980). *A solution to the riddle of dyslexia.* New York: Springer-Verlag.

Levy, J. (1985). Right brain, left brain: Fact and fiction. *Psychology Today, 19*(5), 38–39,42–44.

Levy, R. (1979). General systems theory: A brief commentary. *The Journal of Creative Behavior, 13*(3), 181–193.

Lewis, R., & Tagg, E.D., (Eds.). (1981). *Computer assisted learning: Scope progress and limits.* Exeter, NH: Heinemann Educational Books.

Lieber, A.L. (1978). *The lunar effect.* New York.

Lieber, A.L., & Sherin, C.R. (1972). Homicides and the lunar cycle: Toward a theory of lunar influence on human emotional disturbance. *American Journal of Psychiatry, 129*(1), 69–74.

Liebowitz, M.R., & Klein, D.F. (1979). Hysteroid dysphoria. *Psychiatric Clinics of North America, 2,* 555–575.

Lobe, G.F. (1985). The functional replacement of the ear. *Scientific American, 252*(2), 104–111.

Locke, E.A., & Schweiger, D.M. (1979). *Participation in decision making: One more look.* In B.M. Staw (Ed.), Research in organizational behavior (Vol. 1). Greenwich, CT: JAJ Press.

Loewenberg, P. (1985). *Decoding the past: The psychohistorical approach.* Los Angeles: University of California Press.

Loftus, E. (1980). *Memory.* Reading, MA: Addison-Wesley.

Loftus, E. (1982). The G. Stanley Hall lectures series, Vol. 2. In A.G. Kraut (Ed.), *Memory and its distortions.* Washington, DC: American Psychological Association.

Lomov, B.F. (1982a). Soviet psychology: Its historical origins and contemporary status. *American Psychologist, 37*(5), 580–586.

Lomov, B.F. (1982b). The problem of activity in psychology. *Soviet Psychology, 21*(1), 55–91.

Long, P. (1986). Medical mesmerism. *Psychology Today, 20*(1), 28–29.

Lorayne, H. (1957). *How to develop a super power memory.* New York: Frederick Fell.

Lowell, A. (1930). *Poetry and poets.* Boston: Houghton Mifflin.

Lubin, B., Larsen, R.M., & Matarozzo, J.D. (1984). Patterns of psychological test usage in the United States: 1935–1982. *American Psychologist, 39*(4), 451–454.

Luh, C.W. (1922). The conditions of retention. *Psychological Monographs, 31,* (3, Whole No. 142).

Lumsden, C., & Wilson, E.O. (1981). *Genes, mind, and culture.* Cambridge, MA: Harvard University Press.

Luria, A.R. (1966). *Higher cortical functions in man.* New York: Basic Books.

Luria, A.R. (1976). *The mind of a mnemonist.* Chicago: Regnery.

Lykken, D.T. (1981). *A tremor in the blood: Uses and abuses of the lie detector.* New York: McGraw-Hill.

Lynn, R. (1982, May 20). IQ in Japan and the United States shows a growing disparity. *Nature, 927,* 222–223.

MacLean, P.D. (1949). Psychosomatic disease and the "visceral brain": Recent developments bearing on the Papez theory of emotions. *Psychosomatic Medicine, 11,* 338–353.

MacLean, P.D. (1975). Sensory and perceptive factors in emotional functions of the triune brain. In L. Levi (Ed.), *Emotions: Their parameters and measurement.* New York: Raven.

MacNichol, E.F., Jr. (1964). Three-pigment color vision. *Scientific American, 211,* 48–56.

Marks, L.E. (1975). On color-hearing synesthesia: Crossmodal translations of sensory dimensions. *Psychological Bulletin, 82*(3), 303–331.

Marks, L.E. (1978). *The unity of the senses: Interrelations among the modalities.* New York: Academic Press.

Marsella, A.J., & White, G.M. (Eds.). (1982). *Cultural conceptions of mental health and therapy.* Dordrecht, Holland: D. Reidel.

Maslow, A.H. (1943). A theory of human motivation. *Psychological Review, 55,* 95–107.

Matas, L., Arend, R., & Sroufe, L. (1978). Continuity of adaption in the second year: The relationship between quality of attachment and later competence. *Child Development, 49,* 547–556.

Mather, K.F. (1951). Objectives and nature of integrative studies. *Main Currents in Modern Thought, 8*(1),4–6.

Matlin, M.W. (1983). *Perception.* Boston: Allyn & Bacon.

Mayer, R.E. (1977). *Thinking and problem solving.* Glenview, IL: Scott, Foresman.

Mayr, E. (1978). Evolution. *Scientific American, 239*(3), 46–55.

McAdams, D.P. (1980). A thematic coding system for the intimacy motive. *Journal of Research in Personality, 14,* 413–442.

McClelland, D.C. (1985). *Human Motivation.* Glenview, IL: Scott, Foresman & Company.

McClelland, D.C., Atkinson, J.W., Clark, R.W., & Lowell, E.L. (1953). *The achievement motive.* New York: Appleton-Century- Crofts.

McConnell, J.V., & Shelby, J.M. (1970). Molecular mechanisms in memory and learning. In G. Ungar (Ed.), *Memory transfer experiments in invertebrates* (pp. 77–101). New York: Plenum Press.

McCormick, E.J., & Sanders, M.S. (1982). *Human factors in engineering and design* (5th ed.). New York: McGraw-Hill.

McDonnell Douglas Astronautics Company. (1984). *The human role in space, Vol. II—Research analysis and technical report, MDC H1295.*

McDougall, W. (1908). *An introduction to social psychology.* London: Methuen.

McDougall, W. (1932). *The energies of men.* London: Methuen.

McGrath, J.E., & Kravitz, D.A. (1982). Group research. In M.R. Rosenzweig & L.W. Porter (Eds.), *Annual review of psychology.* Palo Alto, CA: Annual Reviews.

McGuire, W.J. (1969). The nature of attitudes and attitude change. In G. Lindzey & E. Aronson (Eds.), *The handbook of social psychology,* (2nd ed.) (Vol. III) (pp. 136–314). Reading, MA: Addison-Wesley.

McKeon, R. (Ed.) (1947). *Introduction to Aristotle.* New York: Random House.

McLeish, J. (1975). *Soviet psychology: History, theory, content.* London: Methuen.

Mednick, S.A., & Mednick, M.T. (1976). *Examiner's manual: Remote associates test, college and adult forms, 1 and 2; The Test Form 1.* Boston: Houghton Mifflin.

Meeker, M., Meeker, R., & Roid, G. (1985). *Structure of intellect learning abilities test manual.* Los Angeles: Western Psychological Services.

Mehrabian, A. (1972). *Nonverbal communication*. Chicago: Aldine.

Meier, N.C. (Ed.). (1939). Studies in the psychology of art, III. *Psychology Monographs, 51,* No. 5.

Melzack, R., & Wall, P.D. (1965). Pain mechanisms: A new theory. *Science, 150,* 971–979.

Merton, R.K. (1948). The self-fulfilling prophecy. *Antioch Review, 8,* 193–210.

Milgram, S. (1963). Behavioral study of obedience. *Journal of Abnormal and Social Psychology, 67,* 371–378.

Milgram, S., Bickman, L., & Berkowitz, L. (1969). Note on the drawing power of crowds of different sizes. *Journal of Personality and Social Psychology, 13,* 79–82.

Millenson, J.R. (1967). *Principles of behavior analysis*. New York: Macmillan.

Miller, G.A. (1956). The magical number seven plus or minus two: Some limits on our capacity for processing information. *Psychological Review, 53,* 81–97.

Miller, G.A., & Taylor, W.G. (1948). The perception of repeated bursts of noise. *Journal of Acoustical Society of America, 20,* 171–182.

Miller, J.G. (1978). *Living systems*. New York: McGraw-Hill.

Miller, J.G., & Miller, L. (1985). Theoretical trends in psychiatry: General living systems theory. In H.I. Kaplan & B.J. Sadock (Eds.) *Comprehensive Textbook of Psychiatry* (4th ed.), pp.13–24. Baltimore: Williams & Wilkins.

Miller, L. (1986). Some comments on cerebral hemispheric models of consciousness. *Psychoanalytic Review, 73*(2), 129–144.

Miller, N.E. (1978). Annual Review of Psychology. In M.R. Rosenweig & L.W. Poter (Eds.), *Biofeedback and visceral learning*. Palo Alto, CA: Annual Reviews.

Millon, T. (1983). The DSM-III: An insider's perspective. *American Psychologist, 38*(7), 804–814.

Milunsky, A. (1977). *Know your genes*. Boston: Houghton Mifflin.

Mischel, W. (1973). Toward a cognitive social learning reconceptualization of personality. *Psychological Review, 80,* 252–283.

Mischel, W. (1977). Self-control and the self. In T. Mischel (Ed.), *The self: Psychological and philosophical issues,* (pp. 31–64). Totowa, NJ: Rowman & Littlefield.

Mitchell, F.D. (1907). Mathematical prodigies. *American Journal of Psychology, 18,* 61–143.

Mitchell, J.V., Jr. (1983). *Test in print III*. Lincoln, NE: University of Nebraska, Buros Institute of Mental Measurements.

Mitchell, J.V., Jr. (Ed.). (1985). *The ninth measurement yearbook*. Lincoln: University of Nebraska, Buros Institute of Mental Measurements.

Moore, K.L. (1982). *The developing human: Clinically oriented embryology* (3rd ed.). Philadelphia: Saunders.

Moravec, H. (1986). *Mind Children*. Cambridge, MA: Harvard University Press.

Moravec, H.P. (1983). *Locomotion, vision and intelligence*. Pittsburgh: The Robotics Institute, Carnegie-Mellon University.

Morgan, C.J. (1978). Bystander intervention: Experimental test of formal model. *Journal of Personality and Social Psychology, 36*(1),43–55.

Morgan, C.T., Cook, J.S., Chapanis, A., & Lund, M.W. (1963). *Human engineering guide to equipment design*. New York: McGraw-Hill.

Multiple Personality. (1985). *The Harvard Medical School Mental Health Letter, 1*(10), 1–4.

Munroe, R.H., Munroe, R.L., & Whiting, B. (1981). *Handbook of cross-cultural human development*. New York: Garland.

Munsell book of color. (1942). Baltimore: Munsell Color Company.

Murray, H.A. (1938). *Explorations in personality: A clinical and experimental study of fifty men of college age*. New York: Oxford University Press.

Murray, H.A., & the staff of the Harvard Psychological Clinic. (1943). *Thematic apperception test manual*. Cambridge, MA: Harvard University Press.

Muslin, H., & Desai Prakash. (1984, Winter). Gandhi and his fathers. *The Psychohistory Review, 12*(2/3), 7–18.

Naisbett, J. (1982). *Megatrends: Ten new directions transforming our lives*. New York: Warner Books.

National Institute of Mental Health. (1982). *Television and behavior: Ten years of scientific progress and implications for the eighties (Vol. 1: Summary Report)*. (DHHS Publication No. ADM 82–1195). Washington, DC: U.S. Government Printing Office.

National Institute of Mental Health. (1982). *Television and behavior: Ten years of scientific progress and implications for the eighties (Vol. 2: Technical Reviews)* (DHHS Publication No. ADM 82–1196). Washington, DC: U.S. Government Printing Office.

Natsoulas, T. (1978). Consciousness. *American Psychologist, 33*(10), 906–914.

Nauta, W.J.H., & Feirtag, M. (1979, September). The organization of the brain. *Scientific American, 241*(3), 88–111.

Nauta, W.J.H., & Feirtag, M. (1986). *Fundamental neuroanatomy*. New York: Freeman.

Nebylitsyn, V.D., Rozhdestvenskaya, V.I., & Teplov, B.M. (1960). Concerning the interrelation between absolute sensitivity and strength of the nervous system. *Quarterly Journal of Experimental Psychology, 12,* 17–25.

Neisser, U. (1976). *Cognitive psychology.* New York: Appleton-Century-Crofts.

Neisser, U. (1982, May.) In J. Nessel (Ed.), Understanding psychological man: A state of the science report. *Psychology Today,* pp. 40–45, 48–59.

Nesselroade, J.R., Schaie, K.W., & Bates, P.B. (1972). Autogenic and generational components of structural and quantitative change in adult behavior. *Journal of Gerontology, 27,* 222–228.

Newell, A., & Simon, H.A. (1972). *Human problem solving.* Englewood Cliffs, NJ: Prentice-Hall.

Nyhan, W.L. (1976). *The heredity factor: Genes, chromosomes and you.* New York: Gosset and Dunlop.

O'Shea, T., & Self, J. (1983). *Learning and teaching with computers: The artificial intelligence revolution.* Englewood Cliffs, NJ: Prentice-Hall.

Oberg, A., & Woodard, D. (1982, April). Anti-matter mind probes. *Science Digest,* pp. 54–57, 59.

Omenn, G.S. (1978). Prenatal diagnosis of genetic disorders. *Science, 200,* 952–958.

Orne, M.T., & Hammer, A.G. (1975). *Hypnosis.* Encyclopedia Britannica, 15th Ed. Chicago.

Ornstein, R. (1978). The split and whole brain. *Human Nature, 1,* 76–83.

Osborn, A.F. (1957). *Applied imagination* (rev. ed.). New York: Scribner's.

Osgood, C.E. (1980). Things and words. In M.R. Key (Ed.), *The relationship of verbal and nonverbal communication* (pp. 258–299). New York: Mouton.

Osgood, C.E., & Suci, G.T. (1955). Factor analysis of meaning. *Journal of Experimental Psychology, 50,* 325–338.

Osgood, C.E., Suci, G.T., & Tannenbaum, P.H. (1957). *The measurement of meaning.* Urbana: University of Illinois Press.

Overmeier, J.B., & Seligman, M.E.P. (1967). Effects of inescapable shock upon subsequent escape and avoidance responding. *Journal of Comparative and Physiological Psychology, 63,* 28–33.

The Oxford English Dictionary (and supplements). (1933). Oxford University Press, England: Clarendon Press.

Paivio, A., Yuille, J.C., & Madigan, S.A. (1968). Concreteness, imagery, and meaningfulness values for 925 nouns. *Journal of Experimental Psychology Monograph Supplement, 76*(1, Part 2).

Pavlov, I.P. (1927). *Conditioned reflexes.* (Trans., G.V. Anrep) Oxford, England: Oxford University Press.

Pavlov, I.P. (1928). *Lectures on conditioned reflexes.* New York: International Publishers.

Pavlov, I.P. (1960). *Conditioned reflexes: An investigation of the physiological activity of the cerebral cortex.* New York: Dover.

Pearson, K. (1893). Contributions to the mathematical theory of evolution. *Philosophical Transactions,* pp. 71–110. London: Royal Society of London.

Peele, S. (1984). The question of personality. *Psychology Today, 18*(12), 54–56.

Pelligrini, R.J., & Schauss, A.G. (1980). Muscle strength as a function of exposure to hue differences in visual stimuli: An experimental test of the kinesoid hypothesis. *Orthomolecular Psychiatry, 9*(2), 144–147.

Penfield, W. (1955). The permanent record of the stream of consciousness. *Acta Psychologica, XI,* 47–69.

Penfield, W. (1975). *The mystery of the mind. A critical study of consciousness and the human brain.* Princeton, NJ: Princeton University Press.

Penfield, W., & Rasmussen, T. (1958). *The cerebral cortex of man: A clinical study of localization of function.* New York: Macmillan.

Penrod, S. (1983). *Social psychology.* Englewood Cliffs, NJ: Prentice-Hall.

Pervin, L.A. (1984). *Personality: Theory and research* (4th ed.). New York: John Wiley & Sons.

Petty, R.E., & Cacioppo, J.T. (1979). Effects of forewarning on persuasive intent and involvement on cognitive responses and persuasion. *Personality and Social Psychology Bulletin, 5,* 173–176.

Piaget, J. (1952). *The origins of intelligence in children.* New York: International Universities Press.

Piaget, J. (1972). Intellectual evolution from adolescence to adulthood. *Human Development, 15,* 1–12.

Piaget, J., & Inhelder, B. (1969). *The psychology of the child.* New York: Basic Books.

Pierce, J.R., & Karlin, J.E. (1957). Reading rates and the information rates of a human channel. *Bell Telephone Technical Journal, 36,* 497–516.

Piliavin, I.M., Rodin, J., & Piliavin, J.A. (1969). Good samaritanism: An underground phenomenon? *Journal of Personality and Social Psychology, 13,* 289–299.

Pines, M. (1982, March 30). What produces great skills? Specific pattern is discerned. *New York Times,* Section C, pp. 1–2.

Pliner, P., Hart, H., Kohl, J., & Saari, D. (1974). Compliance without pressure: Some further data on the foot-in-the-door technique. *Journal of Experimental Social Psychology, 10,* 17–22.

Plutchik, R. (1980). *Emotion: A psychoevolutionary synthesis.* New York: Harper & Row.

Podrabinek, A. (1980). *Punitive medicine.* New York: Karoma Press.

Porter, A. (1969). *Cybernetics simplified.* New York: Barnes & Noble.

Post, L.A. (1932). Ancient memory systems. *Classical Weekly, VI,* p. 109. New York.

Pribram, K.H., Nuwer, M., & Baton, R.J. (1974). The holographic hypothesis of memory structure in brain function and perception. In D.H. Krantz, R.C. Luce, & P. Suppes (Eds.). *Contemporary developments in mathematical psychology* (pp. 416–457). New York: Freeman.

Pribram, Karl H. (1982). *Languages of the brain.* New York: Random House.

Price-Williams, D.R. (1954). The Kappa effect. *Nature, 173,* 363–364.

Psychological Corporation, Test Service Bulletin. (1955, January). *Methods of expressing test scores.* No. 48. New York.

Puccetti, R. (1981). The case for mental duality: Evidence from split brain data and other considerations. *The Behavioral and Brain Sciences, 4,* 93–123.

Rahmani, L. (1973) *Soviet Psychology: Philosophical, theoretical, and experimental issues.* New York: International Universities Press.

Rao, K.R. (1984). *The basic experiments in parapsychology.* Jefferson, NC: McFarland & Co.

Rapoport, A. (1974). Review of [Irvin Laszlo's A strategy for the future: The system approach]. *General Systems Yearbook, XIX,* 247–250.

Rapoport, A. (1986). *General system theory.* Cambridge, MA: Turnbridge Wells, Kent.

Ratner, S.C. (1967). Comparative aspects of hypnosis. In J.E. Gordon (Ed.), *Handbook of clinical and experimental hypnosis.* New York: Macmillan.

Razan, G. (1965). Russian physiologists psychology and American experimental psychology. *Psychological Bulletin, 63,* 42–64.

Redshaw, M. (1978). Cognitive development in human and gorilla infants. *Journal of Human Evolution, 7,* 133–141.

Reich, W. (1983, January 30). The world of Soviet psychiatry. *The New York Times* Magazine, pp. 20–26, 50.

Reif, F. (1977). Problem solving in physics or engineering: Human information processing and some teaching suggestions. Paper, University of California at Berkeley.

Reif, F. (1979). Cognitive mechanisms facilitating human problem solving in a realistic domain: The example of physics. Paper, University of California at Berkeley.

Reif, F. (1980). Theoretical and educational concerns with problem solving: Bridging the gaps with human cognitive engineering. In D.T. Tuma & F. Reif (Eds.), *Problem solving and education: Issues in teaching and research.* Hillsdale, NJ: Lawrence Erlbaum.

Rensberger, B. (1980, November). Life in limbo. *Science 80,* pp. 36–43.

Restak, R. (1982, May). Islands of genius. *Science 82,* pp. 62–76.

Reynolds, G.S. (1975). *A primer of operant conditioning (revised).* Glenview, IL: Scott, Foresman & Company.

Rhine, J.B., & Pratt, J.G. (1974). *Parapsychology, frontier science of the mind.* Springfield, IL: Charles C. Thomas.

Rhine, J.B., Pratt, J.G., Smith, B.M., Stuart, C.E., & Greenwood, J.A. (1966). *Extrasensory perception after sixty years.* Boston: Bruce Hampheries.

Rhine, L.E. (1977). *Manual for introductory experiments in parapsychology* (2nd ed.). Durham, NC: Parapsychology Press.

Richardson, A. (1969). *Mental imagery.* New York: Springer.

Riegel, K. (1976, October). The dialectics of human development. *American Psychologist, 31*(10), 689–700.

Riegel, K. (1979). *Foundations of dialectical psychology.* New York: W.W. Norton.

Rimland, B. (1978a). Savant capabilities of autistic children and their cognitive implications. In G. Serban (Ed.), *Cognitive defects in the development of mental illness.* New York: Brunner/Mazel.

Rimland, B. (1978b, August). The autistic savant. *Psychology Today,* 69–70, 73–74, 77–79, 80.

Rimland, B., & Hill. A.L. (1984). Idiot savants. In J. Wortis (Ed.), *Mental retardation and developmental disabilities.* (Vol. 13). New York: Plenum Press.

Risser, D.T. (1979, April). A field study of behavioral congruence: Arm crossing in dyads. Paper presented at the Eastern Psychological Association Meeting.

Ristau, C. (1983). Language, cognition, and awareness in animals? In J.A. Sechzer (Ed.), *The role of animals in biomedical research.* Annals of the New York Academy of Sciences (Vol. 406, pp. 170–186). New York: The New York Academy of Sciences.

Robinson, F.P. (1970). *Effective study.* (4th ed.). New York: Harper & Row.

Roebuck, J.A., Jr. (1982). *Space shuttle crew station requirements—past and future.* Rockwell International Corporation #821495, pp. 49–60.

Rogers, C. (1951). *Client-centered therapy.* Boston: Houghton-Mifflin.

Rogers, C. (1951). *Client-centered therapy: Its current practice, implications, and theory.* Boston: Houghton-Mifflin.

Rogers, C. (1961). *On becoming a person.* Boston: Houghton-Mifflin Co.

Rogers, C. (1963). The actualizing tendency in relation to "motives" and to consciousness. In M.R. Jones (Ed.), *Nebraska symposium on motivation* (pp. 1–24). Lincoln, NE: University of Nebraska Press.

Rogers, C. (1980). *A way of being.* Boston: Houghton Mifflin.

Rogers, C., & Dymond, R.F. (Eds.). (1954). *Psychotherapy and personality change.* Chicago: University of Chicago Press.

Roscoe, S.N. (1963). Airborne displays for flight and navigation. *Human Factors, 10*(4), 321–332.

Rosenthal, R., & Jacobson, L. (1968). *Pygmalian in the classroom.* New York: Holt, Rinehart & Winston.

Rosenthal, D., & Quinn, O.W. (1977). Quadruplet hallucinations: Phenotypic variations of a schizophrenic genotype. *Archives of General Psychiatry, 34,* 817–827.

Rosenzweig, M.R. (1984). U.S. psychology and world psychology. *American Psychologist, 39*(8), 877–884.

Rossi, E.L. (1986). Altered states of consciousness in everyday life: Ultradian rhythms. In B.J. Wolman & M. Ullman (Eds.), *Handbook of states of consciousness* (pp. 97–132). New York: Van Nostrand Reinhold.

Rubenzer, R. (1979, Spring). The role of the right hemisphere in learning & creativity implications for enhancing problem-solving ability. *The Gifted Child Quarterly. XXIII* (1), 78–100.

Rubin, Z. (1970). Measurement of romantic love. *Journal of Personality and Social Psychology, 16*(2), 265–273.

Rumbaugh, S.E. Savage-. (1984). Pan paniscus and pantroglodytes: Contrasts in preverbal communicative competence. In R.L. Susman (Ed.), *The Pygmy Chimpanzee.* New York: Plenum.

Rumbaugh, S.E. Savage-, Rumbaugh, D.M., & Boysen, S. (1978, August 18). Symbolic communication between two chimpanzees (Pan Troglodytes). *Science, 201,* 641–644.

Rumbaugh, S.E. Savage-, Sevcik R.A., Rumbaugh, D.M., & Rubert, E. (1985). The capacity of animals to acquire language: Do species differences have anything to say to us? *Philosophical Transactions of the Royal Society of London, 308B,* 177–185.

Rushton, J.P. (1982, April). Altruism and society: A social learning perspective. *Ethics, 92,* 425–466.

Sacks, O. (1985, February 28). The twins. *The New York Review of Books, 32*(3), 16–20.

Sakai, K., & Cespuglio, R. (1976). Evidence for the presence of eye movement potentials during paradoxical sleep in cats. *Electroencephalography and Clinical Neurophysiology, 41,* 37–48.

Savage, J. (1977). *Evolution.* (3rd ed.). New York: Holt, Rinehart & Winston.

Saxe, L., Dougherty, D., & Cross, T. (1985). The validity of polygraph testing, *American Psychologist, 40*(3), 355–366.

Schachter, S.S., & Singer, J.E. (1962). Cognitive, social and physiological determinants of emotional state. *Psychological Review, 69,* 379–399.

Scheerer, M., Rothman, E., & Goldstein, K. (1945). A case of "idiot savant": An experimental study of personality organization. *Psychological Monographs. 58*(4), Whole No. 269.

Scheinfeld, A. (1972). *Heredity in humans* (rev. ed.). Philadelphia: Lippincott.

Schmeidler, G.R., & McConnell, R.A. (1958). *ESP and personality patterns.* New Haven, CT: Yale University Press.

Schneider, B. (1985). Organizational behavior. In M.R. Rozenzweig, & L.W. Porter (Eds.), *Annual Review of Psychology,* pp. 573–611. Palo Alto, CA: Annual Reviews.

Scroggs, J.R. (1985). *Key Ideas in Personality Theory.* St. Paul: West.

Seeman, P., Ulpian, C., Bergeron, C., Riederer, P., Jellinger, K., Gabriel, E., Reynolds, G.P., & Tourtellotte, W.W. (1984). Bimodal distribution of dopamine receptor densities in brains of schizophrenics. *Science, 225,* 728–731.

Segal, M.W. (1974). Alphabet and attraction: An unobtrusive measure of the effect of propinquity in a field setting. *Journal of Personality and Social Psychology, 30,* 654–657.

Selfe, L. (1978). *A case of extraordinary drawing ability in an autistic child.* New York: Academic Press.

Seligman, M.E.P. (1975). *Helplessness.* San Francisco: Freeman.

Selye, H. (1950). The *physiology and pathology of exposure to stress.* Montreal: Acta.

Selye, H. (1956). *The stress of life.* New York: McGraw-Hill.

Selye, H. (1964). *From dream to discovery.* New York: McGraw-Hill.

Selye, H. (1982). History and present status of the stress concept. In L. Golderger & S. Breznitz (Eds.), *Handbook of stress.* New York: The Free Press.

Sexton, V.S., & Misiak, H. (1984). American psychologists and psychology abroad. *American Psychologist, 39*(9), 1026–1031.

Shapin, B., & Coly, L. (Eds.). (1982). *Parapsychology and the experimental method* (Proceedings of an international conference held in New York, November 14, 1981). New York: Parapsychology Foundation.

Sheldon, W. (1954). *Atlas of men: A guide for somatotyping the adult male at all ages.* New York: Harper & Row.

Sherif, C.W. (1982). Social and psychological bases of social psychology. In A.G. Kraut (Ed.), *The G. Stanley Hall lecture series,* Vol. 2, pp. 5–72.

Shiffrin, R.M., & Atkinson, R.L. (1969). Storage and retrieval processes in long-term memory. *Psychological Review, 76*(2), 179–193.

Shirley, M.M. (1933). The first two years. *Institute of Child Welfare Monograph, 7.* Minneapolis: University of Minnesota Press.

Shuldiner, H. (1984, August). Super-smart cars. *Popular Science,* pp. 54–57, 110.

Simon, H.A. (1978). Information-processing theory of human problem solving. In W.K. Estes (Ed.), *Handbook of learning and cognitive processes: Vol. 5. Human information processing.* Hillsdale, NJ: Lawrence Erlbaum.

Simon, H.A., & Newell, A. (1971). Human problem solving: The state of the theory in 1970. *American Psychologist, 26,* 145–159.

Skeels, H.M. (1966). Adult status of children with contrasting early life experiences: A follow-up study. *Monogr. Soc. Research Child Development.* Serial No. 150, *31,* No. 3. Society for Research in Child Development.

Skinner, B.F. (1948). Superstition in the pigeon. *Journal of Experimental Psychology, 38,* 168–172.

Skinner, B.F. (1953). *Science and human behavior.* New York: Macmillan.

Skinner, B.F. (1981, July). Selection by consequence. *Science,* pp. 104–105.

Skinner, B.F. (1984). The shame of American education. *American Psychologist, 39* (9), 947–954.

Slater, E., & Sheilds, J. (1953). Psychotic and neurotic illnesses in twins. *Medical Research Council Special Report.* Series No. 278. London: H.M.S.O.

Smead, F.W. (1983, October). Voice actuated avionics. *Astronautics and Aeronautics,* pp. 54–57, 63.

Smith, D. (1982). Trends in counseling and psychotherapy. *American Psychologist, 37*(7), 802–809.

Smith, D., & Kraft, W.A. (1983). DSM-III: Do psychologists really want an alternative? *American Psychologist, 38*(7),777–785.

Smith, S.B. (1983). *The great mental calculators: The psychology, methods, and lives of calculating prodigies past and present.* New York: Columbia University Press.

Snider, R. (1958). The cerebellum. *Scientific American, 199*(2),84–90.

Social sciences and space exploration. (1984, November). Washington, DC: NASA, EP-192.

Solomon, R.L. & Corbit, J.D. (1974). An opponent-process theory of motivation: I. Temporal dynamics of affect *Psychological Review, 82*(2), 119–145.

Solomon, R.L. (1980). The opponent-process theory of acquired motivation: The costs of pleasure and the benefits of pain. *American Psychologist, 35*(8), 691–712.

Soviet space stations as analogs. (1983). (Contains all of the Soviet (SOV) references). Kent, WA: Boeing Aerospace Company, D180–28182–1, 1983.

Space station habitability design recommendations, (1984, November 15). Vols. I & II. Kent, WA: D180–28402–1.

Space station: The next logical step. (1984). Walter Froehlich, Washington, DC: NASA, EP-213.

Space station/nuclear submarine analogs. (1984). Granada Hills, CA: National Behavior Systems, Kent, WA: Boeing Aerospace Company, # D180–28181–1, 1983. .

Sperry, R. (1986). The new mentalist paradigm and ultimate concern. *Perspectives in Biology and Medicine, 29,*(3), 413–422.

Sperry, R.W. (1968). Hemisphere deconnection and unity in conscious awareness. *American Psychologist, 23*(10), 723–733.

Spiegel, D. (1987, March/April). The healing trance. *The Sciences,* pp. 35–40.

Spiegel, D., Cutcomb, S., Ren, C., & Pribram, K. (1985). Hypnotic hallucination alters evoked potentials. *Journal of Abnormal Psychology, 94*(3), 249–255.

Spitz, R.A. (1945). In Ruth Eissler, et al., *The psychoanalytic study of the child.* Vol. 1, (pp. 53–74); Vol. 2, (pp. 113–117, 313–342). New York: International Universities Press.

Spitzer, R.L., Forman, J.B.W., & Nee, J. (1979). DSM-III field trials: Initial interrater diagnostic reliability. *American Journal of Psychiatry, 136,* 815–817.

Spitzer, R.L., Skodol, A.E., Gibbon, M., & Williams, J.B.W. (1981). *DSM-III case book.* Washington, DC: American Psychiatric Association.

Springer, S.P., & Deutsch, G. (1985). *Left brain, right brain.* (rev. ed.). New York: Freeman.

Sprinthall, R.C., & Sprinthall, N.A. (1981). *Educational psychology: A developmental approach* (3rd ed.). Reading, MA: Addison-Wesley.

Staats, A.W., Staats, C.K. (1958). Attitudes established by classical conditioning. *Journal of Abnormal and Social Psychology, 57,* 37–40.

Standing, L., Conezio, J., & Haber, R.N. (1970). Perception and memory for pictures. Single trial learning of 2500 visual stimuli. *Psychonomic Science, 19,* 23–24.

Statistical Abstract of the United States 1984 (104th Ed.). Population, p. 8. Washington, DC: Government Printing Office.

Staw, B.M. (1984). Organizational behavior: A review and reformulation of the field's outcome variables, In Rosenzweig, M.R., & Porter, L.W., *Annual Review of Psychology,* pp. 627–666. Palo Alto, CA: Annual Reviews.

Steinberg, F. (1980). *Aboard the space shuttle.* Washington, DC: NASA Division of Public Aftairs, NASA EP-169.

Steinbuch, K. (1962, May). *Information Processing in Man.* Paper presented at IRE International Congress on Human Factors in Electronics, Long Beach, CA.

Sternbach, P.D. (Ed.). (1978). *The psychology of pain.* New York: Raven.

Sternberg, R.J. (1984). Toward a triarchic theory of human intelligence. *The Behavioral and Brain Sciences, 7,* 269–315.

Stevens, C.F. (1979, September). The neuron. *Scientific American, 241*(3), 54–65.

Stiles, W.B., Shapiro, D-A., & Elliot, R. (1986). Are all psychotherapies equivalent? *American Psychologist, 41*(2),165–180.

Stone, G. & McCauley, H. (1984, October). *Flight Deck Design Methodology Using Computerized Anthropometric Models.* 1984 SAE Aerospace Congress and Exhibition, Douglas Paper 7508, pp. 1–8.

Stone, J.B. (1958). *Manual: S-O Rorschach test.* Los Angeles: California Test Bureau.

Stone, J.B. (1958). *S-O Rorschach test booklet.* Los Angeles: California Test Bureau.

Strapp, J., Tucker, A.M., & VandenBos, G.R. (1985). Census of psychological personnel, 1983. *American Psychologist, 40* (12), 1317–1351.

Strelau, J., Farley, F., & Gale, A. (1986). *The biological basis of personality and behavior.* New York: Hemisphere/Harper & Row.

Taber, J.I., Glaser, R., & Scheafer, H.H. (1965). *Learning and programmed instruction.* Reading, MA: Addison-Wesley.

Tanner, J.M. (1962). *Growth at adolescence* (2nd ed.). Oxford: Blackwell Scientific Publications.

Tanner, J.M. (1972). Sequence, tempo, and individual variation in growth and development of boys and girls aged twelve to sixteen. In J. Kagan & R. Coles (Eds.), *Twelve to Sixteen: Early Adolescence.* New York: Norton.

Tanner, J.M. (1973, September). Growing up. *Scientific American, 229,* 36–37.

Tayacan, (1984, October 15). *Psychological operations in guerrilla warfare.* Trans. by Language Services, Congressional Research Service, Library of Congress.

Taylor, F.V. (1957). Psychology and the design of machines. *The American Psychologist, 12,* 249–258.

Teplov, B.M. (1962). Investigation of the properties of the nervous system as a path leading to the study of individual differences. In *Psychological Science in the USSR: Vol. 2* (pp. 2–62). Washington Office of Technical Services.

Test Service Bulletin. (January, 1955). New York: The Psychological Corporation, (48), 7–8.

Thalbourne, M.A. (1982). *A glossary of terms used in parapsychology.* London: Heinmann.

Thatcher, R.W., & John, E.R. (1977). *Foundations of cognitive processes.* Hillsdale, NJ: Erbaum.

Thomas, C.A., Davies, I.K., Openshaw, D., & Bird, B.F. (1963). *Programmed learning in perspective: A guide to program writing.* Chicago: Educational Methods, Inc.

Thorndike, E.L. (1898). Animal intelligence: An expenmental study of the associative processes in animals. *Psychological Monographs,* No. 8. Verplanck, W.S. (1957, November) A glossary of some terms used in the objective science of behavior. *Psychological Review 64*(6) (Suppl.), Part 2.

Thorndike, E.L. (1899). *The associative processes of animals.* Boston: Ginn and Company.

Thorndike, E.L. (1909). Darwin's contribution to psychology. *University of California Chronicle, XII,* 65–80.

Thorndike, E.L. (1911). *Animal intelligence.* New York: Macmillan.

Tinbergen, N. (1952). The curious behavior of the stickleback. *Scientific American, 182,* 22–26.

Tomkins, S.S. (1980). Affect amplification: Some modification in theory. In Robert Plutchik & Henry Kellerman (Eds.), *Motion: Theory, research, and experience* (pp. 141–164). New York: Academic Press.

Torney-Purta, J. (1984). Annotated bibliography of materials for adding an international dimension to undergraduate courses in developmental and social psychology. *American Psychologist, 39*(9), 1032–1042.

Torrance, E.P. (1974). *Torrance test of creative thinking: Norms—technical manual.* Lexington, MA: Personnel Press.

Triandis, H.C., & Berry, J.W. (Eds.). (1980). *Handbook of cross-cultural psychology: Vol. 2. Methodology.* Boston: Allyn & Bacon.

Triandis, H.C., & Brislin, R. (Eds.). (1981). *Handbook of cross-cultural psychology: Vol. 5. Social psychology.* Boston: Allyn & Bacon.

Triandis, H.C., & Brislin, R.W. (1984). Cross-cultural psychology. *American Psychologist, 39*(9), 1006–1016.

Triandis, H.C., & Draguns, J. (Eds.). (1981). *Handbook of cross-cultural psychology: Vol. 6. Psychopathology.* Boston: Allyn & Bacon.

Triandis, H.C., & Heron, A. (Eds.). (1981). *Handbook of cross-cultural psychology: Vol. 4. Developmental psychology.* Boston: Allyn & Bacon.

Triandis, H.C., & Lambert, W. (Eds.). (1980). *Handbook of cross-cultural psychology: Vol. 1. Perspectives.* Boston: Allyn & Bacon.

Triandis, H.C., & Lonner, W.J. (Eds.). (1980). *Handbook of cross-cultural psychology: Vol. 3. Basic Processes.* Boston: Allyn & Bacon.

Triandis, H.C., Lambert, W., Berry, J., Lonner, W., Heron, A., Brislin, R., & Draguns, J. (Eds.). (1980–1981). *Handbook of cross-cultural psychology.* (Vols. 1–6). Boston: Allyn & Bacon.

Triplett, N. (1898). The dynamogenic factors in pacemaking and competition. *American Journal of Psychology, 9*(4), 507–533.

Trotter, R.J. (1986, August). Profile: Robert J. Sternberg: Three heads are better than one. *Psychology Today, 20,* 56–62.

Tryon, R.C. (1940). Genetic differences in maze learning in rats. *Yearbook for the National Society for Studies in Education, 39,* 111–119.

Tryon, R.C. (1942). Individual differences. In F.A. Moss (Ed.), *Comparative Psychology* (rev. ed.). Englewood Cliffs, NJ: Prentice-Hall.

Tsukahara, N. (1981). Synaptic plasticity in the mammalian central nervous system. *Annual Review of Neural Science, 4,* 351–379.

Tulving, E. (1972). Organization of memory. In E. Tulving & W. Donaldson (Eds.). *Episodic and semantic memory.* New York: Academic Press.

Tulving, E. (1985). How many memory systems are there? *American Psychologist, 40*(4), 385–398.

U.S. Department of Health and Human Services. (1985). *Electroconvulsive therapy: Consensus development conference statement (Vol. 5, No. 11).* Washington, DC: U.S. Government Printing Office.

Ulrich, R.S. (1984, April). View through a window may influence recovery from surgery. *Science, 222,* 420–421.

Valenstein, E.S. (1980). Who receives psychosurgery? In E.S. Valenstien (Ed.), *The psychosurgery debate.* San Francisco: W.H. Freeman.

Vandenberg, S.G. (1971). What do we know about the inheritance of intelligence and how do we know it? In R. Cancro (Ed.), *Intelligence: Genetic and environmental influences.* New York: Grune & Stratton.

Vandervert, L.R. (1980). Operational definitions made simple, lasting, and useful. *Teaching of Psychology, 7*(1), 57–59.

Vandervert, L.R. (1986). General systems theory. In *Encyclopedic dictionary of psychology* (pp. 115–116). Guilford, CT: The Dushkin Publishing Group.

Vandervert, L.R. (1988). Systems thinking and a proposal for neurological positivism. *Systems Research,* (in press).

Viscott, D.S. (1970). A musical idiot savant: A psychodynamic study, and some speculations on the creative process. *Psychiatry, 33*(4), 494–515.

Viscott, D.S. (1970). A musical idiot savant: A psychodynamic study and some speculations on the creative process. *Psychiatry, 33*(4), 494–515.

Volgyesi, F.A. (1966). *Hypnosis of man and animals: With special reference to the development of the brain in the species and in the individual* (2nd Ed.). Baltimore: The Williams and Wilkins Company.

Voss, J.F. (1976). The nature of the nature of intelligence. In L.B. Resnick (Ed.), *The nature of intelligence.* New York: Lawrence Erlbaum Associates.

Vygotsky, L. (1962). *Thought and language.* Cambridge, MA: MIT Press.

Vygotsky, L. (1979). Consciousness as a problem of psychology of behavior. *Soviet Psychology, 17,* 17, 5–35.

Wagner, M.W., & Monnent, M. (1979). Attitudes of college professors toward extrasensory perception. *Zetetic Scholar, 5,* 7–16.

Wagner, R.K., & Sternberg, R.J. (1986). Tacit knowledge and intelligence in the everyday world. In R.J. Sternberg & R.K. Wagner (Eds.), *Practical intelligence: Nature and origins of competence in the everyday world* (pp. 51–83). New York: Cambridge University Press.

Wahba, M.A., & Bridwell, L.G. (1976). Maslow reconsidered: A review of research on the need hierarchy theory. *Organizational Behavior and Human Performance, 15,* 212–240.

Walberg, F. (1990). *Puzzle thinking.* Philadelphia, PA: The Franklin Institute Press.

Walker, L.J. (1980). Cognitive and perspective-taking prerequisites for moral development. *Child Development, 51,* 131–139.

Walker, S. (1983). *Animal thought.* London: Routledge & Kegan.

Wallas, Graham. (1926). *The art of thought.* New York: Harcourt, Brace & World.

Walster, E, Aronson, V., Abrahams, D., & Rottman, L. (1966). Importance of physical attractiveness in dating behavior. *Journal of Personality and Social Psychology, 5,* 508–516.

Water, E., Wippman, J., & Sroufe, L.A. (1979). Attachment, positive affect and competence in the peer group: Two studies in construct validation. *Child Development, 50*(3), 821–830.

Watson, J.B. (1925). *Behaviorism.* New York: W.W. Norton.

Watson, J.B. (1970). *Behaviorism.* New York: W.W. Norton & Co.

Watson, J.B., & Rayner, R. (1920). Conditioned emotional reactions. *Journal of Experimental Psychology, 3,* 1–14.

Webb, L.J., DiClemente, C.C., Johnstone, E.E., Sanders, J.L., & Perley, R.A. (1981). *DSM-III training guide.* New York: Brunner/Mazel.

Webb, W.B. (1981). The return of consciousness. In L.T. Benjamin (Ed.), *The G. Stanley Hall lecture series, Vol. 1,* pp. 131–152. Washington, DC: American Psychological Association.

Weber, E.H. (1846). Tastsinn Gemeingefuhl. Handworterbuch. *Phys. Wagner, 3,* 481–588.

Wechsler, D. (1955). *Wechsler adult intelligence scale manual.* New York: Psychological Corporation.

Weitz, S. (1977). *Sex roles: Biological, psychological, and social foundations.* New York: Oxford University Press.

Weitzenhoffer, A.M., & Hilgard, E.R. *The Stanford hypnotic susceptibility scale form c.* Palo Alto, CA: Consulting Psyc. Press.

Wertsch, J.V. (1981, December). Trends in Soviet cognitive psychology. *Storia e critica della psicologia, 11,* 219–295.

Wever, E.G. (1949, 1970). *Theory of hearing.* New York: Wiley.

Whitcher, S.J., & Fisher, J.D. (1979). Multidimensional reaction to therapeutic touch in a hospital setting. *Journal of Personality and Social Psychology, 37,* 87–96.

White, B.L. (1984). *The first three years of life: A guide to the physical, emotional & intellectual growth of your baby.* New York: Avon.

White, B.L., & Watts, J.C. (1975). *Experience and environment: Major influences on the development of the young child.* Vol. 1. Englewood Cliffs, NJ: Prentice Hall.

White, R.W. (1952). *Lives in progress.* New York: Holt, Rinehart & Winston.

White, R.W. (1975). *Lives in progress* (3rd ed.). New York: Holt, Rinehart & Winston.

White, W.B. (1975). *Theory and practice of piano construction.* New York: Dover.

Whorf, B.L. (1956). *Language, thought. and reality.* Cambridge, MA: MIT Press.

Wickens, C.D. (1984). *Engineering psychology and human performance.* Columbus, OH: Charles E. Merrill.

Wickens, C.D., & Kramer, A. (1985). Engineering psychology. In Rosenzweig, R.M. & Porter, L.W., *Annual Review of Psychology,* pp. 307–348. Palo Alto, CA: Annual Reviews.

Wicker, A.W. (1979). Ecological psychology. *American Psychologist, 34*(9), 755–765.

Wiener, N. (1961). *Cybernetics: Or control and communication in the man, animal, and the machine.* Cambridge, MA: MIT Press.

Wilkes, J. (1986). Conversation with Ernest R. Hilgard: A study in hypnosis. *Psychology Today, 20*(1), 22–27.

Williams, L.V. (1983). *Teaching for the two-sided mind.* Englewood Cliffs, NJ: Prentice-Hall.

Williams, L.V. (1983). *Teaching for the two-sided mind.* Englewood Cliffs, NJ: Prentice-Hall.

Wilson, E.O. (1978). *Human nature.* Cambridge, MA: Harvard University Press.

Wilson, E.O. (1990, December). The ethical implications of human sociobiology. *Hastings Center Report,* 27–29.

Wing, H.D. (1962). A revision of the wing musical aptitude test. *Journal of Research in Music Education, 10,* 39–46.

Wingfield, A., & Byrnes, D.L. (1981). *The psychology of human memory.* New York: Academic Press.

Winter, D.G., & Stewart, A.J. (1978). Power motivation. In H. London & J. Exner (Eds.), *Dimensions of personality.* New York: Wiley.

Winton, W.M. (1987). Do introductory textbooks present the Yerkes-Dodson law correctly? *American Psychologist, 42*(2),202–203.

Wischnitzer, S. (1981). *Introduction to electron microscopy.* (3rd ed.). New York: Pergamon.

Wolpe, J. & Lang, P.J. (1977). *Manual for the fear survey schedule.* San Diego, CA: EdITs.

Wolpe, J. (1969). *The practice of behavior therapy.* New York: Pergamon.

Wolpe, J., & Lang, P.J. (1969). *Fear survey schedule.* San Diego, CA: EdITs.

Woodson, W.E. (1981). *Human factors design handbook.* New York: McGraw-Hill.

Woolsey, C.N. (1958). Organization of somatic sensory and motor areas of the cerebral cortex. In H.F. Harlow & C.N. Woolsey (Eds.), *Biological and biochemical bases of behavior* (pp. 63–81). Madison: University of Wisconsin Press.

Wozniak, R.H. (1975). A dialectical paradigm for psychological research: Implications drawn from the history of psychology in the Soviet Union. *Human Development, 18,* 18–34.

Yates, F.A. (1966). *The art of memory.* Chicago: University of Chicago Press.

Yerkes, R.M., & Dodson. J.D. (1908). The relation of strength of stimulus to rapidity of habit formation. *Journal of Comparative Neurology of Psychology, 18,* 459–482.

Young, T. (1801). On the mechanism of the eye. *Philosophical Transactions of the Royal Society of London, 91,* Part 1, 23–88.

Zajonc, R.B. (1965). Social facilitation. *Science, 149,* 3681, 269–275.

Zajonc, R.B. (1968). Attitudinal effects of mere exposure. *Journal of Personality and Social Psychology,* Monograph Supplement, *9,* 27.

Zajonc, R.B. (1980). Feeling and thinking: Preferences need no inferences. *American Psychologist, 35,* 151–175.

Zane, M. (1978). Contextual analysis and treatment of phobic behavior as to changes. *American Journal of Psychotherapy, 32,* 338–356.

Zanna, M.P., Kiesler, C.A., & Pilkonsis, P.A. (1970). Positive and negative attitudinal affect established by classical conditioning. *Journal of Personality and Social Psychology, 14,* 321–328.

Zedeck, S. & Cascio, W.F. (1984). Psychological issues in personnel decisions. In Rosenzweig, R.M. & Porter, L.W. (Eds.) *Annual Review of Psychology,* pp. 461–518. Palto Alto, CA: Annual Reviews.

Zeleny, M. (1981). In G. Klir (Ed.), *Autopoiesis: A theory of living organization.* New York: North Holland, The North Holland Series in General Systems Research.

Zellner, M. (1970). Self-esteem, reception, and influenceability. *Journal of Personality and Social Psychology, 15,* 87–93.

Zitrin, C.M. (1982). Combined psychological and pharmacological approach to the treatment of phobias. In R.L. Dupont (Ed.), *Phobia: A comprehensive summary of modern treatments.* New York: Brunner/Mazel.

Zitrin, C.M., Klein, D.F., & Woerner, M.G. (1978). Behavior therapy, supportive psychotherapy, imipramine, and phobias. *Archives of General Psychiatry, 35*(3), 307–316.

INDEX